PERSONAL FINANCE:
TEXT AND CASE PROBLEMS

PERSONAL FINANCE:
TEXT AND CASE PROBLEMS

Second Edition

E. Bryant Phillips
Professor of Economics
University of Southern California

Sylvia Lane
Chairman, Department of Finance
California State College (Fullerton)

JOHN WILEY & SONS, INC.
New York · London · Sydney · Toronto

Copyright © 1963, 1969
by John Wiley & Sons, Inc.

10 9 8 7 6 5 4 3

All rights reserved. No part of this book may be reproduced by any means, nor transmitted, nor translated into a machine language without the written permission of the publisher.

Library of Congress Catalog Card Number: 68-54914
SBN 471 68790 1
Printed in the United States of America

PREFACE

This book is designed to help everyone who is interested in the problem of allocating income and managing personal finances. It does not contain answers to all of the possible questions that may arise in the process of managing one's own monetary affairs, but it does provide an insight into the problems encountered throughout one's lifetime. When applicable, useful techniques have been described, alternate solutions have been weighed, and a course of action has been suggested.

Much of the material in this book is based on concepts and reasoning developed within the disciplines of economics and sociology, but the necessary concepts from finance and accounting are not slighted. As a result, this presentation is interdisciplinary.

This book is directed primarily to college students. A preliminary knowledge of the principles of economics will be helpful to those using it, but this is not absolutely required. Adults who have been dealing with the problems the book describes will find that their own experience and maturity will provide adequate background for their use of this material.

This book is designed for use as a text in a one-semester course. Students may spend additional time on the problems and cases included or on outside readings or projects that will enrich the materials and the coverage of the text.

Topics are arranged in the order in which one becomes increasingly aware of these problems as one progresses through the life cycle. Before solving the problems associated with the management of money, one must have an income. The maximization of income is discussed in the first chapter. Then one must learn to budget and allocate income carefully, use credit, and save and invest wisely. These subjects are developed progressively through the remainder of the book. Since expenditures on housing, automobiles, and medical care are major expenditures that have a marked effect on personal finances, they are carefully considered. The chapters on investments and many of the later chapters assume that college students may expect higher-than-average incomes and that they will be confronted with high taxes and complicated financial problems. Retirement programs and estate planning are saved for the last two chapters.

We are deeply indebted to several specialists who read portions of the manuscript and made a number of suggestions for its improvement. Among these were the following professors from the University of Southern California: Associate Professor Frances L. Feldman, School of Social Work; Professor Kenneth L. Trefftzs, chairman, Department of Finance; Professor Clyde W. Phelps, Economics Department; and Professor James H. Myers, Department of Marketing. We are also grateful for suggestions received from Professor Grant Wells of Ball State University and from the Public Relations Department of the New York Stock Exchange and from several specialists in other financial institutions.

In spite of the advantage of expert counsel provided by dozens of persons whose advice was sought, we make no claims of infallibility for ourselves, and we hereby assume responsibility for errors and omissions that may have crept into the manuscript.

We are also personally indebted to Margaret Starbuck and Elaine Osdick, who typed most of the manuscript in its final form, and to the members of our families, whose patience has been tested for two years: Vi and Colleen Phillips; Ben, Nancy, Reese, and Leonard Lane.

E. Bryant Phillips
Sylvia Lane

Los Angeles, California
September, 1968

CONTENTS

Part I Introduction
1 PERSONAL INCOME AND EXPENDITURES ... 3
2 BUDGETING ... 24

Part II Credit, Saving, and Investment
3 CREDIT AND CREDIT FACILITIES ... 55
4 SAVING AND SAVINGS FACILITIES ... 88
5 FINANCIAL AND INVESTMENT PROGRAMS ... 118
6 ANALYSIS OF CORPORATE SECURITIES ... 145
7 USING INVESTMENT INSTITUTIONS ... 179
8 INVESTMENT COMPANIES ... 218

Part III Major Personal Expenditures
9 EXPENDITURES FOR HOUSING ... 245
10 EXPENDITURES FOR TRANSPORTATION ... 297
11 EXPENDITURES FOR MEDICAL CARE ... 323

12	EXPENDITURES FOR GOVERNMENT SERVICES	352
13	PROPERTY AND CASUALTY INSURANCE	387
14	LIFE INSURANCE	406

Part IV Lifetime Financial Security

15	INCOME-MANAGEMENT STRATEGY	437
16	RETIREMENT PROGRAMS	468
17	ESTATE PLANNING	489

APPENDIX: CHECKLIST FOR EVALUATING A HOUSE	519
AUTHOR INDEX	527
SUBJECT INDEX	528

PART I

INTRODUCTION

1 PERSONAL INCOME AND EXPENDITURES

To earn a little and spend a little less—here is a task for all that a man has of fortitude and delicacy.

ROBERT LOUIS STEVENSON

Ours has been called an affluent society. It produces an abundance of goods and services leading to the highest standard of living known to mankind. In the process, many Americans work hard, earn more than elsewhere, and generally spend more. In fact, after paying their taxes, Americans spend 93 to 94 cents out of every dollar on a vast assortment of goods and services. With what they have left, they buy insurance or, at some later time, housing, appliances, and other consumer durable goods. Sometimes they invest the funds remaining after they have acquired their goods and services.

Because we live in a free society, we may exercise a great deal of discretion in how we spend our money. There is no rigidity to our savings and investment programs. For this reason a textbook on personal finance should include information on many subjects. It should discuss savings institutions and savings plans, various kinds of insurance, expenditures for the financing of homes and consumer durable goods; investments and investment programs; taxes, annuities, social security, and retirement programs; and wills, estates, and trusts. These topics are particularly important to college students who should anticipate saving and investment from above-average earnings.

The large portion of personal incomes normally spent for current consumption suggests that expenditures for goods and services also may deserve attention in a book on personal finance. These types of outlays will be discussed in this chapter and also in the next one, which is devoted to the subject of budgeting. Subsequent chapters will deal specifically with saving, investing, estate planning, the use of personal credit, and major expenditures for such goods and services as automobiles, housing, and medical care. Before returning to the subject of personal expenditures, it seems appropriate to discuss the income from which they derive.

PERSONAL INCOME

An individual's level of personal income largely determines how he lives and what he does. Beyond this, where the populus has freedom to move up and down the social ladder, as in the United States, income is a mark of achievement and a necessary means for the attainment of *status*, or social acceptance. This partially explains the interest of students in how much income they can expect in later years. The other most prevalent means of achieving status in this society are through occupation, education, successful parenthood, and leadership in a group, a firm, or in public affairs. Unfortunately, not all of these assure a high income or even an income commensurate with the status they confer.

The following brief analysis of the subject of personal income poses many questions. Where will personal income come from? How much income will there be? Which groups will have higher and which will have lower incomes? How much income will an individual probably have during his lifetime? How should one go about maximizing one's income? And how do households in the United States spend their incomes?

Sources of Personal Income

Americans received approximately $600 billion in personal incomes in 1967 (see Figure 1-1). Table 1-1 shows each source of income as a percentage of total family incomes. It should be noted that approximately 70 per cent of all personal income derives from wages and salaries. The incomes of young people stem almost entirely from these sources.

Personal Income

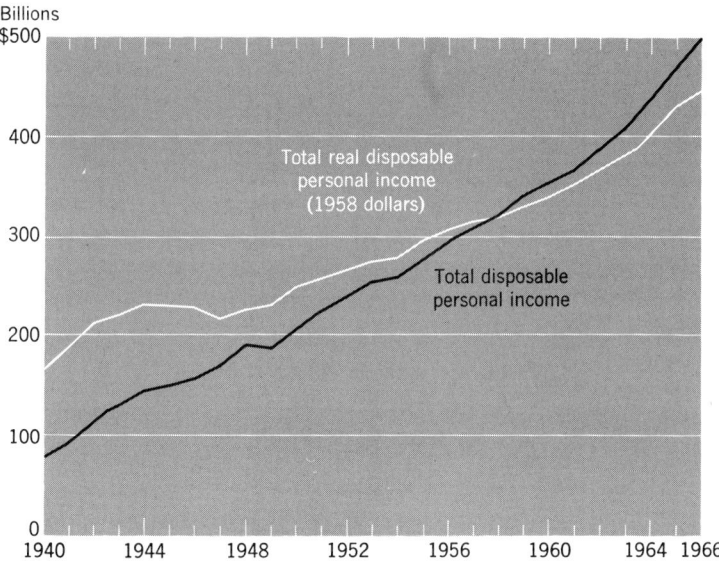

Figure 1-1. **Disposable personal income.** (*Source.* National Industrial Conference Board, Inc.)

In our economy, income is mainly derived from ownership of one or more of what economists call the factors of production. These are *land, labor, capital,* and *entrepreneurship.* Land denotes all of an economy's natural resources. Labor is work by brain or brawn. Capital consists of two kinds: real and monetary. Real capital includes the plant, equipment, and inventories used to produce goods and services; monetary capital covers all such financial claims as stocks, bonds, mortgages, shares in savings and loan associations, etc. Entrepreneurship means being an owner-manager. The commodities produced each year through the uniting of the factors of production go into consumption (C), investment (I), governmental usage (G), or export (X). Households are mainly interested in consumption. Investment enables the economy to add to real capital, which can then be used for further production.

For their use in the production of goods and services (commodities), the factors of production all receive payment. The payment for land is "rent" (rental income in Table 1-1). For labor it is "wages" (wages and salaries and other labor income in Table 1-1). For capital the payment is "interest" (personal interest income). For entrepreneurship it is "profit" (dividends, the household's share of corporate profits, appear in Table 1-1). Because of the many difficulties involved in obtaining an accurate measure of profit, proprietor's income rather than profits appears in Table 1-1.

In the United States, wages and salaries are by far the largest source of personal income. Since 1947 approximately 70 per cent of all personal income

Table 1-1. Sources of Personal Income

	Per Cent Distribution		
Income Type	1929	1947–1957 Average	1965
Wages and salaries and other labor income	59.7	66.7	67.3
Transfer payments	1.6	5.3	7.4
Proprietors' income			
Farm	7.1	5.7	2.7
Nonfarm	10.4	10.3	7.5
Dividends	6.9	3.7	3.6
Personal interest income	8.2	4.7	7.0
Rental income	6.1	3.6	3.5
Total family personal income	100.0	100.0	100.0[a]

[a] Total of 1965 figures do not equal 100 per cent because of rounding.
SOURCE: U. S. Department of Commerce, Office of Business Economics.

has derived from wages and salaries. Proprietor's income, dividend, personal interest income, and rental income shares of personal income have declined since 1929. However, the increase in the share of transfer payments, that is, pensions, social security payments, and other payments for which there are no services rendered in the period in which the payment is made, has offset the declines in the other shares.

Personal income in the United States will continue to increase as the Gross National Product—all that is produced annually—increases. All income basically derives from production, and the higher shares go to factors of production in relatively high *demand* and relatively limited *supply*. Those factors in relatively less demand or in greater supply get lesser shares. Thus if more labor is needed in relation to capital, labor will tend to receive a larger share. If managers speed up automation, the substitution of automatic or semiautomatic machinery and equipment for labor, interest rates rise and the interest income share tends to rise. Interest rates are the price charged for the use of savings with which to buy capital.

The size of any income share results from the interaction in the market place of supply and demand. Supply is the quantity available at various prices and demand is the quantity which will be bought at various prices. To *maximize income* one should own many relatively scarce factors of production that are in high demand and shift each of them into the use in which they will

Personal Income

command the highest price. Having a little monopoly, or even a competitive advantage, in the face of heavy demand, doesn't hurt.

Rising Personal Incomes

Total *personal disposable income*, after taxes, in the United States increased from $83.1 billion in 1929 to $550 billion in 1967. In 1947, after taxes were paid, the median family in the United States had $4,214 in terms of what a dollar could buy in 1964. By 1965, this family income had grown to $6,882, after taxes.[1]

If family incomes continue to increase at the same rate, the average family will have an income of $9,195 in 1964 dollars, by 1975. Since prices probably will continue to rise, although at a slower rate than wages, the actual *real income*, or purchasing power, of the average family will increase considerably. The persistence of this rate of increase into the 1970's and 1980's will result by 1985 in a family income of approximately $11,600 in 1964 dollars.

As income has increased in the United States, the concept of what constitutes *an adequate income* has changed.[2] Income is now considered inadequate if it cannot satisfy the acknowledged physical, cultural, and psychic needs of an individual in his particular environment. If a person with a high income feels that his income is inadequate, it *is* inadequate *for him*. An income of $10,000 a year may not be enough for someone who really believes that he cannot live on it.

As people have more income, they generally seek more goods and services. As Professor George Katona has observed, ". . . it is possible for gratification of needs to result in raising our sights and aspiring for more assets or goods."[3] The components which constitute "the good life" in the United States cost and number more and more as time goes on. Those who want to live in this affluent society have to earn more to keep pace. In recent years they have shown that they are willing to do so.

Distribution of Income

In 1947 approximately 31 per cent of all families in the United States had incomes of under $3,000 a year in 1964 prices (see Figure 1-1A). In 1964 this percentage had fallen to 18 per cent. Over the long period the percentage of families in the lower-income bracket has been declining and the percentage of those in the middle- and upper-income brackets has been increasing. Only 53 per cent of the families in the United States had incomes in excess of $4,000 a year as recently as 1947. Table 1-2 shows the percentages of families according to incomes in 1954, 1959, and 1964.

Only 10 of every 100 families had incomes in excess of $10,000 a year in

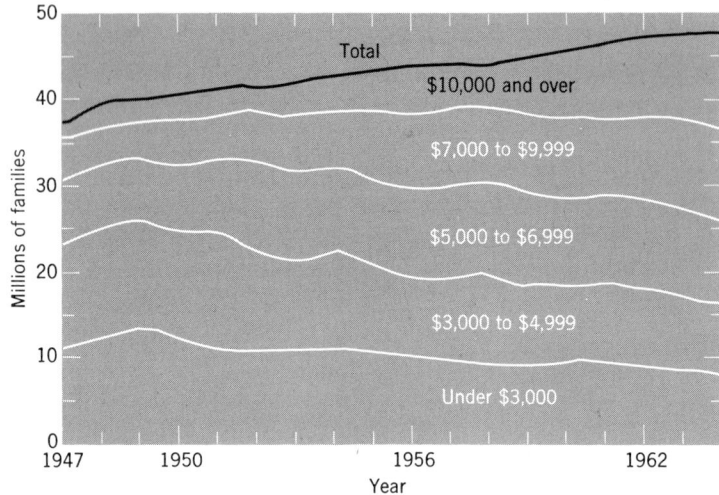

Figure 1-1A. Number of families by family income, 1947–1964 (in constant 1964 dollars). (*Source.* Finance Facts Yearbook, 1966, National Consumer Finance Association, 1000 16th Street, N.W., Washington, D.C. 20036.)

Table 1-2. Family Real Income by Income Groups, 1954, 1959, and 1964

	Percentage		
Family Income	*1954*	*1959*	*1964*
Under $3,000	27	21	18
$3,000 to $4,999	26	20	17
$5,000 to $6,999	22	23	20
$7,000 to $9,999	16	21	23
$10,000 to $14,999	7	11	16
$15,000 and over	2	4	6
Total	100	100	100
Median family income in 1964 dollars	$4,819	$5,773	$6,569

NOTE: Parts may not add to totals due to rounding.
SOURCE: Bureau of the Census.

1962. Only 5 families among every 100 had incomes of more than $15,000.[4] But this 5 per cent received more than 40 per cent of the nation's aggregate family income. Upper-income families received extensive incomes from dividends, interest, rent, and business sources.

Personal Income

Persons who are members of the higher-income groups more often are in families whose heads are between 25 and 55 years old. They are found in the occupational groups classified as professional, semiprofessional, technical, and managerial, or are self-employed, as indicated in Figure 1-2 and Table 1-3.

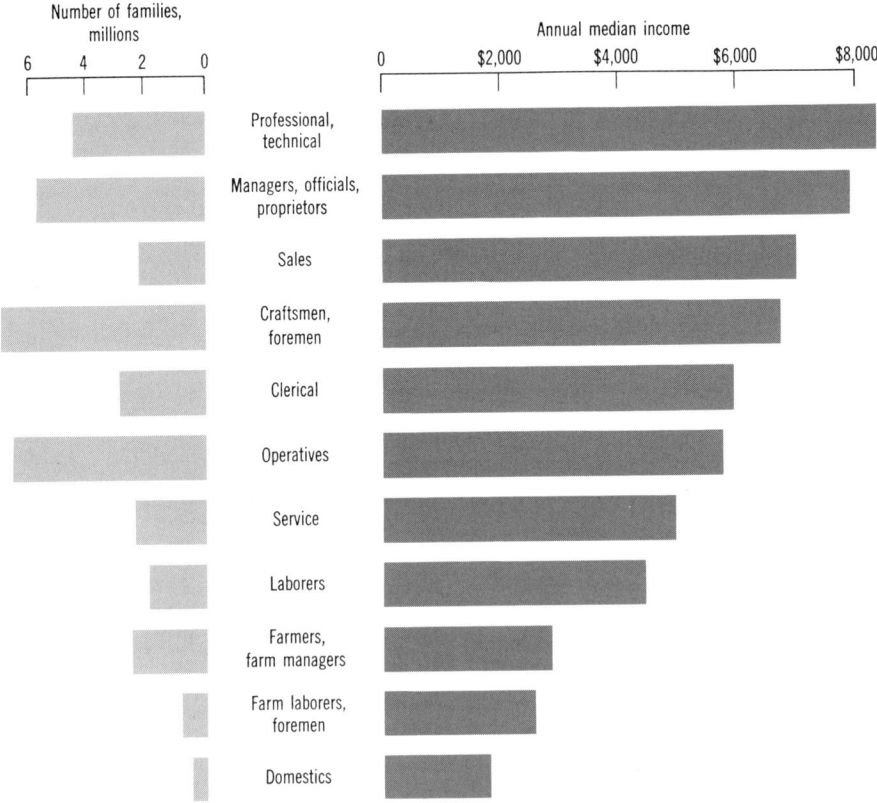

Figure 1-2. Family income, 1960, by occupation of head of family (employed civilians only). (*Source.* "Road Maps of Industry," No. 1366, The Conference Board, New York, March 2, 1962.)

On the other hand, members of the lowest-income groups usually belong to families whose head is between 18 and 24 years of age, or over 65. Their occupation is classified as being in the unskilled labor or service groups, or else the head of the household is retired or operating an unprofitable farm. In some cases, the head of the family may be a woman. Women's earnings, generally speaking, are not as high as men's earnings, even for the same type of work.

The majority of families in the United States are in the middle-income brackets—between $5,000 and $10,000 a year. Approximately 51 per cent of

Table 1-3. Family Income by Age Group, 1964 (Per Cent of Families in Each Age Group)

Family Income	Age of Family Head						
	Under 25	25 to 34	35 to 44	45 to 54	55 to 64	65 and over	All Families
Under $3,000	24.7	11.8	10.5	11.2	17.9	43.6	17.6
$3,000 to $4,999	28.4	18.7	12.7	13.0	16.9	22.9	17.0
$5,000 to $6,999	27.3	24.8	21.4	18.2	17.8	11.7	19.8
$7,000 to $9,999	15.5	28.9	27.1	25.2	21.7	10.4	23.2
$10,000 to $14,999	3.8	12.9	21.1	22.6	17.0	7.2	16.2
$15,000 and over	0.2	3.0	7.2	10.0	8.6	4.2	6.3
Total	100.0	100.0	100.0	100.0	100.0	100.0	100.0
Thousands of families	2,931	9,257	11,151	10,271	7,497	6,728	47,835
Median income	$4,796	$6,577	$7,512	$7,752	$6,696	$3,376	$6,569
Head of family a year-round full-time worker. Per cent of total excluding armed forces	59.8	76.0	78.6	77.2	65.2	15.5	65.5
Median income	$5,670	$7,205	$8,165	$8,513	$7,789	$6,092	$7,720

NOTE: Parts may not add to totals due to rounding.
SOURCE: Bureau of the Census.

them were in this group in 1964. That more families in the United States have been moving into the middle-income and higher-income brackets has been widely commented on and is very encouraging (see Figure 1-3).

Lifetime Earnings

How much a person earns during his lifetime depends, of course, on his annual income and the length of his employment. If a person works 45 years, from the time he is 20 until he is 65, and earns an average of $6,000 yearly, he will have earned $270,000 before he retires. If he wants to earn more over his working life span, he has to increase his worth and find employment in one of the higher-paying vocations or professions. Individuals are investing when they put time, money, and effort into study and training that will help them

Personal Income

develop more valuable skills that command higher rewards. Many people in the United States serve an apprenticeship or attend school for just this reason. Quoting Herman P. Miller of the Bureau of the Census, "the evidence available from recent studies suggests that an investment in schooling pays, on the average, a better return than most other investments."[5]

Importance of a College Education. A college education is necessary for entry into most of the higher-paying vocations and professions. The financial success of the college man usually is impressive. The college graduate can expect a higher lifetime income and a faster rate of pay increases. Between 1949 and 1958 wages for a worker with a high school education increased 47.4 per cent, compared with 66.2 per cent for the college graduate.[6] In addition, college graduates "have peak earnings which, on the average, far exceed initial earnings." College graduates of age 50, on the average, earn 72 per cent more than those who are 30. High school graduates of 50, on the average, earn 28

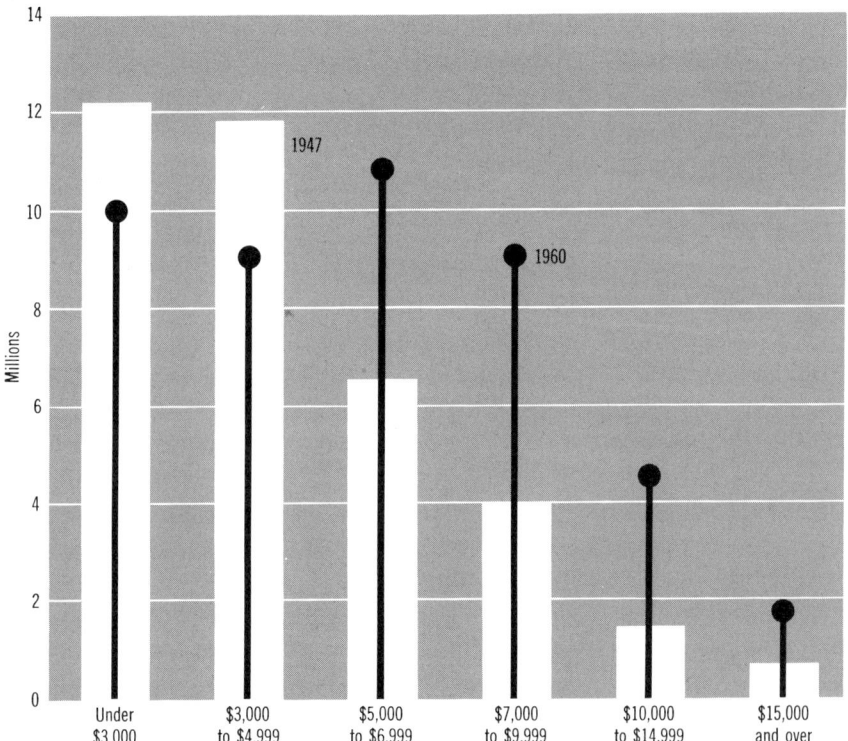

Figure 1-3. Number of families, by income classes. (*Source.* "Road Maps of Industry," The Conference Board, February 23, 1962.)

per cent more than those who are 30; elementary-school graduates earn only 18 per cent more.[7]

Miller also found that:

> In every year for which data are presented, additional schooling is associated with a very substantial increase in lifetime income. . . . The difference between the expected lifetime income of the average elementary school and high school graduate was equally striking. In 1958 the average elementary school graduate could expect a lifetime income of about $182,000 as compared with about $258,000 for the average high school graduate. The expected income differential associated with the four years of high school education therefore amounted to about $76,000 or 42 per cent.
>
> Since a college degree is the "open sesame" to many, if not most, high-paying jobs, it should come as no surprise that the greater income gains associated with additional schooling appear at the college level. On the basis of 1958 data, a college graduate could expect to receive about $435,000 income during his lifetime as compared with $258,000 for the average high school graduate. It can, therefore, be estimated that the approximately 4½ years of schooling beyond the high school level were associated with an increase of about $177,000 in lifetime income or about $40,000 per year of schooling.[8]

But then the fact that the college group generally had higher ability to begin with most probably accounted for a large part of this differential.

Preference for the Professions. Quoting Milton Friedman and Simon Kuznets,

> . . . . Judged by earnings, . . . professional workers are a fortunate group. Their earnings, though less equally distributed than those of nonprofessional workers, are between two and three times as large. . . . Independent practice of a profession tends to be more lucrative than salaried employment; while professional workers, independent and salaried, earn on the average between two and three times as much as all other workers, independent practitioners alone earn about four times as much.[9]

It should also be noted that the median of the earnings of 1,700 top business executives surveyed by *Fortune* was $73,584 a year.[10]

If the highest earning power as a professional is one's chosen goal, then one should plan for an independent professional practice. The financial rewards of various occupations and professions are illustrated in Figure 1-2. It may be noticed that one's chances of reaching a higher income bracket appear better in medicine than in teaching or accounting.

Within each occupation certain specialties and categories command higher salaries than others. For example, orthodontists, with their specialized training in correctional dentistry, earn more than most other dentists who are general practitioners. When the supply of human skill is limited and the demand exceeds the supply, the reward for that skill tends to be high. A topflight pitcher on a major league baseball team may earn $100,000 a year. A few talented actors and musicians may be rewarded very handsomely. But most young people will find that four or more years of college provides entry into the better-paying executive positions and into the professions. Table 1-4 indicates some comparative estimated lifetime earnings for a number of professions.

Other Factors Influencing Lifetime Earnings. An individual's aspirations have a bearing on his income. Sixty-three per cent of a group of college

Table 1-4. **Estimated Average Lifetime Earnings of Professional Men by Level of Education**

Occupation	Lifetime Earnings from Age 18 to 64		
	Average	4 Years of High School	4 or More Years of College
Doctors	$717,000		$721,000
Dentists	589,000		594,000
Lawyers	621,000		642,000
Engineers:			
Aeronautical	395,000	$378,000	418,000
Electrical	372,000	327,000	406,000
Mechanical	360,000	339,000	399,000
Civil	335,000	285,000	380,000
Natural scientists:			
Geologists	446,000		470,000
Physicists	415,000		431,000
Chemists	327,000	274,000	351,000
Biologists	310,000		322,000
Social scientists:			
Economists	413,000		432,000
Psychologists	335,000		345,000
Statisticians	335,000		387,000
Teachers:			
Elementary school	232,000		241,000
High school	261,000		265,000
College	324,000		328,000
Accountants	313,000	286,000	362,000
Clergymen	175,000	156,000	184,000

SOURCE: Bureau of the Census, Bureau of Labor Statistics.

students questioned in an extensive survey during the 1950's expected to be earning over $7,500 a year ten years after they graduated.[11] Approximately 45 per cent expected to be earning over $10,000. Not all of these students, of course, will fulfill their expectations. But aspirations are tied in with the self-image. They are determining factors in the type of occupation an individual will choose and the income he will strive to attain.

A person usually has some concept of his own aptitudes and abilities. Nearly everyone is inherently ambitious. If he is successful as an income provider—and this is appreciated by his dependents, which serves as a reinforcing influence—he usually will try to reach a higher level.

The financial and social status of one's parents often contributes toward a student's level of aspiration. Indeed, these may give him the means of attaining that level. This is increasingly important as education becomes more expensive. If the Office of Education's belief that the cost of attending college will double by 1970 is correct, then four years of college will cost about $13,600 at a public institution and $18,400 at a private university.

Unfortunately, four years of college are not sufficient for some of the professions. The cost of attending medical school, dental school, law school, or the appropriate graduate school must be included in computing the total cost of preparing to enter a particular profession. In addition, there is the matter of limited earnings as one serves an internship, residency, teaching assistantship, or other form of apprenticeship required for entry into a profession. Foregone earnings during the years of training are part of the heavy investment required before substantial returns may be expected. Obviously, one must balance the time, effort, and monetary cost of attending college against the income and prestige rewards to be gained.

PERSONAL EXPENDITURES

Even though income confers status, people want it primarily for what it will buy. Most human wants are satisfied by the things money buys. The individual performs some task for a monetary reward and then spends the money earned for the satisfaction of his wants.

Rising Trend of Personal Expenditures

Along with the rise of all incomes in the United States, personal expenditures for goods and services have increased proportionately. In 1965, outlays for personal consumption reached $428.76 billion. They are increasing at a rate of about 4 per cent a year.[12] This pattern suggests the passing of the $650 billion mark in 1975. In fact, many predictions suggest that personal consumption expenditures may increase even more rapidly. These predictions are based on the assumption that production and incomes, which are increasing rapidly, will continue their rate of growth. They imply that people can be depended on to continue to spend approximately 93 to 94 per cent of their disposable personal incomes. They further imply that spending can be encouraged to provide additional money from which more wages, salaries, rents, dividends, and taxes may be paid. These new and increased incomes will inspire existing firms to expand and induce new firms to come into being. Continued spending depends on the receipt of income, which, circularly, depends on continued spending and continued investment.

Changing Patterns of Expenditure

As income increases, both for the individual family and for the economy as a whole, the amounts and relative proportions spent on different categories of goods and services change. Moreover, both the actual amount of income and the relative proportion saved tend to increase for individual households. Paradoxically the relative proportion of income saved by the economy as a whole over the long period tends to remain the same.

Engel's Law. Christian Lorenz Ernest Engel, a nineteenth century economist and director of the Prussian Bureau of Statistics, published a study in 1857 in which he formulated a much quoted law. Engel's Law stated that as income increased, the proportion spent on food and other necessities decreased. Carrol D. Wright, head of the Bureau of Statistics of Labor in Massachusetts and later United States Commissioner of Labor, integrated Engel's studies with his own. In 1875, he modified the law to state that as income increased, the proportion devoted to food decreased, the part allocated to shelter and fuel remained invariably the same, that allocated for clothing stayed about the same, but the proportion for sundries, to wit, all other categories of consumption, increased.[13] Subsequent studies confirmed the first and fourth of these assertions and showed the invalidity of the second and third in the American economy.

Table 1-5 demonstrates that households[14] in higher-income brackets spend proportionately less for food even though they tend to eat more of the higher-priced foods. Such households spend about the same proportion of their incomes as lower-income households on home furnishings, equipment, and appliances, and on home operation and improvement, until income exceeds $15,000 a year. They spend higher proportions of their incomes for clothing and recreation, and on automobiles and education, until income exceeds

Table 1-5. Percentage Division of Family Expenditures for Current Consumption by Income Class, United States 1960–61*

	All House-holds	Under $1,000	$1,000 to $1,999	$2,000 to $2,999	$3,000 to $3,999	$4,000 to $4,999	$5,000 to $5,999	$6,000 to $7,499	$7,500 to $9,999	$10,000 to $14,999	$15,000 and Over
Food	24.5	28.2	30.6	28.9	26.9	25.8	25.3	24.3	23.9	22.2	19.0
Tobacco	1.8	2.1	2.4	2.4	2.2	2.1	2.0	1.9	1.7	1.3	1.0
Alcoholic beverages	1.5	0.7	0.9	0.9	1.2	1.3	1.4	1.5	1.6	1.8	1.8
Housing	28.4	29.1	30.6	30.6	29.2	28.6	29.0	28.5	27.5	27.0	29.5
Fuel, light, refrigeration, water	4.9	8.3	7.8	6.8	5.8	5.3	5.2	4.9	4.4	4.0	3.5
Household operations	5.6	4.8	5.3	5.2	5.4	5.3	5.3	5.4	5.5	5.9	8.3
Housefurnishings and equipment	5.4	4.4	4.4	4.6	5.1	5.2	5.6	5.6	5.5	5.5	5.4
Clothing, clothing materials, services	10.4	8.1	7.3	8.2	9.0	9.4	9.9	10.6	11.2	11.9	12.3
Personal care	2.9	3.0	3.1	3.2	3.1	2.9	3.0	2.9	2.9	2.7	2.6
Medical care	6.7	10.7	9.4	8.3	7.5	6.7	6.6	6.6	6.3	6.3	6.2
Recreation	4.0	2.5	2.2	2.7	3.3	3.6	3.7	4.1	4.4	4.9	4.7
Reading	0.9	0.8	0.7	0.8	0.8	0.8	0.8	0.9	0.9	0.9	0.9
Education	1.1	0.9	0.4	0.4	0.6	0.6	0.8	1.0	1.1	1.9	2.8
Transportation	15.5	9.9	9.1	11.3	14.5	16.3	15.8	15.7	16.4	16.4	14.4
Automobile	14.0	8.6	7.9	10.1	13.2	15.0	14.7	14.5	15.0	14.6	11.2
Other travel and transportation	1.5	1.3	1.2	1.3	1.3	1.3	1.1	1.2	1.4	1.8	3.2
Other expenditures	2.2	3.9	3.4	2.2	1.7	1.7	1.7	2.0	2.1	2.6	5.0

* Average for all families of two or more persons.

SOURCE: U. S. Department of Commerce, Bureau of Labor Statistics.

$15,000 a year. Whether an individual household varies its expenditures in this fashion as its income increases depends on its own pattern of preferences.

Expenditure Patterns. The proportion of total expenditures devoted to clothing has been decreasing over the years (Table 1-6). The proportion spent on housing and durable goods has increased. More is being spent for housing,

Table 1-6. **Per Cent Distributions of Consumer Expenditures by Major Groups**

	\multicolumn{3}{c}{Distribution Based on Constant (1957) Dollars}		
	1929	1947	1957
Total goods and services	100.0	100.0	100.0
Durable goods	11.7	11.8	14.0
Nondurable goods	50.2	53.2	48.5
Food and beverages	26.1	30.5	26.6
Clothing and shoes	13.5	10.2	8.6
Other	10.6	12.5	13.3
Services	38.1	35.0	37.5
Housing	10.0	10.5	12.5
Other	28.1	24.5	25.0

SOURCE: *Survey of Current Business*, April 1960, p. 3.

as approximately six of every ten nonfarm residences are now owner-occupied, compared with four in 1940.[15] *Durable goods*[16] absorb an increasing share of total expenditures as more and more of these commodities become an indispensable part of the household goods owned by the American family. The washing machine, the built-in range and oven, the refrigerator, the vacuum cleaner, the radio, the television set, and now the clothes dryer, the dishwasher, the garbage disposal, the air-conditioning unit, the freezer, and the two-car garage are all part of this development. The Statistical Abstract revealed that in 1965, 92 per cent of American homes had television sets, compared to 80.6 per cent with telephones. The 1960 census found only 88.1 per cent had either a bathtub or a shower.[17] It would seem that Americans are better entertained than bathed.

A study by the U.S. Department of Commerce during the years 1947–1954 indicated that a 1 per cent change in aggregate income—plus or minus—would produce the following changes in the total purchases in the United States economy, as shown in Table 1-7.[18]

Table 1-7.

Item of Consumption	Percentage Change (Following 1 Per Cent Change in Income)
Food, off-premises consumption	0.9
Furniture	0.6
Medical care	1.0
Housing	1.5
Automobile purchases	1.3

Evidently, additional income, following the war, was more likely to be spent on housing and cars than on food or medical care.

Increasing Similarity of Expenditure Patterns. Table 1-5 notes an important similarity in the expenditure patterns of households at different income levels. It seems that as incomes increase and standards of living rise, the relative expenditure patterns of these income groups become more comparable. Several studies confirm this observation. One, for example, discloses that "the professional and managerial occupations are not radically different from the clerical, skilled, or unskilled workers in the shares of total expenditures going to each broad expenditure category. The findings are quite the same for households of different educational attainments and ages, and for households in different geographic regions although the specific products bought may vary widely."[19]

The reasons for this similarity are not fully known, but studies have shown that most Americans, whatever their income bracket or social status at any particular time, consider themselves members of the middle class.[20] In fact, middle-class prototypes and ideals have become widely known and accepted through mass communication. The wants and attitudes of millions of Americans are influenced by neighbors, by television, the movies, and by dozens of popular magazines and newspapers.

Discretionary Spending. Despite the increasing similarity of expenditure patterns, individual household outlays vary more widely than ever. The wider range of commodities on the market from which they may choose causes this development. Once a family has more than $5,000 or $6,000 a year to spend, the basic necessities are attainable. A family may then use some discretion on how it spends the rest of its income. This remainder, the discretionary spending, makes living more interesting for those in middle- and upper-income brackets.

QUESTIONS

1. What are the cause and effect relationships between income and expenditures? Which seems to exert the most pressure on the other? Is the opportunity for savings threatened because of the relationship between income and expenditures?
2. Why are incomes proverbially inadequate in spite of their rapid increase? Is this inadequacy found at each income level?
3. If personal incomes rise at a rate of 4 per cent annually and the cost of living rises by 3 per cent, what change would occur in the people's real income in ten years?
4. Why do so many college-trained young people seek employment in the professions? Which of the professions is most attractive? Why?
5. Do family income levels make a difference in people's response to income expenditure? In what respects are expenditure patterns markedly uniform?
6. For what purposes do most people spend additional income? Why?
7. What is the connection between the theme of this chapter and the next chapter, which concerns budgeting?
8. Note carefully the key terms in this chapter and be prepared to identify each of them.

SELECTED READINGS

Bureau of Labor Statistics, *Occupational Outlook Handbook*, latest ed., Bulletin No. 1255, U. S. Dept. of Labor, Washington, D. C.
Bureau of Labor Statistics, *Survey of Consumer Expenditures and Income*, U. S. Dept. of Labor, Washington, D. C., published periodically.
Career Booklets, Career Information Service, New York Life Insurance Co., 51 Madison Ave., New York 10, N. Y., free.
Morgan, James N., Martin H. David, Wilbur J. Cohen, and Harvey E. Brazer, *Income and Welfare in the United States*, Survey Research Center, Institute for Social Research, University of Michigan, McGraw-Hill, New York, N. Y., 1962.
Study of Consumer Expenditures, Income and Savings, the Wharton School, University of Pennsylvania Press, Philadelphia, 1956 and 1960.
U. S. Bureau of Census, "Income of Families and Persons in the United States," *Current Population Reports, Consumer Income*, U. S. Dept. of Commerce, published annually.
Vocational Guidance Manuals, Grosset and Dunlap, New York, latest numbers.

NOTES

1. *Economic Report of the President*, January 1967, p. 233.
2. Helen Humes Lamale, "Changes in Concepts of Income Adequacy Over the Last Century," *The American Economic Review*, May 1958, pp. 291–299.

3. George Katona, *The Powerful Consumer*, McGraw-Hill, New York, 1960, p. 137.
4. Statistics unless otherwise indicated are from the Bureau of the Census.
5. Herman P. Miller, "Annual and Lifetime Income in Relation to Education: 1939–1959," *The American Economic Review*, December 1960, p. 963.
6. Data from which percentages were computed from U. S. Bureau of the Census *Current Population Reports*, Series P-60, Nos. 33 and 27, and *U. S. Census of Population*, 1950, Special Report P-E No. 5B.
7. Miller, *op. cit.*, p. 974.
8. *Ibid.*, p. 982.
9. Milton Friedman and Simon Kuznets, *Income From Independent Professional Practice*, National Bureau of Economic Research, New York, 1945, pp. 390, 392.
10. See "1700 Top Executives" in *Fortune*, November 1959, p. 138.
11. Rose K. Goldsen, Morris Rosenberg, Robin M. Williams, Jr., and Edward A. Suchman, *What College Students Think*, Van Nostrand, Princeton, N. J., 1960, p. 34.
12. *Economic Indicators*, prepared for the Joint Economic Committee by the Council of Economic Advisers, U. S. Government Printing Office, Washington, D. C., October 1966, pp. 2, 4.
13. *How American Buying Habits Change*, U. S. Dept. of Labor, U. S. Government Printing Office, Washington, D. C., 1960, pp. 34–37.
14. A household according to the Census definition is one or more persons occupying a common dwelling unit.
15. *Survey of Current Business*, November 1958, p. 5.
16. Consumer durable goods are products which have a life expectancy of one or more years in ordinary household use.
17. Department of Commerce, Bureau of the Census, *Statistical Abstract of the United States*, 1966, pp. 516, 521, and 754.
18. *Survey of Current Business*, September 1955, p. 29.
19. R. H. Ostheimer, "Who Buys What? *Life's* Study of Consumer Expenditures," *Journal of Marketing*, January 1958, p. 265; and L. J. Paradiso and M. A. Smith, "Consumer Purchasing and Income Patterns," *Survey of Current Business*, March 1959, pp. 18–28.
20. William Lloyd Warner, *American Life, Dream and Reality*, University of Chicago Press, Chicago, 1953, p. 105.

PROBLEMS AND CASES

1. Refer to the most recent edition of the U. S. Department of Labor, Bureau of Labor Statistics, *Occupational Outlook Handbook*. How much can you expect to earn annually in your chosen occupation: (1) if you are a student, in the year after your graduation? (2) if you are already employed two years hence? (3) during your lifetime if you plan to work until you are 65? (4) if you will gradually move up into the higher rungs of the occupational ladder in your occupation? and (5) if in addition you will find wages and salaries at all levels increasing 1 per cent a year over the years?
2. Refer to Table 1-3. Considering the costs of training for the various occupations listed, if you anticipate only average earnings, which of the occupations should you choose? Would you choose the same occupation if occupational status is

Personal Expenditures

taken into account? In view of your own interests, would you choose the same occupation?

3. Robert is a college student. He is considering graduate work in electrical engineering. Where should he seek information on the graduate schools in the United States offering master's degrees in the various fields? How can he compare these schools? Where should he find information on the costs involved in attending the various schools? Select three schools that offer high-quality programs in this area. What will his cost per year be at each of these three schools? Which one would you recommend he attend if he can afford all three? Which one would you recommend he attend if he will be dependent on loans and on his own earnings in meeting all costs?

4. Robert is now 23. What is the present value of his anticipated lifetime earnings discounted at 6 per cent if (1) he spends the next two years acquiring his master's degree, starts work the day he is 25, and plans to retire the day he is 65? He plans to spend his entire working life as an electrical engineer and progress normally from junior to senior engineer. What will the present value be if (2) he spends the next four years acquiring his doctorate and then progresses normally, again retiring the day he is 65? By how much does the present value of the doctorate exceed the present value of the master's degree? Where did you obtain your information? You may use engineer's salaries given in the Occupational Outlook. The present value of $1 received annually at the end of each year for N years is:

Years (N)	6%
1	0.943
4	3.465
25	12.783
40	15.046

5. Jane is an attractive college freshman from a high middle-income family who is trying to decide in which subject area to major. She had a B average in high school. She particularly likes mathematics but, as yet, does not dislike any of her subjects. Where should Jane go for information on the various subject areas and the career opportunities in each? Realistically list the pros and cons Jane should consider in deciding on whether to major in (1) mathematics; (2) social work; (3) advertising; (4) education; (5) economics; (6) psychology; (7) biology; (8) retailing; (9) chemistry; (10) English. Where did you find your information?

6. John is an accounting major trying to decide whether to do graduate work in law or accounting. List the pertinent economic and noneconomic factors to consider in making this decision. Where can information concerning these factors be obtained? In light of the information, what would you advise John to do? If John is now a Junior and 20, how much can he expect to earn over his lifetime if he becomes an attorney? How much if he becomes a certified public accountant? Consider the case anew assuming John has an appropriate major and is considering (1) medicine; (2) architecture; (3) library work;

(4) the consular service; (5) teaching on the high school level; (6) teaching on the college level; (7) writing; (8) music (assume he is talented); (9) art; (10) pharmacy; (11) physics; (12) geology.

7. Michael and Irene are 29 and 27 years old, respectively. They are married and have two children, who are 3 and 1. Michael left school after one year in Junior College and is working as a garage mechanic earning $150 a week. He is considering returning to school to major in business administration. Should he plan to return full-time, part-time, or not at all? On what factors should his decision hinge? What are his alternatives and the prospects in each? Irene has a bachelor's degree. She majored in home economics and would like to teach. Should she return to school? List the problems she would encounter if she did and offer possible solutions.

8. Smith has the problem of deciding whether to continue working as a draftsman at $800 a month or setting up his own drafting service. He is 32, married, and has three children and $5,000 in savings. He believes himself to be a capable manager and he has excellent contacts. He can work at home at first and therefore incur little expense other than his own time and materials. What would you advise him to do? On what basis? Would your answer be the same if having the requisite experience and contacts Smith planned to become (1) a consulting engineer; (2) a management consultant; (3) an investment counselor?

9. Cairns argues that both upper-income and lower-income groups are gradually disappearing in the United States and that we shall all be in the middle income group in 20 years. Refer to Figure 1-1A. If present trends continue, what will the shares of the income groups shown be in 20 years. Support or refute Cairns' argument.

10. Barnes is vice-president of a large corporation. Last year he earned $50,000 net after taxes. A week ago on the day he was 45 he was involved in an automobile accident. The fault was the other driver's. If his injuries will prevent him from ever returning to work but will not shorten his life, for how much in lost earnings should he sue? Assume that his earnings will increase at the same rate as aggregate personal disposable income in the United States and use the mortality table on pages 408–409.

11. Barbara is 43. Her youngest child is 18 and away at college. Her other two children are married. She and her husband live in an apartment and she has few household responsibilities. She is a high school graduate and is considering starting college so that she may teach in elementary school. What problems will she face in returning to school? How much will it cost her a year to attend school? Give estimates for both public and private colleges that she might attend in the area where you live. How much will she earn as an elementary teacher in the area in which you live? How many years will she be able to work before the mandatory retirement age? If she starts school this year and graduates in four years how much will her college education cost? How does this compare with the present value of her projected earnings as an elementary school teacher?

12. Thelma is 17 and graduating from high school this year. She would like to be a nurse but her family cannot give her any financial help with her education. Advise her concerning available scholarships. Are there any especially designed

Personal Expenditures

for her as a Negro? Which type of nursing school should she choose, one that is part of a University or one that is part of a hospital? What are the advantages and disadvantages of each? What specializations should she consider? Why?

For the answers to question 1 and for information on colleges and universities in the United States refer to:

1. The College Blue Books, latest edition.
2. Gene R. Hawes, *The New American Guide to Colleges*, Columbia University Press, New York, latest edition.
3. James Cass and Max Birnbaum, *Comparative Guide to American Colleges*, Harper and Row, New York, latest edition.
4. *State Universities and Colleges, a Guide for Prospective Students*, edited by Roy Hoopes, Robert R. Luce, Washington D. C., latest edition.

Those interested in studying abroad should refer to:

International Handbook of Universities, and Other Institutions of Higher Education, The International Association of Universities, 6 Rue Franklin, Paris 16e, latest edition.

For information on careers and prospective lifetime earnings refer to:

U. S. Department of Labor, Bureau of Labor Statistics, *Occupational Outlook Handbook*, Government Printing Office, Washington, D. C., 20402, latest edition.

Present values should be computed with the use of an annuity table.

For information on scholarships refer to:

U. S. Department of Health, Education and Welfare, Office of Education, *Financial Assistance for College Students: Undergraduate, and First-Professional*, Government Printing Office, Washington, D. C., latest edition.

Feingold, Norman S., *Scholarships, Fellowships and Loans*, Bellman Publishing Co., Cambridge, Mass., latest edition.

2 BUDGETING

The wise man is not he who knows only how to earn money, but he who knows how to make the best and most honourable use of it.

DON JUAN MANUEL

A budget is simply a tool for the businesslike management of a household's finances. Unfortunately, the terms budget and budgeting have unpleasant connotations. Those who dislike these words have had little experience in budgeting. Their opposition may be based on the fear of facing budgetary realities, the unpleasant task of keeping a set of books, or the apprehension that self-denial is inherent in the budgeting process. If budgeting means all of these, no wonder so few persons keep a budget. Perhaps the objectives and concepts of budgeting need reexamination.

Is budgeting not an attitude and a set of personal adjustments instead of a discipline enforced by bookkeeping? If a person acquires a practical, flexible attitude towards spending and saving, even if he does not commit his plan to paper, is he not budgeting? Will he not gain more satisfaction from the things he buys and may he not find some pleasure in saving?

NECESSITY FOR BUDGETING

There is a basic necessity for budgeting, which cannot be denied. This need can be demonstrated both for mankind in general and for individuals. In each case, the necessity stems from the fact that the extensive wants of human beings cannot be satisfied by the limited amounts of goods and services available to society.

Insatiable Wants

Nature is bountiful, but not bountiful enough to supply all of man's wants and needs. Using the products of field, mine, and stream, men hew, build, and fashion products that yield real and fanciful satisfaction. If mankind does not produce enough, then some of its wants cannot be fulfilled. This truism has led some persons to speak of economics as the dismal science. Moreover, it seems inevitable that men, like donkeys with carrots on sticks ahead of them, will be forever in pursuit of carrots, or cars, or houses, or the money that buys these things. Among human beings this situation signifies a healthy, continuous increase of objectives that stimulate a growth of economic activity.

As individuals, men are driven to greater productivity by the fact that their wants almost always exceed their incomes. Their wants could be curbed or their incomes might be increased continuously. It seems unlikely, however, that increases in personal incomes will ever provide total satisfaction because wants will have advanced to higher levels in the meantime. An intelligent selection among wants provides the best and only solution to an individual's budgeting problems.

Gradations of Wants. Some wants are primary, some are secondary. Some must be satisfied, some may be postponed or rejected. Some wants are lasting, some are passing fancies. The unimportance of lesser wants may be recognized by the fact that the same person does not consider them as important at different times or under different circumstances; nor are two different individuals likely to assign equal value to them. Obviously there are dozens of gradations of wants.

The Urgency of Wants. Most wants seem very urgent at the moment even though they are destined to fade in importance. One is tempted to overvalue certain wants and, unfortunately, their satisfaction may compel postponement or denial of more important wants later on.

It is normal for people to want more than they have. They want most of the attractive things that they see, and advertisements, displays, and salesmen titillate people and increase their wants. Most people want anything that will increase their own welfare and the happiness of those dependent on them.

Wants and the Family-Life Cycle. Children, as a rule, do not allocate any income they may receive with much discretion or wisdom unless they are carefully taught to do so.[1] Teenagers and pre-teens have definite preferences and tend to use all their income to satisfy them.[2]

A newly married couple needs a car, some furniture, and household appliances, but it makes fewer major purchases of these items than families ten or twenty years older that have more income and more savings.[3] Conveniently located coin-operated washing machines and dryers fill the needs of newly wedded couples. This availability permits them to postpone the purchase of washing machines and other appliances while they spend more money on recreation, clothing, and used automobiles than is spent in the average household in this country.[4]

After the first baby arrives, it becomes apparent that families must allocate more of their incomes to household operations, food, medical care, insurance, and savings. At this stage in the family-life cycle, the young mother usually gives up her job and a financial crisis often ensues. If a house must be furnished and doctor bills paid, it may be necessary to borrow money. This raises a question about the previous spending habits of the young couple; why had they not saved for this crisis? Admittedly, it would have been difficult to prepare for it. Nevertheless, the frequency of this occurrence seems to point to the need for more saving by newlyweds.

A family in the *newly built nest stage*—when members are being added and the children are young—has an unusual number of basic needs. Conscientious mothers of small children, especially if there are several of them, require the advantages of household appliances more than at any other stage of the life cycle. Unfortunately, this is normally the period of low income for the head of the family. Full-time help for the young mother is economically feasible only for those in the higher-income brackets. Fortunately, household appliances are obtainable—on credit.[5]

As a family grows older and approaches or reaches the *full nest stage*, the children eat more and wear more expensive clothes. The mother spends more for personal care, and the family spends more for recreation.

The children's education may be very costly. According to one source, the average child costs his parents $29,204 from birth until college graduation.[6] At this stage in the life cycle families' expenditures are highest.

When the children marry and leave home, a family finally may have surplus income for saving and investing. In many families, saving prior to this time is very limited. The exceptions are for the savings that are built into life insurance and that are destined for the down payment on a house, or for the purchase of such major items as an automobile or an air-conditioning unit.

A couple that is fortunate enough to be in the middle-income or higher-income bracket usually enjoys its peak income when the head of the family is 50 years of age or older. Families in the lower-income brackets reach a peak in their incomes much earlier and often *dissave*—that is, spend more than they earn—at this stage or find themselves in need of financial assistance.[7] This is the phase in the family-life cycle at which retirement plans and savings programs suddenly become important. Table 2-1 shows the categories of consumption expenditure which are highest in percentage for various age groups.

The Permanent Income Hypothesis. Milton Freidman at the University of Chicago has hypothesized that families spend a set amount year after year. He says that they spend a relatively unvarying proportion of what they consider to be their "permanent" income, the income that will be coming in year after year. He believes the family income "horizon," or how far a family looks ahead, in the United States to be about 2½ years. Windfalls, that is, unexpected income, will therefore have no effect on spending or consumption since these do not effect "permanent income." Several other economists disagree.

Extensive Wants and Limited Incomes. Economists have assumed that human wants are unlimited. The major reason that people do not buy endlessly is that incomes are limited. The economists' assumption about unlimited wants is not entirely adequate. Human wants are extensive; still they are limited by the extent of the individual's knowledge. People want only the commodities of which they are aware and then, ordinarily, only those that enable them to do as they wish. Wants are limited also by the amount of time an individual allocates to consumption and the buying of commodities. Of course, the wider an individual's experiences, the more, as a rule, are his needs and wants.

The decision to spend money is based on a person's preferences. These are influenced by external pressures or motivated by the quest for status. Sometimes they are prodded by a desire for *conspicuous consumption*, to use Thorstein Veblen's term.[8] Spending, in our economy, intentionally is made easy, and so the wants that spur spending need not be very strong. Earning, in our economy, on the other hand, is still difficult for many. Consequently, most incomes are far from adequate if an individual, perhaps irrationally but wishfully, aspires to the satisfaction of all of the wants of which he is aware.

Table 2-1. **Age Groups Spending Highest Percentage**

Age Group Spending Highest Percentage (Age of Family Head in Years)	Percentage of Age Group's Total of Expenditures for Current Consumption, U. S. 1960
Under 25	
Tobacco	2.0
House furnishings and Equipment	6.6
Automobiles	18.3
25–34	
Recreation	4.5
35–44	
Clothing	11.4
45–54	
Alcoholic beverages	1.7
Personal care	3.0
Education	1.8
55–64	
65–74	9.7
Transportation other than by automobile	2.4
75 and over	
Food	27.4
Housing	34.9
Household operations	7.2
Reading materials	1.2

NOTE: Table 2-1 shows the age group spending the highest percentage of their total expenditures for current consumption for each of the Bureau of Labor Statistic's major categories of consumer expenditure. The highest percentages in the food and housing categories are spent by those over 75, but many in this group have very low incomes. On the average, food, housing, and household operation took over 70 per cent of the income of this age group, as opposed to some 58 per cent of the income of those between 35 and 44, but households with a head between 35 and 44 years of age averaged total receipts for the year 1960–1962 of $8,962. Those whose head was over 75 averaged $3,678.

SOURCE: *Bureau of Labor Statistics.*

Maximizing Satisfactions

To obtain the most satisfaction from his income an individual must allocate his expenditures so as to derive as much pleasure from the last dollar spent on any single purchase as from spending it on something else. For example, if an individual spent $22 a week on food and $20 a week on rent, but felt that he would enjoy the food that one additional dollar would buy more than the last few square feet of space he had rented, he would allocate his income to better advantage by spending $23 on food, and $19 a week on rent. But this might involve having to hunt for another apartment. Actually, time, energy, and money all must be allocated wisely if one expects to maximize one's satisfactions. The appendix following this chapter explains the process of maximizing satisfactions in economic terms.

Alternative Costs. The economic cost of an item is the value foregone of the best alternatives obtainable so that the limited amount of money may be spent on this item. The economic cost is also termed the opportunity cost. If one is acting rationally according to economic theory, one is constantly evaluating alternatives and shifting the money that is the purchasing power for resources into uses that yield the highest return. Sometimes the alternative cost is the cost of parting with money, which has utility in itself (lose a dollar and you lose the satisfaction obtainable from what it can buy or the satisfaction of having it). The cost of buying an item often involves interest or dividends that could have been earned on money spent. It may also involve as an added cost (cost in the sense of what one pays psychologically not economic cost)— the disutility of having additional debt.

Constellations of Wants. An individual should calculate the satisfaction he will derive from a purchase by considering how that purchase fits with the other things he desires to acquire. Only a few commodities are bought for themselves alone. Total utility and satisfaction are enhanced when the value of all the items purchased is greater than the sum of the parts.

The Concept of Rational Choice. Only a few persons display rationality by thinking appropriately or logically about their purchases. One study found that rational choice was exercised only when items worth $1,000 or more were involved.[10] In other instances, it seemed likely that many people drifted along, subject to advertising and sales pressures, and made their decisions by unpredictable, irrational means. If more thought could be given to purchase decision, experience and logic could become the basis for each succeeding one.

The pitting of one want against another constitutes a realistic and logical way to challenge each of them to see whether either want should be postponed or rejected. In real life, many persons use this device by mediating over the acquisition of an item for some time before they reach a decision. A written *preference list* may be compiled, if desired. A preference list (written or not) implies that a given item must survive the competition with others, or with the possibility of not spending the money. An item that rises to the top of a preference list and remains there probably should be purchased. If it cannot hold that preferred position, its possession probably would yield less satisfaction than something else on the list.

Should one item on a preference list cost less than another, a number of dollars may be added to it until the prospective purchaser reaches a *point of indifference* between this item (plus a sum of money) and the costlier item. Thus, a Chevrolet with an unusual assortment of extra accessories might be compared to another Chevrolet devoid of accessories and $500 in cash. A logical person with a healthy respect for money might find that he is neutral or indifferent between these choices. If, however, he prefers the accessories to the $500, perhaps the purchase should be made accordingly. In decisions of this sort, the expenditure should provide lasting pleasure and happiness.

The Consequences of Inadequate Budgeting

Sometimes, a person must learn that budgeting is wise and necessary. He sees this through the depths to which some families have fallen for lack of budgeting. There are persons whose poor money management has driven them so far into debt that they are threatened constantly by irate creditors and landlords. Financial difficulties often lead to ulcers, loss of friends, and divorce. Sometimes creditors or collection agencies seek to obtain *garnishment* arrangements whereby they attach a fraction of an employee's wages. On occasion, an employer warns his employee that his job will end if additional garnishment proceedings ensue. The unwise and excessive use of installment credit may lead debtors to a dead-end street in which they borrow from Peter to repay Paul.[11]

Debt Counselors and Debt Adjusters. Debt-counseling services have been made available by social agencies, by the joint efforts of those who grant credit, and by private firms who render such service for a profit. Social agencies and jointly sponsored nonprofit debt-counseling organizations generally charge low fees because their costs, as a rule, are subsidized. A private debt adjuster may be a legitimate operator who selects only those customers whom he really can help. Some less conscientious private debt adjusters take payments from distraught clients, provide few counseling services, and retire little of the client's indebtedness. Recently, debt adjusters have been outlawed in New York and a few other states, and they are subject to regulation in an increasing number of states.[12] As there seems to be a real need for this type of service, however, it is likely to continue in most places where it is not prohibited.

In most instances, a debt adjuster charges a fee of 15 per cent on the approximately 40 per cent of a client's salary, which he uses for debt retirement. The debt adjuster frequently is able to appeal to creditors to reduce their claims and postpone their suits against the client so that each creditor may receive payment eventually. In the meantime, the debtor agrees to create no new debts, while living on approximately 60 per cent of his income. Naturally, some budgeting advice and some rigorous budgeting accompanies this ordeal. Not everyone can survive this experience.

Poor Budgeting by Impoverished Persons. Many persons live from one financial crisis to another with little thought for saving to ease the distress certain to accompany their next bout with adversity. Perhaps such things as cigarettes and beer are not as necessary to these people as their long-run salvation from financial hardship. A hurried look at a compound interest table shows that the saving of a few cents a day—perhaps ten dollars a month— would accumulate a sum in excess of $10,000 over the 40-year working life of one member of such a family.

Poor Budgeting by Middle-Income Persons. There are scores of opportunities for observing the consequences of poor budgeting by individuals in the middle-income bracket. Some of these people impoverish themselves by overspending for some things that other persons do not think are important. Some middle-income spendthrifts live beyond their means temporarily by neglecting to provide for emergencies and for their own retirement.

Poor Budgeting by Upper-Income Persons. The majority of persons whose incomes are not high may imagine that others with high incomes do not need to budget. This is a fallacious concept founded on the assumption that the rich have the same level of wants as the poor. This is untrue, of course; individuals tend to upgrade their wants as their incomes rise, if not in advance of income increases. Persons of lower income also fail to realize that many high-income individuals do budget, as indicated by their tendency to save a large part of their incomes.

BUDGET ADMINISTRATION

Even when an individual is convinced that he should begin to budget his income, he must consider several details about budgets and budget administration. First, he and his family should study the family's spending pattern and consider whether they are satisfied with their way of life and its costs. Next, they should schedule their spending for primary commitments for the following month or two. Finally, they should reconsider their budgetary plan after trying it for a short period and change it if necessary. If some expenditures are far out of line, if the budget fails to fit the family's income, if it does not allow for emergencies, major purchases, insurance, medical care, as well as savings and retirement, or if it excludes some things that the family finds it really wants, the budget should be revised. Ideally, a budget should be instituted to improve the family's money management and its living pattern. It should not be used solely to regiment a family or to bail it out of a financial crisis.

Assembling Data on Current Expenditures

Normally a budget plan should begin with a family's current mode of living. Current expenses usually can be estimated, but sometimes a family is surprised to learn from sales slips, check stubs, and other records how much it spends on various items. The gathering of accurate information is important because the amounts spent currently for such things as housing, household operation, food, or transportation become the budget estimates for the succeeding period unless they are specifically revised.

Selecting Budget Categories. As the data on expenditures are gathered, categories manifest themselves. For most families, these categories include food, clothing, shelter, transportation, educational expense, and recreation, among others. Once these groupings become apparent, the assemblage of the data may be facilitated. Expenditures for some items such as music and recreation may overlap. Some arbitrary definitions and assignments may have to be made. In some instances, a number of minor expenditures may have to be lumped into a miscellaneous category. To compare one's own breakdowns with Bureau of Labor Statistics published averages, both for the nation and for each standard metropolitan area, it would be well to use the Bureau's categories as shown on page 28 or 44.

Subcategories. There is some question about how far one should go in gathering detailed data on current expenditures. For example, food, which takes nearly 30 per cent of the average family's income, might be broken into several subcategories such as meat, bread, milk, other goods, and sums spent in dining out. Expenditures for many items, such as cigarettes, often come out of pocket money; hence, they are not easy to isolate. There might be some benefit in gathering data on these separate categories and subjecting them to analysis. However, most persons find this experience too bothersome and embarrassing and therefore do not attempt it.

Setting Up a Budget

Once the expenditure pattern of a family is clear, it is time to review the data and the family's financial position. A tentative budget may then be devised.

Evaluation of Current Expenditure Data. Probably the major achievement of the budgeting process is the attitude that the participants acquire toward each other and toward wise selection among expenditure items. Many hidden issues are resolved when expenditures are out in the open and the wishes of each member of the family are weighed by the others. Exorbitant expenditures and buying for spiteful reasons, or spending just to "get one's share" become obvious. The family conference, or even an informal discussion between the family's senior members, may resolve many personal animosities and revise many estimates of the importance of certain desires in relation to the needs of the entire group. It is probable that this change in a family's attitude has a cause-and-effect relationship to the successful budgeting that almost always follows.

The family should evaluate its expenditure pattern in several respects. First, of course, it should see that the sum of expenditures does not exceed the family's income. If it does, there must be a presumption that something or everything in the budget must be reduced. The possibility of more income might be considered, to be sure, but a family that has been living beyond its means may tend to increase its expenditures still further if its income increases. The soundest approach in this case lies in an attack on expenditures. If certain proposed outlays seem to most family members to be out of line, then it seems likely that these should be pared. The same holds true for expenditures that are far from the norm of families in the same income bracket. If, however, these abnormal outlays represent the choice of the family members who are willing to reduce other ones, the items should be permitted to stand, subject to review at a later date to make certain that this decision really represents the family's wishes.

As Figure 2-1 shows, a family's expenditure pattern should be evaluated also in terms of its provision for future expenditures for insurance, savings, the purchase of major appliances, a home, a car, and even a hoped-for vacation. If provision for all of these is insufficient, the fact should be recognized, and trimming of other expenditures should be anticipated.

Budget Balance Sheet. An easy way to calculate a family's long-range gains or losses is to draw up a budget balance sheet showing the value of the family's *net worth*. This is its total assets minus total liabilities, for each of several years. In making this calculation, the family must take care to use the market value of furniture and the car, the cash surrender value of insurance policies, the cash value of savings, and the like, as indicated in Figure 2-2. If the total value of a family's assets does not increase, the family is neglecting its major purchases, its savings, and its provision for security.

	FOR ONE BUDGET PERIOD	FOR ONE YEAR
Enter INCOME Subtract FUTURE FIXED EXPENSES		
Balance Subtract FUTURE FLEXIBLE EXPENSES		
Balance Subtract PAST-DUE BILLS		
Balance Subtract DAY-TO-DAY LIVING COSTS		
Balance Subtract PERSONAL ALLOWANCES		
SAVINGS FOR WISHES		

Figure 2-1. A planning form. (*Source. Money Management—Your Budget,* Household Finance Corporation, 1950, Chicago, p. 22.

Tentative Budget Schedules. When the chief categories for expenditure have been determined, they can then be evaluated separately and jointly. Unless they are rejected and revised for the reasons already noted, they may comprise the tentative budget. Items that survive this process apparently deserve a place in the tentative budget.

Types of Budgeting

There are many types of budgeting. Some are good, others are not so good. Some involve quite a bit of bookkeeping. Some do not. Budgeting may be considered more than a rigorous discipline enforced by arithmetic and bookkeeping. It is a process or an attitude, whereby one plans, allocates, controls, and weighs outlays habitually and automatically. Once this attitude and sufficient maturity have been acquired, they may be supplemented by the disciplining of one's behavior. As we shall see, the balancing of a budget or the amount saved is not as important as how the money is allocated and the items it covers.

Cash Budgeting. Quite a few people budget on a cash basis. They avoid overdrafts at the bank because they have no bank accounts. They avoid the excessive use of charge accounts and installment credit because these modern

Budget Administration

ASSETS

A. "Fixed Dollar"

		As of _____ 196_		As of _____ 196_	
		In husband's name*	In wife's name*	In husband's name*	In wife's name*

Annual Income

1. Cash
   a. On hand $_____ _____ _____ _____
   b. In checking accounts _____ _____ _____ _____
$_____ c. In savings accounts _____ _____ _____ _____
_____ 2. U. S. Savings Bonds _____ _____ _____ _____
_____ 3. Other bonds and preferred stocks _____ _____ _____ _____
_____ 4. Life insurance cash value _____ _____ _____ _____
_____ 5. Money owed you _____ _____ _____ _____

B. "Equities"

_____ 1. Home (current market value) _____ _____ _____ _____
_____ 2. Business interests _____ _____ _____ _____
_____ 3. Common stocks _____ _____ _____ _____
_____ 4. Real estate _____ _____ _____ _____

C. Miscellaneous Assets

1. Household furnishings _____ _____ _____ _____
2. Personal property (furs, jewelry, cars, boats, etc.) _____ _____ _____ _____
_____ 3. Present cash value of pension or profit-sharing plans _____ _____ _____ _____

Total   Total

LIABILITIES:

Annual Interest

_____ 1. To banks _____ _____ _____ _____
_____ 2. Mortgages payable _____ _____ _____ _____
_____ 3. Life insurance loans _____ _____ _____ _____
_____ 4. Other liabilities
         a. Installment payments _____ _____ _____ _____
         b. Other loans and notes payable _____ _____ _____ _____
_____   Total

Total _____

NET WORTH
(Assets minus Liabilities)

* NOTE: List jointly owned assets under the name of the person who actually provided the funds.

Figure 2-2. Budget balance sheet. (*Source. This Week* Magazine, May 1, 1960, p. 23. Reprinted from *This Week* Magazine.) Copyright 1960 by the United Newspapers Magazine Corporation.

devices are available to them only in very limited amounts. If they can avoid small loans from friends, relatives, and pawnbrokers, they seem to budget; their income and expenditures remain in balance.

Unfortunately such people generally illustrate the worst sort of budgeting. They buy inefficiently and in small quantities. They tend to spend unevenly and unwisely—too much on payday and too little just before the next payday. Usually they neglect savings, insurance, medical care, asset replacement, and provision for major purchases such as a car, a home, and appliances. Their budgeting is good only in the sense that their accounts are balanced. The quality of their purchase decision is open to criticism. A cash-budgeting system might be quite effective, however, if cash sums were sequestered from each pay envelope and placed in sugar bowls or other safekeeping for major expenditures.[13] This would be the simplest way of directing funds from their *sources* to uses.

Budgeting With Check Stubs and Cash. Individuals who have checking accounts tend to accumulate a little money in the bank. With these temporary savings they are more likely to prepare for major purchases, insurance, savings, and medical care. In some respects they, too, are budgeting on a cash basis. As a rule, they do not write a check for each item that they purchase. For this reason, their check stubs do not constitute a complete record of expenditures. Even so, the check stubs may serve as a partial bookkeeping system. To that extent this system is an improvement on cash budgeting.

However, a checking-account budgeting system invites two temptations. First, the balancing of accounts may not be as precise as in cash budgeting because the clearance of checks drawn against an account takes a day or more. This means that some bills may be paid with checks before the money actually is on deposit. Thus, expenditures in one time period very well may exceed income in that same interval. Second, expenditures for various categories may be out of line with scheduled budgetary allotments even though the totals in the checking account may balance. This borrowing among budget categories tends to hide the fact that some expenditures are excessive while others are stinted. The checking account underemphasizes the qualitative control over expenditures and overemphasizes the balancing of total outlays with income.

Cash, Checking-Account, and Installment-Credit Budgeting. A person may increase his purchases of major items when he adds the use of installment credit to his cash and checking-account budgeting. This can be an improvement, or not, depending on the intelligence with which installment credit is used. In some cases, the installment purchases raise levels of living because expenditures for major items replace spending for low-priced items of little consequence. In other cases, the excessive purchase of cars and appliances actually may impoverish a family and unbalance its expenditures by reducing the quality of its food or by reducing its provision for savings and insurance.

Installment credit permits a person to spend future earnings before the earnings are received. To this extent installment buying unbalances income and expenditures for a time. When the first credit is borrowed against the future, a spending binge may follow. After this first binge, however, if his income does not increase, the borrower must budget to prevent the assumption of further monthly payments in excess of his current income. Also, the carrying charges often are high; hence the total amount of goods that can be paid for is reduced by the sum of the financing costs. Many would deny that the use of installment credit constitutes a form of budgeting, yet more people probably practice informal budgeting by this device than in any other way.[14]

Bookkeeping-Budgeting System. A good bookkeeping-budget system probably should utilize coded numbers for expenditure categories. It would set up each account or budget item with a scheduled sum. Against these items it would enter anticipated expenditures as obligations, and would charge actual expenditures against that account.

There are many good budgeting forms to help with the actual bookkeeping involved. These can be obtained for the asking or at a very small cost. The trial budget form contained in *Money Management—Your Budget* may be obtained at any one of a hundred branch offices of, or by writing to, the Household Finance Corporation.[15] A *Budget Book* may be acquired from the New York Life Insurance Company. Budgeting forms may be requested from the Royal Bank of Canada, the Connecticut Mutual Life Insurance Company, the Commercial Credit Corporation, the Institute of Life Insurance, the Department of Agriculture, and from many banks, savings and loan associations, and other financial institutions.

Many advocates of budgeting assume that accounts must be kept if budgeting is to succeed. They are right in the quantitative sense of keeping accurate records by budget categories and tallying the totals. Their system does not provide for the quality of expenditure decisions, however, since these decisions cannot be made in the presence of a set of books. They must be made by people in the market place where the prices and qualitative differences of merchandise may influence judgments.

Budget Revisions

There is nothing more predictable than the probability of change. People change; their wants and interests change; the prices of the things they buy change. The few who dare not veer one degree from their budgetary course are not budgeting intelligently. They are being regimented by a *punitive budget*, which is designed to curb abnormal desires and balance accounts regardless of their shifting preferences. The appeal here is for a higher form of budgeting to permit some choice, provided it is premeditated and rational.

Need for Budget Revision. No budget could remain unchanged indefinitely unless a great many expenditure items were budgeted in a miscellaneous category. This is not good budgeting, of course. If expenditure items are elaborated in much detail, they should be reviewed frequently to be certain that they are reasonable and applicable.

It seems likely that the unpopularity of budgeting arises from the regimentation associated with too much rigidity. If adjustments could be made where the budget pinches tightest, budgeting might regain some of its lost popularity.

Making Budget Adjustments. If some budgeted items seem inadequate at first, it may be necessary to reexamine the basis of the estimates as well as the current expenditures to judge which of the two is out of line. In deference to the idea of holding the line, one should not expect to increase an item that is under pressure unless something else can be cut.

Sometimes individuals may wish to review budget estimates and realign them to conform with normal or typical budgets. This may be wise especially if one wishes to correct a spending abnormality. But the quest for conformity is no more commendable than the adoption by all of the same hobby. Middle-income budgets represent a variety of hobbies, in a sense. If a person has an especially expensive one, his budget need not conform, provided that he continues his hobby at the expense of other things.

Budget Comparisons. Information about average expenditures for differing budget categories may be obtained from the Bureau of Labor Statistics. These may be of interest to persons who intend to set up a formal budgeting system. A typical family may wish to learn how its own pattern of expenditures compares with the average pattern, but the family should not regiment its spending unless drastic budget revision is necessary. A range of acceptable budget variations for families in several income groups may be found in Table 2-2.

Continued Frequent Budget Review. Budgetary items and entire budgets should be reconsidered carefully from time to time. The attention to this review should remind those concerned of the reasons for their decisions. It should make budgeting a device for enabling adjustments, not an instrument for financial enslavement.

Since budget considerations and reviews are an educative process, nearly every member of a family should participate in them. If Johnny wants a pet

Table 2-2. Range of Acceptable Variations in Budget for Family of Four Persons

	Income			
	$2,500	$4,500	$6,500	$12,500
Item	Per Cent Range	Per Cent Range	Per Cent Range	Per Cent Range
Food	28–38	25–35	20–30	15–25
Housing	25–35	25–35	20–30	20–30
Clothing	8–12	9–13	9–15	9–15
Transportation	11–15	16–20	16–20	12–20
Taxes	3–5	6–8	12–15	20–30
Health and insurance	8–10	8–10	7–12	7–15
Savings	—	0–10	0–10	5–15
Advancement	3–10	4–10	5–10	5–15
Installment payments	5–15	5–15	5–15	5–15
Household help	—	0–5	0–10	5–15

Food includes all meals eaten in and out of the home.
Housing may be for rent or home payments. This includes real estate taxes, maintenance, fire insurance, household operations, utilities, and household furnishings. Goods, such as household appliances being purchased on a credit plan, should be included in "installment payments"—and not in this item.
Clothing includes expenses for all members of the family; it covers not only costs for new purchases but also dry cleaning, pressing, and repairs.
Transportation includes public-carrier fares, automobile payments and insurance, repairs, tires, fuel, and other maintenance costs; it covers transportation for work, school, or recreation.
Taxes include federal and other income taxes, whether or not these are withheld by the employer.
Health and insurance include current medical costs and payments for prepaid health plans, health insurance, life insurance, old-age and survivors insurance, and disability insurance.
Savings may consist of bonds, investments, bank, or other accounts.
Advancement includes costs for recreation, charity contributions, education, personal needs, gifts, and personal allowances.
Installment payments include all credit purchases other than monthly charge accounts.
Household help includes sitters, housekeepers, cleaning women, and gardeners.
SOURCE: Adapted from Frances Lomas Feldman, *The Family is a Money World*. Family Service Association of America, New York, 1957, 164 pp., by permission of the author and the Family Association of America. Such percentages are used as "acceptable norms" by many social agencies in the United States.

dog, for example, he should enter into the consideration of the dog's original cost, the expenses involved in its feeding, shelter, medical care, license, kenneling expense when the family is away, and costs of probable damage to rugs and furniture. If Johnny must be told that he cannot have the dog, he deserves to know the reasons why. If the dog is to become a household pet, Johnny's education will not be complete until he is aware of its costs and of the family's responsibility for meeting them.

BUDGETING AT DIFFERENT INCOME LEVELS

Budgeting or failure to budget occurs at various levels of income. Many expenditures are basic and unavoidable at nearly any income level. Others are influenced by the habits and customs of the social and occupational groups with which one associates. Most people have some discretionary income to spend as they please. The temptation to keep up with the Joneses, to buy all sorts of ballyhooed products and services promotes more spending or different patterns of spending. Persons who budget must recognize these influences and face them squarely.

Budgeting for Low-Income Families

Low-income families usually have three handicaps which they must overcome somehow. Their incomes are relatively inadequate, irregular, and uncertain. Their expenditures must be concentrated on the necessities, with little left for discretionary spending, which most families regard as pleasurable. Unfortunately, many members of this group spend with abandon when they have money. By doing so, they deny themselves and their dependents many of the basic necessities of life until the next payday. Budgeting for them should make money available to buy at sales and to buy things that last longer and provide more satisfaction in the long run. Low-income families usually find budgeting and saving quite difficult, yet they must overcome these problems if they hope to rise in the social and economic scale.[16]

Budgeting of Low, Regular Incomes. The hand-to-mouth pattern of spending which accompanies weekly paydays provides a very real challenge to financial planning for most families. It seems so obvious that living from payday to payday is all that this situation requires. Unfortunately, many persons in this category so frequently fall short of this simple goal that there are scores of jokes about people who borrow from other people just before payday.

Quite often the weekly paycheck entails budgeting on a cash basis. A checking account seems unnecessary when another paycheck can be cashed in just a few days. This, in turn, presents another hazard. Cash rattling in one's pocket is an invitation to impulse spending. The tavern keeper, for example, knows that his sales will increase significantly on payday if he provides a check-cashing service. For this same reason many a wife has learned that she had better ask her husband for money for the new hat or beauty treatment on payday. As a consequence of this human frailty, too much of each paycheck is likely to be spent unwisely on the day of receipt, leaving too little for the rest of the week. This constitutes poor budgeting and inefficient spending on both the first and last days of the week, since many things which would be bargains late in the week must be postponed or foregone because of the payday-spending spree.

The employee who is paid every week finds weekly budgeting so simple that he is likely to spend each paycheck with little or no provision for long-range expenditures unless these are made on a costly weekly payment plan. Obviously, the remedy for this weakness of week-to-week budgeting is to introduce a savings element into each week's budget to accumulate sums for expenditures that cannot be financed out of current income.

The Wall Street Journal reported several details about the living expenses of a $90-a-week Levittown, Pennsylvania, metal worker named Tony who with his family regarded themselves as ". . . quite spendthrift, in a conscious sort of way."[17] This family's "voracious" buying proclivities led them to purchase an 8-cubic-foot freezer, which was used extensively for storing out-of-season fruits and vegetables at a carefully calculated cost of $8.29 a month. A new ranch-style tract home was scheduled to cost $68 a month for 29 years. The family has paid $500 down on the house instead of buying a new Lincoln automobile on which they could have had an attractive overallowance on their three-year-old Hudson. Tony carries $15,000 of life insurance and has little savings, so there are months when a new car battery or some similar purchase must come from overtime pay, or a financial crisis arises.

Budgeting of Irregular Incomes. The hourly worker's budgeting problem is complicated by the frequent periods of unemployment and discontinued or reduced income. Somehow, funds must be found for expenditure during the lean periods. Fortunately, for persons in this category, unemployment insurance, severance pay, and union welfare funds are available in many cases. The existence of these funds points to the inability of their recipients to save voluntarily for these purposes. However, if personal savings could be added to these built-in benefits, periods of unemployment might be converted into vacations or into opportunities for self-advancement. There is evidence that a few workers are making this adjustment in their money-management programs.

An assembly line worker in Detroit may save for the unemployment that comes every year at the time of the model changeover, or he may exist on borrowed money and unemployment benefits. If he borrows each summer to meet this emergency, his gross annual wage is reduced by the carrying charge he must pay on the loan. Moreover, his loan payments constitute a lien on his income throughout the winter months. The substitution of a savings plan in place of a loan would add a few dollars of interest to his gross income and provide the worker with some degree of financial security for this and other emergencies. If a worker anticipates one month of unemployment, for example, he should budget 11/12 of his income for living expenses each month and save 1/12 of each paycheck for the period of unemployment. A savings plan for this purpose should be subject to withdrawal without loss of interest when the emergency arises. This year-round budgeting arrangement should replace the financial crisis that otherwise would occur during each period of unemployment.

Budgeting for Relative Necessities. The average American family spends 24– per cent of its income on food. Those in the lower-income brackets spend more than this percentage, especially if the families are large and active. Expenditures for other so-called necessities demonstrate a similar ratio in which little of the poor man's money is left for discretionary spending. This fact, usually known as Engel's Law,* provides many poor persons with an excuse for their failure to budget, since they are inclined to regard nearly everything they buy as necessary anyway. In a primitive society, this would be true, but in our highly productive economy the poorest people enjoy some luxuries. In these circumstances the concept of necessity is relative to the customs and habits of the people. By some standards and by some comparisons, even the poorest Americans have many areas of choice. Budgeting may encourage the application of wisdom in the making of these choices.

Aside from the need for providing funds for the real necessities of life, most low-income families need to earmark more dollars for medical care, insurance, retirement, and savings for the purchase of "big-ticket" items. Once the true list of needs has been determined, budgeting may begin by dividing income among all the items on the list.

Budgeting for Middle-Income Families

There are probably over 100 million Americans living on middle-bracket incomes. These incomes, ranging from $5,000 to $10,000 a year at 1967 prices, supply their recipients with funds for life's necessities and with more for

* See Chapter 1, pp. 15–17.

Budgeting at Different Income Levels

discretionary spending.[18] It is the discretionary spending that requires deliberate decision making or, to put it another way, budgeting.

Budgets are more necessary for middle-income families than might be supposed because of the temptation to stretch their level of living. This tendency is admirable in many respects, but it is achieved sometimes by neglecting savings, insurance coverage, and provision for emergencies. Families in this income group usually spend enough on consumer durable goods such as cars, furniture, or appliances, but generally do not budget for these things; instead, they use installment credit.

The urge to acquire goods and services is so strong among middle-income families that they have difficulty in accumulating sufficient savings to carry themselves through adversity or into retirement. Unfortunately, there is much to be learned about personal savings and the habits of savers. Consumers usually consider their spending for long-lasting items as a form of savings, but the Department of Commerce data on savings do not recognize this distinction.[19]

Middle-income families save temporarily in order to buy cars, make down payments on houses, or start small businesses. Until their families are raised and married, this group for the most part saves little for investment. Under these circumstances, budgeting is usually limited to the collection of funds for the various expenditures, a moderate amount of insurance, and modest savings that are subject to frequent withdrawal.[20]

The range of acceptable percentage variations for ten major categories in a budget for a family of four persons may be seen in Table 2-2. This also illustrates how Americans shift their proportions of income devoted to spending and savings as their incomes increase. Several other studies have reported data that are substantially the same.[21] A budget for a family of four with an income of $6,500 a year whose expenditures were typical in 1961 is shown in Table 2-3.

Budgeting for High-Income Families

High incomes are increasingly common nowadays. The relatively rare $10,000-a-year man of a few years ago might be nearly anyone's neighbor now. The $25,000- and $50,000-a-year men who ride commuter trains live in substantial but unimpressive homes in the suburbs. In fact, nearly anyone with an income above $1,000-a-month may have a new rambling home, a swimming pool, two cars, and other accoutrements of the good life as it is lived in America. Who, then, are the rich? Do they have to budget? How can high-income individuals be distinguished from their less fortunate brethren?

People with high incomes often are prudent individuals. They expect to

Table 2-3. Budget for a Family of Four with an Income of $6,500 a year

Item	Amount Spent per Year	Percentage	Amount Spent per Month
Food	$1,378.00	21.2	$114.83
Clothing	644.00	9.9	53.66
Housing	1,748.50	26.9	145.66
Automobile	273.00	4.2	22.75
Gasoline, tires, repairs	416.00	6.4	34.66
Medical care	442.00	6.8	36.83
Recreation	396.50	6.1	33.04
Interest on debt, legal fees, etc.	429.00	6.6	35.75
Religion, education, and donations	195.00	3.0	16.25
Personal care	110.50	1.7	9.21
Tobacco, liquor	338.00	5.2	28.17
Public transportation, foreign travel, etc.	130.00	2.0	10.83
Total	$6,500.00	100.0	$541.64

NOTE: Percentages are the estimated proportion of total expenditures spent on that category of purchases in the United States in 1961. There is no reason why any particular family should spend exactly this percentage or this amount.

SOURCE FOR PERCENTAGES: *U. S. News & World Report*, December 18, 1961, p. 65. Copyright, 1961.

save some of their incomes; they budget persistently. With saving as a reasonably obtainable goal, budgeting would seem to be simple, but intense desires for high-priced goods frequently neutralize this presumed advantage.

Discriminating Tastes. People with ample incomes are likely to acquire a taste for distinctive flavors and designs. They are likely to prefer their steaks medium rare, their wines of a certain vintage, and their clothes from a reputable tailor or designer. Their discriminating tastes also extend to differences in certain patterns of silverware, china, and furniture. Those who join the cult of the discriminating shopper are constantly on the prowl for *objets d'art* or other evidences of their ability to discover and choose. The homes of many of these people exude an atmosphere that has been captured by a generous expenditure of money coupled with endless attention to minute details.

Examples of High-Income Expenditure Patterns. The Wall Street Journal reported several details about the expenditure patterns of two high-income families.[22] The first family included a 32-year-old physician whose income ranged around $25,000 a year. The family spent $200 a year for country-club dues, $300 to $400 for an annual vacation, and $20 a week for a cook. They owned a $28,000 home subject to a $17,000 mortgage to be amortized in 18 years. Investments were valued at $5,000 or more, but most of this and part of the equity in the house had come from inheritances. The physician carried $70,000 of life insurance but feared the possibility of a disabling illness or a premature termination of his career because he had no retirement pension of any sort.

The other family, an aging Boston family, had received $91,000 the previous year—$53,000 after federal taxes. It kept a town house and a place on Cape Cod for summer living and for projected retirement. Housing costs of $15,060 comprised interest and amortization—$3,000; taxes, etc.—$1,400; repairs and improvements—$3,200; additional land—$1,000; hurricane loss—$1,600; new furniture—$1,040; new appliances—$590; heat—$670; electricity—$360; gardener—$1,170; and cleaning woman—$1,030. This home-oriented family owed no one a cent except for its real estate mortgages. Its one admitted luxury was its habit of trading in the family Cadillac for a new one each year. Last year the car cost $440 for maintenance in addition to the $1,400 "difference money" spent at the time of the trade. The family's food bill was $2,650 last year and its laundry bill at the summer home was $245. Investments and other assets were estimated at $260,000 and liabilities totaled $75,700, leaving a net worth of $184,300.

Prudent Spending. High incomes may be the cause or the result of good financial management. The man who owns a business may be experienced in making exacting value judgments and maximizing benefits per unit of cost.

Some middle-level or upper-level executives in large firms find that promotions depend on large expenditures for homes, cars, and entertainment. In this case, frequent promotions accompanied by transfers from one company office to another may prevent the accumulation of household and other assets that constitute a form of savings.[23] On the other hand, rising executives in large companies are frequently the recipients of company pensions, profit-sharing agreements, and other forms of built-in savings.[24]

Saving. Most high-income families save, and most of the saving is done by persons in high-income or upper-middle-income brackets. In 1959, for example, the Securities and Exchange Commission estimated that the accumulated savings of individuals in the United States aggregated about $775 billion.[25] A very large proportion of all personal saving is done by those with high incomes who are able to save their *marginal dollars*—that is, the extra dollars in each increase of income. The fact that the highest-income group is composed frequently of older, established families may explain their determination and ability to save.

Chapter 4 will delve further into the subject of saving and savings institutions after credit and credit facilities have been surveyed in the next chapter.

QUESTIONS

1. What is the relationship between wants, needs, and the availability of goods and services? Why is budgeting necessary?
2. Trace the shifting and evolution of the wants and needs of (1) young, (2) middle-aged, and (3) aged married couples. Could financial crises be avoided at each of these stages by foresight and budgeting?
3. How should wants be examined to see which should be converted into purchasing decisions?
4. How effective is budgeting as practiced by low-, middle-, and high-income families?
5. What are the consequences of poor budgeting and excessive indebtedness?
6. What are the two basic objectives of a good budget?
7. Describe step by step the method for setting up a budget plan.
8. How and under what circumstances should a budget item or an entire budget be revised?
9. What are the special budgeting problems of low-income families?
10. What are the special budgeting problems of middle-income families?
11. What are the budget objectives and budget problems of high-income families?
12. Note carefully all of the key terms in this chapter and be prepared to define each of them in your own terms.
13. How does one maximize the utility to be obtained from one's expenditures?
14. What is the definition of "permanent income?"

SELECTED READINGS

Burkhart, Roy A., Carl F. Hauver, and James A. Peterson, *Money and Your Marriage*, National Consumer Finance Association, Washington, D. C., 1963.

Consumer Expenditures Study, U. S. Bureau of Labor Statistics and the Wharton School, University of Pennsylvania Press, Philadelphia, 1956, 1957, 1958, 19 vols.

The Family Financial Planner, The Prudential Insurance Company of America, Newark, N. J., 1964.

The Family Money Manager, Institute of Life Insurance, New York, 1959.

Fitzsimmons, Cleo, *Consumer Buying for Better Living*, Wiley, New York, 1961.

"How Other People Spend Their Money," "How to Design a Budget for Your Family," "Family Records: What to Keep," "Money Management at Your House," *Changing Times*, March, 1960, for the American Association of University Women.

Money Management—Your Budget, Household Finance Corp., Prudential Plaza, Chicago 1, Ill., current. Other booklets in this series may also be of interest. Copies may be obtained at nominal cost.

Personal Money Management, American Bankers Association, New York, 1962.

NOTES

1. Sidonie Gruenberg and Benjamin C. Gruenberg, *Parents, Children and Money*, Viking Press, New York, 1933.
2. August B. Hollingshead, *Elmtown's Youth: The Impact of Social Classes on Adolescents*, Wiley, New York, 1949; Paul H. Landis, *Understanding Teen-Agers*, Appleton-Century-Crofts, New York, 1955; and "The Exploding Youth Market," *Printer's Ink*, July 29, 1960, pp. 20–25.
3. *1965 Survey of Consumer Finances*, Survey Research Center, University of Michigan, 1966, pp. 94 and 95.
4. U. S. Department of Labor, Bureau of Labor Statistics, *Consumer Expenditures and Income*, Total United States, Urban and Rural, 1960–1961, pp. 2 and 13.
5. Frances Lomas Feldman, *The Family in a Money World*, Family Service Association, New York, 1957, pp. 24–36; Paul C. Glick, "The Life Cycle of the Family," *Marriage and Family Living*, February 1955, pp. 3–9.
6. *Catholic Digest*, April 1960, p. 39.
7. Herman P. Miller, *Income of the American People*, Wiley, New York, 1955, pp. 69–71.
8. Thorstein Veblen, *The Theory of the Leisure Class*, Macmillan, New York, 1899.
9. Among the most reliable sources of information on consumer goods and services are *Consumer Reports* published monthly by Consumers Union, Mount Vernon, N. Y., the *Consumers Research Bulletin* published monthly by Consumers Research, Washington, N. J., and *Consumers All*, The Yearbook of Agriculture, 1965, obtainable from the Government Printing Office, Washington, D. C., 20402.
10. George Katona, *Psychological Analysis of Economic Behavior*, McGraw-Hill, New York, 1951, p. 67.
11. Charles Neal, Jr., "Bankrupt Debtors Increase," *Des Moines Register and Tribune* Service release, November 20, 1960. See also Helen Arnold, "We Went Bankrupt on the Installment Plan," *Reader's Digest*, January 1961, pp. 30–35; Hillel Black, *Buy Now, Pay Later*, Morrow, New York, 1961.
12. Bud R. Hutchinson, "A Study of Debt Adjustment in Michigan," unpublished doctoral dissertation, University of Southern California, Los Angeles, 1959.
13. E. Bryant Phillips, *Consumer Economic Problems*, Holt, New York, 1957, pp. 42, 43.
14. William H. Whyte, Jr., "Budgetism: Opiate of the Middle Class," *Fortune*, May 1956, p. 172.
15. Household Finance Corporation, Prudential Plaza, Chicago, Ill.
16. A description of some of the difficulties encountered by low-income families Caplowitz, The Free Press of Glencoe, New York, 1963. attempting to maximize satisfaction are found in *The Poor Pay More*, David
17. *Family Fortunes*, reprinted from *The Wall Street Journal*, August 8, 1955.
18. Emily H. Huntington, *Spending of Middle-Income Families*, University of California Press, Berkeley, 1957, p. 12.
19. "Who Spends, Who Saves, Why?" *Business Week*, April 18, 1959, p. 138; See also U. S. Bureau of Labor Statistics and the Wharton School, *Survey of Consumer Finances*, University of Pennsylvania Press, Philadelphia, 1950, 18 vols.

20. "Living on $6,000 a Year," *Changing Times*, February 1959, pp. 8–13; "Quit Kidding Yourself about Your Finances," *Changing Times*, January 1959, pp. 7–13.
21. U. S. Bureau of Labor Statistics and the Wharton School, *Consumer Expenditures, Income and Savings*, University of Pennsylvania Press, Philadelphia, 1956, 19 vols.; J. Frederick Dewhurst and Associates, *America's Needs and Resources*, The Twentieth Century Fund, New York, 1955, pp. 123–467.
22. *Family Fortunes*, reprinted from *The Wall Street Journal*, August 12, 1955 and August 18, 1955.
23. "For Americans Today—Money Is to Spend," *Business Week*, June 16, 1956; *Ibid.*, April 18, 1959, p. 138.
24. Three executive living patterns are described in "How They Live on $20,000 a Year," *Fortune*, December 1966, pp. 186–188, 270, 275–276.
25. *Statistical Series, Release No. 1670*, Securities and Exchange Commission, Washington, D. C., April 8, 1960, p. 1.

Appendix

If we express benefits received as so many *utils* or units of utility or satisfaction, we may ease the difficulty in maximizing. No one has ever been able to measure the amount of utils that any commodity affords in consumption, but it is commonly assumed that additional units of the same commodity will, after a certain point, yield decreasing amounts of satisfaction. This maxim may be recalled as "The law of diminishing marginal utility." Note from Table A-1 that *total* utility is maximized when 5 units are consumed.

Table A-1. **Individual Utility and Quantity Consumed**

Quantity	Total Utility (u)	Change in "Utils"	Change in Quantity	Marginal Utility (MU) Additional Utility Afforded by One More Unit
1	6	6	1	6
2	11	5	1	5
3	15	4	1	4
4	18	3	1	3
5	18	0	1	0
6	16	−2	1	−2

Beyond that our consumer encounters *disutility*. The sixth unit takes two utils or units of satisfaction away from his total utility. He may have overeaten or "had one too many."

Budgeting at Different Income Levels

Armed with knowledge of the marginal utility he will derive from goods, their prices, and the limited amount he can spend in one particular time period, our hypothetical consumer should maximize his purchases as shown in Table A-2.

Table A-2. **Optimum Allocation of Consumer Outlays**

Number of Units Bought	Commodity X (P = $1) MU	MU/$	Commodity Y (P = $2) MU	MU/$	Commodity Z (P = $5) MU	MU/$
1	9	9	22	11	30	6
2	8	8	20	10	25	5
3	7	7	18	9	20	4
4	6	6	16	8	15	3
5	5	5	12	6	10	2
6	4	4	6	3	5	1

	Order of Purchase	Utils Acquired with Purchase per Dollar	Total Utils Enjoyed	Amount Spent
(1)	Y	11	22	$2
(2)	Y	10	41	$4
(3)	Y	9	59	$6
(4)	X	9	68	$7
(5)	Y	8	84	$9
(6)	X	8	92	$10
(7)	X	7	99	$11
(8)	Y	6	111	$13
(9)	X	6	117	$14
(10)	Z	6	147	$19
(11)	X	5	152	$20

First, he should buy 3 units of Y, then one of X since it will yield the same number of utils per dollar of expenditure; then one each of X and Y which both yield 8 utils per dollar; after buying one more unit of X yielding 7 utils, he buys one X, one Y, and one Z. Each of these gives him 6 utils per dollar. Now he has only one dollar left. Either X, the food item, or Z, another square foot of apartment space, would afford him equal satisfaction per dollar spent. But he can enjoy another square foot of space only by renting another apartment for $5 more a month. There are no one-dollar increments in the price of apartment space. This is a *lumpy expenditure*. Having one dollar left, he spends it on X, food, in exchange for another 5 utils.

The formula for maximizing total utility from any given outlay of consumer funds is to allocate expenditures so that

$$\frac{\text{Marginal utility}}{\text{Price of commodity}} \quad \frac{MU_x}{P_x} = \frac{MU_y}{P_y} = \ldots = \frac{MU_n}{P_n}*$$

insofar as possible. The marginal utility of goods or services should be kept as nearly proportional to their prices as possible. As many utils per dollar as possible should be acquired. If Y costs twice as much as X, the utility of the last purchased unit of Y should be about twice as great as that of X.

Approaching a close equality among these ratios is admittedly difficult. It is virtually impossible to make an accurate prediction of utilities to be afforded by various commodities before they have been purchased. But knowing where to find information about merchandise and where to find better values will help to accomplish this maximization.[9]

PROBLEMS AND CASES

1. Compile a record of your expenditures for the month. How do the percentages you spend on each category compare with the percentages shown in Tables 2-2 and 2-3? Do you think you would be happier if you changed the percentages spent on any of the categories of expenditures shown in your budget? If so, prepare the budget you would rather follow next month. If the budget is prepared early enough in the semester, compile a record of expenditures for the second month and compare it with your budget. How well did you conform to your budget? In view of your experiences, make required changes in the budget.
2. Compile a record of expenditures for a family for one month, preferably your own family. How do the percentages expended on each category compare with the percentages shown in Tables 2-2 and 2-3? Do you think this family would be happier if it changed its pattern of expenditure? Why? Prepare a suggested budget for this family that you think would make it happier in the long run in view of its objectives. Justify the percentage change that you recommended.
3. Dennis and Virginia are newly married. Their assets consist of two automobiles, a Volkswagen and an MG, both five years old, their clothing, accessories, and such personal effects as their watches and rings, second-hand television set, and about two dozen wedding presents (china, silver, glasses, linens) worth perhaps $150. They live in a furnished apartment. Prepare their balance sheet. Use market value for assets. (Used clothing and personal effects have little or no market value.) Follow the form in Figure 2-2.
4. Two years later they have $560 in a checking account, only one automobile, the Volkswagen, a like amount of clothing and personal effects, and household

* n refers to the nth or last commodity considered.

Budgeting at Different Income Levels

furnishings, appliances, and accessories with a market value of $1,200. They owe $900 on installment contracts for the household effects. Prepare a balance sheet as of this date. Have they progressed or regressed financially during the two years?

5. Prepare a budget for the first year of their marriage assuming their joint income —all from salaries—to be $9,000 for the year after personal income taxes have been paid. Use the categories and percentages from the latest Survey of Consumer Expenditures and Income for Husband-Wife families. Refer to: U. S. Department of Labor, Bureau of Labor Statistics, *Consumer Expenditures and Income, Urban United States, 1960–61*, Government Printing Office, Washington, D. C., 1964.

6. Revise the budget in Question 3 to reflect shifts that might have been made when they moved to an unfurnished apartment (larger, same rent) and bought the furniture, appliances, and accessories that obligated them to pay $75 a month for 24 months.

7. Revise the budget in Question 4 to accommodate the shifts that might have been made when their first child was born. Their total income was now Dennis' salary which was $6,000 a year after income taxes. (Premiums for "health insurance" are paid monthly—the additional costs for medical care were $50.) The applicable percentages are now in the column Husband-Wife family with oldest child under 6 years.

8. Dennis, some years later, earns $12,500 a year after income taxes. They have two children. They have bought a house and additional appliances and furnishings. They own two cars. Payments on the mortgage are $132 a month. Payments on the installment contracts on the furnishings are $40 a month. Payments on the car that is not yet paid for are $116 a month. Percentages in Table 2-2 may be used.

9. Refer to your own budget. Figure out the percentage spent in each of the Bureau of Labor Statistics' categories. How do you compare with the national average for persons of your educational level? Your type of family? Your income level? People living in areas like your own?

PART II

CREDIT, SAVING, AND INVESTMENT

3 CREDIT AND CREDIT FACILITIES

Remember when people worried about how much it took to buy something, instead of how long?

READER'S DIGEST

Millions of people are buying goods and services on credit. Additional millions borrow from assorted credit institutions in order to pay cash for merchandise that is available at discount prices. Two-thirds of all Americans use credit in one or more of its many forms. During the last 40 years merchandise has been produced and sold to millions of people who lacked the ability to pay cash. Were it not for the wide use of consumer credit, automobile and appliance sales would decline appreciably. In fact, some credit advocates contend that without consumer credit America's high-level prosperity would be replaced by unemployment and underconsumption.

Occasionally, someone decries the trend toward increasing credit usage. We hear that credit is costly, that it corrupts its users, and that it unstabilizes business by borrowing sales from the future. If these charges are valid, the increasing reliance on personal credit constitutes an example of irrational and imprudent behavior by credit users. This chapter may shed some light on these accusations and the counterclaims of those who rise to the defense of personal credit.

In examining this controversial subject, we shall first give attention to the nature and extent of credit usage and to the probability of its increased employment. Next, we shall explore a number of credit-granting institutions, with emphasis on the terms and type of transaction that characterize each. Finally, we shall consider the prudent use of personal credit, and examine its effect on family finances and the business cycle.

THE NATURE OF PERSONAL CREDIT

Good credit is as valuable as a good name; it should be cultivated and protected. Credit is not something that is extended by a friendly lender; it inheres in the borrower and is exemplified by his integrity and earning ability. An individual establishes a reputation for dependability and honesty by the way in which he allocates earnings toward debt settlement, by earning adequate sums for debt repayment, or by limiting his indebtedness to amounts he can retire easily. Credit grantors review an applicant's record by holding a personal interview and by checking his past performance as recorded in the files of a credit bureau.

Since credit is an important asset, it is imperative for individuals to accumulate a number of excellent credit references. In fact, a person who normally pays in cash might be wise to charge something once in a while and establish a favorable credit rating by paying the bill upon receipt.

Increasing Use of Personal Credit

Americans *en masse* are proverbially in debt, and the payment of this debt holds a prior claim over their future expenditures. The total amount of personal indebtedness—*consumer credit*—and the rate of its growth alarms certain experts who advocate a closer link between personal income and expenditures.

Borrowing by individuals is extensive. The outstanding balance of this debt hovers around $96 billion, exclusive of $236 billion of mortgages against dwellings. This personal indebtedness affects the budgeting and expenditures of more than two out of every three American families. The expenditures related to this indebtedness are suggested by Table 3-1, which designates types of credit and amounts outstanding at the beginning of 1967.

Table 3-1 shows that nearly one-third of all consumer credit has been used

Table 3-1. Consumer Credit, January 1968 (Total Credit, in Millions of Dollars)

		Instalment					Noninstalment			
End of Period	Total	Total	Automobile Paper	Other Consumer Goods Paper	Repair and Modernization Loans[a]	Personal Loans	Total	Single-Payment Loans	Charge Accounts	Service Credit
1939	7,222	4,503	1,497	1,620	298	1,088	2,719	787	1,414	518
1941	9,172	6,085	2,458	1,929	376	1,322	3,087	845	1,645	597
1945	5,665	2,462	455	816	182	1,009	3,203	746	1,612	845
1960	56,028	42,832	17,688	11,525	3,139	10,480	13,196	4,507	5,329	3,360
1961	57,678	43,527	17,223	11,857	3,191	11,256	14,151	5,136	5,324	3,691
1962	63,164	48,034	19,540	12,605	3,246	12,643	15,130	5,456	5,684	3,990
1963	70,461	54,158	22,433	13,856	3,405	14,464	16,303	6,117	5,871	4,315
1964	78,442	60,548	25,195	15,593	3,532	16,228	17,894	6,954	6,300	4,640
1965	87,884	68,565	28,843	17,693	3,675	18,354	19,319	7,682	6,746	4,891
1966	94,786	74,656	30,961	19,834	3,751	20,110	20,130	7,844	7,144	5,142
1966										
November	92,498	73,491	30,937	18,945	3,772	19,837	19,007	7,807	6,199	5,001
December	94,786	74,656	30,961	19,834	3,751	20,110	20,130	7,844	7,144	5,142
1967										
January	93,479	74,015	30,689	19,649	3,703	19,974	19,464	7,779	6,472	5,213
February	92,517	73,598	30,530	19,426	3,666	19,976	18,919	7,754	5,824	5,341
March	92,519	73,591	30,527	19,369	3,648	20,047	18,928	7,769	5,809	5,350
April	93,089	73,840	30,635	19,376	3,636	20,193	19,249	7,890	5,923	5,436
May	93,917	74,290	30,852	19,442	3,670	20,326	19,627	8,017	6,231	5,379
June	94,813	75,051	31,208	19,580	3,696	20,567	19,762	8,077	6,334	5,351
July	95,115	75,348	31,364	19,607	3,711	20,666	19,767	8,100	6,346	5,321
August	95,684	75,889	31,455	19,755	3,743	20,936	19,795	8,136	6,368	5,291
September	95,886	76,039	31,296	19,914	3,742	21,087	19,847	8,179	6,387	5,281
October	96,094	76,223	31,237	20,042	3,746	21,198	19,871	8,189	6,471	5,211
November	96,802	76,680	31,217	20,340	3,748	21,375	20,122	8,237	6,614	5,271

[a] Holdings of financial institutions; holdings of retail outlets are included in "other consumer goods paper."

NOTE: Consumer credit estimates cover loans to individuals for household, family, and other personal expenditures, except real estate mortgage loans. For back figures and description of the data, see "Consumer Credit," Section 16 (New) of Supplement to Banking and Monetary Statistics, 1965, and May 1966 Federal Reserve Bulletin.

in the purchase of automobiles, more than 20 per cent for appliances and furniture, and a similar amount for personal installment loans that really represent heavy expenditures for cars and appliances. The remaining columns in the table pertain to other reasonably obvious forms of personal indebtedness. Some of these will be considered later in this chapter.

The increasing use of consumer credit disturbs those who dislike the use of borrowed money for the purchase of nonessential items.[1] The 25 per cent increase in the outstanding balance of credit extended on automobile purchases between 1963 and 1967 and the 40 per cent increase in personal loans during the same prosperous years suggest that credit is not being employed merely to acquire the necessities of life. Men and women utilize personal credit for an increasing array of products and services including cameras, dentures, and overseas trips. Many merchants, by promoting teenage credit, may be involving a new generation prematurely in the use of credit. One witness before a congressional subcommittee, Earl B. Schwulst, chairman of New York's Bowery Savings Bank, stated that "I think this [teenage credit] is something like teaching the young to use narcotics—I think it is very bad, very bad indeed." At the same hearing, A. Leonidas Trotta of the National Retail Merchants Association countered that "We're in a credit economy now, and the sooner these kids know how to handle credit, the better off they'll be."[2]

Types of Personal Credit

Personal credit may be divided into several types. These may be discussed more thoroughly when dealt with separately, even though they overlap in some respects. Nearly everyone avails himself of the *convenience credit* opportunities that most department stores and oil companies offer in the form of 30-day charge accounts. Some people use cash loans to even out the highs and lows in the flow of their spending. They also use them for emergency borrowing or to refinance previous overspending. Many turn to sales financing for the purchase of new cars, furniture, and household appliances. These and other variations of personal credit will be explored in the pages that follow. Housing finance will be discussed in Chapter 9, since it is not customarily included in the subject of personal credit.

Retail Sales Credit

Many retail stores offer convenience credit in the 30-day charge account or one of the other retail sales credit arrangements described in this section.

Thirty-Day Charge Accounts. Department stores and many other retail stores commonly offer charge accounts to customers who can qualify for this

The Nature of Personal Credit

form of credit. The customer promises to pay in full for each month's purchases within 30 days after the purchase in some stores, or within 30 days after the billing date in others. No carrying charge is levied, although the prices set for merchandise and services usually include the cost of extending this form of credit. Retailers have found that they can sell more merchandise to a customer who feels free to use credit to buy sooner or to buy more than on a cash basis.

Retailers often estimate that the credit will justify its cost through added sales to loyal customers. These customers become locked-in financially once they get into a *credit rhythm* in which each month's income is committed in part to payment of past obligations. Theoretically, when a number of competing retailers invite their clients to use credit, markets may become saturated and credit may become an added cost. The consequence is lower profits for the merchants or higher prices for the customers. Nevertheless, a customer who trades at one of these stores might as well use his charge account since he contributes to its support no matter how he pays for merchandise or services.

Many stores offer variations of their 30-day charge-account plans, but these plans involve installments and carrying charges. They will be discussed later under the heading of installment sales credit.

Limited-Purpose Credit Cards. Many merchants and most oil companies encourage their customers to use charga-plates or credit cards. These plastic or metal cards with raised letters identifying a customer and his account number are presented at the time of purchase. The customer's identification is impressed on a charge slip. Until recently, such cards were usable only for purchases from the issuing vendor, hence the term, limited-purpose credit card. Many large-scale merchants have used limited-purpose charga-plates or credit cards for years to facilitate the use of their 30-day charge accounts.

General-Purpose Credit Cards. Small-scale retailers cannot enjoy the advantages of centralized billing and other economies associated with an efficiently operated credit system. Besides, potential customers object to the need for overloading their billfolds with too many credit cards and chargaplates. For these reasons credit cards are issued now by national firms such as the leading petroleum companies; by specialized credit-card firms issuing the Diner's Club cards, Carte Blanche, or the American Express Company credit cards; and by banks such as the Bankamerica card, and others in Chicago and New York. The general acceptance of these credit cards permits the customer to buy for credit from a wide variety of retailers. Conversely, it permits hundreds of small retailers, restauranteurs, and motel operators to bid for the patronage of credit-prone customers. In fact, the use of credit cards has become so common that a cash payment may someday become the equivalent of a "poor man's credit card."

Slow Billing. Some merchants use easy credit as a promotional device designed to accommodate customers, clinch sales, and out-sell competitors. Retailers know that many a customer can be persuaded to buy by the lure of slow billing. Under this practice the sellor promises a delayed bill, or permits the postponement of payments for several months, or both. Sometimes a slow-billing merchant who has no other credit plan finds that his customers prefer a single, postponed payment with no carrying charge to the costly credit plans used by his competitors. Actually, the merchant sets his prices at levels that include the cost of the credit extended and the risks assumed with slow billing. The customers must consider the prices paid for slow-billed purchases in estimating the *hidden carrying charge* in these transactions. Customers must exercise caution, also, lest they be tempted to buy too much on credit extended in this manner. Merchants, on the other hand, must receive prompt payment on due dates; otherwise, slow billing could lead to financial chaos and eventual bankruptcy.

Installment Credit

Installment credit is distinguishable from other types of personal credit by the fact that it usually is *amortized*. It is gradually liquidated by making weekly or monthly payments, each of which includes interest and retirement of some of the remaining principal. This arrangement permits the debtor to meet his obligation with payments from current income. Creditors and debtors are reasonably secure if they arrange for payments that can be made comfortably each month and if the debtor does not enter into other obligations that create excessive total monthly payments.

Americans contract for approximately $85 billion of this form of indebtedness in a typical year and carry an outstanding balance of approximately $76 billion.[3] Let us consider several types of installment credit.

Revolving Credit. A customer may be invited to open a revolving credit or budget account. This permits him to charge purchases up to a specified limit with the privilege of charging additional purchases up to that limit again and again as the balance is reduced. The merchant may impose a schedule of expected monthly payments to reduce the balance or, in some plans, the customer may be permitted to carry his balance at the ceiling level continuously. In either case the customer pays a service or carrying charge of 1 per cent or 1.5 per cent each month on the unpaid balance. A plan of this sort permits many worthy families to manage the purchase of household furnishings and other big-ticket items that are so necessary in American homes today. Unfortunately, the plan is sometimes used unwisely by some customers who acquire excessive indebtedness which they do not feel compelled to retire.

Optional Credit. For the benefit of customers who wish to buy big-ticket items, many merchants permit those qualified to stretch their payments beyond the customary 30-day limit of a typical charge account. There are 60-day, 90-day, 120-day, six-month, nine-month, and 12-month optional credit plans. Under the six-month plan, the customer is expected to retire approximately one-sixth of the balance each month plus a service or carrying charge—again 1 per cent or 1.5 per cent a month—on the unpaid balance. If the customer retires the entire balance within the first 30 days, there is usually no carrying charge. Optional credit is actually a combination of a 30-day charge-account plan and a revolving-credit plan.

Installment Loans. Many people seek cash loans with installment plan repayments in order that they may forestall creditors, meet emergencies, or borrow to finance current purchases. These loans usually are negotiated with a local credit union, a bank, or a consumer finance company. A half-century ago, small-loan companies had no competition in this business. They lent to the needy who frequently met financial emergencies and doctor's bills by borrowing at high percentage rates. In the present generation, emergencies of this sort usually are covered by current expenditures implemented by private insurance, unemployment insurance, or other forms of social insurance. The small-loan companies are now extremely competitive, and the range of their rates is generally subject to government regulation.

Many installment cash loans nowadays are made for the purpose of purchasing additional items at discount prices. In some instances, the discounted price justifies the cost of the loan.

Debt Consolidation. Small cash loans and the financing of low-priced items are relatively unprofitable for lenders. If a borrower has other debts outstanding, he may be induced to borrow more cash. Or he may buy more merchandise in exchange for a new installment contract that will consolidate all his indebtedness into one big contract, which can be paid in a number of easy installments. In many cases the monthly payments on a consolidated debt may be less than they had been prior to the consolidation. This magic may be accomplished, however, only by increasing the total obligation and the carrying charge, and by rescheduling the payments over a longer period of time.

Debt consolidation represents the problem of trying to get out of a hole without making the hole any bigger.

There are a variety of cash-loan plans and percentage rates that will be dealt with in a subsequent section of this chapter.

Sales-Finance Credit. Many people are willing to sign for a series of installment payments in exchange for the immediate possession of their purchases. The temptation is great to drive a new car now and pay later. It is equally great to furnish that new home immediately in exchange for a signature or two on an easy-payment plan. Sales resistance usually is low when the customer is lured by new merchandise, a clever salesman, and an easy-credit plan.

Once a salesman has secured a customer's signature on the installment contract, the dealer is free to sell the contract to a bank or finance company. Some dealers make a few extra dollars by charging the customer the highest of several available percentage rates. The dealer knows that he can get more money from a finance company on a high-percentage rate contract if the customer has made a reasonable down payment or trade-in and if other aspects of the transaction are normal. Most customers do not bother to calculate the percentage rate; they assume that the term "ordinary rate" or "bank rate" implies that the rate is not excessive. For this reason several pages will be devoted later in this chapter to a section on the cost of personal credit.

TERMS OF THE CREDIT CONTRACT

A person who signs a credit agreement has no one but himself to blame if some of the fine-print clauses return to plague him later on. Thousands of credit users pay promptly. They have no occasion to know the legal meaning of the words in their purchase agreements and credit contracts. Nevertheless, it is shrewd to meditate on the obligations one is assuming and the penalties one will draw by failure to pay punctually.

Nearly every clause in a purchase agreement protects the seller, not the buyer; and nearly every clause in a credit agreement protects the lender, not the debtor. This arrangement may be necessary for the protection of sellers and lenders. Without it the increased risks would bring on higher prices and higher carrying charges. However, one might question the reasonableness of contract clauses that assist a vendor in collecting from a customer who has been oversold, or from a borrower who has been induced into borrowing beyond his ability to repay. Fortunately, these abuses are not universal and there is a rising social tide against their recurrence.

Installment Sales Agreements

When a customer pays in cash, he receives some sort of sales slip, receipt, or sales agreement. For durable goods, the sales agreement serves as a legal basis for transferring the title of the item purchased; usually it includes a vendor's warranty of quality. If the customer pays with a check, that fact is entered on the sales slip; if the check is not good, the vendor has several legal courses of action at his disposal. When a purchase involves the use of credit, the buyer cannot renounce the sale; he takes possession of the merchandise and pays taxes on it, but usually he does not hold title until all the payments have been completed.

Conditional Sales Contracts. Vendors' risks are sometimes great because their customers' purchases contain very little *owner equity* in the merchandise. There is little ownership because of low down payment or low trade-in allowance plus low monthly payments. A conditional sales contract offsets the buyer's lack of equity by permitting the seller to retain title to the merchandise until the last payment has been made. The seller, as legal owner, can repossess the merchandise with a minimum of legal expense. He may then resell it to recoup his investment. In most instances, the threat of repossession forces the immediate payment of an installment. Sometimes, if a finance company is involved, a debtor is invited to retain the merchandise, consolidate his debts, and reschedule his payments. In the few cases where repossession is necessary, the buyer is often protected by a state law that requires the return to him of the excess of the merchandise's resale value over legal fees, reasonable financing costs, and the debtor's previous payments.

In Pennsylvania, an equivalent device known as *a bailment lease* is often used. In this agreement, the customer legally leases or rents the purchased item until the final payment is made. Then he receives title for a small fee, which most vendors do not require.

Chattel Mortgages. If the buyer's equity is likely to be very small in a purchase, he may be asked to protect the seller's interest in it by giving him a chattel mortgage on some other possession or possessions that the buyer owns outright. For example, the purchase of a second-hand car with a very small down payment and no trade-in might require the use of a chattel mortgage on the buyer's household furniture in addition to a conditional sales agreement on the car. In this case, the buyer might lose his car *and* his furniture if he failed to make his monthly payments on the car. More than likely, however, the finance company would reschedule the overdue payments at some additional financing charge. It does not really want used cars, used furniture, and the ill will that is associated with repossession proceedings.

Acceleration Clause. If one of the customer's payments is delinquent, an acceleration clause makes all remaining payments due immediately. This clause creates an impossible situation for the purchaser who cannot meet his obligations. An acceleration clause strengthens the position of the creditor. It enables him to use it as a threat to collect at once or to substitute a new schedule of payments including an increase in the total finance charges.

Add-On Clause. Some installment purchase contracts contain add-on clauses. Such clauses specify that an entire series of purchases is subject to repossession if payments become delinquent on any one of the items. Thus, if a family buys a television set on payments and then buys a hi-fi set before all the payments are completed on the television set, both purchases could be subject to repossession because of delinquent payments on the hi-fi unit, even though all payments have been made on the television set.

Wage-Assignment Agreements. When a prospective borrower has nothing more than his job and his personal note to pledge, he may be asked to sign a wage-assignment agreement. This authorizes the taking of a portion of his wages for the satisfaction of a debt if payments become overdue. A wage-assignment clause may lead to a *wage attachment* or a *wage garnishment.* The creditor in such cases may execute a simple document and apply directly to the debtor's employer for periodic payments. In the absence of a wage-assignment agreement, wages may be garnished in some states by creditors who are willing to adhere to legal requirements in an effort to collect on delinquent installment payments. Employers frown on bothersome requests for wage garnishment and on those of their employees who make it necessary.

Cosigner Agreements. In some instances when there is a lack of collateral to pledge, a prospective debtor is asked to get the signature of a friend, relative, or other cosigner who will vouch for completion of the payments. A contract signed by the debtor and a cosigner is frequently known as *accommodation paper.* It is readily acceptable among financiers because of the superior security it provides. Unfortunately, a cosigner often finds himself in debt because of his friend's failure to meet his rightful obligations.

Additional Contract Provisions. An installment contract may appear to be attractive because it cites low monthly or weekly payments. Some states, however, permit a schedule of low payments to be followed by a final *balloon payment* which may be several times as large as each of the other payments. Many customers who buy under an illusion of low payments become disillusioned when they learn of a balloon payment long after their purchase. Frequently, the balloon payment is so high that costly refinancing becomes necessary.

Every installment contract should have a *prepayment clause* which will provide for a fair refund to a debtor who chooses to repay in advance of the final due date. The purchaser of an automobile, for example, might have a schedule of 30 monthly payments on a $2,000 contract including a $250 carrying charge. In case he decided to retire his last 12 payments ahead of schedule, a prepayment clause would guarantee a rate of return of perhaps 3 per cent on the prepaid sums. The debtor could not expect to save all the charges scheduled for his last 12 payments, however, because of the credit grantor's overhead costs including paper work and investigation costs. For lack of a prepayment agreement, many a borrower or purchaser would have no incentive for settling an account ahead of schedule.

THE COST OF CREDIT

Considering the previously mentioned contract provisions, which give assistance to creditors, one might presume that losses would be virtually nonexistent. Actually, losses are infrequent and accounts that have been classified as slow-paying have been about 1 per cent of all credit outstanding during the past decade. Why, then, it might be asked, must installment credit cost so much? One might ask, also, how much does credit usually cost and how can this cost be calculated?

Reasons for the High Costs

Some credit grantors, such as banks, extend credit in large amounts for most of their transactions. By contrast, many installment cash-loan and sales contracts involve small sums, frequent collections, and the necessity for credit investigations. It would not be inaccurate to say that banks and a few other financial institutions are mainly wholesalers of credit, whereas the credit institutions under consideration here extend credit on a retail basis. This difference is especially noticeable when a credit transaction involves frequent collections of small amounts over a short period of time. Actually, a credit grantor's overhead costs as a rule would justify a minimum service charge in addition to a normal interest rate. Since charges are not calculated on this basis, *the percentage rate must be highest when small sums are involved for short periods of time.*

As a generalization, the investigatory work in installment contracts or loans requires the use of costly credit information. Seldom is this information as available or as dependable as the Dun & Bradstreet reports consulted by the banker who is considering a large loan to a businessman. Local credit bureaus do serve credit grantors for a fee, but the information available on any credit applicant is dependent on the completeness and freshness of reports from all other credit grantors. A cautious credit grantor must subscribe to the credit bureau's services, pay an additional fee for a current report on the applicant's recent credit transactions, and then depend on an interview, a character judgment, and perhaps on his own intuition. This is time consuming and costly, of course. The success with which credit is extended to so many persons suggests that this function is being handled satisfactorily. Most people who seek credit are accommodated; most of the deadbeats are culled out; most of the credit grantors are reasonably prosperous.

Dollar Cost of a Credit Transaction

When a prospective seeker of credit subtracts the amount of his original indebtedness from the total number of dollars he must repay, the remainder represents the dollar cost of the credit transaction. The purchase of a $100 vacuum cleaner for 12 monthly payments of nine dollars each involves a total repayment of 12 x 9 or $108, hence the dollar cost of the transaction is eight dollars ($108 − $100 = $8). This eight-dollar cost may seem excessive unless one considers the credit grantor's investigation costs, collection costs, and paper-handling costs on this small transaction.

Two contrasting examples involving dollar costs of credit transactions may be worth noting. In the first example, a $50 power saw might be bought at a well-known mail-order house for six monthly payments of nine dollars each. In this case the four-dollar cost of the credit is primarily a service charge with nothing left for interest as that term is normally understood. By contrast, the financing of a new car costing $2,000—after trade-in allowance or down payment—for $66.66 a month for three years would cost the buyer approximately $400 in finance charges. In this instance, the credit grantor's overhead costs consume a small proportion of the actual cost of the loan. Consequently, his return on this transaction may be relatively high.

Calculating the Percentage Rate

A carrying charge or finance charge is the sum of money paid to the credit grantor over and above the price of the commodity purchased. The percentage rate is the proportion of the principal sum charged for the use of credit for a period of one year. In a *simple interest* problem, for example, the charge for the use of $100 for one year might be six dollars, or 6 per cent. If installment credit were used, however, the problem would become more complex.

The purchase of a $100 vacuum cleaner for 12 monthly payments of nine

The Cost of Credit

dollars each, for example, provides the credit grantor with eight dollars ($9 x 12 = $108 − $100 = $8). However, this eight-dollar carrying charge is not an 8 per cent charge because the $100 of credit is not used constantly throughout the entire year. Actually, the $100 is owed only during the first month. Thereafter, the debt is amortized with each monthly payment of interest and principal, leaving declining balances throughout the year. At the end of eleven months, only nine dollars principal and carrying charge is owed by the debtor. On the average, throughout the year, only a little more than half of the $100 actually is owed by the debtor. Thus the *annual percentage rate* would be nearly twice as much as the apparent 8 per cent rate. If a borrower paid eight dollars for the use of $50 a year, the annual percentage rate would be 16 per cent. In this case, however, the average amount owed throughout the year is a little more than $50; the actual rate thus is 14.7+ per cent when computed by the *constant-ratio formula* shown below.

This annual percentage rate, of course, is not really a true interest rate since it involves heavy overhead costs on a small transaction. Such costs are better covered by a service charge. Theoretically, *residual interest* might be a useful concept to identify any sums remaining after an appropriate service charge has been calculated and deducted from the total financing costs.

Whenever an installment credit transaction involves any period of time other than an even year, the problem becomes still more complicated. It must then be solved by the use of the following *constant-ratio formula* or by using one of the other formulas designed for the same purpose.[4]

$$R = \frac{2mD}{P(n+1)}$$

where

R = the simple interest rate or annual percentage rate
m = number of payments per year
D = dollar cost of the credit
P = principal sum involved
n = number of actual payments

Applying this formula to the example of the $50 power saw purchased for six monthly payments of nine dollars each, we solve the problem the following way:

$$R = \frac{2 \times 12 \times 4}{50(6+1)} = \frac{96}{350}, \quad \text{or} \quad R = 0.274+ \quad \text{or} \quad 27.4+\%$$

This 27.4+ per cent carrying charge, it should be remembered, is not a true interest charge. It includes heavy overhead costs which should be levied as a service charge against the four-dollar cost of the credit. If anything is left from that four dollars, it might be considered as a true interest charge—or as residual interest.

In financing a $2,000 automobile purchase after trade-in, for 36 monthly payments of $65.78 a month, the total interest charge would be $368.10 in a credit arrangement that has been characterized as average.[5] The annual percentage rate amounts to almost 12 per cent:

$$R = \frac{2mD}{P(n+1)} = \frac{2 \times 12 \times 368}{2000(36+1)} = \frac{8832}{74,000} = 0.119+, \quad \text{or} \quad 11.9+\%$$

This annual percentage rate includes some overhead costs, of course. Theoretically, however, this relatively low rate must be linked with the $368 financing costs in judging whether the immediate purchase of a car on these terms may yield more satisfaction to the owner than he might gain by spending this amount of money in some other way.

Summary of Percentage Rate Concepts

As noted, the value of percentage rates is doubtful in judging the fairness of credit costs. A credit grantor may collect too few dollars to cover his costs on a small transaction involving a short period of time, but the percentage rate on these contracts is invariably high, as we have seen. On the other hand, the financing of large sums and over long periods of time incurs proportionately smaller overhead costs that do not justify a relatively high annual percentage rate plus an appropriate service charge. The use of percentage rates as the single basis for evaluating credit terms of varying amounts and duration is indeed fallacious.

The passage of truth in lending acts by several states, prior to a federal act on the same subject in 1968, served a very useful purpose in emphasizing the precise terms and credit charges on installment contracts. The emphasis required by these laws, however, is invariably in terms of percentage rates, which do not account for all of the variables in the contract. Credit costs actually are two-dimensional. They should be judged by looking at the dollar costs and the annual percentage rate. A fair judgment should pertain to both an *appropriate service charge* and a justifiable annual percentage rate. If both costs are just and adequate, then, and only then, may the credit cost be considered fair and reasonable.

COMPARISON OF CREDIT INSTITUTIONS AND TERMS

A person who is about to finance a purchase with a cash loan or an installment contract will find a variety of credit institutions anxious to serve

Comparison of Credit Institutions and Terms 69

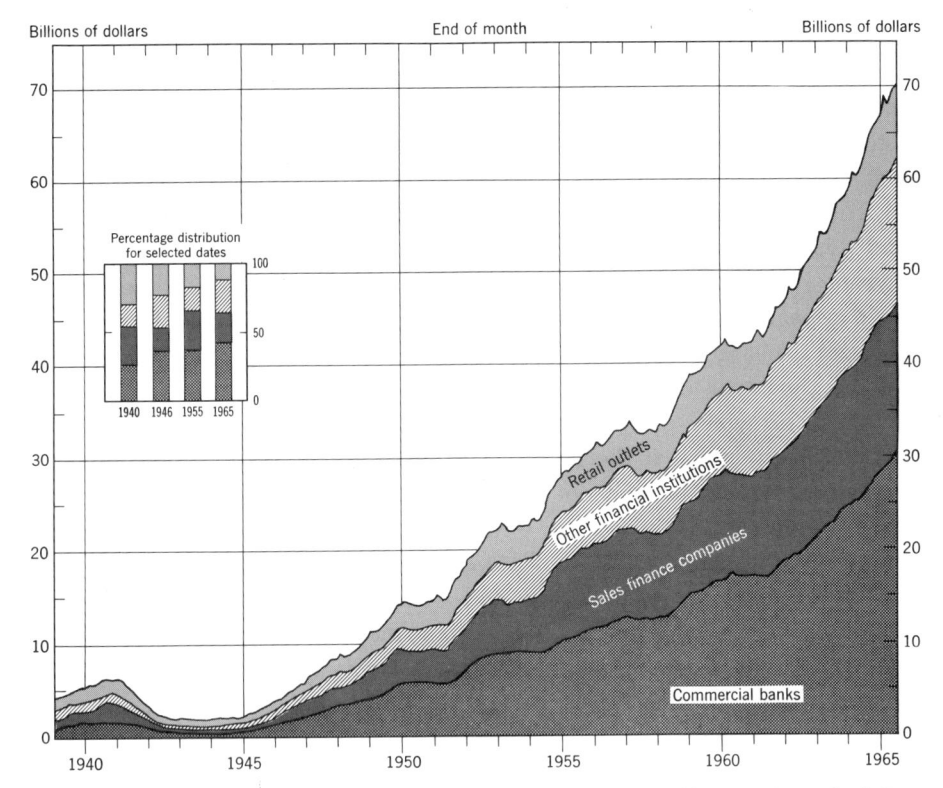

Figure 3-1. **Major holders of consumer installment credit.** (*Source.* Board of Governors Federal Reserve System, *Historical Chart Book*, 1966, p. 64.)

him. Credit grantors deal with a wide variety of customers. Their terms differ because of the credit worthiness of the applicants, the amount of their down payment or trade-in, and the amount of credit requested. In fact, credit grantors specialize: some deal with good credit risks and charge low rates, others deal with poor credit risks and charge high rates. It behooves the credit user, therefore, to examine his own credit worthiness and to shop around for the best terms available to him. To facilitate the search for favorable terms, this section examines credit institutions and the credit arrangements offered by each.

Credit Granted By Banks

Banks lend credit on favorable terms to customers who can qualify for their loans. Less qualified customers may use one of the bank's consumer-loan plans at higher rates.

Bank Loans. Persons who have excellent bank ratings and some collateral to pledge may consult with one of the bank's officers and arrange for a loan at relatively low-interest rates. *Single-payment loans* from banks may fall due within a year, but many banks renew loans regularly on receipt of a token repayment of the principal as quarterly interest payments become due. Customarily, interest is charged in advance by banks, so that a person borrowing at 6 per cent who wishes to have $985 added to his checking account must sign a note for $1,000 to allow for the advance deduction of the first three months' interest. This practice of *discounting a note* has been used by banks for years. It should be noted that a bank-discount note on which the interest charge appears to be 6 per cent actually is more than 6 per cent because the 6 per cent is charged against the face value of the loan, whereas the customer never has the use of this entire amount.

Most borrowers and creditors alike find a single-payment loan burdensome. The very fact that the borrower has had to contract the debt indicates the probability that he will not have enough money at any one moment to settle his indebtedness in a single payment. Conversely, creditors are insecure with this type of loan because they are not certain that the debtor can and will repay on the due date as promised. As a result of these uncertainties, interest rates in past years were notably higher than they would have been if debtors had been permitted to amortize their loans by remitting small sums periodically for the eventual repayment of their loans.

Small Loans from Banks. In recent years, banks have created consumer-loan departments that extend installment credit to persons whose primary qualification includes a steady job, a reasonably good credit rating, and a limited amount of collateral. Bankers have reasoned that since many people have been borrowing on installment contracts at rather high rates, a bank might make the loan and thereby attract credit users to its other banking services. In 1967, for example, banks held $33 billion of installment credit, which was nearly double that held by all sales-finance companies. Commercial banks also held $7 billion of noninstallment credit in 1967, a figure that had nearly doubled in seven years.[6]

Banks discount installment contracts by purchasing them at a portion of face value from furniture, automobile, and appliance dealers. Banks also deal directly with persons who wish to borrow cash for divers purposes. Borrowers may obtain cash from some banks or add to their checking accounts by signing personal notes and presenting evidence of steady employment. Sometimes a wage-assignment agreement may be required. Many banks make loans for the purchase of automobiles if the owner has at least one-third equity in the vehicle and rests the ownership title in the bank's name.

Consumer-loan rates charged by commercial banks usually fluctuate from 5 to 8 per cent. This means that although a 7 per cent percentage rate is applied to the face of the amount due each year on an installment contract, the more accurate figure is likely to approximate 12 per cent simple interest. A few New York banks once extended such loans to their best credit risks for rates as low as 4 or 5 per cent discount. Banks throughout the country have found consumer loans quite profitable, to judge from their rapid expansion of this portion of their business. In addition to the credit cards that many large banks currently issue, there are check-reserve accounts in which an overdrawn depositor may continue to write personal checks, with the understanding that the amount of the overdraft is subject to a charge of one or 1.5 per cent per month. The rapid expansion of this practice and the sending of unsolicited bank-credit cards through the mails is opposed by rival lenders and by persons who fear that it may induce a dangerous expansion of consumer indebtedness.

Consumer-Finance Companies

Basically, consumer-finance companies lend small cash sums that are repaid in installments. The largest of these companies are Household Finance Corporation, Beneficial Finance Company, and Seaboard Finance Company. There are a dozen smaller chains in the business and hundreds of independents. Fifty years ago, there were so many abuses in the small-loan business that the Russell Sage Foundation suggested a uniform small-loan law, which was adopted in three-fourths of the states and is being replaced by the Uniform Consumer Credit Code submitted to the legislatures of various states for adoption in 1968. This law has been known since 1948 as the Model Consumer Finance Act. The basic provisions that govern the policies and charges of consumer finance companies are as follows:

1. Lenders are subject to licensing and supervision by an agency of the state government.

2. No charges for loans are permitted except at percentage rates that are clearly specified in the state law.

3. All financing charges are levied on the unpaid balance only unless there is a specified legal minimum charge.

4. Percentage rates are limited in most states to 3 per cent a month on the first $300, to 21 per cent per year on the balance of the principal between $300 and $1,000; and to 15 per cent on the balance of the principal over $1,000.

5. Full disclosure of all of the loan's terms is required. Borrowers must be informed of actual financing charges and supplied with copies of all portions of the loan agreement.

6. Prepayment of the loan must be permitted and rewarded by an appropriate reduction of the carrying charges.

7. The ceiling limit on loans ranges from $500 to $5,000 in different states.

8. There are limitations on the sale of, or the charge for, credit insurance in some states.

9. Appropriate penalties for violations of the act are specified in the state legislation.[7]

Under the sliding scale of rates that consumer-finance companies charge, borrowers in most states pay a higher rate than to the loan department of a commercial bank. Nevertheless, some borrowers prefer the privacy, friendliness, and counseling provided by the consumer-finance company interviewers and officials.

Consumer-finance companies lend cash to be used for settlement of past commitments or for current purchases that seem imperative or inviting at the moment. Some officials of these companies remind potential borrowers that they may find a retailer's discounted prices for merchandise attractive. Borrowing from a consumer-finance company to take advantage of these prices may make a *shoppers' loan* economically advisable and justifiable.

The preference of a lender to increase the size of a loan suggests that the borrower's best interests may be endangered by the inadequate profit margins permitted on small loans for short periods of time. Many critics of high loan rates overlook the costs of servicing the smallest loans. Consumer-finance company officials are especially anxious to raise the low ceiling limits that some states have placed on their loans. These limits confine their activities to very small loans, which are relatively less profitable.

Unfortunately for the finance company officials, their business has been profitable enough to have attracted too many competitors. As a result, they have to undertake extensive and costly advertising, affect friendly smiles, assume some risks, and offer other accommodations. Actually, some lenders cannot gain enough loan volume—estimated at a minimum $250,000 outstanding—to offset their overhead costs and make a profit. An *imperfect market* exists because some lenders enter the business unwisely and tend to spoil the opportunities for others. From the borrower's standpoint, there is also an imperfect market for small loans. This results from ignorance of his own credit worthiness and his inability or unwillingness to shop for the best terms he can obtain.

Sales-Finance Companies

The major financiers of cars and appliances are the General Motors Acceptance Corporation (GMAC), Commercial Credit Corporation, CIT Financial Corporation, and the leading banks and credit unions. The total amounts of installment credit involved by each type of credit grantor may be seen in Table 3–2. It is obvious that a substantial portion of the outstanding $76.6

Table 3-2. Instalment Credit, in Millions of Dollars

End of Period	Total	Financial institutions Total	Commercial Banks	Sales Finance Companies	Credit Unions	Consumer Finance[a]	Other[a]	Total	Retail outlets Department Stores[b]	Furniture Stores	Appliance Stores	Automobile Dealers[c]	Other
1939	4,503	3,065	1,079	1,197	132		657	1,438	354	439	183	123	339
1941	6,085	4,480	1,726	1,797	198		759	1,605	320	496	206	188	395
1945	2,462	1,776	745	300	102		629	686	131	240	17	28	270
1960	42,832	37,218	16,672	11,472	3,923	3,670	1,481	5,615	2,414	1,107	333	359	1,402
1961	43,527	37,935	17,008	11,273	4,330	3,799	1,525	5,595	2,421	1,058	293	342	1,481
1962	48,034	41,782	19,005	12,194	4,902	4,131	1,550	6,252	3,013	1,073	294	345	1,527
1963	54,158	47,405	22,023	13,523	5,622	4,590	1,647	6,753	3,427	1,086	287	328	1,625
1964	60,548	53,141	25,094	14,762	6,458	5,078	1,749	7,407	3,922	1,152	286	370	1,677
1965	68,565	60,273	29,173	16,138	7,512	5,606	1,844	8,292	4,488	1,235	302	447	1,820
1966	74,656	65,565	32,155	16,936	8,549	6,014	1,911	9,091	n.a.	n.a.	n.a.	490	n.a.
1966 November	73,491	65,046	31,978	16,790	8,480	5,881	1,917	8,445	n.a.	n.a.	n.a.	490	n.a.
December	74,656	65,565	32,155	16,936	8,549	6,014	1,911	9,091	n.a.	n.a.	n.a.	490	n.a.
1967 January	74,015	65,162	32,033	16,814	8,443	5,969	1,903	8,853	n.a.	n.a.	n.a.	488	n.a.
February	73,598	64,966	31,967	16,696	8,429	5,965	1,909	8,632	n.a.	n.a.	n.a.	485	n.a.
March	73,591	65,006	32,068	16,593	8,485	5,951	1,909	8,585	n.a.	n.a.	n.a.	486	n.a.
April	73,840	65,298	32,299	16,590	8,561	5,951	1,897	8,542	n.a.	n.a.	n.a.	490	n.a.
May	74,290	65,733	32,560	16,615	8,665	5,947	1,946	8,557	n.a.	n.a.	n.a.	494	n.a.
June	75,051	66,452	32,966	16,721	8,826	5,995	1,944	8,599	n.a.	n.a.	n.a.	502	n.a.
July	75,348	66,781	33,235	16,747	8,864	6,009	1,926	8,567	n.a.	n.a.	n.a.	506	n.a.
August	75,889	67,273	33,536	16,755	8,991	6,036	1,955	8,616	n.a.	n.a.	n.a.	508	n.a.
September	76,039	67,376	33,637	16,701	9,026	6,067	1,945	8,663	n.a.	n.a.	n.a.	507	n.a.
October	76,223	67,513	33,723	16,698	9,054	6,086	1,952	8,710	n.a.	n.a.	n.a.	506	n.a.
November	76,680	67,763	33,819	16,722	9,113	6,138	1,971	8,917	n.a.	n.a.	n.a.	506	n.a.

[a] Consumer finance companies included with "other" financial institutions until 1950.
[b] Includes mail-order houses.
[c] Automobile paper only; other instalment credit held by automobile dealers is included with "other" retail outlets.
See also Note to Table 3-1.
SOURCE: *Federal Reserve Bulletin*, January 1968, p. A-47.

billion of all installment credit had been created in connection with sales financing and refinancing.

Economic Justification for Sales Financing. Most Americans would agree with the argument that automobiles, appliances, and furniture should be purchased out of income, not out of capital. For consumers with little income or capital this argument may not have much significance. Yet the thought of financing new acquisitions from income seems to represent a substantial achievement. The fact that the income has still to be earned does not deter many persons from indulging in the fantasy that installment purchases of durable goods can be amply justified on economic grounds. The justification must be made, if at all, by comparing the proposed use of the new acquisitions with the purposes that would have been served by other things that the same amount of money would have purchased. By American standards, purchases of durable goods represent a higher utilization of funds. In many other countries, the inflated value that Americans attribute to such goods would be subject to challenge.

Rates Charged for Sales Financing. The customer who is about to sign a sales-finance contract determines his own rates to some extent. He does so by establishing a good or a poor credit rating, by making a high or a low down payment, by being willing to make a large or a small monthly payment, and by shopping or failing to shop for the best credit terms he can acquire. Dealers sometimes induce a buyer to sign financing agreements for rates that are higher than justifiable and necessary, considering the credit worthiness of the buyer. Sales-finance companies frequently provide dealers with several rate cards, thus enabling them to charge the highest rate if the customer unprotestingly accepts it. In many instances, the dealer can sell, or discount, the customer's finance agreement to a sales-finance company for a higher price if the agreement is signed at the highest of several percentage rates. Sometimes, the dealer's advantage results from the low percentage rate he is permitted to pay to the sales-finance company for the financing of his own inventory of cars, appliances, or furniture.

The effect of different rates upon the customer's monthly payment may be observed from the examples in Table 3–3. An alert customer may save several dollars a month on his financing costs by making certain that he receives the lowest percentage rate applicable to the terms of his purchase agreement.

Each monthly payment listed in Table 3–3 includes many things. It covers a retirement of a portion of the indebtedness, a payment for *credit insurance,* which would retire the remaining payments in case of the debtor's premature

Comparison of Credit Institutions and Terms

Table 3-3. **Monthly Payments Versus Quoted Installment Financing Rates**

	\multicolumn{4}{c}{Monthly Payment (at Quoted Rate Below)}
Transaction	6 Per Cent	7 Per Cent	9 Per Cent	12 Per Cent
$ 500 for 12 months	$ 44.52	$ 44.94	$ 45.79	$ 47.06
$1,000 for 12 months	89.04	89.88	91.58	94.12
$2,000 for 12 months	178.08	179.79	183.16	188.24
$ 500 for 24 months	23.73	24.16	25.02	26.32
$1,000 for 24 months	47.46	48.32	50.05	52.64
$2,000 for 24 months	94.93	96.65	108.10	115.29
$4,000 for 24 months	189.86	193.30	—	—
$ 500 for 30 months	19.59	20.02	20.89	—
$1,000 for 30 months	39.18	40.04	41.79	—
$2,000 for 30 months	78.36	80.09	83.58	—
$4,000 for 30 months	156.71	160.19	—	—
$ 500 for 36 months	16.84	17.27	—	—
$1,000 for 36 months	33.67	34.55	—	—
$2,000 for 36 months	67.34	69.10	—	—
$4,000 for 36 months	134.69	138.20	—	—

SOURCE: Adapted from a leading sales-finance company's rate book.

death, and a so-called *time-price* difference, which is the lender's charge for funds extended and services rendered. If $69.10 were paid monthly on a 36-month, $2,000-transaction at a rate of 7 per cent, the debtor actually would return $2,487.60 to the credit grantor. In this instance, the grantor retires the $2,000 debt, provides credit insurance worth 55.97, and has a time-price difference of $431.63. The annual percentage rate calculated by the constant ratio formula actually is more than 13 per cent. The customer would have saved $85 in his total payments if he had agreed to retire his debt in 30 monthly payments of $80.09 each instead of the 36 payments of $69.10 each. If he could have saved an extra $1,000 and reduced his financing requirements by $1,000, he might have been offered a rate of 6 per cent for a 24-month transaction. Here, his total financing costs, that is, insurance plus time-price difference, would have been reduced from $487.60 to $139.04

The Dealer's Pack. Some automobile dealers advertise competitively low prices for their cars and try to make their profit by selling accessories, credit insurance, and several kinds of car insurance. Sometimes these added items are overpriced. Frequently the dealer's commission on them is high. In many states the law requires the purchaser to obtain the car's license through the dealer, also. After adding the extra cost of all these *pack* items to the price of the car, the dealer may levy a rather high carrying charge on the credit transaction. Customers who shop carefully for bargains in cars and in automobile financing would be well advised to pay for their automobile insurance and license fee from current income.

Industrial Banks

Industrial banks, like other credit-granting agencies, seldom are found in a pure, stereotyped form. Originally, industrial banks lent cash to members of low-income groups; rarely have they lent funds to industrialists. In many areas industrial banks charge a flat 10 per cent rate, deducting their fee in advance; they pay up to 4 per cent on savings placed in their care. These banks always have encouraged the accumulation of savings by their insistence on the borrower's purchase of *savings certificates* to vouch for a continuing savings program. Borrowers pay approximately 20 per cent carrying charges on the money actually available to them for the term of the loan. Early in the twentieth century, industrial banks extended loans at rates within the state usury laws but exacted additional fees for such matters as notarizing signatures, investigation costs, and delayed payments. In 1910, Arthur Morris began a new-type institution for low-income borrowers at Norfolk, Virginia. Since then, the Morris Plan banks have become so numerous that the terms Morris Plan and industrial banks have become nearly interchangeable.*

Over the years, usury laws have been supplanted in many states by the Model Consumer Finance Acts and later by the Uniform Credit Code. As a consequence, industrial banks have been overshadowed by formidable chains of consumer-finance companies. In their attempt to compete with the latter, industrial banks have lost some of their distinctive character.

Credit Unions

Members of credit unions may borrow approximately $400 on unsecured loans at rates of 0.5 per cent to 1.0 per cent per month on the unpaid balances.

---

* Under the Morris Plan, a borrower signs a dual contract with an industrial bank. This embraces a loan agreement that contains a flat percentage rate for the period of the loan, plus an agreement to make regular payments on a savings certificate that will be worth enough at maturity to retire the sum owed to the bank.

Collateral usually is required for sums in excess of $400. The monthly rates on the unsecured loans, it will be noticed, range from 6 per cent to 12 per cent a year. The typical annual percentage rate hovers around 8⅓ per cent. Most credit unions are so small that losses are minimized because of the personal relationship between borrowers, officials, and savers. Credit-union rates are low because these institutions do not make a profit, they enjoy tax advantages, and their overhead costs are low since loans usually are approved by unpaid officials who operate in rent-free office space. These advantages have engendered some bitterness toward credit unions by rival credit grantors. The latter feel that the frequent quotation of low credit-union rates constitutes a form of unfair competition.[8]

Unlicensed Lenders

There always have been improvident persons whose dire financial plight has driven them into the hands of unscrupulous lenders. Percentage rates in these circumstances have been so high that in times past the established church and the agencies of government imposed a ceiling over interest rates. Usually this ceiling was 10 per cent per year, which has been known commonly as *usury*. In the Middle Ages many lenders, who were not members of the established church, evaded the usury laws and plied their trade. Basically, these laws were evaded because the 10 per cent ceiling over finance charges did not provide enough of a margin to cover losses, overhead costs, and pure interest on small, short-term loans to the poorest members of society. Unlicensed lenders, benevolent lenders, and loan sharks have flourished ever since because of the urgency for borrowing and lending outside of the law and because of the ingenious practices of some of the breed.

In many instances, an unlicensed lender or a loan shark operates from within a social, fraternal, or occupational organization of which he may be a member. When fellow members need more money before payday or to cover losses at poker, they are likely to be offered five dollars immediately for a promise to return six dollars in, say, two weeks. A five-for-six arrangement of this sort, actually involving approximately 500 per cent annual rate, is not unusual when offered by loan sharks who accommodate their fellow workers in factories or their buddies in the armed services. Loans of this sort are known as *wage buying* if they are made against a borrower's next paycheck and are renewed with accumulating claims against each future paycheck until the borrower is hopelessly and needlessly impoverished. To cover his tracks, a loan shark often employs a fake sale or a wager as a part of each transaction. Seldom does he exact a promissory note or a wage-assignment agreement. Upon occasion, a loan shark's customer may have to be intimidated by strong-arm men. Loan sharks have excellent collection records. Ordinarily, their customers do not report mistreatment because they may wish to borrow again some day.

Pawnbrokers

Persons whose credit worthiness is very low may find occasion to pledge their jewelry, musical instruments, photographic equipment, or clothing as collateral for a small loan at a pawnshop. The pawnbroker must be a good judge of the value of a wide range of pawnable merchandise upon which he will be willing to lend as much as 60 per cent of the resale value. He must lend as much as possible to increase his earnings and his popularity with potential borrowers; yet he must appraise merchandise cautiously, since he may have to recover his loans by selling it later on. With the rise of discount houses, pawnbrokers are having increasing difficulty in appraising merchandise and in pricing unredeemed collateral attractively.[9]

The pawnbroker's customers receive pawn tickets as evidence of the collateral which they may redeem at any time, usually within two months. Upon redemption, the loan is repaid in one lump sum plus a fee of approximately 3 per cent a month. In some states the laws permit a minimum monthly charge of 50 cents. Sometimes a borrower may pay the pawn fee for a month and extend the redemption deadline date. If the collateral is not redeemed within the specified time it is subject to sale by the pawnbroker. Some states require that the merchandise must be held six months or more before it can be sold. Usually, an auction must be held before the pawnbroker holds legal title to the collateral. This so-called auction seldom is attended by borrowers or other outsiders; the pawnbroker bids the amount of his due and eliminates any further claim that the borrower might have in the merchandise.[10]

Some pawnshop customers may be improvident or poor people with nowhere else to turn for a loan. Some may be derelicts. Some may try to pawn stolen goods. If a pawnbroker serves as a *fence* for stolen goods pawned by thieves, the merchandise is subject to forfeiture. A pawnbroker, therefore must judge his customers as well as their merchandise. Pawnbrokers must enter their customers' names and addresses in a register, describe pawned merchandise by code and serial numbers, and assist the police in identifying stolen goods.

The ideal type of customer for a pawnbroker is a law-abiding, middle-income spendthrift who borrows prior to each payday, repays, and borrows again. Thus a pawnbroker may receive and release the same ring or watch or violin once every two weeks and exact a sizeable fee from an habitual credit seeker who has not learned how to budget.[11]

Remedial Loan Societies

Remedial lending by friends, relatives, and religious institutions has existed for centuries, but the excesses of some pawnbrokers and loan sharks explain the rise of remedial loan societies in the 1890's. Most remedial loan societies have been founded by people of means who have been impressed with the need for financial counseling for the improvident and for lower-cost financing for the poor. It is customary for these societies to charge 1 per cent or 1.5 per cent a month on the unpaid balance on loans that average about $50 each. Customers usually deposit jewelry or other collateral, which may be redeemed at any time by presentation of a ticket. Collateral that is not claimed within a year may be sold. The ticket holder may receive a refund if the selling price exceeds the amount of the claim against his account.

The Provident Loan Society in New York City, founded in 1894 by J. P. Morgan and Cornelius Vanderbilt, represents the apex of success among remedial loan societies. Now it has more than 20 branches annually serving 400,000 borrowers who pay only 1 per cent a month on their unpaid balances. The society's loan volume ranges around $40 million a year. Its loans are of such short duration that only a third of the total annual transactions are outstanding at any one time.[12]

The Russell Sage Foundation was founded in 1907 by Margaret Sage, the widow of an unpopular money lender, Russell Sage, who left a fortune valued in excess of $60 million. The Russell Sage Foundation operated as a remedial loan society for a dozen years. Seeing the futility of solving the primary needs of poor people with remedial loans, its officers evolved a uniform small-loan act, which was recommended for adoption by state governments. This act, the Model Consumer Finance Act of 1948, referred to previously, has been adopted in 44 states. It has become the pattern of organization and operation for more than 8,000 licensed small-loan offices, which are known now as Consumer Finance Associations.

With the aid of unemployment insurance and the federal government's stabilization policies, fewer families face dire need now than in earlier times. Remedial loan societies are declining in numbers and in importance. The borrower's needs are being met instead by other lending agencies that cater to sales financing and to cash loans for use in making further purchases.

ECONOMIC RESULTS OF CREDIT USAGE

The advent of personal credit usage has favorable and unfavorable significance in the American economy. Voices have been raised on the issues concerning its benefits and abuses. The impact of such credit is felt throughout the whole economy. It is especially discernible as it affects individuals and families who use it unwisely. Apparently, more education on this subject is needed.

Personal Consequences

There can be little doubt that many families must use credit to acquire cars, furniture, and appliances. In most instances these acquisitions raise the levels of living. Furthermore, the indebtedness is retired promptly, and the net worth of the family is increased. This has become the American way of launching and financing a family through its early stages of durable-goods acquisition.[13] If personal credit were not used, young men would have to postpone marriage and commence working and saving sooner. Families would have to forego or postpone their purchases of durable goods.

Obviously, some families abuse their credit privileges; they cannot resist buying something where no down payment is required; they are *credit prone*. Many merchants are overanxious to sell on loose credit terms.[14] To profit from added overcharges and fees, they solicit business from persons who have been oversold and overburdened with credit before. Many credit grantors extend additional credit too freely after making superficial investigations or none at all. When borrowers, merchants, and credit grantors act selfishly and unwisely, the consequence of this unholy alliance is often a credit-buying binge that may lead to financial disaster. The resort to garnishment proceedings by merchants and lenders was under attack in several states and in Congress in 1968 and, hopefully, credit prone customers would be protected from their own gullibility by legislation. Unfortunately, the borrower is most vulnerable; he is responsible, as observed earlier in the chapter, for all of the self-denying clauses that he signs at the time of purchase. The guilt and the losses are sometimes shared by merchants and credit grantors if the borrower must resort to bankruptcy proceedings. Perhaps the threat of increasing bankruptcies may restrain the appetite to complete transactions. Merchants and credit grantors should institute a thorough check upon each borrower's current *credit buildup*. They should check recent additions to credit since the last report from a credit bureau.[15] If credit grantors and the merchants can exercise moderation, they have the power to curb credit-prone borrowers.

Ultimately everyone's credit transactions must be converted to a costly computer system and made available through credit bureaus if the excesses of credit usage by a few customers, merchants, and credit grantors are to be eliminated. In the meantime, borrowers should be more aware of the contracts they sign and the obligations they assume. Merchants should bear more responsibility for the overselling of their customers and credit grantors should spend more time and money on the counseling services and the credit investigations on which so much of their fee depends.

Social Consequences

The proponents of credit usage sometimes make extreme claims for its continued and further use. How could millions of mass-produced cars and appliances be manufactured and sold in this country without the use of credit, they ask. How many jobs in steel making, highway building, car repair, and furniture making are dependent on installment purchases of consumer-durable goods? The answers seem obvious—we are enjoying high-level prosperity in a credit economy. One might speculate, however, on the alternatives to this arrangement and find them attractive also. If there were little or no personal credit, many debt-beleaguered persons would be better customers. They would pay cash. Also, the masses who now pay substantial sums for credit services presumably would have that much more purchasing power. And finally, if the market for durable goods were to decline for lack of credit, spending might be diverted to other goods and services. Very likely employment and incomes would remain as high as they are now. The economy would be different with the use of less credit, but who is to say that it would be less affluent?

Some advocates of credit usage are quite modest in their statements regarding its impact on the American economy. As one of them sees it:

. . . installment buying is neither as wonderful nor as devilish an institution as its extreme proponents and opponents claim it to be. It is not the cause of the American standard of living but rather one of the many significant factors which influence that standard.[16]

Cyclical Effects. Some persons have held that an economy can be revived or stimulated by a timely addition of credit. This belief, popularized by John Maynard Keynes, the English economist and statesman, has achieved quite a following in America and abroad. However, the creation of credit for infusion into a national economy is one thing. The extension of credit to certain individuals who enhance the employment and prosperity of others by their sudden spurt of spending is something else. Nationally, an economy may be lifted temporarily and, perhaps in the long run, by *deficit financing*. Such financing usually is achieved by increasing the national government's debt and converting it into bank deposits, which may be spent on roads, schools, and unemployment relief, among other things. Unfortunately, when an individual spends borrowed money, the benefits of increased income accrue to others, not to himself. He derives benefits from the use of his purchases, but his own income rarely is affected by the fact that these purchases create increased demand and increased employment. If everybody used credit to buy more goods within a short space of time, they certainly would increase demand and potential incomes. But in a period of full employment they probably would surfeit the market for certain items and drive prices into an inflationary spiral. The benefits from this experience would be spotty. Theoretically, some persons would gain, others would lose.

In a credit economy, such as that in the United States, the real problem is whether a uniform flow of credit can be maintained. Or will the irregularity of the credit flow accentuate boom and recession periods? It seems likely that the use of installment credit increases in certain prosperous years. In 1955 a record number of automobiles were bought in this country. Regrettably, too many cars were bought that year; sales declined in the years that followed because of debt burdens and probably because of tight credit conditions. Finance companies find themselves short of loanable funds in boom years, but have too few credit-worthy customers in recession years. The irregularity of demand has been healthy for neither automobile manufacturers, nor car dealers, nor the economy as a whole.

There is some doubt whether the Federal Reserve System's monetary controls really can regulate the flow of funds into consumer-credit institutions.[17] This problem was the basis for a special study by the Federal Reserve System in 1956. Although no further controls over consumer credit were advocated at that time, the question has reappeared from time to time.[18] Somehow, the flow of consumer credit must become uniform if its effects on the economy are to be neutralized.

Consumer Credit Versus Social Responsibility. When consumer-credit usage becomes fashionable as a consequence of keeping up with the Joneses or the du Ponts, some damage is done to the moral fiber of the nation. A people who becomes accustomed to debt has lost its urge to acquire monetary reserves, and it is subject to recurring financial crises. In these straits individuals are likely to lose their interest in free enterprise. Have-not human beings, like have-not nations, are tempted readily by radical proposals.

If capitalism is to be preserved, the American masses must have a prosperity ethic and a reasonable opportunity to become capitalists themselves.[19] They most certainly will not achieve these objectives by excessive use of personal credit. Successful people save, accumulate, and invest. Because of the importance of these objectives, they become the subjects of Chapters 4, 5, 6, 7, and 8.

QUESTIONS

1. Is credit extended to a credit user as a favor? If not, by what right or merit is credit extended?
2. In what ways can personal credit be used advantageously? Disadvantageously? How can it be abused? Who is responsible if too much credit is used?
3. What are some trend figures that illustrate the increasing use of personal credit? Which forms of credit have been introduced most recently?
4. Name four types of retail-sales credit and state their chief differences.
5. Who really pays the cost of operating a merchant's charge-account system? Is this true in all cases? Explain.
6. Name five types of installment-sales credit and explain their differences. Which has been introduced most recently?
7. Explain the chief clauses that are likely to be found in an installment-sales agreement. Which are designed for the credit grantor's protection? Which are designed for the debtor's protection?
8. In which type of credit usage and with which types of credit facilities are percentage rates on personal credit the highest? Why?
9. In which type of credit usage and with which types of credit facilities are dollar costs of personal credit the highest? Why?
10. Explain why the annual percentage rate on an installment credit transaction is nearly double the quoted rate.
11. Which types of credit users pay the highest rates? Why? Which types of transactions involve the highest rates? Why? Which types of credit facilities charge the highest rates? Why?
12. If a prospective automobile buyer estimates that he can pay $60 a month on installment payments, should he buy the most expensive car on which financing arrangements at $60 a month can be made? Why?
13. Use the formula $R = 2mD/[P(n+1)]$ to solve the annual percentage rate involved in the financing of a $250 television set with a $50 down payment and 12 monthly payments of $18 each. Is this rate excessive? Explain.
14. Describe the type of transaction and the approximate rate structures that characterize (a) industrial banks, (b) commercial bank small-loan departments, (c) credit unions, (d) consumer-finance companies, (e) loan sharks, (f) remedial loan societies, and (g) a pawnbroker.
15. Are the excesses and abuses of credit usage by some persons subject to remedy by (a) legislation, (b) forbearance of credit grantors and merchants, (c) bankruptcy courts, (d) debt adjusters, and/or (e) counselor? Explain.
16. Why might it be beneficial to a nation's economy to curtail credit usage in boom times and increase its usage during recessions? What is actually the practice? Why? With what consequences?
17. Note carefully all of the key terms in this chapter and be prepared to explain each of them in your own words.

SELECTED READINGS

Board of Governors of the Federal Reserve System, *Consumer Instalment Credit*, 6 vols., 4 parts, U. S. Government Printing Office, Washington, D. C., 1957.

Bureau of Federal Credit Unions, *Federal Credit Union Program, 1965 Annual Report*, Washington, D. C.

Bureau of Federal Credit Unions, *Handbook for Federal Credit Unions*, Washington, D. C.

CUNA International, Inc., *International Credit Union Yearbook*, Madison, Wisconsin, published annually.

Federal Reserve Bulletin, "Developments in Consumer Credit," Board of Governors of the Federal Reserve System, Washington, Vol. 52, No. 6, June 1966, p. 769.

Mors, Wallace P., *Consumer Credit Facts for You*, Bureau of Business Research, Western Reserve University, Cleveland, 1955.

National Association of Credit Men, *Credit Manual of Commercial Laws*, New York, published annually.

Provident Loan Society of New York, *71st Annual Report, 1965*, New York, published annually.

Robbins, W. David, *Consumer Installment Loans*, Bureau of Business Research, Ohio State University, Columbus, 1955.

The Industrial Banker & Time Sales Financing, published monthly by the American Industrial Bankers Association, Washington, D. C.

NOTES

1. J. Kenneth Galbraith, *The Affluent Society*, Houghton Mifflin, Boston, 1958; John Keats, *The Insolent Chariots*, Lippincott, Philadelphia, 1958; Vance Packard, *The Hidden Persuaders*, McKay, New York, 1957; Vance Packard, *The Waste Makers*, McKay, New York, 1960; Vance Packard, *The Status Seekers*, McKay, New York, 1959; Hillel Black, *Buy Now, Pay Later*, Morrow, New York, 1961.
2. Sylvia Porter, "Teen Credit Plan Ignites Big Storm," syndicated release, the Hall Syndicate, Inc. (all rights reserved), *Los Angeles Times*, August 15, 1960; *Newsletter*, Council on Consumer Information, October 1960, p. 2; *Wall Street Journal*, August 5, 1960, p. 1; "Touting the Teen-Agers," *Time*, February 2, 1968, p. 68.
3. *Federal Reserve Bulletin*, U. S. Government Printing Office, Washington, D. C., February 1967, p. 292.
4. "Borrowing or Buying on Time? How to Find the True Interest Rate," *Changing Times*, May 1964, p. 16; Roy C. Cave, "Some Consumer Credit Cost Comparisons," mimeographed, Consumer Research Institute, San Francisco State College, 1964; "Consumer Credit Cost Calculator," Household Finance Corporation, Chicago; Richard L. D. Morse, *Consumer Credit Computations*, Council on Consumer Information, University of Missouri, Columbia; *Shopping for Credit*, Council on Consumer Information, University of Missouri, Columbia; *Truth in Lending*, Council on Consumer Information, University of Missouri, Columbia; "Shopping Sense, Ideas for Stretching Food Dollars," President's Committee on Consumer Interests, Washington, D. C.
5. Ford Motor Company, *Buyer's Digest of New Car Facts*, 1961, p. 70.
6. *Federal Reserve Bulletin*, January 1968, A-49.
7. Legislation on this subject has been passed in New York, Michigan, California, and many other states since the promulgation of the Model Consumer Finance Act.

8. Some additional details about credit unions and their use as savings institutions will be considered in Chapter 4.
9. Sol Shockett, "Pawn Brokerage in California," unpublished master's thesis, University of Southern California, Los Angeles, 1958, p. 167.
10. Gunmar D. Kumlien, "Miseries That Pay," *The Commonweal*, LII, December 1, 1950, pp. 194–195.
11. Mary E. Comer, "Cops-and-Robbers in a Pawnshop," *Reader's Digest*, December 1951, pp. 130–132; Edmund Mottershead III, "Pawnshops," *The Annals*, The American Academy of Political and Social Science, Philadelphia, March 1938, Vol. 196, pp. 149–154; Boyden Sparkes, "Is Your Watch at Simpson's?" *The Saturday Evening Post*, February 25, 1937, pp. 86–88.
12. Provident Loan Society of New York, *Annual Report*, New York, 1965.
13. Sylvia Lane, "Socio Economic Study of Marginal Credit Risks," *Quarterly Report*, Personal Finance Law, New York, Vol. 20, No. 3 (Summer, 1966), p. 83.
14. The term "loose credit" has been suggested as a substitute for "easy credit" by Sylvia Porter, a frequent writer on this subject. This substitution has been recommended also by Persia Campbell who served as Consumer Counsel in New York State during the administration of Governor Averell Harriman. See "Governor's Conference on the Cost of Consumer Debt," October 13, 1955, p. 5.
15. James H. Myers, "A Factor Analysis of Retail Credit Application Data," *Journal of Applied Psychology*, Vol. 48, No. 3, June 1964, p. 168; *ibid.*, "Predicting Credit Risk with a Numerical Scoring System," *Journal of Applied Psychology*, Vol. 47, No. 5, 1963, p. 348; *ibid.*, "Numerical Scoring Systems for Retail Credit Evaluation," *Report to Management*, University of Southern California, Graduate School of Business Administration, January 1962; *ibid.*, "Numerical Scoring Systems for Retail Credit Evaluation," *The Credit World*, April 1962; James H. Myers and Edward W. Forgy, "The Development of Numerical Credit Evaluation Systems," *Journal of the American Statistical Association*, Vol. 58, September 1963, p. 799; Clyde W. Phelps, "The Credit Bureau and the Consumer," *ACBofA Management*, February 1967, p. 20; John M. Chapman and Robert P. Shay, *The Consumer Finance Industry: It's Costs and Regulation*, Columbia University Press, 1967.
16. Clyde W. Phelps, *Financing the Installment Purchases of the American Family*, Studies in Consumer Credit, No. 3, Commercial Credit Company, Baltimore, 1954, p. 24.
17. James C. T. Mao, "Is Consumer Credit Immune to General Monetary Control?" *Michigan Business Review*, January 1961, p. 24.
18. Board of Governors of the Federal Reserve System, *Consumer Installment Credit*, U. S. Government Printing Office, Washington, D. C., 1957, 6 vols.
19. Spencer D. Pollard, *How Capitalism Can Succeed*, The Stackpole Company, 1966, p. 104.

PROBLEMS AND CASES

1. Consider the purchase of an automobile for which the asking price is $2,000. The down payment is to be $650. The 12 monthly payments are to be $125 each. What is the annual percentage rate on this purchase? Considering the

rates for such loans charged in your area by banks, would it be cheaper to make a personal loan and borrow the $2,000 needed for the car purchase?

2. Assume you are in immediate need of $500. Investigate the sources in your community from which you may borrow this sum. Determine the percentage rate each would charge if you plan to repay this loan in monthly installments over the 12 months following the contraction of the obligation. Which of the available sources is the most economic?

3. What is the annual percentage rate or "finance charge" on the purchase of a $20 power drill which is to be paid for in six monthly installments of $4 each? By what comparison might this rate be considered rather high? Why must this rate be higher than the rate for financing a car, for example? What costs must the vendor cover from the $4 cost of the loan? Is this financing arrangement apt to be very profitable to the vendor? Why?

4. Why must the impoverished Johnsons pay such high rates on small credit transactions involving a short period of time? Where can they find better terms? Are these low rates subsidized in any way? Name credit-granting institutions that operate at the lowest rates.

5. If a credit-granting institution charges a certain percentage rate per $100, is it natural that it would suggest debt consolidation in order that its average loan would be larger? Would its costs of operation be proportionately less for each additional $100 extended? Would this debt consolidation be to the advantage of the credit seeker? Would the credit grantor's financial counseling probably be sound and unbiased?

6. A pawnbroker lends $5 on a $25 watch. What risks does the pawnbroker take? If a minimum fee of fifty cents a month is applicable, what is the annual percentage rate? If the pawn ticket is not redeemed and the watch is sold for $8 after six months, would its former owner be entitled to a refund? Why?

7. The Jones family owes 15 per cent of its take-home pay every month for installment payments. Upon completion of the 36th payment on its Chevrolet, it will have fewer payments to make. Should it consider trading the car on a new one at that time? Would many persons do this? If the Joneses do it, should the Smiths and Browns get new cars also?

8. If a new Chevrolet is about to be financed and the Joneses paid their previous $90-a-month payments promptly, should they consider a Buick at $110 a month for the next three years? Should they consider a Cadillac at $125 per month for the next forty-eight months? What are the arguments pro and con?

9. If a new car loses nearly one-third of its value when it is driven off the new car lot, how can the dealer accept less than one-third in down payment? If the car was repossessed within half a year, wouldn't the finance company or the dealer lose money on the transaction? Are annual percentage rates designed to be high enough to cover this risk?

10. Mr. Brown and Mr. Smith are very close friends and have often loaned small sums to each other, followed by prompt repayment. Mr. Brown has asked his friend Smith to cosign a note for $500, which will reduce the financing costs of Brown's new color television set. Should Smith sign? Why?

11. If the Joneses can seemingly meet 36 car payments of $100 a month from their budget, how would they be affected by a wartime re-enactment of Regula-

tion W stating that all consumer-installment payments must be limited to amounts that could be completed within fifteen months? How expensive a car could they buy under these provisions? What was the government's purpose in imposing this restriction?

12. If the Bennetts have a choice between borrowing $100 from a bank at 8 per cent "discount" or using a "budget" account to charge $100 worth of merchandise for twelve months at 1½ per cent a month on the unpaid balance, which option would cost the least? Show your arithmetic and explain the basis for each fee.

13. Shop the nearby credit-granting institutions and make a chart of their rates, their services, and other distinctive differences. If you needed credit and could present evidence of credit worthiness, which institution would you use? Why? If your credit were somewhat overextended already, which would you use? Why? From what sources would a credit grantor draw to judge your credit worthiness? How dependable are these sources? How may they be improved? If this information makes a perfect market possible, should a reduction in the cost of credit be possible? Would an improvement in your own information about the market for consumer credit also result in lower rates for you? How?

14. If the Joneses devote approximately 15 per cent of their take-home pay of $10,000 a year to installment credit, the cost to them would approximate $_____ annually. If they could start a savings account and begin to pay cash for the $1,500 of their purchases which had been financed previously, the savings would yield approximately $_____ per year. The sum of the (1) interest on savings, plus (2) the avoidance of finance payments would give the Joneses approximately $_____ for savings, investment, or additional spending.

15. In late 1966 and early 1967, families seemed to be postponing purchases and borrowing less. The installment debt outstanding declined from $74.6 billion in December 1966 to $74 billion in January 1967 and to $73.6 billion in February. Would business have been better if installment credit had increased at a normal rate during these months? If installment credit is a built-in segment of our economy, does not the irregularity of its use constitute an additional problem?

16. Divide a sheet of paper into two columns and list all of the advantages of using consumer credit in one column and all of the disadvantages in the other column. Distinguish between entries pertaining to individuals, families, and society as a whole. Do you conclude that the use of this credit is entirely beneficial, detrimental, or is it a mixed blessing? Why?

4 SAVING AND SAVINGS FACILITIES

A penny saved is a penny that needn't be earned again.

With apologies to BENJAMIN FRANKLIN

Americans may be big spenders. They are also big savers. Since 1968, they have held more than a trillion dollars of liquid or semiliquid assets. These assets which can easily be converted into cash consist of corporate stocks and bonds, government bonds, and currency on deposit at commercial banks, savings banks, and savings and loan associations. In addition, the ownership of homes, cars, personal effects, and insurance and annuities is worth more than another trillion dollars. (See Figure 4–1.) All told, these total savings of Americans are approximately four times greater than the total personal debt of American households and individuals.[1]

We determine the wealth or net worth of an individual by the savings and investments he accumulates over the years less an amount allowed for their depreciation. For the American people as a whole their $2 trillion of savings

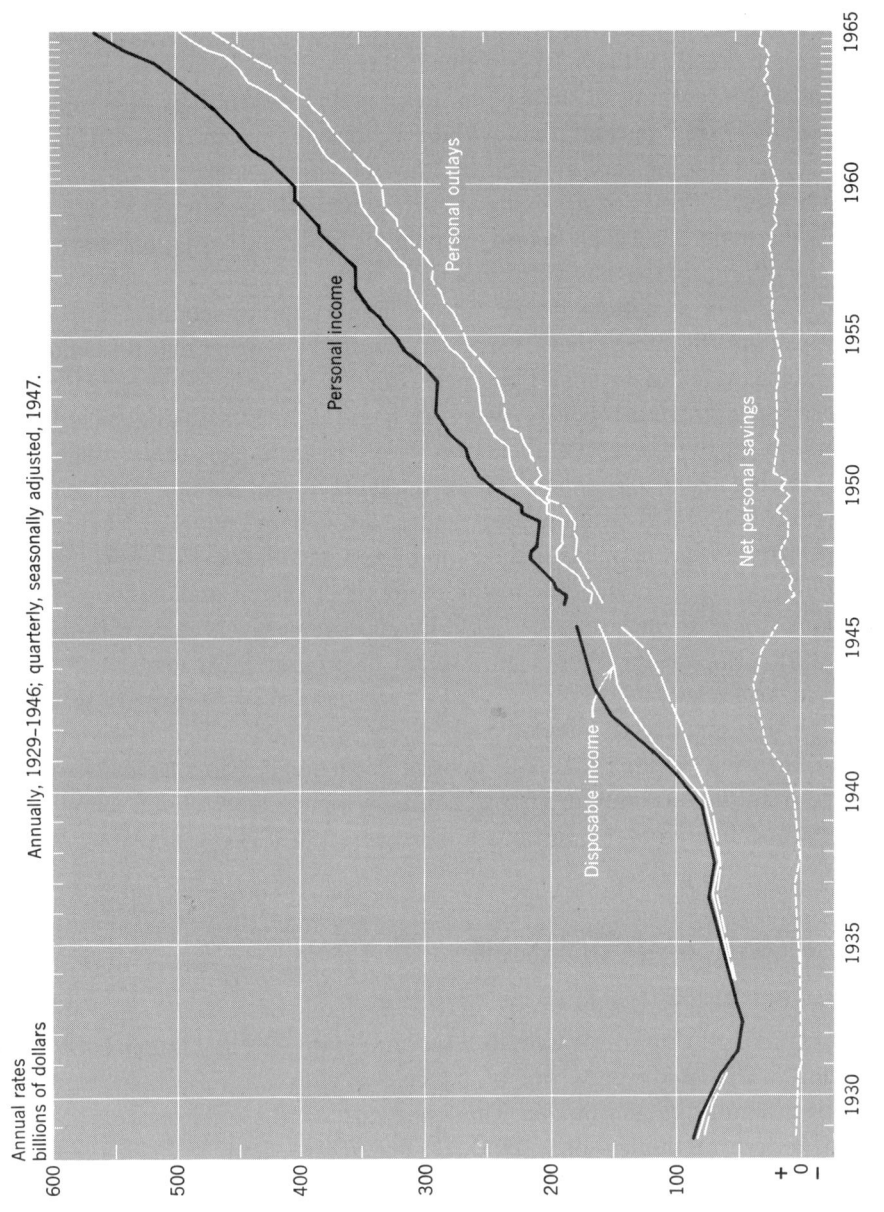

Figure 4-1. Personal income, consumption, and saving. (*Source. Historical Chart Book*, Board of Governors of the Federal Reserve System, 1966.)

grew in 1966 by $108.4 billion. Subtracting a depreciation of $64.4 billion we see that net personal savings for that year totaled $44 billion.[2] In good times most households add to their net worth by increasing their savings and their stock of assets more than they deplete them. But in depression years, unemployed persons add nothing to savings, to investments, and to their accumulation of household items. Instead, they withdraw from savings and do not offset the depreciating value of cars, houses, and household appliances with newly accumulated assets. They are *dissaving*; their savings are negative.

One of the major decisions before individuals and families is whether to spend for something that seems very important at the moment or save for the purpose of spending sometime in the future. For example, should a family deny itself some of the things that it considers necessary now so that its senior members may have more to spend for necessities in their later years? Does saving consist of a mere temporary delay in spending? Does saving include future affluence for the young members of a family in exchange for self-denial now? Does saving have a beneficial effect on savers even though they may never spend the funds they accumulate? Is there a social and national need for saved funds? If so, what happens if the ratio of saving to income is low?

Is there an order of preference to the methods of saving and the devices or institutions where savings may be held? Do most new savers need a target for saving, such as a savings plan or an investment program? Do some savings institutions make savings unusually convenient and rewarding to savers? What are the basic facts relative to interest paid, safety of deposits, and depositor's convenience in using commercial bank savings departments, savings and loan associations, credit unions, mutual savings banks, and government bond savings plans? These and many other questions are answered in this chapter.

SIZE AND COMPOSITION OF PERSONAL SAVINGS

In 1967 the Board of Governors of the Federal Reserve System, the nation's top banking agency, released an important study on the savings habits of individuals.[3] This study grew out of interviews with a carefully selected, representative sample of consumers. The questions sought to determine the nature and pattern of savings of individual consumers. Many of its findings merit attention.

Size of Savings

Savings vary greatly in amount among consumer groups. As Table 4–1 shows, more than half of the consumers interviewed saved from $100 to

Table 4-1. Size of Saving, 1963 (Percentage Distribution of Consumer Units)

Characteristics of Consumer Units	All Units	Saving of $25,000 and Over	$10,000–24,999	$5,000–9,999	$1,000–4,999	$100–999	Saving or Dissaving under $100	Dissaving of $100–999	$1,000–4,999	$5,000 and Over
All units	100	*	2	3	30	27	17	13	6	2
Size of net worth 12/31/62:										
Under $1,000[a]	100	*	*	1	15	31	34	17	2	*
$1,000–$9,999	100	*	1	2	34	31	17	12	4	*
$10,000–$24,999	100	*	3	3	37	27	6	12	8	3
$25,000–$99,999	100	1	4	8	38	17	4	9	12	5
$100,000 and over	100	10	15	15	23	4	5	2	10	16
1963 income:										
0–$2,999	100	*	*	*	5	23	41	23	6	1
$3,000–$4,999	100	*	2	1	19	39	17	15	7	1
$5,000–$7,499	100	*	1	1	35	37	9	11	5	1
$7,500–$9,999	100	*	3	2	54	24	4	6	5	2
$10,000–$14,999	100	*	3	9	54	17	5	6	5	2
$15,000–$24,999	100	3	8	24	39	9	4	3	5	5
$25,000 and over	100	18	17	21	20	4	*	*	6	14
Age of head:										
Under 35	100	*	1	3	33	32	14	12	4	*
35–44	100	1	2	3	35	30	11	11	5	3
45–54	100	*	3	3	40	23	17	8	4	2
55–64	100	1	1	5	25	26	15	17	8	3
65 and over	100	*	2	2	13	25	31	17	7	2
Employment status of head:										
Self-employed	100	4	6	10	29	21	4	9	12	6
Employed by others	100	*	1	3	36	30	13	11	4	1
Retired	100	*	2	1	9	23	37	20	7	2

* Less than one-half of 1 per cent.
[a] Includes negative and zero net worth.
NOTE: Details may not add to totals because of rounding.
SOURCE: *Federal Reserve Bulletin*, January 1967, p. 43.

$5,000. Six per cent dissaved roughly the same amounts. Five per cent saved and 2 per cent dissaved in excess of $5,000. And 17 per cent neither saved nor dissaved as much as $100. Among persons with incomes of more than $25,000, more than half saved at least $5,000. Savings among lower-income groups were more modest. Aged persons saved less than others largely because of their lower incomes.

Composition of Personal Savings

The Federal Reserve study reported that 37 per cent of total saving among these groups comprised equity in automobiles. Another 27 per cent represented increased equity in homes. Overall, 45 per cent of these consumers added to their savings accounts, checking accounts, and savings bonds, whereas 31 per cent dissaved by decreasing their holdings of liquid assets. Other savings items included investments, employee contributions to retirement plans, and the increased net asset value of business firms owned by individuals. In all of these calculations, any indebtedness was subtracted from asset value to attain a net asset figure.[4]

Throughout, the study refers to the composition of personal savings by income, age, and employed versus self-employed groups. As might be expected, the study finds that high incomes correspond with high savings. Young families add more to their automobile, housing, and household appliance equities than do households headed by an older person. Furthermore, 10 per cent of the self-employed included several who saved $10,000 or more contrasted with 18 per cent who dissaved $1,000 or more.[5]

EVOLVING CONCEPTS OF SAVING AND INVESTMENT

Over the years the attitude of people in the United States toward saving has changed. It has evolved from saving and hoarding to saving for permanent investment, to saving for later spending or investment, and to spending first and saving later. It should be obvious that miserly saving to hoard represents an erroneous notion. It dwarfs personalities, lowers living scales, risks the safety of the funds, provides no interest reward, and interrupts the circular flow of funds. It should be equally obvious that persons who take the course of spending first and saving later often pay too high a carrying charge for the pleasure of having things before they are able to afford them. These persons often choose unwisely and spend too much. Their personal financial affairs move from one crisis to another, and they derive less enjoyment out of life than might be expected from a given income. Saving for permanent investment and saving for later spending, on the other hand, both deserve more attention. Moreover, it seems necessary to discuss some aspects of savings plans and investment programs because so many people do not save unless a plan encourages them to do so.

Concept of Saving for Permanent Investment

Once the hoarding of cash or precious gems is dismissed as a poor form of saving, the accumulation of stocks, bonds, land titles, and *earning assets*—that is, factories, buildings, merchandise, and the like—become the chief objectives for permanent investment. Moreover, the true savers of an earlier era seemingly never intended to dip into their capital. They had the idea that money, once saved, should be invested; it should not be spent. It should be passed on intact to one's heirs. During the nineteenth century, many large and middle-sized fortunes were amassed and passed on to responsible and irresponsible heirs in this way.

In times past the emphasis on investment in *earning assets* resulted in a distorted attitude toward other forms of assets that are more in vogue nowadays. Many a thrifty farmer might have had much more pride in his barns than in his home and its meager facilities and appliances. The same attitude might have led him to deny his son a college education in order to devote funds to a new silo or a new tractor. The city banker, in turn, would have been happy to lend him money on such collateral as ownership in land, or factory buildings, or inventories. The banker, however, would not make personal loans to young college people of good character because they had neither earning assets nor collateral to pledge. Similarly, until a generation ago, evidence of ownership in nonearning assets such as household appliances was not commonly considered as acceptable collateral.

Because of income, estate, and inheritance taxes, high-income and middle-income Americans have less opportunity at present to accumulate large holdings of earning assets. It is also likely that many Americans see the fallacy of oversaving by one generation to enable the next generation to enjoy unearned opulence.

Concept of Saving for Later Spending

In the twentieth century, Americans are showing more interest in good living. They prefer a better home, a newer car, and a college education for their children. They save sometimes to buy these things, but only a few of them save for the purpose of making permanent investments.

Saving may be a virtue or it may interrupt spending patterns for necessities, self-improvement, and certain pleasures. It is natural for normal people to place pleasure and self-improvement ahead of saving when income is being divided. It is natural, also, for people to regard expenditures for many things as necessary. Hence, the rationale for saving is destroyed. There are legitimate needs for saving, however. Prudent persons must heed these claims on their current earnings. First, there is the need for an emergency fund to be used for any unpredictable circumstance that may arise later. Second, there will be need for savings for the purchase of big-ticket items costing $100 or more. There will be several stages in the family life cycle when savings will be required: the time when approximately $2,000 will be needed to furnish an apartment or a rented house; the time when a down payment of several thousand dollars will be needed for the purchase of a home; the time when several thousand extra dollars will be needed to provide the children with a college education; or the time when very large sums will be needed to provide financial security in retirement. These and many additional needs must be recognized and anticipated with a savings program that has to compete with each family's urge to spend for current needs and pleasures.

Saving for Medical Care, Emergencies, and Contingencies. Medical care costs the average American family nearly 7 per cent of its income. Yet few families budget and save for this important expenditure. When a family has been spared its normal quota of illness and accident, it should have accumulated enough savings to cover some serious accident or illness in the future. In a similar manner, a family might accumulate savings to cover miscellaneous, unpredictable *contingencies* such as uninsured losses or unemployment. If misfortune occurs, the contingency fund is available for use. If the family avoids these misfortunes, eventually the contingency fund may be devoted to permanent investments.

Saving for Durable-Goods Purchases. Most people require an incentive for saving. They must want something very much, something important enough to offset the natural urge to spend the money for something else. They want cars, household appliances, and other durable goods because of the convenience these durables provide and because they have become status symbols. Why, then, if these people want durable goods so badly should they not set the cost of these things as goals for their savings program and use their wants as incentives toward meeting these goals? If the prospect for buying a new car next year is coupled with this year's savings program, the desire for that new car is likely to provide the incentive for the self-denial that must accompany a savings plan. By using this device for saving *prior* to the purchase, the saver improves his financial position. He accumulates interest from a savings account *before* the purchase instead of paying a high carrying charge *after* the purchase. Moreover, having paid for the car at the time of purchase, he is free to start saving for his next car, for some other purchase, for emergencies, or for retirement. It should be conceded that in the typical American family, the car or household appliance will be bought whether or not the savings program is undertaken before the purchase. The difference lies between *voluntary saving* before the purchase or *enforced* saving at high-percentage rates afterward.

Saving for Alternative Purposes. In order to maximize the satisfaction that income provides, households have to evaluate alternative opportunities for spending and saving. They must choose in order to maximize returns on both the immediate future and over a longer period. If immediate returns are valued more highly than future returns, consumption will tend to be higher than saving. The proportions of income spent and saved are largely determined by expectations. They are also influenced by the household's composition (the number of children, for example), the values placed on spending and saving, which differ among various cultural groups, and the family's "horizon" when viewing its prospects of income. Households usually plan their spending and saving in two- or three-year cycles on the average, especially when predicting their levels of income. In a rapidly changing environment households constitute a highly rational group.

Since many persons are tempted to purchase items from current income, the concept of saving implies the need for funds in the future—for insurance, retirement, and estate building. The holding and safekeeping of these funds leads to the accumulation of financial assets in savings institutions (see Table 4–2). The remainder of this chapter considers the accumulation of financial assets for investment purposes.

Personal Reasons for Saving

During the last two generations there has been a significant change in the attitude toward saving in this country. The precept of Benjamin Franklin that "a penny saved is a penny earned" has been replaced by the concept that America's high-level prosperity depends on continued spending of nearly all of the nation's disposable personal income. To stimulate spending on this scale, an unmatched array of advertising, easy-credit inducements, and selling techniques has been foisted upon the public. The average American may think that he would be wise to "live it up" because of the probability of continued inflation or of an impending nuclear war. Both of these would surely destroy accumulated assets in nearly every form.

Table 4-2. Financial Assets and Liabilities of Individuals: 1950 to 1965 (In Billions of Dollars. As of End of Year.)

Assets and Liabilities	1950	1955	1959	1960	1961	1962	1963	1964	1965
Financial Assets									
Total	472	712	927	936	1,060	1,043	1,171	1,290	1,397
Currency and demand deposits	71	80	82	80	80	83	90	97	105
Time and saving deposits	56	74	96	101	110	125	136	149	164
Savings shares	15	34	58	67	76	86	97	109	118
Securities	246	396	519	504	593	538	618	686	739
U. S. savings bonds	50	50	46	46	46	47	48	49	50
Other U. S. Government[a]	20	19	30	28	27	28	28	30	32
State and local government	16	22	28	30	31	31	33	35	38
Corporate bonds and notes[a]	21	21	20	21	21	21	22	22	23
Investment company shares[a]	5	14	24	23	33	30	35	40	46
Other preferred and common shares[a]	134	272	373	357	436	381	452	509	550
Private insurance and pension reserves	66	100	134	143	157	164	178	194	209
Insurance reserves	54	71	84	88	91	96	100	105	111
Insured pension reserves	6	11	18	19	20	22	23	25	27
Noninsured pension reserves	7	18	32	37	45	47	55	63	71
Government insurance and pension reserves	19	27	38	41	45	48	52	57	62
Liabilities									
Total	59	118	169	185	198	217	239	261	284
Mortgage debt	38	79	118	129	140	152	167	183	198
Consumer debt	18	34	46	51	52	57	63	70	79
Securities loans	3	5	5	5	6	7	8	8	8
Net equity (assets—liabilities)	413	594	758	751	862	827	932	1,029	1,112

[a] Estimated market value. Nonguaranteed Federal agency issues included with "Other U. S. Government."
SOURCE: Securities and Exchange Commission. Published annually in *Volume and Composition of Individuals' Saving* and in the *Statistical Bulletin*. *Statistical Abstract of United States*, 1966, U. S. Department of Commerce, Census Bureau.

In spite of these explanations for the declining popularity of thrift in America, there are a number of reasons why saving must be encouraged. Expanding industries in this country and overseas will need more investment funds. The United States Government needs huge sums to finance and refinance its debt. The people who *do* save may need someday to use their accumulated savings for emergencies, for durable-goods purchases, and for retirement. Because personal incomes are high and rising, it is reasonable to assume that personal saving may be urged to meet these varied needs.

Effect of Thrift on the Thrifty

Thrift should have several objectives. The first two are time tested; they pertain to the character-building and asset-accumulation benefits derived by the saver himself. These two objectives of thrift are as valid as ever. However, advocacy of them has not been as frequent as prior to and during the era of the Great Depression in the 1930's.

Thrift Builds Character. Thriftiness builds moral fiber into people. Those who save demonstrate that they are responsible individuals. They seek to care for their own needs and for the needs of their dependents at present and in the future. If everyone were endowed with this degree of responsibility, there might be less necessity to call on governments to provide social welfare or to bail out people who are in financial difficulty. The freedom of individuals to make their own choices, once abandoned, never may be recaptured. Americans, individually and collectively, might benefit from a new era in which personal thrift is again prevalent and popular.

Thrift Provides Accumulated Funds. Half a century ago, a popular argument for thrift was exemplified in the Horatio Alger novels. The young hero worked and saved, eventually buying out the company for which he had first worked. Americans of the present generation do not choose to work as hard and deny themselves so many things for the hope of eventual success. Nowadays, Americans seem to prefer to enjoy life while they earn; they are content to proceed more slowly toward their financial goals.

Americans in this generation should remember, however, that a patient, methodical saver may achieve financial security through a regular saving program. A 20-year-old young man, for example, who is willing to save ten dollars a month for five years will have $691.06 in his twenty-fifth year if he invests his savings at 5 per cent interest compounded quarterly. A young man of 25 may find a number of uses for the $691.06. If, however, this young man has acquired a pride in his savings account, he may avoid spending this sum and continue to put money away; he will have accumulated savings of

$2,712.87 at 35, $6,035.96 at 45, $11,497.84 at 55. If he continues to save at this same rate until he is ready for retirement at 65, his savings will amount to $20,475.11.

The income available for saving is greater than one might suspect. Within a normal life span, a college man may earn about $435,000, calculated at 1967 price levels. This dollar total will be even higher for men in some professions—and certainly if war or inflation are permitted to interrupt these calculations. If this man and his family save 8 per cent of their lifetime earnings, their estate should be worth $35,000 plus accumulated compound interest at the time of retirement.

Saving Provides Security. From the foregoing, it should be noted that the savings always were available and that they could have been cashed in or used as collateral for loans at any time. This means that a young man might meet unusual and emergency expenditures throughout his lifetime without recourse to borrowing at high percentage rates. In fact, most bankers would welcome him and be happy to extend temporary loans at modest rates. In later years, as the costs of raising a family become a burden, the difference between a family with a savings plan of this sort and one that contracts debt at high interest rates may add as much as 10 per cent to the funds for living expenses for the thrifty family.

National Need for Saved Funds

America must grow strong economically if it is to provide for its growing population and meet the communist challenge by assisting underdeveloped nations. In a period of full employment, if these expenditures and those for military and space rivalry cannot be financed from taxation, corporate savings, and personal savings, the result may be inflation, chaos, and eventually relegation of the United States to the status of a second-rate power. When the nation is prosperous, Americans may help themselves and their country by diverting more of their incomes from nonessentials into savings that could be made available for building new, efficient industries, new transportation networks, new housing, and other essentials.

Need for Personal Savings for Business Expansion. The rate of business expansion has been very rapid in recent years. In the next decade the need for investment funds is likely to be much greater. Personal savings for investment in business enterprise are scarcely adequate to meet these needs. When banks provide these funds they lend either the savings of their depositors or bank credit, which they are authorized to create—within certain limits. In a period of full employment the creation and lending of excessive amounts of bank credit is often inflationary and should be avoided. Hence personal savings loaned directly to business, or the availability of such savings deposited in banks for such loans, is the sound base on which business expansion should be financed. The need for business expansion is great; therefore the need for personal savings is also very great.

Need for Personal Savings for Government Use. Most state and local governments are burdened with a shortage of funds in the face of a need for expansion of government services and facilities into new, rapidly growing areas. Frequently, local taxes are inadequate to finance both current costs and expenditures for these new facilities. This problem usually is solved by floating bonds for new school buildings, storm sewers, or whatever else may be desired. Current tax revenues remain available, then, for current expenditures and for interest on the bonds. If the purchasers of local government bonds buy them with personal savings, they receive not only the interest but also the satisfaction that they have helped to finance community growth in a noninflationary manner.

The United States Government needs money to finance deficits in some years and also money to refinance that part of its bonded indebtedness that becomes due every year. Since so much of the debt is in the form of short-term bonds, it is not unusual for as much as $70 billion to require refinancing within a given year. When personal savings are used for the purchase of these bonds, the buyers benefit from the interest they receive. The Treasury Department is not compelled, moreover, to compete with business for scarce funds in the market or to resort to borrowing from the banks. Since either of these last named forms of treasury borrowing may contribute to inflation, the federal government's debt should be financed and refinanced from personal savings as often as possible.

Savings Related to the Circular Flow of Money

In the depression decade of the 1930's, thrift became unfashionable. It seemed to stop the flow of funds from one person to the next. The halt in this *circular flow* of money was said to be a major cause of unemployment. A sounder version of this same phenomenon is that thrift diverts funds from current spending into savings institutions. There it is available for lending to persons who buy or build machines, houses, factories, merchandise inventories, or other things. In a period of full employment and economic growth, firms see opportunities for borrowing, investment, and profit making. Apart from the possibility of a time lag between saving and investment, the saved funds are spent in ways that ordinarily create as much employment as if the saved dollars had gone into current consumption.

Oversaving by High-Income Groups. The fact that affluent members of society save greater proportions of their incomes than do those with lesser incomes creates several problems. One is that assets are accumulated so rapidly by the rich and near rich that these groups hold a concentration of economic power. Another is that the lack of current spending, which accompanies the thriftiness of high-income persons, is believed to disrupt the circular flow of funds to current consumption goods and services. The consequent *overinvestment* in new industry and *underconsumption* of consumer goods and services are held by some persons to be causes of business failures and recessions. Current thinking contends that a proper proportion of savings is necessary for an economy to function efficiently at any particular level.

Undersaving by Low-Income Groups. The people with low incomes, who tend to save so little, lag behind the wealthy in the accumulation of worldly goods and investments. This accentuates the problem of the haves and have-nots unless tax legislation and other laws level incomes and wealth to some extent. The lack of saving by low-income groups accounts for much of their lack of morale and for their feelings of insecurity. A family without savings is at the mercy of friends, relatives, and creditors if serious illness, unemployment, or an unanticipated financial emergency strikes. The family with some savings may face these same adversities with more confidence in its ability to survive the crisis.

SAVINGS DEVICES

The accumulation of financial assets requires the availability of a variety of savings devices and savings institutions for beginners, for intermediate savers, and for habitual savers. Each of these devices and institutions will be examined and evaluated in the remaining pages of this chapter.

Cash-Savings Devices

A piggy bank, a toy cash register, or a coin holder may be ideal for the first saving experiences of a young child. The handling of bright coins and the thrill of hearing them tinkle as they hit bottom in the piggy bank seem to provide offsetting rewards for their having been removed from circulation. It is doubtful, however, if many youngsters comprehend the significance of this experience. That they frequently attempt to retrieve their coins and play with them again suggests that this form of saving is a mere game. It may become saving, however, if it becomes a habit, which can be transferred later from the piggy bank to other savings institutions.

Savings Devices

Over the years, many adults have kept coins and currency hidden in old sugar bowls or under the mattress. In many a sparsely settled community the sugar bowl on the mantel has been the most accessible savings institution. Unfortunately, piggy banks and sugar bowls have been plundered for years.

Safeguarding the Funds. The saving of small cash sums is usually a mere holding operation. These funds always are designated for spending or for investment later on. Banks and other savings institutions protect the depositor against loss from fire and theft; on that score they have rendered the piggy bank, the sugar bowl, and the mattress obsolete. Most savings institutions also belong to a deposit-guarantee plan, which protects the depositor against loss in case the institution becomes insolvent.

Cash Saving as a Form of Hoarding. When cash—coins or currency—is saved and held as cash, it is out of circulation. Idle cash savings earn no interest because they are not available for investment in earning assets such as factories, buildings, or merchandise inventories. Thus the saver loses his interest and the economy may lose a new industry. Ideally, the saved funds should be deposited in a bank or savings institution. In this way the savings of many people may be combined into funds sufficient for investments that may increase economic activity in the community.

Passbook Savings Accounts

Passbook savings are created when cash or its equivalent is exchanged for an entry in a passbook at a bank or savings institution. The individual's deposit immediately loses its identity as all savings deposits become bookkeeping entries subject to investment in interest-bearing assets. Depositors, in turn, receive interest for the use of their funds. Everyone gains as long as the funds are invested profitably. In nearly all cases, depositors are insured against loss whether the investments are profitable or not.

Passbook savings accounts may result from the actual deposit of coins, currency, checks, money orders, or drafts. They may also be created by the voluntary or involuntary withholding from an individual's income at its source. *Voluntary withholding* requires a signed authorization by the person who agrees to the deduction from his income of a specified sum to be paid to the savings institution at regular intervals. This form of savings is practical for many persons. These people abide by the agreement they make and learn to live within their actual take-home pay. *Involuntary savings* occurs only when a court or an executor orders the saving of a portion of the income of a minor or an incompetent person who might otherwise misuse his funds. Voluntary savings plans may become somewhat involuntary, since the decision to save need not be renewed with each successive withholding of income.

Nonmonetary Savings

Persons who have accumulated savings accounts, property, or stocks and bonds may reinvest their interest and continue their accumulation of assets indefinitely. Since this reinvestment need not involve the cashing and reinvestment of interest checks, the process may be called a form of nonmonetary savings.

In the case of certain *growth stocks*, which will be examined further in Chapters 5, 6, and 7, dividends are small. Most of the corporation's earnings are plowed back into the business in the form of research or new plant expansion. The owner of a growth stock can expect to benefit from higher dividends and the increased value of the stock in later years. The foregoing of current income, in anticipation of higher dividends and stock values constitutes a form of nonmonetary *built-in savings*.

Miscellaneous Forms of Savings

The homeowner who enjoys landscaping a newly purchased residence and planting a variety of hedges, flowers, and grass spends extra dollars in the process. These dollars may bring joy to him and to his neighbors. They also may become *invested dollars*, which will be returned with interest if the property eventually proves attractive enough to bring a good price.

Another form of savings is practiced by the small businessman who works longer and harder for himself than he would be likely to work for anyone else. Moreover, in the first few years of any small businessman's struggle to launch his firm, his efforts seldom are well rewarded. Those who do succeed are likely to reinvest much of their earnings in the business. Unfortunately, the sacrifice and reinvestment, which are common among most small businessmen, are not always rewarded. Many of them are not successful in the first years of their initial attempt at proprietorship. The few successful ones owe much of their achievement to the practice of a form of built-in savings and reinvestment with deferred rewards.

SAVINGS INSTITUTIONS

Half a dozen types of savings institutions are available for use by individuals who are ready to employ them. All of these institutions perform three major services for their customers: first, they accept small sums and thereby help the customer to accumulate larger sums; second, they hold and safeguard the customer's funds; third, they pay interest to the customer from the earnings received through the investment of a portion of his funds. These institutions differ in their historical background, their legal foundations, and the plans they offer their customers. The customers also vary in the emphasis that they place on safety, liquidity, and high returns. It behooves the customer, therefore, to distinguish carefully between types of savings institutions and to deal with those that are best fitted to his needs.

Commercial Banks as Savings Institutions

Commercial banks are the ordinary banks and branch banks that most people deal with regularly. Commercial banks have many functions of which customer savings is of relatively minor importance. Individuals do save in their checking accounts, however, and many of them save regularly in the savings department of their bank. Each of these savings vehicles deserves further consideration.

Checking-Account Savings. An ordinary checking account in a commercial bank may serve as a depository for the safekeeping of funds.* It is also a convenient device for transferring sums with checks and a place where small funds may accumulate until their size suggests the wisdom of investing them elsewhere. The most important use of a checking account is for the deposit of monthly or weekly paychecks and the writing of checks for the payment of small bills. If the depositor reduces his account to nearly nothing each month, the bank has little of his money on hand for lending. Hence, the bank must collect a *service charge* to cover its costly check-clearing operations. When, on the other hand, the customer leaves a sizeable minimum balance in his checking account, the service charge is less or nonexistent. In this instance, the bank can collect some interest on the funds it can lend.

Bank service charges are composed usually of a *flat rate* of about 50 or 75 cents a month, plus a *measured rate* of five to seven cents per check.[6] Thus a depositor may pay a service charge of nearly two dollars if he writes 20 checks a month and permits his minimum balance to drop below $100 sometime during the month. To avoid a service charge altogether, a depositor who writes 20 checks a month might have to have a minimum balance of approximately $1,000. With this balance, it will be noted, the customer who avoids a service charge receives the equivalent of interest at the rate of two dollars a month or $24 a year for the bank's use of his $1,000 minimum balance. Thus the depositor who builds up his balance not only accumulates funds, but also

* Deposits insured up to $15,000 by the Federal Deposit Insurance Corporation.

receives a modest interest for the use of his money. At some place in a service-charge schedule, however, the depositor with a high minimum balance reaches diminishing returns; then he should divert his surplus funds to some other savings outlet or investment that will pay an interest rate. He may decide, for example, to seek a greater return from his $1,000 minimum balance by placing it in the bank's savings department where it may earn from $30 to $40 a year; or he may deposit it in a savings and loan association account where it will earn from $40 to $50 a year. Either of these amounts, it will be noted, exceed the service charges that are likely to be assessed against the depositor's checking account. Perhaps the increasing use of computers will reduce bank costs in handling checking accounts with the result that service charges can be reduced.

Commercial Bank Savings Accounts. When a checking account becomes larger than necessary, a depositor may be wise to transfer some of his funds into a commercial bank savings account that will pay an interest rate ranging from 2.5 to 4 per cent compounded semiannually or oftener. Funds that remain in the bank for several months are known as *time deposits.* The bank can lend these funds with confidence and is therefore able to pay a higher interest rate. Thus a commercial bank depositor who has both a checking and a savings account may endear himself to his banker while feathering his own nest.

A bank's interest rate on savings accounts is payable only if the funds are left in the account for the full quarterly or semiannual period. A customer who withdraws funds prior to these terminal dates must forfeit the interest for the time period. Depositors are permitted sometimes to make several withdrawals a month in some bank-savings departments. As a consequence of these frequent withdrawals, depositors forfeit a considerable portion of their interest. Bankers have had to condone this practice in some places or even to calculate interest on a daily basis in order to meet the competition of savings and loan associations. The latter often have accommodated customers who sought to make frequent withdrawals.

Mutual Savings Bank Savings Accounts

Mutual savings banks are organized to accept small savings, which are invested as advantageously as possible. After necessary operating expenses are deducted, the profits accrue as income to the depositors or as a surplus designed to protect the interests of the depositors. Frequently these institutions are operated by a self-perpetuating board in behalf of the members. By 1967 there were more than 506 mutual savings banks in 18 states with deposits of $59 billion and total assets of $66 billion (Table 4–3). Counting branch offices, there were 1,195 savings banks in 1967. The majority of these institutions are located in New England and south along the coast to Maryland.

Table 4-3. Mutual Savings Banks (Amounts in Millions of Dollars)

End of Period	Loans Mortgage	Loans Other	Securities U.S. Government	Securities State and Local Government	Securities Corporate and Other[a]	Cash	Other Assets	Total Assets—Total Liabilities and General Reserve Accounts	Deposits[b]	Other Liabilities	General Reserve Accounts	Mortgage Loan Commitments[c] Number	Mortgage Loan Commitments[c] Amount
1941	4,787	89	3,592	1,786		829	689	11,772	10,503	38	1,231	—	—
1945	4,202	62	10,650	1,257		606	185	16,962	15,332	48	1,582	—	—
1960	26,702	416	6,243	672	5,076	874	589	40,571	36,343	678	3,550	58,350	1,200
1961	28,902	475	6,160	677	5,040	937	640	42,829	38,277	781	3,771	61,855	1,654
1962	32,056	602	6,107	527	5,177	956	695	46,121	41,336	828	3,957	114,985	2,548
1963	36,007	607	5,863	440	5,074	912	799	49,702	44,606	943	4,153	104,326	2,549
1964	40,328	739	5,791	391	5,099	1,004	886	54,238	48,849	989	4,400	135,992	2,820
1965	44,433	862	5,485	320	5,170	1,017	944	58,232	52,443	1,124	4,665	120,476	2,697
1966													
November	46,953	1,131	4,848	254	5,644	799	1,029	60,658	54,326	1,463	4,869	91,634	2,072
December	47,193	1,078	4,764	251	5,719	953	1,024	60,982	55,006	1,114	4,863	88,808	2,010
1967													
January	47,484	1,076	4,679	247	6,053	969	1,062	61,570	55,456	1,259	4,855	88,479	2,013
February	47,692	1,137	4,700	249	6,251	1,041	1,051	62,122	55,788	1,428	4,906	90,223	2,055
March	47,973	1,136	4,645	246	6,480	1,140	1,081	62,701	56,538	1,249	4,914	91,125	2,172
April	48,236	1,075	4,481	243	6,803	1,069	1,076	62,982	56,739	1,381	4,863	88,295	2,242
May	48,493	1,261	4,433	235	7,062	1,095	1,074	63,654	57,185	1,546	4,923	92,754	2,495
June	48,771	1,226	4,336	249	7,313	1,140	1,108	64,143	57,836	1,379	4,929	95,187	2,657
July	49,010	1,144	4,396	246	7,642	1,084	1,116	64,639	58,169	1,563	4,908	91,559	2,647
August	49,322	1,210	4,367	242	7,910	1,034	1,117	65,201	58,499	1,732	4,969	n.a.	2,592
September	49,557	1,152	4,406	243	8,054	999	1,147	65,559	59,066	1,525	4,967	n.a.	2,724
October	49,827	1,169	4,299	228	8,080	959	1,134	65,696	59,257	1,489	4,950	n.a.	2,710
November	50,046	1,243	4,397	222	8,107	915	1,130	66,061	59,462	1,597	5,002	n.a.	2,684

[a] Also includes securities of foreign governments and international organizations and nonguaranteed issues of U. S. Govt. agencies.
[b] See note 4, p. A-7.
[c] Commitments outstanding of banks in N.Y. State as reported to the Savings Bank Assn. of the State of N.Y. Data include building loans beginning with Aug. 1967.

NOTE: National Assn. of Mutual Savings Banks data; figures are estimates for all savings banks in the United States and differ somewhat from those shown elsewhere in the BULLETIN; the latter are for call dates and are based on reports filed with U. S. Govt. and State bank supervisory agencies. Loans are shown net of valuation reserves.

SOURCE: *Federal Reserve Bulletin*, January 1968, A-31.

Savings Accounts. Although most savings accounts in mutual savings banks are small, there is an assumption that the funds will be left to accumulate. Passbooks are used commonly to make deposits and withdrawals. Earnings from investments generally are sufficient for the declaration of 4 or 6 per cent dividends and the building of an adequate reserve account. Yet the average rate of dividends hovers below 3½ per cent in a typical account after allowances are made for deposit and withdrawal activity.

Safety of the Funds. Over the years, mutual savings banks have increased their reserves and few of them have failed. Most of them belong to the Federal Deposit Insurance Corporation, which insures their individual deposits for amounts up to $15,000. Several states, notably Massachusetts, New York, and New Hampshire, regulate and inspect these institutions with such vigor that these states have been willing to set up insurance systems for the protection of mutual-savings-bank deposits. In several European countries, the respective governments have gone one step further to nationalize the savings institutions that formerly had been mutual or cooperative banks.

Saving in Savings and Loan Associations

Persons with savings amounting to several hundred or several thousand dollars may find a locally owned savings and loan association the most suitable place for their savings.* These associations pay roughly 4 to 6 per cent on savings that usually are loaned on local real estate at 6½ per cent, more or less. Since there are approximately 8,000 savings and loan association offices or branch offices, compared with about 14,000 banks and branch banks, savers frequently can find a savings and loan office in their nearest shopping center.

Savings and loan associations, formerly known as building and loan associations in some communities, are controlled vaguely by the saving and borrowing "members." In some of the state-chartered savings and loans associations, there are permanent capital stockholders who acquire a proprietary interest in the direction of policies, in the control of reserves, and in the absorption of losses.

Traditionally, a savings and loan association member purchased "shares" in the association, which paid dividends ordered by its elected board of directors. Aside from reserves that were withheld, the "earnings" were divided among the shareholding members in the same way as in a mutual association. The term "share" and the terms "dividend" or "earnings" are still used by many associations. Nevertheless, the earnings rates tend to remain uniform in large communities, and the small shareholder has virtually no proprietary interest in

* Deposits insured up to $15,000 by Federal Savings and Loan Insurance Corporation.

the association's accumulated reserves. In many of the state-chartered associations, the pretense of a mutual association is less noticeable.

In California, for example, the term "share" or "shareholder" has been replaced by the term "holder," and the term "earnings" by the word "interest." The fact that earnings or interest rates usually are uniform among rival associations suggests that the mutual division of earnings is passing. Competition is more likely to manifest itself in the size of reserve accounts, in the growth rates of rival associations, or in the prizes given by some associations to persons who open new accounts.

Passbook Savings Accounts. The act of depositing funds or buying shares in a savings and loan association is confirmed by making an entry on the association's records and in a passbook. The passbook is then given to the depositor or "member," depending on the type of association. The passbook must be used to make further additions to or subtractions from the account. Many savers add to their accounts whenever they wish, although a few associations have plans that require definite amounts to be deposited at stated intervals. Interest, or a "dividend," is paid semiannually or quarterly by many associations; premature withdrawals result in forfeiture of the interest for the amount withdrawn for the three-month or six-month interval. It should be noted, however, that withdrawals usually must be made in person and that such withdrawals are scarcely 10 per cent as many as would be made normally in a typical commercial bank checking account.[7] Since some savers regard this as the only important difference between the services offered by a bank and a savings and loan association, commercial banks show concern over this new type of competition.

Investment-Certificate Plan. Savers who wish to invest several thousand dollars may purchase investment certificates in even thousand-dollar amounts. Years ago, savings and loan associations paid interest on these certificates more often than on the passbook accounts. Recently that distinction has disappeared in many instances. Usually the bonus interest rate on investment certificates is paid nowadays by check, whereas the interest or "dividend" on ordinary savings is merely added to the principal and compounded in a passbook account.

Security of the Funds. All federally chartered and most state-chartered savings and loan associations are members of the Federal Savings and Loan Insurance Corporation. This organization insures each account up to $15,000 in a manner similar to but not identical with the insurance of commercial bank deposits by the Federal Deposit Insurance Corporation. However, the financial

Table 4-4. Savings and Loan Associations (in Millions of Dollars)

End of Period	Assets				Liabilities					
	Mortgages	U.S. Government Securities	Cash	Other[a]	Total Assets[b]— Total Liabilities	Savings Capital	Reserves and Undivided Profits	Borrowed Money[c]	Loans in Process	Other	Mortgage Loan Commitments[d]
1941	4,578	107	344	775	6,049	4,682	475	256	636	775	—
1945	5,376	2,420	450	356	8,747	7,365	644	336	402	356	—
1960	60,070	4,595	2,680	4,131	71,476	62,142	4,983	2,197	1,186	968	1,359
1961	68,834	5,211	3,315	4,775	82,135	70,885	5,708	2,856	1,550	1,136	1,908
1962	78,770	5,563	3,926	5,346	93,605	80,236	6,520	3,629	1,999	1,221	2,230
1963	90,944	6,445	3,979	6,191	107,559	91,308	7,209	5,015	2,528	1,499	2,614
1964	101,333	6,966	4,015	7,041	119,355	101,887	7,899	5,601	2,239	1,729	2,590
1965	110,306	7,414	3,900	7,960	129,580	110,385	8,704	6,444	2,198	1,849	2,751
1966 December	114,192	7,772	3,361	8,672	133,997	114,010	9,256	7,464	1,272	1,995	1,512
1967											
January	114,229	7,883	3,170	8,442	133,724	114,194	9,084	6,708	1,189	2,549	1,661
February	114,395	8,079	3,364	8,554	134,392	114,957	9,073	6,107	1,217	3,038	1,925
March	114,797	8,058	3,544	8,754	135,153	116,414	9,064	5,441	1,365	2,869	2,269
April	115,233	7,950	3,638	8,936	135,757	116,911	9,062	5,027	1,503	3,254	2,699
May	115,909	8,072	3,859	9,376	137,216	118,041	9,055	4,630	1,710	3,780	3,081
June	116,944	7,987	3,997	9,232	138,160	119,976	9,268	4,559	1,918	2,439	3,250
July	117,676	8,378	3,412	9,169	138,635	120,031	9,270	4,456	2,019	2,859	3,420
August	118,674	8,857	3,127	9,221	139,879	120,677	9,265	4,399	2,130	3,408	3,443
September	119,529	9,017	3,078	9,158	140,782	121,870	9,255	4,382	2,158	3,117	3,337
October	120,362	9,171	3,040	9,217	141,790	122,365	9,256	4,373	2,213	3,583	3,310
November	121,127	9,424	3,068	9,352	142,947	122,947	9,248	4,455	2,241	4,070	3,287
December	121,905	9,323	3,416	9,117	143,761	124,559	9,559	4,863	2,280	2,500	3,035

[a] Includes other loans, stock in the Federal home loan banks, other investments, real estate owned and sold on contract, and office buildings and fixtures.
[b] Before 1958, mortgages are net of mortgage-pledged shares. Asset items will not add to total assets, which include gross mortgages with no deductions for mortgage-pledged shares. Beginning with Jan. 1958, no deduction is made for mortgage-pledged shares. These have declined consistently in recent years from a total of $42 million at the end of 1957.
[c] Consists of advances from FHLB and other borrowing.
[d] Commitments data comparable with those shown for mutual savings banks would include loans in process.
NOTE: Federal Savings and Loan Insurance Corp. data; figures are estimates for all savings and loan assns. in the United States. Data beginning with 1954 are based on monthly reports of insured assns. and annual reports of noninsured assns. Data before 1954 are based entirely on annual reports. Data for current and preceding year are preliminary even when revised.
SOURCE: *Federal Reserve Bulletin*, February 1968, p. A-32.

108

strain caused by the interest rate rivalry with commercial banks in the mid-1960's has prompted savings and loan associations to seek relief. They have requested authority to make installment loans on automobiles and appliances. so they can increase their earnings.

Saving at a Credit Union

Persons who work in a company that has 500 or more employees usually will be invited to join the local credit union. One joins by purchasing one or more "shares," which generally sell for five dollars each. Savings of any amount may be made thereafter. A credit union is a cooperative organization that divides earnings among its shareholders on a share-for-share basis. Actually the shareholders are likely to receive from 4 to 6 per cent for the use of their funds. If earnings justify more than 6 per cent, the credit union may reduce the percentage rates charged of borrowers or it may add the remainder to its reserve funds.

It is natural that employees find it convenient to save at the credit union where they work. They choose the credit union for their saving, also because of the opportunity for low-interest loans. They may wish to use these loans for financing their next baby, household appliance, or automobile.

Credit unions have enjoyed several advantages, which have created animosity on the part of some rival credit institutions. In most cases, a credit union is welcomed by employers who are thereby relieved of requests for frequent advances on paychecks. In return for this advantage, management usually provides desk space, some free publicity, and a few moments of company time for credit-union officers to devote to their collecting and bookkeeping chores. Since members, officers, and borrowers all work for the same employer, losses on loans are usually inconsequential, earnings are dependable, and funds are secure.

In 1966 there were 17,000 credit unions with assets of $10 billion. The fact that these organizations seek to make no profit, enjoy extremely low-operating costs, and lend at low-interest rates accounts for their popularity. It also explains their ability to attract savings in spite of high interest rates offered by rival organizations. It should be noted, of course, that rival credit institutions must pay additional taxes, pay heavy operating costs, and seek to make a profit. Consequently, the success of any one credit union should be measured only in comparison with other credit unions.

Government Bonds for Savers

Saving plans can be built rather easily around the purchase of United States savings bonds. Thousands of Americans respond readily to the appeal to support their government's needs while achieving a guaranteed 4 to 5 per cent yield on their investment. There are in current use several dozen types of United States Government bonds and several hundred state and local bond issues. Of these, the three that are most commonly bought in relatively small holdings will be discussed here.

Series E Bonds. Series E bonds may be bought through payroll withholding or by direct purchase at any bank. An individual who is new to saving is likely to buy Series E bonds for these reasons: first, they are sold in low denominations; second, they are promoted and sold by many agencies; third, their redemption values are guaranteed; and fourth, they are popular because $18.75 invested in a $25 bond creates the illusion of immediate affluence or gain.

The inclusion of accumulated interest in the final value of these bonds distinguishes Series E *appreciation bonds* from most other bonds called *current-income* bonds that pay interest periodically. Since Series E bonds are designed to be sold for three-fourths of their face value, the time necessary for their maturity becomes the variable by which their actual interest rate may be changed. At first the rate was approximately 3 per cent and the bonds were redeemable in ten years. More recently the redemption time has been reduced to 7¾ years and then to seven years, thus increasing the bond's current interest rate to 4¼ per cent. It may be expected that this time-interest rate ratio will be subject to further change. Moreover, the purchase of these bonds is now tied in with the right to acquire high interest bonus *Freedom bonds* as the Treasury Department seeks to keep its Series E bonds competitively priced and attractive enough to induce continued purchases. Incidentally, the built-in interest in Series E appreciation bonds must be acknowledged as taxable income, either as the bonds appreciate or at the time of their redemption.

Series H Bonds. When a person has saved a thousand dollars he may be interested in purchasing a Series H bond. These bonds pay 4¼ per cent interest, payable by check semi-annually; hence, they are known as *income bonds* as compared with the Series E appreciation bonds. In 1965 the interest rate on these bonds was raised from 3¾ per cent. The Treasury Department is determined to keep this rate competitive with interest rates offered by other savings institutions.

Treasury Bills and Notes. There are many types of government bonds (see Table 4–5) that a person might use to safeguard his accumulating funds. Three-month and six-month treasury bills and five-year treasury notes may be purchased from a bank which acquires them from its nearby Federal Reserve Bank. Treasury bills are bought in $1,000 lots at discounted prices; this permits

Savings Institutions

Table 4-5

(left)
Source: *Wall Street Journal*, February 9, 1968, p. 20.

(Right)
Source: *New York Times*, February 22, 1968, p. L49.

their owner to realize from 3½ to 5½ per cent on his investment. Treasury notes may be purchased in one- to five-year maturities bearing a fixed-interest rate. They are priced so that their actual return equals an interest rate comparable to other bond rates at the moment.

State and Municipal Bonds. A so-called municipal bond is issued by a state, county, city, school district, water department, sewer district, or toll highway. Usually, these bonds are backed by a pledge of tax revenues and some bonds are graded higher than others where the taxing authority is only mildly encumbered with obligations against the tax base. Some of these issues on toll bridges or on water districts are known as *revenue bonds* since the revenues derived from the service are expected to pay their interest and pay for their eventual retirement. The tax district pays these charges only if and when the operating revenues fail to meet these requirements.

The particular significance of municipal bonds is that the interest they pay is not subject to the federal income tax, hence they are bought readily by persons with middle and upper-bracket incomes. Because they are bought so readily, the issuing authorities usually can issue them at relatively low-interest rates. An investor's high income-tax bracket, for example, may entice him to buy a 3½ per cent municipal instead of a 5 per cent corporation bond because his after-tax earnings would be higher on the former investment. For this reason, many a city or county is tempted to attract new industry by financing plant construction with low-rate *municipal-industrial bonds.* This recent development is meeting some opposition, since it appears to rival firms, rival cities, and some investment bankers as a mere subterfuge to issue tax-exempt corporate bonds.

Life Insurance as Savings

Life insurance is frequently a device that induces individuals to start saving and to continue saving habits. Many persons save this way and no other; hence, the cajolery of insurance agents may be expedient sometimes.

It should be noted, first, that *term insurance* protects only against the financial tragedy that accompanies an untimely death. All other types of insurance include some savings in addition to basic insurance. It is the savings element of these straight life, limited-payment life, and endowment policies that is considered here; other aspects of life insurance will be discussed in Chapter 14.

A Locked-In Savings Plan. Because losses will be sustained if an insurance plan is dropped, the insured individual is inclined to continue his payments even though some of them present a hardship. It seems apparent, nevertheless, that many customers do not understand the savings features of the insurance plans they have bought. As a consequence, the average insurance policy is kept less than ten years, and the customer seldom reaps the full benefit of his savings plan.

The Disadvantages of Life-Insurance Savings. When a person buys insurance, he should be most concerned with the need for protecting his dependents against financial losses that may accompany his premature death. This kind of protection can be bought in the form of term insurance. Term insurance is priced low in the insured's earliest years since the probability of death is lowest at that time. When a young family's needs for insurance protection are greatest, it may not be wise to add a savings feature to the insurance program at the cost of reduced insurance coverage. Unfortunately, many persons are underinsured because they embark on a savings program that contains too little insurance coverage.

The customer who buys a straight life, limited-payment, or endowment insurance policy acquires an asset against which he eventually may borrow or collect someday if he surrenders his policy. These savings, plus the insurance protection in the meantime, make these policies very popular. However, insurance as savings is not and cannot be a very remunerative investment, since insurance companies are compelled to invest so cautiously that their earnings are scarcely 5 per cent. Most insurance companies pay the customers only 4 per cent on the savings portion of insurance premiums. Thus it may be concluded that there are other places to invest one's savings at a higher rate of return.

Other Savings Institutions and Plans

At some point, a savings institution and a savings plan become primarily investment institutions and plans. Investment constitutes the major subject of Chapters 5 to 8; hence the emphasis here should be on savings. Several of the institutions and plans included here, especially those involving the purchase of government bonds, might be contained appropriately in the chapters on investments. In addition, some of the institutions and plans that follow below also may belong in those chapters. Even though many families may save routinely all their lives and never consider the purchase of government bonds, corporate securities, or rental real estate, all the institutions and plans that might be considered by such families have been treated in this chapter as savings institutions. Several others remain to be covered briefly.

Home Investments as Savings. A family saves in two ways when it purchases a home. It saves by investing money in landscaping, furniture, and added facilities. This investment is almost always over and above the payments associated with the mortgage on the home. If the added investment is made at the expense of other things that would have been bought and the family has acquired a salable asset, it has really saved. It should be noted also that most families spend long hours of toil on their newly acquired properties; in this sense their "sweat equity" provides a salable asset, and they also save.

Borrowing to Save and Invest. Sometimes small-scale investors are invited to borrow to finance an investment that yields a very high return. Frequently the vendors of speculative investments, including second mortgages or second trust deeds, have offered to assist their customers in financing these purchases. If the investment proves to be successful, the customer has acquired an asset that has a value in excess of the debt against it. In that sense the customer has saved and earned by going into debt. If the investment proves to be unsound, the value of the asset will not equal the indebtedness, and a loss will have been sustained.

Savings by Investing in One's Future. Many unmarried young people forego other pleasures and work part time to be able to stay in school and further their careers. Many a newly married husband attends night school for the same reason. Young doctors in medical school or in internships or young men who embark on a graduate program leading toward an M.A., M.S., M.B.A., D.B.A., or Ph.D. degree usually may live a miserly, hermit-like existence while they invest everything in their education.

There are many things to be said for the financial and psychic values that accompany investment in one's self. First, this type of investment is unique in the sense that it cannot be lost or taken away. Second, it becomes part of the person who has committed himself to this venture. And finally, most people thrive because of the challenge of a respected profession; moreover, their lives are enriched because of the struggle, the sacrifices, and the eventual achievement.[8]

QUESTIONS

1. What constitutes saving according to the Federal Reserve study cited in this chapter?
2. Distinguish between consumer assets and financial assets. Why is the latter term needed in discussing savings institutions and stock market investments?
3. Explain and illustrate how people can benefit financially and in other ways as a result of personal habits of thrift.

Savings Institutions

4. Explain the effect of personal savings on the national economy. How are these savings used?
5. What are the consequences if some people save too much and others save too little?
6. If saving is not limited to investment in earning assets, then what are the logical objectives for saving?
7. How do children or primitive people save? What are the more mature ways in which savings should be held or invested?
8. Check the term-insurance rates and straight-life rates which you would pay on an insurance policy for the next 20 years. Note the death benefits, loan value, and cash-surrender value of each policy. Which policy would you buy and why?
9. Inquire about housing values and determines whether owners are being rewarded for the time and money which they spend on their properties.
10. Under what circumstances might one accumulate savings by going into debt?
11. How could you invest profitably in your own career? What monetary return and what psychological return could be expected for the projected expenditure of time and money?
12. Note carefully all of the key terms in this chapter and be prepared to define each of them in your own words.

SELECTED READINGS

Bureau of Federal Credit Unions, *Report of Operations, Federal Credit Unions*, U. S. Dept. of Health, Education, and Welfare, latest ed.

CUNA International Inc., *International Credit Union Yearbook*, Madison, Wisconsin, published annually.

Croteau, John T., *The Economics of the Credit Union*, Wayne State University Press, Detroit, 1963.

Dougall, Herbert E., *Capital Markets and Institutions*, Stanford University, 1965.

Duesenbery, James S., *Income Saving and the Theory of Consumer Behavior*, Oxford University Press, New York, 1967 (paperback).

Friend, Irwin, *Individuals' Saving: Volume and Composition*, John Wiley, New York, 1967.

Goldsmith, Raymond W., *The Flow of Capital Funds in the Postwar Economy*, National Bureau of Economic Research, Columbia University Press, New York, 1965.

Goldsmith, Raymond W., *The National Wealth of the United States in the Postwar Period*, National Bureau of Economic Research, Princeton University Press, Princeton, 1962.

Goldsmith, Raymond W., and Robert E. Lipsey, *Studies in the National Balance Sheet of the United States*, Vol. I, National Bureau of Economic Research, Princeton University Press, Princeton, 1963.

Goldsmith, Raymond W., et al., *A Study of Savings in the United States*, 3 vols., National Bureau of Economic Research, Princeton University Press, Princeton, 1956.

Savings and Home Financing Source Book, Federal Home Loan Bank Board, Washington, D. C., latest ed.

Savings and Loan Fact Book, United States Savings and Loan League, Chicago, latest ed.

Securities of the United States Government, The First Boston Corporation, Boston, published annually.

NOTES

1. Raymond W. Goldsmith, *The Flow of Capital Funds in the Postwar Economy*, National Bureau of Economic Research, Columbia University Press, New York, 1965, p. 34; Raymond W. Goldsmith and Robert E. Lipsey, *Studies in the National Balance Sheet of the United States*, Volume I, National Bureau of Economic Research, Princeton University Press, Princeton, 1963, pp. 260–261.
2. *Federal Reserve Bulletin*, Board of Governors, Federal Reserve System, Washington, January 1967, p. 148.
3. "Size and Composition of Consumer Saving," *Federal Reserve Bulletin, Ibid.*, pp. 32–50.
4. *Ibid.*, pp. 35–37.
5. *Ibid.*
6. A depositor who writes very few checks each month pays a sizeable service charge because of the aforementioned flat rate. A "ten-plan" or "twenty-plan" account costing about 12 cents a check usually will be less costly for an account of this sort.
7. From 30 to 180 days' notice may be demanded by a savings and loan association if withdrawals are to its disadvantage.
8. Marguerite C. Burk, "On the Need for Investment in Human Capital for Consumption," *The Journal of Consumer Affairs*, Vol. 1, No. 2, Winter 1967, pp. 123–138.

PROBLEMS AND CASES

1. Inquire about service-charge schedules at several commercial banks and estimate what minimum balance would have to be held in the bank to avoid a service charge in a normally active checking account. Find out how much interest could be expected on that minimum balance if it were invested in (1) a bank savings department, (2) a credit union, (3) a mutual savings bank, (4) a savings and loan association, or (5) some other type of savings institution. What conclusion can be drawn concerning the most economical way to use a checking account?
2. Get the latest information about interest rates, guarantee plans, and withdrawal privileges offered by the several types of savings institutions in your community.
3. Find out how much a Series E bond will be worth if cashed in (1) three years after its purchase; (2) five years after its purchase; (3) six years after its purchase. In view of the currently prevailing level of interest rates offered by the insured savings institution paying the highest interest rate on savings in your community, when is it and when is it not advisable to buy Series E bonds? Find out about Freedom bonds: Their earnings and the conditions of their sale.
4. Go to a bank or to a savings institution and find out how much you would have to deposit a month to accumulate $3,000 in ten years at the current rate of interest compounded quarterly. How much would your savings amount to after

Savings Institutions

20 years at the same rate of saving? What would you probably do with that money after ten years? After 20 years? What other advantages would the account provide even if it is not cashed in during this period?

5. Is it the FDIC or FSLIC insurance of up to $15,000 that really safeguards a bank deposit or a savings deposit, or is it the nature of investments that these institutions make and the reserves that they keep? If you were a bank examiner and already knew that a bank's assets balanced liabilities plus net worth, what would you really examine to judge the soundness of the bank? If, as a potential saver, you wished to judge any savings institution, what would you inquire about? What could the institution's balance sheet reveal?

6. In former years when bankers demanded a pledge of earning securities as collateral, how or from whom could consumers borrow? What collateral have consumers to pledge? Would you want your savings loaned to businessmen, to consumers, to housing, or to college students who are preparing for professional careers? Which of these is likely to earn and to pay the highest interest return? Which is most needed by the borrower? Which provides the greatest social benefit? Is there an evolution in our thinking about saving and lending and the nature of acceptable collateral?

7. Based upon savings data provided by the Federal Reserve, which population segments in this country (1) save, (2) dissave, (3) neither save nor dissave? Approximately what percentage of financial advantage should accrue to the savers because of (1) the interest received, (2) avoidance of finance charges, and (3) both of these financial advantages? Is there evidence that the nonsavers can or will catch up? If not, what are the probable socioeconomic consequences of this spread between the "haves" and the "have-nots"?

8. Do the statistics seem to indicate that nonsavers catch up in years of prosperity or do they find more occasions to buy on installment credit instead of adding to savings?

9. Do high interest rates seem to induce saving and low rates discourage saving? If so, why do some segments of the population fail to respond to interest-rate inducements? What are the other explanations for extensive saving by some of the people and the lack of saving by others?

10. How do credit unions invest their money? Do they get a high rate of return commensurate with the risk they assume? Should they pay a higher percentage rate on savings? Why?

11. If the last dollars of the annual income of a man who is 5 years away from retirement are in a 30 per cent income-tax bracket, show that he might be wise to invest his next $1,000 in Series E bonds instead of some other savings plan that pays 5 per cent annually. Why would Series H bonds paying the same rate as Series E bonds not yield the same result?

12. In an affluent economy, is there need for people who are anxious to save more than the national average? Should not ambitious young people aspire to own more than an average share of investments in American industry? How much could they have after saving ten dollars a month for ten years at 5 per cent interest compounded quarterly? How much if they saved ten dollars a week?

5 FINANCIAL AND INVESTMENT PROGRAMS

The way to get money is to work for it, and the way to have money is to keep it by investing soundly.

JOHN C. CLENDENIN

With savings one may be ready to embark on an investment program. Unfortunately, the sobering responsibility that confronts a prospective investor raises many questions. How much should an individual have accumulated before he commences to invest regularly? How much of his worldly assets should remain in liquid or cash form? What are the elements of a satisfactory investment program? Does a novice investor dare to risk his rainy-day fund or the down payment on the home he hopes to buy? Should an investment program consist of a savings account, common stocks, or government bonds, or should the investor start his own small business? These and a number of other questions may suggest the emphasis of this chapter.

PROVIDING FOR FINANCIAL SECURITY

Provision for financial security including debt management, a savings account, life-insurance buying, and the acquisition of a home is recommended as the first stage of an investment program. This approach draws heavily on budgeting, the use of personal credit, and saving. These topics constitute the broadest possible approach to the study of an investment program.

Elements of a Satisfactory Investment Program

There are three necessary steps leading to investment. First, one has to have a surplus beyond his needs. Second, one requires the willpower to forego the use of some of his own funds. And finally, one must be willing to part with his savings and allow their use for purposes other than his own. Usually, an investor starts by saving, rather than by spending some apparent windfall. Otherwise, saving is a habit that must be cultivated the hard way.

Many persons who never buy a stock, a bond, or a trust deed are the owners of bank accounts, insurance policies, and other assets. These assets actually create funds for others to invest. Thus a person who has certain types of life insurance is actually an investor, indirectly.

A paradox develops. Many persons do not save, in the familiar sense of the word; thus it would seem that very few are in a position to make investments. As we have seen, however, the term saving may be understood to include net investment in consumer durable goods. Hence there is the possibility that people invest more than at first might be presumed. Moreover, as consumer durable goods sometimes are purchased on the installment plan, many investments of this sort have not been preceded by saving.

Stages of a Satisfactory Primary Investment Program

The various stages of a financial program will be reviewed in the approximate order in which they should be undertaken. Bear in mind, however, that younger families with unusual financial responsibilities may not progress beyond the first stage of the program. But since such families usually outlive periods of financial stress, they may be wise to keep the long-range program in mind. They can then work toward it whenever they are able to do so.

Savings in Commercial Bank Accounts. A checking account in a commercial bank would seem to be the first step in a financial program. A checking account is convenient and safe, it may be used in a budgeting system, and check stubs facilitate simple record keeping. These facts commend it for the consideration of persons who hope to achieve a degree of financial independence in later years. Although not a financial program in any important way, a commercial bank account is the basis on which such a program may be built. Individuals who do not have such accounts are not likely to enter into the advanced stages of a financial program.

The objectives for the individual or family to achieve with a checking account are the building up of a bank account and its maintenance at a level of several hundred dollars. It may be advisable to keep the balance at an amount that makes service charges unnecessary for the average number of checks written against the account each month. In most communities this amount is likely to range between $600 and $1,000 for most persons. If, however, a constant balance of $800 is necessary to avoid service charges, and the account has reached a level of $900, the last $100 may be removed and placed in a savings account or perhaps in a savings and loan association. A financial program is then under way. However, many persons never reach this goal.

Commercial bank accounts provide safety for a prospective investor's funds and *liquidity of funds*—that is, immediate withdrawal is permissible. Each of these advantages is important to those whose primary concern must be the security of their funds.

An Adequate Insurance Program. The financial security of a family is so important that it is quite necessary for the chief income provider to be insured adequately. This becomes urgent even before the checking account can be built up to a favorable level. Insurance is an intricate subject about which a considerable amount of detail will be included in Chapter 14. The only purpose for referring to insurance here is to consider its proper place in a financial program. Actually, when any young man undertakes to provide financial support for the young lady he marries he is normally obligated to carry life insurance, naming her as the beneficiary. With the arrival of children, the mother can scarcely be expected to seek gainful employment while caring for her youngsters. In consequence, the husband and father is obligated to carry an adequate amount of life insurance. In a typical case, a young family man should carry more than $30,000 worth of life insurance. The average man in this country carries half that amount nowadays.

The financial tragedy affecting families when early death removes the husband and father may be so great that it can impose unusual sacrifices on the survivors. Certainly, the level of living is seriously depressed. The widow may face a losing and hopeless financial struggle, and her children are almost certain to be underprivileged. Since this tragedy may occur, life insurance becomes a necessity. It is the family's defense against adversity. It is a vital part of the financial program.

A Savings Account. When a commercial bank account reaches a satisfactory level, it is advisable, as stated previously, to transfer some funds into a savings account. This assumes that the family has adequate life-insurance coverage, of course. It also assumes that proper insurance is carried against accidents, fire, and other hazards.

There are quite a few institutions that are worthy of recommendation as depositors for savings. Ordinarily banks usually maintain savings departments for this purpose, but as a rule they pay only 3, 4, or 5 per cent interest. Money must be left in these accounts for three- or six-month periods to draw interest, ordinarily. Only the convenience of having a savings account in the same institution with one's checking account seems to justify its use for most persons. Special savings projects such as "Christmas savings clubs" are commendable, though not for the interest that they yield.

Savings and loan associations are found in almost every community. As noted in the preceding chapter, they pay a higher-interest rate normally than savings banks or the savings department of a commercial bank. Savings banks usually lend money for housing and for personal loans. Savings and loan associations lend most of their money for housing. In either case, the institution is probably quite safe in normal times because its investments are reasonably sound. And since the federal government tends to buttress the building trades and the housing industry in depression periods, these investments are supported, at least indirectly, in that way. So, for a generation at least, investments in savings banks and savings and loan associations have been quite secure. Also, as explained previously, deposits in most of these institutions are insured up to $15,000.

Home Ownership. For a family that is reasonably certain to remain in a given community, home ownership may be recommended. A home serves as a primary link in a family's way of life. Home ownership provides a family with stability and security. The stability lies in the family's increasing equity in the property as a portion of each monthly payment is applied toward retirement of the mortgage indebtedness. Although it is hoped that the family will not have to borrow against the equity in its home, the possibility of such borrowing constitutes a measure of financial security. The same security probably would not have been attained if the same family had been tenants. A number of other facets of this subject will be included in Chapter 9.

Investment in Government Bonds. Many individuals have acquired investments in government bonds, especially during the years of the Second World War. Frequently these investments have not been part of a planned financial program. Rather they have been expedients undertaken at the behest of an employer or of a bond-selling committee. Through them the government sought to eliminate inflation by depriving ordinary individuals of some of their excess purchasing power at a time when civilian goods were noticeably scarce in the market. Since the government has not really been retiring this indebtedness, there is a tendency for many persons to retain government bonds as a form of long-range investment.

Considering the inflationary price trend of the last two decades, the holding of Series E bonds by individuals has not been particularly profitable. A $75 investment in Series E bonds is repaid with $100 about seven years later. Unfortunately, the $100 may fail to buy as much as the original $75 had bought seven years earlier. This is not to say, however, that the individual should not have bought these bonds. He did force himself to save money that otherwise might not have been saved. The facts that these bonds are a safe, low-income investment and that they are *liquid*—that is, cashable at any bank, 60 days after their purchase—indicate that they contain the necessary elements of a safe, nonspeculative, primary investment.

Government bonds come in assorted sizes, guarantees, and rates of return, as noted in the preceding chapter. A novice investor may be wise to consider their purchase. A few well-chosen corporation bonds also may serve as safe investments for individuals whose primary concern must be for the safety of their funds. Corporation bonds will be discussed further in the next chapter.

Necessity for Secure, Low-Income Investments

There is a tendency for persons of little means to try to catch up financially. These people play the "long shots" at the races or seek a high return on their few dollars by investing in oil stocks, in uranium mines, or in the stocks of small, new companies engaged in fledgling enterprises.

The less a person has to invest, however, the less risk he can afford. Deviations from this basic rule are costly to individuals or to governments. Obviously, the antidote lies in the willingness of each individual and family to formulate and follow a sound investment program. Risk taking and its twin associates, higher returns and higher taxes, may come later in the second stage.

If a family can acquire savings, life insurance, and a home while holding its routine expenditures in check, it may accumulate sufficient financial resources to be ready to enter into the second stage of an investment program. Many persons, unfortunately, risk their essential reserve funds. Savings that may be necessary for emergencies or for retirement may find their way into the stock market. In this instance, if investment is undertaken, the emphasis should be on the safety and liquidity of these funds. That is, bonds and gilt-edged stocks most likely should be selected even though their rate of return may be very low.

Investments in stocks and bonds that are listed on a stock exchange may be converted into cash at any time. The risk is that their selling price may be low rather than high at the moment that their owner urgently may need cash. Investors who have urgent reasons for emphasis on liquidity and security might better place their money in government bonds, in a commercial bank, in a savings and loan association, or in carefully selected corporate bonds. With these investments, the need for safety and liquidity is likely to be met, but the rate of return is destined to be relatively low.

INCOME AS AN INVESTMENT OBJECTIVE

For those ready to embark on the second stage of an investment program, some risks may be taken in the hope of obtaining greater returns. Investments in government bonds and low-return, gilt-edged corporate securities may be replaced by a vigilant search for half-hidden facts that may lead to unusual investment opportunities with high-income potentials. Obviously, opportunities of this sort are difficult to find, otherwise the securities would be *overpriced*. They would be sought by so many persons that their purchase price would tend to be bid up excessively. For this reason, sharp investors who seek high returns must expect to spend a considerable amount of their time in search of promising opportunities. Obviously, there is quite an element of risk involved because the investors are actually wagering that the situations that they have uncovered will result in substantial returns.

It should be noted that most investments of this sort focus on the prospects of *increment*, or increase in the value of the shares. In many cases, the investors also seek high dividends. Thus, if a privately owned firm has a phenomenally prosperous year, it could be sold to a new owner for a high price. If the company is incorporated, the value of its shares will increase sharply because of the expectation of high dividends. The value of the shares may also rise, despite a modest dividend, because the earnings are high. Because of this possibility, the investor watches a corporation's earnings as well as its dividend record. He also watches the trend of its business, the efficiency of its management, the long-run potentiality for its products, and the diversity of its activities. Then, too, he explores its prospects in wartime or in various phases of the business cycle, its accumulated reserves, its outstanding indebtedness, and the nature of its competition. Most of all, an investor watches the reports about a company and the general market trend. The price of a stock will surely go up if enough people expect a rise and buy the stocks; conversely, the price of a stock will go down if enough people expect a decline and sell the stock.

Recent theory has it that the price of a stock depends primarily upon earnings—whether or not they are paid out in dividends. Only a small proportion of stockholders—mainly institutions, trusts, and wealthy individuals—are interested in dividends, which are taxed at the rate applicable to other taxable income rather than at the capital-gains rate.

The price that rational investors pay for a stock is the present value of the income stream they expect from the security, discounted at an appropriate rate. To illustrate, an investor will gladly put down $.92 today to receive $1 a year from today. For another $.85 he will also get $1 two years from today. Thus, if he expects a security to yield an 8 per cent return for the next decade, he will be willing to pay $6.71 in order to receive $1 at the end of each of the next ten years.

According to economic theory, each rational investor seeks to maximize the present value of his wealth. He plans his investment program so that the value of each investment is the highest that is possible with respect to his preference for risk. Therefore, he *shifts his holdings so as to increase the discounted income stream from each of his investments up to the limit imposed by his wish to avoid higher risk.* Thus he is maximizing when he has arranged his portfolio of investments so that he can obtain the highest possible return in accord with his risk preference from each dollar invested.

The term *yield* is frequently used with reference to bonds, although it may be applied to any investment. The yield of an investment is the quotient of the annual dividend or interest paid divided by the market price of a security. Thus, if American Telephone and Telegraph shares paid an annual return of $9 and the shares could have been bought for $150, the yield would have been $9 ÷ $150, or 6 per cent. If the same security had been selling at $180, the yield would have been only 5 per cent: $9 ÷ $180 = 0.05 or 5 per cent. Since the traditional yield expected of this security by the experts was approximately 6 per cent, the experts preferred not to recommend its purchase at a price above $150. It is the common jargon of the market place to speak of a security as if it were *priced to yield* a certain percentage. Thus, if American Telephone and Telegraph had been priced to yield 6 per cent, that price would have been $150.

Types of Investment Risks

Investors who are willing to assume risks in exchange for increased income should consider several types of risks and the possibilities of minimizing them. John C. Clendenin in his *Introduction to Investments* lists the following investment risks:[1] (1) the *business or functional* risk in which declining investment values are caused by waning patronage, reduced earning power, uncontrollable costs, management error, unforeseen government action, and other business hazards; (2) the *market risk* in which the market prices of securities decline even though their earnings are normal; (3) the *money-rate risk* in which the attractiveness and price of certain securities diminish because of the shifting availability of money and the general change in interest rates; and (4) the *price-level risk* in which the value of an investment such as government bonds will be affected adversely by rising prices and a corresponding decline in the value of the dollar because of the bonds' promise of settlement in a specified number of dollars.

Minimizing Investment Risks

Since so many persons seek higher incomes from their investments in spite of the risks involved, it seems appropriate to examine several ways in which these risks may be offset or minimized. First, there is the business risk relative to a company's management and its level of earnings. This risk can be minimized by a careful selection of companies whose securities are to be purchased. Moreover, by spreading one's investments over a number of types of companies and between bonds and stocks, an individual may diversify his investment. Unfortunate selections are thus offset by better ones. *Diversification*, that is, the holding of a variety of types of investments, is valuable also in offsetting the market risk.

The money-rate risk may be reduced by combining well-chosen common stocks and bonds in the same *portfolio*, or group of security holdings. This risk and the price-level risk may be tempered by purchasing securities at uniform intervals throughout the business cycle. Such a practice involves *dollar averaging*, which means the investment of an equal number of dollars at specified times in a given security or group of securities. Sometimes the ill effects of changes in the price level may be offset by *buying or selling* futures, that is, the *purchase* or sale is completed with delivery postponed for as much as 12 months. Thus, if a flour miller anticipated increasing wheat prices, he might buy wheat on the *futures market* six months in advance of his needs. If an ordinary investor holds a number of bonds and fears that he might lose purchasing power because of inflation and the price-level risk, he might *hedge* against receiving a fixed-dollar settlement by purchasing common stocks or some kinds of real estate whose market prices should reflect the inflationary movements. Conversely, a person whose investments consist largely of common stocks or real estate should hedge with bonds if he expects a serious recession to affect the market price of his holdings. No hedge can be perfect, of course,

INVESTMENT IN GROWTH STOCKS

Many investors who have provided amply for the security of their families often desire to own and *manage* a growing business or so-called *growth stocks*. The value of growth stocks, it is hoped, will increase materially over the years. By such investments, an individual may build up a sizable estate as the stocks or the business increase in market value. Investors in growth stocks are often successful men, thirty to sixty-five years old. They seek no more current income because of the high tax bracket in which additional income would fall.* In place of current income they want capital gains derived from rising stock prices. The capital gains are not taxed until the stock is sold—perhaps during low-income retirement years. If the stock is passed on to heirs, there is an additional tax advantage, which will be explained in Chapter 17.

Investors who are interested in growth stocks are searching constantly for firms whose line of business or unique management or research program suggests a phenomenal rate of growth. Among many small companies, earnings in the early years of the firm's existence are reinvested in the business. An investor is on the trail of a good growth situation when he has found a company with high or potentially high earnings accompanied by a modest dividend policy. He is likely to find dramatic growth in a company that has an excellent research department engaged continually in the development of new products that diversify the company's output.

A rational investor is interested in the maximum present value of the stream of *anticipated income after taxes*. Dividends are subject to the personal income tax at the full rate.** Appreciation of the security's market price is subject to the less costly capital-gains rate only if the security is held longer than six months (see Chapter 12). An investor in one of the higher tax brackets can maximize his present wealth or present net worth by investing in nondividend paying stocks, on which he anticipates the highest earnings. Because of high demand, the price of growth stocks is often very high in relation to their earnings.

INVESTMENT IN A SMALL BUSINESS

Many individuals who are in a financial position to make investments sometimes consider buying or starting a small business. There are nearly ten

---

* An alternative long-term tax rate of 25% may be used, however.
** Subject to dividend exclusion as explained in chapter 12.

million business units in the United States.[2] Most of them are small-scale, individually owned enterprises. Business ownership may demand the investor's total resources and energies, or it may be a sideline in which the investor may become a silent partner of the individual who actually manages the firm. In some cases, this latter arrangement may be practical. However, an investor should exercise caution in the choice of associates and the risks he assumes in business ventures, since he may become more deeply involved than anticipated.

Why do people go into business for themselves? What determines whether they will succeed or fail? How much capital is needed? Where may it be obtained? What skills does managing a business entail? What are the advantages and disadvantages of individually owned firms, partnerships, and corporate organizations? The detailed answers to these questions pertaining to the operation of a small business may be especially important. Many of the same business-management problems on a magnified scale affect the corporations in whose affairs many stockholders have a vested interest.

Reasons for Starting and Managing a Small Business

People decide to start and manage small businesses for various reasons. They may prefer working for themselves to working for others; they may believe that they can make more money in business for themselves than in any other way; they may be confident that the enterprise will be a sound investment, or they may have no other alternative.

There are many persons who enjoy responsibility and independence. The owner-manager of a small firm has untold responsibilities and ordinarily is free to stand or fall on the consequences of his own decisions. Success stories have pointed the way for others; realistically or not, each person believes that his business will prosper. Among some groups in our society, there is enough status in being the owner of a business to compensate for the struggles of the initial phases of proprietorship, for the long hours, and for the lower earnings than those obtainable by working for others. For many, and these include the handicapped, the socially unemployable, and many older, semiretired people, this is the only feasible way of earning a living.

Success or Failure in Business

On the average the business life of firms in the United States is from six to eight years.[3] Few go bankrupt, but many close their doors because their owners can earn more in some other type of employment. Yet as fast as firms die, others are born; so the number of firms in the United States continues to grow, slowly but steadily. The most common causes of business failure are listed and classified in Table 5–1.

Table 5-1. Why Businesses Fail: Year Ended June 30, 1966 (Per Cent)

Apparent Causes	Manufacturing	Wholesale	Retail	Construction	Commercial Service	Total
Neglect	3.0	4.7	4.2	4.0	3.1	3.9
Fraud	1.7	2.7	1.2	1.8	0.8	1.5
Inexperience, incompetence	92.2	90.3	91.2	91.5	92.8	91.5
Inadequate sales	42.5	41.5	43.9	20.8	40.5	38.7
Heavy operating expenses	15.3	8.6	5.1	35.1	15.4	13.7
Receivables difficulties	13.8	20.5	5.7	14.5	5.0	9.9
Inventory difficulties	3.5	6.7	9.0	2.2	1.4	5.9
Excessive fixed assets	6.8	2.3	3.6	3.8	8.0	4.4
Poor location	1.0	1.6	6.6	0.6	3.1	3.8
Competitive weakness	19.5	20.3	25.9	19.5	24.3	23.1
Other	7.2	6.9	3.6	6.1	4.9	5.1
Disaster	2.2	1.1	1.4	0.6	0.8	1.3
Reason unknown	0.9	1.2	2.0	2.1	2.5	1.8
Total number of failures	1,863	1,275	6,010	2,448	1,315	12,911

SOURCE: Compiled by DUN & BRADSTREET, Inc. Classification based on opinion of creditors and information in credit reports. Since some failures are attributed to a combination of causes, percentages do not add up to 100 percent. *Dun's Review*, September 1966, p. 15.

The success of an owner depends on four factors: first, whether there is a large-enough market for his product or service at the price at which it is offered; second, whether an adequate amount of capital can be found; third, whether the business can be run as efficiently as that of its competitors; and fourth, whether the owner-manager can adapt well enough to any circumstance to keep his business operating profitably.

Ease of Entry. A major reason for the high failure rate is the ease with which a firm may be established in our economy. Anyone with an idea who can raise the necessary capital to take out a business license and who can arrange for the facilities, labor, and materials or merchandise inventory needed to "open the doors" becomes an owner and manager of a firm.

Importance of a Business Survey. Too many persons who start business ventures undertake little or no preliminary investigation of the problems related to the management of a business. Asking a few questions of friends and looking over the scene is hardly a valid method of finding out whether there will be enough customers for the product or service at the price they will set for it. Some of those who have had previous business experience may do some market research or they may conduct some economic research, that is, find out the unit cost of production and whether the firm is likely to prosper.

Importance of Business Experience. The cheapest and easiest way to acquire the necessary contacts and a knowledge of a business is to work for someone else who is in the same endeavor. A knowledge of business techniques and procedures, wherever it may have been acquired, also may prove profitable. An understanding of accounting, and management and marketing techniques in particular, is imperative. Personal qualifications are important too. Experience normally will point out which of these are especially required in any given business. Experience is a good teacher, but only if one's objectives are clear and one is capable of both observing and analyzing. Without awareness of one's objectives, it is entirely possible to work for years and ignore useful information. It is also possible to work under supervision for years and not realize that one lacks the initiative or the capacity to make decisions necessary to insure the success of the self-owned business.

A leading cause of business failure is incompetence. This may or may not be discovered through experience. The next three causes of failure—unbalanced experience, lack of managerial experience, and lack of experience in the line—all stem from insufficient experience in the particular business or from not having had the right kind.

Adequacy of Capital. The most frequent excuse given for business failure is lack of capital. In many cases this is a valid reason. However, the amount of capital needed usually may be calculated. Moreover, the difficulty of obtaining it also can be anticipated with some degree of accuracy.

Many aspiring owners of businesses find themselves hard pressed to raise the capital required to start or to stay in business. Banks ordinarily will not furnish *venture capital*, for the risk is too great; and lenders who assume the risks connected with new ventures charge high rates of interest for doing so. Banks lend money only to firms that can show a record of success and evidence of ability to make a profit. Most small firms must depend on capital that their owners have saved or can borrow by pledging their personal assets as collateral. They also depend on capital that the owners can borrow without collateral from friends and relatives. Unless the business can show a profit before the initial capital has been exhausted, the chances are that the investment and the owner's time may be lost. One-third to one-half of all retail businesses are discontinued within two years.[4]

Different business ventures vary in the amount of capital required. To build a "Breakfast House" costs approximately $75,000. To lease it, complete with an operating franchise, and the opportunity to buy it over a period of time from the profits necessitates only $5,000 to $10,000 in initial capital. The $10,000 will include working capital for the first month of operation. Normally, the proceeds from the venture will be sufficient to meet expenses after the first month. If the location is chosen properly, with the franchise and sponsorship help, there should be profits before the second month has passed.

There are many types of franchises available to those who want to go into business for themselves. Ordinarily, since a parent organization can offer much assistance, acquisition of a franchise is both a safer and more feasible way of investing in a small business. It is one of the least expensive ways of acquiring experience, expert assistance, and of going into business on someone else's capital. The probability of record returns from this sort of venture, however, is reduced by the fact that too many enterprising persons may wish to share in the opportunity.

If a business can operate profitably for a period of months, the bank may become an excellent source of additional capital, particularly *working capital.* That is the money needed to buy additional raw material or inventory, to meet the payroll, and to pay such overhead items as rent, electricity, and office expense, until customers pay for the goods or the services that the enterprise produces and sells. Many small firms are compelled, however, to get credit from suppliers. Some of them *factor* their accounts receivable, that is, when a shipment is made to a customer, the firm's owner takes the invoice—the evidence of the shipment to the factor, a finance company or the factoring department of a bank—and receives the amount that the customer has promised to pay, less a discount for the factor's services.[5] If the enterprise stands a reasonable chance for success, but the lack of capital hinders its growth, it may apply for a loan to one of the private lending corporations whose loans are sponsored by the government's Small Business Administration.

Most small firms are granted credit by suppliers. If they fail to avail themselves of cash discounts by paying, for example, $98 on or before the tenth day following the date of the invoice for a $100 shipment (if the terms are 2/10 net 30), they pay a high price for not utilizing this credit. In the example cited, paying $100 on the thirtieth day from the invoice date means that they have paid $2 more for having $98 worth of merchandise for twenty days without having paid for it. This is the equivalent of an annual interest rate of close

Investment in a Small Business

to 37 per cent. There are more than 18 twenty-day periods in a year and they are paying $2 in interest for each such period for the loan of $98 worth of goods.

Managing a Business

The successful management of a business necessitates the possession and use of information about the business and its environment. This includes knowledge of its competitors, its functions, and its operations. Successful management also demands the proper business strategy, efficient organization, and direction of its operation toward its predetermined goals—of which the most important is the maximization of its profits. Further, it requires supervision of its operation so that it meets necessary standards, control of the business to keep it on its predetermined course, and having a staff adequate to do what has to be done. Information on all these phases of business activity, especially on management techniques, may be obtained from the Small Business Administration.[6]

Accounting as a Management Tool

It is essential for anyone who is going to invest in a business to understand accounting if he is to manage effectively. The two fundamental accounting statements, which must be understood, are the balance sheet and the profit-and-loss or income statement.

Balance Sheet. The condition of a business may be observed from a balance sheet. Issued annually, or more frequently, every balance sheet shows the value of the firm's assets, the amount of its liabilities, and its *net worth*. The assets less the liabilities equal the net worth. Table 5–2 illustrates the balance sheet of a hypothetical business enterprise.

Most of the specific items on a balance sheet are self-explanatory. *Inventory* consists of the stock of materials, merchandise, or products in some stage of production. *Accounts payable* are owed to creditors; *notes payable* are owed to banks. The Small Business Administration (SBA) note included in the balance sheet in Table 5–2 represents a sum owed to the Small Business Administration.

The balance sheet illustrated in Table 5–2 concerns a corporation. An owner who owns one or more stocks is known as a shareholder in the business. In the case of an individual enterprise or a partnership, the share of the net worth owned by the owner or owners is shown as *owners' equity*, or as the net worth of the firm.

Table 5-2. **A Balance Sheet: Assets = Liabilities + Net Worth**

Assets		Liabilities and Net Worth	
Current assets		Current liabilities	
Cash	$ 10,000	Accounts payable	$ 20,000
Inventory	20,000	Notes payable	10,000
Fixed assets		Long-term liabilities	
Equipment	20,000	SBA[a] note	10,000
Building	50,000		
		Net worth	
		Stock	
		Retained earnings	60,000
Total	$100,000	Total	$100,000

[a] Small Business Administration.

Profit-and-Loss Statement. The profit-and-loss statement* reports the income received, the expenses incurred, and the resultant profit or loss of the business for a specified period of time. Table 5–3 represents a profit-and-loss statement of a small corporation. Most of the items, once more, are self-explanatory. *Depreciation*, however, needs some explanation. Over the lifetime of any fixed asset, a portion of its value deteriorates or vanishes each year until the asset is shown to be worthless—or fully depreciated. A fixed asset may be depreciated on the books of a company at a rate that is more or less rapid than the actual rate of the physical impairment of the asset itself. The *addition to surplus* in Table 5–3 is an item representing earnings not paid out as dividends that will be added to the net worth of the firm in the next balance sheet.

Different types of firms include slightly different items on their profit-and-loss statements. A wholesale or retail firm will show no manufacturing costs, but it will show inventory and depreciation. A service firm may have neither manufacturing costs nor inventory. A professional person may list his income under the heading of fees.[7]

Many firms release work-in-progress reports and other financial reports to indicate the current status of the company's operation. The balance sheet and the profit-and-loss statement are used universally, however, and should be understood by everyone who contemplates management responsibilities. Prospective investors who have a stake in the management of a corporation also should learn to use balance sheets and income statements.

* Sometimes called the income statement.

Investment in a Small Business

Table 5-3. **Profit-and-Loss Statement**

Net sales (after all discounts and rebates)		$100,000
Less: Manufacturing costs		
Materials	$20,000	
Labor costs	40,000	
Depreciation charges	10,000	
Miscellaneous operating cost	2,000	
Total manufacturing cost	72,000	
Add: Beginning inventory	20,000	
	92,000	
Deduct: Closing inventory	20,000	
Equals: Manufacturing cost of good goods sold		72,000
Gross profit (or gross margin)		28,000
Less: Selling and administrative costs		2,000
Net operating profit		26,000
Less: Fixed interest charges and state and local taxes		1,500
Net earnings before income taxes		24,500
Less: Corporation Income Taxes		4,000
Net earnings after taxes		20,500
Less: Dividends on stock		10,000
Addition to surplus		10,500

The Prospect of a Profit

A prospective businessman can anticipate a profit only when *total revenues exceed total costs*. This can be demonstrated by the simple break-even graph in Figure 5–1. The vertical axis represents costs and the horizontal axis represents quantity or volume of sales. The line AB represents fixed costs including rent or ownership costs of facilities, heat and lighting costs, etc. The wedge between AB and AD represents the addition of variable costs such as raw materials and the power used for operating machines. The line AD represents the sum of fixed and variable costs or total costs. If total revenues XY rise steeply enough, they will overcome the handicap of fixed costs and they will equal total costs at the point Z, which is known as the break-even point. At Z, total revenue (quantity sold times price) finally equals total costs (fixed plus variable costs

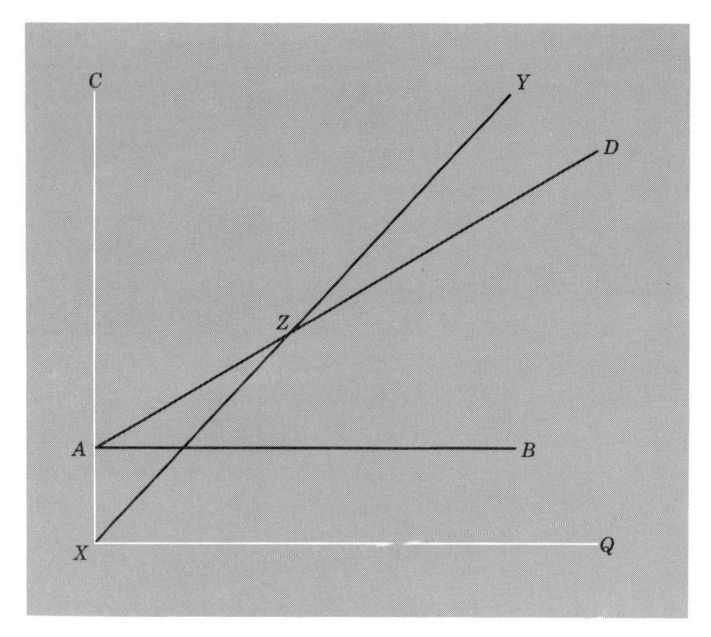

Figure 5-1. A simple break-even graph.

times quantity). Prior to reaching Z, the firm suffers losses. After Z is reached, profits commence.

Many small firms never reach the break-even point. All firms must control costs and achieve a sufficient volume of sales if they are to make a profit. These are the basic risks of going into business. In a free market, private enterprise economy, a profit is not guaranteed. *The businessman has only the prospect of a profit.* If that prospect is good, if he has energy and know-how, and if circumstances are favorable, he may become very prosperous, indeed.

FORMS OF BUSINESS ORGANIZATION

Many persons who would never deign to launch business firms of their own might be willing to enter business with a partner. They also might be interested in buying stocks in a corporation. The majority of people invest in business indirectly because they have deposits in banks or savings institutions. A few individuals prefer to invest directly. Most of these choose corporate enterprises because of advantages that we shall consider.

The country's largest firms tend to be incorporated and financed by the sale of corporate *securities*, that is, stocks and bonds. Corporations and their

Forms of Business Organization

securities usually comprise the substance of investments. However, it is appropriate to examine other forms of business enterprise first, since they serve as an introduction to the corporation and the methods of its financial operation.

An Individual Proprietorship

Most firms in the United States are individual proprietorships. One person owns and operates the firm. The profits belong to him, the losses are his also. He has *unlimited liability* for all debts contracted by the business. All of his property, with the exception of a small minimum that varies from state to state, can be attached by law to meet the debts of the business. In many instances an individual owner of an enterprise will borrow directly from a bank or other lender. He thus retains the business under his own control as long as the enterprise can produce enough money to meet operating costs and permit frequent payments on the debt. Eventually the business may thrive free of debt and solely owned, but during the period of incubation and growth the owner may take little out of the firm.

This is the American dream. It has been repeated so often that the nation has thousands of successful businessmen who "started on a shoestring," and built thriving industries that have provided employment and new products. Seldom are outsiders invited to share in individually owned enterprises, except as money is borrowed temporarily by small enterprisers.

Unhappily, many new industries are destined for failure, since any enterpriser is subject to a number of risks that may cause financial losses. The individual proprietor may "lose his shirt" or his home, and he usually has so little to lose that a short period of business adversity may impoverish him (see Table 5-4).

A Partnership

Partnerships may be formed by any two or more people who wish to engage in a joint business enterprise. Each partner agrees to provide some part of the services or capital and to share some part of the profits, losses, or debts. The agreement to form the partnership may be informal and oral, but it is better practice to have it written and formal. A thrifty partner, for example, may risk the loss of his home and other assets, whereas some less thrifty and less affluent partners may risk little more than their time. Some of the losses of partners and individual enterprisers may be covered by insurance and avoided by several legal arrangements, but the principle of *unlimited liability* involving responsibility for debts and losses is basic in unincorporated business enterprises.

Partnerships normally can raise more capital than individual proprietor-

Table 5-4. **Age of Business Failures by Functions in 1964 (Per Cent)**

Age in Years	Manu-facturing	Whole-sale	Retail	Con-struction	Service	All Con-cerns
One year or less	2.3	1.6	3.5	1.3	2.8	2.6
Two	13.6	10.3	20.0	11.0	14.3	15.8
Three	14.4	13.1	18.6	14.5	17.2	16.5
Total: three years or less	30.3	25.0	42.1	26.8	34.3	34.9
Four	12.1	13.4	12.1	11.3	13.0	12.2
Five	8.4	8.5	8.5	10.9	8.9	8.9
Total: five years or less	50.8	46.9	62.7	49.0	56.2	56.0
Six	7.4	6.5	6.4	7.5	8.4	7.0
Seven	4.1	4.8	4.1	6.1	4.8	4.5
Eight	3.9	4.4	3.6	4.8	4.7	4.0
Nine	3.2	4.1	2.4	3.9	3.3	3.1
Ten	3.1	3.1	2.3	3.8	3.0	2.9
Total: six-ten years	21.7	22.9	18.8	26.1	24.2	21.5
Over ten years	27.5	30.2	18.5	24.9	19.6	22.5
Total	100.0	100.0	100.0	100.0	100.0	100.0
Number of failures	2,254	1,392	6,239	2,388	1,226	13,501

SOURCE: *The Failure Record Through 1964*, Dun & Bradstreet, Inc.

ships, since there are more persons involved. There is no limit to the number of partners; in the brokerage business, for example, there are some firms with more than 100 partners. Obviously, partnerships are flexible; they consolidate business skills and experience, but they also may bring together persons whose dispositions and financial responsibilities may not be well matched.

The major disadvantages of partnerships are: *unlimited liability*, since each partner is liable without limit to the full extent of his personal assets for all debts contracted by the partnership; *mutual agency*, a doctrine under which each partner has broad powers to act as an agent and commit the whole partnership by his acts; and the fact that each time a new partner is admitted, or a partner dies or resigns, a whole new partnership must be formed. In some instances, the liability of certain partners may be limited by agreement or by use of insurance arrangements.

Corporate Form of Business Organization

When a group of men decide to incorporate a business enterprise, they obtain a corporation charter from one of the states. Then they issue and sell corporate securities, and cast votes at a rate of one vote for each share of stock for a board of directors. From security sales they allocate funds for the purchase of plant, equipment, and current operating expenses. Further, they select corporate officials and hire managers and employees to operate the business. Each year they provide the stockholders with a financial report, which includes a balance sheet and an income statement.

The corporation has marked advantages over the other two forms of business organization. Its primary advantage is that investors have *limited liability*. A person buying stock in a corporation can lose only the amount that he paid for the stock; his purchase merely buys a share of the ownership of the firm. The second major advantage of the corporate form is that corporations can obtain far more capital than either a single proprietorship or a partnership.

A corporation is a fictitious legal person created by the state. Unless the corporation charter issued by the state is revoked or restricted to a limited period, the corporation may continue as long as it is in business, irrespective of what happens to the individuals who own or manage it.

There are disadvantages as well as advantages in the corporate form of business organization. The most important of these is the tax disadvantage. Under the federal corporate income tax laws, most corporations pay from 22 to 50 per cent of their earnings in taxes. Corporate stockholders also must pay a personal income tax on nearly all of the dividends they receive. The earnings of individual proprietorships and partnerships are not subject to corporate income taxes.

The Corporation Charter. Many investors are aware of the fact that corporations usually obtain their charters from states that issue them with vague or lenient provisions. Most corporations, for example, obtain charters that are purposefully vague about the nature of the corporation's business activities. If a corporation's research leads to new activities, or if it is to shift from unprofitable into profitable lines, it needs the freedom to expand and grow. From an investor's standpoint, it is preferable that a corporation charter should be perpetual or issued for 100 years or more. Then the corporation need not fear the threat of a costly liquidation, or the necessity for merging with another corporation in possession of a satisfactory charter. Some corporation charters contain specific and limiting clauses concerning the total amount of authorized stock, the different classes of stock, maximum dividend rates, par value of the stock, total number of shares, and voting and other stock rights.[8]

The Corporate Structure. Each corporation has its own charter, its own board of directors, and its own dividend policy. Legally, a corporation is a separate entity that is subject to the will of its voting stockholders. Actually, corporate independence may be compromised because the voting control of some corporations resides in other corporations or their chief stockholders. A *parent corporation*, for example, may hold the largest *block of stock*—perhaps 25 per cent—in a *subsidiary corporation* whose policies obviously are subjected to the interests of the controlling corporation or stockholder group. In some instances, investment in a subsidiary may earn less or pay lower dividends than investment in the parent company, which uses the subsidiary to develop a doubtful new product or a doubtful new territory. Then, when the doubt is resolved successfully, the subsidiary may become wholly owned or merged with the parent company.

For sound investing, an investor needs information about corporations within a group and their interrelationships with each other. This information is available in a corporation's *prospectus*, which presents basic facts when new shares are offered for sale in interstate commerce. The information is available also in brokerage offices, in *Moody's Manual of Investments*, and in *Standard & Poor's Standard Corporation Records*. Any indication that one corporation's prosperity depends on the wishes of another corporation or on a special-interest group should indicate the need for caution in investment.

Corporate Securities. A so-called *public corporation* issues securities that it sells to the public at large in exchange for funds that are then invested in the corporation's plant and facilities.* A corporation may issue all of its securities in the form of common stocks. This arrangement divides the risks and the opportunity of financial rewards proportionately among the stockholders. Each stockholder has a percentage share in the business represented by the ratio of his holdings to the total number of shares outstanding. The absence of bonds in this situation constitutes a safety factor for the stockholders, since there will be no bondholders to file prior claims against the corporation's assets in case of bankruptcy. If a $100 million corporation has one million shares outstanding and its annual earnings amount to $12 million, then the earnings minus approximately $5.5 million of corporate income taxes would leave $6.5 million or 6½ per cent on the investment available for dividends. Normally, the corporation's Board of Directors would declare something less than 6½ per cent in dividends and "plow back" the remainder in the form of new investment in plant and facilities.

Since the board of directors is elected annually by the stockholders, the

* A *private corporation*, by contrast, is wholly owned by an individual or by a family.

board has a motive for declaring attractive dividends. However, a corporation needs money for expansion, so the dividends seldom approximate the full earnings. The difference between the earnings available for dividends and the actual amount paid out, however, is not lost by the stockholders when it is employed for reinvestment in new facilities, research, or other profitable corporate activities that result in an increase in the price of the stock.

The share of each stockholder in the capital contribution plus his share in these reinvested funds is known as the *stockholder's equity* in the business. Thus, the one million stockholders in a $100 million corporation hold shares worth approximately $100 each, assuming that there are no outstanding liabilities. If a $100 million corporation plows back $2 million of its $6.5 million after tax earnings, its total assets of $102 million divided by one million shares would indicate that each share now represents its original capital contribution of $100 of value plus an additional $2. The stockholder's equity is now $102 per share.

A prospective investor might prefer a higher dividend, and the market price of his shares might rise rapidly because of the prospect of continued high dividends. However, a conservative dividend policy with the profitable reinvestment of undeclared earnings should be recognized as the safer and better policy. The stockholder's equity may be determined, also, as follows:

$$\text{Stockholder's equity} = \frac{\text{firm's assets minus liabilities}}{\text{number of shares outstanding}}$$

Potential investors who watch earnings reports as well as dividend reports will recognize the stockholder's equity in a stock and bid for it at a price commensurate with its real and potential value, that is, the present value of the income stream it will engender.

Most corporations are financed with a combination of some stocks and some bonds. This arrangement may involve more risk for the stockholders, since the bondholders will receive their interest first in poor business years as well as in good years. Moreover, the bondholders will have a prior claim on the corporation's assets in case the business fails completely. Because of these facts, an investor in common stocks needs to know the extent to which his interests as a stockholder are subordinated to the interests of bondholders.

There is a good reason, however, why the directors of a profitable corporation may choose to include some bonds among the securities comprising the corporation's *capital structure* as in Table 5–5. The fact that a corporation's earnings record is good, suggests that it may borrow by issuing bonds at low-interest rates. Thus, if half of a $100 million corporation's financing can be obtained in the bond market for 5 per cent or perhaps less, and if it earns 12 per cent on the total investment, then the sum of $2.5 million is available to pay the interest on the 5 per cent bonds and $5 million (after corporate income taxes of approximately $4.5 million) is available for 10 per cent dividends. Alternatively, $2 million may be plowed back into the business and a 6 per cent dividend made payable to the stockholders, or there may be any other possible combination of dividends and reinvestments.

Table 5-5. **Corporate Capital Structure**

Corporation A	Corporation B
$100 million—common stock	$50 million—common stock
— bonds	$50 million—5% bonds
$100 million—total capitalization	$100 million—total capitalization
$12 million—assumed earnings	$12 million— assumed earnings
5.5 million—corporate income tax	2.5 million—interest on 5% bonds
	4.5 million corporate income tax on $9.5 earnings
$ 6.5 available for 6.5% dividends	$ 5 million available for 10% dividends
or	or
$2 million plowed back into the business	$2 million plowed back into the business
$4.5 million declared as a 4½ % dividend	$3 million declared as a 6% dividend
or	or
any other possible combination of dividends and retained earnings	any other combination of dividends and retained earnings

This arrangement, which is highly favorable to common stockholders, entails little risk in a profitable corporation and it provides additional dividends or additions to stockholder's equity. This latter advantage is known as *leverage* because a small amount of common stock supported by a core of bonds may create attractive earnings for the benefit of the stockholders. Shrewd common stock buyers must judge a corporation's capital structure compared with its earnings record and discover whether the existence of bonded indebtedness adds a degree of risk that is more than offset by a higher degree of anticipated earnings.

Significance of Corporation Securities to Investors

Most investors prefer the freedom from management responsibilities which is theirs when they invest in a corporation's securities. Investors are protected from loss by the corporation's limited liability which protects the investor's home and other assets from loss. Many investors protect themselves further by *diversifying their investments*, that is, by purchasing a variety of securities in order to have some assurance that all is not likely to be lost at once. With these assurances, investors by the millions enter the market for securities in this country. In prosperous years, new waves of investors plunge into the market and the additional weight of their buying pressure bids stock prices upward. This causes other investors to enter the market because stocks held by their friends are quoted at higher and higher prices. Eventually, a market of this sort may represent more speculation than investment. Because of the danger in this situation, Chapter 6, on corporate securities, will delve further into the details of various types of corporate securities and their interrelationships with each other. It is hoped that investment need not be replaced by speculation if enough American investors learn to distinguish between the two.

QUESTIONS

1. Why must a family's financial and investment program be so closely related to its affluence? How does the family life-cycle affect the opportunity for investment?
2. What expenditures and investments should be included in the primary security stage of a family's financial program? Justify each.
3. Why must people with the least affluence limit their investments to low-income-type securities? Do they?
4. What type of person should seek high-income investments even though they involve increased risk? What are these risks? How can they be minimized?
5. What is a growth stock? What type of investor is most interested in it? Why?
6. Under what circumstances should a person consider investing in a business of his own? How should he judge the business opportunity and his own attributes?
7. Why do so many small business firms fail?
8. Why is accounting described as a management tool? What are the important elements of a balance sheet? Of an income statement? Which items in these two accounting instruments are likely to be ignored by a careless, untrained manager in a small business?
9. What are the advantages and disadvantages of each of the three forms of business organization?
10. How are corporations organized, governed, and financed? What are a stockholder's obligations and rewards?
11. Why should a stockholder concern himself about the corporation's capital structure? What combination of stock versus bonds may be most advantageous to him? Why?

12. Note carefully the key terms in this chapter and be prepared to identify each of them.

SELECTED READINGS

See the list of selected readings at the end of Chapter 6.

NOTES

1. John C. Clendenin, *Introduction to Investments*, McGraw-Hill, New York, 4th ed., 1964, pp. 4–7.
2. U. S. Bureau of the Census, *Statistical Abstract of the United States: 1966*, Washington, D. C., 1966, p. 486.
3. Betty C. Churchill, "Rise in the Business Population," *Survey of Current Business*, U. S. Dept. of Commerce, Washington, D. C., May 1959, pp. 15–19 and 26; Betty Churchill, "Age and Life Expectancy of Business Firms," *Survey of Current Business*, U. S. Dept. of Commerce, Washington, D. C., December 1955, pp. 15–19 and 24; and Kurt B. Mayer and Sidney Goldstein, *The First Two Years; Problems of Small Firm Growth and Survival*, Small Business Administration, Washington, D. C., 1961.
4. Betty Churchill, *loc. cit.*
5. Clyde William Phelps, *The Role of Factoring in Modern Business Finance*, Commercial Credit Co., Baltimore, Md., 1956; and same author and publisher, *Accounts Receivable Financing as a Method of Business Finance*, 1957.
6. Small Business Administration, *Loan Sources in the Federal Government*, Management Aid No. 52, Washington, D. C., and Jack Zwick, *A Handbook of Small Business Finance*, Small Business Administration, Washington, D. C., latest edition.
7. Small Business Administration, *Small Business Bibliography*, Washington, D. C., 1965.
8. Clendenin, *op. cit.*, p. 44.

PROBLEMS AND CASES

1. Set up a savings and investment program for a family of four, consisting of a husband, wife, and two children aged 2 and 4, whose annual income is now $10,000, and annual expenditures, including rent, $8,000. The husband has no insurance other than his GI term insurance in the amount of $10,000 on which he pays an annual premium of approximately $100, much of which has been returned to him in the form of a dividend most years. Assume that the wife is not employed and that the husband's income will increase at the rate of 4 per cent a year during the next 30 years—the duration of his employment. The objective of your program is the highest possible yield consistent with maximum security.
2. If the Brown family of four has an income of $5,000 a year, what should the family's financial program include? What if the income is $10,000? What changes would occur if the income were $20,000? How would the ages of the Browns influence this decision?
3. If the $20,000-a-year Browns have net assets of $10,000 how much should be in the form of cash and checking accounts? Why not more or less than the

Forms of Business Organization

amount stated? In what form can some of the assets be nearly liquid even though they are in the form of an earning asset? Why would the percentage rate of earnings be low in this instance?

4. The Joneses are nearly fifty years of age and they have saved virtually nothing. If they received a thousand dollar inheritance, how should they invest it? What should be their investment objective?
5. If a "blue chip" common stock is qouted at $90 and pays an annual dividend of $2.70, what is its yield? Should its quotation rise further if it is already paying out most of its $3.30 per share of earnings in dividends? What probably caused the market price to rise so high?
6. If a nation's effective money supply and its price and wage levels were rising twice as fast as its rate of productivity increase, should an investor switch from stocks to bonds? Or vice versa? Why? How might he hedge to cover his position in case the situation deteriorated rapidly?
7. At what stage in the Browns' family life cycle should they be especially interested in research-conscious companies with high earnings and low dividends? Why?
8. Call on the Small Business Administration office nearest you. Ascertain which type of small business has been most profitable during the past year and why. It also may be well to inquire about the prospects and pitfalls associated with any business in which you may be interested. What information do they make available that will be helpful if you plan to start a business? If you plan to maximize the rate of growth of an established business? Where is the listing of their publications available?
9. Make up a balance sheet and a profit-and-loss statement for your own household, treating it as a going concern. If the data are obtainable, make up a balance sheet and a profit-and-loss statement for a business with which you are familiar.
10. "Pop and Mom" can't find employment. Should they invest half of their $4,000 savings in a small grocery store in which they might work and make $5,000 a year? What are the advantages and what are the risks? Would they be working too hard and "too cheap"?
11. Use a break-even graph to illustrate that a small business must have revenue and volume before it begins to earn money. How are overhead costs represented on this graph? How might Pop and Mom gain enough customers to bring success to their grocery store? At what cost? Is it not likely that some of their remaining savings might be lost before the store began to provide earnings?
12. Smith and his wife have saved and acquired a few assets. Smith's partner, Jones has saved nothing. If their variety store begins to lose money, who will pay the creditors? Is there any way to avoid this eventually?
13. By what rationale could a widow with an estate of $20,000 invest in the common stocks of ten reputable companies? What risk is she assuming? How do limited liability and diversification strengthen her position?
14. What would be the advantages and disadvantages of a simple corporate capital structure with no bonds and no preferred stocks? Why do very strong companies have bonded indebtedness?

15. At what stage in their family life cycle should the Browns be especially interested in buying corporate bonds? How can they acquire information about various bond issues? Should they buy convertible bonds? Why?
16. Show your own savings and investment program that will apply if all works out according to your life plan. Include the savings institutions you will be utilizing and the amounts you will have saved in each, the types of investments you will make and the approximate worth of each of these types of investments (*a*) five years hence; (*b*) ten years hence; (*c*) twenty years hence.

6 ANALYSIS OF CORPORATE SECURITIES

Never invest your money in anything that eats or needs repainting.

BILLY ROSE

The desire to put surplus funds to effective use has brought many individuals into the various markets for corporate securities. Some see these markets as an avenue to quick riches, but the wise and prudent investor is not affected by avarice. His objective is a fair return on his invested funds and the prospect of some increase in the market value of the securities he buys. To achieve this end, the responsible prospective investor should undertake a broad analysis of the various types of securities available for sale before choosing. He may choose between stocks and bonds, among the securities of companies in different types of industries, and among either the stocks or bonds of the vast number of enterprises whose securities are offered to the public. Moreover, the investor should consider the timing of his investments. And he should search carefully for special investment opportunities if he hopes to make the best use of his extra funds.

Several questions present themselves for the attention of a prospective investor. Must he gather information about a company's earnings history and dividend record before deciding to buy its common stock? Is it necessary for a common-stock buyer to have knowledge about the company's preferred stocks and bonds? What are the different types of bonds and preferred stocks, and what preferences or priority rights have they over common stocks? When should a corporation's earnings be regarded as adequate to meet the requirements of bond interest and stock dividends? How does an investor recognize and take advantage of special investment situations? These and a number of other questions will suggest the contents of this chapter.

TYPES OF CORPORATE SECURITIES

The term securities comprises stocks and bonds of various types. As each type is discussed in the following pages, its liquidity, safety, income, and growth attributes will be described in brief. These distinct types of investment should be matched, as far as possible, with the needs and desires of potential investors in terms of their differing incomes, ages, and interests.

Corporation Bonds

Corporation bonds, in effect, represent a loan of funds to the borrowing firm which usually pledges certain properties as *collateral* for their repayment. Unless there are prior claims against the collateral, the bondholder is reasonably assured of the safety of his capital. Furthermore, in most cases the interest on the bonds must be paid regularly and promptly, or the bondholders as a group can foreclose the pledged property and force the company into bankruptcy or receivership. It should be noted, however, that the court supervising the receivership may, by order, delay payment of the bond interest even though it has appointed a receiver. Under these circumstances, secured bonds often lose value.

First-Mortgage Bonds. A pledge of corporation assets or collateral may be described in a legal document known as a *bond indenture*. If the collateral is pledged as security for eventual repayment, holders of these securities have a prior claim, or *first mortgage*, on the described assets. The holders of other types of bonds or stocks are *residual* claimants; their claims may be satisfied, or partially satisfied, only after the first-mortgage bondholders have exercised their claim.

Normally, the first-mortgage bondholder is virtually certain of the return on his investment. The exception occurs when unpaid bills and claims or poor earnings followed by the issuance of *Receiver's Certificates*, which are debts created by a receiver with the court's approval, take prior claim. Basically, however, the degree of safety associated with these first-mortgage bonds, also known as *senior bonds*, generally raises their popularity but reduces their interest rate. An investor, in other words, gets about what he pays for. In this instance, he gets low returns because of the relative certainty of the return of his investment.

Second-Mortgage Bonds. Investment in second-mortgage bonds, sometimes called *junior bonds*, is quite similar to investment in the senior issues. The exception is that the holders of these securities have a second priority claim on the property described in the official bond indenture and pledged to the first-mortgage bondholders. Because the investment is less secure, the interest rate on second-mortgage bonds is approximately 1 per cent higher than on comparable senior bonds.

Bond-Rating Services. Two firms, Moody's Investment Service, Inc. and Standard & Poor's Corp., rate municipal and some corporate bonds as they are issued and sometimes at a later date also. These ratings, AA, A, B, etc., convey to both buyers and sellers of bonds the rater's estimate of the financial soundness of the issuer. Obviously, the issuer whose rating is not high will have to offer a higher rate of interest to induce investors to buy its bonds. Or, failing to offer a high-interest rate, it must expect that the bonds will be sold at a discount. The ratings generate ill will in many instances, but it must be admitted that investors are better informed because of them.

Obviously, the assumption of the added risk in a second-mortgage bond implies that certain persons should not consider their purchase. Yet there are instances in which the first-mortgage bonds have been so nearly retired that the second mortgage virtually constitutes a first mortgage on the assets in question. In such cases, some persons with extremely sharp pencils and the patience to read the fine print can uncover excellent investment opportunities. Needless to say, the holder of second-mortgage bonds needs to know a great deal about the first-mortgage bonds that are senior to his investment. He also needs to know a great deal about the company's earning ratios, its reserves, and its ability to withstand adversity.

Other Type Bonds. Several other types of bonds deserve comment because they are used frequently. There are *income bonds* and *debentures*; these are not secured by a mortgage on specifically designated assets. Never-

Table 6-1

New York Stock Exchange Bond Trading

SOURCE: *New York Times*, February 22, 1968, p. L-49.

theless, like other bonds, they have a claim on a corporation's assets and earnings prior to the claims of the stockholders. There are also *guaranteed bonds* issued by one company and guaranteed by another. The investor needs to know a great deal about both companies and about all the securities senior to this issue. There are *collateral-trust bonds* that pledge a corporation's collateral or holdings in other corporations. There are *blanket-mortgage bonds*; these pledge any property of the issuing company not already covered by mortgages. A blanket mortgage might be used in desperation by a weak company. On the other hand, it might be used by a strong company that prefers it to the issuance of additional common or preferred stocks and to the disturbance of existing bond-mortgage arrangements.

Unfortunately, the brief reference to bonds in a daily newspaper (see Table 6-1) does not reveal enough detail for the formulation of investment decisions. Prudent investors will usually seek the aid of investment counsel or of a broker when they enter the market for bonds.

Bond Yields. The matter of yield is especially significant to investors in the bond market. It is quite complicated by the inclusion of *terminal dates*, or due dates, which affect the calculation of a bond's *yield to maturity*. If a person pays $800* for a $1,000 bond promising 4 per cent interest, for example, he actually receives 5 per cent yield on the $800 he invests: $40 of annual interest equals a 5 per cent return on $800. This is known as *current yield*. In the bond yield table, Table 6-2, current yield appears in the last column as current income. If the bond's maturity date were five years away, the purchaser would receive $1,000 at that time, $200 more, in fact, than he paid for the bond. This $200 *increment* is the equivalent of an extra $40 for each of the five intervening years; hence the annual return can be ascertained by a glance at the *bond yield table* or calculated more laboriously as follows:

Annual interest ($1,000 × 4 per cent)	$40
Annual share of increment from $800 to $1,000	40
Total annual return	$80

The effective yield of the bond, or the *yield to maturity*, equals the annual return divided by the average investment. This average is computed by adding the actual price of the bond to its maturity value and dividing the sum by two. In this example, the $80 return is divided by the average investment of $900—that is, $800 plus $1,000 divided by two—for a quotient of 0.888 +, or a yield

---

* Since the prices of corporate bonds fluctuate in the markets, investors may purchase them at less or more than their redemption price. In this instance, the bond is bought at four-fifths of its value at maturity—or *par* value.

Table 6-2. Bond Yield Table—4 Per Cent Bond

Price	3 Years	3½ Years	4 Years	4½ Years	5 Years	5½ Years	6 Years	Current Income
74	15.094	13.578-	12.448	11.575-	10.879-	10.312-	9.841-	5.405
74½	14.838	13.357	12.254	11.401-	10.721-	10.167-	9.707-	5.369
75	14.585-	13.139-	12.062-	11.228	10.564	10.023	9.574-	5.333
75½	14.333-	12.922-	11.871-	11.057-	10.409-	9.881-	9.442-	5.298
76	14.083	12.707-	11.681	10.887	10.255-	9.739	9.311-	5.263
76½	13.835	12.493	11.493-	10.719-	10.102-	9.599-	9.181	5.229-
77	13.590-	12.281	11.306	10.551	9.950-	9.460-	9.052	5.195-
77½	13.346-	12.071	11.121	10.386-	9.799	9.321	8.924	5.161
78	13.104-	11.863-	10.937	10.221-	9.650-	9.184	8.797	5.128
78½	12.864-	11.656-	10.755-	10.057	9.501	9.048	8.671	5.096-
79	12.625	11.450	10.574-	9.895	9.354	8.913	8.546	5.063
79½	12.389-	11.246	10.394	9.734	9.208	8.779-	8.422	5.031
80	12.154	11.044	10.216-	9.574	9.063-	8.646-	8.299	5.000
80½	11.921	10.843	10.039-	9.416-	8.919-	8.514-	8.177-	4.969-
81	11.690	10.644-	9.863	9.258	8.776-	8.383-	8.056-	4.938
81½	11.461-	10.446	9.689-	9.102-	8.634	8.252	7.935-	4.908-
82	11.233	10.250-	9.516-	8.947-	8.493	8.123	7.815	4.878
82¼	11.120-	10.152	9.429	8.870-	8.423	8.059-	7.756-	4.863
82½	11.007	10.055-	9.344-	8.793-	8.353	7.995-	7.697-	4.848
82¾	10.895-	9.958-	9.258	8.716	8.284-	7.931-	7.637	4.834-
83	10.783-	9.861	9.173-	8.640-	8.214	7.867	7.579-	4.819
83¼	10.671	9.765-	9.088	8.564-	8.145	7.804-	7.520-	4.805
83½	10.560-	9.669-	9.003	8.488	8.076	7.741-	7.462-	4.790
83¾	10.449	9.573	8.919	8.412	8.008-	7.678-	7.403	4.776
84	10.339-	9.478	8.834	8.337-	7.939	7.615-	7.345	4.762-
84¼	10.229-	9.383	8.751	8.262-	7.871	7.552	7.287	4.748-
84½	10.119	9.289-	8.668	8.187	7.803	7.490	7.230-	4.734-
84¾	10.010-	9.194	8.585-	8.113-	7.736-	7.428	7.172	4.720-
85	9.901	9.100	8.502	8.038	7.668	7.366	7.115	4.706-
85¼	9.793-	9.007-	8.420-	7.964	7.601	7.305-	7.058-	4.692
85½	9.685-	8.914-	8.337	7.891-	7.534	7.243	7.001	4.678
85¾	9.577	8.821-	8.255	7.817	7.467	7.182-	6.944	4.665-
86	9.470-	8.728	8.174-	7.744-	7.401-	7.121-	6.888	4.651
86¼	9.363-	8.636-	8.092	7.671-	7.335-	7.060	6.832-	4.638-
86½	9.256	8.544-	8.011	7.598	7.269-	6.999	6.776-	4.624
86¾	9.150	8.452	7.930	7.526-	7.203-	6.939	6.720-	4.611-
87	9.044	8.361-	7.850-	7.453	7.137	6.879-	6.664	4.598-
87¼	8.939	8.270-	7.769	7.381	7.072-	6.819-	6.609-	4.585-
87½	8.834-	8.179	7.689	7.310-	7.007-	6.759	6.553-	4.571
87¾	8.729	8.089-	7.610-	7.238	6.942-	6.699	6.498	4.558
88	8.625-	7.999-	7.530	7.167-	6.877-	6.640	6.443	4.545
88¼	8.521-	7.909-	7.451-	7.096-	6.812	6.581-	6.388	4.533-
88½	8.417	7.819	7.372-	7.025	6.748	6.522-	6.334-	4.520-
88¾	8.314	7.730	7.293	6.954	6.684-	6.463	6.279	4.507
89	8.211	7.641	7.215-	6.884	6.620	6.404	6.225	4.494
89¼	8.109-	7.553-	7.137-	6.814-	6.556	6.346-	6.171-	4.482-
89½	8.006	7.464	7.059-	6.744	6.493-	6.288-	6.117	4.469
89¾	7.905-	7.376	6.981	6.674	6.430-	6.230-	6.063	4.457-
90	7.803	7.289-	6.904-	6.605	6.367-	6.172-	6.010-	4.444
90¼	7.702-	7.201	6.827-	6.536-	6.304-	6.114	5.956	4.432
90½	7.601-	7.114-	6.750-	6.467-	6.241	6.057-	5.903	4.420-
90¾	7.500	7.027	6.673-	6.398	6.179-	5.999	5.850	4.408-
91	7.400	6.941-	6.597-	6.330-	6.116	5.942	5.797	4.396-
91¼	7.300	6.854	6.520	6.261	6.054	5.885	5.745-	4.384-
91½	7.201-	6.768	6.445-	6.193	5.993-	5.829-	5.692	4.372-
91¾	7.102-	6.683-	6.369-	6.125	5.931-	5.772	5.640-	4.360-
92	7.003-	6.597-	6.293	6.058-	5.869	5.716-	5.588-	4.348-
92¼	6.904	6.512-	6.218	5.990	5.808	5.659	5.536-	4.336
92½	6.806	6.427	6.143	5.923	5.747	5.603	5.484-	4.324
92¾	6.708	6.342	6.069-	5.856	5.686	5.548-	5.432	4.313-
93	6.611-	6.258	5.994	5.789	5.626-	5.492-	5.381-	4.301
93¼	6.513	6.174-	5.920-	5.723-	5.565	5.436	5.329	4.290-
93½	6.416	6.090	5.846-	5.656	5.505-	5.381	5.278	4.278
93¾	6.320-	6.007-	5.772	5.590	5.445-	5.326	5.227-	4.267-

Types of Corporate Securities

Table 6.2. (*Continued*)

Price	3 Years	3½ Years	4 Years	4½ Years	5 Years	5½ Years	6 Years	Current Income
94	6.223	5.923	5.699-	5.524	5.385-	5.271-	5.176	4.255
94¼	6.127	5.840	5.625	5.458	5.325	5.216	5.125	4.244
94½	6.032-	5.758-	5.552	5.393-	5.265	5.161	5.075-	4.233-
94¾	5.936	5.675	5.479	5.327	5.206	5.107-	5.024	4.222-
95	5.841	5.593-	5.407-	5.262	5.147-	5.053-	4.974	4.211-
95¼	5.746	5.511-	5.334	5.197	5.088-	4.998	4.924-	4.199
95½	5.652-	5.429	5.262	5.133-	5.029	4.944	4.874	4.188
95¾	5.558-	5.348-	5.190	5.068	4.970	4.891-	4.824	4.178-
96	5.464-	5.266	5.119-	5.004-	4.912-	4.837	4.775-	4.167-
96¼	5.370	5.185	5.047	4.940-	4.854-	4.784-	4.725	4.156-
96½	5.277-	5.105-	4.976	4.876-	4.796-	4.730	4.676-	4.145
96¾	5.184-	5.024	4.905-	4.812-	4.738-	4.677	4.627-	4.134
97	5.091-	4.944-	4.834-	4.748	4.680-	4.624-	4.577	4.124-
97¼	4.998	4.864-	4.763	4.685-	4.622	4.571	4.529-	4.113
97½	4.906	4.784	4.693-	4.622-	4.565-	4.518	4.480-	4.103-
97¾	4.814	4.705-	4.623-	4.559-	4.508-	4.466-	4.431	4.092
98	4.723-	4.625	4.553-	4.496-	4.451-	4.414-	4.383-	4.082-
98¼	4.632-	4.546	4.483-	4.433	4.394-	4.361	4.334	4.071
98½	4.540	4.468-	4.413	4.371-	4.337-	4.309	4.286	4.061-
98¾	4.450-	4.389	4.344-	4.309-	4.280	4.257	4.238	4.051-
99	4.359	4.311-	4.275-	4.246	4.224-	4.206-	4.190	4.040
99¼	4.269	4.233-	4.206-	4.185-	4.168-	4.154-	4.142	4.030
99½	4.179	4.155-	4.137-	4.123-	4.112-	4.102	4.095-	4.020
99¾	4.089	4.077	4.068	4.061	4.056-	4.051	4.047	4.010
100	4.000	4.000	4.000	4.000	4.000	4.000	4.000	4.000
100¼	3.911-	3.923-	3.932-	3.939-	3.944	3.949-	3.953-	3.990
100½	3.822	3.846-	3.864-	3.878-	3.889-	3.898	3.906-	3.980
100¾	3.733	3.769	3.796	3.817	3.834-	3.847	3.859-	3.970
101	3.645	3.693-	3.729-	3.756	3.779-	3.797-	3.812-	3.960
101¼	3.557	3.617-	3.661	3.696-	3.724-	3.746	3.765	3.951-
101½	3.469	3.541-	3.594	3.636-	3.669-	3.696	3.719-	3.941-
101¾	3.382-	3.465-	3.527	3.576-	3.614	3.646-	3.672	3.931
102	3.294	3.389	3.460	3.516-	3.560-	3.596-	3.626	3.922-
102¼	3.207	3.314-	3.394-	3.456-	3.505	3.546	3.580-	3.912-
102½	3.121-	3.239-	3.327	3.396	3.451	3.496	3.534-	3.902
102¾	3.034	3.164-	3.261	3.337-	3.397	3.447-	3.488	3.893-
103	2.948-	3.089	3.195	3.278-	3.343	3.397	3.442	3.883
103¼	2.862-	3.015-	3.129	3.218	3.290-	3.348	3.397-	3.874
103½	2.776	2.940	3.064-	3.160-	3.236	3.299-	3.351	3.865-
103¾	2.690	2.866	2.998	3.101-	3.183-	3.250-	3.306-	3.855
104	2.605	2.792	2.933-	3.042	3.130-	3.201	3.261-	3.846
104½	2.435	2.645	2.803-	2.925	3.023	3.104-	3.170	3.828-
105	2.267-	2.499	2.674-	2.809	2.918	3.007-	3.081-	3.810-
105½	2.099-	2.354-	2.545	2.694-	2.813	2.911-	2.992-	3.791
106	1.932	2.209	2.417	2.579	2.709-	2.815-	2.903	3.774-
106½	1.766-	2.065	2.290	2.465	2.605	2.720-	2.815	3.756-
107	1.601-	1.922	2.164-	2.352-	2.502-	2.625-	2.727	3.738
107½	1.437-	1.780	2.038	2.239-	2.399	2.531-	2.640	3.721-
108	1.274-	1.639-	1.913-	2.126	2.297	2.437-	2.553	3.704-

NOTE: Yields in per cent per annum, correct to the nearest five ten-thousandths of 1 per cent, interest payable semiannually.

SOURCE: David Johnson, Caleb Stone, Milton C. Cross, and Edward A. Kircher, *Yields of Bonds and Stocks*, Prentice-Hall, New York, 1938.

to maturity of 8.9 per cent. This figure becomes 9.063 per cent, if compounded semiannually, as may be seen in Table 6–2.

Callable Bonds and Yield Rates. The 4 per cent bond in the foregoing example might be *callable*, or payable, at the company's option. This could be perhaps one year before the bond's due date. If the company redeems or pays the bond by calling it four years after its purchase, the $200 increment would be absorbed in four years instead of five and the annual share of the bond's enhancement would increase to $50 instead of $40. The yield to maturity would then become 10.216 per cent instead of 9.063 per cent.

It should be obvious, however, that a company in a poor financial position will not be likely to call its bonds one year ahead of the terminal date unless the 4 per cent rate imposed too heavy a burden on its resources. If, on the other hand, the company's finances permit early redemption, and if the bond market suggests the wisdom of such action, many shrewd investors might discover the callable high-yield bond and bid for it at prices considerably above $800.

When a company's financial position is excellent and its bonds are rated AA, or nearly as high, the bonds actually might sell at a price slightly above the $1,000 maturity or *face value*, provided that the 4 per cent rate is considered satisfactory. If someone pays $1,050 for a $1,000 five-year 4 per cent bond that does not contain a callable clause, this actual yield will be reduced to 2.918 per cent because he must recapture the extra $50 in five years (see Table 6-2). By adding a callable clause, which is effectuated always at the company's option, the 2.918 per cent yield is further endangered and the bond will be salable only at a loss.

Convertible Bonds. When an investor prefers bonds to stocks because he believes that the immediate future is not very bright, he may gain the long-run advantage of stock ownership by buying convertible bonds. A convertible bond has the usual security features of an ordinary bond, plus the bondholder's option to convert or exchange it for a specified amount of common or preferred stock. Usually, the conversion is spelled out in detail. For example, a $100 bond might be convertible into two shares of common stock at $50 per share after three years. In this instance, the investor has the relative safety provided by his bonds for three years. Then, if business and profits drive the market quotations of his company's stocks above $50 per share, he is free to convert to common stocks and enjoy the benefits of the rising market. Obviously, in a certain phase of the market, convertible bonds are popular. Their issuance is quite common with companies in need of additional capital at a moment when they can obtain more from a convertible bond issue than they would from an issue of common stock.

Preferred Stocks

The implied preference in the term "preferred stocks" is likely to mislead inexperienced investors. Actually, preferred stocks have some preference over common stocks issued by the same company. Otherwise, they lie approximately halfway between bonds and common stocks in regard to the safety of invested funds and the rewards that they offer to the investor.

Preferential Claim on Assets. Most preferred stocks have two significant advantages over common stocks. First, they have a preference in the order of priority of claims on the company's assets. This is extremely important if the company goes bankrupt. It should be noted, however, that preferred stocks rank behind all bonds in priority.

Preferential Claim on Earnings. The second preference of preferred stocks over common stocks is the priority of their claim for dividends. Usually, no common-stock dividends may be declared unless preferred stock dividends also are declared. Also, where the shares are *cumulative preferred*, a dividend that has not been paid in any one year may accumulate to be paid in later years, presumably. This is not to say that this accumulated obligation, or *arrearage*, always is paid, but as a rule no common stock dividend can be distributed again until the cumulative preferred stock obligations have been accommodated. Relatively speaking, this dividend preference over common stocks is important. However, many preferred stocks are *noncumulative*, which means that they lack this added attraction. Actually, the fine print in a preferred stock certificate discloses which preferences are included.

Participating Preferred Stocks. Another variation, which should be mentioned, is the right of holders of some preferred stock, known as participating preferred stock, to share in dividend declarations that exceed a specified amount of dollars or a fixed percentage. Thus, if a nonparticipating preferred share calls for a 6 per cent dividend, that is the maximum that ever could be declared. But owners of participating preferred stock might join with the common stockholders in sharing an unusually attractive dividend. The cumulative aspect of a 6 per cent cumulative participating preferred share, therefore, offers a semiguarantee that the dividend will become an arrearage if it falls below 6 per cent. The participating characteristic promises that it may very well exceed that figure.

There are all sorts of gradations of dividend participation. In some, for example, the participating preferred stockholders share equally with the common stockholders in a substantial dividend. In 50 per cent participating preferred, they may share only half the difference between the stipulated preferred stock dividend rate and any higher amount declared to the common stockholders.

The addition of a participating clause or a cumulative clause in a preferred stock enhances its value and its price. These clauses are likely to be added by a rather weak company to tempt investors, or by any company when market conditions are unfavorable. Thus a prospective investor might consider buying 6 per cent cumulative preferred shares or 6½ per cent noncumulative shares in the same firm. If the firm is apt to be in financial difficulty, the investor probably should consider sacrificing the ½ per cent differential and buy the 6 per cent cumulative preferred. If business conditions are good and the company is prospering, the small risk entailed suggests the wisdom of purchasing the 6½ per cent noncumulative preferred. Likewise, a participating clause in a preferred stock issue is of little value in a weak company, but it may be so valuable in a strong company in good times that the investor may be wise in paying a premium price for the stock.

Relatively few preferred shares are issued currently because dividends on preferred stock are a fixed cost and are usually as high or higher than interest on bonds. Most firms that can issue preferred stocks can also issue debentures, which are favored because interest on them is deductible from the taxable income on which the federal corporate income tax is paid. Two groups of firms still commonly issue preferred stock: (1) public utilities when state-regulating commissions require additions to their equities because their debt/equity ratios are too high; (2) firms that cannot issue bonds because they are in financial difficulty. However, many seasoned preferreds are on the market in relatively small quantities generally as a leftover from the 1920's when preferreds were extremely popular.

Common Stocks

Persons who own common stocks in a corporation share all the residual claims on remaining earnings and assets after bondholder and preferred stockholder claims have been satisfied. These so-called *equity* claims of the stockholders may be virtually worthless in a bankrupt corporation because so many bondholders and preferred stockholders hold prior liens. But when a corporation is noticeably successful, equities increase and the stockholders thrive.

The price of common stocks rises and falls sharply in relation to a corporation's success and general business conditions. For this reason, those who buy securities in quest of an increase in their value are more likely to buy common stocks than any other form of security. For this reason also, common stocks occupy the mainstream of published market quotations and the conversation of persons who are interested in securities as investments.

Most investors or speculators are *long on the market*. That is, they hope to buy low and to sell high after a rise in the market. When they succeed at this venture, they pocket the difference between the buying and selling prices, less two commissions, one brokerage fee for buying and one for selling.

Many persons who are long on the market merely play the business cycle. They buy the stocks of reputable companies in the recession phase of the business cycle and wait for increased earnings and better business generally. A business recovery customarily is accompanied by an upsurge of quotations in the stock market, which provides an opportunity for investors to sell at a profit. Actually, the market price of shares in a few companies may follow seasonal cycles or some other cyclical variations. Shares in air-conditioning companies usually reach their highest quotations in March and their lowest quotations in October, for example.

A few professionals enter the market for a "short rise," which may involve only a matter of hours or days. Thus, a five-dollar net gain on a $100 share provides a phenomenal rate of gain if the entire transaction is completed within a week. The professional who moves his money in and out of transactions of this sort with a high percentage of winning ventures represents the epitome of success in the market. Obviously, such persons diversify their investments and play the law of averages; they cover a few losses with a number of gains, obtaining a net return from their overall purchases and sales. Unfortunately, however, the tax is about twice as high for *such short-term capital gains* achieved in less than six months as for long-term gains.

It is as important to have as thorough a knowledge of corporate senior securities, which have prior claims on company earnings, as of common stocks and the companies they represent. This is indeed a most exacting task, but the rewards are high for those who succeed; the losses are virtually limitless for those who fail. On the average, the losses cancel out the gains, which are reduced still further by the cost of brokerage fees. In view of this net result, the probability of successful market venturing by average persons who are compelled to match investment decisions with professional investors is apt to be low.

Par Value. Some common stocks have a normal or *par value* of $100. Although the corporation issuing them may receive somewhat less than this amount, many persons estimate the stock's value in relation to its par value. Some corporation shares have no par value; their market price depends to some extent on a calculation for their net-asset value and also on the amount of demand for the stock by investors. Since a par value of $100 is often misleading, many corporations assign to their shares a mere one dollar par value.

When a share's price climbs considerably, the corporation frequently issues additional shares to its present stockholders, *splitting the shares* in some predetermined ratio, such as two-for-one. This may be accomplished, also, by declaring a *stock dividend* of one share for each share that is *outstanding*, or in the possession of stockholders. The difference between a stock split and a stock dividend is explained by the fact that funds from retained earnings are transferred to the capital stock account when a stock dividend is declared, whereas a stock split leaves the retained earnings untouched. The stock split merely lowers the market price of each share to a more attractive range. Stockholders do not receive an additional claim to assets or earnings by virtue of either a stock dividend or a stock split. Consequently, it is not surprising that when the publicity effects are dissipated, the stock prices tend to return to a designated proportion of their previous level. If there are now two shares instead of one, each will be worth approximately half. (For example, if one share of stock sold for $100 before the stock dividend or the stock split, each of the two shares thereafter will, within a short period, sell for about $50 each.)

Voting Rights. Ownership of common stocks in a corporation usually includes the right to a vote for each share held. Each corporation is governed by a board of directors chosen by the common stockholders. Other security holders in a corporation usually have no right to vote. Occasionally, nonvoting common stocks are bought because most common stockholders are not particularly interested in voting rights. Only rarely are there contests for the control of corporations, at which time the holders of small numbers of shares of common stocks are invited to transfer their voting rights by *proxy* to interested owners of large blocks of shares.

The common stockholders have it within their power to choose the board of directors and, in effect, to run the corporation. They thus are able to protect their own interests in several ways. When one group of stockholders, or proxy holders, casts the largest block of votes polled, it chooses the board of directors, which, in turn, selects the officers and management of the corporation. In practice, the board of directors may expect to remain in control. If the management is inept or unpopular, the board is subject to overthrow at any of the company's annual meetings.

FUNDAMENTAL APPROACH TO SECURITY ANALYSIS

Once a prospective investor has determined whether his financial position permits the purchase of corporate securities, his interest should turn to the type of industry in which his investment dollars should be placed. Having decided to invest his funds, he should investigate firms within each industry in the hope that his analysis will lead to the best investment opportunities. A balanced investment program should include ownership of both stocks and bonds scattered among several industries and a variety of firms. The search for better-than-average investments requires security analysis, investment timing, and a little luck. Each investment should be analyzed thoroughly, whether it involves all or only a few of one's investment dollars.

Analysis of Industries

Industries rise and decline in importance, in profitability, and in the favor of investors. Half of the industries listed in Table 6–3 represent very few firms that had stocks on the market a generation ago. Railroad securities, which dominated the market until about 1920, have lost their glamor in recent years. Some industries, such as shipbuilding, aircraft, and the electrical industries, are dependent on military contracts and rumors of war; others, such as foods and retail trade, contain firms only slightly affected by war scares, political situations, and the business cycle. A few industries, such as petroleum, rubber, and steel, are diverting their attention to new products and sidelines in an attempt to promote growth and increased profits in the future. Some industries, especially automotive and building, are notably dependent on the business cycle and on the public's spending mood. Table 6–3 shows the earnings record of firms within 26 industrial groups, plus railroads and utilities.

As industries arise, they seem to pass through several identifiable phases. Since 1960, for example, the electronics industry has been in an awkward stage in its evolution. Electronics firms usually are small, dependent on military contracts, and subject to rapid rise if a single important new invention or discovery is found. If their research does not bear fruit, these firms decline. Small electronics firms cannot afford research programs to assure that they will have marketable products year after year; hence there is little stability in the industry; mergers are frequent. Eventually, this industry will settle into a few large, stable firms. Until this evolution has occurred, investments in stocks in electronics firms will be faced with wide price fluctuations, bankruptcies, and occasional mergers.

Railroads have thrived, matured, and declined in this country. The causes to which this evolution is commonly attributed are stodgy management, featherbedding labor practices, excessive taxes, and roadbed and terminal costs that are not borne in like manner by competitive transportation modes. For a generation, railroad securities have reflected the poor earnings and unpromising future of the carriers. Investor bias against railroad securities—the *rails*—has grown so strong that one may be unwise to buy them even when they are

Table 6-3

: Corporations' Profits Again Seem
ɔm One Quarterly Record to Another

Fourth-Quarter Profits of 581 Concerns Rose 5.2% From Level of Like '66 Period

The columns below show by industries earnings reported for the fourth quarter of 1967 and those for the like quarter of 1966, with percentage changes. Where individual company reports cover three-month periods other than calendar quarters, the nearest comparable periods have been used.

	Fourth Quar. 1967	Fourth Quar. 1966	% Change
12 Aircraft Makers	$ 70,282,000	$ 66,062,000	+ 6.4
10 Airlines	45,161,000	68,604,000	− 34.2
17 Autos & Equipment	720,678,000	655,835,000	+ 9.9
14 Building Materials	54,374,000	46,454,000	+ 17.0
8 Building Supplies	50,215,000	42,336,000	+ 18.6
6 Cement Companies	4,159,000	4,118,000	+ 1.0
23 Chain Stores	47,546,000	44,142,000	+ 7.7
6 Apparel & Clothing	4,270,000	3,638,000	+ 17.4
5 Drugs	7,012,000	6,574,000	+ 6.7
12 Grocers	36,264,000	33,930,000	+ 6.9
19 Chemicals	226,520,000	229,057,000	− 1.1
18 Department Stores	166,096,000	157,026,000	+ 5.8
6 Distillers	52,084,000	50,061,000	+ 4.0
13 Drug Manufacturers	123,972,000	112,845,000	+ 9.9
27 Elec Equip-Electronics	161,837,000	148,190,000	+ 9.2
10 Broad-Line Companies	121,346,000	101,705,000	+ 19.3
17 Specialty Companies	40,491,000	46,485,000	− 12.9
5 Farm Equipment	40,563,000	55,613,000	− 27.1
11 Finance Companies	37,993,000	33,494,000	+ 13.4
22 Food Products	126,109,000	119,560,000	+ 5.5
21 Mining & Metals	155,764,000	258,452,000	− 39.7
6 Aluminum Companies	72,156,000	82,627,000	− 12.7
15 Copper & Other Metals	83,608,000	175,825,000	− 52.4
8 Office Equipment	253,886,000	190,328,000	+ 33.4
21 Petroleum Products	1,351,903,000	1,177,594,000	+ 14.8
10 Publishing Companies	19,689,000	20,676,000	− 4.8
22 Pulp & Paper Prducts	134,716,000	149,919,000	− 10.1
10 Railway Equipment	23,742,000	27,818,000	− 14.7
30 Steel Manufacturers	276,779,000	274,278,000	+ 0.9
19 Textiles	65,348,000	65,626,000	− 0.4
6 Tobaccos	85,689,000	76,083,000	+ 12.6
23 Tools & Machinery	62,285,000	64,414,000	− 3.3
132 Other Industrials	670,913,000	627,165,000	+ 7.0
Total 499 Industrial Cos	4,973,929,000	4,719,296,000	+ 5.4
25 Railroads	209,773,000	229,471,000	− 8.6
57 Utilities	440,660,000	398,755,000	+ 10.5
Total 581 Concerns	$5,624,362,000	$5,347,522,000	+ 5.2

SOURCE: *Wall Street Journal*, February 13, 1968, p. 23.

priced attractively. The bias against the industry may prevent the resale of these securities at reasonable prices.

From decade to decade, one industry or another gains the favor of investors. For example, petroleum stocks, which were popular during the early 1950's, were replaced by the so-called *chemicals* late in that decade. Uranium mining and the electronics industries enjoyed brief periods of prosperity during that time. Earnings data generally are available to substantiate investor preference for the securities of one industry over another, but sometimes these statistics become available too late to explain this favortism.

Analysis of the Firm

After an investor has chosen several industries that he deems suitable for his investment dollars, his next task is to select the best firms within these industries. A brief analysis of several firms will suffice to exemplify the most desirable approach to the problem. The illustrations chosen assume a primary interest in the purchase of common stocks.

Airline Stocks. Ten years ago the airline stocks seemed to be worth an investor's attention. Shares in three major airlines—United, American, and Pan American could be bought for around $20. At this price their yield was approximately 5 per cent. Another airline, Trans World Airlines (TWA), was large and, with its favorable continental and overseas routes, it seemed to have a promising future. Unfortunately, its earnings were negative; it had paid no dividends for years; and its stock was selling below $9 a share at that time. Account executives in more than one brokerage house made no effort to promote "that dog," TWA. Three long magazine articles maligned the company's management. Perhaps, that was just the time to buy TWA. Perhaps the stock was a "sleeper."

In 1960, TWA needed additional financing for its newly purchased jets. Failing to get the funds, the airline lost its control to a committee of financiers who employed new managers. The line's efficiency increased noticeably, its earnings exceeded that of any other airline, and its stock rose to a range of $60 to $80 per share—practically the same as the market price of United, American, and Pan American. Finally, Howard Hughes who owned three quarters of the TWA shares gave up his attempt to regain control of the airline and arranged with Merrill, Lynch, Pierce, Fenner & Smith to sell off his 6,584,937 shares in the second largest secondary stock distribution in American history. The transaction was handled successfully. Institutional buyers joined the man in the street in scooping up the offering. Hughes sold out for $550 million at the top of the market. TWA fell off a few points, as did United, American, and Pan American, then all four began to rise again before they leveled off and declined after 1966.

Railroad Stocks. A well-diversified portfolio might contain a few well-chosen railroad stocks as a wartime hedge since the rails tend to thrive during a mobilization period. Investigation reveals that a few railroads, namely, the Union Pacific (U.P.), the Atchison, Topeka, and Santa Fe (Santa Fe, or A. T. & S. F.), and the Norfolk and Western (N. & W.), have had excellent earnings records over the years and apparently comprise the best investments among the rails, except when some others are underpriced temporarily. Some other lines have had irregular earnings records, whereas most railroads have had very poor dividend records. The three railroads mentioned have diversified their holdings by investing their own reserves in other rail lines, oil properties, and other facilities. There have been several years, for example, in which the Union Pacific earned more from its investment in oil properties than from its rail operations. The Norfolk and Western is a major coal-hauling railroad. This operation has provided excellent earnings in the past. In some recent years, subsidized coal exports have provided profitable operations for the road.

Rail lines saddled with unprofitable commuter service may enjoy increased earnings if they can discontinue or obtain a subsidy for that service. Long-haul passenger and freight service has been more profitable to the Santa Fe and the Union Pacific than to any other lines. However, the increased use of trucks and the increased popularity of air travel inevitably must reduce the profitability of the long-haul railroads.

Ideally, prospective investors should judge a company by its continuity of dividends over a period of ten or twenty years. On this score, these railroads have excellent records. The earnings of both the Union Pacific and the Santa Fe have justified recent stock splits and continuous dividends of approximately 6 per cent. Norfolk and Western's dividend approximates only 4 per cent, but the public acceptance of its shares is so good that the shares hover around $100 on the market. The shares are held often by institutional investors and recommended by reputable brokers in counseling their clients.

Chemicals. Among the chemical firms, Du Pont certainly deserves consideration by a potential investor. This well-managed giant among the chemicals holds a leading position in the production of synthetic fibers, which account for 36 per cent of its sales and half of its profits. The remainder of Du Pont's business is divided among several dozen chemical products in which its research provides the key to the company's success. Unfortunately, rival firms are encroaching upon the market for man-made fibers, so that Du Pont's dominant share of that market has slipped from 70 per cent in 1955 to 45 per cent in 1967.

For years, Du Pont was a favorite among investors. Its own leadership in a lively new field was supplemented with earnings from the huge block of General Motors shares that it held. By court order, Du Pont had to dispose of its holdings in General Motors. This divestiture, although conducted in an orderly manner, cast some doubt upon Du Pont's future earning ability. Then, with Du Pont's sagging share of the synthetic chemicals, along with generally declining market quotations in 1966 and 1967, Du Pont shares skidded from $240 in mid-1966 to $148 in the spring of 1967. The company's earnings per share dropped in that interval from $8.63 per share to approximately $7, and although the earnings and dividends were nearly adequate to support a price of $151 per share, there was little basis for the shares to rise above that figure unless or until the company regained its earlier preeminence in the field of man-made fibers or in some of its other chemical products.

Special Investment Situations

A company's earnings and dividends are most likely to increase because of new and improved management. They may also increase because of technological improvements resulting from a fruitful research and development program. In either case, the investor who has a better-than-average knowledge of corporate policies seeks a company with a low-risk, high-profit potentiality and some obscure assets. In a book entitled *Special Situations in the Stock Market*, Maurece Schiller has written that these prospects are most likely to develop in new-era companies, in old companies in new fields, or in companies involved in liquidation, mergers, acquisitions, reorganizations, and recapitalizations.[1]

New-Era Companies. Technology-based industries with generous expenditures for research and development are likely to harbor the new-era companies. Some of these companies, such as the Polaroid Corporation, International Business Machines, and a number of electronics firms, have enjoyed an annual growth rate in excess of 9 per cent in recent years; that was three times the national growth rate.[2] In some instances these companies have pioneered new fields; sometimes they have had ample basic research and the good fortune to be on the spot when the missile era came along. The best of these companies have proved excellent investments, characterized by capital gains resulting from growth in asset value.

Old Companies in New Fields. Old, established companies often absorb weak, new companies or develop new lines as the outgrowth of their own research and development policies. Many of them diversify their own holdings by adding new products; sometimes the new products transform the company's former business, its volume, its growth rate, and its profitability. Often the public image of an older company becomes out of date. At such times, an informed investor may buy a company's securities anticipating that their value will rise in the market. For example, many investors in railroad-equipment companies have profited in recent years because these firms have diversified and thrived despite the severe decline in railroad-equipment orders. The leading petroleum stocks have been able to advance despite overproduction of petroleum and adverse market conditions. They have done so primarily because these companies have introduced chemical by-products that have become a part of the petroleum business.

Companies in Financial Reorganizations. Occasionally, a company's securities may be undervalued when compared to their possible market price following a financial reorganization, liquidation, merger, or recapitalization. The acquisition in 1961 of Capital Airlines by United Airlines is such an example. Capital Airlines' $1,000 debentures, selling at $640, were to be exchanged for 20 shares of United Airlines stock which was then selling at $32 a share. Before the date of the actual transfer, however, public interest in United Airlines stock ran high as the company paid a 3 per cent stock dividend. United Airlines stock rose to $47 and the Capital debentures increased correspondingly to $940. This enabled investors who had shown foresight and courage in purchasing these debentures during the period of uncertainty prior to the acquisition of Capital Airlines to partake of an increment of 50 per cent.[3] In a similar manner, a shrewd investor might have profited by investing in Hudson and Manhattan Railway bonds, Pittsburgh Railway Company stocks, or Los Angeles Railway Company stocks.

Checklist: Fundamental Approach to Security Analysis

Those intending to invest should investigate before buying, and the persons who already own securities should analyze the current position of each item in their portfolios at frequent intervals. This will tell them whether any particular security should be sold or retained. Although several analytical tools already have been reviewed in this chapter, it seems appropriate at this point to present a step-by-step checklist, as in Figure 6–1. Our list uses the *fundamental approach to security analysis*. This approach should be distinguished from a *technical approach* that is based on a use of charts, which will be explored presently. The fundamental approach proceeds with a methodical analysis of bonds, preferred stocks, and common stocks.

Fundamental Approach to Security Analysis 163

Name of Company_____

Type of Security_____

Analysis	Pertinent Data	Evaluation

	High	Average	Low

1. Investigation of the industry
   Public image_____
   Immediate prospects_____
   Long-run prospects_____
2. Investigation of the firm
   Public image_____
   Research and development_____
   Quality of management_____
   Immediate prospects_____
   Long-run prospects_____
3. Adequacy of earnings (price-earnings ratio)
   Bonds_____
   Preferred stocks_____
   Common stocks_____
4. Investment yield
   Bonds_____
   Preferred stocks_____
   Common stocks_____
5. Asset coverage
   Bonds_____
   Preferred stocks_____
   Common stocks_____
6. Special analysis of common stocks
   Dividend regularity_____
   Leverage factor_____
   Book value_____
   Market price trends_____
   Investment market image_____
   Immediate prospects_____
   Long-run prospects_____

Figure 6-1. **Checklist for security analysis.**

Bond Analysis. Prospective buyers of any type of security issued by a company should scrutinize its bonds because of the bondholders' prior claims to earnings and assets. A bond may be regarded as a good investment if it rates favorably in the following categories:

1. Adequate earnings—earnings must be ample and sufficient to pay interest regularly. They must also be able to set aside reserves for interest payments in poor years and to make funds available for preferred-stock and common-stock dividends. Depending on the ratio of bonds to stocks, a company should earn enough to cover its bond interest at least two to perhaps five or ten times.

2. Investment yield—as explained previously, a bond must be bought at a price low enough to permit the investor to obtain an attractive return on his actual investment. This rate of actual return, or yield, must take into account the terms under which the bond may be called or converted in order to determine its yield to maturity. An investor must make these calculations before buying or selling at the market price. For example, a highly rated bond that yields 3.5 per cent on its face value may be worth less than that value in a market that is paying interest rates of 4 per cent or more.

3. Asset coverage—a group of bondholders accepts a low rate of return in exchange for safety. This safety takes the form of a company pledge of certain assets, which may be claimed and sold if the company fails to pay its interest on schedule or fails to redeem the bonds on terminal dates. It behooves the purchasers of bonds to ascertain whether the pledged properties will cover their claims against the company adequately in case its business fails. Liquidation sales yield low prices. Bondholders, therefore, must guard jealously their claims against pledged assets. If they do not, the property itself may suffer devaluation or the legal title to it may deteriorate from erosion or counterclaims of other security holders.

4. The market image of the bonds—what is the reputation of the company and of this bond issue? Has the company always met its obligations promptly? Are the company's bonds rated "B" or higher? Has the company paid stock dividends regularly, thus indicating that it has had a reservoir of earnings more ample than the sums needed for bond interest? What prediction, consequently, may be made about the company's future earnings and its ability to meet its obligations to its bondholders with ease and certainty?

Preferred Stock Analysis. Since preferred stockholders have the next claim on a corporation's assets after the bondholders, it is important for them to know their exact situation compared with the claims and rights of other security holders. A preferred stock may be regarded as a good investment if it satisfies the following requirements:

1. Adequacy of earnings—enough to permit the declaration of regular preferred stock dividends plus additional earnings to cover common stock divi-

dends. Preferred stockholders must recognize that their own dividends are threatened when a company fails to declare common stock dividends. No general statement applies to the amount of earnings that should surround preferred stock dividends because the ratio of preferred stocks to common stocks is not uniform. Some investment specialists insist, however, that the company's earnings must be at least three times as much as the preferred stock dividends.

2. Investment yield—a preferred stock should be bought at a price that permits the investor to realize an attractive rate of return on his investment. The current yield on a cumulative preferred share with a $6 regular dividend, bought for $120, would be $6 ÷ $120 or 5 per cent, for example. A similar preferred stock without the cumulative clause might be bought for $100, thereby yielding 6 per cent on the investment. If a company's dividends are irregular, an investor has more to gain from the cumulative clause than from the higher yield. But if a company is financially strong, he might be wise to forego the cumulative clause and seek the 6 per cent dividend.

A preferred stock yield may be affected also by the terms of a conversion clause. If, for example, a preferred stock paying a $6 dividend and costing $100 might be converted after three years into common stock that might be worth $103, the $3 gain divided into three years would add $1 a year to the $6 dividend, thus providing a yield of 7 per cent for the three-year interval. However, the value of the right to convert the preferred share into a share of common stock cannot be determined in advance, since one cannot estimate the market price of the common shares three years beforehand. An investor can only watch the market price of the common shares and choose to convert or not convert after the three years have elapsed.

Some preferred shares are callable at a specified price at the option of the company on a stipulated date. If a company chooses to call a $100, 6 per cent preferred share at $105 in five years, the investor's effective yield becomes 7 per cent. It consists of the annual $6 dividend plus an additional $1 per year ($105 − $100 = $5 ÷ 5 years = $1 per year).

Obviously, an investor might pay more willingly and accept a lower yield on a preferred share containing a favorable conversion clause. Conversely, he might wish to pay less for a preferred stock with a callable clause that the company might elect to exercise for its own advantage. Sometimes, however, a company is so intent on eliminating an issue of preferred stock that it buys back the stock at a price that is distinctly favorable to the stockholder.

3. Asset coverage—preferred stockholders have no asset protection, except as their claims in the event of liquidation are residual to bondholders' claims. Usually they have priority over the claims of common stockholders.

For preferred stockholders to be satisfied, the liquidation value of the company's assets should be large enough to cover the claims of both bondholders and preferred stockholders, at least. Preferred stockholders must be vigilant in defense of their interest in a company's assets should liquidation become necessary, since their asset claims precede those of the common stockholders and their dividends are proportionately lower.

4. The market image of the preferred stock—has the company paid its preferred stock dividends regularly and promptly for a period of years? Has the trend of the stock's market price been sufficiently upward in recent years to indicate the probability that it will be a good investment in the future?

Common Stock Analysis. A prospective buyer of common stocks should have investigated the company's bonds and preferred stocks because of their prior claims over common stocks. If this analysis is encouraging, a common stock may be regarded as a good investment if it meets these specifications:

1. Adequacy of earnings—if a corporation and its investors prefer that dividends be paid regularly, earnings available for common stock dividends must be more than sufficient for the payment of such dividends after all operating costs, bond interest, corporate income taxes, and preferred stock dividends have been covered. A rule-of-thumb ratio based on the performance of a number of dividend-paying corporations in this country suggests that the earnings available for common-stock dividends should approximate twice the dividends to be declared. This permits the corporation's board of directors to set aside reserves so that regular dividends may be paid in lean years. This practice of retaining earnings also permits *internal financing* of plant expansion and increases the stockholder's equity in the business. Needless to say, these stocks are destined to increase in market price; and when the company's investment in physical plant and research reaches significant proportions, the shares may be characterized as growth stocks or the stocks may be split, with additional shares—although no additional value—accruing to the stockholders.

In judging the adequacy of earnings, one should investigate them over a period of at least ten years. By calculating the average yearly earnings per share and noting the trend, future earnings and dividends may be estimated.

The company's dividend policy should be analyzed to ascertain whether dividends are uniform year after year—that is, *regular*—or whether they follow the fluctuations in the company's earnings. The market price of stocks may be influenced by dividend policies, since some buyers are less cognizant of earnings than they should be. Stability of dividends is regarded by some as the mark of a good investment; it implies the existence of adequate reserves. Yet

Fundamental Approach to Security Analysis

an erratic dividend policy does not necessarily suggest that an investment is inferior. The company may have valid reasons for reducing dividends in some years to finance the expansion of its plant or to develop new products, or it may require an additional supply of cash for a number of different purposes. Moreover, an investor who shrewdly predicts changes in earnings and dividends is in a position to profit from his forecast by buying the stock at a low price and later selling it at a higher price.

2. The *price-earnings ratio* of a stock—if a stock sells at ten or twelve times a corporation's annual earnings, the stock is considered conservatively priced, although in the 1960's many investors would have considered a price-earnings ratio of 15 or 20 to one as normal and conservative. If a stock that earns $10 per share and pays $5 as a dividend can be bought for $70, the investor's yield is 7.14 per cent ($5 ÷ $70 = 0.0714), and it is protected by a low price-earnings ratio of 7 to 1. If the market price of this stock should rise to $100, as it probably will, the yield would drop to 5 per cent and the price-earnings ratio would change to 10 to 1. The investor who purchases this stock at $70 and sells it at $150 enjoys a good yield and an $80 increment in value. The investor who acquires the stock at $150 could expect a 3⅓ per cent yield, but his chances for further increment would tend to be limited unless the stock became speculative at higher prices and a higher price-earnings ratio.

There is no general agreement as to the precise point at which a stock ceases to be a good investment and becomes speculative. Many shares sell readily at 40 times their earnings. For example, the stock cited above might sell at $200, although cautious investors might regard it as overpriced. If the market were in a speculative mood some persons would ignore the 2.5 per cent yield and 20 to 1 price-earnings ratio and buy it at $200, hoping to sell it soon for $210 or $220. A boom market permits short-term capital gains of this sort, but eventually public optimism wanes and the market price of a stock like this one will fall to $200, or even lower.

3. Leverage—low-interest bonds and low-dividend preferred stocks that form part of a corporation's total capitalization enhance the earning ability of the common stock. Investors should be cognizant of this *debt-equity ratio* even though fixed-dividend preferred stocks are sometimes regarded as debt. The shifting of preferred stocks from the numerator to the denominator of the ratio and back can play havoc with this fraction and with the debt-equity concept. Sometimes, of course, a high leverage factor may be desirable. With leverage, a high proportion of a corporation's earnings belongs to the common stockholders, if a large amount of the company's capitalization has been acquired with low-interest bonds and low-dividend preferred stocks, as Figure 6–2 illustrates.

For purposes of elucidation, suppose we hypothesize that, after corporate taxes have been paid by the two corporations represented in Figure 6-2, a sum of $100,000 remains for distribution to the security holders of each. Corporation A, having no leverage, would be able to declare to its common stockholders, its *only* security holders, a 10 per cent dividend, or perhaps a smaller one and retain the balance of the earnings for corporate needs. In Corporation B, however, $25,000 must go to the bondholders and $15,000 to the preferred stockholders, leaving $60,000 for distribution to common stockholders or for dividends and reserves, as its board of directors may prefer. But the residual $60,000 in this instance represents not 10 per cent but 24 per cent of the face value of the common stock. Thus the higher the leverage of the common stock, the greater is the portion available for dividends. In a prosperous corporation, a high leverage or debt-equity ratio is an attractive inducement to the prospec-

Corporation A		*Corporation B*
$1,000,000	Common stocks	$ 250,000
—	6% preferred stocks	250,000
—	5 per cent bonds	500,000
$1,000,000	Total capitalization	$1,000,000

Figure 6-2. **Leverage.**

tive investor. In a struggling corporation, on the other hand, high leverage is dangerous since the available earnings are apt to have been devoured by the bondholders and preferred stockholders as prior claimants.

4. *Book value*—a common stock has a book value per share which can be calculated precisely and used as one of the measures of reasonableness of the market price. Specifically, book value per share equals the total assets less the liabilities, and the liquidation value of preferred stocks, divided by the number of common shares. When, for example, General Motors had total declared assets of $8.5 billion and liabilities (debts—mainly bonds and preferred stocks valued at $2.6 billion), its invested capital of $5.81 billion divided by 285 million shares indicated a book value per share of $20.39 in 1961. The actual market price of General Motors common stock ranged at that time from $40 to $50 per share.

5. The market image of the stock—has the stock enjoyed enough investor preference over the years to have been traded heavily at relatively high prices? Has the market price fallen less than the price of other stocks when business has been depressed? Has the price rallied earlier than the prices of most other stocks? Has the price of the stock been consistently higher than the stock's book value and has the price-earnings ratio been high? If the price of the stock fluctuates considerably, can the pattern of its fluctuations, as compared with

earnings, the business cycle, or the various market indices, be detected? What seem to be the immediate and long-range prospects for high and rising quotations on this stock?

TECHNICAL APPROACH TO SECURITY ANALYSIS

Another approach to security analysis is composed of the charts drawn by analysts to represent the movement of stock prices—largely the common stocks. These prices, in turn, reflect the day-to-day struggle between buyers and sellers; they indicate the rise or fall of investor confidence. For example, a stock may sell for fifteen times earnings at one time and twenty times earnings a few days later. From his incisive attention to market prices, the *chartist* believes that he can sense the moment when prices of a single stock or of the market as a whole will "break out" into a decisive rise or decline.

Point-and-Figure Charts

One type of chart is the point-and-figure variety. A chartist constructs such a chart by placing an X on a sheet of graph paper in a left-hand vertical column at the point that represents the dollar price of the stock being charted. In Figure 6–3, the first price of $50 per share is represented by the X in the left-hand column next to the $50 mark. As the price rises dollar by dollar or, in investment parlance, point by point, to $55, an X is posted for each point above the original $50 mark. Some chartists record only three-point changes.

As long as the price trend moves in one direction, new postings are made in the same column. When the trend reverses, the next X is posted in the

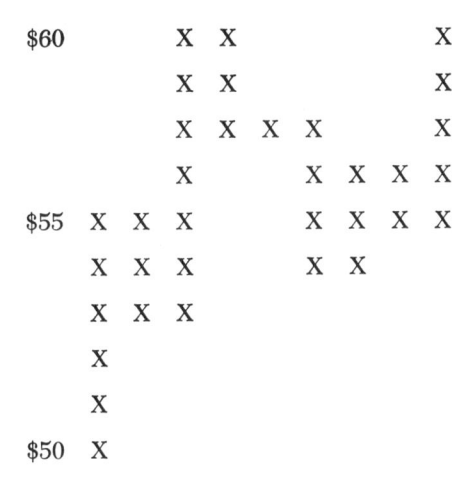

```
$60         X X                 X
            X X                 X
            X X X X             X
            X       X X X X
$55  X X X          X X X X
     X X X          X X
     X X X
     X
     X
$50  X
```

Figure 6–3. **Point-and-figure chart.**

adjacent column. In Figure 6–3 the series of X's in the second column shows a price decline from $55 to $53 followed in the third column by a subsequent price rise from $53 to $60 per share. A continuation of this pattern, rising several points, falling back a little, and rising several points again, suggests to the chartist that investor confidence is strong enough to overcome minor setbacks. The stock seems destined for a substantial rise. Other patterns suggest other influences.

Wave Cycles

Another type of chart is the wave cycle. Daily price movements mean little, say some chartists, but the long-term movements of a single stock or of the entire market has considerable significance. To these chartists, who have delved into the past record of a particular stock, the stock may move in a five-wave cycle as indicated by Figure 6–4. If this analysis is correct, the stock in question should rise through three more waves before its upward force has been spent.

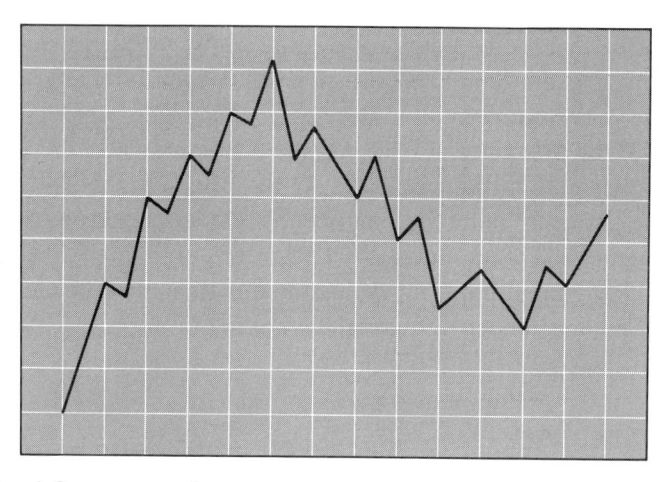

Figure 6-4. A five-wave cycle.

There are additional charting tools used in the technical approach; they consist primarily of confidence index charts, plotting of central values, and combinations of all of these approaches. At some point the technical approach merges into or incorporates the *Dow theory* and other tools of analysis. The technical approach to security analysis may be a useful tool in the hands of specialists for confirmation of their findings from the fundamental approach. Individual investors may find the charts too complicated for their own use and subject to many interpretations.

The Dow Theory

Followers of the Dow theory believe that an upward market trend will be indicated when a market-price peak and trough are higher than the preceding upward swing. Conversely, the primary market trend is believed to be downward if a market-price peak and trough are lower than in the preceding downward market swing. The theory notes, also, that investors gain most by following a primary upward or downward market, and that a primary trend is indicated when industrial stocks on the Dow-Jones list, followed by railroad stocks, break through their previous high or low quotations (Fig. 6–5).

PORTFOLIO MANAGEMENT

No single investment is ideal under all circumstances and at all times. A common stock investment that earns 7 per cent should probably be sold if most other common stocks are earning 9 per cent and bonds of the same companies are yielding 5 per cent or more. Investment opportunities and special investment situations must be weighed against the question of selling or retaining each and every item in one's investment portfolio. Indices must be watched; trustworthy information must be gleaned from dozens of sources; predictions must be made; buy-and-sell orders must be given. This task and responsibility, however difficult, may be lightened by utilizing some of the following guides.

Achieving a Balanced Portfolio

An investor may average his losses without noticeably penalizing his chance for gains by balancing his portfolio. This requires a proper assortment of investments diversified between the bonds and stocks of several well-chosen firms in selected industries. Some risks must be taken, however, if income from earnings and capital gains is to be average or above average.

A shrewd investor must review his investment position continually. Is he overloaded with equities in anticipation of a business boom which may not materialize? Does he hold convertible debentures which should be exchanged for common stocks? Each investment must be subject to constant review to see whether its prospects suggest its disposal or retention. Most of these investment decisions are dependent on proper timing.

Investment Timing

No one really knows the precise moment for buying or selling a security. Some investors plunge into the market, making good and bad decisions because of haste. Others are too timid or hesitant; their mistakes consist most often

172   Analysis of Corporate Securities

The Dow-Jones Averages

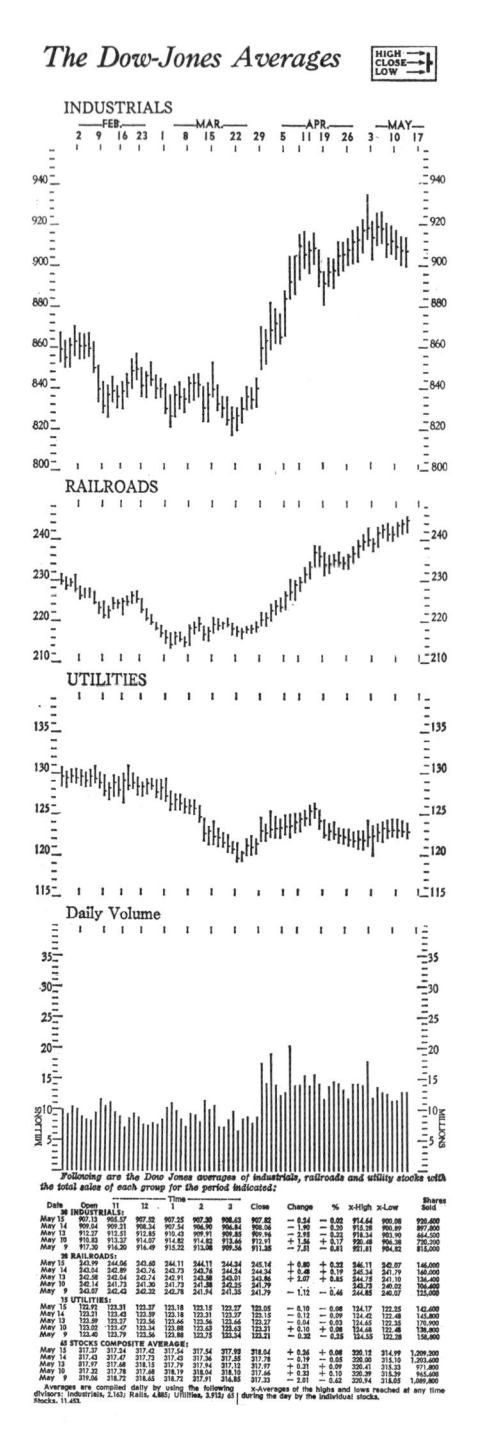

The Dow-Jones Average Stocks

INDUSTRIALS

Allied Chemical	General Electric	Sears Roebuck
Aluminum Co	General Foods	Std Oil of Calif
Amer Can	General Motors	Std Oil of NJ
Amer Tel & Tel	Goodyear	Swift & Co
Am Tobacco	Inter Harvester	Texaco
Anaconda	Inter Nickel	Union Carbide
Bethlehem Steel	Inter Paper	United Aircraft
Chrysler	Johns-Manville	US Steel
Du Pont	Owens-Illinois	Westinghouse El
Eastman Kodak	Procter & Gamble	Woolworth

RAILS

Atchison	Gulf Mobile & Ohio	St Louis-San Fran
Canadian Pacific	Illinois Central	Seab Cst L RR
Ches & Ohio	Kansas City Sou	Southern Pacific
Chi & NW	Louisv & Nash	Southern Railway
Del & Hudson	Missouri Pac	Union Pacific
Den & Rio Gr W	Norfolk & West'n	Western Pacific
Great North Ry	Penn Central	

UTILITIES

Am Elec Power	Consol Nat Gas	Panhandle EPL
Cleveland E Ill	Detroit Edison	Peoples Gas
Colum Gas Sys	Houston Lt & Pw	Phila Elec
Comwlth Edison	Niag Mohawk P	Pub Serv E&G
Consol Edison	Pacific Gas & El	Sou Cal Edison

YEARLY HIGHS AND LOWS OF DOW-JONES AVERAGES

	—Industrials—		—Railroads—		—Utilities—	
	High	Low	High	Low	High	Low
1967-68	943.08	786.41	274.49	205.16	140.43	120.97
1966	995.15	744.32	271.72	184.34	152.39	118.96
1965	969.26	840.59	249.55	187.29	163.32	149.84
1964	891.71	766.08	224.91	178.81	155.71	137.30
1963	767.21	646.79	179.46	142.03	144.37	129.19
1962	726.01	535.76	149.83	114.86	130.85	103.11
1961	734.91	610.25	152.92	131.06	135.90	99.75
1960	685.47	566.05	160.43	123.37	100.07	85.02
1959	679.36	574.46	173.56	146.65	94.70	85.05
1958	583.65	436.89	157.91	99.89	91.00	68.94
1957	520.77	419.79	157.67	95.67	74.61	62.10
1956	521.05	462.35	181.23	150.44	71.17	63.03
1955	488.40	388.20	167.83	137.84	66.68	61.39
1954	404.39	279.87	146.23	94.84	62.47	52.22
1953	293.79	255.49	112.21	90.56	53.88	47.87
1952	292.00	256.35	112.53	82.03	52.64	47.53
1951	276.37	238.99	90.08	72.39	47.22	41.47
1950	235.47	196.81	77.89	51.24	44.26	37.40
1949	200.52	161.60	54.29	41.03	41.31	33.36
1948	193.16	165.39	64.95	48.13	36.04	31.65
1947	186.85	163.21	53.42	41.16	37.55	32.28
1946	212.50	163.12	68.31	44.69	43.74	33.20
1945	195.82	151.35	64.89	47.03	39.15	26.15
1944	152.53	134.22	48.40	33.45	26.37	21.74
1943	145.82	119.26	38.30	27.59	22.30	14.69
1942	119.71	92.92	29.28	23.31	14.94	10.58
1941	133.59	106.34	30.88	24.25	20.65	13.51
1940	152.80	111.84	32.67	22.14	26.45	18.03
1939	155.92	121.44	35.90	24.14	27.10	20.71
1938**	158.41	98.95	33.98	19.00	25.19	15.14
1937	194.40	113.64	64.46	28.91	37.54	19.65
1936	184.90	143.11	59.89	40.66	36.08	28.63
1935	148.44	96.71	41.84	27.31	29.78	14.46
1934	110.74	85.51	52.97	33.19	31.03	16.83
1933	108.67	50.16	56.53	23.43	37.73	19.33
1932	88.78	41.22	41.30	13.23	36.11	16.53
1931	194.36	73.79	111.58	31.42	73.40	30.55
1930	294.07	157.51	157.94	91.65	108.62	55.14
1929	381.17	198.69	189.11	128.07	144.61	64.72
1928†	300.00	191.33	152.70	132.60	....	....
1927	202.40	152.73	144.82	119.29	....	....

**From June 2, 1938, the Utility Average was based on 15 stocks instead of 20 as formerly.
†On March 7, 1928, the list of rails was increased to 20 from 12.

Figure 6-5. Dow-Jones averages. (*Source. Wall Street Journal,* March 8, 1968, p. 23.)

of the stocks not bought when prices are lowest and securities not sold when prices are highest. These people become confirmed fence sitters; they become, in fact, observers of the market, hypnotized into inaction.

When to Buy and When Not to Buy. If the general level of stock prices seems to be rather high according to the Dow-Jones Averages or some similar indicator, perhaps one should refrain from buying in such a market. Nevertheless, a *bull market** in the latter phases of a boom period attracts a great number of novices by its spectacular rise in market prices, even though this suggests the probability that prices will go down before long. If prospective investors are guilty of pushing a market beyond a reasonable price range, they very well may suffer losses when it reacts and caves in on them.

Ideally, investments should be made when market prices are low in the recession phase of the business cycle. Few persons, however, have sizable sums available or the courage to invest at such times unless they sell other securities or other assets when selling prices are as low as buying prices.

Shifting Between Bond and Stocks. If an investor were wise enough, able to buck the mob psychology, and lucky, he might buy stocks at the bottom of the business cycle. Holding them until the peak of the boom phase, he would switch to high-grade bonds to be held during the impending recession. Another switch would be made by selling the bonds and buying stocks when the latter seem to have reached their lowest price during the recession. With good fortune, an investor can have dividends and capital gains from both the stocks and the bonds during the period each is held.

Dollar Averaging. The investor who lacks knowledge of the business cycle and has neither stocks nor bonds to sell may invest in harmony with the business cycle by *investing an equal number of dollars in successive time periods*, a practice known as dollar averaging. Thus, for $100 a month a novice investor might buy three shares of General Motors during a recession, two shares during a moderately prosperous period, and one or one-and-a-half shares in the boom phase of the business cycle, or when the market is up for GM shares. Short of shewd buying when prices are low and abstinence from buying at other times, dollar averaging is designed to provide a moderate price per share over the cycle, except that it entails small purchases involving high commission rates. Unfortunately, there is no corresponding arrangement for selling a stock in some way that averages the effects of the business cycle and its accompanying market-price changes.

* In a bull market there is more buying than selling pressure, thereby pushing up prices of securities.

When to Sell and When Not to Sell. Much less has been written about the selling of securities than about their purchase. Presumably a security should be sold when its market price is highest, but how does one recognize this high point in the market? Moreover, if an investor sells in the boom phase of a business cycle, how shall he invest his funds without buying some other overpriced securities? How may his taxes on capital gains be minimized?

If an investor can sell his holdings at high prices and get out of the market, he will have made a capital gain and be ready to enter the market again, eventually, when prices are appreciably lower. If he can repeat this process through several market cycles, he can count his gains in sizable figures. But few are sure when to sell and when to buy; prices zigzag and trends are uncertain. Besides, investing is a challenging endeavor, and many persons are not temperamentally inclined to sell and leave the market, once they have entered it. Finally, where would an individual invest his money safely and gainfully during the months in which he has withdrawn from the market—and would not the tax be high on a short-term capital gain of less than six months? This manner of investment might be profitable, but it is not typical; it does not constitute the pattern of portfolio management suggested by most of the specialists in this subject.

Portfolio management is a task that challenges every investor, although most often it confronts older, richer investors who have acquired a knowledge of the market and an eagerness for the test it offers. These investors continuously reevaluate their portfolios for income and growth possibilities, switching from one investment to another as their needs may dictate. They sell and buy, sometimes with abandon. Eventually, they leave their holdings—perhaps in a trust agreement*—to their wives, their children, and their favored charities. Once a trust arrangement has been made, the management of an investment portfolio passes into professional hands.

The next two chapters continue this subject. One deals with investment institutions and the other with investment companies.

QUESTIONS

1. Name several types of corporate bonds. Which are secured and which have prior claims over others? What is the position of debentures in relation to all other types of securities?
2. How would a callable clause probably affect bond yields of a very successful company? Why?
3. Name and explain several preferential clauses in preferred stocks. How are these preferences likely to affect the market price in boom times? In depressions? With successful companies? With unsuccessful companies? Why?

* See Chapter 17, pp. 504–509.

4. What are the advantages of common stock ownership? When and why should common stockholders be especially concerned about interest payments to bondholders and dividend payments to preferred stockholders?
5. Why do certain industries rise and others decline in the favor of astute investors? Which have been the favored industries in recent years?
6. When and why may a new, small firm's securities be a poor investment even in a favored industry?
7. What must a company's management do to make its common stock attractive to shrewd investors if the company is in a moderately unsuccessful line of endeavor?
8. Use Du Pont, TWA, United Airlines and several other stocks to illustrate the relationship between their respective market images. How do the securities of these companies differ in (a) earnings, (b) yields, (c) asset coverage, (d) book value, and (e) leverage?
9. What special investment situations are likely to attract astute investors? Why?
10. How do the fundamental approach and the technical approach to security analysis differ? Should they be used jointly? Which is more adaptable for use by amateur investors? Why?
11. When is a portfolio balanced? Why does balance and diversification require frequent purchases and sales? Why is timing very important? Why is portfolio management especially important for a wealthy, aged investor?
12. Is portfolio management too difficult for a typical investor? What are the alternatives?
13. Note carefully the key terms in this chapter and be prepared to identify each of them.

SELECTED READINGS

Amling, Frederick, *Investments, An Introduction to Analysis and Management*, Prentice-Hall, Englewood Cliffs, N.J., 1965.

Badger, Ralph E., *Investment Principles and Practices*, 5th ed., Prentice-Hall, Englewood Cliffs, N. J., 1961.

Ball, Richard E., *Readings in Investments*, Allyn and Bacon, Inc., Boston, 1965.

Baumol, William J., *The Stock Market and Economic Efficiency*, Fordham University Press, Bronx, 1965.

Bellemore, Douglas H., *Investments, Principles, Practices, and Analysis*, South-Western Publishing Company, Cincinnati, 1967.

Bernhard, Arnold, *The Evaluation of Common Stocks*, Simon and Schuster, New York, 1959.

Bogen, Jules I., and Herman E. Krooss, *Security Credit*, Prentice-Hall, Englewood Cliffs, N. J., 1960.

Brown, F. E., and Douglas Vickers, "Mutual Fund Portfolio Activity, Performance, and Market Impact," *Journal of Finance*, May, 1963, p. 377.

Bullock, Hugh, *The Story of Investment Companies*, Columbia University Press, New York, 1959.

Casey, William J., *Mutual Funds and How to Use Them*, New York Institute of Business Planning, New York, 1959.

Calkins, Francis J., *Cases and Problems in Investments*, Prentice-Hall, Englewood Cliffs, N. J., 1955.
Clarkson, Geoffrey P. E., *Portfolio Selection: A Simulation of Trust Investment*, Prentice-Hall, Englewood Cliffs, N. J., 1962.
Clendenin, John C., *Introduction to Investments*, 4th ed., McGraw-Hill, New York, 1964.
Coe, James Clarence, *Common Stocks for Investors and Traders*, Vantage Press, New York, 1961.
Cootner, Paul H., *The Random Character of Stock Market Prices*, Massachusetts Institute of Technology Press, Cambridge, 1964.
Dowrie, George William, Douglas R. Fuller, and Francis J. Calkins, *Investments*, 3rd ed., Wiley, New York, 1961.
Farrar, Donald Eugene, *The Investment Decision under Uncertainty*, Prentice-Hall, Englewood Cliffs, N. J., 1962.
Eiteman, Wilford J., Charles A. Dice, and David Kurt Eiteman, *The Stock Market*, 4th ed., McGraw-Hill, New York, 1966.
Fortune—List of 500 Leading Corporations, annually in July.
Galbraith, John Kenneth, *The Great Crash 1929*, Houghton Mifflin, Boston, 1961.
Graham, Benjamin, *The Intelligent Investor*, 3rd rev. ed., Harper, New York, 1965.
Hayes, Douglas A., *Investments: Analysis and Management*, 2nd ed., Macmillan, New York, 1966.
Jordan, David F., and Herbert E. Dougall, *Investments*, 7th ed., Prentice-Hall, Englewood Cliffs, N. J., 1960.
Kooros, Ahmed, "The Theory of Investment Programming: A Suggested Econometric Model," unpublished doctoral dissertation, University of Southern California, Los Angeles, 1960.
Loll, Leo M., Jr., and Julian G. Buckley, *The Over-the-Counter Securities Markets: A Review Guide*, Prentice-Hall, Englewood Cliffs, N.J., 1961.
Manne, Henry G., *Insider Trading and the Stock Market*, Free Press, Macmillan, New York, 1967.
Markowitz, Harry Max, *Portfolio Selection: Efficient Diversification of Investment—Cowles Commission Monograph 16*, Wiley, New York, 1959.
Moody's Handbook of Widely Held Common Stocks, Moody's Investors Service, latest edition.
Robbins, Sidney, *The Securities Markets, Operations and Issues*, The Free Press, Macmillan, New York, 1966.
Robinson, Roland I., and Robert W. Johnson, *Self-Correcting Problems in Finance*, Allyn and Bacon, Inc., Boston, 1965.
New York Stock Exchange, *Fact Book 1966*, New York.
Prime, John H., *Investment Analysis*, 4th ed., Prentice-Hall, Englewood Cliffs, N. J., 1967.
Schiller, Maurece, *Special Situations in the Stock Market*, American Research Council, Larchmont, N. Y., 1961.
Smith, Ralph Lee, *The Grim Truth About Mutual Funds*, G. P. Putnam's Sons, New York, 1963.
Sobel, Robert, *The Big Board*, The Free Press, Macmillan, New York, 1965.
Wiesenberger, Arthur, *Investment Companies*, Wiesenberger, New York, published annually.

Wu, H. K., and A. J. Zakon, *Elements of Investments,* Holt, Rinehart and Winston, New York, 1965.

Refer to the footnotes in Chapters 5, 7, and 8 for excellent additional sources for further reading in this subject.

NOTES

1. Maurece Schiller, *Special Situations in the Stock Market,* American Research Council, Larchmont, N. Y., 1961, pp. 5, 6, *et seq.*
2. *Ibid.,* pp. 18–20.
3. *Ibid.,* pp. 36–39.

PROBLEMS AND CASES

1. Assume that you have the opportunity to purchase a corporate bond for $950. Its face value is $1,000 and it matures five years hence. It pays 5 per cent per annum in interest. Compute the current yield on this bond and its yield to maturity or effective yield.
2. For $900 Fred Jones buys a $1,000 five-year second-mortgage bond paying 4 per cent. Use Table 6–2 to determine (1) the current yield he will receive, and (2) the yield to maturity. Weigh the strength of these bonds if most second-mortgage bonds are priced to yield 5½ per cent at the present time. What yield to maturity can Jones anticipate if his bond should be called a year before its terminal date?
3. For $1,025 Jones buys a $1,000 five-year 4 per cent first-mortgage bond in the same company. What (1) current yield and (2) yield to maturity will he receive? Assess the strength of these bonds if most first-mortgage bonds are priced to yield 5 per cent at present. What yield to maturity can Jones anticipate if his bond should be called a year prior to its terminal date? Is that likely to occur? Why?
4. Why does exercise of the callable clause benefit the bondholder in one of the foregoing instances and harm him in the other? Based upon the evaluation of these bonds and of the issuing company, what are the prospects that it will exercise its call option in each instance?
5. Get in touch with an investment broker in your area or use available financial publications. Obtain an industry analysis and an analysis of the prospects of a particular firm whose securities are being offered for sale. How thorough are these analyses? Are they adequate for the careful investor?
6. Refer to the financial page of a newspaper. Chart the average selling price of a particular stock listed on the New York Stock Exchange over the past month. Can you find any particular reason why any trend apparent from your chart should continue? Any guarantee that it will?
7. Obtain, if possible, the price movements and the dividend record of a particular stock over a period of three years. (Reference may be made to financial publications or to investment brokers who have these data.) What is the relationship between the dividend paid on this stock, its yield, and its price currently? Has this relationship varied over the three years? To what extent would you conclude that expected yield has affected the price of this stock?
8. Refer to Figure 6–1. Complete this analysis for a specific security of a specific

firm. (Data may be obtained from financial publications, the firm itself, and brokers, as long as care is taken to assume their authenticity.)

9. You have $100,000 to invest. Purchase stocks and bonds with one objective—maximizing income. Determine how your securities fared over the period of 6 months by referring to financial publications. How much were your earnings? What rate of return did you achieve?
10. In what stocks would you invest $100,000 now if your goal was purchasing stocks that will have a maximum accretion in value over the next year? Why did you choose these particular securities?
11. List facts about (1) the company, and (2) business conditions generally, that a prospective investor in a convertible debenture would need to investigate.
12. Jack Adams can buy cumulative preferred stocks in a weak company for $99 per share. The comparable noncumulative preferred shares are selling for $95. Which should he buy? Why?
13. Smith can buy participating preferred shares in a strong company for $107, whereas comparable nonparticipating preferred shares are selling for $102. Which should he buy? Why?
14. A series of 5 per cent first-mortgage bonds in a strong company has been nearly retired and the $1,000 bonds are selling at $1,010 five years before their terminal date. A comparable issue of second-mortgage bonds has a quoted price of $1,000. Which should be bought? Why? What is the difference if the first issue is callable at $1,003 in three years?
15. Should Widow Smith pay $40 a share for common stocks with a price-earnings ratio of 10 to 1 if there is a two-year arrearage on the cumulative preferred? Why? Could this be a sleeper? What other factors should be investigated?

7 USING INVESTMENT INSTITUTIONS

How is it possible to budget for solvency in dealing with matters of chance?

GEORGE BERNARD SHAW

A prospective investor will probably glance curiously at some published market quotations for the previous day. From that moment he begins to learn. Hopefully, he should learn a great deal before he enters the market as a novice.

In Figure 7–1 the reader will observe several things about the previous day's market on the New York Stock Exchange. The names of companies are entered in abbreviated or shortened form. It is assumed that the listings refer to common stocks, unless otherwise indicated. Using Wheeling Steel, for example, the reader will note that the market price of its common stock ranged between 15½ and 22¾ during the previous fourteen months and that 1,600 shares changed hands on the previous day. On that day, the market price ranged between 18¼ and 18⅜ which means $18.25 to $18.37½ per share. The

New York Stock Exchange Stocks

Continued From Page 26

—1967-68— High	Low	Stocks	Div.	Sales in 100s	Open	High	Low	Close	Net Chg.
33½	27	Wn Banc	1.20	60	32¾	32⅞	32⅜	32½	....
41¾	26⅜	Wstn Md	1.60	2	28⅜	28⅜	28⅜	28⅜	− ⅛
38½	31	WstnPac	2.20	7	33½	34	33⅜	33¾	+ ¼
46⅝	30	WnUTel	1.40	72	32⅞	33	32¼	32⅝	...
45⅞	30⅜	WghABk	1.80	473	41	41½	40	40⅛	−1⅜
79⅛	46⅜	WestgEl	1.80	232	61⅛	63⅞	61⅛	63½	+2¼
80	63½	WestE	pf3.80	z20	68¾	68¾	68¾	68¾	.....
33⅞	18⅜	Weyberg	1.20	5	30⅛	30⅛	30⅛	30⅛	.....
47¾	33¼	Weyerhr	1.40	139	36¾	36¾	36⅜	36½	+ ⅛
22¾	15½	Wheelg Steel		16	18¼	18⅜	18¼	18¼	.....
67¼	49⅛	Wheel Stl pf		z350	53	53	52	52⅞	+ ¼
57	31¾	Whirl Cp	1.60	103	48¾	50	48⅝	50	+1¼
74½	36¼	White Cn	.15r	112	41½	43½	41½	43½	+2½
40⅜	36½	WhiteC	pf2.75	1	39¼	39¼	39¼	39¼	+ ½
35¼	23¼	WhiteCrss	.40	7	30⅛	30⅛	30	30	− ⅛
60½	40⅝	White Mot	2b	23	48⅛	48¼	47⅞	47⅞	− ¼
94⅜	53¾	Whittaker Cp		388	65¾	66	64⅜	65½	+1
32⅛	18	WickesCorp	1	20	31½	31½	30⅜	30⅝	− ⅝
78¼	34	Williams Bro		66	59½	61½	59½	61½	+2½
35	26¾	WinnDix	1.50	244	30⅜	30¾	30⅛	30⅛	− ¼
29¾	23	WisElPw	1.32	33	24½	25¼	24½	25¼	+1
116¾	99½	Wis ElP	pf 6	z10	103½	103½	103½	103½	+ ¾
20½	17⅝	WisPSvc	1.02	6	19	19	18¾	18¾	− ⅛
39½	27	Witco Ch	1.20	27	36⅜	37	36	37	+1
71	55¼	WitcoC	pf2.65	1	64¼	64¼	64¼	64¼	.....
27⅞	14	Wolv WW	.50	46	15	15¾	15	15⅝	+ ⅝
24	10⅞	Wometco	.48	21	19¼	19⅞	19⅛	19⅝	+ ¾
36	23⅝	WoodwIr	1.60	12	29⅞	30	29¾	30	+ ½
32⅜	19⅝	Woolworth	1	125	22¾	22⅞	22½	22¾	+ ¼
41⅞	16⅛	World Airwy		51	19⅛	19⅜	18⅝	18⅞	+ ⅛
122¾	103¼	Wrigley	3a	12	107½	107½	107	107	− ¾
36	18⅛	Wurlitzer	.80	10	18⅝	19½	18⅝	19½	+1⅞
314¼	197¼	XeroxCp	1.40	389	242	250	240½	245¾	+6¾
36⅝	26¾	YngstSht	1.80	79	30	30⅞	30	30⅝	+ ¾
27¼	17½	YngstSD	1.20	18	21½	21½	21¼	21⅜	− ⅛
43⅜	28⅛	Zayre Corp		42	32⅞	33¼	31	31	−1¼
72¼	47¾	ZenithR	1.20a	88	55	56¼	55	56	+1¾

z—Sales in full.

Unless otherwise noted, rates of dividends in the foregoing table are annual disbursements based on the last quarterly or semi-annual declaration. Special or extra dividends or payments not designated as regular are identified in the following footnotes.

a—Also extra or extras. b—Annual rate plus stock dividend. c—Liquidating dividend. d—Declared or paid in 1967 plus stock dividend. e—Declared or paid so far this year. f—Payable in stock during 1967, estimated cash value on ex-dividend or ex-distribution date. g—Paid last year. h—Declared or paid after stock dividend or split up. k—Declared or paid this year, an accumulative issue with dividend meeting. r—Declared or paid in 1968 plus stock dividends in arrears. n—New issue. p—Paid this year, dividend omitted, deferred or no action taken at last dividend. t—Paid in stock during 1968, estimated cash value on ex-dividend or ex-distribution date.

cld—Called. x—Ex dividend. y—Ex dividend and sales in full. x-dis—Ex distribution. xr—Ex rights. xw—Without warrants. ww—With warrants. wd—When distributed. wi—When issued. nd—Next day delivery.

vj—In bankruptcy or receivership or being reorganized under the Bankruptcy Act, or securities assumed by such companies. fn—Foreign issue subject to interest equalization tax.

Year's high and low range does not include changes in latest day's trading.

Where a split or stock dividend amounting to 25 per cent or more has been paid the year's high-low range and dividend are shown for the new stock only.

Figure 7-1. **Market quotations.** (*Source. Wall Street Journal*, **March 8, 1968, p. 26.**)

opening quotation, the highest quotation, the lowest quotation, and the closing quotation for the day are all given. There was no net change in price at the close of the market day compared with the closing price of the previous day. In the next line down, Wheeling Steel preferred is listed, and similar information is included. The preferred shares have a different price range and their response to market changes may vary much less than the price range of the common shares for a number of reasons that depend somewhat on the nature of the preferences included. Since Figure 7-1 represents companies at the end of the alphabet, the footnotes, which are included, explain a number of items that do not pertain to the 32 issues shown here.

The individual investor need not depend entirely on his own intuition and his own investment surveys. There are thousands of brokers and dozens of investment services waiting to provide their clientele with investment counsel.

Behind the brokers and investment services lies an assortment of stock exchanges, investment specialists, commodity exchanges, odd-lot dealers, investment bankers, and underwriting syndicates. This array of investment institutions may have evolved in a haphazard manner, but it is fully integrated to provide investors with a unified, speedy service for a relatively low fee.

Originally there were just a few investors and they bought and sold directly in the exchanges. The exchanges have grown in number and size, but now the average investor seldom enters one of them; he deals with a broker or a broker's representative in his community. To understand the operations of a brokerage office, the customer must go behind the scenes and examine the origins, the motives, and the contributions of a number of investment institutions.

PRIMARY DISTRIBUTION OF SECURITIES

When a corporation decides to raise capital by selling an issue of securities, it may open its stock subscription book and sell directly to the public, or it may sell to the public through brokers, agents, investment bankers, or underwriters. Thus, in one way or another, an original or primary issue of securities will be distributed to individual investors.

Direct Distribution to Investment Bankers and Traders

In rare instances, investment bankers, stock traders, or other groups may purchase an original issue of securities from a corporation, for their own use, not for resale purposes. This means of distributing securities was very common in earlier times when investment bankers were permitted to accept deposits that they invested in well-chosen new issues and in huge blocks of voting stock. Investment banks have lost their glamor since the passage of the Banking Act of 1934, which eliminated their right to accept deposits. They lost their influence and some of their money as well, because they held so many foreign securities in an era of declining colonialism and uncollectable international accounts.

Frequently, nowadays, investment bankers are security traders who specialize in certain new issues and in special investment situations. Sometimes they buy and vote their holdings; often they buy for the purpose of selling again at a higher price. Sometimes they do not buy; they merely act as agents in the attempt to sell a corporation's securities.

Underwriting Syndicates

In the last 50 years, new issues of securities usually have been "launched" or "floated" by underwriters. An underwriter is an investment banker who has previously acquired the securities from the issuing corporation at a discounted price in exchange for an obligation to sell the entire issue to the investing public. As corporations grew larger, the responsibility for the successful marketing of large new security issues was shared by a number of underwriters who formed an underwriting syndicate. The syndicate members share the risks and profits resulting from a single underwriting assignment. As Figure 7–2 will indicate, several dozen firms may form one of these underwriting syndicates for the issuance of listed securities.

A corporation that is about to float an original or an additional issue of securities will seek investment counsel from one or more underwriters. The underwriter recommends an appropriate selling price and gives advice about the receptivity of the current market for various types of securities. Sometimes several underwriters bid on an entire issue, but frequently a syndicate of underwriters is formed to take the issue at a discounted price. Underwriters usually discount an issue at 2 per cent to 10 per cent in exchange for the promotional services and the market-price stability they provide.[1] Underwriters and syndicates are able as a rule to dispose of an issue through their branch brokerage offices and through affiliated brokers. An underwriter or an underwriting syndicate stakes its reputation on its ability to sell each issue that it has agreed to promote. Needless to say, most issues are successfully sold within a period of a few days or weeks. A few issues, such as the first public issue of Ford stock in 1956, have been oversold immediately and each prospective investor had to be satisfied with a percentage of the shares that he had sought to buy.

> This advertisement is neither an offer to sell nor a solicitation of an offer to buy any of these Securities. This offering is made only by the Prospectus.

New Issue   March 6, 1968

100,000 Shares
The Connrex Corporation
Common Stock
(Without Par Value)

Price $12 per share

Copies of the Prospectus may be obtained in any State from only such of the undersigned as may legally offer these Securities in compliance with the securities laws of such State.

Schwabacher & Co.	Joseph, Mellen & Miller, Inc.
Estabrook & Co.	Putnam, Coffin & Burr–Doolittle, Inc.
	Affiliate of Advest Co.
Fulton, Reid & Staples, Inc.	Hayden, Miller & Co.
McDonald & Company	Prescott, Merrill, Turben & Co.
Cooley & Company	Chas. W. Scranton & Co.
Murch & Co., Inc.	Crowell, Weedon & Co.
Singer, Deane & Scribner	J. N. Russell & Co., Inc.

Figure 7-2. A syndicate offering. (*Source. Wall Street Journal,* March 8, 1968, p. 17.)

THE CONTINUING MARKET FOR SECURITIES

Once a corporation's securities are in the hands of individual investors, the corporation is not directly concerned with the fact that the securities are bought and sold over and over again. These later sales, referred to as the *secondary distribution of securities,* require the use of stock exchanges and brokerage houses, which comprise the major subject of the remaining pages in this chapter.

Individuals who have purchased securities may wish to sell them quickly; or they may wish to sell a certain security and buy another. The fact that anything may be bought and sold freely enhances its value and makes it more attractive. This is known as *marketability*. The market for stocks and bonds is very well organized. Securities can be bought or sold usually within an hour. The depth of the market for stocks, involving stock exchanges, brokers, and millions of investors, assures that many buyers and sellers are almost certain to be bidding for any given security at any given moment.

Over-the-Counter Market

The over-the-counter buying and selling of *unlisted securities*—that is, securities not registered for trading on an organized exchange—represents a very simple form of security buying and selling. In many instances, securities representing local or regional companies are not listed and sold through a regular stock exchange because they are owned primarily by local investors. If American Express common stock is traded on the over-the-counter market, for example, a potential buyer might find that the most recent "bid" or buying quotation was $146½ a share and that the most recent "asked" or selling offer was $148 per share, as in Figure 7–3. This spread of 1½ points between bid and asked quotations is common in over-the-counter markets and indicates the upper and lower ranges within which the next transaction is likely to be negotiated. Actually, the prospective investor, through his broker, will buy American Express stock from a dealer who "makes a market" for it and buys and sells it freely. Obviously, over-the-counter trading is time consuming and costly when compared with the ease of trading in an organized stock exchange.

Stock Exchanges

When stock exchanges first evolved, they were composed of members who met in a coffee house where shares in merchant ventures and securities were bought and sold. For years, some exchanges operated on the sidewalk or curb near a building in which the "buy" and "sell" orders were executed. For a generation, now, each exchange has had its own building which usually includes a trading floor, a visitors' gallery, communications facilities, and executive offices. Members of the exchange have the exclusive right to send their men onto the floor to trade for the member firm or its clients. Needless to say, most member firms, which have paid a high price for their membership seats, trade for clients for a commission, and many of them have branch offices or affiliated brokers in the country's leading cities so that more clients may be serviced and more commissions collected. A few exchange members are mere *traders* who buy and sell exclusively for their own account.

A visitor to one of the leading exchanges is invited to look down on the trading floor from a visitors' gallery. On the trading floor are several trading posts, each serving as a center for buy-and-sell orders for specified securities. At each trading post the visitor will see the men representing various member firms who have orders for the securities being traded. Each of these busy men, sometimes called floor traders, is in continuous communication with his firm, which relays new orders to be executed. Around each trading post there is a din of shouts, accompanied by signals and gestures that indicate acceptance or rejection of each new buying or selling offer. Behind the scenes, in each member firm's office, a stream of new orders arrives from branch offices and affiliated brokers throughout the country.

The computerization of stock exchange transactions has been partially completed. Transactions flow faster, reports and billing are expedited with less clerical labor, and at long last it is possible to trace market activities so that buyers, sellers, and market pressures can be identified. Eventually, this information will be available for an appreciable number of years. Then, perhaps in five years, some of the mystery may be eliminated from the market.

The leading stock exchanges in the United States may be characterized briefly as follows:

New York Stock Exchange. The largest organized securities market in the United States is the New York Stock Exchange with 1,366 exchange members, 4,901 allied members, 29,500 registered representatives, and 57,684 other employees of the members. Actually, the New York Stock Exchange (NYSE) encompasses thousands of employees in 3,962 member offices scattered among 798 cities in the United States and in two dozen foreign countries.[2] In a trading day, 3 to 20 million shares are bought and sold on the *big board*, which is a complimentary term whose use is synonymous with the New York Stock Exchange. In 1929, a "seat" or membership sold for $625,000. In 1967, the top price was $450,000.

The 1,253 corporations whose common stocks are listed on the NYSE comprise a fraction of 1 per cent of all stock-issuing corporations, but these corporations represent 30 per cent of the total capital, 21 per cent of the employees of all American corporations, and gross sales or revenues of $395 billion.

The NYSE's rigid listing requirements specify that each initial listing must represent a company with (1) at least one million shares divided among 2,000 or more shareholders, (2) at least $10 million of tangible assets, and (3) at least $2 million of annual earnings. The exchange's 33-member Board of Governors has revised and strengthened the listing rules until it can be said that most of the large prestige corporations now list their securities on the NYSE.

The physical plant of the New York Stock Exchange includes a trading

Figure 7-3. **Over-the-counter market.** (*Source. Barron's*, **March 4, 1968.**)

March 4, 1968 *BARRON'S*

OVER-THE-COU

March 1, 1968

These quotations are supplied by the National Association of Securities Dealers. They do not represent actual transactions. markup, markdown or commission. Year's highs and lows are approximate ranges of bid prices from the time of each

Name of Stock and dividend	Latest Interim or fisc yr earns	1967-68 High Bid	1967-68 Low Bid	Over Counter Bid	Over Counter Asked	Wk ago Bid
A						
A-G Foods	67Dec1.47	52	46	51½	53½	50½
AAICorp	66Dec.24	29½	10½	16	18	16½
AberdnMfg.50d	Sep39w.91	14	8⅜	8⅜	8⅞	8⅜
AcmeElectric.16	Dec6m.57	24¾	16½	16¾	17¼	18
AcmeInd	67Dec.54	8¾	4¾	7½	8¼	7½
AcmeVisible.10e	Dec3m.42	64½	30	48½	50½	51
AcushnetProc.50b	67Dec1.69	28½	14½	24¼	25¼	26¼
AddisonWes.10	67Nov.43	31	16	16	17	17¼
AdleyCp	Sep36wD2.04	8¼	2½	7⅜	7⅞	7½
AdvanceRoss	Sep9m.18	26½	11½	19	19½	20
Aero-Chat	Dec6m.38	30½	2⅜	19½	20	21
Aerosonic.05	Nov6m.22	17½	6¾	10¾	11½	11¼
AffHospProd.40	Sep9m.69	25	14½	18¼	19¼	20
AirCalifornia	Jun14mD1.98	23¼	12	12¼	12¾	12⅞
AirIndustries	Dec6m.45	20⅞	16¼	16¼	16¾	17
AirborneFght	Sep6mD.21	19⅞	8	10⅞	11⅛	12¼
AirliftInternat'l	Sep3m.04	12⅛	3⅛	5½	5¾	5⅝
AitsInc.		41	30	31	34	33
Al-TennNG.80	Sep12m.95	14½	12⅝	13	13⅜	13
Albertson'sB.36	Dec39w.56	14⅝	8⅞	14⅝	15	13
AlcoStd.20g	67Sep2.26	49½	12¼	37½	38½	39
Alcolac.30	Dec6m.09	8¾	4½	6½	7	8
AlconLabs.40	Jan9m1.20	54½	22	39½	41	43½
AlicoLandDevCo	67Aug.01	11⅛	7½	10½	11	9¾
AlisonAyers10g	67July1.02	9⅞	2⅞	7½	8	7⅞
AllTechInd	67Oct.55	14¾	6	12¾	13¼	12⅜
AlegPepsi.40	Sep9m1.35	14½	6¾	13	13½	13¼
AllenOrgB.15b	67Dec.68	18¼	9	9½	10½	9½
AlliedEquities	Sep9m.86	21¼	10¼	12¼	12¾	12½
AlliedMain.60	Dec9m1.54	45	13	36½	37½	37
AlliedRadio	Apr36w1.11	20¾	8	....	....	15½
AlliedTherm 1.50b	67Dec4.28	43	34	37	39	37
Allyn&Bacon.40	67Apr.96	30¼	18¾	23½	24½	23¼
AloeCremeLabs	67JulyD.10	10¾	4¾	6¾	7¼	7¼
Alphanumeric	66DecD.46	144	63	64	68	84
AlpineGeo	Oct6m.19	43	15½	22¼	23¼	23½
AmAutVend.20	Aug6m.47	16¼	6¾	14¾	15¼	15
AmElLab	67Nov.42	22½	15½	17½	18½	17
AmExpress 1.40	67Dec4.76	189	89¼	146½	148	148½
AmFinan.15b	Sep9m1.11	31½	13¾	26½	27½	29
AmFurniture.24	67Dec.65	7¾	5⅜	6½	6¾	6⅜
AmGreetA.60	Nov12m1.47	38½	35¼	35¼	36¼	37¾
AmHerPub.40	Dec6m.42	25¼	10½	12½	13½	13
AmInstDev	66Dec.02	41	17½	32½	34½	38
AmMaizePrd.50	Sep9m.49	37	19¾	21	22	21¾
AmMedEnt.10d	Nov3m.19	48	29	29	30½	35
AmNuclear	67May.29	36½	9⅝	24	25	24½
AmMusicStrs.15e	Oct3m.46	14½	10¾	12½	13	13¼
AmPipe&Cons.50	67Nov1.45	17½	10⅛	16¼	16¾	15¾
AmRealtyTr.24e	67Sep.35	6¾	4¼	6⅜	6¾	6¼
AmRub&Plas.80a	Nov9m1.18	17¾	12½	17½	18½	16½
AmSGobain	Sep9mD1.54	8¼	4	5¼	5¾	5⅜
AmStG5%pf		16½	10	10½	11	10
AmTechMch.05r	67Dec1.21	21¼	14	16¼	17	15½
AmWld&M.80	67Nov2.22	26½	22	22¾	23¾	23
Amoskeag 2.00		50½	38½	49	50	48
Ampeg		6	2½	4¾	5¾	5
AmtelInc.40	Sep9m.99	40	5⅞	33	36	33
Anadite	67Oct2.10	63	31	34	36	35½
AnchorCpB1.60	67Dec2.65	40	17¼	33¼	34¼	33¼
AndersonLabs	Nov9m.45	20¼	4½	14½	15½	15¾
AnhBusch 1.30	67Dec3.27	90½	54½	80½	81½	84¼
ApbaumFd.36	Jan39w1.05	22¼	7⅞	21¾	22¾	20
AppliedDataR	67Dec.43	30	3⅛	26	28	25
AppMagnetics	Dec3m.10	36	24	28½	29½	29½
ArcsIndS3%e	Nov9m.46	13	4⅝	7⅛	7⅝	7½
ArdenMay.40g	Dec13w.20	15½	10⅞	13⅛	13⅝	12
ArdenMayfair pf 3.00		50½	38	40	42	40
Aries Corp	67DecD.42	30½	12¾	15½	17	18
AristoFoods	67Sep.54	20½	19	19	20	20⅜
ArizonaBiochem		25¼	7¼	12½	13½	13¼
ArkMoPw.52	Sep12m.72	14¼	9½	11⅝	12	11⅞
ArkValInd	Dec9mDef	13⅜	6¾	10⅛	10⅝	10⅝
ArkWstGas.60	Sep12m.90	15⅝	10½	11	11⅜	10⅞
ArkwinInd	Oct6m.17	12⅞	9¼	11⅜	11⅞	12¾
ArmstgAJ	Jun6m.002	8¾	5	7¼	7¾	6½
ArnoldConst	67JanD2.82	7¼	3¾	5½	6½	5½
ArrowHart 2.80	67Dec5.07	71	45¼	61¼	62¼	60
ArtMetalInc.80	Aug3m.37	34¾	26¼	31½	32½	30¾
ArvidaCorp	Jun6m.19	11⅛	5¾	10¾	11	10⅝
AsgrowSeed.60	Sep12m1.00	17¼	9½	15⅜	15⅞	15½
AssoCocaCola.72	Sep9m1.31	23¾	13⅛	22⅝	23⅛	22⅞
AssocMtg S5%g	67Sep1.03	9½	5¼	8¼	9	8¼
AthloneInd	67Dec2.27	30	5½	24½	25¼	28
AtlGasLt.88	Nov12m1.43	18⅝	15⅜	16⅜	16⅞	16⅝
AtlImprov		21	15½	19½	21½	17
AtlUtilities		13	4⅝	13	14	13
AutBldCmp	Oct9m.42	13	11	12	12½	12¾
AutoInd	67Dec1.23	52	26	43½	44½	46¼
AutoBanking S4%g	67Sep.11	6¾	3¾	4	4¾	5⅛
AVMCorp.25g	67Dec2.51	34½	12⅛	31	32	33¼
AztecOilGs S6%g	67Dec.59	21¾	14⅝	15⅝	15⅞	16
B						
BabcockElec	Nov6m.40	22⅞	5½	16	16½	17⅞
BaqdadCp.30	Sep9m.71	18½	13½	16¼	16¾	16¼
BairdAtomic	67SepD1.10	12⅞	5	11	11⅜	12½
BaltPt&Ch.20	67Aug.59	8½	3⅜	6	6½	6
BangHydro 1.16	67Dec1.62	20⅝	18	18¾	19¾	18¾
BardCR.25	67Dec.80	41½	29	33¾	34¾	35
Barden 1.20	Jan3m.32	48¼	28½	28½	30½	31
Barnes-Hind	Dec12m1.43	53¾	25½	43¼	44½	40¼
BarryRG	Jun25w.43	17¾	9½	15	16½	16
BasicProp.50		7	3⅛	6½	7½	6
BassettFurn 1.20	May6m1.30	35	33½	34	35	34
BaylessMkt.60	67Dec.53	10¾	7⅞	10⅜	10⅞	10¾
BeauCounsel.60	Sep9m.67	23¾	8¼	22½	23	22½
BeelineFash.20	67Dec.71	33½	18	21½	22¼	22½
BehlenMfgCo.80	Nov36w.73	14¾	9⅜	14¼	14¾	13⅜
Belknap.15e	66Apr1.01	11½	8⅝	10¾	11¼	11
BelleIsle.3282e		15⅞	11¼	14½	15	14½
BlmIrWr	67Nov4.19	39	14½	26	30	28
BlmtS&L	67Dec.54	8	3½	6½	7	6½
BeneficialCp 1.20a	Jun6m.69	29¾	19¼	27¾	28½	28
BrgstmPap 1.00	67Dec1.62	25½	18	20½	21½	20½
BerkshGas 1.30	Sep12m1.77	22½	19	20½	21¼	20½
BerkHathwy.10g	July9m.13	21¼	16¼	21	21¾	21
Bernz-O-Matic	Oct6m.07	9¾	3½	7½	8	8⅛
BetzLabs.40	67Dec1.02	45¾	27	39¾	40¾	39¾
BibbMfg 1.20	67Aug2.30	29	20½	22	22¾	22
BigDrum.60	Sep9m1.26	16⅛	8⅜	12½	13	12⅞
BillupsWestPet.50	Oct6m.69	9⅛	6⅝	8¼	8½	8⅜
BioDynamics.16	Nov9m.52	66	30¼	54	56	61½
Bird&Son 1.40a	Sep9m3.38	42½	31¼	42	43½	41
BirtcherCp	Jun6m.16	19¾	2⅜	12¼	13	13
BlkHillP&L 2.04	Oct12m2.69	38½	32½	32½	33¼	33¼
BlairJohn.80	67Dec2.02	35	15½	24¾	25½	26½
BlasiusInd	67May.47	7⅞	7¼	7⅞	8⅜	7¾
BlockHR .60	67Apr1.05	78	31¼	70	74	67
BogueElec	66Dec.34	14¾	2½	7¼	7¾	9¼
BoltBeranek&New	Dec6m.11	30	8¼	17¼	18¼	19¾
BostonCapital.05e	Sep6m.80	20¼	5⅞	17	17½	17⅜
BostonHerT S3%e	67Dec.27	72	40	50	54	50
Bowser pf 1.61		22	19	20½	22	20
Braden-Aer.05e	Dec6m.29	7½	4¾	7½	8	7½
BrandonAppliedSys		13¼	9	9	10½	10½
BraunEng.24	67Dec1.25	23½	12	13¾	14½	13¾
BrencoInc.30	67Dec1.68	33¼	24½	27⅛	27⅝	27⅛
BridgptHyd 1.12	Jun6m.48	29½	23½	25	26	25½
BristolBr 1.00	67Dec2.35	29¾	13½	22	23½	27
BristolDyn	Jun3m.25	13¼	2⅝	9½	10	9¾
Bro-DartInd	Sep3m.45	48½	30	36	38	43¾
BrockGlass 1.00	Dec3m.86	43¾	27	27	29	27½
BrownFintb.60	Sep9m.74	22¾	9¾	15¼	16¼	16
BrowningArms.50	67Dec1.61	20⅜	7½	18¼	18¾	18⅜
BrunswigDr 1.00a	67Dec1.90	21	17¼	19½	20	19½
BrushBeryllium	67Dec1.25	42½	18¼	29	29¾	32¼
BuckbeeMears.60	67Dec2.12	48¾	31	34½	35¼	35¼
BuckInt'l 1.60	67Dec5.09	49½	25½	48½	50¼	48½
BuehlerCp S5%e	Sep9m.76	20½	9¼	15	15¾	13¾
BusinessFds.10g	Sep6mNil	7¾	4¼	5⅝	5⅞	5¾
ButlerMfg 1.20	67Dec5.40	60½	37½	48½	49½	49½
C						
CabotCorp 1.00	Dec3m1.53	61¼	42	57¾	58¾	60¼
Calbiochem	Sep9m.13	27¾	9¼	20½	21¼	19¾

Figure 7-3. (*continued*)

NTER MARKET

Quotations are bids and offers quoted by over-the-counter dealers to each other; they do not include retail issue's inclusion in Barron's. Symbols are shown at the top of the first page of "Stock Market at a Glance."

Name of Stock and dividend	Latest Interim or fisc yr earns	1967-68 High Bid	1967-68 Low Bid	Over Counter Bid	Over Counter Asked	Wk ago Bid
CalWtSvc 1.50	Jan12m2.27	25⅞	22	25⅛	25⅝	25⅛
CamcoInc.20	Oct3m.50	42½	10	32½	33½	34
CamlFast.80	Sep9m1.06	28½	14	20	25	20
CanMillscm 3.60	66Dec10.74	97	77	79	82	82
CanMillsB 3.60	66Dec10.74	91	75	77	81	79
CanogaElec	Jan3m.07	22	5¼	13½	14½	15¾
CapitalBchrs		11¾	7½	8¾	9¾	9
CapitalSowest.20	Sep6m.22	20⅜	9	17¾	18⅛	18⅛
CapW&Cab.40	Dec9m1.51	37½	15	26½	27	27
CapitolFood.08g	Nov6m.07	10⅝	6¼	8⅛	8⅝	8½
CapitolInt'lAir	Sep9m.80	29¾	13¼	14½	15¼	15¼
CapitolProdCp	67Oct.45	9¾	3¾	8½	9	9
CapTechInc	67Mar.23	19¼	4½	14	14½	14¾
Caressa.10e	Dec3m.26	14½	3	13	13¾	12¾
CarhartPhoto.10	Sep52w.61	14⅛	8½	10	10½	10¾
CarolinaFrght.68	Sep9mNil	13½	10½	12¾	13½	13¼
CarolinaP.60	Dec12m1.12	17½	13⅛	16½	17½	16¾
CarsonPScott.90	Oct52w2.24	28	17½	22½	23½	23½
Cascade.25g	Oct3m.08	24¾	16⅛	16⅛	16⅝	17¼
CascadeNG.64	67Dec1.10	16¾	12	12¼	12⅝	12⅝
Cavitron	67Sep.51	16	6	12½	13	11¼
Cellu-Craft	66Dec1.23	22¾	8¼	21½	22	22¾
CenterLab.12d	Dec6m.15	9½	3⅜	5½	6	6¼
CenLaEl.88	67Dec1.14	25¾	18⅝	22½	23	22⅞
CenTrans.28	Dec3m.57	36½	25¾	28	29	31
CenVerPS 1.28	67Dec1.84	25⅛	19⅛	23⅜	23¾	23½
ChampionProd.13e	Sep9m.97	20⅛	15½	16¼	17	16
ChanceAB 1.00	67Dec2.10	46½	24¼	29½	30½	29¼
Chandler.10d	Dec6m.37	21¾	9½	19¼	20	19½
ChanngFin.32	66Dec.43	20¼	10¼	17½	18	18¼
ChattGas.36	Nov12m.74	8	6½	8	8⅜	7½
ChemLeaman.50	67Dec.30	14⅛	10⅛	11½	12¼	12⅜
ChesapUtil.60b	Sep12m1.45	18	14	15½	16½	15¾
ChesterElecLab	Dec6m.52	37¾	22½	31	32	33
ChiBr&Iron 1.40	Sep36w3.04	78	39	65½	67½	66
ChristSec 1.25e	67Dec5.30	174	142	145	150	156
ChristSec pf 7.00	Jun6m293.36	130	113	113	115	113
CinnEnquirer 1.40	67Sep2.28	29	26	28	30	28
CitadelInd	66Dec.48	15	10½	11	12	13
CitizUA S4.1%g	Sep12m1.21	28½	19¼	22¾	23¼	23¼
CitizUtilB 1.02	Sep12m1.21	26⅛	19¼	22½	23	23¼
CityNews.12½e	Sep9m.76	13¾	9⅞	12¾	13¼	12½
ClarkJL.80	67Nov1.81	24	14¾	19	20½	19
ClaytonCorp	Sep9m.05	7¼	1¾	4⅜	4¾	4⅜
ClintonOil.20g	Jun6m.33	8¾	5¼	5⅞	6¼	7⅛
ClowCorp 1 25	67Dec2.95	39	19¾	32½	33½	31¾
CocaCLA 1.40	67Dec3.18	62¼	30	52½	53½	53½
ColecoInd.16	67Dec1.31	31	25	29	31	29½
ColemanEng	67Jun.07	13¼	7⅞	8¼	9	9
ColStores 1.40	67Dec2.48	26	20¾	25¼	26¼	24½
CombPaper.80	Aug6m1.52	32	24	30	33	31
CommerC1H.60	67Dec1.75	68½	33	54½	56½	54½
CommrS&S 1.00b	67Oct3.49	39½	34½	37½	38½	37½
ComwGas.19	Jun6m.43	10¼	16¾	9	9½	9⅜
ComwNG 1.30	67Dec2.23	33¼	25⅝	29½	30	29¾
ComwTel.92	67Dec1.59	42½	27½	30½	31½	30¾
ComwThea.12	Oct6m.32	6⅞	1¾	5½	5¾	5½
Components Am	Dec39wD.12	8¼	6¼	6¼	7	6¼
ComputerDiode		14½	8¼	10¾	11¾	11
ComputerEquip	67Dec.23	17	12	12	12½	12¾
ComputrUsge.20	Dec3m.21	72	20¼	39	40½	43
Computing&Soft	67Oct.89	56	8½	36½	38½	42
ConnC.G.Ltd.20	Oct6m.20	18½	12⅛	13⅜	13⅞	13¼
ConsoAirborne	67May.51	11⅜	5	7¼	7¾	7⅞
ConsPapers 1.40	67Dec3.20	38¾	26½	26¾	27¾	26½
ConsRockProd.80	Jun6m.67	23	16¼	19	20	19
ContScrew.80	Dec6m1.16	29½	18	24½	25	25¾
ContTranLns.10e	Sep36wD.59	14	9¾	12¼	13	11⅜
Contrafund		12¼	10⅜	10⅜	10⅝	10⅝
Conwed.30	67Nov1.06	14¾	7¼	14½	15¼	14½
CooperLab		23¼	16½	18	19	20½
Corenco.80	67Dec1.29	29¼	16	17¼	18¼	17
Cornelius.40	67Dec1.80	84	23	46	48	44
Corporate Ent		23¾	17	17½	18½	18¾
CosmeticallyYours	July6m.27	19¼	6⅛	15	16	16
CosmoBook	Dec6m.20	8⅞	3	6¾	7¼	6⅝
CountrySet.52	Sep9m1.31	15½	8¼	14¾	15¼	14½
CredithriftFin 1.30	Dec3m.72	27	20¾	22	23	22½
CrescentTech	Sep6m.01	8⅞	5½	6	6½	6
Crompton 1.40	Dec3m.09	41½	23	28¼	29¼	30
CrossCo.40	67Sep3.98	44¾	23¼	33	34	33¼
CryplexInd		60	13½	50	53	53
Cutler-Fed S3%g	Sep9m.36	15½	3¾	10	10¾	10
CyberTronics	67Apr.10	19	4¾	12¼	13¾	14¼
D						
DallasAir.50	Nov9m1.17	37	8⅞	25¾	26½	26
DamonCreation.50	Oct6m.61	13¼	11⅛	11⅛	11⅝	12¾
DanlyMCp.50	Dec6m.28	27¼	14½	14½	15¼	15
DasaCorp	66Oct.27	23	9½	12½	13¼	13
DataDesign.05g	Dec6m.11	22	6½	13¼	13¾	14
DataProd	Dec9m.17	23⅜	2½	15¼	15⅝	16¾
DataTrends		15½	3⅜	9½	10½	11½
DaytonCp.20e	Oct12m2.10	53½	45	48	49	48¾
DaytonMall.80	Dec3m.95	39½	25¾	33¼	34¼	34½
DCInt.60	Sep9m 69	20¼	15⅛	18½	19	18¾
Decitron	Jun6m.40	25	5¼	15½	16¼	16
DelhiAustPet	Jun6mD.14	10⅜	6¾	9⅛	9⅜	9⅛
DelhiTaylorOil.051e		3⅛	1½	2½	2¾	2¼
DeluxeCheck.80	67Dec2.00	41¾	17	32½	34½	34
DenverRealEst.60	66Dec.50	11⅜	8⅞	11⅜	11⅞	11⅜
DeroR&D	AugD.11	20¾	12½	13½	14½	12½
Designatronics	67Aug.70	19	10½	11½	12½	12¼
DetrexChem.60	Sep9m1.20	23¾	14½	15¼	16¼	15½
Det&CanTun 1.30	67Oct1.49	19¾	16¾	17¾	18½	17½
DetIntlBr 1.20	67Dec1.81	22	15½	19½	20½	19
DeweyGC.05d	Dec6m.23	12	3	9¾	10¼	10⅜
Dexter.07½e		25¾	21	23⅜	24¼	25
DialFin.50	67Dec1.05	12¼	8¾	10	10⅜	9⅜
DiaCrSlt.40b	Dec9m.78	19½	12½	15¾	16¼	15⅜
DiapulseCorp	66Dec.09	32	4½	8½	9	9¾
DickeyWS.72	Jan3m.15	18¼	14	14¾	15½	14¾
DicksonElect	July26w.16	34½	11	14	15	11
DigitronicsCp	67MarD.53	27½	6	19¼	20¼	20
DillonJ.S. .50	Dec6m.50	16½	12½	14½	15	14½
Diversa	Mar3mD.01	9⅜	3¾	4⅞	5¼	4¼
Diversa pf.93¾g		20½	11½	13	14	11½
DixieDinettes.28	Dec6m.45	6⅛	4⅛	6	6⅜	5¾
DixJCuc 1.50	Jan6m1.99	48½	29½	44	47	43
DollyMad.60a	Feb3m.51	16¾	9⅛	14¾	15¼	16½
DomesticAirExp	Sep9mD.08	20½	11⅝	12	14	13
Donaldson.60	Oct3m.23	30	21¾	22½	23¼	23
Donkenny.26	Jun6m.40	9¼	6	6¼	6¾	6¼
DorchGasS	Sep9m.80	16⅜	11⅜	14¼	14¾	14⅝
DoricCorp.40	67Dec2.03	27	18	23	25	23
DorsettElec	67Dec.13	8	5⅛	5¼	5½	5¼
DowJones 1.20	67Dec2.03	88½	50½	74	76	78
Downtowner.14	67Dec.36	10¼	4⅜	8¼	8¾	8½
DoyleDane.80	67Oct2.30	54¾	25⅛	34½	35½	34½
DPAInc	67Nov.30	17⅜	4¼	13¼	13¾	14½
DravoCorp 1.20	67Dec3.51	36¾	30	30¾	31¼	31½
DrewProp.03e		7¼	3⅛	6⅜	7½	7
Ducommun 1.00	67Dec2.71	38¾	35¼	36¼	37	36¼
Dun&Brad.90	67Dec1.81	45¼	32	40¼	40¾	43⅝
DuncanElec 1.20	67Feb2.01	90	35	68	73	78
DuplexProd	Jan3m.23	21¼	9¾	11½	12	11⅝
Duriron 1.00	67Dec3.13	39⅝	21	33½	35	35
DynamicInst	July9m.32	19¼	7⅛	13½	14½	15¾

PERFORMANCE OF SELECTED NEW ISSUES

	Offering Price	Recent Bid	Recent Asked
Canoga Electronics	17½	13¾	14½
Dorne & Margolin	8	5¼	6
Dunkin' Donuts	20	32¾	33½
Kings Electronics	9⅞	10⅛	10⅝
Laribee Wire	9	7	7½
Mogul	17¼	23	23½
Nathan's Famous	8	15⅛	15⅝
Pharmaceut. Sav. Plan	5	6½	7
Planet Oil & Mineral	10	12¾	13¼
Seaway Food Town	18¼	17½	18
Supreme Equip. & Sys.	9	13¼	13¾
Yuletide Enterprises	7	8	8¾

Figure 7-4. Trading post, New York Stock Exchange. (*Source.* New York Stock Exchange *Fact Book 1962*, cover page.)

floor (see Figure 7-4) as large as a football field in a stately building at the corner of Broad and Wall Streets in New York's Financial District at the lower end of Manhattan Island. Within the building are executive offices, a visitors' gallery, and a network of communication facilities. Within a few blocks of the New York Stock Exchange may be found the leading financial houses in the United States. The exchange is the center and heart of the Wall Street community.

The American Stock Exchange. Just four blocks away from Broad and Wall Streets stands the American Stock Exchange building on Trinity Place. The securities of more than 1,000 corporations are listed on the American Stock Exchange. The listing requirements are lower than those of the NYSE with the result that the number of listed middle-sized corporations has increased rapidly in recent years. Unlisted stocks also are traded. From two to ten million shares are exchanged in a trading day. With this level of activity AMEX has more than half the volume of NYSE.

The American Stock Exchange (AMEX) floor-trading area is adequate, but crowded and noisy as in all exchanges; the visitors' gallery is small. Executive offices occupy the upper floors of the building. The AMEX is the second largest stock exchange in the United States. It has more than 500 regular members, more than 300 associate members, and a listing of 1,040 securities. Trading and the receipt of commissions were profitable enough in 1929 to induce the purchase of a "seat" or membership on the AMEX for a quarter of a million dollars. Many brokerage houses and NYSE member branch offices buy and sell shares on the American Stock Exchange. Trading by associate members and abuses of regulations led to a reorganization of the American Stock Exchange and corrective action in 1962 and 1966. An interesting innovation at AMEX is the so-called New Average for New Market Insights, which charts the rising quotations of stocks that are more speculative than the blue-chip Dow-Jones industrials. In 1966, for example, this index rose precipitously, but declined only slightly more than the Dow-Jones industrials. The AMEX Breadth-of-the-Market index is designed to provide information similar to Dow-Jones information.

The National Stock Exchange. New York City's third stock exchange, the National Stock Exchange (NSE), was opened in 1962, the first exchange to be registered with the Securities and Exchange Commission since 1934. The trading procedures on the NSE are similar to those on the Big Board, although it does not trade issues that are listed on other exchanges. Currently the NSE is the primary market for thirteen small companies.

Regional Stock Exchanges. As communications and the handling of orders have improved, there has developed less need for local stock exchanges outside of New York City. A few local issues are listed on these exchanges and a number of NYSE and AMEX stocks are traded on an unlisted basis, but many buyers outside of New York City find brokerage offices and branch offices so convenient that they seldom visit their local stock exchange. Less than 10 per cent of the trading volume of the registered security exchanges in America is traded in the 11 regional exchanges. Civic pride and the natural urge to perpetuate these institutions accounts for their continuation, however.

Regional stock exchanges are frequently primary markets for certain issues that are of local importance. Moreover, it is argued that the regional exchanges' splitting of the market for certain nationally important securities permits the sale of a large number of shares of a certain security with less distortion in the marketplace. And finally, the time difference on the Pacific Coast Exchange permits two hours of additional transactions for the nationally important issues that can be traded on that exchange.

Fortunately for the regional exchanges, the two large exchanges in New York are subject to transactions taxes designed to raise revenues for the City of New York. New York Stock Exchange officials threatened to leave the city in 1966; currently some of their activities are housed in New Jersey. This has resulted in some increase in trading on the regional exchanges.

The foremost of the regional exchanges is the so-called Midwest Stock Exchange in Chicago. It is the result of a merger of former exchanges in Chicago, Cleveland, St. Louis, and New Orleans, where branch offices are still in existence.

The Pacific Coast Stock Exchange is the result of a merger between the former exchanges in Los Angeles and San Francisco. Offices of the Pacific Coast Exchange have been retained in each city with open-circuit communications between the two exchange facilities.

The Philadelphia-Baltimore Stock Exchange has replaced exchanges in these two cities, has added Washington, D.C. to its trading area, and maintains trading facilities in all three cities.

In addition to the foregoing exchanges, there are stock exchanges in Boston, Cincinnati, Detroit, Pittsburgh, and Salt Lake City, in addition to the Chicago Board of Trade, which specializes in grains and commodities. There are also *unregistered exchanges* in Colorado Springs, Honolulu, Richmond, and Wheeling. This latter group of exchanges has been exempted from registration by the Securities and Exchange Commission.

The exchanges in Toronto and Montreal are also worth the attention of citizens of the United States. And exchanges or bourses in the leading capital cities of Europe are important, even though rates of exchange, special taxes, and U.S. restrictions against capital movements often preclude the use of many of these exchanges by Americans.

Brokerage Houses

The typical investor will buy and sell securities through a broker, not directly through an exchange. Some brokerage offices are actually branch offices of one of the New York firms that maintains memberships in the leading exchanges in that city. Many brokerage offices outside of New York City are so-called *independent brokers* who maintain a correspondent relationship with a member firm in New York City. In either instance, a brokerage office often may be identified by an electronic "quote" board where stock quotations are recorded* and seats where spectators are free to linger in comfort while they survey the price changes of their favorite stocks. Nearby, there are apt to be booths where *account executives* or *customers' men* may confer directly or by phone with investors. Adjoining offices are likely to house a manager, some consultants, a switchboard, and the personnel who are responsible for billing and collections. Brokerage offices tend to be concentrated in financial areas, resort areas, or in upper-income suburbs. Most investors select a broker because the office is conveniently located or because of a personal recommendation by friends.

There are 5,000 brokerage offices in the United States. The largest of them, with respect to volume, is Merrill Lynch, Pierce, Fenner & Smith, which has 165 offices including offices in 16 foreign countries. Merrill Lynch as the firm is popularly known, belongs to forty-one stock exchanges, its offices are connected by 285,000 miles of private wire, it transacts 12 per cent of the round-lot business and 19 per cent of the odd-lot business on the New York Stock Exchange.[3]

Other brokerage firms, although smaller, are eager and well prepared to serve their clients. An investor may be attracted to one of the large brokerage firms because of the prevalence of its advertising and because of the availability of research reports on leading issues. Actually an investor's relationship with his customer's man is likely to form the basis of his judgment of the firm. Needless to say, the customer's man or account executive must have a suitable background, experience, and tact. Once an account executive is assigned to a prospective investor, he must ascertain whether the customer's investment goals, inclinations, and fortune suggest emphasis on safety, income, or growth. Then the account executive may recommend certain securities designed to fit these objectives and inform the investor so that he may make the decision himself. In only a few instances does a customers' man manage a customer's portfolio—that responsibility is usually reserved for the customers themselves or assumed by investment counselors in trust companies.

Investors must learn to accept suggestions from customers' men without becoming dependent on them. Sometimes, it is alleged, an investment counselor may be guilty of *churning accounts*, that is, urging the needless sale of some stocks and the purchase of others, because of the commissions which may be collected from the transactions. Sometimes a broker who is either trading on his own account or involved in underwriting new issues may urge customers to purchase those of his wares which he needs to market. These practices, involving a conflict of interest, were very common 60 or even 30 years ago.[4] Today they are denounced by the Securities and Exchange Commission, by the rules

* A desk unit known as "stockmaster" or a "quotron" is often used to determine the latest quotation, the dividend, the yield, the earnings, and the price-earnings ratio.

of the larger stock exchanges, and by the National Association of Security Dealers.[5]

Use of Brokerage Services

An investor who wishes to utilize a brokerage office for buying and selling securities first must open an account; he will be asked a few questions about his assets, his occupation, and bank references. The account and any securities purchased may be in the investor's name or it may be a joint account with the right of *survivorship* to a designated person. In the latter case, the investor's wife, if designated as the survivor, could sell the securities without difficulty following the death of her husband. In many instances a new account designates that the purchased shares shall not be delivered to the investor, but rather that they shall remain with the broker in a so-called *street name*. In this instance the broker collects dividends and credits them to the investor's account. This is a practical arrangement for investors who anticipate frequent sales of securities that they do not wish to hold in safety deposit boxes. Investors of this sort prefer to call their customers' man, order the stock sold, and avoid the bother of retrieving the stock certificates from a safety deposit box. A proposal in 1968 indicates that IBM may soon be used in place of stock certificates.

Placing "Buy" or "Sell" Orders. In issuing a buying or selling order, most investors inform themselves of the market price at the moment, then they merely call the customers' man and tell him to buy or sell *at the market*. If the order is for a *round lot*—an even hundred-share unit—and if the stock is being traded freely, the order should travel through channels to the proper exchange so rapidly that the customer could be notified of the transaction within five or seven minutes. An *odd-lot* transaction—for less than a hundred shares—might consume 15 minutes. Over-the-counter transactions may take several hours. All accounts owed to brokers must be paid on the fourth business day following a purchase. All sums owed to a customer following a sale of securities will be credited to the customer's account and will be payable on the fourth business day following the transaction. If stock certificates are to be registered in the customer's name, he should not expect delivery for approximately two weeks.

Sometimes an investor prefers to give his account executive a *limited order* that will order a purchase at a designated price or below, or a sale at a designated price or above. Thus a limited order to buy General Motors at 50 must be held until GM drops to 50 before the order will be executed. Limited orders may be *open orders* that are held until canceled, but most often the broker will insert a time factor and cancel the order if it cannot be executed before the deadline.

A *stop-loss* order may be issued if an investor wishes to minimize a possible

The Continuing Market for Securities

loss. Thus an order to buy at the market may be coupled with an order to sell if and when the stock drops two points. This type of order indicates that the investment is being traded for a quick rise and that the customer cannot risk much of a decline.

Puts and Calls. An investor who believes that the market price of a stock will rise may purchase a *call* option through his broker. For a fee, this option permits the purchase of the stock within a stated period, usually 30, 60, or 90 days, at a designated price. The permissible buying price usually approximates the market price at the time the call was purchased. Hence the investor's fee constitutes a penalty for postponement of the purchase and an interesting speculation on whether the rise in price may or may not exceed the cost of the call. Thus, if an investor bought a call option for $425, he would be certain of his right to buy 100 shares of Eastman Kodak eight weeks later for $136 per share according to the Godnick & Son Inc. "Put and Call" offer in Figure 7-5. In this case, for a $425 fee, on March 8, 1968, the investor might have bought

PUT AND CALL

SPECIAL OPTIONS
PUTS PER 100 SHARES

32¼	Allis Chalmers .. 30	June 10	$225.00
42⅞	Gulf & Western . 41⅛	6 mos.	425.00
36	Murphy Oil 37½	May 20	487.50
32¼	Occidental Pet. . 31¾	6 mos.	412.50
29¾	Purex 28⅛	June 10	225.00
17	Saturn Ind. ..... Mkt.	6 mos.	262.50
42¼	SCM 43¼	6 mos.	550.00
22	Seaboard Wd Air. 21¼	6 mos.	262.50
46¼	Sperry Rand 45⅜	6 mos.	550.00
39⅜	U.S. Steel 39	6 mos.	225.00

CALLS PER 100 SHARES PLUS TAX

17¼	Am. Photocopy .. 17⅜	6 mos.	387.50
19⅞	Commonwlth Oil 20	6 mos.	325.00
133½	Eastman Kodak .136	May 6	425.00
21⅜	Flying Tiger 21¼	6 mos.	362.50
69⅞	Gen. Foods 69¾	May 7	350.00
36	Murphy Oil 37½	May 20	450.00
32¼	Occidental Pet. . 31⅜	June 10	375.00
20	Struthers Wells .. 21½	Aug. 29	287.50
100	Teledyne 99½	6 mos.	1750.00
29½	Warner 7 Arts . 30	1 Year	650.00

Subject to Prior Sale or Price Change
FREE BOOKLET: "THE ABC OF PUT & CALLS"

GODNICK & SON INC

Established 1932
Members Put & Call Brokers & Dealers Association, Inc.
223 South Beverly Drive, Beverly Hills, Calif.
BR 2-0271   CR 4-8675
NEW YORK • DALLAS • MIAMI BEACH

SPECIAL OPTIONS
CALLS
PER 100 SHARES (PLUS TAX)
Subject to Prior Sale or Price Change

Last Close & Stock	Price	Period	Cost
35¼ Avnet 32	June 10	$575.00
44⅞ Am. Brdcst. 50	May 31	187.50
50⅞ Am. Tel & Tel. . 50.15	21 mos.	587.50
44½ Am. Export 53¾	May 27	137.50
11½ Alside 11⅞	June 10	137.50
107½ Digital Equip. ..112¾	May 3	1187.50
13⅞ Gale Ind. 17	Aug. 26	225.00
95⅛ Itek 111	May 2	825.00
80½ Kresge 84.78	Apr. 15	287.50
95½ Ling Temco 98.42	May 6	825.00
43⅛ Monsanto 43¾	June 7	387.50
40½ Metro Goldwyn . 42⅜	5 mos.	525.00
44⅝ Stokley Van Cp. . 50	June 6	187.50
54⅞ Schenley 56¾	Apr. 22	325.00
160¼ Solitron 180½	Apr. 15	587.50
100 Teledyne 91⅛	6 mos.	2175.00
62 U.S. Smelting ... 62½	Apr. 26	487.50
17⅞ Wean Ind. 17.95	May 15	212.50

Free Informational Booklet on Request
THOMAS, HAAB & BOTTS
50 BROADWAY, N.Y. 212-269-8100
Member Put & Call Brokers & Dealers Assn.

Figure 7-5. Put and call options. (*Source. Wall Street Journal,* March 7, 1968, p. 27.)

the shares for $136 anytime before May 6th if their price had gone above $136, or he might elect to ignore his option and lose the $425.

When an investor purchases a stock, he may pay an additional fee and purchase through his broker a *put* option. The *put* option permits the sale of that stock at a designated price within the stipulated 30, 60, or 90 days. A *straddle* is an option to *call* or to *put*, whichever serves the investor's purpose when the market turns sharply up or down. Calls and puts are really options to buy and to sell. They become legal rights to be exercised at the option of the investor. They are used primarily by professional traders. Average investors might use them more, with increased profit, or with a minimization of loss.

Margin Trading. An investor buys on margin by opening a margin account with his broker. Under current regulations early in 1968, an investor could put up 70 per cent of the price of his purchase and borrow the remaining 30 per cent from his broker, who holds the stock in a street name. The 70 per cent *margin requirement* was raised again in 1968 by the Board of Governors of the Federal Reserve System because a low margin requirement may have inflationary influences since an investor is tempted to buy more shares on margin than he would buy for cash. Obviously, if stock prices continue to rise, an investor holding more stocks will make more money in capital gains simply because he holds more shares.

A margin account with a broker requires a minimum of $2,000 which may be applied to the initial purchase. As an investor's holdings rise in market value he may have increasing margins which may be applied to new purchases. Thus, if an $8,000 margin deposit is used to purchase $10,000 worth of stock at an 80 per cent margin ratio, a 10 per cent increase in market price to $11,000 would permit the purchase of $200 worth of additional stock with no further commitment of cash. New York Stock Exchange rules require that the equity value of a margin account must be maintained at a minimum of 25 per cent of the current value of the stock. If a stock declines in market price, a *margin call* may be issued by the broker who must demand the required margin coverage at current market prices, else he must sell the stock to protect the interests of the creditors who have supplied the previously borrowed funds. Thus, if the $10,000 worth of stock declined rapidly to a market value of $8,000, for example, the lender's grubstake would be endangered and more margin would be required. In case the additional margin were not forthcoming, the stock would be sold for what it would bring. If the stock had to be sold for a mere $2,000, the investor may have lost his entire investment, since the $2,000 would be required for repayment of the loan. In addition to the usual margin trading requirements, the New York Stock Exchange has expanded its disciplinary powers. These include the so-called antispeculation rule which requires collateral or cash up to 100 per cent of the purchase price of certain designated stocks.

Because of the 6 or 7 per cent interest charged for margin loans and because of the threat of a margin call and the threat of being sold out in a declining market, margin trading comprises a jittery market situation. Investors who buy on margin hope to profit hastily and with relatively little capital investment. They may absorb large losses, however, if the market declines only a few points.

Selling Short. A few experienced investors are able to make money in a declining market by selling short (see Figure 7-6). Strangely, they sell first and then they buy later to cover their short sale. Actually, an investor deals closely with his broker in a short sale in the following manner. The order to sell is given and executed. The sale must be on an "uptick," that is, at an eighth of a point or more above the preceding quotation of the stock. The broker requires collateral to insure the eventual purchase of shares to cover the short position, and he borrows shares at a small fee to deliver along with the sale that has been completed. In perhaps 60 days, the investor hopes that he will be able to purchase the desired shares at a low market price. If this is possible, he gains the difference between his buying and selling prices, less a buying and a selling commission and the interest on the loan of the borrowed shares. If the stock cannot be bought for a low price, he must buy it anyway, even if the transaction ruins him financially. Sometimes, an expert can gain time and hope for a market decline that will eventually rescue him from his short position. Only a few investors engage in selling short. This is one investment strategy that should probably be left to the professionals.

An ingenious variation of selling short is known as *selling against the box.* In this maneuver, the investor sells short a stock that he already holds—a stock that has made a profit that will be protected by selling against the box. Thus if the investor owns a hundred shares of a given issue, he will sell short another hundred. If the market price rises, he can deliver his own shares or he can make a profit currently and in the future by keeping them, although this gain will be reduced because he will have to buy an additional hundred shares to cover his short position. If the price falls, he simply buys a hundred shares to cover his short position at a profit.

Commission Rates. The commissions charged for stock transactions are as low or lower than fees charged for any other form of property transfer. These rates change from time to time because of increasing costs. In the late 1960's,

BARRON'S   February 26, 1968

Short Interest Ratio on New York Stock Exchange Advances to 1.77; Daily Trading Volume Decreases

Short interest on the New York Stock Exchange on February 15 decreased to 19,445,204 shares from 20,107,917 shares the previous month. Average daily trading for the period retreated to 11,005,052 shares from 11,920,030 shares, and the short interest ratio rose to 1.77 from 1.69. On February 15, short interest in odd-lot dealers' accounts amounted to 151,162 shares, compared with 148,796 shares the preceding month. Of the 1,702 stock issues listed on the Exchange, there were 242 issues in which a short position of 20,000 or more shares existed, or in which there was a change of 10,000 or more since the last report. The totals which exclude odd-lot dealers' short positions were:

	2-15-68	1-15-68
	Shares Listed	
Adams Mills	44,840	60,681
Addressograph-Multig	35,205	23,129
Admiral Corp	59,114	48,186
Air Products & Chem	22,066	28,471
Air Reduction	10,632	22,092
A J Industries Inc	27,625	27,015
Allied Products	65,025	42,642
Amer Airlines	20,892	26,135
Amer Hoist & Derrick	22,536	8,806
Amer Hospital Supply	22,216	27,260
Amer Motors Corp	229,880	246,928
Amer Photocopy Equip	198,624	55,675
Amer So Africa Inv	92,940	49,555
American Standard	27,670	50,196
t-Amer Telephone & Tel	63,376	71,827

	Shares Listed	2-15-68	1-15-68
		798,480	
		8,030,506	
		5,150,322	
		4,781,127	
		1,107,146	
		3,458,121	
		1,553,553	
		20,232,559	
		1,317,611	
		9,316,849	
		19,269,359	
		8,022,336	
		2,400,000	
		1,709,936	
		541,189,396	

	2-15-68	1-15-68
Hunt Foods&Indust	22,497	14,855
Income&Cap Capital Sh		10,000
Inter Business Mach	48,256	37,654
Int Flavors&Fragrance	28,876	17,301
Inter Minerals&Chem	32,894	34,440
Int Rectifier Corp	52,150	36,245
tInter Tel & Tel	417,513	317,402
Inter Utilities Corp	37,569	9,469
Itek Corp	91,282	86,841
Kaiser Alum & Chem	54,962	52,646
Kerr McGee Corp	27,741	56,606
Kidde (Walter) & Co	23,513	40,447
tKinney Nat Service	112,573	81,670
Lab for Electronics	22,537	41,493
Lehigh Valley Indust	26,745	11,740
Libby McNeill&Libby	3,006	16,472
Ling-Temco-Vought	63,199	55,740
Lionel Corp	91,390	90,200
Litton Industries	217,676	169,084
Loews Theaters Inc	r30,032	s9,195
Lukens Steel	29,795	36,331
Macy (R H)	5,784	16,036
tMadison Fund Inc	105,689	85,980
Madison Sq Garden	57,150	35,105
Magnavox Co	30,365	42,540
Massey-Ferguson Ltd	18,100	6,879
Mattel Inc	46,725	27,809
McDonald's Corp	18,423	4,264
McDonnell Douglas	95,930	114,649
McGraw Hill Inc	71,977	64,567
Merck & Co Inc	57,397	64,539
Mid-America Pipeline	25,812	9,320
Mo Kans Texas RR	49,175	34,191
Monogram Industries	42,158	69,349
Motorola Inc	55,305	28,966
National Airlines	84,195	91,863
Nat Cash Register	30,719	49,364
National General Cp	25,025	21,394

	Shares Listed	2-15-68	1-15-68
Allied Artist Pictures	6,899,325	24,420	20,608
Alloys Unlimited Inc	1,510,011	76,759	73,725
Amco Industries	56,134,575	16,600	21,400
American Safety	10,884,712	35,830	22,944
Applied Devices Corp	9,621,112	22,227	22,586
Argus Inc	2,599,482	28,388	24,774
Associated Laundries	23,549,000	13,900	2,468
Associated Oil & Gas	6,949,684	129,714	156,508
Astrex Inc	2,239,634	24,915	7,582
Astrodata Inc	17,297,663	42,584	54,551
Baldwin-Montrose Chemical	7,382,940	44,433	82,613
Barnwell Industries	4,317,726	6,184	16,420
Bell Electronic	1,333,117	20,356	16,808
Bunker-Ramo Corp	1,201,314	124,188	71,657
Burma Mines Ltd	5,503,708	102,482	45,037
Buttes Gas & Oil Co	5,572,073	71,152	17,690
California Computer	4,726,103	128,527	150,897
Cameo net	2,560,245	51,033	
Against the box	23,636,431	7,410	
Gross	4,756,657	58,443	58,271
Canadian Export Gas	2,851,784	63,561	72,038
Castleton Industries	9,033,797	18,600	7,700
CBK Industries Inc	11,080,054	8,500	18,700
CCI Corp	7,526,525	9,948	20,645
Chief Consolidated Mining	15,444,098	40,223	64,694
Coburn Corp of America	18,120,770	22,884	13,340
Commonwealth United C A	2,757,786	122,865	41,965
Compudyne Corp	2,629,250	29,705	45,555
Computer Applications	27,265,294	59,141	88,943
Computer Sciences	21,515,808	87,925	120,680
Condec Corp	35,624,879	28,162	36,652
Consolidated Oil & Gas	1,993,212	36,271	32,464
Continental Materials	1,956,058	26,950	26,100
Crestmont Oil & Gas	3,713,794	23,945	40,956
Cubic Corp	6,150,613	23,544	15,210
Data-Control Systems	8,606,377	47,665	65,160
Data Processing Financial net	8,925,065	121,370	
Against conv debs	3,713,336	4,332	

AMK Corp	114,707	104,875	1,978,585
Ampex Corp	45,298	64,427	9,605,818
Amphenol Corp	30,606	57,983	3,252,905
AMP Inc	42,440	42,815	12,480,000
Anaconda Co	20,750	21,618	21,918,741
Anken Chemical & Film	63,996	66,096	1,106,480
Arizona Pub Service	....	12,200	8,500,000
Armstrong Cork	12,213	28,506	10,768,737
Ashland Oil & Ref Co	23,666	15,075	18,803,146
Atlantic Richfield	52,686	39,091	11,789,922
Atlas Corp	58,078	48,529	13,915,740
tAutomatic Sprinkler	122,694	121,613	4,780,095
Avco Corp	33,323	45,337	14,112,794
Avnet Inc	r88,209	s78,693	4,963,732
Avon Products	58,070	52,318	28,719,137
Bangor Punt aCorp	27,608	43,146	1,972,726
Bausch Lomb Inc	53,453	52,638	2,371,938
Baxter Laboratories	23,563	15,986	12,519,567
Beckman Instruments	27,450	16,811	3,410,571
Becton Dickinson & Co	88,513	104,608	10,774,015
Belco Petroleum Corp	23,888	24,005	5,913,295
Bell & Howell	37,298	32,086	4,747,611
Benguet Cons Inc	125,795	109,800	13,500,000
Berkey Photo	18,482	7,933	2,488,758
Berman Leasing Co	20,966	33,041	1,300,403
Boeing Co	88,324	81,241	21,609,872
tBoise Cascade Corp	170,190	224,327	10,668,805
Boise Cascade 140 pr	26,271	34,825	4,468,615
Braniff Airways	31,308	35,320	5,896,238
Bristol-Myers	93,476	100,935	27,700,040
tBrunswick Corp	122,735	111,561	18,417,592
Bunker Hill Co	39,496	17,935	1,606,000
Burlington Indust	20,525	19,500	25,581,420
Burroughs Corp	78,573	46,339	8,210,803
Carrier Corp	86,184	51,502	7,576,706
Caterpillar Tractor	32,726	28,276	56,824,530
Chadbourn Gotham	51,014	40,449	2,397,762
Chi & Northwest Ry	26,979	22,753	1,735,574
Chrysler Corp	183,074	191,269	46,426,117
City Investing	22,952	25,911	2,526,207
Collins Radio Co	30,975	51,152	2,949,754
Columbia Bdcasting	90,911	141,470	23,665,797
Columbia Pictures	r39,287	s15,555	4,498,729
Combustion Engneerng	19,580	8,775	4,003,562
Commercial Solvents	23,918	22,320	3,109,670
Comm Satellite Corp	45,194	35,152	10,000,014
Continental Air Lines	89,800	97,680	10,016,807
Continental Tel Corp	32,809	86,579	19,452,868
tControl Data Corp	271,284	272,762	8,835,961
Crowell Collier&Mac	33,557	22,930	4,999,200
Cudahy Co	42,310	13,490	1,544,988
Curtis Publishing	60,012	51,494	3,555,568
Deere & Co	31,461	35,149	14,792,514

Northwest Airlines	47,906	56,443	9,149,628
tOccidental Petroleum	245,526	246,348	14,740,566
tOgden Corp	163,907	215,318	7,945,818
tPan Amer World Airwy	116,616	102,996	33,747,182
tPenn NY Central Trans	132,406		23,021,544
tPepsico Inc	131,815	136,077	20,987,796
Perkin Elmer Corp	123,711	95,765	6,300,724
Phillips Petroleum	42,875	42,193	35,949,057
Pitney Bowes Inc	30,855	11,725	4,586,385
Polaroid Corp	187,644	201,826	15,831,135
Purex Corp Ltd	20,022	17,023	8,547,452
Radio Corp of Amer	56,767	41,243	62,693,405
Ralston Purina Co	60,990	18,572	30,714,625
Rayette-Faberge Inc	47,110	53,505	2,804,997
Raytheon Co	26,687	47,351	7,262,516
Reliance Elec & Eng	17,675	29,138	3,009,141
Republic Corp	81,746	73,504	3,049,096
Rexall Drug & Chem Co	21,364	18,879	13,429,978
Rex Chainbelt Inc	8,203	18,693	2,891,658
Reynolds Metals	65,655	69,177	16,688,909
Ritter Pfaudler Corp	21,759	19,134	8,639,893
Rohr Corp	38,283	39,117	3,504,792
Safeway Stores	7,061	20,082	25,533,302
Sanders Associates	28,386	41,893	4,617,473
St Regis Paper	75,104	59,280	13,428,707
SCM Corp.	76,852	114,332	8,297,831
Scientific Data Sys	86,420	59,071	3,910,943
Seaboard World Airls	69,287	77,681	4,679,310
Sears Roebuck	50,618	62,424	153,023,393
Skil Corp	24,333	21,700	1,731,174
Sola Basic Indust	19,866	9,111	2,382,479
Southern Cal Edison	7,170	22,486	38,982,889
Spartans Indust	25,926	53,390	5,360,068
Sperry Rand Corp	178,287	197,579	33,878,313
tSprague Electric Co	105,771	100,004	3,383,568
Sterling Drug	18,841	8,683	24,467,704
Stokely Van Camp	23,939	30,613	3,220,785
tStudebaker-Worth	116,848	155,016	6,202,346
Sunbeam Corp	48,483	42,171	7,446,551
Sundstrand Corp	40,855	48,573	4,131,621
Swingline Inc	4,911r	22,968s	5,711,260
Tandy Corp	16,234	34,680	1,696,574
Tektronix Inc	130,357	107,713	8,082,080
tTeledyne Inc	138,911	131,814	8,658,224
tTenneco Inc	120,430	139,729	53,507,762
Texas Eastern Trans	11,567	24,383	20,694,655
Texas Gulf Sulphur	60,701	46,642	11,520,000
Texas Instruments	206,781	205,368	10,913,627
tTextron Inc	125,546	127,931	26,929,316
Time Inc	64,045	61,097	7,016,967
Tractor Supply Co	16,825	6,500	1,313,923
tTransamerica Corp	139,315	93,888	23,912,188
Transitron Electrnic	85,882	38,630	8,192,533
Trans World Airlines	48,210	46,012	9,898,801

Gross	125,702	91,790
Dixilyn Corp	22,350	22,465
Dynalectron Corp	142,133	138,220
EDO Corp	42,540	48,632
Electronic Assistance	54,204	58,759
Equity Corp	24,864	17,520
Equity Funding Corp	27,802	18,924
Exquisite Form Cl A	26,300	24,600
Frontier Airlines	22,160	27,292
Gale Industries Inc Net	272,794	....
Against the box	9,180	......
Gross	281,974	300,908
Garan Inc	13,349	38,972
G C Computer Corp Net	61,616	43,497
Against conv debs	68,714	236,804
Gross	130,330	280,301
Gearhart-Owen Industries	17,129	4,487
Giant Yellowknife	23,211	12,225
Gray Mfg Co	22,826	23,472
Great American Industries	33,480	35,650
Great Basins Petroleum	37,200	27,200
Grow Chemical Corp	23,013	27,620
Gulf & Western	23,062	....
H&B American Corp	35,377	31,950
Harvard Industries	41,931	39,095
Hoe (R) Co	28,283	32,286
Holly Corp	28,364	1,912
Husky Oil Canada	36,199	47,304
Hydrometals Inc	85,423	86,404
Intex Oil Co	5,670	19,274
Irvin Industries Inc	13,282	....
Kaiser Industries	22,072	17,251
Kaltman (D) & Co.	113,100	108,419
La Maur Inc	20,500	20,500
Leasco Data Processing	28,768	27,882
Levin-Townsend net	42,923	....
against conv debs	8,354	....
gross	51,277	56,822
Lodge Shipley Co	81,114	85,814
LTV Aerospace net	51,042	33,389
against conv debs	21,035	115,437
gross	72,077	148,826
LTV Ling Altec Inc.	20,522	6,152
Magellan Petroleum	41,710	112,399
Marley Co	22,520	21,800
Martin Marietta wts	47,229	27,126
Mary Carter Paint Cl A	52,015	53,440
McCulloch Oil Corp	20,638	43,020
McCrory Corp wts new	14,684	88,719
Microdot Inc	22,332	21,195
Microwave Associates	35,300	55,070
Mohawk Data Sciences	22,623	20,183
Molybdenum Corp	55,671	59,698

Figure 7-6. **Short interest.** (*Source. Barron's*, **February 26, 1968, p. 38.**)

198

Delta Air Lines	148,292	156,024	19,125,000	tTRW Inc	122,412	91,754	11,196,483
Diamond Shrk 120cv prd	6,965	19,184	3,697,832	Twentieth Cent Fox	56,676	25,203	7,035,182
Diamond Shamrock	29,734	59,089	6,302,293	Union Oil of Calif	36,214	12,620	31,774,182
Disney Productions	27,349	29,829	4,106,644	Union Tank Car	46,000	46,100	3,646,368
tEastern Airlines	125,057	85,652	11,422,457	United Air Lines	30,770	44,481	18,378,421
Eastman Kodak	34,890	28,716	80,772,718	United Gas Corp	36,634	18,371	12,594,006
tEG&G Inc	192,033	149,240	4,186,576	United Nuclear Corp	23,361	27,289	4,558,851
El Paso Natural Gas	14,844	29,231	26,907,532	United Park City Mns	25,355	16,300	4,317,516
Electronic Assoc Inc	41,464	16,477	2,557,944	US Gypsum	108,168	42,055	8,234,183
Electronic Specialty	21,700	19,511	1,784,334	US Industries Inc	26,427	26,344	3,740,152
Elec & Mus Indus Ltd	98,300	1,400	5,893,585	US Plywood-Champ Pap	56,544	35,836	10,448,646
Emerson Elec Co	67,781	42,659	9,581,515	US Smelt Ref Maine	47,872	43,471	2,356,058
Emery Air Freight	43,592	40,615	3,734,176	United Utilities Inc	20,316	18,795	25,408,788
Emporium Capwell Co	7,460	27,290	5,398,355	Universal Oil Prod	26,696	18,575	3,613,347
Fairchild Camra&Inst	204,293	234,997	4,304,990	Varian Associates	68,898	76,023	6,416,179
Fairchild Hiller Cp	28,131	29,538	4,534,320	Villager Inc	27,119	37,218	3,234,866
Fansteel Metal Corp	28,866	14,995	1,652,102	Vornado Inc	47,091	48,137	5,865,995
Fedders Corp	17,433	38,477	2,141,624	Ward Foods Inc	28,876	27,951	2,232,115
Financial Federation	50,697	46,857	2,720,149	Wean Industries	21,033	933	2,503,717
First Charter Fin Cp	55,854	41,290	9,396,365	Webb Del E Corp	49,043	34,793	6,606,062
Flying Tiger Line	153,284	138,804	4,538,138	Western Union Tel	11,415	35,105	7,527,702
Ford Motor Co	28,678	29,003	65,488,845	Westinghouse Elec	25,918	74,777	38,205,609
Foremost-Mc Kesson	29,784	26,549	10,730,844	White Cons Ind	39,159	16,752	3,459,746
Foxboro Co	21,927	23,078	4,246,680	tWhittaker Corp	178,418	162,068	4,915,952
Freeport Sulphur	26,859	13,075	15,499,190	Williams Brothers Co	32,855	9,510	2,743,678
Gen Acceptance Corp	15,771	26,148	3,107,452	World Airways Inc	2,896	14,886	10,000,000
General Aniline & Film	22,015	23,365	13,342,085	Xerox Corp	179,762	184,027	21,968,596
General Electric	22,935		91,310,465	Youngstwn Sheet & Tube	34,020	3,100	10,680,852
Genl Host Corp	30,050	3,950	1,688,343	Zenith Radio	54,104	58,908	18,852,730
tGenl Instrument	123,267	66,405	4,005,363	r-New; s-Old; t-Short positions may have been af-			
General Motors	64,194	51,497	287,520,261	fected by arbitrage situations; z-Revised.			
Gen Precision Equip	11,516	22,299	3,944,170				
Gen Tel&Electronics	86,462	71,719	100,915,245	Short Interest Decreases			
General Time Corp	40,521	12,355	2,112,629				
Georgia Pacific Corp	34,880	38,303	19,072,064	At American Stock Exchange			
Getty Oil Co	74,699	91,891	20,221,374				
Giddings & Lewis Inc	31,800	31,660	3,319,818	The American Stock Exchange reported a		
Glen Alden Corp	496,164	1,760,949	11,576,386	short interest of 9,038,502 shares as of February		
Global Marine Inc	44,523	62,460	3,877,290	15, a decrease of 775,036 from the revised total		
Grace (WT) & Co	55,294	54,640	38,232,237	a month earlier. In February 1967, the short in-		
Great Westrn Financl	23,054	16,632	12,952,553	terest amounted to 3,834,550 shares. Of the 1,080		
tGulf&Westrn Ind	71,082	33,857	9,151,928	stocks and warrants traded on the Exchange,		
Gulton Industries	897,900	757,692	13,136,603	short positions existed in 291 issues. A list of		
Helmerich & Payne	31,241	36,925	3,004,787	those issues with a short position of 10,000 or		
Hercules Inc	20,045	20,275	1,939,316	more shares included:		
Hess Oil & Chemical	25,005	27,695	9,802,912				
Hewlett Packard Co	73,067	66,675	10,033,021	Aeronca Inc		2-15-68	1-15-68
High Voltage Eng	147,989	90,986	12,482,035			27,925	38,594
Holiday Inns of Amer	182,753		2,461,952	Alaska Airlines		37,917	38,118
Honeywell Inc	45,107	48,195	8,812,889				
Hooker Chem Corp	28,624	23,624	14,582,564				
Howard Johnson Co	42,253	49,117	9,710,295				
	60,012	30,897	4,962,717				

National Equipment net against conv debs gross	12,023	18,351
	13,449	11,326
National Video Corp	25,472	29,877
Nuclear Corp of America	378,604	297,257
Nytronics Inc	30,620	63,235
Oxford Electric Corp	40,852	68,415
Ozark Air Lines	25,100	13,300
Pacific Data wts	40,951	48,698
Pancoastal Pete vtc	178,180	183,080
Planning Research	59,373	137,272
Potter Instrument	56,699	55,732
Ramada Inns Inc	10,679	23,900
Rapid American Corp	5,608	26,154
Rath Packing Co	28,876	61,216
Reserve Oil & Gas Co	41,179	44,826
Retail Centers of America	67,166	55,637
RIC Group Inc	10,777	29,892
Royal American Industries	16,700	5,000
Rusco Industries Inc	17,439	4,903
Ryan Consolidated	86,036	99,208
Scurry-Rainbow Oil	37,849	64,558
Siboney Corp	28,945	49,816
Signal Oil Gas Co Cl A	28,845	36,700
Silicon Transistor	271,725	301,400
Silvray-Litecraft	2,121	16,595
Solitron Devices	45,490	42,501
Statham Instruments	21,044	30,662
Stanrock Uranium	25,751	40,955
Sterling Precision	28,495	28,900
Stylon Corp	23,652	15,306
Susquehanna Corp	14,987	32,810
Syntex Corp	23,135	6,080
Talley Industries	104,310	123,823
Technical Tape Inc	25,183	14,299
Technicolor Inc	108,185	152,622
Textron Inc wts	29,446	14,691
Thompson-Starrett Co	26,950	26,110
Trans Investing	215,039	203,527
Transogram	61,286	62,573
Unexcelled Inc	34,648	40,780
United Industrial Ws net	62,821	61,965
Against the box	18,200	
Gross	195,264	161,345
Vernitron Corp.	21,732	29,311
Volume Merchandise	12,708	32,861
Warner Bro-7 Arts	39,537	17,072
Westates Petroleum	108,555	106,073
Westec Corp. net	20,021	20,856
against the box	12,464	13,664
gross	32,485	34,320
Wyle Laboratories	45,705	54,361
Zapata Off-Shore Co.	16,665	26,926
Total	9,038,502	9,813,538

Figure 7-6. (continued)

the rates of the NYSE, which were generally followed elsewhere, are shown in Table 7–1.

Table 7-1

Purchase or Sale	Commission
$100 to $399.99	2% plus $3 (minimum fee of $6)
$400 to $2,399.99	1% plus $7
$2,400 to $4,999.99	1/2% plus $19
$5,000 or more	1/10% plus $39 (maximum = $75 for 100 shares)

Odd-lot purchases add ⅛ point (¼ point in shares selling at $55 or above) to the purchase price and subtract ⅛ point or ¼ point from the price when sales are made. The odd-lot differential is $2 more than the round-lot rate with a minimum of $6 for transactions of $100 or more.[6] Incidentally, the odd-lot firms, Carlisle & Jacquelin and Coppet & Doremus, have both computerized their operations to permit the execution of odd-lot orders on the floor of the NYSE. This operation promises to reduce the costs of odd-lot trading.

Over-the-counter dealers extract their fees from the spread between their "bid" and "asked" prices. Thus if one of the dealers bids $25 and asks $26 for a certain share, his commission for a purchase *and* a sales transaction is the one-point spread between the "bid" and "asked" quotations. If a buy *or* a sell order is taken by this dealer, his commission is approximately half of this spread or 50 cents per share.

The So-Called Third Market.

An interesting development in the market involves the off-floor trading of large numbers of shares that are listed on NYSE or AMEX. This market evolved to avoid the dumping of thousands of shares on the market by mutual funds, pension funds, estates, or insurance companies, which would cause the market price to decline gradually or precipitously until buyers appeared to clear the market of the huge offering. On the contrary, if large-scale purchases of a given security were ordered by a large institutional investor, the market price would rise gradually or precipitously until enough security holders were tempted to sell. In either instance, the market for that issue would be distorted by the size of the single "buy" or "sell" order and huge commissions would have to be paid by both buyers and sellers. To avoid this disturbance, a large non-member firm may take over an entire transaction and sell off the issue directly to its clientele. This trading of listed securities off the floor is resented by the organized exchanges. It escapes the regulations and the customary commissions imposed by exchanges and also is subject to abuses by the professional traders who are involved in "making the market" for these securities, which are being marketed outside of the market. The third market dealers insist that they are merely providing a form of healthy competition for the exchanges.

COMMODITY MARKETS

A farmer or businessman who wishes to avoid risks about future prices may *hedge* by entering into a futures contract in a commodity market. Cattle feeders, for example, may buy cattle for feeding at today's prices and sell their contracts for cattle to be fattened and delivered three or six months hence at today's future prices. Thus the buying and selling prices are known, and the cattle feeder devotes his attention to the business of cattle feeding without the hazard or speculation of price changes. Someone with speculative inclinations and money will buy the farmer's futures contract at today's prices and sell it several months later at a price that will be higher or lower depending upon unexpected changes in the weather, the international situation, governmental policies, or consumer preferences. The person who buys and sells future contracts in grains, cattle, metals, or anything else is a speculator, not an investor. His gain or his loss is dependent upon the uncertainty or unpredictability of many price determining variables.

Commodity Exchanges

Commodity markets have evolved to serve as a clearing house for all who wish to buy or to sell contracts for the future delivery of a variety of commodities such as those listed in Figure 7-7. The chief of these markets include the Chicago Mercantile Exchange, the New York Mercantile Exchange, the New York Produce Exchange, the New York Cotton Exchange, the Chicago Board of Trade, the Commodity Exchange, Inc. (New York), and many others. Brokerage houses and some banks around the country will arrange for the sale and purchase of futures contracts. Merrill Lynch, Pierce, Fenner & Smith Inc., for example, has set up commodities account executives in many of its branch offices.

Speculative Commodities

Certain commodities become highly speculative at times. In 1967 and 1968, for example, the contract for delivery of a 76-pound flask of mercury changed from $525 in February 1967 to $400 in May, to $525 in late December, to $605 in February 1968. These price changes were attributed to increasing

Commodity Markets

Futures Prices

Figure 7-7. Future prices. (*Source. Wall Street Journal*, February 15, 1968, p. 22.)

demand for the metal combined with a sharp drop in output in Spain, the chief source of mercury ores. The price declined or levelled off periodically as the General Services Administration in Washington released 11,000 flasks of mercury from its stockpile.

Coffee prices soar or decline because of weather conditions in the South American republics unless these prices are held in check by "coffee agreements" between major countries. Copper prices are affected by wartime demand and by lengthy strikes. Silver and gold bullion prices vary with production rates, new discoveries, and a "run" on either or both of the metals caused by adverse balances in the balance of payments between various nations. Thus the passage or nonpassage of additional tax legislation in Britain or in the United States might affect the price of silver or gold bullion.

Increasing Interest in Commodity Markets

A few investors are prepared to assume some measure of risk as they seek to "clean up" in the stock or commodity markets. Others sell off their stocks when the market is high and buy commodity contracts because they find few stocks attractively priced. The commodity exchanges expand their trading list when there is need for establishing a market for additional metals, minerals, grains, or what not. If the stock market lacks glamor, as it did for much of 1968, investable funds find their way into the commodity markets.

INVESTMENT INFORMATION

It is hoped that the prospective investor may learn to rely on better information than market tips, rumors, unjustified infatuation for certain glamor stocks, and an inherent tendency to play the one and two dollar "cats" and "dogs" as if they were long shots at the horse races. There is an abundance of research and market information available to those who wish to use it. Many of these resources provide original, basic information about business in general, about the trends in certain industries and companies, about management decisions, and about financing plans. Some investment information consists of estimates and reports of research concerning the probable market-price trends that may be expected for certain securities and the price range at which these issues should be bought or sold if certain investment objectives are to be met.

Financial News in Daily Papers

Most newspapers carry news that may inform investors about general business conditions, unusual news about business firms, unusual management changes, and governmental activity that is likely to affect the future of one or more corporations. Scattered throughout these newspapers, one finds news items about local firms, financial leaders, new inventions, financing promotions, labor relations, and corporate policy changes. These items are important news to stockholders and prospective investors.

Financial Sections of Metropolitan Papers. Newspapers in the larger cities usually devote several pages to the subject of investments in each edition. These financial sections, as may be seen in Figure 7–8, originally include stock quotations from several stock exchanges in New York, from a local exchange, and from the national and local over-the-counter markets. Some news of commodity exchanges and foreign investments is also commonly included. Usually a local financial editor comments on the previous day's market; sometimes these comments are supplied by a press release or by a syndicated writer. Special feature articles often cover subjects involving specific security issues, corporation financing, or the effects of taxation on various investment situations.

An entire section of the Sunday edition of a typical metropolitan newspaper may be devoted to finance and investments. This financial section is likely to recapitulate the range of stock market quotations for the past week with a complete listing of quotations that may not have been included in some of the daily newspapers. Market analysts summarize, analyze, and predict with special zeal in the Sunday editions. Corporate promotions are portrayed in articles and advertisements; articles, aimed at the uninitiated, expound the virtues and advantages of thrift and suggest various investment programs, especially for beginners.

Among the better financial sections in American newspapers is that of *The New York Times* with its New York Times Market Index and an excellent set of articles on market analysis.

The Wall Street Journal. No paper has been as singularly devoted to the field of investments on such a grand scale as the *Wall Street Journal*. This publication is printed five times a week in six American urban centers. It circulates for early morning delivery to a million subscribers whose interests are whetted by this investment-oriented newspaper.

The *Wall Street Journal* devotes three page-one columns in each edition to items of general interest to investors—items on such subjects as changes in the national income, anticipated consumer-spending patterns, savings institutions and savings data, medical aid, or information about specific industries or firms. The remainder of the customary two-dozen pages contains industry and firm information, proposed financing plans, worldwide monetary and exchange information, and a complete reporting of the country's leading stock exchange and commodity exchange quotations.

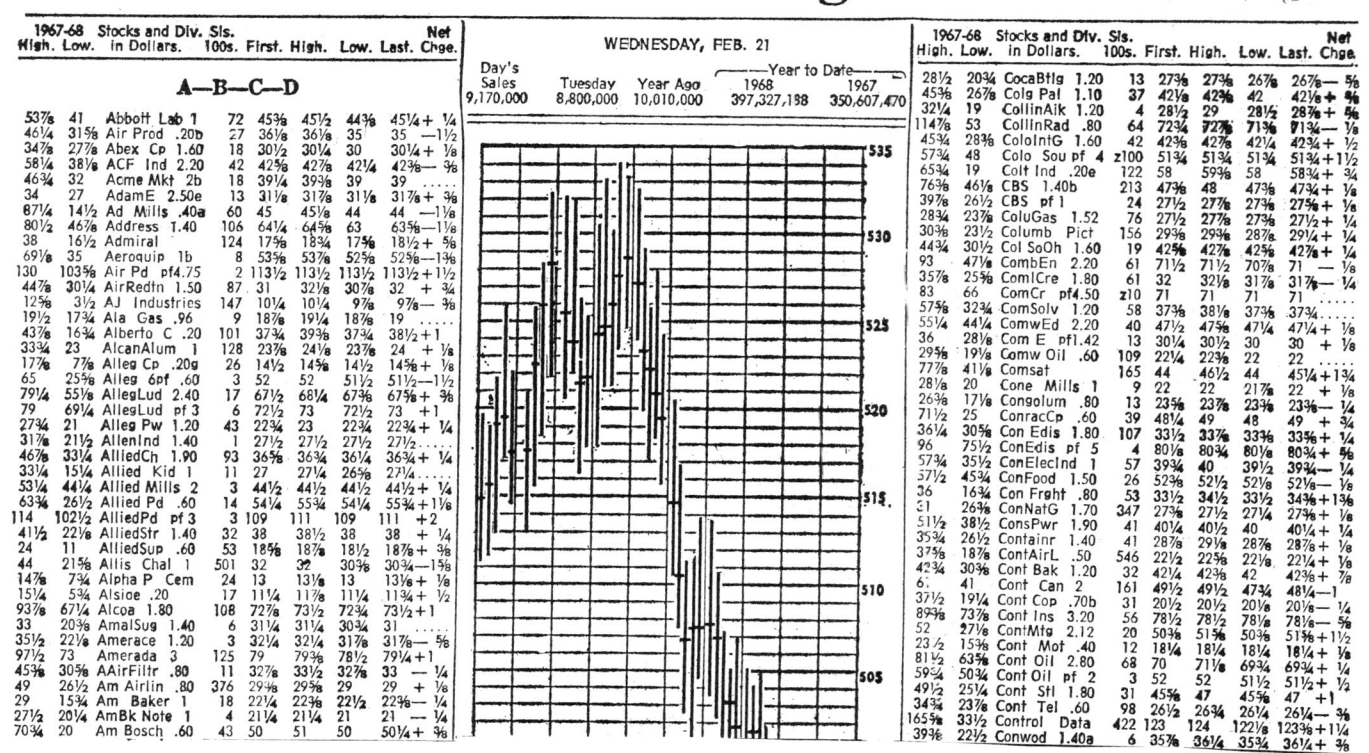

New York Stock Exchange Transactions

A—B—C—D

1967-68 High.	1967-68 Low.	Stocks and Div. in Dollars.	Sls. 100s.	First.	High.	Low.	Last.	Net Chge.
53⅞	41	Abbott Lab 1	72	45⅜	45½	44⅜	45¼	+ ¼
46¼	31⅝	Air Prod .20b	27	36⅛	36⅛	35	35	—1½
34⅞	27⅞	Abex Cp 1.60	18	30½	30¼	30	30¼	+ ⅛
58¼	38⅛	ACF Ind 2.20	42	42⅝	42⅞	42¼	42⅜	— ⅜
46¾	32	Acme Mkt 2b	18	39¼	39⅜	39	39	.....
34	27	AdamE 2.50e	13	31⅛	31⅞	31⅛	31⅞	+ ⅜
87¼	14½	Ad Mills .40a	60	45	45⅛	44	44	—1⅛
80½	46⅞	Address 1.40	106	64¼	64⅝	63	63⅝	—1⅛
38	16½	Admiral	124	17⅝	18¾	17⅝	18½	+ ⅝
69⅛	35	Aeroquip 1b	8	53⅝	53⅞	52⅝	52⅝	—1⅜
130	103⅝	Air Pd pf4.75	2	113½	113½	113½	113½	+1½
44⅞	30¼	AirRedtn 1.50	87	31	32⅛	30⅞	32	+ ¾
12⅝	3½	AJ Industries	147	10¼	10¼	9⅞	9⅞	— ⅜
19½	17¾	Ala Gas .96	9	18⅞	19¼	18⅞	19	.....
43⅞	16¾	Alberto C .20	101	37¾	39⅜	37¾	38½	+1
33¾	23	AlcanAlum 1	128	23⅞	24⅛	23⅞	24	+ ⅛
17⅞	7⅞	Alleg Cp .20g	26	14½	14⅝	14½	14⅝	+ ⅛
65	25⅝	Alleg 6pf .60	3	52	52	51½	51½	—1½
79¼	55⅛	AllegLud 2.40	17	67½	68¼	67⅜	67⅝	+ ⅜
79	69¼	AllegLud pf 3	6	72½	73	72½	73	+1
27¾	21	Alleg Pw 1.20	43	22¾	23	22¾	22¾	+ ¼
31⅞	21½	AllenInd 1.40	1	27½	27½	27½	27½	.....
46⅞	33¼	AlliedCh 1.90	93	36⅝	36¾	36¼	36¾	+ ¼
33¼	15¼	Allied Kid 1	11	27	27¼	26⅝	27¼	.....
53¼	44¼	Allied Mills 2	3	44½	44½	44½	44½	+ ¼
63¾	26½	Allied Pd .60	14	54¼	55¾	54¼	55¾	+1⅛
114	102½	AlliedPd pf 3	3	109	111	109	111	+2
41½	22⅛	AlliedStr 1.40	32	38	38½	38	38	+ ¼
24	11	AlliedSup .60	53	18⅝	18⅞	18½	18⅞	+ ⅜
44	21⅝	Allis Chal 1	501	32	32	30⅜	30¾	—1⅝
14⅞	7¾	Alpha P Cem	24	13	13⅛	13	13⅛	+ ⅛
15¼	5¾	Alside .20	17	11¼	11⅞	11¼	11¾	+ ½
93⅞	67¼	Alcoa 1.80	108	72⅞	73½	72¾	73½	+1
33	20⅜	AmalSug 1.40	6	31¼	31¼	30¾	31	.....
35½	22⅛	Amerace 1.20	3	32¼	32¼	31⅞	31⅞	— ⅝
97½	73	Amerada 3	125	79	79⅜	78½	79¼	+1
45⅜	30⅝	AAirFiltr .80	11	32⅞	33½	32⅞	33	— ¼
49	26½	Am Airlin .80	376	29⅜	29⅝	29	29	+ ⅛
29	15¾	Am Baker 1	18	22¼	22⅜	22½	22⅜	— ¼
27½	20¼	AmBk Note 1	4	21¼	21¼	21	21	— ¼
70¾	20	Am Bosch .60	43	50	51	50	50¼	+ ⅜

WEDNESDAY, FEB. 21

Day's Sales	Tuesday	Year Ago	Year to Date 1968	Year to Date 1967
9,170,000	8,800,000	10,010,000	397,327,138	350,607,470

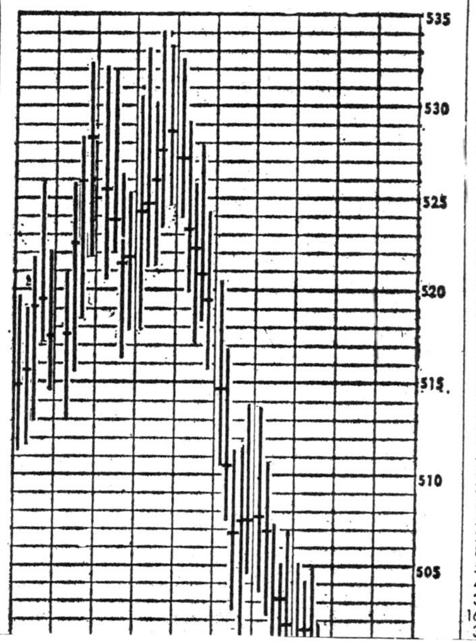

1967-68 High.	1967-68 Low.	Stocks and Div. in Dollars.	Sls. 100s.	First.	High.	Low.	Last.	Net Chge.
28½	20¾	CocaBtlg 1.20	13	27⅜	27⅜	26⅞	26⅞	— ⅝
45⅜	26⅞	Colg Pal 1.10	37	42⅛	42⅜	42	42⅛	+ ⅜
32¼	19	CollinAik 1.20	4	28½	29	28½	28⅞	+ ⅝
114⅞	53	CollinRad .80	64	72¾	72⅞	71⅜	71¾	— ⅛
45¾	28⅜	ColoIntG 1.60	42	42⅜	42⅞	42¼	42¾	+ ½
57¾	48	Colo Sou pf 4	z100	51¾	51¾	51¾	51¾	+1½
65¾	19	Colt Ind .20e	122	58	59⅜	58	58¾	+ ¾
76⅜	46⅛	CBS 1.40b	213	47⅜	48	47⅜	47¾	+ ⅛
39⅞	26½	CBS pf 1	24	27½	27⅞	27⅜	27⅝	+ ⅛
28¾	23⅞	ColuGas 1.52	76	27½	27⅞	27⅜	27½	+ ¼
30⅜	23½	Columb Pict	156	29⅜	29⅜	28⅞	29¼	+ ¼
44¾	30½	Col SoOh 1.60	19	42⅝	42⅞	42⅝	42⅞	+ ¼
93	47⅛	CombEn 2.20	61	71½	71½	70⅞	71	— ⅛
35⅞	25⅝	ComlCre 1.80	61	32	32⅛	31⅞	31⅞	— ¼
83	66	ComCr pf4.50	z10	71	71	71	71	.....
57⅝	32¾	ComSolv 1.20	58	37⅜	38⅛	37⅜	37¾	.....
55¼	44¼	ComwEd 2.20	40	47½	47⅝	47¼	47¼	+ ⅛
36	28⅛	Com E pf1.42	13	30¼	30½	30	30	+ ⅛
29⅝	19⅛	Comw Oil .60	109	22¼	22⅜	22	22	.....
77⅞	41⅛	Comsat	165	44	46½	44	45¼	+1¾
28⅛	20	Cone Mills 1	9	22	22	21⅞	22	+ ⅛
26⅜	17⅛	Congolum .80	13	23⅝	23⅞	23⅜	23⅜	— ¼
71½	25	ConracCp .60	39	48¼	49	48	49	+ ¾
36¼	30⅝	Con Edis 1.80	107	33½	33⅞	33⅜	33⅝	+ ¼
96	75½	ConEdis pf 5	4	80⅛	80¾	80⅛	80¾	+ ⅝
57¾	35½	ConElecInd 1	57	39¾	40	39½	39¾	— ¼
57½	45¾	ConFood 1.50	26	52⅜	52½	52⅛	52⅛	— ⅛
36	16¾	Con Frght .80	53	33½	34½	33½	34⅜	+1⅜
[illegible]1	26⅜	ConNatG 1.70	347	27⅜	27½	27¼	27⅜	+ ⅛
51½	38½	ConsPwr 1.90	41	40¼	40½	40	40¼	+ ¼
35¾	26½	Containr 1.40	41	28⅞	29⅛	28⅞	28⅞	+ ⅛
37⅝	18⅞	ContAirL .50	546	22½	22⅝	22⅛	22¼	+ ⅛
42¾	30⅜	Cont Bak 1.20	32	42¼	42⅜	42	42⅜	+ ⅞
6[illegible]	41	Cont Can 2	161	49½	49½	47¾	48¼	—1
37½	19¼	Cont Cop .70b	31	20½	20½	20⅛	20⅛	— ¼
89⅜	73⅞	Cont Ins 3.20	56	78½	78½	78⅛	78⅛	— ⅝
52	27⅛	ContMtg 2.12	20	50⅜	51⅝	50⅜	51⅝	+1½
23½	15⅜	Cont Mot .40	12	18¼	18¼	18¼	18¼	+ ⅛
81½	63⅝	Cont Oil 2.80	68	70	71⅛	69¾	69¾	+ ¼
59¾	50¾	Cont Oil pf 2	3	52	52	51½	51½	+ ½
49½	25¼	Cont Stl 1.80	31	45⅝	47	45⅝	47	+1
34¾	23⅞	Cont Tel .60	98	26½	26¾	26¼	26¼	— ⅜
165⅝	33½	Control Data	422	123	124	122⅛	123⅜	+1¼
39⅜	22½	Conwod 1.40a	6	35⅞	36¼	35¾	36¼	+ ⅜

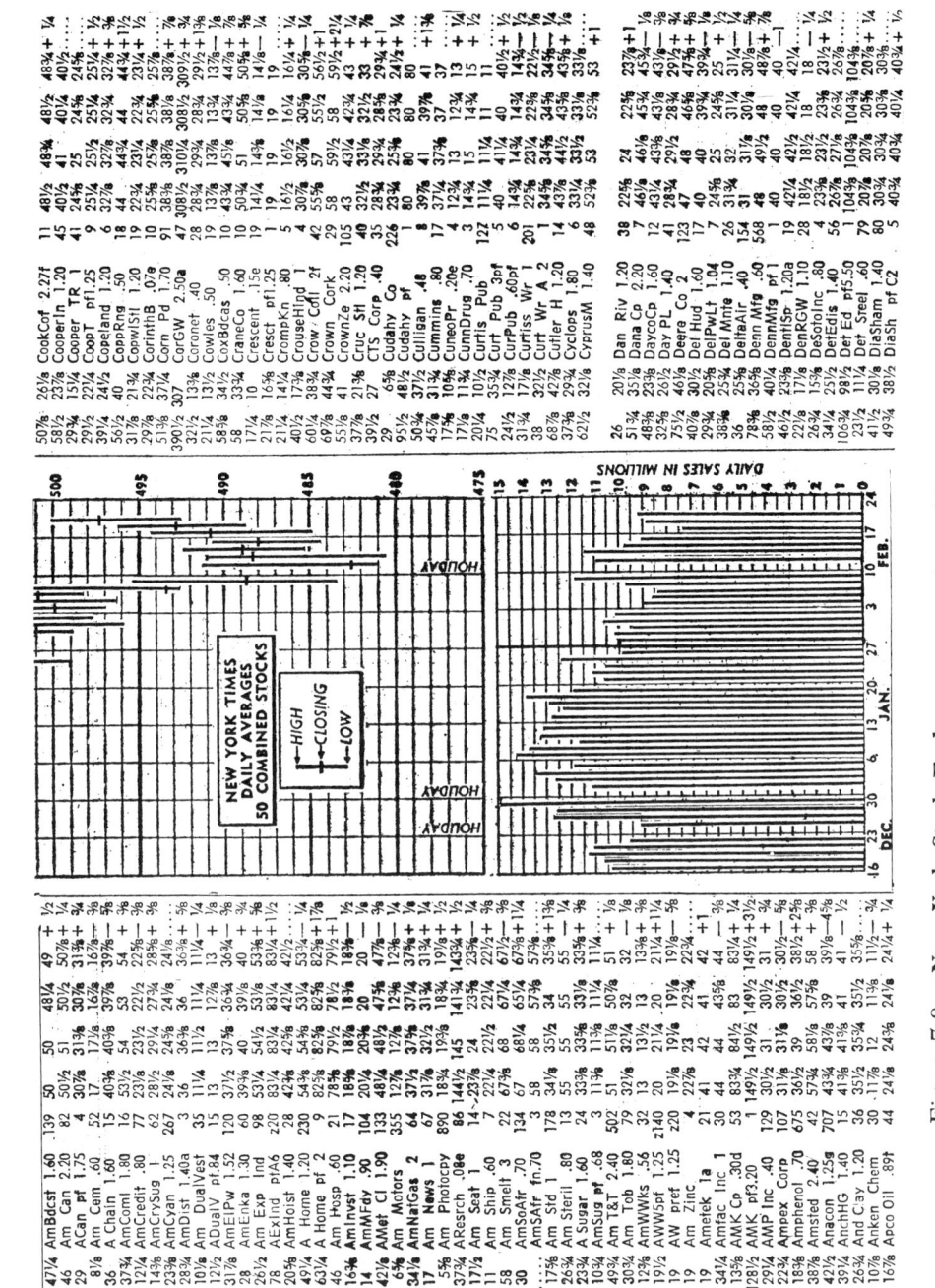

Figure 7-8. New York Stock Exchange transactions. (*Source. New York Times*, February 22, 1968, p. 47.)

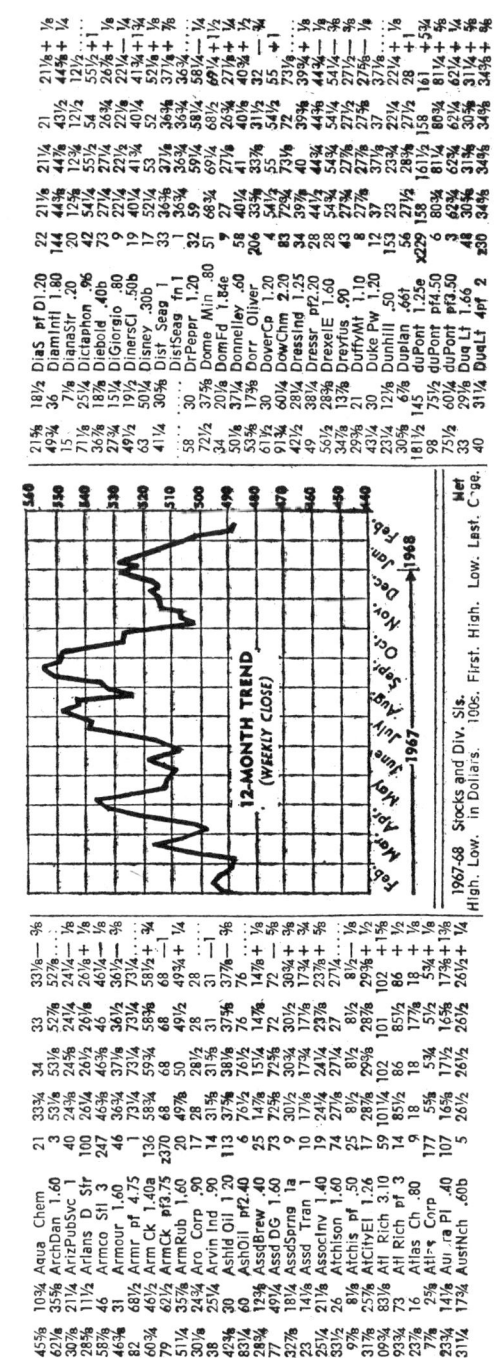

Figure 7-8. (*continued*)

Listed prominently on the next-to-the-last page, as in Figure 6–5 in the last chapter, is a large reproduction of the Dow-Jones Averages, a product of the Dow-Jones Company, which also publishes the *Wall Street Journal.* The Dow-Jones Averages provide running comparisons of industrial stocks, railroad stocks, and utility stocks. The changed average of the market prices for selected stocks in each group provides a usable spot estimate of market trends. However, it should be borne in mind that the Dow-Jones Averages embrace only 65 stocks and that they continue to use a number of security issues that no longer are representative of the market.

In the *Wall Street Journal,* the advertisements are usually newsworthy and informative. Nearly every stock promotion or bond offering is likely to be included in these ads.

Periodical Coverage of Investment Information

Many periodicals report and summarize the news each week, including generalized information about business conditions and specific information about certain firms, their policies, and their financing, which are important to investors and potential investors. News of this sort is found every week in *Time, Newsweek,* and *U.S. News & World Report. Business Week* specializes in business news. These magazines keep investors abreast of events, since investments are influenced by external factors such as international trade, labor relations, antitrust actions, and by investors' interpretations of recent news about these things.

Among the monthly magazines, there is *Fortune* whose articles, usually the result of investigation and research, present detailed information for the specific fields they cover. *Changing Times* also carries investment advice in some of its articles. The scholarly bimonthly *Harvard Business Review* and the quarterly *Journal of Finance* contain occasional articles that bear on the subject of investments.

Barron's. Under its full name of *Barron's National Business and Financial Weekly,* Dow-Jones publishes this periodical of approximately 64 pages each week. Its contents include special reports and signed articles relating to trends in specific industries, and others on governmental, monetary, taxing, and regulatory policies. There are a number of reports on the most popular stocks, the most promising growth stocks, and on dividend news and expectations. There is also a weekly summary of the several American and Canadian stock exchanges and commodity markets. *Barron's* reports the Dow-Jones Averages and runs a comparative series called Barron's Market Laboratory (see Figure 7–9). This series includes Dow-Jones comparisons, foreign stock indexes, and Bar-

February 5, 1968

• MARKET LABORATORY

Week's Market Statistics

	Last week	Prev. week	Last year
Shares traded, thous:			
Total sales NYSE	50,225	54,632	54,132
Total sales ASE	26,948	34,425	19,273
Dow-Jones groups:			
65 Stks, th shs	4,295	5,061	4,144
30 Ind, th shs	3,054	3,587	3,161
20 RR, th shs	534	641	446
15 Util, th shs	707	833	537
20 Most Active Stocks:			
Average price	41.24	50.61	36.19
Ratio vol to tot vol, %	17.59	16.05	15.53
20 Low Priced Stocks-v:			
Index	410.2	385.5	234.3
Volume, th shs	658.1	813.9	1,492.8
% of vol to D-J Ind vol	20.80	23.29	47.06
Odd-lot trading week ended Jan. 19:			
Purchases, th shs	3,495	3,568	3,315
Purchases, th $	176,176	185,985	162,538
Sales, th shs z	3,559	3,553	3,426
Sales, th $ z	180,270	181,486	173,769
Short sales, no shs	36,110	33,756	41,970
Member trading, week ended Jan. 12:			
% total	24.06	25.57	24.62
Purchases, th shs	14,966.7	11,748.0	12,914.9
Sales, th shs-z	16,762.6	13,340.8	13,814.8
Short sales, th shs	3,975.3	2,558.0	3,439.5
For week ended Friday:			
Bond vol, NYSE, th $	74,720	77,168	79,261
Brokers' loans mil $-nw	2,364	2,316	1,543
Bond offerings, th $	367,193	416,985	272,195
Stock offerings th $	12,581	7,700	1,200
Bk clrgs, NYC, mil $-v	41,159	41,074	36,268
Barron's 10 Hi-Gr bond yields-v	6.13	6.10	5.18
Spread between yields for Barron's Hi-Gr Bonds & D-J Ind Stk Avg.	—2.65	—2.63	—1.46
Ratio to D-J 40 Bonds (Confidence Index)	94.9	94.6	95.2
Prices and Yields (which include stock dividends) on Dow-Jones Averages:			
30 Ind	863.56	865.06	857.46
30 Ind, %	3.48	3.47	3.72
30 Ind, % (cash only)	3.44	3.43	3.52
20 RR	228.31	231.75	228.03
20 RR, %	5.08	r5.00	4.99
15 Util	129.54	130.24	138.90
15 Util, %	4.58	4.55	4.22
40 Bonds, %-v	6.46	6.45	5.44
10 Hi Gr, %-v	6.43	6.35	5.41
10 2d Gr, %-v	7.03	6.99	5.87
10 Ind, %-v	6.09	6.09	5.28
10 Util, %-v	6.27	6.35	5.22
Municipal Bond, yield, %	4.25	4.28	3.38

n-N. Y. City, excluding government bond loans. r-Revised. v-Week ended Thursday. w-Week ended Wednesday. z-Includes short sales.

Foreign Stock Indexes

	—1967-68— High	Low	Feb. 2 Close	Week's Change
Australia	485.92	320.66	485.92	+ 20.60
Austria	2,196.00	1,863.00	1,885.00	— 11.00
Belgium	118.90	93.50	113.70	+ .40
Canada	171.45	147.65	156.57	— 3.10
France	109.00	85.20	107.20	— .60
Italy	7,571.00	6,526.00	6,927.00	— 31
Japan	1,506.27	1,250.14	1,318.11	+ 5.07
Netherl.	373.50	268.00	368.20	+ 2.50
Switzer.	246.60	167.30	240.10	— 2
U.K.	428.30	308.60	428.30	+ 14.00
U.K. Kaffirs	71.10	45.50	71.10	+ 4.50
[illegible]	108.78	68.96	108.73	— 1.15

20 Most Active Stocks

1967-68 High	Low		Sales	High	Low	Close	Chg.
22½	5⅝	Am Photo	1,133,800	22½	19	19⅛	— ⅛
120⅜	67⅛	Litton Ind	674,700	75⅝	67⅛	73⅜	—1½
15⅞	6⅝	Am Motors	578,400	14½	13⅛	13⅞	+ ⅞
143⅞	93¾	Teledyne	543,500	117⅞	100	103⅞	—13⅛
65⅛	28⅛	Sperry Rnd	536,800	53	46	47⅜	—4¾
165⅝	33½	Control Dat	513,200	133	115½	118½	—14⅞
57¾	26¾	Bunker Hill	402·300	56	46½	55¼	+4¾
25¼	14	Am Mch Fd	400,100	23	20⅛	22⅞	+2½
33⅜	14⅞	Unit EngFd	396,000	30	27⅝	28⅞	— ⅛
59	28½	McDonnD	36,300	56⅝	50⅛	52¼	—3¾
11⅞	2¼	Benguet	361,800	10¾	9⅝	10⅜	— ⅛
62¾	49¾	Am Tel Tel	357,200	53¼	51	51⅞	+ ⅜
34¼	24¾	Int Paper	345,000	31½	29¼	29¾	—1⅜
19⅝	9¾	Glen Ald	344,000	14⅞	13½	13½	—1
66⅛	30⅝	Gulf Wn In	340,200	58⅜	53	53½	—4⅝
35½	32⅝	Occident wi	335,900	35½	32⅝	33⅞	......
81¾	44⅝	Monog Ind	320,400	66¼	53⅝	56¼	—10¼
7¼	3½	Elect Music	302,200	7¼	6¾	6¾	......
18⅝	8⅝	Gt W Finan	294,900	18⅝	16¼	17⅝	+ ⅞
17⅝	7	Brunswk	290,600	17⅜	16	16	—1

Barron's 50-Stock Average

	Feb. 1 1968	Jan. 25 1968	Feb. 1967
Price	353	356	339
Projected quarterly earn	6.00	6.00	5.55
Projected annual earn	24.00	24.00	22.20
Ratio price to proj an earn	14.7	14.8	15.3
5-year average earnings	23.16	23.16	22.17
Ratio price to 5-yr av earn	15.2	15.4	15.3
Earn for year just ended	23.50	23.47	25.89
Ratio price to yr end earn	15.0	15.1	13.1
Earn yield yr ended earn	6.67	6.60	7.65
Bond yields	6.13	6.10	5.15
Bond-stock ratio	.92	.92	.68
Divs paid in year ended	14.30	14.30	14.33
Div yield in year ended	4.05	4.02	4.23

New York Stock Exchange Diary

	Jan. 29	30	31	Feb. 1	2
Issues traded	1,477	1,491	1,463	1,452	1,482
Advances	587	401	339	602	583
Declines	698	873	903	612	671
Unchanged	192	217	221	238	228
New highs 67-68	50	27	17	13	23
New lows, 67-68	20	31	34	28	21

Weekly

Issues traded	Advances	Declines	Unchanged
1,641	514	984	143

New 1967-68 highs last week 90; new lows 67.

American Stock Exchange Diary

Issues traded	963	965	966	964	961
Advances	379	223	239	339	334
Declines	441	596	580	470	435
Unchanged	143	146	147	155	192
New highs, 67-68	48	36	19	16	27
New lows, 67-68	11	11	14	11	7
Sales th shs	5,560	5,920	5,280	4,820	4,921

New 1967-68 highs last week 94; new lows 26.

Bond Averages and NYSE Bond Sales

40 Bonds	76.42	76.43	76.34	76.26	76.28
10 Hi-Gr RR	65.32	65.32	65.03	64.76	64.86
10 2d-Gr RR	76.52	76.37	75.63	75.66	75.68
10 Util	80.24	80.29	80.94	80.79	80.77
10 Ind	83.62	83.77	83.80	83.83	83.83
U.S. Govts.	82.81	82.71	82.71	82.65	82.81
Income RR	64.38	64.40	64.06	65.05	64.17
Sales, ths $	14,780	15,860	13,860	14,890	15,340

Odd-Lot Trading

	Jan. 26	29	30	31	Feb. 1
Purch, th shs	600.6	658.6	621.4	594.3	594.2
Sales, th shs	517.1	588.9	618.4	589.7	590.3
Short Sales, sh	5,237	8,960	12,534	13,382	13,968

Figure 7-9. **Market laboratory.** (***Source.*** ***Barron's*, February 5, 1968, p. 46.**)

ron's 50-Stock Average that reports the monthly prices, dividend rates, projected annual earnings, and earnings ratios of these 50 stocks. Toward the end of each year, the magazine draws short-run and long-term comparisons of stock market prices in ten countries by inclusion of the major index in each of these countries. All this may be of use to the experienced investor and the novice alike.

Other Financial Publications. The other publications include *Forbes* magazine, the *New York Journal of Commerce*, the *Financial World*, the *Magazine of Wall Street*, the *United States Investor*, the *Commercial and Financial Chronicle*, and others. Each of these publications has its loyal band of followers who find in it the facts, the analyses, and the interpretations they evidently need to make their investment decisions.

Financial Reporting Services

Several financial services are distinguishable from the others because of the thoroughness with which they report the earnings, dividends, and other relevant news of corporations. An investor might try to acquire the same information by accumulating a myriad of corporate *annual reports* that contain income statements and balance sheets. The financial reporting services are more useful, however. They include earnings and dividend records for 10 or 20 years back and adequate accounts of each corporation's financial history, its interrelated subsidiaries, and its bond obligations. With this information at hand, an investor may base his security analysis on timely and pertinent information.

Two of the three major financial reporting services, Moody's and Standard & Poor's, publish basic information manuals. These large and cumbersome publications, Moody's *Manuals* and Standard & Poor's *Standard Corporation Records*, will be found in most large libraries and should be used by students who wish to analyze the securities of one or more corporations. Professional investors and many libraries also subscribe to one or more of the loose-leaf services provided by Standard & Poor's, by Moody's, or by the Fitch Investment Service. These loose-leaf services are especially useful because they provide the latest information about certain corporations. A good stock analysis should utilize both annual reports and at least one of the loose-leaf supplements.

Financial Advisory Services

The Fitch *Weekly Survey*, Moody's *Stock Survey*, Moody's *Bond Survey*, and *Standard & Poor's Outlook* are advisory services that are available weekly to investors who are willing to pay a substantial fee. In their service reports, the publishers necessarily express opinions and make recommendations. Other advisory services include *Forbes Guide to Common Stock Profits*, the *Investors Intelligence Inc.* service, the *Value Line Weekly Summary-Index*, and advisory reports by a number of leading brokers, dealers, and investment houses. Several of these services will provide their clients with a limited number of analyses of specific stocks as part of the advisory service.

The Value Line advisory service uses charts extensively to set upper and lower limits of ranges within which each stock is expected to move within a period of five years. Other services use professional chartists extensively to project market situations. Many of the services hire scores of experts who use orthodox methods of analysis; it is obvious that professional analysts who limit their attention to a small group of stocks can project market-price trends better than individual investors who are mere novices by comparison. But very often the experts who are often wrong but never uncertain are in disagreement, forcing individual investors to rely on their own analysis and judgment.

The Security and Exchange Commission improved its rules for supervising financial and advisory services in 1962. It is possible that testimonials, exaggerated statements, and deceptive claims will be abandoned by advisory services as they seek to enlarge their list of fee-paying clients.

REGULATION OF INVESTMENT INSTITUTIONS

Inexperienced investors certainly need all the protection they can get. Otherwise, they might succumb to the enticements of the purveyors of securities and of financial services. Actually, no rules or laws ever could be enacted to protect some persons from the consequences of their own misjudgments. The purpose of present regulations is merely to eliminate misrepresentation and duplicity. Security dealers and stock exchanges have adopted a variety of regulations designed for the protection of the investor. In addition, several states and the federal government have enacted a number of statutes for the same purpose, and specialized agencies have been created for their enforcement.

Self-Regulation

Over the years, a minority of security dealers and exchange members have been guilty of overselling their clients and of the churning of accounts. Some reputable security dealers, investment counselors, and exchange members have become so incensed at these actions that punitive rules have been made and professional standards have been improved.

National Association of Security Dealers. Because of some misrepresentation, some churning of accounts, and a few instances involving fraud, security dealers have formed a professional organization with restricted membership and a code of ethics. By now the profession is reputable; a salesman who is a member of the National Association of Security Dealers (NASD) may be depended on to represent the high standards of his profession. Notwithstanding, the investor who is "sold" securities by a dealer must expect that some of the advice received will be biased by the dealer's desire to sell. Ideally, an investor should decide for himself what and when to buy; he should not be "sold."

Stock Exchange Regulations. Over the years, stock exchanges have increased the rigor of the rules that their members must obey at the risk of expulsion. In these same exchanges, the regulations pertaining to the listing of securities also have been tightened. Generally speaking, exchange members have been forced by the regulations of their exchange to deal with increasing fairness with their clients and fellow members, and with security dealers who do not have seats on the exchange.

In like manner, it can be said that the listing of a security insures an increasing degree of authenticity of the factual representations made about it. This has been especially true of securities listed on the New York Stock Exchange.

Basically, stock exchanges require their members to agree to a set of regulations that are binding on them. Investors benefit indirectly from the proper performance of a well-ordered stock market, which accounts for the investor's interest in the rules adopted by the members. To prevent various forms of chicanery, all transactions must be in the open and recorded. Spot checks of a member's transactions may be requested by the exchange, and periodic reports may be required of the members. The functions of *brokers* or *dealers* who buy and sell for clients, of *specialists* who seek to make a market for specific securities, and of *underwriters* who launch new issues on the market, are carefully differentiated. Otherwise an overlapping of these functions might lead to a conflict of interest that might be detrimental to the interests of clients and of other members. As these words are written, the better exchanges have cleaned their houses quite well. A scandal in the American Stock Exchange in 1961, related to trading in unlisted stocks, the function of specialists, and an overexpansion of newly listed issues, led to reorganizations of that exchange in 1962 and 1966, thereby confirming the proposition that standards of ethics are rising in stock exchanges generally.

Government Regulation

When gaps have occurred in the self-regulation of security dealers and stock exchanges, public opinion has demanded that these gaps should be filled with governmental action. Local governments and states have passed *blue sky laws* whose purpose was to drive from their borders all unscrupulous oil-stock promoters and fly-by-night purveyors of Canadian uranium-mine stocks. Since the 1930's several federal laws and the Securities and Exchange Commission (SEC) have dominated the governmental regulation scene. The practices that the SEC and its supporting legislation have eliminated, in part or totally, merit further consideration.

Adequate Disclosure of Information. For years, new issues had been offered on the market with biased claims in support of the corporation's earnings, business volume, and assets. The Securities Act of 1933 required that sworn statements be given in support of all such claims. Moreover, the act provided penalties enforceable by the newly created Securities and Exchange Commission for evident misrepresentations. This "truth in securities" legislation has had a sobering effect on the entire financial community.

Banning of Manipulative Activities. The Jay Goulds and Jim Fisks of another era no longer can spread rumors or keep corporate accounts in such a manner than they cause market prices of stocks to rise or fall, thus enabling themselves to buy or sell shares at great profit. A more common form of manipulation occurred when a group bought a certain stock extensively, then sat back to wait until the "suckers" bought it and pushed it higher, whereupon the original instigators of the manipulation quietly sold out, took their gain, and left the others to suffer the stock's decline.

Under the term of the 1934 Securities Act, enforced by the SEC, market manipulations became definitely illegal and punishable in several ways. SEC experts now watch quotations and investigate the cause of any unwarranted change in market price. Manipulation of stock prices has been virtually eliminated. Dealers and specialists who seek to make the market for certain issues are scrupulously regulated.

National Regulation of Listed Securities. The Securities Act of 1934 required that all securities listed on an exchange also had to be registered with the SEC and subject to its rules. This requirement has tended to fill a void that might have resulted from the laxness of some of the exchange listing specifications. It also may have discouraged the listing of some doubtful securities and strengthened the control of exchanges over their remaining, list which was authorized for trading. Actually, the listed securities on several small exchanges have been exempted from this requirement and many unlisted securities are admitted for trading on exchanges with the notable exception of the New York Stock Exchange.

Basic Inadequacy of Regulation. If self-regulation by securities dealers and stock exchanges were adequate, there would be no need for government regulation. Each has its proper sphere of activity, yet gaps remain. Fraudulent practices of investment purveyors and advisors virtually have been eliminated, but investors still must weed out worthless or untimely information, or both. Investors often are influenced to buy too much, too often, or unwisely; they may be induced to sell something good and buy something else. The investor's proverbial questions—what to buy, when to buy, what to sell—are never in want of answers; he can get the information for a fee from one investment adviser or another. However, the investor in search of advice needs more counsel on how to ferret out and use the assistance that is available. Since 1962, the Securities and Exchange Commission has registered and supervised the services that sell financial advice.

Investors' Need for More Information

The need for educating investors is threefold. First, new groups of prospective investors appear and require guidance along with inducements to invest. If these groups cannot be absorbed into the investment community with each new generation, the country's capital formation may be threatened. To prevent each new investor from having to learn his lessons the hard way, caution and wisdom have to be passed along with the basic information that is so essential for effective investment. Maturity or experience has to be transferred, if possible, to the new generation of investors. Thus young persons and others who have acquired surplus funds will be able to invest them without fear of impoverishing themselves and spoiling the market by unpredictable and unwise decisions.

Second, the increasing complexity of the economy, the business scene, and corporate finance. Evidence of this complexity may be seen in the increasing difficulty of predicting the business cycle. Some corporations have split their stocks so many times that true values and earnings per share have become harder to evaluate. The science of business management has evolved so far that few can keep abreast of it. Then, also, new inventions must be understood, as they are vital to many a corporation's success. There is the further fact that wage and tax increases often squeeze profits. Annual reports frequently conceal the truth of these matters from stockholders and prospective investors alike. Hence the investor needs to be able to distinguish fact from fiction in order to analyze securities in a proper manner.

Third, coping with the moods of the stock market; the market does not always follow facts and logic. It is buoyant, overoptimistic, depressed, or overly pessimistic. It overprices some issues and underprices others at any given moment. There are rumors that cause buying and selling orders to swamp an exchange; then come the facts, and the corrective action causes further activity. How can any investor, experienced or inexperienced, adapt his decisions to this unpredictable, illogical, capricious performance?

Available Courses

What shall prospective investors do, considering their lack of preparation for the vagaries of the securities markets? There seem to be three courses.

1. Bold Invetment Policy. Investors may barge headlong into the market exercising their best judgment and hoping for a stroke of luck. As long as stock prices reflect some of the general price increases that characterize our economy, typical investors who buy quality issues and hold them for several years will make 6 per cent or 8 per cent from their ventures—enough to justify the risks assumed. Without inflation, most of these investors probably would lose money in the market or make less than enough to justify the risks. It is to be hoped that prospective investors who are determined to enter the market will avail themselves of every opportunity to increase their knowledge and sharpen their judgment so that they may succeed in their investment endeavors.

2. Leave the Market Alone. Some prospective investors are likely to realize their own inadequacies and to cringe in the face of the frightening responsibilities associated with investment decisions. Such individuals often shy away from the market; they are not part of it. By nature they are timid; they deliberate too long; they do not relish decision making and hasty reevaluations involving hundreds or thousands of dollars. Such persons may be wiser to invest in banks, savings and loan associations, or investment companies, where they relinquish to others the responsibility for making decisions.

3. Invest in a Mutual Fund or Investment Company. The next chapter will survey investments in mutual funds and investment companies. This sort of investment may meet the needs of individuals who want to invest but prefer to let someone else make the investment decisions. By contrast with other choices available to investors, this arrangement would seem practical for novices, and it merits serious consideration. Its disadvantages, however, leave many of the investor's questions unresolved; therefore, investment companies apparently do not really serve, as we shall see, as panaceas for typical, inexperienced investors.

QUESTIONS

1. Distinguish carefully between the primary and secondary distribution of securities.
2. What service does an underwriting syndicate perform?
3. How are stocks actually traded on the floor of an exchange? How may a brokerage office outside of New York City be used for a transaction that is completed on the New York Stock Exchange?
4. What are the chief differences between the NYSE, AMEX, the NSE, and any one of the leading regional stock exchanges?
5. Indicate the close relationship between an investor and an account executive. Why does an investor have an account with his broker?
6. Explain the advantages and dangers of margin trading.
7. What can a prospective investor learn from (a) a metropolitan newspaper, (b) the *Wall Street Journal,* (c) weekly and monthly magazines.
8. What are the methods used by financial advisory services in analyzing securities? Why is this probably better than the analysis of a typical investor? What are the dangers inherent in the offerings of these advisory services?
9. How do securities dealers and stock exchanges regulate their own activities? Why has government regulation seemed necessary? What are the chief responsibilities and activities of the SEC? Are investors adequately protected now against (a) fraud, (b) misrepresentation, (c) their own acts and decisions?
10. Is investment a science which can be mastered by experts? If some persons are inadequately prepared to make investment decisions, should they (a) invest boldly anyway, (b) abstain from investing, (c) invest in an investment company? Why?
11. Is the stock market, from investors through brokers to exchanges, well organized and efficiently operated? Do the participants respond to normal self-interest based on adequate information? Does it represent a free play of supply and demand forces?
12. Note carefully all the key terms in this chapter and be prepared to identify each of them.

SELECTED READINGS

See list of selected readings at end of Chapter 6.

NOTES

1. Underwriters' commissions ranging from 0.65 per cent to 8.00 per cent were reported in 1963. John C. Clendenin, *Introduction to Investments,* McGraw-Hill, 1964, pp. 171, 172.
2. See *New York Stock Exchange Fact Book,* issued annually, and *Understanding the New York Stock Exchange*; publications of the New York Stock Exchange.
3. T. W. Wise, "How to Choose a Broker," *Fortune,* December 1961, p. 213;

Time, August 19, 1966, p. 67; *Wall Street Journal,* November 28, 1966; *Newsweek,* March 1, 1965.
4. Lewis Corey, *The House of Morgan,* Watt, New York, 1930, pp. 255–259.
5. Wise, *loc. cit.*
6. *Understanding the New York Stock Exchange, op. cit.,* p. 33.

PROBLEMS AND CASES

1. Refer to a financial publication. Find a stock listed on both a national exchange and a regional exchange. On that day is its closing price the same on both exchanges? Will it always be? If not, why not? Explain.
2. If there is a stock exchange in your area, pay the exchange a visit. Determine how many stocks are listed on this exchange, its monthly sales volume, and the number of brokerage firms represented on the exchange.
3. Stock worth $20,000 when it was bought declines in value to $12,000. If the stock was bought on 80 per cent margin, how much will the broker demand in additional margin? Would the broker have waited this long? Why?
4. Under current New York Stock Exchange rates, how much commission must be paid on the purchase of $3,000 worth of stock; $6,000 worth?
5. Select a corporate security and read the reports about it in Moody's and in Standard & Poor's publications. Use the historical account, the capital structure data, and the earnings and dividend data to make a fundamental analysis of this security as suggested in the previous chapter.
6. If an institutional investor is selling off 50,000 shares of stock that has been selling at $100 a share, its quotation will presumably drop sharply, then rise again after the market stabilizes. How does a trader who is a "specialist" in this particular issue prevent this damaging, temporary price slump? If he did not support a price of, say $98, on the down swing, what effect might it have on the price of other shares? On the entire market? Is he risking his money by buying heavily at $98 when the price would probably drop below $95 if he did not? May not his purchase at $98 lead to a capital gain if and when the shares rise again to $100? Does he perform a service? Should he be condemned if his gains are substantial in "making a market" for this stock?
7. If Brown must pay odd-lot commissions in order to achieve diversification and his investments are only moderately successful, may he not be more successful paying regular round-lot commissions with less diversification? If Brown holds his shares several years, on the average, before selling, is not the disadvantage of higher commissions diminished? Isn't it likely that odd-lot buyer Brown is a relative novice who should "play the market" for the long-run anyway? How much more would he have to know to play the market successfully for short-run gains?
8. If professional investor Smith feels certain that the market will decline and he sells short 10,000 shares of a cyclical, speculative stock at $90 a share, how much will he make (minus commissions and other charges) if he can buy at $80 per share within ninety days and cover his short sale? How does he fare if the shares do not go below $90? How does he fare if he has to buy ninety days later at $95?
9. If you had had $6,000 in February 1968, would you have bought six-month

futures on 10 flasks of mercury in a commodity exchange? What circumstances would have made possible the resale of this contract at a profit six months later? At a loss six months later? From the financial pages, determine the spot price and quotations in future contracts in wheat at the time you are reading this and estimate the profitability of having bought the futures contract in 1968 (see Figure 7–7).
10. If the publication of an investment service arrives at Brown's office five days after it was compiled, what are the prospects that its contents will lead to profitable investments for Brown? For the compilers of the information? How can Brown hope to be informed immediately if a good investment opportunity develops?
11. Does the principle of "adequate disclosure of information" in the prospectus for new issues provide sufficient protection for a novice investor who is seeking to double his money within a year? How should such a prospective investor be advised? Why? By whom?
12. With 2 or 3 per cent of inflation annually, are not most stocks destined to attain higher levels? In the long run, has this proved to be the case? Doesn't this phenomenon cover up some mistakes and raise the odds for successful long-run investments? Is there danger that this upward momentum may become contagious and lead to an overpriced market? Do price-earnings ratios, external factors, and other indicators justify current market levels as indicated by the Dow-Jones industrial averages? Explain the reasons for your judgment.
13. In consideration of the variety of facts and factors affecting market quotations, how can a novice hope to call the upward or downward turn of the market? With inexact information, how should one decide what to buy and sell, and when? Is there any limit to the time one might wish to spend or the amount of information one might wish to acquire in order to be a successful investor? Do the financial rewards and other satisfactions indicate that investment as a profession or as an avocation merits the attention of many young people? Does it suggest, also, that many young people who comprehend the risks and uncertainties involved will reject this way of making a living or increasing one's assets?
14. Would the novice investor's probable lack of diversification, odd-lot commissions, lack of information, and lack of investment acumen suggest buying investment company shares to offset these disadvantages, even though the buying-in fees range from 5 to 8½ per cent and their annual management fee often amounts to 0.5 per cent of the portfolio valuation?

8 INVESTMENT COMPANIES

An investment company security is a wise choice only if the diversification and management advantages which it offers are worth the added cost.

CLENDENIN

The decision to turn investor is not an easy one. It necessitates a careful self-assessment of whether an individual is qualified to take on the job of managing his own investment affairs. The prospective investor often hesitates because he doubts his ability to make intelligent investment decisions. He doubts the adequacy and authenticity of the information available to him. In addition, he may not want to spend the time required to partake of this type of activity. He may prefer buying the stocks of investment companies, that is, firms that use the proceeds from the sale of their shares to buy other securities. He may, for example, invest in what is popularly known as a *mutual fund.*

Investing on this basis seems to offer a possible solution to the problems raised in the two preceding chapters. This chapter concentrates on a myriad of details concerning investment companies and attempts to discover whether they solve the problems of typical investors.

One strong argument in support of investment companies is the claim of many of them that they produce a 7 per cent or an 8 per cent annual return over a period of years. Few investors can match this record, especially if they have to buy in odd lots to achieve diversification. The superiority of investment company earnings results from the sizable funds at their disposal that permit good management, selectivity, and diversification. The element of diversification, according to advocates of the funds, adds a safety factor that prevents or reduces losses in a declining market. For persons who dislike the responsibilities of making investment decisions, the arguments of investment company proponents seem very convincing.

Investment companies have mushroomed on the American scene in the last four decades. During the 1920's there were a few sound plans, but there were many others that led to losses and congressional investigations in the 1930's. The Investment Company Act of 1940 ushered in a new era for this form of investment. In the late 1960's, investment company plans attracted approximately six million investors. The holdings totaled $35 billion divided among 300 investment plans, and new plans were being announced every month. Actually, the proliferation of investment companies is aided by the fact that their founders collect their sales commissions and management fees irrespective of the gains or losses in the fund's portfolio.

CLASSIFICATION OF INVESTMENT COMPANIES

Mutual funds have become so numerous and so popular in the last decade that masses of American investors use the term as synonymous with all other forms of investment companies. Actually, a mutual fund is an open-end company with other attributes that enable it to expand rapidly (see Figure 8-1). To clarify this distinction, it will be necessary to examine many legal and structural forms of investment company organization.

One of the first questions that a prospective investor must ask about investment companies concerns the type of company in which he wishes to place his funds. These companies differ in regard to their form of business organization and whether they are *open-end* or *closed-end* companies. Three other types of investment companies are examined here even though they appear only infrequently. The Securities and Exchange Commission (SEC) requires investment companies to register under one or more of its classifications. So-called investment companies that exist to hold voting control of other companies are not classified as investment companies by the SEC. They need not be dealt with in this discussion.

Mutual funds paid dividends of $ 72,098,000 in 1948
Mutual funds paid dividends of $ 87,493,000 in 1949
Mutual funds paid dividends of $111,540,000 in 1950
Mutual funds paid dividends of $129,572,000 in 1951
Mutual funds paid dividends of $147,087,000 in 1952
Mutual funds paid dividends of $173,645,000 in 1953
Mutual funds paid dividends of $200,102,000 in 1954
Mutual funds paid dividends of $240,036,000 in 1955
Mutual funds paid dividends of $284,694,000 in 1956
Mutual funds paid dividends of $322,381,000 in 1957
Mutual funds paid dividends of $372,291,000 in 1958
Mutual funds paid dividends of $419,023,000 in 1959
Mutual funds paid dividends of $479,789,000 in 1960
Mutual funds paid dividends of $520,414,000 in 1961
Mutual funds paid dividends of $552,679,000 in 1962
Mutual funds paid dividends of $587,846,000 in 1963
Mutual funds paid dividends of $694,601,000 in 1964
Mutual funds paid dividends of $797,336,000 in 1965
Mutual funds paid dividends of $875,113,000 in 1966

Figure 8-1. Mutual funds: growth and dividends. (*Source.* Investment Company Institute, an advertisement in *The New Yorker*, April 15, 1967, p. 133.)

Organizational Structure

The Investment Company Act of 1940 used the term "investment company" to include several forms of companies that provide approximately the same services. Formerly, investment trusts with a trust indenture and trustees were so common that the term "investment trust" was used carelessly and commonly to denote several other types of investment companies as well. Since the 1930's, most investment companies have been chartered corporations. For this reason, perhaps, the term investment company has supplanted the term investment trust in popularity.

Massachusetts Trusts. A few investment companies are organized as Massachusetts Trusts or *Boston Trusts*. These trusts are administered by a board of trustees that determines policies within the limitations of the terms of the trust indenture. Usually these terms limit the types and amounts of securities to be held in the company's portfolio.

Originally, these *investment trusts* divided their portfolios into units that were sold to individuals who thus acquired a share of the trust agreement. Now, many investment companies that are organized as trusts may use their discretion in choosing and managing their investments, or they may contract for management services. Even though these companies presumably are subject to supervision of a court, their regulation has become the responsibility of the Securities and Exchange Commission under the terms of the Investment Company Act of 1940.

Incorporated Investment Companies. Following several decades of evolution, most American investment companies are now incorporated. The company has a charter that prescribes its activities; it has a board of directors whose members are elected, subject to limitations concerning their affiliations with other companies. Normally a chartered investment company is free to buy and sell securities, manage its portfolio, and offer a choice of several investment plans to utilize more fully the services of its research and management staffs. Such a company refers to each of its separate investment plans as an *investment fund*.

Investment Management Firm. Investment companies often contract with an *investment management firm* for management counsel that includes research services and management of the investment company's *portfolio*, that is, the securities that the investment company owns, on which its earnings depend. The Securities and Exchange Commission, in administering the Investment Company Act of 1940, tries to prevent a conflict of interest that may arise when officials of management-counseling firms become members of an investment company board of directors. As a further safeguard, investment company board members are not permitted to represent underwriting companies, traders, or brokers who sell investment company shares. In spite of these precautions, there are instances in which an investment management firm may provide research and management services for several investment companies that appear to be captives of the management firm.

Closed-End Versus Open-End Companies

The investor will find a number of important differences between closed-end and open-end investment companies. These differences affect his buying and selling price, his opportunity for a share of capital gains, the ease of marketing his shares and, the investment company's virtual freedom to acquire several classes of securities and to manage its portfolio of investments. Closed-end and open-end companies must be examined briefly if one is to understand these differences.

Closed-End Investment Companies. An investment company is known as closed-end when it has a relatively fixed capitalization. Once the company's shares are sold to investors, they may be traded, thereafter, on the market at whatever price they will bring. In 1964, for example, closed-end shares were commonly discounted, some of them by 10 per cent or more. The company does not promise to redeem the shares or to issue additional shares. A closed-end company may be either a trust plan or an incorporated investment company.

Closed-end companies appeared originally as *unit trusts* in which a list of securities held in a common-law trust were divided into units. Certificates were issued and sold as shares in the trust. Originally, in Great Britain, the typical trust agreement restricted the trustee to specific investments and even to specific proportions of each. As closed-end trusts and closed-end companies evolved, they often acquired the right to select and trade the securities in their investment portfolios. In the United States, a small fee usually is charged for administration of the fund and for management of the portfolio of investments.

The unique feature of many closed-end companies is their *multiple capital structure*; they issue bonds or preferred stocks in addition to common-stock shares. Thus, by using leverage, investment companies provide a higher rate of earnings for their stockholders than for their bondholders or preferred stockholders, if the investment portfolio shows satisfactory returns. Multiple capital structures were quite common during the 1920's, and losses were catastrophic when the stock market crashed in 1929. Since 1940, however, the issuance of bonds by a closed-end investment company has been accompanied by a required asset coverage of at least 300 per cent, and preferred stocks have had an asset coverage of at least 200 per cent. No closed-end company may have more than one class of bonds or preferred stocks.

Open-End Investment Companies. An investment company that is required to redeem its own shares, usually at asset value, and one that continuously issues new shares is known as a *mutual fund.* Such a company is an open-end investment company. In recent years nearly nine-tenths of the new investment companies have been of this variety.

An open-end investment company is permitted to have only one class of shares. Since investors usually buy their shares at asset value and sell at asset value, they divide the earnings and capital gains on a mutual basis. To cover the company's sales, bookkeeping, and portfolio management expenses, a fee of approximately 8 per cent is charged at the time an investor purchases his shares. For this fee, investors obtain diversified portfolios managed by experts, a share of current earnings plus a share of capital gains, quarterly or semi-annual reports on the specific contents of the portfolio, and twice-daily evaluations of the asset value of each share. Many investors grumble about the high fee, but few of them could obtain the diversification and other advantages at a lower price.

With rising stock prices and high-level prosperity in the years following the end of the Second World War, investors have bought shares in the mutual funds avidly. In response to this interest, the mutual funds have merely expanded their portfolios as more of their shares have been sought by investors. The closed-end companies have not shared a similar growth rate for lack of this built-in means of expansion (see Figure 8–2).

The eventual success of the mutual funds depends on successful portfolio management, since so many shares are being purchased. Management experts fully recognize that people have bought mutual fund shares because of the funds' favorable record of performance since 1940. This success has been associated with the sharp rise in stock market prices in the 1940's and 1950's. Early in the 1960's these market prices reached record historic highs, which portended that their rise would not be likely to continue indefinitely. How these mutual funds will thrive in an era in which investors no longer could count on perpetual capital gains at such high rates remains to be seen.

Miscellaneous Investment Company Classifications

Three other types of investment companies have been recognized and classified by the Securities and Exchange Commission since 1940. Most in-

Mutual Funds

March 8, 1968

Price ranges for investment companies, as supplied by the National Association of Securities Dealers:

	Bid	Asked	y-Latest 12 Mos. Payments From Income	w-Cap. Gains
Aberdeen Fd	2.86	3.13	.047	.131
Advisers Fd	7.92	8.70	.175	.43
Affiliated Fd	8.21	8.88	.32	.66
All Amer	1.14	1.25	....	....
Amer Bus Sh	3.44	3.72	.16	.35
Am Div Inv	10.83	11.83	....	....
Am Grth Fd	7.61	8.27	.16	....
Am Inv Fd	v33.14	33.14	.11	3.35
Am Mutual Fd	9.39	10.26	.31	.89
Am Pac	6.71	6.71	....	....
Assoc Fd Tr	1.52	1.66	.066	.107
Axe-Houghton:				
Fund A	7.75	8.42	.141	.759
Fund B	9.95	10.82	.33	.68
Fund Stk	7.10	7.76	.02	.68
Axe Science	19.81	21.53	.30	4.90
Babson	v7.29	7.29	....	....
Blue Ridge	12.33	13.48	.318	.702
Bondstock	6.55	7.16	.18	.14
Boston Fd	8.49	9.28	.345	.22
Broad Street Inv	13.70	14.81	.49	1.06
Bullock Fd	14.19	15.55	.44	.81
Can Gen Fd	8.12	8.87	.215	.30
Canadian Fd	16.16	17.49	.45	.75
Cap Inc	x8.29	9.08	.40	.23
Capitol Life Ins	6.27	6.87	.051	.099
Century Sh Tr	8.97	9.80	.195	.30
Channing Funds				
Balanced	12.26	13.46	.40	.71
Com Stk	1.83	2.00	.05	.18
Growth	15.75	17.21	.16	2.16
Income	7.91	8.64	.34	.45
Special	2.88	3.15	.01	.35
Chase Fd Bos	11.23	12.27	.06	....
Chemical Fd	16.87	18.44	.285	.70
Citadel	2.88	3.15	....	.19
Cstl Sec Inv	1.49	1.61	....	....
Colonial Fd				
Col Equity	4.79	5.23	.015	.263
Col Fd	12.69	13.87	.43	.83
Col Growth	8.93	9.76	.10	.835
Com Stk Fd SB	4.70	.511	....	....
Commonwealth Funds:				
Capital	17.90	19.56	.17	1.52
Income	9.79	10.70	.44	.36
Investm	9.70	10.60	.32	.50
Stock Fd	9.68	10.58	.21	1.02

	Bid	Asked	y-Latest 12 Mos. Payments From Income	w-Cap. Gains
Guard Mut	v25.90	25.90	.56	2.00
Hamilton	5.08	5.55	.1025	.295
Hartwell	14.99	14.99	....	....
Hor Mann	14.25	14.84	....	....
Hubshman	v10.80	10.80	....	....
Imperial Cap	9.49	10.32	.205	.41
Imperial Grth	7.34	7.98	.05	....
Income Found	12.57	13.74	.45	.85
Income Fd, Bos	7.48	8.17	.44	.20
Indepen	10.60	11.58	.08	1.00
Ind Trend	13.69	14.96	.17	.33
Ind Fd Am	6.66	7.28	.04	.59
Ins & Bk Stk Fd	5.10	5.57	....	....
Invest of Am	12.96	14.16	.34	1.13
Inv Tr of Boston	12.51	13.67	.28	.61
Investors Group:				
Mutual	10.84	11.78	.428	.26
Stock	20.11	21.86	.5875	.49
Selective	9.40	10.10	.5075	.0125
Variable Pay	7.85	8.54	.146	.525
Invest Rsch	18.85	20.60	....	2.05
Istel Fund	22.48	23.17	.66	2.30
Ivest	14.58	15.93	.03	.72
Johnston Mut	v19.10	19.10	.29	.70
Keystone Custodian:				
Inv Bd B-1	21.11	22.03	1.06	....
Med G Bd B-2	22.36	24.40	1.23	....
Disct Bd B-4	9.68	10.56	.64	....
Inco Fd K-1	8.78	9.58	.48	.10
Grth Fd K-2	6.03	6.59	.09	1.05
Hi-Gr Cm S-1	20.73	22.62	.39	.20
Inco Stk S-2	10.49	11.45	.33	....
Growth S-3	9.13	9.97	.14	1.18
LoPr Cm S-4	6.30	6.88	.04	1.09
Keystone Int Fd	14.09	15.24	.04	2.57
Knickrbok Fd	7.08	7.76	.16	.25
Liberty	7.31	7.99	.17	....
Lexngtn Inc Tr	9.79	10.70	.42	.17
Lex Resch	14.17	15.49	.16	2.16
Liberty	7.31	7.99	.17	....
Life Ins Inv	5.96	6.52	.07	.10
Life Ins Stk	4.24	4.63	.041	....
Loomis Sayles Funds:				
Canadn	32.17	32.17	.57	2.60
Cap Dev	11.23	11.23	.19	.91
Mutual	14.65	14.65	.53	1.00
Manhattan	9.50	10.38	.07+S3%	

	Bid	Asked	y-Latest 12 Mos. Payments From Income	w-Cap. Gains
Sec Inv	7.96	8.70	.32	.51
Selected Am	10.65	11.52	.24	1.18
Sharehl Tr Bos	11.82	12.92	.43	1.01
Sigma Cap	8.70	9.51	....	....
Southwstn Inv	9.11	9.85	.245	.875
Sovereign Inv	14.86	16.28	.48	.68
State St Inv-a	45.86	46.33	.92	2.40
Steadman Funds:				
Am Ind	11.50	12.57	.155	425
Fid	7.75	8.47	.10	.55
Sci & Gr	6.52	7.13	.07	.72
Stein Roe Funds				
Balanced	v19.63	19.63	.55	1.30
Int'l	v14.47	14.47	.34	1.18
Stock	v12.95	12.95	.24	.90
Sterling Inv	12.46	13.47	.47	.39
Suprv Inv Gr	6.04	6.62	....	....
Teachrs	11.99	12.49	....	....
Technology	8.83	9.62	.17	1.12
Temple Gr Ltd	16.50	18.03	.25	....
Texas Fund	10.76	11.76	.165	1.01
20th Cent Grth	5.01	5.48	.022	.74
20th Cent In	5.21	5.69	.192	.505
United Funds:				
Accum	7.25	7.92	.21	.50
Incom	13.29	14.59	.31	.64
Science	8.39	9.17	.12	.46
Un Fd Can-Int	6.05	6.61	.055	....
Value Line Funds:				
Val Line	8.26	9.05	.09	....
Income	6.17	6.76	.26	.505
Spl Situa	7.91	8.67	.01	.17
Vanguard	4.13	4.51	....	....
Varied Ind	5.40	5.87	.145	.15
Viking Gr	6.68	7.26	....	....
Wall St Inv	11.42	12.48	.28	.10
Washington Mut	12.69	13.87	.43	.32
Wellgtn Fd	12.19	13.25	.49	.43
Western Ind Shs	7.62	8.33	....	....
Whitehall	13.70	14.81	.41	.86
Windsor Fd	17.65	19.18	.41	2.37
Winfld Gr Fd	12.17	13.30	.02	1.37
Wisc Fd	7.06	7.72	.15	.60
Worth	4.68	5.10	.05	2.07

a-Fund's redemption price. d-Ex-distribution. r-Ex-rights. v-Net asset value. w-Includes all payments other than those made from Income. y-Payments are on the basis of stock of record date. z-Fund not reporting.

CLOSED-END FUNDS

Friday, March 8, 1968

Following is a weekly listing of unaudited net asset values of closed-end investment fund shares, reported by the companies as of Friday's close. Also shown is the closing listed market price or a dealer-to-dealer asked price of each fund's shares, with the percentage of difference.

	N.A. Value	Stk Price	% Diff
Abacus	17.66	15¾	—10.8
AdmExp	31.36	32¾	+ 4.4
AmEuro	39.44	34½	—12.5
AmIntl	17.70	16	— 9.6
Amoskeag	67.72	52	—23.2
Am-SoAf	35.83	74¾	+108.6
Carriers	34.66	28¾	—17.1
Dominick	27.12	26⅞	— 0.9
Eurofund	18.18	24⅞	+36.8
GenAInv	34.04	23½	— 1.6
GenPubS	6.86	6⅜	— 7.0
IntlHold	18.48	14⅝	—20.9

	N.A. Value	Stk Price	% Diff
Japan	12.90	11½	—10.9
Lehman	17.90	20¼	+13.1
Madison	19.75	25⅝	+28.4
NatlAvia	31.52	36⅛	+14.6
NiagraSh	23.21	23⅜	+ .7
OseasSec	8.14	18½	+127.3
PetroCp	21.90	21¼	— 3.0
StdSh	24.95	21¾	—12.8
Tri-Contl	31.25	27⅝	—11.6
United	12.19	11	— 9.8
US&For	37.64	31⅛	—17.3

Commonwealth Trust:				
Plan A&B	v1.59	....	....	....
Plan C&D	v1.77	....	....	....
Composite B&S	10.28	11.15	.21	.54
Composite Fd	10.87	11.82	.23	.71
Concord Fd	v19.43	19.43	.28	....
Consol Inv Tr	12.00	12.37	.38	.26
Consumers Inv	5.59	6.11	.07	....
Convertible Sec	9.87	10.79	.40	2.00
Corporate Ldrs	15.78	17.29	.301	.3585
Cntry Cap	11.50	12.43	....	....
Crown West D-2	6.76	7.40	.19	.36
deVegh Mut	v69.63	69.63	1.46	9.78
Decatur Inc Fd	12.58	13.75	.50	1.20
Delaware Fund	14.27	15.60	.24	1.905
Divers Grth Stk	13.19	14.45	.12	1.01
Divers Invest	9.08	9.95	.355	.35
Dividend Shs	3.60	3.95	.11	.13
Dow Th Inv F	7.38	7.98	.14	.45
Drexel Eq	v15.03	15.03	.30	2.00
Dreyfus Fund	13.23	14.44	.265	.445
Eaton & H Bal	10.94	11.88	.44	.50
Eaton & H Stk	14.86	16.14	.3875	.72
Eberstadt	12.52	13.69	.16	.78
Emplyr Gp	13.49	14.66	.24	.18
Energy Fd	v15.22	15.22	.23	1.09
Enterprs Fd	7.45	8.14	.60	.02
Equity Fd	10.03	10.84	.284	.591
Equity Gr	15.02	16.46	.05	.95
Explorer	24.12	25.66	....	....
Fairfield	12.59	13.76	....	.32
Farm Br Mt	v11.09	11.09	.20	....
Federat Gr Fd	13.91	15.20	.20	1.58
Fidelity Cap	12.65	13.75	.21	1.44
Fidelity Fd	16.98	18.36	.46	1.85
Fidelity Tr	27.02	29.37	.39	3.14
Financial Program:				
Dynam	5.73	6.27	....	....
Ind	5.02	5.50	.12	.428
Ind Inc	6.70	7.33	.24	.519
First Inv Gr	8.75	9.59	.06	.10
First Inv Stk	9.86	10.81	.28	.50
Fletcher	14.47	....	.03	.79
Fla Grth	6.86	7.49	.125	.45
Founda Lf	4.63	5.06	....	....
Founders Mut	8.09	8.83	.255	....
Foursquare Fd	12.51	13.67	.28	.74
Franklin Custodian:				
Com Stk	6.82	7.47	.15	.76
Utilities	6.90	7.52	.23	.15
Income	2.59	2.84	.155	.12
Fund of Am	9.82	10.73	.05	.25
Fundmtl Inv	10.27	11.25	.25	.90
Gen'l Inv Tr	6.80	7.39	.30	.16
Genl Sec	v11.25	11.25	.16	.84
Group Securities:				
Aerospace	9.45	10.33	.10	1.21
Com Stk	13.17	14.40	.57	.61
Fully Admin	9.07	9.92	.41	.30
Growth Indus	20.85	21.48	.39	.63
Gryphon	17.75	19.40	.13354	2,06246

Mass Fd	x11.46	12.52	.36	.60
Mass Inv Grth	11.09	12.12	.183	.274
Mass Inv Trust	15.10	16.50	.50	1.092
Mates Inv	5.79	5.79	....	....
McDonnell Fd	10.84	11.88	.075	.80
Mid Amer	6.73	7.36	.05	....
Moodys Cap	15.26	16.68	.24	1.20
Moodys Fd	13.07	14.28	.20	.18
Morton Funds:				
Growth	11.82	12.95	.19	1.10
Income	4.21	4.61	.215	.225
Insuran	6.30	6.90	.08	.17
M I F Fund	17.63	19.06	.70	1.40
M I F Growth	5.70	6.16	.17	.38
Mutual Shares	v17.86	17.86	.16	2.59
Mutual Tr	2.56	2.61	.117	.083
NEA	10.75	10.97	.22	.17
Nation-W Sec	10.42	11.28	.43	.34
National Ind	11.71	11.71	....	....
National Inv	7.14	7.72	.13	.35
National Securities Series:				
Balanced	10.92	11.93	.45	.15
Bond	5.94	6.49	.26	....
Dividend	5.07	5.54	.22	.16
Preferred	7.57	8.27	.36	....
Income	5.89	6.44	.27	.25
Stock	8.73	9.54	.34	.40
Growth	11.11	12.14	.24	.92
Nat Western	5.75	6.30	....	....
New England	10.42	11.26	.385	.424
New Horiz	v23.28	23.28	.15	1.43
New World	12.56	12.73	.27	.88
Northeast Inv	v16.86	16.86	.92	.315
100 Fund	13.28	14.51	....	....
One William St.	v15.43	15.43	.31	.61
Oppenheimer	6.97	7.62	.0066	1.30
Penn Square	v16.49	16.49	.60	.804
Philadelphia	13.71	15.02	.37	.36
Pilgrim	9.30	10.33	.04	.22
Pilot	6.62	7.23	....	....
Pine St.	v11.40	11.40	.37	.83
Pioneer	12.80	13.99	.315	.55
Planned Inv	12.34	13.49	....	1.66
Price T R Grth	v21.79	21.79	.39	.43
Provident Fd	5.62	6.14	.20	.37
Puritan Fd	10.78	11.65	.45	.40
Putnam Funds:				
Equities	10.50	11.48	...	....
George	14.36	15.67	.48	1.08
Growth	11.39	12.45	.14	1.79
Income	7.11	7.77	.42	.27
Invest	8.72	7.13	.155	.79
Rep Techn	5.63	6.15	.035	.33
Revere Fd	13.72	14.99	....	2.65
Scudder Funds:				
Int Inv	v14.07	14.32	.33	.75
Balan	v15.61	15.61	.48	1.09
Com	v10.59	10.59	.25	.39
Spec	v35.70	35.70	.31	3.74
Sec Div	12.95	14.00	2.12	.30
Sec Equit	14.97	16.35	.07	.74

TAX-FREE EXCHANGE FUNDS

	Net Asset Value Per Share Mar. 8	Mar. 1
Capital Exchange Fund	25.90	26.06
Centennial Fund, Inc.	12.93	13.20
Congress Street Fund, Inc.	137.94	138.77
Constitution Exchange Fund	52.77	53.16
Depositors Fund of Boston	20.37	20.58
Devonshire Street Fund, Inc.	14.96	15.23
Diversification Fund	28.53	28.61
Empire Fund	27.69	27.93
Exchange Fund of Boston	36.31	36.46
Exeter Fund	53.83	54.30
Exeter Second Fund	55.27	55.65
Exeter Third Fund	48.15	48.93
Federal Street Fund	69.66	70.16
Fiduciary Exchange Fund	21.17	21.33
Fifth Empire Fund	21.94	22.41
Fifth Presidential Fund	46.51	46.71
Fourth Empire Fund	25.52	25.84
General Exchange	25.90	26.17
Industries Exchange Fund	18.80	19.06
Investors Capital Exchange	115.84	117.49
Ohio Capital	23.78	24.09
Presidential Fund	44.73	44.98
Scudder Duo Vest Exchange Fund Corp.	450.75	473.42
Scudder Duo Vest Exchange Fund Inc.	502.98	502.49
Second Centennial Fund	16.46	16.86
Second Congress Street	32.45	32.76
Second Empire Fund	20.01	20.20
Second Federal Street	32.24	32.10
Second Fiduciary Exchange	37.26	27.50
Second Presidential Exchange Fund	42.60	42.65
Sixth Empire Fund	19.93	20.40
Third Empire Fund	17.49	17.60
Westminster Fund	15.21	15.33

DUAL-PURPOSE FUNDS

Friday, March 8, 1968

Following is a weekly listing of the unaudited net asset values of dual-purpose, closed-end investment funds' capital shares as reported by the companies as of Friday's close. Also shown is the closing listed market price or the dealer-to-dealer asked price of each fund's capital shares, with the percentage of difference.

	Cap. Shs. Price	N.A. Val-a Cap. Shs.	% Diff.
Am DualVest	10⅞	12.80	−15.0
Gemini	11¼	12.64	−11.0
Hemisphere	9¾	10.66	− 8.5
Income and Cap.	9¼	10.57	−12.5
Leverage	10	12.21	−18.1
Putnam Duo Fund	8¼	8.26	− 0.1
Scudder Duo-Vest	7⅝	8.04	− 5.2

a-After giving effect to arrearages, if any, of cumulative dividends and amortization of any difference between original paid-in capital and the redemption price of income shares.

Figure 8-2. **Mutual funds, closed-end funds, exchange funds, dual-purpose funds. (*Source. Barron's*, March 11, 1968, pp. 44, 58, 65.)**

vestors will have no occasion to deal with them, but these companies deserve brief mention at this time in spite of their relative unimportance.

A Unit Trust. During the late 1920's unit trusts attracted some attention. Under this arrangement an individual or organization set up groups of well-diversified securities as units and deposited them with a custodian such as a bank or trust company for a period of years. The sponsor of the units would sell as many of them as possible, keeping the securities in a depository, and issuing certificates accordingly. The purchaser's gain or loss was tied closely to the asset value of the securities, although the unit trust might be traded at some other price, depending on the mood of the market.

Face-Amount Certificates. An investor may purchase face-amount certificates by making installment payments over a period of time. The issuer of the certificates pledges, in return, to pay a stated amount on the terminal date. Usually the face amount includes built-in compound interest, which is partially forfeited if the investor's payment schedule is interrupted. The issuing company's investments have been subject to SEC regulation under terms of the Investment Company Act of 1940. Sometimes these face-amount certificate plans are accompanied by borrowing privileges or group insurance for the investor, or both.

A Regulated Company. Some investment companies can qualify for the right to avoid payment of the 25 per cent capital-gains tax. They then pass these gains directly to their shareholders whose incomes may be low enough to require less than a 25 per cent capital-gains tax rate on their own incomes. The rigid requirements that such a company, a regulated investment company, must meet, however, and the lack of interest by low-income investors have relegated this arrangement to minor use.

A TYPICAL AMERICAN INVESTMENT COMPANY

To paraphrase a descriptive account by an experienced mutual fund manager, a typical American investment company would be a mutual fund with a single class of shares, fully paid and fully voting. There would be the proviso that the company would repurchase the shares at asset value whenever the investor chose to sell.[1] The company would not acquire debt; it would not buy on margin; it would not sell short; it would not underwrite its own securities. The corporation's directors—probably seven—would be elected by the stockholders; the officers would be elected by the board of directors. Nearly half of the directors of this typical company would represent the investment management company that provided research and investment counseling. The other directors would probably include a well-known economist, two prominent industrialists, and a security specialist. No banker could serve on this board of directors.

The typical mutual fund would invest in approximately 100 common stocks with no more than 5 per cent of the original investment in any one corporation's securities. These securities, plus some cash and a few government bonds, would be placed in a bank that would act as custodian of the fund's approximately $75 million worth of funds. Additional deposits of securities, bonds, or cash would be required if and when additional shares were issued.

Dividend checks would be issued quarterly by the bank designated as paying agent. These checks would represent each stockholder's share of the fund's income less operating expenses. Once a year, stockholders could elect to take their portion of the fund's capital gains in cash or additional shares. Stockholders would report their capital-gains income to the Bureau of Internal Revenue as a long-term capital gain, whereas their quarterly dividends would be reported as short-term gains. Full publicity about the fund's portfolio of securities would be supplied to the stockholders every three months.

The typical investment company's operating expenses would include the dividend payments, a fee to the custodian bank, auditor's fees, legal fees, taxes, office and mailing expenses, and a management fee. The annual management fee for research and investment counseling services would amount to approximately 0.5 per cent of the asset value of the portfolio. The other costs and fees would bring the total annual operating costs to approximately 0.7 per cent of the portfolio's asset value. There is a controversy over the cost of investment-management services. Perhaps the fee is too high, especially where very large investment portfolios are concerned.

This typical investment company would deal with an underwriting firm that would buy the investment company's shares at asset value and sell them to investors at a premium of 8 per cent. This premium pays the dealer's commission and provides for the underwriter's promotional and overhead expenses.

INVESTMENT COMPANY PORTFOLIOS

The investor who selects an investment company because he seeks refuge from decision making will find that he still has some very important decisions to make among classifications of investment companies and types of investment funds. In this section, we shall explore the different types of investment portfolios and the investor's stake in each of them. To be sure, the investor benefits from diversification and expert management of an investment company portfolio, but there are funds of varying degrees of diversification and also specialized funds from which to choose. An examination of these differences follows.

Diversified Portfolios

The typical investment company owning securities in a hundred corporations may easily divide its holdings among different types of securities or among many companies. The spreading of investments among industries and firms is a relative, not an absolute, concept, and perfection cannot be achieved. Portfolio managers may be satisfied with a distribution of investments that approximates the current importance of each industry. On the other hand, they may prefer to scatter their investments on the basis of estimates of the future importance of these industries. Some of these experts would disagree with others about the rise and fall of certain industries and firms. Therein lies the art or the science of good diversification and good portfolio management.

A closed-end investment company with a diversified portfolio of common stocks and a significant number of senior securities is sometimes known as a *balanced fund*. Such a fund may be managed to vary the proportion of bonds to common stocks in anticipation of market swings and business cycle changes. Thus, bonds would replace some of the common stocks when declining stock prices were anticipated and vice versa. "The balanced fund is the most completely managed diversified investment available, since the management decides on both portfolio tactics and choice of securities,"[2] wrote John Clendenin. The balanced fund's formula is not unique; its success depends on timing and fortunate selections within both the bond and the stock groups.

Specialized Funds

Portfolio managers whose success depends on their estimates of the future growth and earnings of industries and firms may as well abandon diversification for advocacy of specialized funds composed only of stocks in the most promising companies. These, almost certainly, would be mutual funds. If the managers of these funds can achieve their objectives, their clients may anticipate higher earnings than derive from well-managed diversified funds. For this reason the specialized funds deserve careful consideration.

Common Stock Funds. A specialized common stock fund reflects a purposeful abandonment of diversification. The fund, composed exclusively of common stocks, does not have the balance that the inclusion of preferred stocks or bonds could provide. Such funds are chosen for the evident reason that common stocks tend to enjoy sizable capital gains in companies enjoying growth and prosperity. The weakness of the common stock fund lies in its inability in view of its character to switch to bonds when stocks are likely to decline. The best known common stock funds in the late 1960's included the Bullock Fund, Chemical Fund, Dreyfus Fund, Fidelity Fund, Fundamental Investors, Investors Stock Fund, Keystone S-4, Massachusetts Investors-Growth, National Investors, and the Television-Electronics Fund.

Blue-Chip Funds. Several investment funds are known as blue-chip funds because their portfolios contain nothing but common stocks in companies that are widely conceded to have had the very best earning and dividend records. As continuity of dividends is the characteristic of the blue chips, they tend to maintain their prices relatively well during recessions. Blue-chip stocks often are overpriced, however, because of the institutional and public demand for them; consequently, they are likely to yield low returns during periods of prosperity. Obviously, the blue-chip funds reveal the same advantages and disadvantages as the blue-chip stocks, and therefore the management of such a portfolio requires adeptness at selecting investments with income, growth, and special situation potentialities. The best-known blue-chip investment fund is Keystone S-1. Several other funds have a conspicuous number of blue chips in their portfolios.

Income Funds. Investors living in retirement often wish to buy shares in investment companies that earn and pay out sizable dividends. Several investment company funds have portfolios that are selected on precisely this basis. The income stocks in these portfolios must represent thriving companies whose stocks have not been overissued and that do not reinvest excessive amounts of their earnings in their own enterprises. The selection and management of such a portfolio entails the use of research into the financial and management policies of thousands of business firms. Most individual investors could not hope to equal the investigatory and management facilities of the better investment companies and their management companies. Income funds may be found among both closed-end or open-end investment companies. Some of the best known include Keystone S-2, the United-Income Fund, Institutional Shares-Income Fund, and National Securities-Income Fund.

Growth Funds. For investors with high incomes who seek the postponement of additional current income in favor of future capital gains, growth stocks seem to be the answer to their needs. Investment companies may serve this purpose by not paying out the capital gains from their portfolios. In this instance, the investor may sell his shares when he retires or he may place his nest egg into one of the so-called *withdrawal plans* that continues to earn while it pays out a specified number of dollars per month to the investor. Other investment company growth funds sell off portions of their portfolios in any one year, with the company or its stockholders having to pay the capital gains taxes incurred. Actually, there were some investment companies with growth funds that quadrupled in asset value between the 1950's and 1960's. The best-known growth funds include the Chemical Fund, Massachusetts Investors Growth, National Investors, Television-Electronics, Diversified Growth Fund, Florida Growth Fund, Growth Industries Fund, Institutional Shares Ltd.-Growth Fund, Keystone K-2 Growth Fund, National Securities-Growth Fund, and Putnam Growth Fund, among others.

Dual Funds. Late in 1966, several investment companies borrowed the "Split-capital trust" concept from England and offered it in the United States as closed-end dual funds. Each of these dual funds is divided into equal amounts, with one half sold as income-oriented and the other as growth-oriented. The income shareholders receive income from both segments of the entire portfolio, while the growth shareholders receive the capital gains or losses from both segments of the entire portfolio. Obviously the holders of the growth shares may expect sizable gains during a sustained period of industrial growth. Usually, the income shareholders are assured of 5 to 7 per cent return since this represents a mere 2½ to 3½ per cent income on the entire portfolio. In 1968, the leading dual funds were Scudder's Duo-Vest Fund, Wellington's Gemini Fund, Chase's Income and Capital Shares, American Dual Vest Fund, and Vance, Sanders & Company's Leverage Fund of Boston, (see Figure 8–2).

Industry Funds. Dozens of specialized investment company funds confine their holdings to carefully selected securities in a single industry. They serve the investor who wants his money placed in one industry's offerings. In life insurance he may choose among Life Insurance Investors, Capital Life Insurance & Growth Stock Fund, B. C. Morton Insurance Fund, and several others. In electronics his choices lie among Electronics Investors, Aviation-Electronics, Managed Funds-Electric, and others. For those who wish to concentrate their investment dollars, there are funds in metals, in petroleum, in Canadian enterprises, and in many other categories. The purchase of any of these funds signifies that an investment decision has been made to abandon diversification, but to retain portfolio selection and management services. In this small arena, it is unlikely that investment companies still may have very much to offer the investor.

Leverage Funds

A closed-end company may have in its capital structure so many bonds drawing low-interest rates, or preferred stocks with low-dividend rates, that most of the company's earnings may be available for common-stock dividends. In leverage funds of this type, common stocks tend to earn more in a rising or prosperous market; their losses, conversely, could be catastrophic in a falling market. An open-end investment company may achieve leverage indirectly by buying stocks in corporations whose capital structures are so laden with bonds, preferred stocks, or both, that the composition of the capital actually provides leverage.

Many investment companies used the leverage principle extensively in the 1920's. Sometimes the common stocks held by these companies actually were pyramided on debt. Among these companies were some like the Insull Utility Investments, Inc., the Shenandoah Corporation, and the Alleghany Corporation that brought financial losses to many of their shareholders and disrepute to investment companies in general. In recent years, leverage situations have been found in some closed-end companies, but these are neither conspicuous nor numerous.

The Hedge Funds. In the early 1960's, A. W. Jones & Co. managed two investment partnerships that spawned the idea of the highly speculative Hubshman "hedge fund" in 1966. The partnerships actually bought on margin, placed perhaps a fifth of their assets into bonds, and sold short upon occasion. The partnership operation was unusually successful and attracted attention to the new fund. It seems likely, however, that the managers of the fund, although sponsored by the Jones group, will exercise much more caution than they have with the partnership investments.[3]

The Proliferation of Mutual Funds. In the mid-1960's, mutual funds were launched by several insurance companies, by Sears Roebuck & Co., and by a Swiss company, Investors Overseas Services, Ltd. This last venture managed a fund that bought into several other funds in the United States and elsewhere. Known as the Fund of Funds (FOF), this venture could potentially control one or more U.S. funds. But since that would require registration with and supervision by the Securities and Exchange Commission, FOF did not seek to expand its holdings beyond a minority position held in several U.S. funds.[4]

Capital-Exchange Funds. A new investment pattern was introduced in 1960 with the Centennial Fund of Denver. This was followed immediately by the Congress Street Fund of Boston and by a number of others (see Figure 8–2). The so-called centennial-type fund, or capital-exchange fund, is closed-end. It is aimed at wealthy investors who seek diversification of their holdings and minimization of their capital-gains taxes. The Centennial Fund started by exchanging $25 million worth of its own shares, tax free, for $25 million worth of stock held by the investors. Generally, these funds insist on exchanging no less than $15,000 worth of securities; they charge a fee of 1 per cent to 4 per cent for each transaction depending on its size.

Between 1960 and 1967, the tax liability of an investor who held stock with a market enhancement of $95,000 at the time of his exchange would be postponed, according to an Internal Revenue Service ruling, until he sold his capital-exchange fund shares. In the meantime, he would have postponed taxes and achieved diversification as well. Many wealthy, aged investors also could have left these shares to their heirs in a trust agreement and delayed or avoided capital-gains taxation.

The capital-exchange funds are not permitted to sell additional shares, once the fund has been set up, and the shares may not be liquidated by resale to the company. An investor liquidates his holdings in these funds by selling them on the market for what they will bring.

Early reports on the original Centennial Fund and on the other funds indicated that their portfolios, containing a wide variety of stocks, had increased in asset value from their inception. The best known of these funds were Centennial Fund I, Centennial Fund II, Congress Street Fund, Federal Street Fund, Westminster Fund, Devonshire Street Fund, and Investors Capital Exchange Fund.

The capital-exchange funds, commonly known as "swap funds," were subject to envy and criticism because of their inherent tax benefit. Several times, prior to 1967, the shareholders were reassured that the Internal Revenue Service's ruling would not be reversed. Then, early in 1967, the IRS ruled that the thirty swap funds in existence and six in process of formation would not be nullified, but that the tax-exempt capital-gains advantage could not be permitted after a cut-off date late in 1967. This ruling, which had been anticipated, meant that virtually no new exchanges would be made into the so-called swap funds.

Special Situation Funds

A few funds engage in investments in special situations that produce a short-term advantage through a corporation's liquidation, merger, reorganization, or new-product introduction. The managers of these funds ferret out potential situations and calculate the probable risks and gains in them. They play the law of averages by entering into a number of these special situations simultaneously. Many other types of funds participate occasionally in special situations. For example, Atlas Corporation, a closed-end investment company, acquired nearly 10 per cent of Consolidated Vultee Aircraft Corporation in 1947 and entered into its management. A few years later, Atlas sold its interest at a profit to other groups that wanted control of Vultee. Among the investment companies, Value Line's special situation fund is noted for this type of investment.

INVESTMENT COMPANIES IN EVOLUTION

In spite of the high rate of returns enjoyed by the owners of investment company shares during the 1950's, the funds were under attack as the 1960's began. Reforms and new regulations followed in rapid succession in 1961 and 1962. The funds had benefited from an illusion of glamor caused by a dozen years of uninterrupted success. Perhaps the illusion had tarnished or had turned to disillusion as capital gains began to decline. It was hoped by the investment profession that the attacks and doubts would subside so that the funds might be recognized once more as a likely device to develop a "people's capitalism" in America.

Performance Record

The investment companies are most vulnerable to a charge of poor performance. This charge, if it can be sustained, challenges the efficacy of the fund managers and the validity of the fees collected. Moreover, it undermines the very idea that some advantage may be gained by pooling investments and investment knowledge. Few authors on this subject actually will make a flat statement in praise of investment company earnings. Most of them do recognize the general worth of the investment company concept, but they are inclined to qualify their statements about earnings with comments about the disbursement of capital gains, the tax advantages of investment in certain funds, the possibility of buying closed-end funds below their asset value, and the effect of fees on the net yield from the investment.

During prosperous periods, the investment companies have thrived, their customers have increased in numbers and in holdings, and the complaints about their fees have been less vehement. When stocks turn downward, however, there are dozens of dissenters against the investment companies. Hugh

Bullock, an apologist for investment companies, concedes the poor showing of these companies during the great depression, blaming pyramiding, poor judgment, and a few instances of fraud.[5] He summarized his views by quoting from the SEC findings on the subject:

> It can, then, be concluded with considerable assurance, that the entire group of management investment companies proper failed to perform better than an index of leading common stocks and probably performed somewhat worse than the index over the 1927–1935 period.[6]

During the mild recession of 1960 the sale of mutual fund shares declined, then revived in 1961 as the stock market revived. It would seem that many investors may have been merely "good weather friends" of the mutual funds. Perhaps, on the other hand, these were the marginal buyers who entered and dropped out of the market with the turn of stock prices and of their own fortunes. Or perhaps they had been oversold by the funds' stock distributors. Or, had more investors matured in 1960 and become ready to make their own investment decisions?

During the sharp decline in market quotations in 1962, the situation was different. The mutual funds declined more than either the Dow-Jones 30 industrial stocks or Standard & Poor's 500-stock index. The decline of the growth stock funds ranged from 20 per cent to 30 per cent in net-asset value in the first half of 1962, while the decline of the balanced funds ranged from 10 per cent to 22 per cent.[7]

As the stock market thrived during the mid-1960's, investment company shares thrived and sold in ever-increasing amounts. Claims and counterclaims were advanced to attest the superiority of the funds in this bull market. On the average, the funds gained nearly 19 per cent in asset value in 1965 compared with 14 per cent for stocks on the Dow-Jones industrial average list. The growth funds were especially popular. When the market began its decline in 1966, however, earnings and asset values tumbled, and fund sales fell off sharply. Growth funds were especially vulnerable. Even though new funds were being launched in the late 1960's, the myth of superior performance seemed to have been subjected to serious doubt.

Attacks on Management Firms

There was a strong inference that portfolio management for investment companies by management firms was less than effective if the funds failed to thrive and grow in periods of prosperity and adversity. Magazine articles began to challenge the current investment company practice of purchasing research and management responsibilities from others.[8] This practice seemed to be particularly objectionable when members of the management firm sat on the board of directors of the investment company; nor was this practice denied by Hugh Bullock, as we have noted, in his description of the typical American investment company.[9]

Late in 1960, at least fifty stockholder suits were brought against investment companies for payment of allegedly excessive fees to management companies. It was shown that eight management firms had averaged gains of approximately 100 per cent during 1961. Nevertheless, investment company proponents maintained that the paring of management fees would have had only a temporary effect on the funds.[10] A Delaware court immediately dismissed one of the key suits.

Sliding-Scale Fees. In settling a stockholders' suit in 1962, Affiliated Fund attempted to counter the attacks. The Fund proposed a compromise scale of fees that it would pay to its investment adviser, Lord, Abbett & Company. The Fund devised a sliding scale to consist of a rate of 0.25 per cent on the first $600 million of the Fund's $804 million assets and 0.2 per cent on the excess. It was hoped that the use of sliding-fee scales would reduce the fees paid by investment companies to management firms. This would remove at least one of the major objections raised by the critics of investment company management. Thereafter, management company fees were placed on a sliding-scale fee basis with increasing frequency and the Security and Exchange Commission virtually insisted upon this arrangement late in the 1960's.

Attack on Distributing Companies

Among its important provisions, the Investment Company Act of 1940 denied registered investment companies the opportunity to underwrite their own shares. This rule seemed necessary to prevent the overissuance of shares. Currently an investment company issues shares to an underwriter for sale to the public only after it has placed its securities in the hands of a custodial bank. The business of underwriting, promoting, and selling investment company shares has been transferred to distributing companies and brokers. In 1960, when these distributing companies came under attack, fifteen were identified as thriving corporations whose own stocks had risen rapidly on the over-the-counter market, in spite of the fact that their sales of investment company shares had not been good that year. As late as 1967, many persons looked askance at the distributing companies, and the Securities and Exchange Commission challenged the necessity for the size of the fees they were charging.

Accumulation Plans. The promotion and sale of investment company shares by distributing companies has led to a number of accumulation plans in which salesmen try to induce investors to buy shares in a plan by making payments at regular, frequent intervals. Some of these plans are so-called *voluntary plans*; the investor is free to decide each time a payment becomes due whether he will add to his accumulated holdings. Other plans are involuntary, *contractual plans*; the investor agrees in advance to continue the periodic payments on an installment basis for the duration of the contract.

As a reward for the sale of a contractual accumulation plan, the distributing company, its salesmen, the broker, or all of them become eligible for a large fee or commission on the face amount of the plan. This *front-end load* incites promoters and salesmen to sell intensively, using high-pressure tactics at times. Several investment companies, in the early 1960's, actually have raised their fees to 8.5 per cent of the face amount of the contract in the expectation that promoters and salesmen will persuade more investors to buy their shares. As a matter of fact, a huge front-end load may devour as many as the first half-dozen of the investor's payments. His holdings in the fund do not begin to accumulate until the fee has been extracted; should he drop the plan before its completion, no part of the fee will be returned. This aspect of the investment company business has rankled many a student of the subject. Quite a few investors and potential investors, in fact, are still unaware of its existence.

Level-Load Funds. In 1962, Lehman Brothers' One William Street Fund announced a contractual plan in which each payment made by an investor would bear a proportionate share of the total sales charge. The selling incentives were not dimmed, however, because dealers and salesmen were to be rewarded by means of advanced commissions on the investor's total contract. If the investor failed to fulfill his contract, he would be held responsible for half the difference between the sales charge he had paid and the cost of a front-end load. It was hoped that this level-load plan would be acceptable in the ten states that had outlawed contractual purchase plans because of the front-end load that they included.

No-Load Funds. Since 1949, no-load funds have appeared. Their chief characteristic has been that they could be bought without payment of the usual 8 or 8½ per cent fee. The no-load funds often are sponsored by investment management firms that collect their management fee, forego the services of distributing companies, and sell at cost. On occasion, the charge for selling and promoting these funds has been 1 per cent for acquisition of shares and 1 per cent for liquidating them. The lack of fees for dealers and brokers has retarded the sale of no-load fund shares, of course. But these funds have been sound and have grown moderately; the investors have saved money on fees. Among them, the best known are listed in Table 8-1.

Table 8-1. **Leading No-Load Mutual Funds**

Fund	Location	Recent Price per Share
American Investors	Larchmont, N. Y.	$36.38
Concord		15.83
de Vegh	New York	79.77
Energy	New York	15.44
Guardian Mutual	New York	27.55
Johnston Mutual	New York	20.40
Loomis-Sayles	Boston	—
Canadian Fund		29.86
Capital Development		11.79
Mutual		15.95
Mutual Shares	New York	17.26
Northeast Investment-Trust	Boston	17.42
One William Street	New York	16.10
Penn Square	Reading, Pa.	18.18
Pine Street	New York	12.63
Price G		23.22
Scudder	Boston	—
Balanced Fund		18.46
Common Stock		12.23
Special Situation		32.87
State Street		50.74
Steadman		21.51
Stein, Roe & Farnham	Chicago	—
Balanced Fund		21.44
International		14.03
Common Stock		14.00

SOURCE: *Wall Street Journal,* April 3, 1967, p. 21.

New Rules

In 1962, the SEC issued new rules requiring reports and full publicity about investment-advisement contracts with the mutual funds. The agency demanded the names of persons associated with these contracts and statements about the fees they received from the mutual funds. It also required the names of brokers and a statement of any reciprocal business arrangements made by them with the funds.

Self-Regulation. That same year, responsible leaders within the industry's trade association, the Investment Company Institute, agitated for a self-imposed code known as the *Guide to Business Standards, 1962.* The code covered five basic practices of special concern to Institute leaders.

First, mutual fund officers were warned against profiting from the use of inside information. This was prevalent in the practice of buying for their personal accounts the same securities bought and sold by the funds with which they were associated. Nor was this inside information to be revealed to brokers, dealers, and others until the buying or selling transactions had been completed.

Second, mutual fund officers also were warned against seeking and accepting favors from brokers and dealers who marketed their funds and also dealt in new stock issues.

Third, the funds were cautioned against buying securities just prior to dividend payments unless the purchase was made for other considerations. Funds were advised to seek the best execution of all buying and selling orders in order to attain the best price at the lowest commission.

Fourth, brokers and dealers were instructed to accept nothing of material value from a mutual fund except the usual compensation available to all brokers and dealers.

Finally, investment companies were urged to spell out in detail the information about their dividend policies and capital-gains distribution. Untimely announcements of these details were to be condemned because they merely confused the investors.

No doubt the responsible members of the Institute will abide by this code; their standards would have been above reproach without it. By 1970, the efficacy of this attempt at self-regulation may be judged by appraising the conduct of all members of the Investment Company community.

In 1965, unfortunately, the SEC reported a general laxity in the performance of the investment companies. It pointed especially at the fees charged by the management companies and the distributing companies. The SEC allegations met with resistance and the industry offered to modify certain practices and fee schedules. It is to be hoped that the funds will clean their own house and avoid the imposition of additional regulations and penalties. If this change transpires, the funds may yet become the most convenient and profitable way for novice and small investors to enter the market.

So much, then, for credit, savings, and the fine points of investment. In the next several chapters, we shall turn attention to the major personal expenditures, those related to housing, transportation, medical care, governmental services, and insurance.

QUESTIONS

1. List and discuss the advantages which shareholding in an investment company may have over independent investment by individuals.

Investment Companies in Evolution

2. Characterize investment companies and their growth before 1940 and after 1940.
3. What are the Securities and Exchange Commission's chief classifications of investment companies?
4. Distinguish between a Massachusetts trust and an incorporated investment company.
5. What are the functions of an investment management firm? Of a distributing firm? How may these be interrelated with the management of an investment company? What are the dangers in this arrangement?
6. List and discuss several important differences between a closed-end and an open-end investment company. What good and what controversial features do these two have in common? What are the chief characteristics of a typical American investment company?
7. List and briefly describe each of the nine important types of investment company portfolios which are described in this chapter. Which are diversified? Which are specialized? What are the advantages and disadvantages of each?
8. Has the performance of the funds justified their cost to investors over the years? Recently? In depression periods?
9. What is the nature of the controversy about management fees? Brokerage fees? Underwriting and trading fees? Front-end loading? What recent reforms have been attempted regarding these controversial points?
9. Do you believe that the mutual funds or anyone connected with them exercises an unusual influence on the stock market? On the American economy? What are your reasons for this belief?
10. Which of the following is likely to lead to effective reform in the investment company industry: (*a*) attempts at self-reform, (*b*) new SEC rules, (*c*) new types of investment company plans? Why do you hold this belief?
11. Note carefully all the key terms in this chapter and be prepared to identify each of them.

SELECTED READINGS
See the list of selected readings at the end of Chapter 6.

NOTES

1. Hugh Bullock, *The Story of Investment Companies,* Columbia University Press, New York, 1959, pp. 165–167.
2. John C. Clendenin, *Introduction to Investments,* McGraw-Hill, New York, 1964, p. 400.
3. "Those Fantastic 'Hedge Funds,' Personal Investing," *Fortune,* April 1966, p. 237; "Wall Street: Hedge Funds," *Newsweek,* December 5, 1966, p. 85; *Business Week,* April 12, 1966, p. 108.
4. *Business Week,* June 12, 1965, pp. 146–152.
5. Bullock, *op. cit.,* pp. 27–35, 47–55, 75–77.
6. Report of the Securities and Exchange Commission, *Investment Trusts and Investment Companies,* Part 2, Appendix J, p. 905, as cited in Bullock, *op. cit.,* p. 76.
7. *Business Week,* July 14, 1962, p. 98; *Wall Street Journal,* June 13, 1962, p. 1.

8. George B. Bookman, "How Good Are Mutual Funds?" *Fortune*, June 1960, pp. 144–196.
9. Bullock, *op. cit.*, p. 166; Edward S. Herman, "Mutual Fund Management Fee Rates," *Journal of Finance*, May 1963, pp. 360–376; Jack L. Treynor and Kay M. Mazuy, "Can Mutual Funds Outguess the Market?" *Harvard Business Review*, July-August 1966, pp. 131–136; Jack L. Treynor, "How to Rate Management of Investment Funds," *Harvard Business Review*, January-February 1965; Carol J. Loomis, "Where Manny Cohen is Leading SEC," *Fortune*, December 1966, pp. 163–220.
10. *Business Week*, December 16, 1961, p. 110.

PROBLEMS AND CASES

1. Obtain the prospecti of several mutual funds. Determine whether each of these is a corporation or an *investment trust*, and whether it is an *open-end* mutual fund or a *closed-end* investment company.
2. From the same prospecti, determine whether each of these funds is a *balanced fund* or a *specialized fund* and, if it is a specialized fund, what type of a specialized fund it is.
3. Refer to a financial publication. Find the prices of the shares of each of the investment funds referred to above that are listed for one month. How do their price movements compare with the movements of the Dow-Jones averages?
4. Which of the funds referred to above are *front-end-loading* funds; *level-load* funds; *no-load* funds?
5. Refer to the daily listing of Mutual Funds in *The Wall Street Journal*. Note that the no-load funds have identical "bid" and "asked" quotations. Note, also, that many of these no-load funds are offered by investment companies that have other funds.
6. What reasons can be given to account for the very rapid rate of growth of the Mutual Funds (see Figure 8-1)? Does their performance justify this growth?
7. Refer to Figure 8-2 or to a recent Monday morning issue of *The Wall Street Journal* or to any issue of *Barron's* and note in the listing of closed-end funds that many of them are selling at a discount from net asset value. Are the closed-end funds increasing in number? Are these funds permitted to increase the size of their portfolios?
8. How does a closed-end leverage fund differ from a nonleverage fund? What are the advantages? The disadvantages?
9. How can an open-end fund achieve leverage?
10. List the basic advantages offered by the funds. How long, approximately, would one have to hold a fund investment to reduce the buying fee to a point where it is comparable with commissions charged when one invests in stocks for one's own portfolio? How different would this answer be if the portfolio purchases must entail odd-lot fees?
11. What is a balanced fund? What are its advantages and disadvantages? How can a fund provide balance that a small investor cannot hope to achieve with his own portfolio?
12. If a balanced fund provides a hedge against certain risks, containing perhaps

50 per cent bonds and 50 per cent common stocks, would not the balanced fund's performance be mediocre if either inflation or deflation prevails?
13. If specialized funds, industry funds, common-stock funds are sought to avoid the mediocre performance of a balanced fund, are not the buyers' decisions similar to those of an investor who must select his own portfolio?
14. What controversy surrounds the flat percentage rate fees charged annually for management of the funds? If sliding-scale fee rates are to be charged in the future, will this be an advantage to the largest funds and their clients? If a management company manages several funds, should its combined fees be on a sliding-scale basis?
15. What controversy surrounded the fees charged by the distribution companies that promote the sale of the funds? How is this controversy illustrated in the case of (1) the front-end load, (2) level-load funds, (3) no-load funds? Do the poor sales of the no-load funds indicate that some promotional effort is necessary and that a reasonable charge for promotion may be justified? Ideally, shouldn't an investor search out those investments that seem to merit his attention, or should he wait for an investment to "be sold" by someone who comes to him?
16. If the Brown family's income-tax bracket is so high that it wishes to avoid taking capital gains, should it consider the growth segment of a Dual Fund? Explain. Should it have considered an Exchange Fund when they were still available? Explain. Would buying shares in a growth fund and holding them until retirement serve the Browns' goals? How and when do most funds distribute their capital gains? With what effect upon the taxes of high-income shareowners?
17. If the Smiths have a very low income, should they investigate the regulated funds? Explain.

PART III

MAJOR PERSONAL EXPENDITURES

9 EXPENDITURES FOR HOUSING

The best security for civilization is the dwelling; and upon adequate and attractive dwellings depends more than anything else the improvement of mankind. Such dwellings are the nursery of all domestic virtues, and without an adequate and attractive home the exercise of those virtues is impossible.

BENJAMIN DISRAELI

Without question, a home is the most important single purchase the average family ever makes. If present trends continue, the majority of American families will buy a home at least twice and will sell one at least once.[1] The expenditure for housing or, more exactly, the expenditure for occupancy, operation, maintenance, and furnishing of personal dwellings constitutes close to one-third of total consumer outlay in the United States.

Although everyone requires a dwelling, the size and type of accommodation chosen varies. These depend, for the most part, on income. They also depend on the proportion of income to be spent on housing, the purchaser's wants and preferences and the size and type of accommodations available at various prices.

The proportion of incomes that people spend on housing normally reflects the importance they place on the subject. To most people in the United States, their home is one of their most important status symbols. If they own their home, it is usually their principal possession.

Numerous psychological and social factors enter into the formulation of the concepts that determine the houses people want. They desire those houses that they can see themselves living in, the ones that they consider esthetically satisfying and socially acceptable.

The housing available on the market reflects what those who produce it believe can be sold at a high enough price and in a large enough quantity to make production profitable. However, housing units that are the most profitable to produce, or from whose ownership the greatest returns derive, may not be the ones that provide the best solutions to personal or family housing problems. Poor housing contributes to the spread of disease and the breeding of personal and social problems. Yet over 30 million people lived in housing classified as "deteriorating" or "dilapidated" by the Bureau of the Census, in 1960.[2] Generally they lived in these houses because they could not afford adequate housing.

The median values of existing homes whose mortgages were insured by the Federal Housing Administration—for example, standard one-family homes —increased over 70 per cent between 1950 and 1965.[3] However, incomes also rose, and those who could afford to continued to buy homes. More than 60 per cent of the American people own their own homes, although most of the homes are mortgaged.[4]

Expenditures for housing are increasing and in all probability will continue to do so in the foreseeable future. Housing remains associated with personal, social, technological, and economic problems that are growing in importance and in complexity. In consequence, to maximize the utility of the expenditures on housing will require a growing body of information.

COST OF HOUSING

The price of a typical low-cost, three-bedroom, two-bathroom, conventionally built home containing 1,415 square feet of living space was $18,678 in September 1964.[5] The average cost of constructing a single family dwelling in 1965, excluding the cost of land, was $16,250.[6] The median sales price of a new single family dwelling in 1965 was $19,300.[7] Looking at Table 9–1, it may be

Table 9-1. Monthly Costs of Housing

Selling Price	Mortgage[a]	Amortization[b]	Taxes[c]	Insurance[d]	Maintenance[e]	Utilities and Heat[f]	Total	Annual Income Required[g]	Percentage Able to Buy in 1964[h]
$12,000	$10,800	$ 61.34	$17.04	$2.04	$19.92	$22.00	$122.34	$ 7,340	43.1
16,000	13,800	78.38	22.72	2.72	26.56	26.00	156.38	9,383	27.3
20,000	16,800	95.42	28.40	3.40	33.20	30.00	190.42	11,425	19.5
25,000	20,550	116.72	35.50	4.25	41.50	35.00	232.97	13,978	9.5
30,000	24,300	131.75	42.50	5.00	50.00	44.00	270.25	16,215	5.0

[a] The mortgage is figured at 95 per cent of the first $9,000 of valuation and 75 per cent of the value above $9,000.
[b] Amortization is computed over a 30-year period at an interest rate of 5% per cent.
[c] Taxes are estimated at 1.7 per cent of value annually. This estimate will be far from the actuality in many cases.
[d] Hazard is estimated at 0.2 per cent of value annually.
[e] Maintenance is allowed for at the rate of 2 per cent of value annually.
[f] The estimate for utilities and heat is arbitrary. Heat will cost less in the South, more in very cold areas.
[g] Annual pre-tax income required is figured at five times the total cost of housing, including utilities and heat. This should be refigured in specific cases in terms of the actual percentage of its income the family wishes to allocate to housing.
[h] Family incomes are for 1964 from the Current Population Reports, Bureau of the Census.

SOURCE: The National Housing Conference, and the Bureau of the Census.

reasonably estimated that less than 22 per cent of the families in the United States in 1964 could afford the "typical" low-cost house described in the preceding sentence, if one-fifth of each family's income was to be used for housing, including utilities and heat. Actually, there is no hard and fast rule that obliges families to allocate one-fifth of their incomes to housing. They may spend as much as they wish on housing, provided that they consider their other wants in proper proportions.

Demand for Housing

The demand for a dwelling is not merely a demand for *new* homes. Many people want *used* houses, apartments, or mobile homes. Effective demand requires a purchaser who wants a particular commodity and is willing and able to pay the price for it. The demand for housing comes from many different persons wanting different types of dwellings and willing and able to pay many different prices.

Bachelors and spinsters, married people without children, divorcees, widows, widowers, and older couples whose children have left home generally do not buy houses. They prefer apartments, rooms in dormitories, hotels or boarding houses, or mobile homes. These groups are growing both in absolute numbers and as a percentage of the population of the United States. In contrast, in the next 25 years, the number of persons who have been buying homes in the suburbs, notably couples between 30 and 49 years of age with growing children, are expected to increase very little.

However, the Survey Research Center of the University of Michigan reported that about 40 per cent of American families would like to move to different homes. Of those who have moved in recent years, about two thirds have done so because they wanted a better home in a more attractive neighborhood.[8] This trend may very well continue. In the 1960's the number of children under 18 was expected to grow faster than the total number of households. Moreover, the teenage population, located mainly in families whose head was between 40 and 55 years old and frequently able to afford more expensive housing, would be growing in number at an even faster rate. To this group, a better home was often of the utmost importance. As a result, the market and the prices of better homes would tend to be sustained by strong demand. In fact, the market for replacements, that is, "better" homes, has been estimated at 625,000 units a year throughout the 1960's.

Sherman Maisel of the University of California has pointed out that actual physical scrappage of houses and apartments would average 300,000 units a year during the 1960's. Some are scrapped because of slum clearance. An additional number are destroyed by fire. More than 200,000 additional units a year would be removed from the supply to decay as the population of the United States continued its shift from farm to city and from the slums to better neighborhoods or to the suburbs. In all, about 687,000 units were removed annually in the period from 1965 to 1969 from the supply of housing, according to the National Association of Home Builders. The organization estimates that about 720,000 will be removed each year in the years between 1970 and 1974. It has been estimated that mobility patterns, household formation, and replacement needs would sustain a demand for 1,700,000 housing units in the second half of the 1960's. New construction would not be that high, however, because part of the demand—roughly 200,000 units a year—could be satisfied by converting old homes and apartments into multiple units, and by production of house trailers and seasonal bungalows.[9]

Housing Needs. Behind the demand for housing are actual housing needs. People buy homes because they need an enclosed area. Here they can keep warm and dry, eat, drink, sleep, dress; take care of personal hygiene, cosmetic, and sanitation needs; and take care of children and their needs. Here they prepare and preserve food, wash, iron, and store clothes and belongings, read, write, study, listen to music, watch television, work, play games, pursue hobbies, converse, entertain, sit and look out of the window, work on cars, plant flowers, and undertake the countless things that people do at home. This habitation must contain enough space, equipment, and facilities to permit the pursuit of these activities. Both the needs and the form that housing takes are determined largely by the cultural pattern, but within the accepted cultural norms there is much personal variation in the United States. No two individuals and no two families have exactly the same housing needs. Such needs, wants, and space requirements change with the particular individual or family patterns of activity in and around the housing unit. They change also with the belongings that the individuals wish to accommodate, with their personal tastes, and with the impression they desire to convey.[10]

Nevertheless, the American Public Health Association prepared a schedule of minimum floor space requirements in 1950 that took account of both health and living requirements. Table 9-2 contains the specification. It does not include all the possible functions of a home; nor does it divide the area into rooms. It does not make any differentiations because of diverse patterns of household composition. It does, however, provide a rough standard for measuring whether a family or a certain number of persons has enough floor space in a home.

The table indicates that as family size increases, the total floor space required does not increase proportionately. The reason for this is that, no

Table 9-2. Percentage Distribution of Minimum Floor Space Required for Basic Household Activities, by Number of Persons in Household

Household Activity[a]	1 Person Square Feet	1 Person Per Cent	2 Persons Square Feet	2 Persons Per Cent	3 Persons Square Feet	3 Persons Per Cent	4 Persons Square Feet	4 Persons Per Cent	5 Persons Square Feet	5 Persons Per Cent	6 Persons Square Feet	6 Persons Per Cent
Total:	380	100.0	765	100.0	989	100.0	1159	100.0	1420	100.0	1550	100.0
Sleeping and dressing	74	19.5	148	19.3	222	22.4	296	25.5	370	26.1	444	28.6
Personal cleanliness and sanitation	35	9.2	35	4.6	35	3.5	35	3.0	70	4.9	70	4.5
Food preparation, preservation	8	2.1	76	9.9	97	9.8	97	8.4	118	8.3	118	7.6
Food service and dining	53	13.9	70	9.1	91	9.2	105	9.1	119	8.4	146	9.4
Recreation, self-improvement	125	32.9	164	21.4	221	22.3	286	24.7	357	25.1	383	24.7
Extra-familial association	17	4.5	17	2.2	34	3.4	34	2.9	51	3.6	51	3.3
Housekeeping	48	12.6	91	11.9	110	11.1	127	11.0	146	10.3	149	9.6
Care of the infant or ill	...	...	124	16.2	124	12.5	124	10.7	124	8.7	124	8.0
Circulation between areas	20	5.3	20	2.6	35	3.5	35	3.0	45	3.2	45	2.9
Operation of utilities	...	...	20	2.6	20	2.0	20	1.7	20	1.4	20	1.3

[a] The space requirements for each activity are adjusted for overlapping area uses.

SOURCE: American Public Health Association, *Planning the Home for Occupancy*, Public Administration Service, Chicago, 1950, p. 15.

matter the size of the family, some space needs remain constant. Space demands for food preparation, for service areas, and for housekeeping, although they increase in actual feet required, decline in proportion as families grow larger. Space needs for sleeping, dressing, and social activities—"recreation" and "extra-familial association," in Table 9–2—increase in actuality and percentage.

The American Public Health Association's estimates of the minimum number of rooms required by families of varying sizes may be seen in Table 9–3. The association allows a minimum of one room per person. Beyond that, the requirements depend largely on the size and layout of the rooms, how they are used, and the composition of the household. A six-person household would need only three bedrooms, for example, if the family consisted of two parents, two girls reasonably close in age, and two boys reasonably close in age. Another six-person household of father, grandmother, two boys aged 21 and 9, and two girls aged 12 and 4 would need six bedrooms, according to the APHA standards. Maximum density standards, that is, the maximum number of people that can live in one room and maintain health, the Bureau of the Census has said, lie between 1.51 and 1.01 persons per room. However, much depends on the size and layout of the room.[11]

John Mabry has written:

> So little is known of the actual minimum space required for the maintenance of physical and emotional health that it is difficult to find exact estimates or precise criteria for determining housing spatial adequacy.[12]

In a study of 90 typical single-family homes representative of residences in the $13,000–$18,000 price range in the central New York area, Mabry found no home inadequate on the basis of the 1.51 persons-per-room ratio. When his index of spatial interaction took into account the number of square feet available for each two-person grouping among family members, he discovered many homes with inadequate dimensions. All three-bedroom homes in the sample,

Table 9-3. Minimum Size of Dwelling Unit, by Number of Rooms and Size of Household

Number in Household	Number of Rooms	Number in Household	Number of Rooms
1 person	1–2	4 persons	4–6
2 persons	2–4	5 persons	5–7
3 persons	3–5	6 persons	5–8

SOURCE: American Public Health Association, *Planning the Home for Occupancy*, Public Administration Service, Chicago, 1950, p. 39.

for example, were adequate for three-person families, but 31 per cent of the two-bedroom, single-family homes were inadequate for them. As family size increased, the proportion of adequate homes for six-person families declined to 3 per cent among two-bedroom dwellings and 37 per cent among three-bedroom types. Mabry found that sleeping and dressing were the two most common life activities for which space in two-bedroom homes was inadequate.[13]

Of the dwellings existing in the United States in 1960, 10.3 per cent lacked flush toilets; 11.9 per cent had no bathtub or shower; 7.1 per cent had no piped water within the structure; and 1.7 per cent had no heating.[14] As housing for people in this country, these dwellings were clearly inadequate.

Satisfaction of Housing Needs. How well housing needs may be satisfied depends largely on the amount of income available. It depends further on the percentage apportioned for housing and especially on the intelligence and ingenuity shown in maximizing the use of housing dollars. All too few individuals and families analyze their housing requirements carefully. All too few know how to achieve the most satisfaction from existing technology. Very few consult architects or employ them to design homes to fit their specific needs. Fewer know how to *buy* a house or rent an apartment. Real estate men feel that those who do know constitute less than 10 per cent of their customers.[15]

Fashions in Dwellings. Fashions in dwellings are influenced to a large extent by the consumer "home" magazines. *House Beautiful* and *Better Homes and Gardens* are two of these. The Home Magazine Section distributed with Sunday newspapers has influence similar to these "home" magazines. The magazines cater to every level of taste. Since the United States does not have any deeply embedded cultural prototypes for the proper home for specific social groups, the editors of these publications become arbiters of taste and wield a strong influence on both builders and buyers. Some of the magazines, *Arts and Architecture* for one and *Parents'* for another, indicate by comment or commendation what they consider to be well-designed or well-built homes. The commendations often serve to give houses "status" in a buyer's eyes. They reassure the prospective, relatively uninformed owner that he is buying a "good" house. To the extent that these houses satisfy the needs of specific families for homes that make them happy and comfortable, that wear well, and that are not too difficult to maintain, they may be said to be "good" houses. However, only the family that lives in a house can analyze specifically what it needs and wants in a home.

Homes are bought generally because they are in the "right" neighborhood.

They look impressive or attractive, they are in fashion, they are priced right, they are large enough, and people are tired of house hunting. Nonetheless, the magazines have served to make many home buyers demand such appliances as garbage disposals, dishwashers, ranges, and ovens as part of the finished house. They have, moreover, incited a desire for separate family rooms and living rooms, in the larger homes, and for an outdoor eating area. In short, they have standardized tastes so much that the large-scale builders, with their trade associations and their trade publications to guide them, have a good idea of what is fashionable before they produce their "models."

Homes designed by innovators or originators among the architects may set the trend in home fashions. Often these may accord with the ideas of their clients. Those that incorporate innovations in design, construction, or the use of materials are generally publicized. However, if the idea, technique, or new materials is too advanced for the majority of potential home buyers, or if it is too expensive, it will be slow to gain wide acceptance. Large-scale builders will, at least for a time, shy away from it. On the other hand, if the innovation fits prevailing living patterns, adapted versions of it may become widespread. The enlarged master bedroom and the ornate bathroom, found only in the most expensive homes a few years ago, have become commonplace in tract houses.

The wide acceptance of row houses, shell houses, prefabricated houses, cooperative apartments, and ornate, essentially stationary "mobile" homes* followed by some time their introduction by innovators. They were found to be good solutions to existing housing problems and were widely publicized. The publicity tended to reinforce the advertising of their marketers.

As the income level and the mobility of the population of the United States has increased, the housing market has become more and more like the automobile market. Individuals and families have replaced their houses, apartments, or trailers, trading them or buying new and more fashionable dwellings ever more frequently.

The Supply of Housing

In over six million housing units in the United States in 1960 occupancy was greater than the generally acceptable maximum of one person for each room.[16] But even more than increasing the quantity of housing proportionate to population growth, the problem in the United States is to improve the quality of both housing and neighborhoods. Too many still live in tenements and in slums, urban and rural; that is why, as income increases, the demand for better housing is so insistent.

* See pp. 340 and 341.

The building industry has been fairly responsive to anticipated demand. In fact, the supply of housing, insofar as new units have been concerned, has been rather elastic. The quantity of houses or apartments built and offered for sale has increased greatly and rather rapidly when builders have thought that they could sell them at high enough prices and sell a large enough number of units to obtain a profit. New units can be built and offered for sale within 60 days after the start of construction. The result is a periodic oversupply in some areas and some decreases in price from time to time. More often, however, rather than reducing prices, builders simply add attractions to make the houses or buildings more salable. Whether these add to the value of the home depends on the buyer's appraisal.

The Housing Industry. Most builders of housing units in the United States are entrepreneurs. They buy the land, arrange for plans and specifications to be drawn, let the contracts to subcontractors, pay for the construction, negotiate for any financing they may need, and commit themselves for the payment of the debt. Speculative builders of housing units frequently are land developers as well. They pay for the costs of preparing the sites on which the houses will be built, and arrange to have streets, street lighting, sewers, and water pipes installed. They also arrange to have the public utilities put in gas lines, equipment for the furnishing of electricity and telephone service, and means of rubbish disposal. Some then hire contractors; others do their own contracting and building and only hire subcontractors, such as plumbers or electricians, whom they may not have in their own organizations. The high-volume developers and builders, of whom there are only a handful, have men of all skills on their own building staffs. These men, plumbers or painters, for example, progress from one house or building to another performing the same operations. Since these buildings—tract houses for the most part, although apartments are built in this way, too—are semimass-produced, the costs of constructing them may be considerably less than for the custom-built or few-of-a-kind building.

Conversely, custom-built houses or buildings are constructed individually for the owner. No matter how efficient the contractor, the cost of building only one of a kind normally will be much higher than for the mass-produced or semimass-produced standardized unit. This is the premium paid for being able to specify one's exact wants.

Small-scale builders cannot utilize many of the advanced techniques or much of the expensive construction equipment that enables volume builders to operate so economically. They are also unable to buy materials in quantities large enough to reduce unit purchase costs. Often they may be prejudiced, in addition, against the use of factory-built components. These cost less but are not exactly the products they have been accustomed to using.

The large-scale tract builders, on the other hand, erect a salable house at a relatively low price. Their price reflects the prevailing level of taste of a large enough group of potential buyers to provide a sufficient market. They build standardized houses, even though floor plans and exterior trims may vary, or there may be a choice of paint colors. Naturally, it pays them to utilize the advanced techniques akin to those familiar to other industries for many years. For example, they purchase standard sections cut to standard sizes that can fit into standardized frames. A shell of a house using these sections can be assembled in a few hours. The number of houses built simultaneously makes the use of these techniques and the buying of expensive mechanized equipment feasible. This enables the builders to cut down on the cost of labor and produce at lower prices. Yet despite the technological advances made by the large-scale builders, the housing industry as a whole is still notoriously backward.

Building Codes. Most cities, counties, and other incorporated localities in the United States have building codes that are more or less archaic, depending on how recently they have been revised and who had a hand in the revision. If a new material is substituted for a material in which the locality has an economic interest, the code may prohibit its use. Or, if a new technique cuts down on the hours of work required on a house by a local union, its use may be barred. "Any attempt to change a code brings a cry from labor unions and trade associations."[17]

Needed in the interest of safety, codes often cause a building to be far more expensive than it otherwise would be. Still, building codes are not alone in raising the cost of building. The Federal Housing Administration's standards, which have to be met by any dwelling before its mortgage will be insured by that agency, may act to discourage practicable innovations that will result in "more house for less money." Yet, that agency's standards were established so that uninformed home buyers would be protected against poor construction and shoddy materials. In this respect, the standards have served well.

Availability and Use of Sites. Since 1950, land prices for home building have soared anywhere from 100 per cent to 3,760 per cent.[18] For the most part, this has been the result of tract builders bidding up the price of the cheapest land to build on and then the next cheapest as cities have spread out. Much land that is harder to build on has been by-passed, and much good land has been held off the market by speculators. The results are that most cities tend to sprawl rather haphazardly over the landscape; close-in sites that are easy to build on are generally in short supply; neighborhoods are quite different from what they could be if suitably planned; and housing is in greater demand and more expensive than it need be.

Availability of Financing. When money is cheap and lenders are willing to make loans at relatively low rates of interest, builders find that the cost of borrowing the money to pay for land, labor, and materials is lower. Builders normally work with little money of their own. Low-interest rates give them an added possibility of making higher profits and, in consequence, they will tend to increase the number of houses they build. In addition, a lower-interest rate for mortgage loans makes buying a home less costly and therefore more attractive. If other factors are not offsetting, builders can hope to sell more homes when interest rates are low. At such times the number of housing starts, that is, the number of houses that builders start to build during a given period, increases as builders eye the prospect of profit.

Types of Housing. In some localities the supply of housing for some minority groups is severely limited. Prices of homes increase and housing becomes relatively expensive when one of these groups moves into such a neighborhood and others move out. The shortage in low-priced, adequate housing for families in minority groups as well as for low-income families has been solved to some extent by the building of row houses, shell houses, prefabricated houses, mobile housing, and public housing.

Row houses are built with no space between the houses. Consequently, land costs for each house are less, and they can sell for as little as $9,000.

Shell houses are unfinished houses. The buyer purchases a structure that usually has a foundation, exterior shell, roof, walls, ceilings, floors, plumbing, electrical wiring, heating system, closets, windows, and a door. Beyond that, he finishes the construction of his house. He paints, finishes the floors, lays tile, or both; installs the plumbing and electrical fixtures; pours and lays the cement for walks, driveway, and other cemented areas; buys and installs cabinets, the kitchen sink, and all the appliances, puts in shelves, and does whatever else he wishes to finish the house to make it livable. In addition, he may buy a shell garage and finish that as well. Unfinished houses may be purchased with a site or, in some areas, may be moved by the owner to his own lot. In either case, they are relatively inexpensive.

Prefabricated houses are houses whose components have been cut, shaped, processed, and assembled as much as possible at the factory. The purchase, which includes the preassembled sections of walls, exterior siding, foundations, and other components, is shipped to a prepared site where the house is completed. Such houses usually cost at least one sixth less than a similar house entirely constructed on the site.

Mobile homes were originally small house trailers. They were meant to be towed to locations where they could be parked while the occupants spent the night or a relatively short vacation period before moving on or going home. House trailers, however, soon were found to be an inexpensive type of housing for those who could tolerate cramped quarters, whether the occupants were itinerant or not. Trailer parks, which had been established to cater to travelers and itinerant workers, found themselves with more or less permanent residents who stayed for months or years in one location. Many trailer parks have been designed for these long-term residents. Especially in California and Florida, there are many with playgrounds for children, swimming pools, various other types of recreational facilities, laundry facilities, snack bars, and some of the atmosphere that used to be associated only with country clubs.

The mobile homes themselves frequently have complete bathrooms, hot water, and two bedrooms. Many of them now sell for as much as $8,000 and, once located on a site, are not meant to be moved. In fact, many can be moved only if towed by large trucks. Supplementary units to make the mobile home L-shaped, picture windows, and fireplaces are available to make these units seem even more like permanent homes. In many states, trailer dwellers are now being taxed on their homes, even though at a much lower rate than for conventional homeowners. In 1966 there were an estimated 2 million mobile homes in use in the United States. They housed about 6 million people and were located in or shuttling between nearly 20,000 trailer parks. Mobile home shipments were estimated at 20.7 per cent of total single-family residential "starts" in 1965, a not inconsiderable proportion.[19]

A stationary mobile home and its parking lot can be bought in some mobile-home communities for a 25 per cent down payment. The balance is covered by a mortgage similar to a real estate mortgage and subject to 7 per cent interest. Originally, all trailers were financed through the use of costly chattel mortgages, and many still are. These usually terminate after five to seven years and are subject to a 6 per cent discount, which is the equivalent of about 11 per cent simple interest. The improvement in mobile-home financing undoubtedly will mean that more units will be sold for retirement housing and for housing for low-income families. But, unless one buys a parking space, the rent for the space in the "mobile home park" is generally between $25 and $125 or more a month. This outlay must be considered when comparing the cost of living in a mobile home to the cost of living in a house or an apartment.

Public housing, or housing built for and managed by governmental units, consists for the most part of federally owned housing projects for the families of servicemen, or of federally aided, state or municipally owned, multiunit projects to provide housing for low-income families and "senior citizens." Some cities are building single-family homes; like the multiunit projects, these are being located in previously blighted areas or on vacant land. In 1965, there were almost 750,000 dwelling units in low-rent housing programs under the Public Housing Administration of the Housing and Home Financing Agency of the federal government, and in recent years they have been increasing at the average rate of approximately 38,000 a year.[20]

The families living in public-housing units pay low rents and have better quality housing than would be available to them otherwise. This is because the community is paying for it, in part, by way of taxes. Even when the housing project is financed through a bond issue, the interest that must be paid on the bonds reduces the revenue from the projects, which may or may not be self-supporting and self-liquidating. Still, it must be remembered that the social costs resulting from human maladaptations caused by inadequate housing may be much higher than the taxes paid to prevent the problems that occasion these costs.

Philosophically, both political parties are committed to checking urban blight. However, local tax structures, economic and social disadvantaging of certain groups, inadequate city planning, and inadequate enforcement of health and safety codes continue to contribute to the decay.

Housing projects for the elderly are either apartment houses or courts comprised of single-unit dwellings in a landscaped setting. Those who no longer want the responsibility of homeownership or cannot afford it and want to live with a group of their peers seek out these quarters.

Cooperative apartments are units in multifamily dwellings. Their occupants ordinarily have bought a proportionate number of shares in a corporation, a proportionate interest in a trust of which they are then the beneficiaries, or a proportionate share in a cooperative. The corporation, the trust, or the cooperative owns and manages the apartment buildings. The occupant pays monthly carrying charges that cover his share of payments on the mortgage, taxes, and maintenance costs.

In a *condominium*, occupants purchase apartments to which they obtain deeds of ownership. In addition to owning their own apartments, they also own, as a result of purchase, a proportionate share of the common elements of the building, its land, roof, utility system, entry, and halls. The occupants as owners are taxed on their apartments and on their fractional interests in the common elements of the building. The condominium owners must agree among themselves how to manage the building and share maintenance costs.

Cooperative apartments and condominiums or the so-called planned unit developments have proven to be popular in areas where land is relatively scarce. For one thing, they give the older people who constitute a large number of their occupants a place where they would rather be. For another, they may house them among groups of the same kind and provide opportunity for socializing. For a third, there is the lessened responsibility for and expense of upkeep; because of the cooperative arrangement, the amount paid tends to be less than is required for a house or, often, for a comparable apartment. And, finally, for many such dwellers, both in cooperatives and condominiums, there is the tax advantage similar to that enjoyed by homeowners.

However, there are disadvantages to this type of housing arrangement. The owner assumes the risk of ownership. He loses his apartment if he cannot meet the payments. He loses the interest he might be earning on his down payment. This factor should be taken into account when making the comparisons on which to base the decision to go into this type of arrangement. So should the facts that property ordinarily depreciates, that there is a legal liability connected with being the partial owner of a building or the owner of a part of one, and that one may have difficulty in selling one's interest in the cooperative or one's "unit."

Rental housing, most often apartments in multiunit high-rise buildings but also "flats" in row houses or other older buildings, or garden-type buildings, exists in every urban area. Its supply tends to increase when demand is expected to increase or there is a shortage and building and interest costs are low enough to permit competitive rates of return to be earned on completed buildings.

Cost of Adequate Housing

Only an individual or a family can decide what constitutes adequate housing in the light of his or its needs. Having done so, either one's commitment for housing will result only partially from subjective decision. The prices of various types and amounts of housing depend on the supply and demand in the locality chosen. The individual or the family is confronted with what is available at diverse prices. From this array, either may accept or reject the housing for sale or for rent, or may choose to build.

Prices of Homes. The median price of the new one-family homes with a mortgage insured by the Federal Housing Administration in 1965 was $16,190. This was $4,077, or about one third more than the average of $12,113 in 1955. The average price of a new one-family house carrying a conventional mortgage granted by a savings and loan association in 1965 was $23,700 as compared with an average of $12,928 in 1955.[21]

Mortgages increased correspondingly, from a median value of $10,634 on new FHA homes in 1955 to a median value of $15,574 in 1965; and from an average of $8,135 on new or existing conventionally mortgaged homes in 1955 to an average of $18,106 on new homes in 1965. However, down payments on the FHA homes decreased from an average of 15.1 per cent in 1955 to 5.7 per cent in 1965; from 5.3 to 2.2 per cent on homes whose mortgages were guaranteed by the Veterans' Administration; and from 37.1 to 24 per cent on new and existing homes carrying conventional savings and loan association mortgages.

The typical first-mortgage loan made in 1965 was at least one-third larger than in 1955 because of higher prices for homes and the higher loan-to-price ratio on houses financed by mortgages. Since demand for one-family homes may not always be as strong as it was during this period, prices may not always rise as rapidly. Yet, as prices for houses rise, mortgages probably will tend to rise, too, both in absolute amounts and as a proportion of the purchase price. However, down payments may decrease concomitantly. Thus, despite the continuing rise in house prices, more people should be able to afford homes and, in more cases than at present, down payments will cease to be required.

The average size of the houses bought increased from 900 square feet in 1955 to 1,415 square feet in 1964, or over 57 per cent. Moreover, there was a proportionately greater increase in the number of houses bought that had basements, garages, and two or more bathrooms.[22]

The higher prices of homes over the years can be attributed to various causes. They can result from rising costs, from more houses being bought, from the liberalization of credit terms that have enabled more people to meet the payments on higher-priced homes, and from the reductions in down payments that have enabled more people to afford them. It should be noted perhaps that the median income of the buyers of one-family homes advanced at a rate comparable to the increase in prices of these homes between 1946 and 1966.

Breakdown of the Price of a House. Why are housing prices at present levels? Rents charged for housing units and prices paid for houses or trailers tend to settle where supply and demand are in equilibrium. When apartments or houses are scarce relative to the demand for them, their prices are relatively high. When they are in plentiful supply, their prices are relatively low. Unless builders can cover their costs and obtain loans, they will not build. Supply will be curtailed, and prices will tend to rise until costs are covered.

What are the builder's costs? Table 9–4 shows the typical costs for a three-bedroom, two-bathroom, conventionally built house in 1966. This is an "average" house. Total monthly costs on this house would approximate $205.* Almost 30 per cent of the cost of the house pays for the lot, which is about

* See Table 9-1.

Table 9-4. Typical Costs of Average Single-Family Merchant-Built Three-Bedroom, Two-Bathroom Conventionally Built House in 1966[a]

Item	Cost to Buyer (Dollars)	Per Cent
Lot	6,000	27.3
On-site labor		
Erection, painting, etc.	4,000	18.2
Electricity	400	1.8
Plumbing	1,000	4.5
Heating and air conditioning	1,800	8.2
Appliances	800	3.6
All other components and materials	4,000	18.2
Financing and legal fees (construction mortgage, financing, closing fees)	1,000	4.5
Builder's overhead	1,000	4.5
Sales cost	1,000	4.5
Builder's profit	1,000	4.5
	22,000	100[b]

[a] Air-conditioned 1,650 square foot house.
[b] Per cents do not sum to 100 because of rounding.
SOURCE: *House and Home,* August 1966, p. 63.

average. A little less than 50 per cent covers the labor, component, and material costs, excluding appliances, and slightly less than 5 per cent remains as the builder's profit. Many volume builders of tract units work on an even slimmer profit margin. Labor costs are less on shell houses and prefabricated houses, which accounts in part for their lower prices.

Additional Costs. Only in very exceptional cases does the price of the new house include complete landscaping. An additional 3 to 5 per cent of the cost of the house is required ordinarily for this purpose, but this may range even more, depending on the landscaping desired. Many homeowners do most of the work involved themselves, which cuts down on this outlay to some extent.

In a new area, special assessments for sidewalks, sewer lines, streets, street lighting, trees to border the street, and wider access roads to accommodate the increased flow of traffic, may be more than likely. Then, too, some thought should be given to the cost of furnishing the house and buying the necessary appliances, which in this case are not included in the purchase price.

Cost of Operation and Maintenance. A careful study concluded: "A typical home costs its owner about 10 per cent per year,"[23] that is, 10 per cent of the value of the home. The costs included are maintenance and improvement, taxes, insurance, interest on the mortgage loan, amortization of the mortgage, and imputed interest on the investment in the house, which is the amount that the same sum of money could have earned from another investment. This accords roughly with the National Housing Conference figures in Table 9–1.

The study noted that "many of the costs of homeownership [were] subject to the owner's control, but [that] the time of their occurrence and their amounts [could not] be readily anticipated."[24] It would consider the 2 per cent allowed for maintenance in the National Housing Conference table as too low. The types and frequency of maintenance expenditures, which it found that a typical homeowner incurs, may be seen in Table 9–5.

Maintenance costs may be lower for homeowners who are adept at making their own repairs. For that matter, many homeowners who are skilled in the particular types of work required may improve their property at modest cost. Hiring outside labor for home maintenance or improvement projects may be very costly. Still, the by-passing of competent craftsmen when maintenance

Table 9–5. **Types and Frequency of Maintenance Expenditures Incurred by a Typical Homeowner**

Frequency	Type of Expenditure
Every 4 years	Painting all interior rooms
	Restoring or improving lawn and plantings
	Painting and exterior of house
	Making major repairs to hot water heater
Every 5 years	Completely renovating lawn and plantings
	Replacing hot water heater
	Repairing plumbing and/or fixtures
	Repairing roof and drains
Every 6 years	Repairing, replacing, or installing heating unit
	Replacing plumbing (pipes) and/or fixtures
	Repairing roof and drains
	Treating the foundation for termites
Every 7 years	Replacing and/or painting screens
	Repairing plumbing (pipes)
	Repairing chimney
	Replacing, repairing and/or installing walks
Every 8–12 years	Replacing roof and drains
	Repairing the foundation
	Oiling or painting roof

SOURCE: Fred E. Case, *Cash Outlays and Economic Costs of Homeownership*, Bureau of Business and Economic Research, University of California at Los Angeles, 1957, p. 8.

work is necessary may be even more costly. In fact, an ounce of prevention—against termites, for example—may save hundreds of dollars. The alert homeowner develops a sense of timing as he accumulates the experience that enables him to make better decisions concerning when and how to care for maintenance economically.

There have been many instances, to be sure, of firms, engaged in home maintenance or improvement activities, that have misrepresented services to be performed and that have persuaded unwary homeowners to sign contracts for unwarranted sums. As an antidote there are excellent government publications on the care and repair of the home.[25]

Costs of home operation, over and above those already mentioned, average more than 10 per cent of a family's annual expenditures.[26] These include the amounts paid for utilities, that is, gas, electricity, water, telephone service, and garbage and waste disposal; for household help, for household and gardening tools and equipment, for cleaning supplies, for plants and seeds, and for other things. They vary widely and are higher for some houses and in some localities than for others. Besides these, there are the costs of home furnishings, which total about another 15 per cent per year of the expenditures of American families.

Fire insurance on the home and its furnishings, insurance against wind and storm, theft insurance on valuable personal property, and insurance against liability due to accidents that may occur on the property are considered essential. This probably will cost another 2 per cent of the value of the house.[27] In addition, it may be prudent to take out mortgage insurance—insurance designed to pay off the mortgage in case the head of the family dies. Rates charged by different insurance companies vary, as do rates in different localities and the coverage provided by different policies. Consequently, it pays to shop for homeowner's insurance, just as it does for any other type of insurance.*

All in all, the costs of homeownership are not low, and there are questions to be answered by each person in every case: Is it worth it to me? Can I afford it without giving up something I want more?

Rents. Rents vary with the prices of homes. The consumer price index for residential rent in the United States reached 110 in 1966.[28] The index for the average rent paid in 1957–1959, the base years, was 100. Looking back over the entire period since the Second World War, one finds residential rents have risen faster than prices as a whole.

Rents are higher for luxury apartments, not only because they contain more space but because of their location in fashionable areas that command

---

* For an extended discussion of such insurance, see Chapter 13.

high rents, the status of the address, the appearance of the building, the appurtenances, and the services offered. The lowest-priced units are in shanties and slums, not in public housing. However, since public housing is subsidized, many of the best values in housing are to be found in these projects. Ordinarily only those in the lower-income groups are eligible, and the locations are not particularly desirable.

The question as to whether to buy or rent is considered later in the chapter.

HOUSING FINANCE

Only a small percentage of those who buy real estate can afford to pay the entire purchase price in cash. Most people in the United States make a down payment and raise the rest of the money needed to buy the property by mortgaging it.

Mortgages

A mortgage is a conveyance of property, either real or personal, as security for the payment of a debt. The lender gives the borrower who wishes to buy the property the money after the borrower has signed a note secured by the mortgage on the property. When the note is paid, the mortgage is released. The person who mortgages his property is called the *mortgagor*. The person to whom the mortgage is given, that is, the lender, is the *mortgagee*.

The straight mortgage,* the most common form of mortgage loan until about twenty years ago, has now generally given way to the direct-reduction or amortized mortgage loan.

The Amortized or Direct-Reduction Mortgage. This type of mortgage specifies that the borrower make a fixed monthly payment that includes the interest on the loan, a partial reduction of the principal and, in many cases, a prorated portion of the annual taxes and insurance charges. As time passes, the interest portion of the monthly payment decreases and the amount available for the repayment of the principal correspondingly increases, as may be observed in Table 9–6.

Since interest is paid on a diminishing principal, which averages one-half of the original sum borrowed, total interest charges paid on this type of mortgage loan are considerably less than those paid on the nondiminishing principal of the straight mortgage. The main advantage of this type of mortgage,

---

* A straight mortgage requires only that interest be paid during the term of the mortgage. When the mortgage comes due, the entire principal is due and either has to be paid or refinanced.

Table 9–6. Illustration of Monthly Amortized Loan Payments: Amount Borrowed, $10,000; Interest Rate, 6 Per Cent; Term of Loan, 20 Years

		Monthly Payment			Balance Due at End of Month
Years	Months	Total	Interest Portion	Principal Repayment	
0	1	$71.70	$50.00	$21.70	$9,978.30
0	2	71.70	49.90	21.80	9,956.50
0	3	71.70	49.80	21.90	9,934.60
3	1	71.70	45.70	26.00	9,120.40
3	2	71.70	45.60	26.10	9,094.30
3	3	71.70	45.50	26.20	9,068.10
10	1	71.70	32.20	39.50	6,404.10
10	2	71.70	32.00	39.70	6,364.40
15	1	71.70	18.40	53.30	3,635.60
18	1	71.70	8.00	63.70	1,530.60
19	10	71.70	0.90	70.80	116.10
19	11	71.70	0.60	71.10	45.00
Final payment		45.20	0.20	45.00	0.00

however, is that the fixed monthly payment is easier for most families to budget and meet. It does not require them to discipline themselves as rigorously to plan and save for quarterly or semiannual interest payments on the straight mortgage, or to accumulate and put aside the principal during its life.

First and Second Mortgages. If a mortgage loan cannot be obtained in an amount sufficient to cover the difference between the down payment and the full cost of the property, the prospective purchaser may try to obtain a second mortgage. This is simply a second-mortgage loan secured by the same piece of property, and its claim in the event of foreclosure would be subordinate to that of the holder of the first mortgage. On second mortgages lenders may demand as much as 8, 10, 12, or 14 per cent per annum in interest because of their weaker claim against the property. If two loans are not enough to bridge the gap between the down payment and the full price of the property, the borrower may negotiate a third-mortgage loan, in exceptional cases. Since these loans entail an even greater risk than second-mortgage loans, interest rates on them tend to be yet higher. Interest rates have to be high enough to make the lender feel the risk is worth taking.

Trust Deeds. A trust deed is a deed to property held, in trust, by a third party as security for a note. Thus it takes the place of a mortgage. This form of security for a loan is used extensively because it renders the note it secures negotiable, that is, salable for cash. Just as there are first, second, and third mortgages, so there are first, second, and third *deeds of trust*, or trust deeds.

Open-End Mortgages. On an open-end mortgage loan, the lender may increase the amount of the loan after it has been in effect for a time. The amount of an ordinary mortgage, to the contrary, is fixed. The advantage of having an open-end mortgage is that additional funds may be obtained from the same lender, once he has been convinced of the borrower's integrity and ability to pay. This is usually easier and cheaper than obtaining a loan from another source.

Early Repayment. At buyers' insistence, the repayment contract on the mortgage loan may contain a clause that permits them to pay off the loan in its entirety before the expiration date and thereby save themselves the interest they would have had to pay during the remaining life of the loan. If this clause is not included, they may be liable for interest for the entire term of the loan, even if they pay it off before it becomes due; or a penalty may be exacted for early repayment.

On anything as important financially as a mortgage loan, an attorney familiar with real estate law and practice should be consulted to make sure beforehand that the terms of the contract are as favorable as any that might be obtained. Few laymen are experts in real estate law and finance.

Sources for Mortgage Loans

Mortgage loans are made by several types of investors—commercial banks, mutual savings banks, savings and loan associations, life insurance companies, mortgage companies, and private noninstitutional lenders. Currently, commercial banks hold about 14 per cent of the mortgage loans on homes in the United States.[29] Mutual savings banks located in 17 states, predominantly in the northeastern section of the United States, also hold about 14 per cent of the outstanding home mortgage loans.

Savings and loan associations (also known as savings associations), building and loan associations, cooperative banks, and homestead associations, of which there are approximately 6,200 throughout the United States, have about 44 per cent of the mortgage loans on homes. About 85 per cent of their assets are tied up in home-mortgage loans. These associations operate under a Federal Home Loan Bank Board charter or under special state charters designed for this type of business, but primarily they are local in character. They are the main source for conventional loans not insured by the government, still the most prevalent form of mortgage loan in the United States.

Life insurance companies hold another 14 per cent of the home-mortgage loans. If one of these companies does not have a branch office in a particular area, a mortgage firm or mortgage broker acts as the company's representative to arrange for the loan. Mortgage companies or mortgage bankers, as their names imply, are in business especially to make mortgage loans. Some lend out their own funds. Some have access to or are agents for firms or persons with money to invest in mortgages. Many specialize in making loans on more profitable second mortgages. In addition, any person with money to invest may make a loan secured by a mortgage or may buy a mortgage; many have done so. Approximately 10.5 per cent of the loans secured by mortgages on nonfarm homes in the United States are held by mortgage companies or private individuals.

Mortgage loans at lower interest rates, because they entail less risk or because a government agency such as the Federal Housing Administration or the Veterans' Administration has set the rate that may be charged, are available mainly from banks and mortgage companies. Because of their volume of lending, these institutions may find loans at lower rates of interest profitable (see Figure 9–1). However, owing to competition, the interest rates charged on loans entailing about the same amount of risk tend to be nearly equal.

Interest Rates

Interest is the price paid for the use of money. In the case of the private lender, interest repays him for foregoing the use of his money in some other manner for the length of time it is out on loan. In the case of a bank, most of the money lent is depositors' money. As a matter of fact, the money loaned by any lending institution will be depositors', investors', or borrowed money on which interest must be paid. The institution must charge a high enough interest rate to enable it to pay interest to its depositors or to those from whom the money was borrowed originally and still make a profit.

Interest partially repays a lender for taking the risk that the money may be lost. Those who borrow pay the interest, on the other hand, because they expect to derive a benefit from the use of the money equal to or greater than the cost of the interest. For every type of loan and every degree of risk there is a certain amount of money available at each interest rate. The less the risk, the lower is the rate of interest. The lower the interest rate, the larger is the number of prospective borrowers willing and able to pay it. For a particular type of loan with a specific degree of risk, the interest rate at a particular time will tend to settle at the level at which the amount of money available at that rate meets the amount of money required. Here, too, as elsewhere, the laws of supply and demand prevail to establish the rate of interest. Rates of interest fall when the

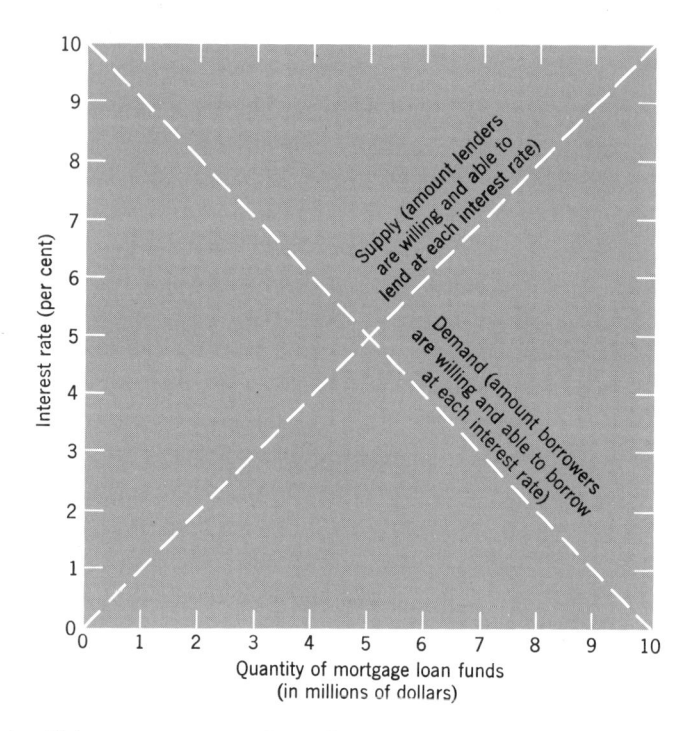

Figure 9-1. **If interest rates are low, the demand for mortgage loans increases; if interest rates are high, the supply of funds for mortgage loans increases.** Here, the market is in equilibrium when the interest rate is 5 per cent. At this rate, 5 million dollars will be lent.

supply of money at a specific rate exceeds the demand; they rise when the demand at that rate outweighs the supply.

Closing Costs

In general, borrowers assume all of the costs incurred by the lender in making a loan on property. Such costs are called closing costs. They generally include the cost of making the appraisal; a survey of the property by a licensed surveyor; the report on the credit rating of the borrower; the search for evidence of clear title; the recording of a certificate of title; the policy of title insurance; the recording of the trust deed or any other deeds involved and of any necessary assignments or conveyances of title; and the drawing of any necessary documents; in addition to any legal fees, notary fees, transfer fees, escrow fees, and any and all other loan-origination costs. The latter may include brokerage fees. Sometimes the parties resort to escrow. An escrow is the holding of all of the money and documents involved in a transaction by a neutral third party who takes all necessary steps to make sure that the parties discharge their contracted responsibilities so that the property may be conveyed from the seller to the buyer in accordance with the law. Some of the legal terms that apply to property transactions will be explained presently. Closing costs, in most cases, have to be paid in cash before the sale of the property is completed. Points (a point is 1 per cent of the purchase price) charged by lenders to offset the difference between established rates on government-insured or guaranteed loans and rates obtainable on conventional mortgage loans are generally included in the closing costs.

THE GOVERNMENT AND HOUSING FINANCE

Both the federal and state governments have established agencies to encourage the building and financing of housing. The Federal Government's Department of Housing and Urban Development includes the Federal Housing Administration and the Public Housing Administration; the Veterans' Administration; the Federal National Mortgage Association; and the Federal Home Loan Bank.

Federal Housing Administration

The Federal Housing Administration, established in 1934, a major constituent agency of the Department of Housing and Urban Development, is the main governmental agency responsible for improving the housing of families in the United States. This agency primarily insures mortgages, but it also encourages improvement in housing standards and conditions. To begin with, it sets standards that any house approved for an FHA loan must meet. It inspects and appraises property before it qualifies the property for a loan. The agency provides information on its approved methods for locating, planning, and developing subdivisions. It also supplies analyses of local markets for housing to avert overbuilding, facilitates financing at better rates than those otherwise available, and exerts a stabilizing influence on the mortgage market.

The Federal Housing Administration operates like an insurance company. It insures the repayment of mortgage loans and charges the holders of mortgages a premium on every loan it underwrites. This income, together with fees and interest on investments, pays all of its operating costs and maintains its insurance reserves to provide against future losses. Mortgages and property-improvement loans insured by FHA must require repayment in periodic installments. They are amortized mortgage loans.

FHA provided the first standardized mortgage instrument that made possible the purchase and sale of insured, direct, amortized home-loan mortgages on a national scale. The fact that the lender could sell the mortgages made them more acceptable and made for the decline in importance of the straight-mortgage loan.

The monthly payment on an FHA-insured mortgage covers principal, interest, the FHA mortgage-insurance premium computed at 0.5 per cent annually on outstanding balances of principal, and fire and other hazard insurance premiums, plus real property taxes, special assessments, and ground rent, if any. All this is prorated throughout the year on a monthly basis.

Interest rates on insured mortgages are changed from time to time because of the availability of mortgage funds or because the Housing and Home Finance Agency wishes to encourage building starts or home buying. In 1966 the maximum FHA interest rate was 6 per cent.

Home-Mortgage Insurance. The principal activity of the Federal Housing Administration is the insurance under the National Housing Act of mortgages on one- to four-family homes. Under Section 203-b, mortgages on one-family dwellings are insured in amounts up to $30,000; on two-family dwellings up to $32,500. Within these limits, when the mortgagor is both owner and an occupant, the agency insures mortgages that represent up to 97 per cent of $15,000 of the property value as appraised by its staff, plus 90 per cent of the next $5,000 of appraised value, plus 80 per cent of anything remaining. Thus, an owner who will be an occupant, who buys a new house with an FHA appraised value of $25,000 and a first mortgage to be insured by the agency, may borrow:

97 per cent of	$15,000	$14,550
90 per cent of	5,000	4,500
70 per cent of	5,000	4,000
	$25,000	$23,050

When the application for the insurance is made after construction has started but within a year after its completion, the maximum that may be underwritten is 90 per cent of $20,000 of appraised value, plus 80 per cent of the remainder of the dwelling's value. When the borrower does not occupy the property, the mortgage generally is limited to 85 per cent of the amount that would be available to an owner-occupant.

The down payment made by any borrower on any dwelling whose mortgage is to be insured by FHA must be at least 3 per cent of the agency's estimate of the total cost of the property. Incidentally, a mortgagor who is at least 62 years of age may borrow the down payment and closing costs from a person or corporation approved by the FHA commissioner.

In addition to underwriting mortgage loans on new homes, the FHA insures mortgages to finance the replacement of homes destroyed or extensively damaged by major disasters. It also insures the financing of rental projects, mobile home courts, housing projects for the elderly, cooperative housing projects of the ordinary or condominium types, and urban renewal projects.[30]

FHA-insured mortgages may be open-end mortgages. However, extensions made on them may not increase the outstanding balance beyond the original mortgage amount unless the money is to be used to add rooms or other enclosed space to the dwelling. For insuring an open-end addition, the lender is required to pay to the FHA a charge of 0.5 per cent per annum on the combined amount of the increase and the balance due on the original loan.

Many borrowers who pay off their mortgages insured under Section 203 receive *participation payments* from FHA. These cash payments are similar to dividends. They represent the excess of premium charges over FHA expenses, insurance losses, and provision for insurance reserves for such mortgages.

Insurance of Property-Improvement Loans. Under Title I of the National Housing Act the Federal Housing Administration is empowered to insure lending institutions against loss on loans made to finance alterations, repairs, and improvements to existing structures. The FHA's liability is limited to 90 per cent of the loss on any individual loan. Title I loans are made by approved lending institutions to borrowers with satisfactory incomes and credit records. The borrowers own the property, are buying it on contract, or have a lease on it expiring not less than six months beyond the maturity of the loan.

Loans to improve single-family homes may be made up to $3,500. The interest charge is a "5 per cent discount" on the first $2,500 and a 4 per cent discount on the amount over $2,500. On the average loan the total is equivalent to about 9.4 per cent simple interest per annum on the unpaid balance of the amount borrowed. The principal and interest are repayable in equal monthly installments over a period not exceeding five years. Larger loans in amounts from $2,500 to $10,000 are obtainable at 6 per cent plus the FHA insurance premium of 0.5 per cent and are repayable in equal monthly installments over a period of as long as 20 years.

The availability of property-improvement loans has made for a marked increase in enhancement of existing housing. The result has been an upgrading of properties and an improvement in their value and livability.

FHA's greatest impact has been on the market for relatively low-cost housing. Buyers could afford to pay for homes under FHA-mortgage terms, and builders could construct them at a profit and sell FHA-insured mortgages on a favorable basis because of the lessened risk involved. Thus, relatively low-priced homes in the suburbs became the stereotype for a single-family dwelling in the 1950's. By 1966, the FHA had written insurance on the mortgages of over seven million homes.[31]

Veterans' Administration Loans

Since 1944, when Congress passed the Servicemen's Readjustment Act, eligible veterans or their widows have been enabled to apply for loans guaranteed or insured by the Veterans' Administration. These loans, known popularly as "GI loans," have to be used to purchase, construct, or improve a home; to buy a farm; to buy a business; or to go into business. The act has been amended several times. Veterans of later military engagements were made eligible for substantially the same benefits as veterans of the Second World War.

GI Loans from Private Lenders. Ordinarily, eligible veterans must make their own arrangements for home loans through conventional lending channels. Sometimes a builder will relieve a veteran of most of these details. The veteran who qualifies for a GI loan then simply signs the necessary papers, pays the fees, and assumes the responsibility for mortgage payments. Under the *guarantee plan*, there is no limit to the price of the home or size of the loan, but there is a maximum amount that can be guaranteed. The VA warrants the lender against loss up to 60 per cent of the outstanding balance on the loan; in no case may this amount exceed $7,500. In a practical sense, therefore, a lender is not likely to advance more than $12,500 to an individual veteran on these transactions. The VA-guaranteed mortgage, unlike the FHA-insured mortgage, requires no premium for the warranty. Nevertheless, recent loans to veterans who have served in the armed forces since February 1955 require a 0.5 per cent loan fee to be paid when the loan is made. The proceeds from the fee go into a fund to protect the Veterans' Administration from loss through default in mortgage payments.

Under the *insured plan*, the VA protects the lender against loss on loans to veterans under principles very much like those prevailing for FHA-insured mortgages. For each loan a lender makes he receives an insurance credit of 15 per cent of the loan's face value, with a maximum credit of $4,000 on any one loan. His total credits may be used to indemnify him against loss sustained on any of his transactions. The prudent lender, of course, will weigh his applications for money. He wishes to minimize the likelihood of not being insured against all possible losses. Although, in theory, loans of this kind may apply to the purchase of a farmhouse or the repair, altering, or improving of an existing home or farmhouse, the VA insurance plan has not been used much in real estate. It is reserved more for business ventures. The maximum lent under this plan to any single veteran is $26,666.

The interest rate on VA-guaranteed or VA-insured realty loans may not exceed 6¾ per cent per year on the unpaid balance. The repayment period or maturity of GI home or home-improvement loans may be as long as 30 years. However, since the loans are made by private lenders, the lending institution makes the decisions as to the terms of the loans. The amount of down payment and the length of the repayment period are matters to be agreed on between the veteran and the lending institution. The Veterans' Administration does not require a down payment, but the banking institution may. The veteran is required to pay the closing costs which are often several hundred dollars. If a veteran defaults on his payments on a loan and the Veterans' Administration has to pay the lender, the veteran still owes the government the amount the Veterans' Administration has had to pay out for him.

Unless the home to be purchased by the veteran was completed at least a year before he applied for a loan, it must meet or exceed the minimum requirements of the Veterans' Administration for planning, construction, and general acceptability. On new homes being financed with GI loans, builders are required to give veteran-buyers a one-year warranty that their homes have been constructed in "substantial conformity" with VA-approved plans and specifications.

A veteran must certify that he intends to live in the home he is buying or improving with a GI loan. However, he may sell his home and be released from liability to the agency if the person to whom he is selling the property obligates himself by contract to buy the home and assume the veteran's debt. The Veterans' Administration must be assured that the purchaser is a good credit risk, for it continues to remain liable on the guarantee.

As the principal of the GI loan is reduced, the VA's guarantee remains 60 per cent of the unpaid balance of the principal and is proportionately reduced. If the borrower still owes $8,000 on a $10,000 loan, the VA then guarantees payment of only $4,800 instead of the original $6,000. Veterans who have not used the entire $7,500 guarantee to which they are entitled may obtain additional guaranteed home loans until the guarantee is used up.

Interest rates on GI home loans are lower than those on most comparable home loans. Veterans with this type of financing, therefore, have an advantage when they wish to sell their homes. In addition, a veteran who has used his guarantee and then, through no fault of his own, has had his home destroyed or taken away, or has been forced to sell because of a health failure, a change of jobs, or some other equally compelling reason, could obtain a new GI loan under the same maximum conditions. The Veterans' Administration, however, has to be relieved of liability on the old guarantee, and the veteran must apply for another loan before the expiration of his eligibility.

Direct Loans. In those areas where the Veterans' Administration has determined that private mortgage financing at its maximum rate of interest is not available, eligible veterans may borrow directly from the Veterans' Administration in order to buy, build, or improve homes. The maximum amount on such loans is $13,500 and the interest rate is the same as on other GI home loans. There is no down payment required on these loans but, as in the case of other GI home loans, the veteran must pay the closing costs.[32]

The Federal National Mortgage Association

The Federal National Mortgage Association, or "Fannie Mae," as the agency is called, operates as a stabilizer of mortgage funds. First, it carries out an orderly liquidation of FHA-insured and VA-guaranteed mortgages acquired before November 1954. This activity is intended to prevent a disruption of the mortgage market. Second, it provides special assistance in financing such programs as housing in urban renewal areas, military housing, and housing in regions affected by natural disasters. Here it uses its resources to prevent a decline in home building that could threaten the economy. Third, and most important, it maintains a secondary market facility for the buying and selling of home mortgages. In so doing, it balances the distribution of mortgage funds.

In practice, Fannie Mae purchases FHA-insured and VA-guaranteed mortgages from private lenders in places where there is a shortage of mortgage capital and resells them where there is an abundance of mortgage funds. When money is tight, and the demand for loans is heavy in the face of official desires to curb the use of credit, Fannie Mae's purchases of mortgages softens the impact on the housing industry. Lenders thus acquire new funds for additional investment in housing; mortgage money becomes more plentiful.

When mortgage credit is ample, Fannie Mae pares its holdings by selling mortgages to mortgage companies, banks, savings and loan associations, and insurance companies. The lending institutions, which at such times encounter difficulty in making mortgage loans, buy mortgages from Fannie Mae as an investment of their own. As Fannie Mae observes an abundance of such buying and a corresponding diversion of funds from home loans, it increases the selling price of its mortgages. The fall in interest yields prompts the lenders to redirect their funds into mortgage-loan channels in preference to buying investments from Fannie Mae. Thus, if Fannie Mae raises the price of a $1,000 mortgage to $1,100 and still pays $60 a year, the yield drops from 6 per cent to 5½ percent. The lender shifts his money back to making mortgages when they yield a higher return.

The Federal Home Loan Bank

The Federal Home Loan Bank lends funds to eligible mortgagees so that they can make conventional mortgage loans more readily available. Its principal clients are the savings and loan associations. Conventional loans, which are secured by mortgages that are not insured by a government agency and therefore entail more risk, generally are made at higher interest rates than FHA and GI loans. They are the only loans available for those buying homes or property who are ineligible for government-insured mortgages. Consequently, the number of housing starts in the largest segment of the housing market is heavily dependent on the availability of conventional loans.

When conventional loans are easy to obtain at relatively low-interest rates, and the Federal Home Loan Bank detects an inflationary trend in the mortgage market, the bank may raise its interest rate on loans to mortgage lenders. This makes the bank less attractive as an additional source of funds, and mortgage lenders, discouraged from making as many loans, ordinarily will raise the interest rates on such loans. When the bank detects a deflationary trend in the conventional mortgage market, it can and normally will lower its interest rate to make funds more cheaply and readily available to mortgage lenders. They, in turn, usually relax their loan qualifications and lower their interest rates. Thus the bank acts to stabilize the market for conventional loans.

In 1966, approximately two-thirds of the one-to-four-family dwelling nonfarm mortgage debt outstanding was conventional mortgage debt; 20 per cent had been financed with FHA-insured mortgage loans and 14 per cent with VA-guaranteed mortgage loans.[33] Since most housing units in the United States are financed with conventional mortgage loans, the Federal Home Loan Bank is a powerful institution in the housing market.

In its effort to encourage the building and sale of housing units that lower-income-bracket families can afford, the federal government often has acted to make mortgage funds more readily available. Interest rates on conventional mortgages have therefore tended to remain about 1 per cent higher than those legally allowed on FHA-insured mortgage loans.

However, down payments required on property financed by a conventional mortgage loan are generally considerably higher than those required on property financed by FHA- or VA-insured mortgage loans. In the former case, down payments may reach 20 to 25 per cent of the value of the property. Thus, fewer people can afford to buy property financed with conventional mortgage loans.

State Agencies

California's Division of Farm and Home Purchases of the Department of Veterans' Affairs will lend veterans as much as $15,000 directly on homes that they appraise at $25,000 or less. The title to the property remains with the State of California until the veteran repays the loan, but the interest rate on these loans are considerably below the market rate. Other states, and New York deserves particular mention, have similar arrangements. It behooves the individual buying a home, especially if he is a veteran, to investigate and find out if he can finance his house at a lower rate by borrowing from the appropriate state agency.

The Government's Role

The housing industry is an important segment of the economy, on which personal and social welfare heavily depends for adequate housing. Unaided, the industry cannot always provide profitably for all of the population. So the government has played, and will continue to play, a more and more important role in the encouraging and subsidizing of the building of adequate housing. To the extent that the individual, the housing industry, and the private sector of the economy effectively solve housing problems, the government's role is lessened. To the extent that groups with a voice that can be heard by Congress are not able to obtain adequate housing at prices and on terms they can afford, the role of government will grow.

BUYING, SELLING, OR BUILDING A HOUSE

Anyone who faces the necessity of finding a place to live is confronted with two sets of questions in need of answers before the hunt for housing may truly begin. The first of these has to do with taste—what type of accommodations are desired and in what locality? The second concerns the pocketbook—how much can the individual or family afford for housing, and is it more economic to buy, build, or rent?

How much anyone can afford is a personal matter, depending on how he wishes to allocate his income. However, if the individual, or the family, wishes to use a residual approach and allocate to housing what is left after all other expenses are met, he may employ the budget form in Table 9–7.

Buy or Rent?

For the couple without children and pets or for persons living alone, apartments, trailers, rented units in duplexes or triplexes, or rented houses may constitute adequate housing. Such housing generally provides the additional advantages of requiring less cleaning and maintenance. It takes less expense and effort to maintain and beautify the surrounding area. Homeowners tend to be

Table 9-7. **Budget Form**

Item of Expense	Amount	Total
Housing expenses, monthly		
Estimated payment on mortgage loan (lending agency can supply this figure)	_____	
Hazard-insurance premiums (fire, earthquakes)	_____	
Taxes and special assessments, if any	_____	
Maintenance and repairs	_____	
Utilities		
Electricity	_____	
Gas	_____	
Water	_____	
Telephone	_____	
Trash collection, etc.	_____	
Total housing expenses		_____
Living expenses, monthly		
Food	_____	
Clothing	_____	
Household furnishings, equipment and supplies (if these are bought for cash)	_____	
Automobile (depreciation, license, operation, repairs)	_____	
Other transportation, if any	_____	
Medical and dental	_____	
Education (tuition, books, etc., if any)	_____	
Insurance premiums (life, theft, automobile, liability, accident, health, etc.)	_____	
Recreation and entertainment	_____	
Emergencies	_____	
Contributions	_____	
Miscellaneous (dues, dog license, traffic tickets, etc.)	_____	
Total living expenses		_____
Fixed obligations, monthly		
Installment payments	_____	
Other debt payments	_____	
Retirement fund, pension payment, or other commitments	_____	
Miscellaneous (support of parent, alimony, or court-ordered child support, etc.)	_____	
Total fixed obligations		_____
Total income, monthly, after taxes		_____
Surplus or deficit		_____

families with children.[34] The reasons they give for buying are summarized in Table 9–8.

The major advantages of homeownership ordinarily are more space for the same amount of money, more privacy, additional indoor and outdoor space in which children may play, the tax advantage and, in some cases, more pleasant surroundings. The major disadvantages are the loss of mobility, the added responsibility, and the high cost.

Table 9-8. **Reasons for Buying**

Reason	Per Cent
Buying is an investment	24
Rents too high: ownership cheaper	24
Ideal of homeownership	22
Forced to buy: could find no place to rent	19
Desire for independence: security	11
"Found just the right place"	4
Reasons of location	2
Other reasons	7

SOURCE: "Why People Buy the Houses They Do," *Housing Research*, Housing and Home Finance Agency, Washington, D. C., October 1952.

The high cost of buying may be recalled from Table 9–1. On an $18,000 house, with a $2,700 down payment and a 30-year FHA-insured mortgage for $15,300 at 5¼ per cent interest, monthly costs will total about $173.40. An adequate apartment or, in the South or West, an adequate house, could be rented for this amount.

Apparently, people buy homes because they want homes of their own. They *think* ownership is cheaper than renting, whether it actually is or not. They feel that they are investing in a home. To the extent that they make down payments and pay off the principal of their mortgage loan, they acquire an equity in property, which, in essence, becomes an investment. However, homes are not always the most profitable investments. The average home does not appreciate as much as even the blue chips among common stocks and, if the neighborhood deteriorates, it may not appreciate at all.

The economic advantages will vary in relation to the income of the homeowners. On federal income tax returns, for instance, those owning their own homes may deduct from their adjusted gross incomes the interest paid on their mortgage loans, property taxes, and any casualty losses not compensated by insurance. Thus their taxable net incomes will be less then otherwise. In itself, however, this tax advantage is not usually sufficient justification for buying a house. Yet, by obligating themselves to meet the payments on a home, some people save more than they otherwise might. Often the ownership of a house means that there will be an estate for their children. The same amount, or even less, paid out in rent simply would have been a necessary current consumption outlay that vanished with its payment.

The search for a rational answer to the question of whether to buy a house should include in each case a personal or family listing, weighing, and evaluating of needs and wants. It should assess the satisfactions and dissatisfactions and the advantages and disadvantages, financial and nonfinancial, that will accrue from renting and from homeownership. It also should include a careful comparison of what is available on the new and resale housing markets. The objective is to acquire the housing that will be enjoyed the most at the lowest possible price.

Buy or Build?

Ordinarily, building a house is more expensive than buying an existing house that often has depreciated to some extent. In some cases, however, especially in localities that are growing more desirable, houses may appreciate in value. In such instances, the difference between buying a house that is already built and building one may not be very great. In each case, only a specific comparison can provide the answer.

Actually, the chances of finding exactly what one wants in an existing house are rare. Yet, because of the problems involved and the patience required, Consumers Union advises: "Build only if you can't find what you want in existing houses."[35] Few people who have not built a house have the background and experience to anticipate the problems that such a project entails. *Mr. Blanding Builds His Dream House*[36] was no exaggeration.

BUILDING A HOUSE

In all building, four steps are involved. First, plans and specifications are drawn. Second, a building permit is obtained. Third, contracts are drafted and let. Fourth, there is the actual building. For the first step, an architect's advice is helpful. For the second and fourth steps, an ethical building contractor proves valuable, and the third step benefits from the aid of an attorney and an architect.

Stock Plans

"Stock" plans from housing magazines, drafting services, or agencies that specialize in their sale may be utilized. Rarely, if ever, however, will they fit the specific requirements of the persons for whom the house is being built. Furthermore, it is usually difficult for many people to visualize from plans exactly how the finished house will look. It is well to see another house constructed from the same plans before deciding whether plans are suitable. Revising plans is a relatively expensive procedure. Consequently, "stock" plans that require radical revisions generally prove costly. Nevertheless, it is cheaper to make changes on plans than to make changes once construction of the house is underway.

Hiring an Architect

If a house is to be designed for a specific person or family, if it is at all out of the ordinary, or if it constitutes a relatively large expenditure, the prospective owners should consult a licensed architect. Architects' fees for complete services are normally 12–15 per cent of the finished cost of the house. For this, architects act as the owner's representative in all matters, including supervising the construction and authorizing the disbursement of construction funds when work has been satisfactorily completed. The selected architect should have tastes in design similar to those of the prospective owner. This may be determined from looking at houses he has designed and from talking with his former clients before deciding to work with him.[37]

Hiring a Contractor

Consumers Union has cautioned: "Unless you are qualified by experience, don't try to be your own contractor, and don't let the subcontracts yourself." Moreover, it is well to be sure beforehand that the money for each contractor or workman will be available at the time needed. The construction schedule should be discussed with the person or financial institution providing the funds.

BUYING A HOUSE

The process of buying a home usually begins with the hunt for an available one within one's price range in the area or neighborhood preferred. When it has been found, the next task is to obtain an appraisal and evaluation for one's own purposes so as to make the most of the relatively large expenditure.

Then the necessary loan must be negotiated, and all the legal and other necessary requirements have to be met to insure that one acquires clear title to the property.

Finding a House

In considering the area or neighborhood in which to buy a house, Consumers Union recommends the consideration of the following items:

1. Convenience and cost of commuting. If commuting by rail is involved, impending rate increases and possible curtailment of services should be investigated.
2. Traffic patterns and chronic rush-hour tie-ups.
3. Schools. Also, are children of the same age within walking distance?
4. Houses of worship.
5. Community facilities—that is, meeting places, playgrounds, other recreation facilities, including swimming places—theaters, museums, and libraries.
6. Shopping location, hours, and variety of stores. If the family car is needed for transportation to and from work, shopping for food and household supplies is difficult in some suburban areas.
7. Utilities and services. Police and fire protection, road maintenance, sewerage availability, snow removal, trash collection.
8. Assessments and taxes. The possibility of increases in tax rates for such services as new schools, sewers, or roads should be taken into account.
9. Zoning—that is, protection against undesirable industries and residential overbuilding.
10. General character and stability of the neighborhood.

Since houses will depreciate in value far more quickly than a surrounding area or neighborhood depreciates, it is well to select an area that is likely to appreciate rather than run downhill. This necessitates ascertaining which areas are *becoming* desirable—that is, people want to move into them. It is no longer merely a question of knowing the right from the wrong side of the tracks. It is a question of finding out where the social leaders are locating. Housing in these localities commands higher prices because they are known as "good neighborhoods." There is a hierarchy of locations in every community and good neighborhoods are more in demand. If neighborhoods remain good, property in them may appreciate. Few do so, however, for any long period of time. If a neighborhood contains houses that will go out of fashion, if its houses are not maintained well, or if they are on relatively small lots, its chances of deteriorating are greater. In any area, prices of new houses are ordinarily firmer than those of older houses, but if houses are not selling, all prices will tend to drop. If there is a strong demand for a particular type of housing that is in relatively short supply, its price will rise.

Evaluating the House

Whether someone likes or does not like a house is something that only an individual can decide. It is impossible to evaluate a house subjectively in terms of the satisfaction that it will bring to another person. However, it is possible to appraise the market value of a house in terms of the prices of similar houses. They can also be evaluated in terms of houses that contain similar or equivalent components in a like amount of space and that are located in comparable areas. Moreover, it is possible to appraise the market value of the land on which the house is located. The land will be compared with equivalent lots in the same area, and the prices at which they have sold most recently will determine the value of the lot in question.

Houses normally are appraised at an amount that lies between their original cost and their replacement value. This pertains to a completed house with all of its equipment, less its depreciation, or plus its appreciation if it is in an area where property has appreciated in value. Much depends on the judgment of the appraiser, who tends to gain skill with time.[38]

No matter how much one may like a house because of its appearance or personality or how high it has been appraised, it is still well to inspect it carefully before buying. Every house that has been lived in will have been damaged to some extent, and every house that falls short of the ideal will have some faults. Faults vary in importance. Some are slight; others are not negligible, but may be remedied at a price. Some, however, may be regarded as so serious as to disqualify the house from consideration.

When considering the purchase of a particular house, it is well to use a checklist that includes most of the faults that might be found in a house. Such a checklist is shown in Appendix 2 at the end of the last chapter. Old houses and those with unfinished attics and cellars are the most revealing and the easiest to inspect. In many cases, only the owner or the builder can answer the questions—if he will.

By assigning demerits to the various faults in accordance with the evaluation of their importance, the purchaser may have a quantitative score useful for purposes of comparison. A 1-2-4 scale such as is shown in Appendix 2 has been found to be informative, as a rule, even though it does not correspond to the costs of correcting the defects. No scale will fit all the situations encountered. Yet if the same scale is used for comparative evaluation of all the houses being considered, it will serve its purpose.

Special Faults of Masonry Houses. A masonry house is one in which walls of stone, concrete, brick, or similar hard material bear a significant load. Masonry veneer, such as a single thickness of standard brick, may be used in place of wood siding, but this does not make it a masonry house.

Almost all the faults of wood houses may exist in masonry houses. In addition, masonry has its own peculiar defects. Because of its greater weight, masonry allows less margin for error than does wood-frame construction. Consequently, its faults for the most part are serious.

Arranging the Financing

In attempting to ascertain if one can afford the estimated payment on a mortgage loan, it might be well to refer again to the budget form presented in Table 9–7. No matter what type of personal or mortgage loan for which, an individual may apply, he usually has to fill out a similar form and substantiate it. Even though the form shows the prospective borrower to be eligible for a mortgage loan of a certain amount, this does not necessarily imply that the lending agency will grant the loan. The amount an agency is willing to lend, the actual interest rate it will charge, and the down payment it will require is governed by its supply of funds at the time of the loan application and the other opportunities available for the investment of these funds (see Figure 9-1).

As to mortgage limits, many financing agencies use a rule of thumb and lend no more than twice the borrower's regular gross income when mortgage funds are relatively scarce. The family whose income before taxes is $10,000 a year may borrow up to $20,000. When mortgage funds are plentiful, the agencies will relax their requirements and may lend as much as two-and-a-half times the amount of gross annual income. Many banks and insurance companies decide on eligibility for a particular loan by using a form much like the one in Table 9–9.

The weighting of the various items is interesting. *Nonprofessional* wives under 38 and professional wives under 32, for example, are believed to be more likely to have first or additional children and leave their outside-of-home employments. The proportion of "annual carrying charges to effective annual weighted income" is arbitrary and will vary from one lending institution to another. Each sets a maximum figure on the basis of its own past experience.

There is no set rule or formula for determining exactly how much of a mortgage a family can afford. It depends largely on how big the monthly payment is to which it is willing to commit itself.

Longer- or Shorter-Term Mortgages. Whether a buyer should seek the longest-term mortgage loan obtainable to bring down the monthly payments,

Table 9-9. Income Computation Form to Determine Eligibility for a Mortgage Loan on a Residence[a]

Determine weighted annual income as follows:		
Regular wages or commissions	$10,000 × 1	$10,000
Additional income from employment	300 × ⅓	100
Income on investments	1,000 × ½	500
Wife's earnings if under age 32	4,800 × 0	
Wife's earnings if from age 32 to 38	× ½	
Wife's earnings if over age 38	× 1	
Wife's earnings if professional and under age 32	× ½	
Wife's earnings if professional and over age 32	× 1	
Gross weighted annual income		$10,600
Less installment debts		2,600
Effective annual weighted income		$ 8,000
Carrying charges for $16,050 mortgage at 5½ per cent for 30 years on $19,000 home:		
Mortgage payment		$ 91.16 per month
Taxes (approximately)		26.98 per month
Insurance (hazard)		3.23 per month
		$ 121.37 per month
		× 12
		$1,456.44 per year
Proportion of annual carrying charges to effective annual weighted income (acceptable maximum = 20 per cent)		18.2 per cent

[a] This is a typical but not an actual form.

even though the interest for the longer period of time is more, or whether a shorter-term loan with higher monthly payments and less interest to be paid better suits his purpose is a question that should be given full attention. If being in debt does not give rise to psychological problems, the buyer should consider the advantages of longer-term mortgage loans (see Figure 9–2).

First, less interest is paid on mortgage loans than on almost any other type of loan. Second, the money not being used for house payments can be spent on commodities with higher priorities on the list of wants. Third, the service charges—to be mentioned shortly—and other costs related to the loan are the same or almost the same on the shorter as on the longer loan, and often the interest rate is higher on shorter loans. Fourth, it is usually easier to sell a house with a longer or larger mortgage than one with a shorter or smaller loan. The buyer does not have to make as big a down payment. The equity created by a down payment cannot be considered a current asset until the house is sold. It may not even serve as collateral for loans, since lenders favor more liquid

Buying a House

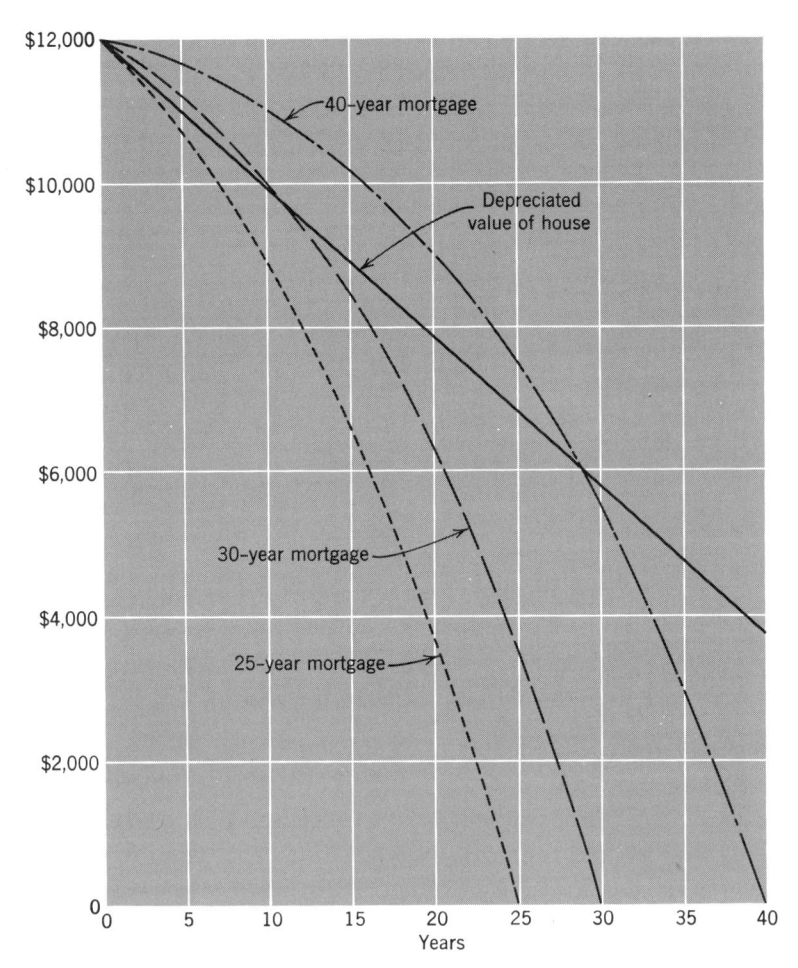

[Figure: Graph showing $12,000 to $0 on y-axis vs Years 0 to 40 on x-axis, with curves for 40-year mortgage, 30-year mortgage, 25-year mortgage, and Depreciated value of house]

Figure 9-2. *Source. Changing Times*, September 1961, p. 19.

assets. All in all, obtaining the longest-term mortgage available at the lowest rate of interest to be found usually results in minimizing current outlays for housing.

Two major financial disadvantages of longer-term mortgage loans are: first, more interest is paid over the life of the loan and, second, during a large part of the life of the mortgage loan, the size of the loan may exceed the value of the mortgaged property. The first point may be illustrated by Table 9–10. The hypothetical example is a $12,000 mortgage loan at 5½ per cent interest. The amount over $12,000 is interest, for instance, $17,708 on the 40-year loan. As previously noted, interest on a mortgage loan, like rent, is current outlay that does not result in any increase in assets. However, it is tax deductible.

Table 9-10. Varying Terms for a $12,000 Mortgage Loan and Corresponding Costs

Term of the Loan (Years)	Total Payments (Dollars)	Term of the Loan (Years)	Total Payments (Dollars)
15	17,649	30	24,528
20	19,811	35	27,066
25	22,107	40	29,708

The second point is illustrated by the chart in Figure 9-2. Note that it is assumed that this house will last 50 years; this is not always a reasonable assumption. If the house depreciates faster, the value line moves down and to the left. A 40-year mortgage on this house would result in the owner's indebtedness exceeding the value of the house for the first 30 years of the loan. Unless the house appreciates for some reason, the owner cannot count on getting his money out during this period. In effect, his house payments, again exactly like rent, must be regarded as current payments for shelter. The question, then, is whether to maximize the housing that may be enjoyed for the lowest possible monthly outlay or whether to build up an equity in a house as an investment.

Service Charges. To cover the costs entailed in processing the various forms and in determining if the prospective borrower is eligible for a mortgage loan, the lending institution imposes a service charge. This charge changes from instance to instance and from institution to institution. It must cover the costs incurred in each case and is one of the costs the borrower must expect to pay.

LEGAL MATTERS: DEEDS AND TITLES

The deed is a document conveying title to real estate. The person or firm shown on the deed as the one transferring the title to the real property is known as the *grantor*. The person or firm to whom or to which the title is being transferred is known as the *grantee*. A *grant deed* simply conveys title from the grantor to the grantee.

Forms of Deeds

A grant deed conveys the title held by the grantor and any title to the property which he may later acquire. A warranty deed also conveys the title held by the grantor but, in addition to the conveyance, it contains a warranty from the grantor that his title to the property and his right to transfer it are unencumbered and not defective in any manner. If a warranty deed is used when title to the property is transferred, and it is later discovered that the title the grantor held was defective, the grantee may sue for breach of warranty and recover what he paid, as well as recompense for the resultant damages. In addition, there are many special forms of deeds used for particular purposes in the various states. The *deed of trust* commonly used instead of a mortgage in California conveys title to a trustee until the loan is paid.

Title Protection

To assure himself that he is receiving good title, a buyer may obtain an *abstract, a certificate of title,* a *Torrens certificate,* or he may take out *title insurance.*

An abstract is a condensed history of the ownership of the property. It is a formal legal document prepared by the attorney or the title-guaranty company that undertook the responsibility for the necessary research. If there are any liens or claims of record still outstanding against the property, they will be listed and described in the abstract. There will be a list and description also of the legal proceedings, deeds, mortgages, sales, or other documents and matters of record related to the particular property. Even though the abstract does not indicate or guarantee that the title is free from defect, it will show that no unsettled claims of record have been found. Thus it may serve to reassure the buyer, especially if he is confident that a careful, thorough, and honest search of the records has been made.

A certificate of title, a certification by an attorney that he has examined all the records affecting the property and that to the best of his knowledge and belief there are no unsettled or prior liens or claims outstanding against it, is used in some areas instead of an abstract. The attorney who signs the certificate certifies that, in his opinion, the buyer is receiving a valid title, but this is not a guarantee. Should a claim that impairs the title come to light at a later time, the certifying attorney cannot be held liable for the resultant damage if he exercised due care when making the search of the records affecting the property.

A Torrens certificate is issued by an official recorder or registrar after he has placed an official notice in the newspaper inviting anyone who has a claim or a lien against the property to file suit. If no one sues within a given period of time, a court orders the registrar to record the title in the new owner's name and to issue a Torrens certificate to this effect. In a few states Torrens certificates are still issued but, for the most part, they have fallen into disfavor.

Title insurance protects against loss from the possibility of defects in a title, with the exception of losses described in the policy. Before a policy is issued, the title-guaranty company will search the records to ascertain if a clear title is being transferred. Subsequently, if the title is challenged, the title company appears in court for the insured defendant and pays any costs and expenses. Title insurance may be obtained in most cities in the United States.

Before completing a purchase of property, buyers might well have the titles to the property judged valid by attorneys or title-guaranty companies who have searched the relevant records. If a loan is involved, the lending institution generally insists on this and will, in addition, take out title insurance covering the amount of the loan for its own protection. This insurance is charged to the buyer. However, the buyer would do well to take out his own title insurance for the full cost of the house. Normally he is interested in protecting his own equity, and the title insurance held by the lender protects only the lender.

Recording a Title

Deeds and mortgages are recorded customarily in the appropriate registers at the courthouse in the county in which the property is situated. Recorded deeds and mortgages take legal precedence over those not recorded, even though the unrecorded deed or mortgage would have been valid had it been set down, and even though it preceded the recorded deed or mortgage. Legally, anyone is entitled to rely on the validity of titles as disclosed by the public records.

Forms In Which Titles May Be Held

Tenancy. One or more persons may hold title to real property jointly or separately. If one person alone holds title, he has an *estate in severalty*. If two or more people hold the title to the property, they may be *joint tenants* or *tenants in common*. If two or more persons take title to property under the legal instrument, that is, if the recorded deed bears all of their names, under common law they are joint tenants. If one of the joint tenants dies, the others fall heir to his share of the property. The heirs of the deceased joint tenant have no claim to the property.

Under more recent state statutes, which have superseded the common law in most states, persons own property under a *joint tenancy with rights of survivorship* or, if they are husband and wife, under a *tenancy by the entirety* or as *community property*. As far as the effects of these statutes are concerned, there is little change from the common law. If one of the joint tenants dies, the entire property still becomes the property of the surviving tenant or tenants. However, under *tenancy by the entirety* or the *community property laws*, neither the husband nor the wife can transfer any interest in the property while both are alive without the consent of the other.

If two or more persons hold property as *tenants in common*, under separate legal instruments or under one instrument that shows that each has a separate or individual interest in the property, the heirs of a tenant who dies will inherit his share of the property. It may be noted that a corporation may be a common tenant but never a joint tenant. In most states, the statutes now provide that all transfers of property to two or more persons are tenancies in common unless they are specifically designated as joint tenancies. Those inheriting property now generally receive it as tenants in common.

Dower or Curtesy. In some states, a married man or woman cannot sell his or her interest in any property, even though he or she is the sole owner of that property, without having his wife or her husband join in the deed to release *dower or curtesy*. These are legal anachronisms. By common law, dower is the wife's right to a life interest in one-third of her husband's real property, should he die. Curtesy is, according to the common law, the husband's right to his deceased wife's property if they had a child. It still applies if the child died before the mother. In most states, these rights have been modified by statute. In states having community property laws, property acquired by married persons becomes the joint property of husband and wife, unless it is designated as being his or her separate property.

Homestead. In some states, people may legally declare their home to be their homestead. Thus protected, it may not be seized or attached if they do not pay their debts. The amount of property exempted under the right of homestead differs in the various states that permit this type of exemption, and it may vary within the state. Some allow higher exemptions in one area than in another; some fix a maximum value that can be exempted. In most cases, homesteaded property cannot be sold without the consent of the spouse of the person who wishes to sell. In some states, if the husband dies, his widow and minor children automatically remain protected by the homestead.

SELLING A HOUSE

Selling a house involves finding a buyer, agreeing on a price, and arranging the terms of sale, the financing, the escrow, the conveying of title, and the collecting of the money. Real estate brokers are experienced in all these matters. Ordinarily they know how to attract buyers through advertisements or other devices. They know how to show a house to its best advantage and how to persuade prospects to buy. They know prices of comparable property and how to make a price seem fair. They are familiar with necessary down payments for various types of loans, loan sources, and the interest rates being charged for various types of loans. Their handbooks tell them the monthly payments on various priced houses with differing down payments and interest rates.[39] As a rule, they can arrange for financing more readily and on more favorable terms than an individual homeowner because they have the necessary contacts with banks, insurance companies, mortgage brokers, and lending institutions. They know escrow procedure and escrow companies. They know the problems involved in ascertaining the validity of a title and whom to designate to conduct the title search. As a third party, even if not always a neutral one, the broker can deal with both parties to a transaction in matters where the two do not want to deal with each other directly and where a third party is better able to effect the desired result.

Generally, brokers charge 6 per cent of the transaction's value for their service. The seller who can sell his home without using the services of a broker can set his price at 6 per cent less and obtain the same amount.

"Adequate" shelter is a culturally determined requirement. As incomes and cultural levels rise, housing tends to become more complicated and perhaps more aesthetically desirable; but then it invariably becomes more expensive.

QUESTIONS

1. If families devote one-fifth of their incomes to house payments, utilities, and heat, what percentage of American families today can afford a $20,000 house? Use Table 9–1 for required payments.
2. Barring a major recession, why can prices of homes in the United States be expected to increase?
3. According to the American Public Health Association, what is the minimum number of rooms needed by four people? What determines how much space a family will need in a house? What determines how many rooms they will need in a house?
4. As far as a particular family is concerned, what is the usual reason why a house becomes "too small"?
5. What determines how well housing needs can be satisfied?
6. Who sets the fashions in housing? How are they promulgated?
7. Is housing currently in short supply? Is any particular type of housing currently in short supply in your area? Why?
8. Why are prices of houses as high as they are? List some of the factors that keep prices relatively high.
9. Can the housing industry produce as efficiently as the automobile industry? Compare and contrast the two. (Refer to the chapter on transportation.)
10. What are the major costs categories that are included in the price of a finished house? What proportion of the price are each of these cost categories?
11. In addition to house payments, list some of the additional costs of home ownership.
12. Why is the mortgage loan currently most used known as an amortized direct-payment secured loan?

13. How does a second mortgage differ from a first mortgage?
14. What is a trust deed or deed of trust?
15. What are the sources of "conventional" mortgage loans? What other types of mortgage loans are available? From what sources?
16. What government agencies insure mortgage loans?
17. How do the Federal National Mortgage Association and the Federal Home Loan Bank make mortgages easier to obtain?
18. In making the decision as to whether to buy or rent, what factors should be considered?
19. When is one well advised to build a house?
20. What should be considered in deciding on the area or neighborhood in which to buy or build a house?
21. How is the value of a house determined? What are some of the factors to consider in deciding whether to buy a particular house?
22. What determines how large a mortgage the prospective purchaser of a house can obtain?
23. Which form of deed is the safest? What is title insurance?
24. Define community property; tenants in common; homestead.
25. What is an architect's customary fee? For what services is he paid?
26. What are the advantages and disadvantages of dealing with a real-estate broker when selling a house?

SELECTED READINGS

Beyer, Glenn H., *Housing and Society*, Macmillan, New York, 1965.
Brown, Robert K., *Real Estate Economics*, Houghton Mifflin, Boston, 1965.
Case, Frederick E., *Real Estate*, Allyn & Bacon, Englewood Cliffs, N. J., 1962.
Changing Times, The Kiplinger Magazine, various issues.
FHA Home Mortgage Insurance, Federal Housing Administration, Washington, D. C., latest edition.
FHA Home Owner's Guide, Federal Housing Administration, Washington, D. C., latest edition.
Hebard, Edna L. and Gerald S. Meisel, *Principles of Real Estate Law*, Simmons-Boardman, New York, 1964.
Hoagland, Henry E. and Leo D. Stone, *Real Estate Finance*, 3d ed., Irwin, Homewood, Ill., 1965.
Maisel, Sherman J., *Financing Real Estate*, McGraw-Hill, New York, 1965.
North, Nelson L. and Alfred A. Ring, *Real Estate Principles and Practice*, 5th ed., Prentice-Hall, Englewood Cliffs, N. J., 1960.
Rogers, Tyler S., *The Complete Guide to House Hunting*, Charles Scribner's Sons, New York, 1963.
Savings and Loan Fact Book, United States Savings and Loan League, Chicago, latest edition.
The Story of Modern Home Financing, United States Savings and Loan League, Chicago, latest edition.
What You Should Know Before You Buy a Home, United States Savings and Loan League, Chicago, latest edition.
Your Shelter Dollar, Household Finance Corp., Chicago, 1963.

NOTES

1. Consumers Union, *Consumer Reports, 1961 Buying Guide Issue*, Mt. Vernon, N. Y., December 1960, p. 184.
2. Bureau of the Census, *Statistical Abstract of the United States 1966*, Washington, D. C., p. 753.
3. *Ibid.*, p. 747.
4. *Ibid.*, p. 752.
5. United States Savings and Loan League, *Savings and Loan Fact Book 1966*, Chicago, Ill., 1967, p. 31.
6. *Ibid.*, p. 29.
7. Housing and Home Finance Agency, *Housing Statistics, Annual Data*, Washington, D. C., 1965, p. 22.
8. "Spotlight on Housing," *Business in Brief*, Chase Manhattan Bank, May-June 1959, p. 4, and *Savings and Loan Fact Book 1966, op. cit.*, pp. 42–45. In 1965, approximately 63 per cent of the existing occupied dwelling units were owner occupied; 37 per cent were rented.
9. Michael Sumichrast and Norman Farquhar, *Net Removal Rate from Housing Inventory*, National Association of Home Builders of the U. S., Washington, D. C., 1967, p. 281.
10. See Edward T. Paxton, *What People Want When They Buy a House*, U. S. Dept. of Commerce, Housing and Home Finance Agency, Washington, D. C., 1955.
11. Louis Winnick, *American Housing and Its Use*, Wiley, New York, 1957, p. 21.
12. John H. Mabry, "Toward the Concept of Housing Adequacy," *Sociology and Social Research*, November-December 1959, p. 89.
13. *Ibid.*, p. 91.
14. *Statistical Abstract of the U. S., 1966, op. cit.*, p. 754.
15. Arthur Whitman, "Don't Let Them Sell You a House," *The American Weekly*, April 9, 1961, p. 10.
16. *Statistical Abstract of the U. S., 1966, op. cit.*, p. 755.
17. *Time*, December 5, 1960, p. 82.
18. *House and Home*, August 1960, p. 101.
19. *Savings and Loan Fact Book*, United States Savings and Loan League, Chicago, Ill., 1966, p. 28.
20. *Statistical Abstract of the United States, op. cit.*, p. 455.
21. *Ibid.*, pp. 747 and 758 and *Savings and Loan Fact Book, 1966, op. cit.*, pp. 91 and 132.
22. *Savings and Loan Fact Book, 1966, op. cit.*, p. 31.
23. Fred E. Case, *Cash Outlays and Economic Costs of Homeownership*, Bureau of Business and Economic Research, University of California at Los Angeles, 1957, p. 4.
24. *Ibid.*, p. 5.
25. See Vincent B. Phelan, *Care and Repair of the House*, National Bureau of Standards, U. S. Dept. of Commerce, Washington, D. C., 1950.
26. Bureau of Labor Statistics, *Consumer Expenditures and Income*, Urban United States, 1960–1961, Washington, D. C., 1964, p. 10.
27. See "House Insurance," in *Kiplinger's Family Buying Guide*, Prentice-Hall, Englewood Cliffs, N. J., 1959, Chapter XI.

Selling a House

28. *Statistical Abstract of the United States, op. cit.*, p. 356.
29. *Savings and Loan Fact Book, 1966*, p. 33. All figures in this and the next paragraph are from various pages in this source.
30. Information on all types of FHA loans may be obtained from FHA offices, which are located in all major cities in the United States, or in small towns and cities from local lending institutions that have been certified as authorized agents for FHA. A convenient library reference is the Federal Housing Administration's *This Is the FHA*, Washington, D. C., latest edition.
31. *Savings and Loan Fact Book, 1966, op. cit.*, p. 131.
32. Veterans wanting further information about GI home loans or other benefits for which they are eligible should inquire at the nearest regional office of the Veterans' Administration. The pamphlet entitled *Questions & Answers on Guaranteed and Direct Loans for Veterans*, obtainable from the Veterans' Administration, Washington, D. C., contains answers to most questions asked by veterans concerning GI loans. GI home loans are granted under Title 38 of the United States Code. For answers to specific technical questions, direct reference to the code is recommended.
33. *Federal Reserve Bulletin*, January 1967, p. 130.
34. Some 72 per cent of the families in the United States with a youngest child of six or over owned their own homes in 1960. Of the total population, 63 per cent owned their own homes (Survey Research Center, University of Michigan, *1960 Survey of Consumer Finances*, Ann Arbor, 1961, pp. 50, 51, and *1965 Survey of Consumer Finances*, p. 118.
35. Consumers Union, *1961 Buying Guide Issue*, p. 185.
36. Eric Hodgins, *Mr. Blanding Builds His Dream House*, latest edition, Simon and Schuster, New York, 1946.
37. Those planning to build homes should refer to Waldo A. Kirkpatrick, *The House of Your Dreams: How to Plan and Get It*, McGraw-Hill, New York, 1958; and to Francis D. Lethbridge, "Architecture for the Home Builder," *Journal of American Institute of Architects*, January 1960, pp. 31–35.
38. The authoritative reference on real estate appraisal is American Institute of Real Estate Appraisers, *Appraisal of Real Estate*, Chicago, 1952. Those concerned with the appraisal of homes should refer to Percy E. Wagner, "Appraisal of Single Family Homes," in *Real Estate Appraisal Practice*, American Institute of Real Estate Appraisers, Chicago, 1958, pp. 63–80.
39. Before dealing with a real estate broker or salesman, it would be well to read: *Real Estate Salesman's Handbook*, National Association of Real Estate Boards, Chicago, latest edition.

PROBLEMS AND CASES

1. Refer to Table 9–1. If a family devotes 15 per cent of its income to housing, how much annual income must it have to afford a $15,000 house; a $20,000 house; a $25,000 house? If it devotes 20 per cent of its income to housing? If it devotes 25 per cent of its income to housing?
2. The Smiths are interested in purchasing a $25,000 home. Using Table 9–1, compute their monthly payment if it includes taxes and insurance. Note their total monthly housing expense. If the Smiths receive $1,200 a month what percentage would they be spending on housing? If their income is relatively

certain would you recommend that they buy the house? Would you recommend the same decision if their income fluctuated from month to month between $900 to $1,500?

3. The Crawfords are a family of five: the parents, one girl, age 12, and two boys, ages 9 and 3. What is the minimum number of rooms they require according to the American Public Health Association? Would this number change if their grandmother came to live with them? Would it be different if all three children were boys? What is the minimum number of square feet they require according to the Association? How many more will be required after their grandmother arrives?

4. The Crawfords are considering building a 2,000 square-foot house. If there will be six persons living in the house, how many square feet should they allocate for each of the household activities listed in Table 9–2? (Use the percentages in the last column.) How should they arrange the house to best provide for these activities? Will this arrangement minimize costs?

5. Refer to Table 9–2. What is the minimum floor space required by your family? How does this compare with what you have? Do you feel crowded? Why or why not?

6. Using the maximum density standards of the Bureau of the Census, indicate whether or not the tract home most commonly built in your area is adequate for a family of five. Using Table 9–3, is the house adequate if two of the children are boys and one a girl? Is the house still adequate if the wife or husband's mother comes to stay?

7. Refer to Table 9–2. For which of the activities listed does the house in Question 3 have adequate space and for which ones does it not?

8. The Brights have three teenage girls. They live in a 2,000 square-foot, three-bedroom, two-bathroom, typical tract home. For which "life activities" would this home probably be inadequate as far as this family is concerned? How might this be remedied?

9. Interview a custom builder in your area. Ascertain to what extent he subcontracts for work on the houses he builds and how he arranges for financing.

10. Interview a builder of tracts. Ascertain to what extent he subcontracts for work on the houses he builds and how he arranges for financing. Contrast his manner of operation with that of the custom builder referred to in Question 5.

11. Interview an architect. Ascertain if he thinks housing in your area meets the needs of the area's residents adequately. If not, what measures does he think should be taken? Do you agree? Why or why not?

12. Ask an architect and a contractor what measures should be taken to improve the efficiency of the housing industry. Referring to library references, what additional measures may be added to these lists?

13. Obtain the building code for the area where you live. Determine if it permits the use of plastic pipe for plumbing; dry wall construction; erection of prefabricated homes by factory crews. Are any of the provisions of the code outdated? Which ones? Will any of the provisions cause a home to be more expensive than it would be otherwise? Which ones? What revisions would you recommend in the code? Why?

14. What percentage of a lot may be covered by a building in the area where you live? This information is obtainable from the planning commission or the build-

ing department. What effect does this regulation have on the appearance of your neighborhood? On the value of the property in the area? Should the regulation be changed? If so, why and how?

15. Price similar-sized vacant lots: one near the center of a city, one in a metropolitan residential area in the same city, one in a suburb of the city, and one in an outlying portion of the same metropolitan area. How do they compare in price? Determine, if possible, why the first three lots were "passed over" when that part of the area was developed.

16. Interview a land developer. Ask why he selects the land that he does to develop. What costs influence his decisions the most? How do local tax rates in the area and his personal and business taxes influence his decision? How could the government encourage the development of areas closer to the central core of the city?

17. How is your local community effecting urban redevelopment? What programs and projects are in progress, if any? Why? How are they being financed? Could they be financed otherwise? Why or why not?

18. The Brooks are interested in building a home. They are shopping for a lot. Their net disposable income is $17,500 a year, and they have decided that their house and lot should have a total cost of no more than $40,000. How much should they pay for their lot? (A rule of thumb, which should not and need not be followed dogmatically, is usually stated as ¼ on the lot, ¾ on the house.) They have to have the lot paid for before they start building (a customary requirement). If they have $8,000 in their savings account would this change your answer? Where should they look for a lot in their price range— near the center of the city? in an existing middle class suburb? in a new development? Where will lots be likely to be better buys? Why?

19. Refer to Table 9–4. Make a similar breakdown for the costs of a house recently built in your area. Why are they higher or lower than the costs shown in the table?

20. How much will it cost currently to operate and maintain in your area the house referred to in Problem 9?

21. Interview four or five sources of mortgage loans in your area. How much will each of them lend on the house referred to in Question 9? At what rate of interest? For how long? How much down payment does each of them require? If there are differences in the answers to any of these questions, why do they differ? How many will not handle the loan if it is an FHA loan? A VA loan? Why?

22. Using the budget form in Table 9–7, and considering your income and expenditure pattern, how much of a monthly outlay can you conveniently afford as a payment for housing? Using Table 9–1, what price house can you afford to buy? Can you afford a house that is adequate for your needs?

23. Refer to Problem 18. If the Brooks can obtain from the bank an 8½ per cent discounted construction loan for one year to be repaid by a 6 per cent 20-year mortgage on 90 per cent of the value of the house, how much interest will they pay on the construction loan? Thereafter, what will their monthly payment be on the house? Would they be better off financially buying or building? Why? If not, why would they go ahead and build?

24. The Davises are a family of five. Their total income is $6,000 a year. If they

decide to buy a tract house, how much can they afford to pay for it? (Refer to Table 9–1 and allocate 20 per cent of their monthly income for housing.) Should they buy or rent? If older homes in the community where they live are available for a minimum of $8,000 and they can obtain a second mortgage at 8½ per cent interest on the unpaid balance, would this change your answer? Would your answer change if they had six children? Why?

25. If the lowest-priced tract homes available to veterans in an area are $15,000 and mortgage interest rates are 5¾ per cent on 30-year mortgages, what is the minimum income required to buy a home if you are a veteran? Should a childless young married veteran whose income is $450 a month buy a tract home or rent an apartment? Why?

26. Determine what rents are being charged for the various types and sizes of apartments available in your area. (Consider age of building and neighborhood as well.) Again in view of your needs, would it be more economical for you to buy a house or rent an apartment? Make a list of the costs involved in each case.

27. Determine what rents are being charged for the various types and sizes of houses available in your area. (Again also consider age of house and location.) Once more in view of your needs, determine if it would be more economical to buy or rent a house in your case. List the advantages and disadvantages of buying and renting as far as you are concerned, as well as the costs.

28. Should you build a house? List the pros and cons of buying versus building in your own case. Which would be the more economical for you?

29. Determine whether homes in the neighborhood in which you live are appreciating or depreciating and the reasons therefor.

30. Refer to Table 9–9. Evaluate the house in which you live. In view of the evaluation, would you buy it?

31. Refer to Table 9–9. What is the maximum mortgage loan on a residence for which you would be eligible?

32. As far as you are concerned, if you obtained the maximum loan referred to in Problem 31, what would the optimum term of the loan be? Why?

33. Refer to Problem 18. Compute the interest the Brooks would pay if they obtained a 25-year mortgage; a 30-year mortgage for $30,000, both at 6 per cent. Should they obtain the 20-year, 25-year, or 30-year mortgage loan? Why? If Mr. Brooks has been averaging a consistent return of 8 per cent on his investments, would that change your answer?

34. Interview a real estate broker. Have him show you a file containing all of the documents pertaining to a particular real estate transaction involving a residence and describe just what he did in effecting the transaction. Do you think he earned his fee? Why or why not?

35. Mr. Smith, of the family referred to in Problem 2, has been informed he will be transferred to a distant city by the company for which he works. He has six months before the date of transfer. Should he attempt to sell his house himself or utilize a real estate broker? Give the advantages and disadvantages of each course of action. How should he go about finding housing in the city to which he is being transferred?

10 EXPENDITURES FOR TRANSPORTATION

Every year there are more station wagons and fewer stations.

BILL VAUGHAN, Bell Syndicate

Americans travel more than 850 billion miles a year without leaving the country. They cover almost 90 per cent of this distance in private automobiles. In 1963, they traveled approximately 18.6 billion miles on railroads, more than 20 billion miles on intercity bus lines, and over 42.7 billion miles on airlines.[1]

Since 1925, the use of public transportation has steadily declined and the use of the private automobile has correspondingly increased. But this trend may now be reversing itself. Ordinarily it is less economical to drive a car, especially for short trips taken alone, than to make use of public transportation facilities. Nevertheless, an automobile usually provides a faster and more convenient way of reaching one's destination.

There are now more than 72 million passenger cars registered in the United States and each of them is driven about 10,000 miles a year.[2] As a result, highways built when automobiles were fewer in number and were being driven much less speedily are now frequently inadequate; there are not enough highways to meet current needs, and certainly not enough to meet future needs. Traffic congestion is commonplace and increasingly becoming more a problem in many localities. But as yet the wider use of public transportation is not generally held to be anything but a hoped-for partial solution to this problem.

If the current trend prevails, every spending unit in the United States can anticipate buying an automobile at least once during his or her lifetime. Some buy new cars, but many more buy used cars. Either way, buying an automobile is rarely a simple process. An automobile is a complex commodity and the second largest single purchase made by most people in the United States. The automobile market has grown increasingly more ramified over the years.

In short, it is no longer a simple task to maximize the benefits that derive from expenditures on transportation and transportation facilities.

THE DEMAND FOR TRANSPORTATION

People do not live within walking distance of the places to which they wish to go. They need some means of transport. This circumstance leads to the current demand for transportation in the United States. As the automobile has increased mobility, many people have moved farther and farther away from the centers of cities and have become increasingly dependent on transportation.

Need for Transportation

Transportation is needed mainly by those who leave home to earn a living. About 46 per cent of motor-vehicle use, according to one study, is for the purpose of going to and from work. Some 69 per cent of all people who require transportation to go to work use an automobile but 14 per cent are passengers in cars driven by others. Approximately 85 per cent of suburbanites who work in the city drive to work; 95 per cent of those who live and work in the suburbs use their automobiles to go to and from their jobs.

About 19 per cent of all privately owned motor-vehicle use is for the purpose of attending to family business; 34 per cent goes for transportation needed in order to participate in social and recreational activities, and 3.7 per cent covers transportation needed in order to participate in educational, civic, and religious activities.[3]

Those without cars require transportation for much the same reason as those with cars. An estimated 16 to 18 million families in the United States depend on public transportation by streetcar, bus, subway, or elevated lines for intraarea mobility.[4] As fewer people live in the cities and more in the suburbs, more transportation has become necessary.

Social Patterns

The typical American family is pictured as owning at least one automobile. Affluence is associated with owning at least two. Public transportation is used most often now by those who cannot afford a car or cannot drive, or by those who commute.

Typically and increasingly, the family that can afford to do so lives in a suburb. As time goes on, more will be farther from the central core of the city. Industry, trade, social, recreational, civic, educational, and religious facilities have grown in number in the areas outside the central districts of cities. But they have not grown as rapidly as resident population has increased in these areas. In consequence, there has been no visible decline in the number of people who travel to the center of the cities for one reason or another.

The move away from the central areas of cities is partially due to the increase of places of work in the suburbs. As recently as 1954, 65 per cent of the jobs were in city centers; 35 per cent in the suburbs. By 1975, the estimates are that jobs in the city will decrease to about 44 per cent; 56 per cent will be in the suburbs. However, there has been an increase in the number who travel from the cities to the suburbs and from one suburb or rural area to another.

As population and its supporting cultural institutions increase and become more and more dispersed, travel also increases. Travel patterns grow in number and become more diffused. Driving 20 miles from one suburb to work in another is now quite common. A relatively small proportion of the population living in outlying areas goes downtown to shop; for the most part, it drives to shopping centers. Children increasingly do not walk to school because it is too far. They go to school on the bus. The family visiting friends or relatives may drive ten, twenty, or two thousand miles. Increasingly, also, people travel for recreation.

Because of the growing population and increased needs and wants based mainly on changes in patterns of living in the United States, consumer expenditures on transportation have grown tremendously. In 1929 Americans spent $2.6 billion for transportation services and $3.2 billion for automobiles and parts. By 1965 they spent $12.2 billion and $29.9 billion on these same categories.[5] All of these amounts are expressed in current dollars, that is, they are the amounts people actually spent in those years. Even if the increase in the prices of these commodities is taken into consideration, consumers still bought more than twice as much transportation service in 1965 as they had in 1929 and almost five times as many automobiles and parts.

The Supply of Transportation

The supply of transportation for consumer use in the United States has been augmented to the extent that it has in recent years, mainly because of an increase in the number of automobiles. Although an index of consumer transportation expenditures, with the amount spent in 1957–1959 designated as 100, had risen from 77 in 1949 to 110.6 by 1965, the number of transit riders fell by over one half in this period during which automobile registrations virtually doubled.[6]

Automobiles

The number of automobiles registered in the United States has been increasing steadily. As a result, problems due to traffic congestion, inadequate highway systems, and inadequate parking facilities also have been increasing; but they have not had any appreciable effect in slowing down the rate of increase in the number of automobiles. It is anticipated that 88 million automobiles will be registered in the United States in 1975—one car for every 2.5 people.[7] By 1960, this ratio had already been achieved in Los Angeles County. In the early 1960's, about three-fourths of all families in the United States owned a car. By 1966 over 78 per cent of all families in the United States owned a car. Approximately 18 per cent owned two cars.[8]

Public Transportation

Means of public transportation have not kept pace with the demand for public transportation. They have lacked adequacy of conveyances at the time wanted, provision of enough routes, and quality.

Inadequacies of Urban Public Transportation. The public transportation companies operating intraurban and interurban transportation systems are, for the most part, caught in a dilemma. As more and more people own and use their automobiles the use of public transportation decreases. Public transportation firms cannot afford newer and better means of conveyance. Yet as their facilities deteriorate—and many buses, streetcars, elevated railways, subways, and commuters' trains have done so—fewer and fewer people make use of them.

Second, most people use public transportation during the "rush" or peak hours. Thus the companies find that having enough equipment to meet the demand adequately during these hours means that they will have idle equipment most of the time. The equipment continues to depreciate, even if it is not being used, and the costs of storage space and maintenance must be met even if it is producing no income. Enough idle equipment for enough time can wipe out any profits made on equipment in use.

Third, public resistance and the action of the public utility regulatory bodies that must approve any increase in rates charged often prevent transportation companies from raising fares high enough to make operation of the system profitable. If they do raise fares, they frequently find that patronage decreases. Again the operation of the system becomes unprofitable.

The opening of new routes to suburbs where population is more dispersed than in the more centralized areas frequently is not economically feasible. Consequently, many parts of these areas have no means of public transportation.

Since those dependent on public transportation must be served in the public interest, many cities now subsidize transportation companies or own their transportation systems. Still, many urban public transportation systems are far from adequate. They are wanting in both the quantity of equipment in relation to needs during the hours of peak loads and the quality of equipment in use. Systems that are well patronized and profitable are mainly those operating newer and faster equipment in densely populated areas.

Daniel Suits has written:

The stimulation to automobile ownership initiated by the high level of postwar incomes resulted in increased difficulties for public mass transportation systems. The reduction of service by the latter resulted in an increased need for automobile ownership at all income levels. This in turn contributed to the troubles of public transportation. It is hardly surprising that the result is an economy from which public transportation has all but disappeared, and in which ownership of an automobile is a necessity for most families.[9]

Problems of Intercity Transportation. Because of the relatively high prices for travel as a first-class passenger and the required maintenance of unprofitable routes, there is an oversupply of carriers and facilities in intercity transportation in relation to the effective demand. The Interstate Commerce Commission, a federal agency, regulates the routes, the services offered, and the rates charged for transport of passengers in more than one state. Once a carrier assumes the responsibility of offering transportation over a particular route, it can abandon that route only if it can show the commission both that it is no longer profitable to service the route, and that there is no further need on the part of any appreciable number of persons for transportation over it. Nor can the carrier seriously curtail the amount of service offered without the consent of the commission. Consequently, many trains, buses, and boats travel over their assigned routes more than half empty. This is especially true on off days or during off hours, and for the higher-priced first-class accommodations. Lower-priced accommodations, such as "economy" trains and intercity buses, carry relatively more people. Since they are more in demand, they can be furnished profitably in a larger number of cases.

Airlines and firms furnishing helicopter service generally turn to the Civil Aeronautics Board for permission to charge higher fares when their operations are unprofitable. The higher fares inevitably curtail demand to some extent. If demand is *elastic*—that is, if it does not remain relatively the same even if the price is increased—and if it does not increase due to other factors, revenues fall off and profits dip.

In 1964, profits before corporate income taxes totaled about $92 million for the nation's intercity bus lines. For the nation's domestic airlines, they were $263 million. The nation's railroads, on the contrary, lost approximately $389 million on their passenger service,[10] but this was less than losses in previous years.

Automobile Versus Public Transportation

Within a metropolitan area, decisions on whether to use automobiles or public transportation usually are based on availability, cost, convenience, and time. As to availability, many persons do not own automobiles or drive. In many areas, however, means of public transportation other than taxis, which are a relatively expensive form of transport, are not available.

If total costs per mile driven are considered, public transportation ordinarily is less expensive than driving, unless several people share the costs of making a trip in an automobile. However, few consider the entire cost of driving a car. In most cases, they already own a car and intend to maintain it. Therefore, if they consider costs at all, they usually consider only the *marginal* or extra costs, such as for gasoline and oil, associated with the trip. For a 20-mile trip these costs average approximately 60 cents—less than the cost of public transportation.

If public transportation leaves the passenger a considerable distance from his destination with no other means of transportation, it cannot be said to be convenient. Unless there is a public transportation route within walking distance, or unless a suitable parking place for one's car is available, public transportation may not be convenient.

Time enters into this consideration, as well. Public transportation, to be convenient, mut be available when needed. An automobile that is in operable condition always is available as a means of transportation; it can be driven from one's point of origin to one's destination. In short, it is a very flexible form of transportation. For some city dwellers, however, having to take an automobile out of a garage some distance away, or having to wait for it, makes the use of public transportation for short trips more convenient. In most instances, of course, the automobile enables one to reach one's destination faster.

Socially, the costs of controlling traffic congestion, building highways, accidents, and other factors occasioned by the greater use of an increasing number of automobiles may be high. Yet automobile owners, even though they may be aware of these costs, cannot be expected to return to the use of public transportation in large numbers unless public transportation systems are greatly improved. Actually, when all costs are considered, it may be far less expensive to use public transportation than to drive one's car.

As Warren Gramm has written:

Recurrent studies of the problem in major metropolitan areas reiterate one general . . . recommendation . . . substitution of rapid transit for automobiles. Although the alternatives of social versus individual means of meeting the problem have been clearly specified from the side of technology, unfortunately no similar clarity or consensus has appeared concerning the economics of such a reversal. The problem is much more deep-seated than either the "public" remedy—establishment of a rapid transit authority or of state or federal subsidies to local transit units, public or private—or the market solution which is to urge increased use of automobiles and consumption of gasoline to render profitable private investment decisions of the past.

Success of the rapid transit solution would depend on offering service that is comparable to the private automobile in cost and convenience. Such success . . . involves nothing less than a basic redistribution of consumer expenditures between automobiles and alternative transit media, as well as of related investment expenditures. Given the strategic position of the automobile in our economy and culture at large, the weighting would appear to be on the side of a private, individualistic solution. Public action to date has been confined virtually to the construction of a highway net to accommodate . . . the private automobile.[11]

Increased federal subsidies to public transportation, recommended by many who appraise the accruing benefits as greater than the costs, may serve in part to encourage an increase in these facilities. For many in the low-income brackets who have no automobiles, they will unfold broadened opportunities for employment "beyond walking distance."

THE COST OF TRANSPORTATION

The cost of transportation will be considered in three parts: the cost of owning and operating an automobile; the cost of public transportation in metropolitan areas; and the cost of public transportation for longer journeys.

The Cost of Owning and Operating an Automobile

The average cost of operating a new car has been estimated at approximately twelve cents a mile.[12] This figure includes both the direct operating expenses—that is, gasoline and oil, maintenance, and tires—which vary with the number of miles driven, and depreciation, insurance, and license fees, which remain the same irrespective of the number of miles driven. These average costs are shown in Table 10–1.

The actual cost of operating a particular new car rarely conforms to the average. Taxes and license fees differ from one locality to another. Insurance costs vary with the type and the value of the policies and the companies from which the policies are purchased. In some cases, inadvisable though it may be, the car owner may not carry insurance. Since there is a wide range in automobile prices, there is also a wide range in annual depreciation charges.

Table 10-1. **Annual Cost of Operating a New Car**

Cost Items	Cost in Cents per Mile for 10,000 Miles
Variable costs	
Gas and oil	.0261
Maintenance	.0074
Tires	.0041
Total	.0376
Fixed costs	
Fire and theft insurance	.0030
Property damage and liability	.0117
License fees	.0024
Depreciation	.0633
Total	.0804
Total Cost	.1180

SOURCE: American Automobile Association, 1965.

Other factors influencing the cost include speed—the faster one travels, the lower the gas mileage and the higher the cost of gasoline, oil, maintenance, tires, and depreciation—road design and surface type, and the degree of traffic congestion. Frequent start and stop are a cause of rapid deterioration.

How safely one drives also affects costs. Insurance rates may be lower for safe drivers whose repair and maintenance costs also are less.

If a family budgets 10 per cent of its disposable income for the cost of operating its car, and the car is driven the 10,000 miles during the year as shown in Table 10–1, and no more, the family spends roughly $1,180, on the average, on its operation. Presumably the family has a disposable income of $11,800 for the year. Operating costs are increasing, primarily because of higher depreciation charges as car prices rise, but also because all of the other operating costs are rising. Between 1955 and 1965 costs of owning and operating an automobile increased 29 per cent.[13] As a result, many families are economizing by buying used cars on which depreciation charges are less; however, repair and maintenance costs may be higher. Then, too, many are buying foreign cars, which may be lower in price to begin with and more economical to operate.

American Cars Versus Foreign Cars. An example of the difference in operating costs of two cars may be seen in Table 10–2. The first is a used, four-door sedan of one of the widely sold, lower-priced makes. To economize, its buyer bought a six-cylinder, standard-shift model in one of the more inexpensive series. He averaged 15 miles per gallon using "regular" gasoline. The second is a Volkswagen.

The cash value of the first buyer's four-year-old car was $850, including radio and heater but not including state taxes. The Volkswagen came equipped

Table 10-2

Cost Items	U. S. Car (4 Years Old)	Volkswagen (New)
Price paid	$ 850	$1,775
Variable costs		
Gasoline @ 32¢/gallon	$1,600 (15 miles/gallon)	$ 828 (29 miles/gallon)
Oil @ 60¢/quart	57 (5 quarts to fill)	42 (2.7 quarts to fill)
Tires @ $28 each	336 (20,000 miles per set)	112 (40,000 miles per set)
Antifreeze	45	—
	$2,888	$2,757
Fixed costs		
Depreciation	850	875
Insurance	730	610
License Fees	95	95
	$1,675	$1,580
Total costs for 5 years	$4,563	$4,337
Total annual operating costs (15,000 miles per year)	$ 577.60	$ 551.40
Total annual costs (15,000 miles per year)	$ 912.60	$ 867.40

Source: American Automobile Association and Volkswagen of America, Inc., 1966.

with a heater, but the cost of a radio was appended to its price, bringing its cash value to $1,567, excluding taxes, freight, and other accessories, or a total price of $1,775.

The cost of operating the used American car for a year was more than the cost of operating the newer Volkswagen. Admittedly, a fairer comparison could have been made with an American compact car. In fact, not all foreign cars, even small ones, may depreciate as slowly as the Volkswagen. Nevertheless, the lower initial cost and the low operating cost of many imported cars make them worthy of consideration. For some foreign cars, however, maintenance and repair costs are higher than for comparable American cars because parts may not be as easy to obtain, mechanics who understand the cars may be fewer, and it may be more difficult for one reason or another to service the car or to make the necessary repairs. If this is the case, total operating costs per year may be higher for the foreign car. However, many a foreign car is bought because of the special characteristics of its design or performance, which generally are not available in American cars. There is no feasible way of evaluating how much these special features are worth to any individual except by observing how much he is willing to pay for them.

New Cars Versus Used Cars. The main advantage of buying a used car is that at least part of the depreciation at higher rates, which occurs in the earlier years of an automobile's life, has been borne by the previous owner. Under current depreciation rates, a new car originally priced at $3,000 will decline about 50 per cent in value during its first two years. The first year's depreciation is at the highest rate—normally at a rate of about 30 to 40 per cent for most American cars. During the second year, these vehicles depreciate between 15 and 25 per cent, on the average; during the third year they lose between 10 and 15 per cent more of their original value. During each ensuing year the depreciation will occur at a decreasing rate.

Not all cars depreciate at the same rate. Among the low-priced American cars, the less expensive lines of each manufacturer generally depreciate more, at least during the first years, than do the higher-priced, more glamorous lines. Among the medium-priced and high-priced cars, the reverse is true; the higher-priced models show greater depreciation, both in percentage rates and dollar amounts, than the less expensive lines of the same manufacturer.

The type of engine makes a difference in the depreciation rate. "Sixes" depreciate more rapidly than "V-8's."

Since depreciation is such a large part of operating cost in the case of any automobile, and since depreciation rates vary, a used car buyer must understand rates, causes, and patterns of depreciation in order to maximize the "value" or "utility" of his outlay. Studying the "Blue Book,"[14] which all automobile dealers use in evaluating particular cars, may be advisable.

The exact depreciation rate that will apply in any one case will depend on many things. These include the age of the automobile, its price class, its make, line, and model, its engine, its mechanical condition, the mileage, the condition of the frame and body, its appearance, plus any added attraction it may have, and current conditions in the automobile market. Consumers used to be concerned, for the most part, with current outlays. Now that they own homes, appliances, and automobiles to the extent that they do, they are almost equally concerned with capital costs as their fixed assets depreciate.

The Cost of Public Transportation in Metropolitan Areas

The cost of public transportation in metropolitan areas, which has been increasing, can be expected to continue to rise. Transportation systems now cover greater distances, and land, labor, and equipment costs have mounted, all contributing to higher costs of operation. These costs can be covered only by increased fares or federal subsidies.

The Cost of Public Transportation for Longer Journeys

Railroads have lost passengers to bus lines, which may be more convenient, and to airlines, which are faster, if more expensive. Few railroads still operate their passenger-carrying trade profitably.

All in all, over longer distances, bus lines and airlines operate most profitably because they provide economical transportation for the lower-income groups in the one case, and high-speed transportation in the other.

BUYING AN AUTOMOBILE

Despite the costs involved, people do buy cars. Buying an automobile often is undertaken in the spirit of adventure. Nevertheless, it involves some careful and often difficult decisions if the fullest satisfactions are to be derived from its purchase. Choices have to be made as to exactly the type of car wanted, the specific make and model, and when and where to buy. If one is buying a used car, it is extremely important to determine the condition of the car and whether the price for it is the lowest possible.

What Type of Car?

Deciding which car to buy requires answers to the following questions. Is it to be a new or used car? A small, medium-sized, or large car? A light or heavy car? A sedan, station wagon, hardtop, convertible, or sports car? A foreign or domestic car? Or should it be a car with a low-, medium-, or high-horse-power engine? The following matters should be considered in formulating the answers.

Particular Need for a Car. Is a car essential for transportation to and from work? Is it necessary for business? Is it important as an all-around family and family-errand car? Will it be used mostly for pleasure?

Number Who Will Ride Regularly. Will the car be shared with others for shopping, or riding to work or to school Are there several small children or older people who frequently will ride in it?

Conditions of Normal Use. Is the regular driving in city traffic, on open highways, or on mountain or rough country roads? What kind of weather will the car be driven in most of the year?

Importance of Prestige and the Latest Model Car. Is a new car each year or two important? Does the buyer's standard of living require the latest? For some salesmen, for example, a new car each year is necessary to maintain business and social status and to serve as a concrete symbol of achievement, that is, to show they have been doing well.

Price and Payment Terms. What price is the buyer willing to pay and what will his budget allow? Will he pay cash or finance the car? What amount of money is available for a down payment? Will he buy on a trade-in? Will he buy a new or a used car?

Costs of Ownership and Operation. The costs of car ownership and operation, as discussed earlier in this chapter, are one of the major items in the budget of any car-owning family or individual.[15] In addition, the most important consideration usually turns out to be whether it is a car that the prospective purchaser can see himself or herself driving. Cars, like clothes and houses, are selected by people in accordance with their own conceptions of themselves, to project the image of themselves they want others to see, and to fit the roles they are called on to play.

Which Make and Model?

Several publications maintain staffs to test and evaluate models of each make of car that appear on the American market. Reading their findings and evaluations to learn if a car has those attributes in which one may be interested can be profitable. Before relying too heavily on such evaluations, however, it is necessary to know how accurate and trustworthy they are likely to be. Some are more reliable than others. The prospective buyer must know what he is interested in finding in a car so that he can compare specific attributes. Then he can determine which make and model will give him the most of what he wants for the lowest cost. Relatively reliable sources for information that may be used in comparing the various makes and models of automobiles include:

Consumer Reports Annual Auto Issue.[16] This appears each April. All models of American-made passenger cars are evaluated. The evaluations are reliable, but care must be taken to see whether they consider the particular attributes in which the buyer is interested. They are not particularly cognizant of the image conveyed, fashion, or the psychological interaction between the car and the driver or owner. The major criteria on which their evaluations are based are usefulness as transportation, primarily for family use, quality of workmanship and materials, mechanical efficiency, fuel economy, potential durability, safety, and optimum driver control. In addition, *Consumer Reports* evaluates foreign cars on the American market and station wagons in separate issues and used cars in its *Annual Buying Guide*, which appears in December of each year.

Consumer Bulletin Annual Auto Issue.[17] This appears each July. Full-sized cars are listed in five price groups and compared. The *Annual Compact Issue* appears each May and, throughout the year, information about and ratings of various models are included in the monthly issues. The *Consumer Bulletin's* major criteria for comparison are quality of workmanship and materials, mechanical efficiency, potential durability, and safety.

In addition, *Popular Mechanics*[18] and *Mechanix Illustrated*[19] test and compare the automobile models that appear on the American market each year. Neither of these are as critical as are *Consumer Reports* or the *Consumer Bulletin*.

Which Size of Car?

Normally, the larger the car, the more its initial cost and the more it costs to operate. The problem with some of the compact cars is that they do not cost appreciably less to operate than standard-size cars and, in a few cases, they may depreciate more quickly than the standard-size models. Like some foreign cars, moreover, they may be more expensive to maintain and repair. In short, the purpose for which the car is to be used; its costs of operation, maintenance, and repair; its depreciation; and its probable recovery value when traded or sold—all should be considered when deciding which size of car to buy.

When to Buy

Based on careful studies, the average fleet-operated automobile owned by a governmental agency or a private firm is traded in every three years. This does not imply that every individual should acquire a new car that often.

Questions that bear on the decision of when to buy or replace a car include the following considerations. If the individual or family already owns a car, how much has the car been driven and what type of driving has it had? In what condition is the car? What will be the probable cost of maintenance and repairs during the next year or the next two years. How much has the car depreciated? Is the equity in the car enough to constitute the down payment on the car to be acquired? Will the payments be the same as they have been or will an additional amount have to be budgeted for them? If a car is being bought for the first time, are funds available for the down payment and is income sufficient to meet the anticipated monthly payments, in addition to all of the outlays that are to be made? How important is the prestige or status anticipated from having a new or newer car, and how much is this increment to prestige or status worth? Does the household need a second car? If so, can the car owned presently serve this purpose if another car is acquired?

Specific families and individuals may have additional questions that should be answered before deciding to buy or to replace a car.

Where to Buy

Most new-car dealers are *authorized dealers* who have received a franchise or authorization from a manufacturer to sell and service one or more of its particular lines of cars in a defined area. Price competition among authorized dealers generally takes the form of variance in the amount deducted from the price as a *trade-in allowance.*

Independent dealers ordinarily specialize in the sale of used cars, but they also may sell new cars which they may have bought at wholesale. Frequently, authorized new-car dealers having more cars than they can sell at retail will sell some of them at wholesale.

Individuals often offer their cars for sale. In this way they can sell them at the retail market price. If, instead, they sell their car to a used-car dealer and do not trade it in on another used car or a new car, they cannot expect to receive more than the current wholesale price for the car.

Buying a Used Car

Buying a used car intelligently is more difficult than buying a new one, because determining the exact condition of the car and buying it at the lowest possible price both entail an expenditure of effort and the making of careful evaluations.

Determining Condition. Consumers Union advises:

No matter how new and shiny a late-model car may look, nearly every used car has something the matter with it; careful examination, together with all the testing you can give it (or an expert mechanic with access to all the requisite testing equipment can give it) is required to determine how well the particular car you are contemplating has retained the attributes CU noted when it was new.[20]

It may be added that the testing is needed also to determine what repairs it is likely to need, and what parts will require replacing, and how soon.

Obtaining the Lowest Possible Price. Buying a used car for the lowest possible price involves careful shopping and astute bargaining. If at all possible, the *Blue Book*[21] should be consulted for the wholesale price of any car under consideration. If the car is purchased from an individual seller who is not in the automobile business, a small margin above the wholesale price should be added when the offering price is computed. Used-car dealers, as a rule, will pay individuals the wholesale price of a particular used car or a little less.

In addition, the prices shown for a particular car in the classified advertisements of newspapers may serve as a basis for comparison.

Occasionally a car may be offered as a *leader* by an automobile dealer at close to the wholesale price. Those who are attracted by the offer may come in and buy another car on which there is a greater margin of profit. From time to time some automobile dealers may have to unload some cars to improve their cash position or to pay off indebtedness. That is when they may offer cars at close to their wholesale prices.

The price quoted for a used car is not always a firm price. In most cases, bargaining and the use of sophisticated bargaining techniques is necessary if the lowest possible price is to be obtained.

Buying a New Car

To minimize the price one generally should:

1. Ascertain the wholesale cost or dealer's cost of the automobile from the Blue Book or the American Automobile Association and then compute the dealer's margin on sales. The rule of thumb is a 21 per cent "markup" on com-

pact cars, 25 per cent on regular lines, and 27–29 per cent on luxury models. The markup is given as a percentage of the "list" or retail price. A 25 per cent markup on retail price is a 33⅓ per cent markup on cost; one-third of the cost to the dealer is being added to establish the retail price. (Retail price—$1.00; markup—.25; cost—.75. Markup on retail price—25 per cent; markup on cost—33⅓ per cent.)

2. Determine your trade-in value in actual worth to the dealer. This may be found in the *Automotive News*.[22]

3. Consider these additional facts:

(a) Large dealers with a high turnover can sell for less. A dealer selling more cars per time period who is "turning over" his inventory faster can spread his fixed expenses over a greater number of units. Frequently a "discount house," a cooperative, or a "buying service" is able to arrange for substantial discounts. By sending in customers they are reducing the dealer's sales cost.

(b) Factory installed "extras" are marked up 21–25 per cent, whereas dealer-installed extras are marked up close to 40 per cent.

(c) Different models in the same series are basically the same. The higher price of some is due to the trim.

(d) All dealers receive a factory rebate of 5 per cent on models that have not been sold at the time the new models are introduced. Just prior to the introduction of new models, manufacturers generally have contests that allow dealers larger rebates on the number sold over and above a certain quota. Consequently, dealers are generally willing to accept lower prices during the contest period.

Financing an Automobile

Consumer automobile installment credit outstanding in 1968 amounted to about $32 billion, roughly one-third of total outstanding consumer credit. Over 60 per cent of automobiles purchased new are bought on credit. In addition, about 50 per cent of used cars are bought on credit.

On a new car bought on a typical 36-month installment contract, the charges for interest and insurance provided by an independent finance company—often better known as a consumer-finance company—average over $400. These charges comprise more than 20 per cent of the net cash price of the car and in some cases may amount to as much as 25 per cent.

Minimizing Financing Costs

To avoid paying interest, a car buyer has to have the difference *in cash* between the trade-in allowance he is granted on the car he owns and the price

Buying an Automobile 313

of the car he is buying. (That is, providing he has a car to trade in; otherwise, he has to have the entire price in cash.) It should be noted that, while he was accumulating this sum he could have been earning interest from it. Consumers Union advises:

If at all possible, pay cash, particularly for a used car. If you must finance the purchase, here—by way of guidance through the tangled and sometimes shady world you are entering—are some points it would be well for you to remember:

1. Shop for your loan as thoroughly as for the car itself. The best loan source is usually a bank or credit union; avoid dealer financing if possible.

2. Try to limit the contract to 18 months, or two years at most, to avoid paying additional interest.

3. Buy your insurance separately, not as part of the time-payment sales contract; if it is part of the contract, it will almost certainly cost you more.

4. Read all the fine print. Do not sign either a car-purchase agreement or a loan agreement until all details are written in and you understand them all. Get an explanation of anything that is not clear. *Never sign a blank contract.*

5. Get and keep in your possession a *signed* copy of the contract, any other papers that you sign, and all insurance policies you buy.

6. If you are convinced later on that the dealer or the finance company didn't act in good faith, get in touch with your local Better Business Bureau.[23]

Financial agencies contend that the rates they charge have to be higher in the case of older cars. Should these vehicles have to be repossessed, always a costly process, they might be worthless and, in addition, they would be more difficult to resell. The individual buying an older car usually has less income and poorer prospects; consequently, there is a greater chance that he will not be able to repay the loan.* Buyers making lower down payments or having poor credit ratings are considered greater risks and, in consequence, have to pay higher interest rates.

However, when funds available for automobile financing are plentiful, interest rates tend to be lower and all types of lenders incline toward leniency regarding terms and down payments. When loanable funds grow scarce, interest rates rise, loans become more difficult to obtain, down-payment requirements tend to stiffen, and the periods in which the loans have to be repaid contract.

Sources of Financing

The normal sources for auto loans are banks, automobile clubs, consumer-finance companies, automobile dealers, and credit unions.**

* Furthermore, the interest charge must be higher when smaller sums are involved for shorter periods of time. See Chapted 3, p. 65.
** Except for automobile clubs, the sources for auto financing are discussed in Chapter 3. See pp. 68, 72–76.

Automobile clubs and associations usually make loans to members at rates of interest only slightly higher than banks. Many of these associations are mutual associations; what profits they make come primarily from the sale of insurance to members. They have an advantage over other credit sources in that membership fees may offset many of their operating costs. When loanable funds come from excess insurance reserves, their interest charges can be highly competitive.

Bank, automobile club, finance company, and dealer interest rates on loans to be used for the purchase of new cars range from 4 to 7 per cent on the full amount of the loan. Most credit unions charge 1 per cent interest per month on the unpaid balance. On December 31, 1965 outstanding consumer automobile installment credit was distributed as shown in Table 10–3.[24]

Table 10-3

	Credit Outstanding (Millions)	Per Cent of Total
Commercial banks:		
Purchased contracts	10,310	35.8
Direct loans	5,721	19.8
	16,031	55.6
Sales-finance companies	9,241	32.0
Auto dealers	447	1.6
Other (primarily credit unions and automobile clubs)	3,124	10.8

The repayment record on automobile loans is excellent. Less than 2 per cent of new car buyers have their cars repossessed and, in the last 30 years, the figure has rarely been much higher than 3 per cent for all car buyers.[25]

Comparing Financing Costs

In shopping for the lowest price for financing, it is well to use a comparison sheet like the one shown in Table 10–4. In many states, financing organizations are required by law to make the following facts known to would-be purchasers before they sign the purchase contract: the cash sale price; the amount of trade-in allowance; the exact cash balance due; the number of payments and the amount of each payment; total charges for financing; and the kind, amount, and cost of insurance.

If the cost of insurance is included in the amount to be financed, interest has to be paid on the amount lent to cover the insurance premiums. In addition to the customary types of automobile insurance, the car buyer usually is sold

Table 10-4. **Comparison Sheet**

Item	Hypothetical Figures from First Source	Second Source	Third Source
Down payment	⅓ down		
Payment period	24 months		
Interest rate quoted	5 per cent per year on total owed		
True interest rate (figure or ascertain this rate)	Over 10 per cent annually		
Total cost of automobile (include all extras and taxes)	$3,000		
Deduct down payment:			
Trade-in allowance. $1,500			
Cash 500	$2,000		
Balance due	$1,000		
Insurance payments on automobile during payment period	240		
Fee for credit investigation and processing transaction	10		
Total to be financed	$1,250		
Financing charge over payment period (2 years at 5 per cent)	125		
Total owed	$1,375		
Number of monthly payments	24		
Monthly payment	$57.29		

credit life insurance; this indemnifies the seller for the unpaid balance on the car should the buyer die before completing payment.

INSURING AN AUTOMOBILE

Since automobile accidents are numerous and increasing in frequency, it is imperative that every automobile owner carry insurance against claims that may be made on him. These claims originate because of injury to persons or damage to property. He should also be insured against costs which he may incur because of injuries or property damage that he may suffer. In some states, an automobile may not be registered until the owner shows proof that he carries liability insurance. In other states, if a driver is involved in an accident, he must be able to show that he carries liability insurance, or he must *post bond*, that is, deposit a sum of money or deeds to property with an appointed agent of the state. Either course gives assurance that he will pay any costs and damages for which he may be held responsible. Automobile insurance is discussed in Chapter 13. Insuring an automobile should be regarded as insuring an investment.

To Buy or To Lease

Leasing a car may be preferable to buying one:

1. If you feel you need to drive a new car or a more expensive one than you can afford to buy.

2. If you cannot or do not want to tie up funds in an automobile. Remember that any returns that may be earned on the down payment are foregone if the funds are used to buy the automobile.

3. If you live in an urban area where owning a car is more trouble than it is worth (disutilities outweigh utilities). Some leasing companies offer free parking, a convenient place to service the car while it is not being used, all the necessary maintenance as part of the lease price, another car to drive while the leased car is being serviced, and other amenities.

4. If you have computed the costs and benefits of buying versus leasing accurately. Tax considerations enter here.

Whether one owns or leases a car, an owner of a busines or an employee may deduct the costs of operating the automobile associated with its business use on his federal income tax return. These costs qualify as a business expense or as an expense connected with his employment. Leasing companies provide statements of miles driven during the year and payments made for tax purposes.

The offsetting considerations are the following ones.

1. It generally costs an individual *more* to lease a car than to buy one. One pays for all services received, such as maintenance.

2. There are several types of basic leasing plans. Those with relatively lower monthly payments may have a high "balloon" payment at the end. Leasing contracts must be read carefully.

The leasing of automobiles by individuals appears to be increasing rapidly. In 1964, according to a survey by the magazine, *Automotive Fleet*, 38 per cent of all leased automobiles were hired by individuals. And, according to American Motors, upward of 70 per cent of all lessors sign a second contract when the first one expires.[26]

The Lease. Under all automotive leases, the lessor chooses the automobile and the lessee, i.e. the leasing company, generally a new-car dealer, buys it. Leases differ in how the lessor pays for insurance, maintenance, and most important, depreciation.

Under a straight lease, also termed a "closed end" or "walk-away" lease, the lessor makes a fixed monthly payment for the stipulated period, frequently 12 or 26 months, plus, in some instances, a charge per mile over a certain mileage. The monthly charge includes the cost of depreciation. When the lease expires there are no further obligations. If the lessor signs a full maintenance lease, which is one form of the straight lease, all connected charges, except those for gas and oil are included in the monthly fee. This is probably the most popular and convenient lease for individuals. Under a *net lease*, the monthly fee covers depreciation, but the lessor pays for maintenance and all operating expenses.

Under a finance lease, also termed an "open end," "cost-plus," or "contingent liability" lease, the leasing company's monthly charge covers a prorated amount for a depreciation reserve and its profit. When the lease expires, the lessee will sell the automobile, and at that time the reserve should cover the depreciation. If the sale brings in more than was expected, the lessor receives a refund; if less, he pays the difference. Most of the sales are made on the wholesale market, resulting in a greater depreciation loss than would occur if the lessor sells the automobile at retail.

Under some contracts the leasing company is entitled to part of the refund, the so-called "overage bonus." In some instances the lessee charges a fee for selling the car. In effect, these are additions to the depreciation loss incurred by the lessor. Properly used, the finance lease is the more economical of the two lease forms. Maintenance, insurance, and other services may be included for an additional fee.

The third leasing arrangement, the *lease-sale*, not too commonly used, as yet, provides for a monthly payment that covers the rental fee plus operating expenses for the automobile. It further provides that the lessor will buy the automobile from the leasing company for a designated price at the end of the contract term. The Internal Revenue Service regards a lease-sale as a contract sale and will not allow business users to deduct these lease payments as expenses.

Leasing companies prefer "normal" automobile users with A-1 credit ratings. Most contracts contain an excessive-abuse clause which holds the lessor responsible for anything the leasing company considers beyond "ordinary wear and tear."

The Cost. The dealer generally figures the monthly payment as follows:

Hypothetical cost of car to dealer	$2,750
Markup on sale to own leasing company (3–4 per cent)	85
Taxes and miscellaneous charges, about	60

Leasing company's own markup (generally 14–17 per cent
on so-called "capitalized cost") 345

"Capitalized Cost" (or about what you should expect to
pay him if you bought this automobile new) $3,240

The monthly payment is determined by the capitalized cost. The amount for the depreciation reserve is generally 2 per cent of the capitalized cost per month or about $62.80

The "service-finance" charge is generally 0.6 per cent per month (7.2 per cent per annum), or in this case 19.44

Thus, the amount of the monthly payment on this *finance lease* would be $82.24

As noted above, an additional payment will be required at the expiration of the lease if the depreciation reserve does not cover the lessor's depreciation loss. Under a *straight lease*, an additional charge will be added to cover this contingency.

A study comparing the costs of leasing or buying for three cars all of which listed for about $3,300 and actually sold for $3,000 is shown in Table 5. The costs will vary somewhat in different areas but not by very much. The cost of owning the automobile is exclusive of operating costs and includes depreciation, a 7 per cent finance charge (or an effective rate of about 14 per cent), and ordinarily associated miscellaneous expenses.[27]

Table 5

Monthly Costs for Buying the Car Using Installment Credit and Selling after 24 Months (Dollars)		Under a Maintenance Lease (Dollars)	Under a Net Lease (Dollars)	Under a Finance Lease (Dollars)
Chevrolet (Impala)	59.50	107.50	97.50	82.50
Ford (Galaxie)	68.00	116.00	106.00	91.00
Plymouth (Fury)	72.00	110.00	110.00	95.00

Under the maintenance lease, $10 a month or $120 a year is added to the payments. This should be compared with the national average for maintenance costs on automobiles—less than half a cent a mile, or about $40 a year for 10,000 miles.

As this chapter has indicated, maximization of the use to be made of outlays for transportation and from investments in means of transportation no longer can be accomplished without making decisions about increasingly complex matters. For the truth is that expenditures for transportation, like expenditures for almost every other major item in the American budget, may be expected to increase as prices continue to rise and the demand for the commodity grows even greater as a concomitant of the changing social patterns.

QUESTIONS

1. Why has the demand for transportation grown as it has in the last 40 years? Can this increase be expected to continue for the next 40 years? Why? On what factors do you base your answer?
2. Why are the number of automobiles in the United States increasing, despite the problems engendered by their growing number? What are some of the problems engendered by the growing number of automobiles?
3. What are some of the problems faced by urban transportation companies? List possible solutions to these problems. Explain why you think these will work.
4. How much per mile does it cost to operate a standard-sized car in the community where you live? (Automobile clubs and leasing agencies will have data that can be used in answering this question.)
5. Why may total operating costs per mile for a foreign car such as a Volkswagen be less than for a comparable American car? Why might they be more?
6. When does a car depreciate most rapidly?
7. What are the advantages and disadvantages of buying a used car?
8. List some of the factors that will have a bearing on how fast a car will depreciate.
9. Why have transit fares been increasing in recent years? Can they be expected to continue to increase? Why?
10. What questions should be answered before deciding which type of car to buy?
11. What are two reliable sources of published information that may be used when comparing various makes and models of cars? List ten of the attributes that are considered in the comparisons made. Are these the attributes that are of the most importance to you?
12. What are some of the factors to consider when deciding which size car to buy?
13. List some of the questions to be answered before deciding to buy a new car.
14. What is meant by an "authorized dealer"? What other automobile dealers are there?
15. Why must one be especially cautious in buying a used car?
16. How may a car buyer minimize interest charges to be paid on the amount of the price that he finances?
17. When is it advisable to lease rather than buy a new automobile?
18. What is meant by a "straight" automobile lease? A "finance" lease?
19. Which form of automobile lease is most popular among individuals? Why? Is this a "straight" or a "finance" lease?

SELECTED READINGS

Keats, John, *The Insolent Chariots*, Lippincott, Philadelphia, 1958.
Owen, Wilfred, *Automotive Transportation; Trends and Problems*, The Brookings Institution, Washington, D. C., 1949.

Owen, Wilfred, *The Metropolitan Transportation Problem*, The Brookings Institution, Washington, D. C., 1956.
Smerk, George M., *Urban Transportation: The Federal Role*, Indiana University Press, Bloomington, Ind., 1965.
Westmeyer, Russell E., *Economics of Transportation*, Prentice-Hall, Englewood Cliffs, N. J., 1956.
Your Automobile Dollar, Household Finance Corp., Chicago, 1956.

NOTES

1. *Statistical Abstract of the United States*, U. S. Department of Commerce, Bureau of the Census, Washington, D. C., 1965., p. 559.
2. *Ibid.*, p. 569.
3. Frank Donovan, *Wheels for a Nation*, Thomas Y. Crowell Co., New York, N. Y., 1965, p. 276.
4. Wilfred Owen, *The Metropolitan Transportation Problem*, The Brookings Institution, Washington, D. C., 1956, p. 68.
5. *Economic Report of the President*, January 1966, Washington, D. C., 1966, p. 219.
6. *Statistical Abstract of the United States*, 1965, *op. cit.*, pp. 361, 569 and 578.
7. Owen, *op. cit.*, p. 40.
8. *Statistical Abstract of the United States*, 1965, *op. cit.*, p. 573.
9. Daniel B. Suits, "Exploring Alternative Formulations of Automobile Demand," *The Review of Economics and Statistics*, February 1961, p. 69.
10. *Statistical Abstract of the United States*, 1965, *op. cit.*, pp. 579 and 592.
11. Warren S. Gramm, "Criteria for Public Investment," *Proceedings of the Thirty-Fifth Annual Conference of the Western Economic Association*, held at Stanford, Calif., August 24–26, 1960, p. 63.
12. *Business Week*, March 27, 1965, p. 162.
13. Releases of American Automobile Association.
14. *Official Guide*, Kelly Blue Book, Los Angeles, Calif., issued annually. Each major city has its own.
15. *Money Management, Your Automobile Dollar*, Money Management Institute, Household Finance Corp., Chicago, Ill., 1956, p. 4.
16. Issued by Consumers Union, Mount Vernon, N. Y.
17. Issued by Consumers' Research, Inc., Washington, N. J.
18. Issued by The Popular Mechanics Co., Chicago, Ill.
19. Issued by Mechanix Illustrated, New York, N. Y.
20. *Consumer Reports 1961 Buying Guide Issue*, Consumers Union, Mount Vernon, N. Y., December 1960, p. 350.
21. *Official Guide*, *op. cit.*, see latest year.
22. *Automotive News*, Slocum Publishing Co., Inc., 965 E. Jefferson, Detroit, Mich.
23. *Consumer Reports 1961 Buying Guide Issue*, *op. cit.*, p. 350, and see Chapter 3.
24. Theodore O. Yntema, *A Statement on Proposed Legislation Prohibiting Automobile Manufacturers from Offering Finance and Insurance Services to Dealers and Car Buyers*, Ford Motor Company, Dearborn, Mich., pp. 3, 4, and 12.
25. Clyde William Phelps, *Using Installment Credit*, Commercial Credit Company, Baltimore, Md., 1955, pp. 46 and 47.

Insuring an Automobile 321

26. *Changing Times*, The Kiplinger Magazine, August 1965, p. 29.
27. *Ibid.*, pp. 30 and 31.

PROBLEMS AND CASES

1. How much does it cost to operate your car or your family's car per week? Per month? Keep a complete record of all expenses for a week. How much is it costing per mile? (Keep a record of the exact number of miles driven during one week.) Considering all other costs (payments including interest paid, insurance, and depreciation), what are your total costs per mile? What are your fixed costs (those that do not change, no matter how much you drive)? What are your variable costs (those that change with the number of miles you drive)? What are your marginal costs (the cost of driving one additional mile)? What is the relationship between your variable costs and your marginal costs?

2. If a family has an income of $10,000 a year, how expensive a car can it afford, if it budgets 10 per cent of its income for the ownership and operation of a car, drives 6,000 miles a year, and plans to pay for a car by putting one third down and liquidating the balance over a 12-month period? The family will be paying 5 per cent on the unpaid balance of any amount it finances.

3. If this family wants to buy a second car for $2,000 and plans to drive it 5,000 miles a year and finance it as it did the first car, how much additional income will the family need if it is not to increase the amount allocated to automobile ownership and operation to more than 10 per cent?

4. The Townsends are considering buying a second car since Mrs. Townsend needs a car for shopping, taking the children to their various groups, etc., while Mr. Townsend is away with the family car during the day. They are undecided between an older, domestically manufactured car and an imported car. Counsel them by giving them the advantages and disadvantages connected with both. If the final choice is between a three-year-old Ford Mustang and a new Volkswagen (price both) what will be the probable costs of owning and operating these cars for one year? Over a period of three years? Which one would you advise the Townsends to buy? Why?

5. The Beatons need a replacement for their car. They are undecided whether to buy a new or a used car. Their income from all sources is $6,800 a year. Can they afford a new car? Which one? Can they finance it? How? How much would the payments be each month on the least expensive new car they could buy—domestic or import? How much would the payment be on a four-year-old used "low-priced" domestic automobile? On a "less well known" four-year-old lower-priced import? Which should they buy? Why?

6. John Lea is a salesman. He drives over 10,000 miles a year on business. His problem is whether to buy or lease a new car. Investigate the leasing arrangements available for three domestic cars. What types of leases are being offered? How much would his monthly payments be if he bought one of these three cars? What is the difference in each case between the monthly payment if he bought the car and the payment on the lease? What accounts for the difference? Is there any tax advantage to Lea in leasing? If so, what is it?

7. What are some of the problems faced by intercity carriers? List possible solutions to these problems and explain why you think they will work.

8. List some of the factors on which the decision as to whether to use an automobile or public transportation may hinge. If all private and social costs are considered, which of the two would be the logical choice? Why?
9. If you were deprived of your automobile for a week, by what means of transportation would you reach your usual destinations? What would your costs for for transportation be during this week? Is this more or less than it costs you to operate your car, considering all costs? Would any of your activities be curtailed? Do you think this experience might result in your using your car less? Why or why not?
10. You are offered the choice of buying or leasing a new Ford. The net price of the car to you is $3,500. Using the percentages and estimates given in the text, how much would you estimate the difference in your monthly payments would be between what you would pay if you bought the car and what you would pay under a maintenance lease, a net lease, a finance lease? Interview an automobile dealer and determine how close your estimates were.
11. Interview the city or regional official most concerned with transportation. Determine from him if he thinks intra-area and interarea transportation needs are being adequately met for your locality. If not, what does he think can be done to improve the situation? Do you agree with him? Why or why not?

11 EXPENDITURES FOR MEDICAL CARE

Gold that buys health can never be ill spent ...

JOHN WEBSTER

Everyone is concerned about health. Americans were sufficiently concerned to spend $30 billion on personal medical care in 1966. This was about 3½ times the amount they spent in 1950 and about ten times the amount they spent in 1929. Part of this increase may be attributed to the growth in population and to the larger proportion of children and older people; these are the two groups that normally require more medical care than others. Most of this increase, however, stems from wider utilization of medical care and the higher prices for it. In consequence, per capita medical expenditure rose from $27 in 1929 to $136.92 in 1965. It is this rise, compounded by the inherent uncertainty of medical expenses, that has brought the problem of financing medical care to its present proportions.[1]

DEMAND FOR MEDICAL CARE

The demand for medical care obviously comes from those who are seriously ill or injured. Yet more often it comes from those who have less serious disabilities but desire treatment, and in recent years it has been coming increasingly from those who desire preventive care.

Incidence of Disability

Between July 1, 1966 and June 30, 1967, there were about 318 million statistical instances of illness in the United States in which acute conditions restricted the activities of individuals or required medical attention. In all, these persons spent a total of 1,536 million days in bed. Table 11-1 shows the distribution of the causes of their disabilities. On the average, during this 12-month period, every person in the United States spent approximately six days in bed. Respiratory illnesses alone caused 590.8 million days of restricted activity. Besides, 50 per cent of the population were reported to be suffering from one or more chronic conditions.

Table 11-1. **Distribution of the Causes of Illnesses, 1967**

Condition	Per Cent of Total
Infectious and parasitic diseases	14.0
Respiratory conditions	43.0
Digestive system conditions	4.0
Injuries	23.6
All other acute conditions	15.4
Total	100.0

SOURCE: Public Health Service, U. S. Dept. of Health, Education, and Welfare.

A total of 54.1 million persons were injured in 1967. Over 100,000 died. Roughly 16 per cent of these injuries occurred at work, 15 per cent involved a motor vehicle, and 44 per cent happened at home. Altogether about 29 million persons were admitted to hospitals; this is one out of every seven people in the United States. On the average, every person in the United States visited or was visited by a doctor 4.5 times during that year. In any one year, every American can expect to be disabled to some extent owing to illness or injury, and everyone will need some medical care.[2]

Demand for Preventive Care

To prevent disabilities and stay healthy, Americans have been told to see their doctors at least once a year and their dentists twice a year. Children, pregnant women, those engaged in particularly strenuous or hazardous occupations, and those in their later years normally need more medical attention for preventive care. In addition, immunization against an increasing number of diseases has become possible, popular, and prevalent over the last 20 years. More and more, healthy people are demanding medical care to help them keep and improve their health.

Other Factors Affecting This Demand

"Health is now considered a right, it's no longer a question of whether people get it, it's simply how."[3] The miracles of modern medicine have been widely publicized; in consequence, many now regard as unnecessary and intolerable the disabilities that their grandparents regarded as inevitable. Admittedly, doctors and dentists cannot perform miracles in every case, but they can and do alleviate a greater number of disabling conditions more effectively than they did 30, 20, or even 10 years ago. As more people appreciate the benefits of medical care, more take advantage of it. In addition, increased incomes and wider health-insurance coverage have resulted in more people being able to afford more medical care. Consequently, about two-thirds of the population now see a doctor at least once during the year. Thirty years ago it was less than half the population. Moreover, the number of visits per patient has risen 40 per cent.[4]

SUPPLY OF MEDICAL CARE

There are approximately 300,000 practicing physicians in the United States and more than 2,000,000 persons employed by the health services industry. However, the increase in the supply of the services and facilities devoted to health care has not kept pace with the demand for them. Between 1900 and 1950 the number of doctors increased by only slightly more than half. During the same period, total population just about doubled. The number of nurses increased fiftyfold; dentists, one-and-a-half times; and pharmacists, more than five times. Nonetheless, because of increased demand, there is still a shortage in every one of these occupational categories.[5] In the case of physicians, the shortage in some areas is serious.[6]

Between 1910 and 1955, as the American population grew by 80 per cent, hospital beds increased by 280 per cent. Yet the demand for hospital care expanded more rapidly, causing an acute shortage of specific types of hospital facilities, and of hospital beds in certain areas.[7]

In the attempt to meet the still increasing demand for medical care, many steps are being taken to utilize health services and facilities more efficiently. Doctors carry heavier patient loads. In most cases, the lone physician no longer attempts to render complete medical care. Generally, this has grown beyond any one individual's knowledge and skill and often has become financially infeasible as well.[8] The capital investment required to equip and operate an adequate office has become high and is going higher. Most doctors work collaboratively with others, formally or informally in groups, and refer patients to the appropriate specialists for treatment. Almost without exception, they join the staffs of hospitals or establish working relationships with hospitals.

Most doctors, dentists, opticians, and practical nurses nowadays maintain private practices. Some pharmacists own their own pharmacies. However, over 1.5 million members of the health-service industry are employed by various governmental and private agencies and firms in the field. The nurse, the laboratory technician, the therapist, the rehabilitation counselor, the administrator, the dietician, and the patient's doctor or doctors are all members of the team employed to maintain or restore health.

The team can handle more patients than its members could as individuals. It can do more for patients and operate more competently. As in any industry in which operations can be standardized, analyzed, and broken down into their component functions, specialization in the health field increases productivity.

COST OF MEDICAL CARE

Private medical expenditures were $7.6 billion in 1948 and $24.8 billion in 1964. Medical expenditures comprised 4.3 per cent of total consumer expenditures in 1948 and 6.2 per cent in 1964.[9] There is little doubt that this percentage will continue to increase. Over the years there has been a change also in how each medical care dollar is spent. Table 11–2 illustrates this point.

Increasing Costs of Medical Care

Costs of medical care have been rising rapidly in recent years. Between 1950 and 1964, the Bureau of Labor Statistics' Consumer Price Index for all items increased a little less than 25 per cent of the prices in 1957 to 1959. The medical care component of the index, in contrast, rose by about a half in the same period—twice as much—and more than any other category of expenditures. Transportation expanded 30.3 per cent, but no other category increased

Table 11-2. Distribution of the Consumer's Medical Care Dollar

	1949	1959	1964
Hospital services	.24	.30	30.4
Physicians' services	.32	.27	27.3
Medicine and appliances	.25	.26	21.7
Dentists	.11	.11	9.4
Other services	.08	.06	11.2
Total	1.00	1.00	1.00

NOTE: Other services include nursing homes or, more accurately, extended care facilities, which have been taking a growing proportion of the consumer's medical care dollar: 1.3 cents in 1950, 3.2 cents in 1964; and the net cost of insurance to consumers, which has also been increasing. They were 3.5 cents of each dollar spent for medical care in 1950, 4.6 cents in 1964.
SOURCE: Social Security Administration, U. S. Dept. of Health, Education, and Welfare.

by as much as 32 per cent. The Bureau of Labor Statistics' subordinate indices for the various medical care items included in the overall medical care index show that, by 1964, hospital room rates had increased 100 per cent from 1947, general practitioners' fees 47 per cent, dentists' fees 41 per cent, prescriptions and drugs about 19 per cent, and optometric examinations and eyeglasses 10 per cent.[10]

Hospital Rates. Hospital care is the fastest growing and most expensive area of medical service. But, whereas hospital room rates have increased drastically and in all probability will continue to do so,[11] modern methods of medical treatment have provided an offsetting factor by reducing the average length of stay in the hospital. Between 1946 and 1964 alone, the average length of stay was reduced by 15 per cent.[12] More important, more lives are being saved and health is being restored more often than even a few years ago.

Doctor's Fees. Fees for doctors' services have risen, particularly since 1950,[13] and they are continuing to do so. But they are not rising as rapidly as they might for a number of reasons. These include the competition in some areas, the greater efficiency resulting from group practice, the publicizing of standard fee schedules, and patient resistance to higher costs.

Although doctors have a partial monopoly of the services they render and enjoy a sellers' market to some extent, in some of the populous urban areas there is a relative oversupply of doctors in some specialties.[14] Yet, in many cases, instead of producing a reduction of fees charged, this has simply resulted in each doctor seeing fewer patients. Not all doctors are equally popular, however, and not all of them are fully employed. In consequence, there are many who do feel the effects of competition.

Group practice ordinarily results in medical services being made available at lower fees. Dr. Russel Lee, head of the 80-patient Palo Alto Clinic, has observed:

> I know from experience that a group can profitably give complete medical service at $5 per person per month. The Palo Alto Clinic has such a deal with the Masons. We take care of all their old people at that price. Old people, remember aren't supposed to be insurable. And these Masons are from 65 to 105 years old. Yet, we give them complete care for $5 a month.
>
> Q. And you don't lose money?
>
> A. One year . . . we kept a careful check. At $5 a month we took in $234 more from them than we would have earned on a straight fee-for-service basis. If it can be done for old folks, it can be done for anybody.
>
> Q. Can a solo practitioner do it?
>
> A. The solo practitioner can't afford complete prepayment because he can't give comprehensive care.[15]

And it is not only a matter of price. As Selig Greenberg has said, "Group practice looks like the most promising mechanism yet devised for controlling both the efficiency and quality of medical care."[16] The economies of group practice impressed the Twentieth Century Fund. The private medical needs of the American people in 1960, it predicted, could have been met for approximately half the cost incurred under prevailing methods of organization.[17]

Standardized publicized fee schedules have come into wider use. The government-approved fee schedules under *Medicare* and for the beneficiaries of several other programs are open to public inspection. According to the Social Security Administration, these fees are "reasonable" and "customary." They are based on the individual doctor's customary charge and the prevailing charge in the locality where, in turn, they affect the prevailing level of fees. Some groups now post the fees charged for visits and common medical procedures in their waiting rooms. There, patients may see them before they see the doctors. The increase in health insurance has also promoted the adoption of standardized fees because physicians cannot always submit charges to the insurance companies or plans on the basis of individual cases.

This is a far cry from the day when fees were discussed in hushed tones, and discriminatory pricing based on ability to pay was practically the only method used by physicians.[18] It is still used to some extent, but a statewide Michigan State Medical Society survey showed that, in setting their own fees, nearly two-thirds of the doctors gave most weight to "the usual fee in the community." Slightly more than one-fifth considered the doctor's own "evaluation of his professional ability" as the best criterion, while 14 per cent depended primarily on the "economic potential of the patient."[19] Moreover, doctors sometimes charge higher fees if they know that a patient does have insurance.

An interesting development in the standardization of fee schedules is the *Relative Value Schedule* that attempts to relate the value of various medical procedures to each other. In California, the state schedule has been adapted at varying price levels to the California Medicare program, the state public-assistance program, and many private health-insurance programs. In Michigan, such a schedule is used in determining Blue Shield fees. The American Medical Association hopes soon to have a nationally accepted schedule. Under these schedules, there are no set prices or fees for specific services, but a particular service might be shown as being worth twice as much as another. In the California schedule, for example, the relative value of an appendectomy is 35.0, and the relative value of a tonsilectomy is 15.0. Thus, if the physician charges $175 for an appendectomy, he should charge $75 for a tonsilectomy.

Patient resistance to higher prices has resulted in the neglect of health needs by families who cannot or will not pay the prices asked. It has also occasioned nonpayment or very slow payment of medical and hospital bills. Historically, the doctor has been the last man to be paid.

Drug Prices. In the case of many drugs, patients are a captive market. They are buyers who have no choice and who must pay for prescriptions in cash. In most cases, doctors do not prescribe drugs by generic name. Generally they prescribe the branded products they know, which frequently cost many times what the similar, nonbranded product may cost. Drug prices are high because their ingredients and manufacture are costly; because the research and product development behind their discovery and marketability are expensive; "because there is no competition on many products for which particular companies hold patents"; and because their distribution and promotion costs are steep.

Undoubtedly economies are possible in distribution and promotion. Prices of many products would be lower if there were more competition in the industry. They would also be lower if the products were not fair-traded, that is, if their minimum retail price were not protected by law, and if drug markups, the amount the seller adds on to the cost, were not so high. Charges for prescriptions have increased significantly since 1947–1949.[20] Although they may not increase as drastically in the future because of heightened public resistance to higher prices, they will continue to be a major part of the high cost of adequate medical care. Moreover, they are still not generally covered by insurance.

The Cost of Adequate Medical Care

Medical expenses are rarely average for most people or most families. They may vary widely in different years. Illness or injury generally occurs when it is not expected. In any one year, the chances are one in five that medical bills will exceed 10 per cent of the family income; they are one in fifty that they will exceed half of income.[21] A catastrophic illness may result in bills that are four times the family's income. Donald B. Straus has pointed out that "most American families simply are not able to pay for modern medical care."[22] He has maintained that:

. . . there is a growing consensus that a family should be able to get these services, when needed:

(1) Hospitalization up to 120 days a year in semi-private accommodations.

(2) Unlimited access to doctors' services for diagnosis and preventive care, as well as treatment of illness.

(3) Drugs.

(4) Enough dental care to keep the mouth healthy, though not necessarily beautiful.

(5) Miscellaneous necessities, such as braces, appliances, and private nursing in serious illness.

Here is what these things now cost, in a typical big city, according to the best available estimates. (You should give or take 20 per cent, to account for local variations—and keep in mind that these are averages; any given family in any one year might spend far less, or more.)

Hospitalization (insured)	$150
Doctors' care (insured)	150
Drugs	100
Dentistry	100
Miscellaneous	50
Total	$550[23]

A tidy sum!

FINANCING MEDICAL CARE

The average family does not and apparently will not budget and save to meet its medical expenses. Neither will it put aside a reserve to offset the loss of income that occurs when illness or injury incapacitate the wage earner. Instead, its members resort to one of the following courses: they wait until illness or accident strikes, and when it does, they use up their savings and borrow if need be; for them preventive care is largely neglected. Or they take out insurance against the costs of medical care and the loss of income as a result of illness or injury; some still take out a form of insurance that indemnifies them only against the loss of a part of parts of the body and the loss of their earnings because of this disability. Or they become members of groups or prepayment plans that provide medical care, insurance, or both, at lower rates to those who qualify.

In some cases, employers and unions pay part of the cost for medical care or health insurance. In many cases—servicemen, for example—the government pays for medical care. By 1964, about 151 million Americans were making payments or having premiums or payments paid for them to insurance organizations or prepayment plans. Thus they would not have to finance the entire cost of maintaining health when they made use of health services or the costs of restoring health when injuries or illnesses occurred.[24] In addition, for the "medically indigent" who are eligible for medical assistance under the provisions of the various state laws, aid is provided in meeting their medical expenses under Title 19 of the Social Security Act, the so-called "Medicaid" provisions. The federal government pays at least 50 per cent of the cost of Medicaid for some of the higher-income states and up to 83 per cent of the cost for states with the lowest tax revenues. The groups ordinarily receiving Medicaid are the blind and disabled, the elderly, dependent children, and families considered "medically indigent." The last are families with insufficient income to meet medical expenses in addition to other living costs ($3,600 for a family of four in Illinois, for example). To qualify for federal reimbursement, the state programs are required to provide five basic benefits: hospital care, outpatient hospital care, doctors' services, nursing home care for adults, and laboratory and X-ray services, but the amounts of benefits and the scope of the programs vary among the states. Minnesota, noted for the breadth of its program, covers "whatever the doctor orders."

Health Insurance

The term "health insurance" is misleading. Ordinarily this type of insurance is not bought to protect health but to alleviate the impact of the hospital, surgical, and other medical expenses related to the regaining of health when illness or injury occurs. It is a relatively high-priced form of indemnification.

Normally other types of insurance are bought to protect the insured against an event that is not an ordinary occurrence. The chances of the event's happening to any one person in the total group insured can be computed accurately. Then the insured need pay only enough to cover the costs incurred by the insurance company in satisfying claims in the relatively *small proportion* of cases in which the event does occur and in meeting overhead.* For example, a

* See Chapter 13, p. 388.

$25,000 house can be insured against fire for about $25 a year. In a lifetime, premiums will amount to only a fraction of the cost of replacement of the house, because ordinarily relatively few houses burn down.

In contrast, most persons suffer one or more major illnesses and many minor ones in a lifetime. Consequently, it costs from $270 to $300 a year in the early 1960's to buy insurance protection against hospital and doctors' bills alone, which accounted for less than 60 per cent of all personal health expenditures.[25] Since illness and injury are a certainty in almost everyone's life, they are not low-cost insurable risks in the same sense as fires, floods, and other catastrophes which have a relatively rare occurrence rate.

Extent of Coverage. About one-quarter of our nation's total personal medical bill is now financed through health insurance. About four-fifths of the people in the United States have insurance against hospital expenses. About 70 per cent of the hospital bills in the United States are paid by the insurance. By 1964, almost 141 million had protection against some surgical expenses, about 109 million had some protection against regular medical expenses, and 47 million were protected to some degree against major medical expenses, those hospital and medical costs resulting from a catastrophic or prolonged illness or a disability due to injury. Almost 40 per cent of the doctors' bills in the United States were paid by insurance.[26]

About a fifth of the population has no health insurance; more than half are insured against charges for medical care only while in the hospital, and less than 5 per cent are enrolled in plans that provide comprehensive physicians' services.[27] Then, too, since so few nonhospitalized illnesses are covered, the prevailing forms of insurance that exclude diagnostic, preventive, and convalescent services have a tendency to pyramid costs incurred by illness or injury by encouraging excessive hospitalization. This adds monetary pain, if not insult, to the injury. Those who have health insurance have been paying higher premiums before the onset of illness or the occurrence of injury and then have been liable, despite broadened coverage, for a greater difference between the amount covered by insurance and the total bill. If coverage offered is further broadened in response to vociferous demands, and if policies are written to indemnify the insured against the costs of services only minimally covered now, premiums inevitably will be higher still. As a result, many more people may find themselves unable to afford health insurance. Despite rising incomes for the population in general, those who need health insurance and cannot afford it are steadily increasing in number.

Types of Insuring Organizations. In 1964, more than 1,900 insuring organizations in the United States provided protection against the hospital, surgical, and medical expenses arising from illness or injury and also against the loss of income accompanying disability.[28] Of these, 972 were insurance companies. The 100 leading companies in the field issued 85.4 per cent of the contracts in 1959.[29] The other organizations providing insurance were 78 Blue Cross Plans, including Puerto Rico, 75 Blue Shield Plans, and nearly 800 independent plans.[30] The premiums written and the claims incurred by these organizations are shown in Table 11-3. Obviously group policies and Blue Cross, Blue Shield, and independent plans pay out much larger proportions of their income in benefit payments than do private insurers. The health-insurance business is clearly one of the nation's major industries.

Table 11-3. Subscription or Premium Income and Benefit Expenditures of Private Health Insurance Organizations, 1964

Organization	Income (in Millions)	Per Cent	Benefit Expenditures (in Millions)	Per Cent
Blue Cross-Blue Shield Plans				
Blue Cross	2,697.6	30.1	2,592.8	33.2
Blue Shield	1,087.5	12.1	981.6	12.6
Total	3,785.1	42.3	3,574.4	45.8
Insurance companies				
Group policies	3,297.0	36.8	3,024.0	38.7
Individual policies	1,355.0	15.1	739.0	9.5
Total	4,652.0	51.9	3,763.0	48.2
Independent plans	521.0	5.8	470.0	6.0
Total	8,958.1	100	7,807.4	100

SOURCE: *Social Security Bulletin,* December 1965, p. 20.

Types of Insurance Policies. *Hospital-expense insurance* provides benefits to be applied against hospital daily room and board charges. These policies have an allowance that may be applied against charges for the use of the operating room, laboratory fees, X-ray and fluoroscopic examination fees, drugs and medications, and some miscellaneous charges for hospital services such as special nurses' fees. Allowance for hospital "extras" are frequently $150. Hospitalization policies usually provide a specified number of dollars a day. In some plans they sanction as much as $18, for a specified number of days, typically 30 per year or per illness, but in some policies as many as 70, 120, or 365 days. Allowances for dependents are a little lower. As competition within the industry increases, there is a tendency toward an increase in both the allowance and the number of days covered.

Surgical expense protection provides benefits to be applied against the cost of operations and particularly against surgeons' fees. The various companies have differing lists of allowances that are payable for the various surgical procedures. The maximum allowance has increased surgical procedures. The maximum allowance has increased steadily to a current average of $250. Table 11-4 illustrates some of the maximum indemnities for a typical policy.

Table 11-4. **Surgical Benefits**

Surgery	Amount (Dollars)
Appendectomy	150
Appendectomy, ruptured appendix	200
Cholecystectomy (gall bladder)	200
Herniotomy, single	100
Herniotomy, bilateral	150
Hemorrhoidectomy (internal)	100
Prostatectomy	200
Hysterectomy	200
Tonsillectomy and adenoidectomy	50
Fractured humerus, reduction of	80
Fenestration	300

Regular medical-expense insurance indemnifies the insured against the costs of visits to the doctor or the doctors' visits to the insured at home or in the hospital. Most companies usually pay from $3 to $5 per visit. The maximum number of calls for each illness or injury usually is specified in the contract. The majority of these policies apply only to nonsurgical doctors' visits in the hospitals. Many insuring organizations will not write this specific type of policy; instead, they indemnify the insured against these costs in their combination medical-surgical, or comprehensive, policies.

Major medical-expense insurance, unknown before 1951, provides benefits that may be applied against virtually all types of hospital and medical expenses incurred by catastrophic or prolonged illness or by injury. Costs of all types of medical treatment prescribed, whether in or out of a hospital, X rays, drugs, medications, and appliances all are covered beyond an initial amount, which the insured agrees to pay. If it is a $50 *deductible* policy, the insured pays the first $50 of his medical bill, other than for hospital room and board. Thereafter, on a typical policy that costs $81 a year, the insurance company will pay the first $250 for room and board on a hospital bill, and 75 per cent of the remainder, up to a specified maximum. The company also will pay 75 per cent of any other medical or hospital costs incurred in connection with the illness or injury. This can be much-needed assistance. However, having to pay the first $50 plus 25 per cent of any hospital and medical bills, apart from the initial $250 for room and board, means that this policy will not help offset the usual run of medical costs.

Higher-cost major medical-plan policies pay more. A typical policy costing $128 a year pays $1,000 of the first $1,500 of hospital charges for room and board and 80 per cent of any balance in excess of this amount, up to a stated maximum. After the insured pays the first $50 of the expenses connected with the illness or injury, other than hospital expenses, he is indemnified for the remainder of his expenses, up to the stated maximum.

Typically, major medical-expense protection policies have high maximum limits—some as high as $20,000—that may apply to any one illness or injury or to the total expense in any one policy year. They normally carry deductible provisions. These may range from $50 to $500. The higher the deductible amount, the lower the premium. These serve to eliminate the small claims that are costly to process. Therefore the insuring organization can afford to offer this type of insurance at lower rates. The *coinsurance* provisions, which require the insured to pay part of his medical and hospital bills, also are included in all policies of this type and serve to reduce claims. If one has to pay part of the costs stemming from illness or injury, there is an incentive to keep these costs down.

Comprehensive medical-expense insurance plans came into being in 1954. They provide in one policy indemnifying protection against hospital, surgical, and regular medical expense incurred by short-term or long-term illness or injury. Since this helps to solve so many more problems than the other types of health insurance, it is the fastest growing one. Comprehensive policies contain the deductible and coinsurance provisions found in major medical policies. The deductible provisions, however, may not call for quite as high an amount. They normally cover the greater part of all hospital, surgical, and medical expenses during short stays in the hospital; a lesser proportion of these expenses during a longer stay, up to a stated maximum; and expenses incurred for physicians' home or office visits, nursing care, drugs and medications, and medical appliances. For an individual, this type of policy may be rather expensive, costing as much as $300 a year.

Insurance against loss of income, one of the oldest forms of health insurance, provides benefits when the insured is unable to work because of illness or injury. This was the type of insurance needed in the early years of the twentieth century. In those days the general practitioner flourished, medical bills were low, and the question of where income would come from until the wage earner was well enough to return to work was the major problem connected with illness or injury that did not permanently disable. Policies of this type issued by insurance companies may pay the individual up to 75 per cent of his normal income, usually after a stipulated waiting period. Insurance companies reason that if they were to replace the entire income lost while the insured was not at work, many of those carrying such insurance might malinger, feign illness, or suddenly become accident-prone.

Policies that provide for a longer waiting period generally provide also for higher payments for a longer period of time. Again, as with other types of insurance policies containing a deductible or coinsurance clause, the insurer, by eliminating a number of small claims, can afford to pay more in the case of eligible ones. Loss-of-income policies usually also provide for a stipulated payment to the beneficiary in case of the accidental death of the insured individual and payment of an indemnity to the policyholder if he should lose an arm, a leg, an eye, or some other part or parts of his body.

Insurance for groups. Insurance rates for those paying for medical, surgical, or hospital insurance as members of groups are lower than those for individuals carrying the same types of insurance offering comparable benefits. One reason why the insurance company can give the lower rate to members of groups is that it does not incur the sales costs necessary to solicit that number of persons as individuals. Another reason is that it has to write or issue only one policy for the entire group. Third, and most important, the risk of any one member of the group's acquiring a disability is far lower than the risk of an individual's doing so.

Many firms pay all or part of the premiums on this type of insurance for employees and deduct the payment from taxable income as a business expense. Thus, for corporations paying a 48 per cent corporate income tax, the government is, in effect, foregoing in tax revenue and thus subsidizing 48 per cent of the premium. This is one of the popular fringe benefits that are appended to wages, and unions have negotiated for and accepted it in lieu of wage increases. Under these plans, employees are not only insured and do not have to pay income tax on the amount of the premium, as with a wage increase, but also any premium they pay usually is deducted from their paychecks, making the payment relatively painless. Under some of these plans, the firm, the insurer, the union, or the organization pays the doctor or the hospital directly. The employee's only responsibility is to take care of any unpaid difference.

As of December 31, 1964, approximately 176,891,000 members of employee groups, trade association groups, fraternal groups, or other groups were insured by private insurance companies in the United States against some portion of the hospital, surgical, or regular medical expense. On the same date, there were about 86,817,000 individual policyholders carrying the same types of insurance in the United States.[31] The figures are as high as they are because they include duplication. One person may have two or three policies. Still, roughly twice as many Americans have health insurance under group plans as buy and carry it individually.

Prepayment Plans

Let us now dwell on plans, other than those designed by the insurance companies, that provide for the payment for medical care for those who pay in advance of need. Many of these are service plans; the enrollee makes the payments to the group sponsoring the plan and the group pays the doctors, hospitals, or whoever furnishes the needed medical service. However, a plan may not pay all the costs involved in every case. Plans vary. Many of them, like the plans of the insurance companies, simply provide payments against covered medical expenses incurred. Some of them include a combination of prepaid services and indemnities. The best known of these plans is Blue Cross.

Blue Cross. The Blue Cross plans are the nonprofit plans for hospitalization insurance approved by the American Hospital Association. There were 78 of these plans in the United States and Puerto Rico in 1965 with a combined enrollment of nearly 60.5 million members.[32]

Insurance against the expenses resulting from being hospitalized were first offered in some individual income-loss-due-to-disability policies as early as 1904. It took the form of an increase in benefits while the disabled policyholder was hospitalized. Indemnities to the policyholder against expenses due to hospitalization or surgery were first offered by private insurers to groups in 1928. In 1929, the local teachers' organization in Dallas, Texas, worked out a plan with the Baylor University Hospital. Each teacher who wanted to participate in this arrangement paid $3 per semester to the hospital. In return, the hospital agreed to provide 21 days of hospital care, room and board only, to any one of the teachers who had paid and needed it. This was the first of the Blue Cross plans.

As this plan was publicized, many hospitals realized that prepayment of hospital bills would solve one of their knottiest problems: what to do about the large percentage of people who did not, generally because they could not, pay their hospital bills. They began actively to organize group plans for the prepayment of hospital expenses. In 1932, the first citywide Blue Cross plan was tried out with a group of hospitals in Sacramento, California. By 1937, there were a number of these plans, and the Health Service Commission, now known as the Blue Cross Commission of the American Hospital Association, which serves as their coordinating body, was organized. By then, Blue Cross membership had reached well over half a million. The reason was that people were and still are afraid of large hospital bills.

Since 1946, the American Hospital Association has allowed the plans to use its seal if they meet its requirements, largely concerned with the plans' financial soundness and the keeping of adequate statistics. The plans are incorporated under special state-enabling acts relating to nonprofit medical-service corporations. These generally stipulate that contracts with subscribers and hospitals be approved by the state insurance commissioner. Blue Cross plans are usually controlled by local hospitals, but increasingly representatives of community and consumer interests are found on their boards of directors.

Plans coordinate their public relations, research, and enrollment activities through the Blue Cross Commission. However, the individual plans independently set the rates and determine the services and indemnities in their contracts. Consequently, the rates charged and the payments made for similar cases and services differ from plan to plan. The local plans make their own arrangements with local member hospitals that furnish hospital care to subscribers. Nevertheless, firms or other groups that are national in scope or operations may arrange for Blue Cross coverage for their members or employees.

Hospitals in any part of the United States will be reimbursed for charges incurred by a member of a plan in another area through Blue Cross's Inter-Plan Bank. A foreign department makes payments to hospitals in countries other than the United States to cover charges incurred by Blue Cross members.

Most Blue Cross members are insured under group contracts, but almost all of the plans admit individuals at higher rates. Conversion from group to nongroup coverage usually is permitted on liberal terms. As a result, the proportion of nongroup subscribers has been steadily increasing. Normally, those who move from one locality to another may transfer from one plan to another.

Although the rates and indemnities, or the services, differ among plans, a general pattern may be discerned from looking at a number of plans. For covered disabilities, most of the minimum-price plans allow for the full cost of a semiprivate room and board at the hospital, plus a limited number of services for 21 to 30 days a year, or 21 to 30 days for each admission to the hospital, whichever is greater, plus 50 per cent of the hospital's charges for room and board and the stipulated services for 180 additional days. Some, instead, provide a per diem payment of $10 a day to the hospital for the stipulated period. However, the exclusions are many. Excluded are admissions for diagnosis, convalescence, and rest. Costs of blood, blood-donor services, and blood plasma

Financing Medical Care

are excluded. Limitations on the costs incurred as a result of tuberculosis, long-term, chronic, and mental illnesses vary, but they are excluded to a greater or lesser extent in all of the plans. Very few plans cover hospitalization resulting from dental problems. Maternity care costs are covered only for group subscribers under some of the plans. In others, this type of coverage is available at higher rates. In most plans, the subscriber must have been a member, or the dependent of a member, for nine to twelve months preceding the date of any expense connected with pregnancy or childbearing, if any of the expense is to be paid; and yet most younger families need this type of coverage more than any other.

Higher-priced Blue Cross certificates or contracts provide full coverage of hospital costs up to 120 days or even 365 days a year, and have fewer exclusions. In any case, and under any of the plans, Blue Cross rarely if ever covers the entire hospital bill for a major disability. Still, it must be remembered that the Blue Cross plans are nonprofit. Approximately 96 per cent of the premiums collected by the organizations are paid out to members who have made claims.[33] Clearly, Blue Cross rates are as high as they are and the coverage as limited as it is because hospital charges are so high, and both rates and charges are still rising. Many Blue Cross plans now pay member hospitals their regular rates less 10 per cent. Under some plans, marginal hospitals receive an additional rebate. Hospitals that charge Blue Cross wholesale rates are growing fewer, and the Blue Cross plans have not been able to do much to control the quality of hospital care or the hospitals' costs and their resultant charges.

Blue Shield. Blue Shield plans are the medical-society-approved, nonprofit plans for medical care. There are 75 of these plans in the United States and Puerto Rico. The beginnings of Blue Shield have been traced to the 1920's when local medical societies in Oregon and Washington sponsored medical-service bureaus to offset allegedly poor quality of care offered by private group clinics and hospital associations. Officially, however, the first Blue Shield plan, California Physicians' Service, was formed in 1939.[34] This and the other Blue Shield plans organized in the 1940's arose primarily in response to the need for financing medical and surgical costs for persons in the lower-income brackets. Again, these were the ones who did not and often could not pay their bills. In addition, among the medical societies, composed almost solely of private practitioners, there was some fear of the government's playing a larger role in furnishing medical care to those who could not afford it.

The first Blue Shield plans were primarily service contracts. The attached fee schedules specified a list of allowances payable for different surgical procedures, which constituted full payment by the insured to his doctor. Only groups were insured. There was no coverage of dependents. If the insured earned more than a stated amount, $2,500 to $3,500 a year in most of the plans, the doctor was authorized to charge more than the scheduled fee. However, the income limit in the early California Physicians' Service plan excluded only about 10 per cent of the population from full service benefits.[35]

The physicians found this type of contract unsatisfactory. The contracts gradually abandoned the service principle in most of the plans, primarily by permitting income limits to become obsolete as incomes generally rose, but also by changing over to straight indemnity insurance. As of October 1965, only six plans, small in membership, provided service benefits to all subscribers regardless of income. Thirteen plans were on an indemnity basis—that is, the participating physicians did not undertake to accept the plan's payments as full payment for their services. The largest number of plans (55), with about three-fourths of the total membership, provided mixed service-indemnity benefits. Under these, the participating physicians agree to accept the plan's scheduled payments or allowances as full payment for their services to subscribers with incomes under specified ceilings; the benefits for these subscribers are thus on a service basis. To subscribers with higher incomes the physicians, if they wish, may make additional charges; for these subscribers, benefits were on an indemnity basis.

The ceilings or limits for service benefits under the mixed service-indemnity plans are typically $4,000 for a single person and $6,000 for a family. As of October 1965, the limit for a single person was under $4,000 in 12 plans, $4,000–$5,000 in 29, and $6,000–$12,000 in 14. For a family, it was under $6,000 in 12 plans, $6,000–$7,999 in 33, and $8,000–$12,000 in 10.

Thirty-four of these plans had two sets of ceilings for their service benefits (that described and one or two lower ones); they also had two (in a few instances, three) schedules or allowances or fees. The ceilings under the lower schedules generally were $2,500–$3,000 for a single person and $4,000 for a family.

A nationwide study by the National Association of Blue Shield Plans in 1965 found that, for all plans and all certificates, "in 67 per cent of all claims the Blue Shield payment covered the doctor's charges in full, and that plan payments met 77 per cent of total charges under all claims."[36]

Blue Shield is interested in insuring groups. Experience has shown these to be profitable policies if rates are properly adjusted to take care of claims that can be anticipated rather accurately. The commercial insurance companies are interested primarily in this type of insurance as well, and therefore competition for these policies has been keen. In consequence, in California, Blue Shield has offered insurance for dependents since 1942; it has relaxed restrictions on the coverage of preexisting conditions since 1943 and has liberalized age limitations since 1945. Coverage of medical care for nonsurgical conditions for members and their families and individual memberships for families not affiliated with any group were made available in 1949. Other Blue Shield plans followed suit at about the same time.

Blue Shield plan presentations stress the fact that the subscriber may choose any physician he wishes. Under the plans that provide for hospital care, he may also choose any licensed hospital he desires, with few if any limitations on his range of choice among those that are available. Opponents of Blue Shield point out that when it comes to choosing a physician or a hospital, the layman is all too often not a particularly enlightened consumer. Consequently, having a free choice may not be of the utmost importance.

Some Blue Shield plans offer very liberal remuneration to physicians; for example, $12.60 to $25.00 for a consultation is not uncommon. Payments for hospital and surgical services tend to equal those of Blue Cross, and the exclusions are almost identical. Benefits available under Blue Shield group contracts can include doctors' services both in and out of the hospital, surgical and hospital benefits, and coverage for catastrophic illness. Some Blue Shield plans also offer package plans to groups, which include life and accidental death and dismemberment insurance underwritten by commercial insurance companies.

Like the Blue Cross plans, the Blue Shield plans are nonprofit corporations beset with many of the same problems. Increasingly, members of their boards of trustees are interested members of the community who are not physicians. It should be noted that Blue Shield has one overwhelming advantage in dealing with private physicians—it is their own plan for the prepayment of medical expenses.

The "Independents." The one attribute that the approximately 400 independent plans that provide health insurance have in common is that they are all nonprofit. Most of them are self-insurers, but some cooperate with Blue Cross or a private company and offer their members hospitalization insurance under a joint arrangement. Most of them are not part of any national organization, but many of those that offer their enrollees comprehensive care under a group-practice arrangement are members of the Group Health Federation of America. Some may be properly classified as industrial; these restrict their membership to those who are in a particular employee group. For example, they may be composed of members of a sponsoring union, such as the International Ladies' Garment Workers or the United Mine Workers, or of individuals who work for a railroad or a particular firm. The nonindustrial plans are open to the general public and include community plans such as HIP (Health Insurance Plan of Greater New York), Kaiser Foundation Health Plan, known as Permanante, the California group; cooperative plans such as the Group Health Association of Washington, D. C., and the Group Health Cooperative of Puget Sound; and various private, group-practice clinics such as Ross-Loos in Los Angeles, the Gunderson Clinic in La Crosse, Wisconsin, and the Palo Alto group referred to earlier in the chapter.[37] The "strength" of the independents is greatest in New York, Ohio, Connecticut, and California. Opposition to them on the part of the medical profession has mainly centered in New York and California, but has not been confined to these areas.

Virtually unknown until 1929, independent plans now enroll approximately nine million, or about 8 per cent of the total American health-insurance enrollment.[38] Nonindustrial plans account for over three-fifths of this total and, within this group, community plans account for over two-fifths of the enrollment. Union plans are dominant in the industrial group and account for about one-fourth of the total. According to Anne and Herman Somers:

> The most significant distinguishing aspect of this type of carrier is the extent to which "comprehensive" benefits are provided. About 3.5 million enrollees have hospital, surgical, medical and diagnostic benefits and another 2.4 million have comprehensive out-patient services without hospital benefits. The latter generally have B.C. (Blue Cross) or other hospital coverage. Nearly 4 per cent have dental insurance. These proportions contrast conspicuously with the usual hospital-surgical coverage available through "Blue" or commercial insurance. It is related to the fact that nearly 2/5 of independent enrollees receive medical care through group-practice.[39]

Alternate Systems for Provision of Medical Care

Both the form of organization and the method of financing whereby the quality of medical care is maximized are still matters that provoke heated discussion. Private practitioners refer to doctor-patient relationships and infer that this relationship is somehow impaired under independent group-practice plans. Groups have presented convincing evidence to the contrary.

There is no question that uninsured individuals who do not have access to free or governmental care do not, as a whole, use the medical facilities as effectively as those who are insured or belong to covered groups.[40] Medical care costs money and too often is needed when money is not available. In addition, groups often educate their subscribers on the more effective use of medical care. There is also evidence to show that many people will pay more and feel better if they visit private practitioners, because they are afraid that they will not get as much individual attention or as high a quality of care from the doctor who is a member of an organized practicing group.

Currently, however, there is general agreement on what constitutes an

Financing Medical Care

adequate system of medical care. Two well-known authorities in this area have written:

> Most people would agree that any system of medical care should first make full use of all the modern knowledge and equipment available to produce the scientifically accurate diagnosis and treatment we call good care. It should offer a worthy and dignified role as well to the professional practitioners who are to provide that care. Also, and by no means to be taken as academic, it should be so constituted that prospective patients will choose to take full advantage of the benefits offered by such care (and feel they can afford it).
>
> There is general agreement on these objectives. But a controversy hinges on the form of organization by which they may be achieved.[41]

They continue:

> The popular fear of governmental or private large-scale medical service seems to be based on the fear of loss of personal attention in a bureaucratic setting. Team practice (the experimental team was composed of an internist, a pediatrician for children under 13 years of age, a public health nurse, and a social worker who was, however, not to be a part of future teams. Parents had an annual personal conference with members of the team on the entire family's health problems) . . . seems to provide the attention desired, even though the setting is bureaucratic, since the patients expressed a high degree of personal satisfaction with the care they received.[42]

One type of team-practice solution to the controversy is being tried out under HIP in New York. Subscribers who choose to may be patients of the team at no additional charge. It is not too early to prophesy that medical care will be furnished increasingly under prepayment plans by groups of practicing physicians and by teams functioning under the supervision of the group of which they are a part. The custom of going to see the private family doctor, or of calling him and paying him when he sends his bill or when that bill can be conveniently paid, is fast vanishing.

Dr. Howard B. Sprague has written:

> Get used to dealing with teams of doctors. The trend in medical care is toward big medical centers at the core, with teams of doctors practicing in their "office-islands" close to each center even in our smaller and medium-sized communities. This is the way it's got to be if you are to benefit from all the complex advances of modern medicine. The team approach, too, will permit you to spend more time with the doctor who can serve you best.[43]

And Dr. Eveline M. Burns adds:

> Governmental involvement in the financing and organization of our health services is here to stay, and there is every indication that it will increase.[44]

The general or acute as well as the long-term hospital components of the medical center usually exist because they could be financed with a relatively low-cost loan obtained under the provisions of the Hill-Burton Act.

Nonetheless, the lone physician in private practice will remain an important member of the health-services structure for many years, but increasingly his fees will be coming from tax-supported programs.

Comparative Prices

Premiums for health insurance differ with the type of carrier, the type of policy—group or nongroup—the range and type of benefits, the geographic differences in hospital charges and doctors' fees, the characteristics of the particular insured group or individual risk, and a host of other factors. In recent years there has been a movement away from communitywide pricing, originally employed by all the Blue Cross and Blue Shield plans. Now the trend runs to differential pricing or experience-rating pricing as developed by the insurance companies.

Under community rates, premiums are set on the basis of the medical expenditures of a cross section of the community. The good risks help to pay for the poor risks. Under differential or experience-rating techniques, good risks are rewarded for their anticipated or actual low claims experience by lower initial rates, annual refunds, dividends, or some other form of a downward adjustment from the standard premium. Thus the preferred risks pay lower prices, and the poorer risks, higher.

The intense pressure of competition for the profitable group policies has resulted in a steady trend toward experience rating among all three types of insurance carriers—commercial, Blue Cross, and independent nonprofit. As a result, their rates have moved closer together and it behooves the subscriber to any of these plans or the individual buyer to shop and compare. Policies should be read carefully and exclusions of what is not insured and under what conditions should be noted. Waiting periods, that is, the length of time that must elapse before any indemnities will apply, may decrease the worth of the policy to the insured. Table 11-5, which gives illustrative annual premiums under some of the representative major group health-insurance plans and comprehensive prepayment plans, may be of help in making preliminary price comparisons.

There is no nicely packaged solution for the family that wishes to prepay completely for adequate medical care covering all likely contingencies plus adequate preventive care. There are, however, several partial solutions. Each family or individual, of course, is still responsible for choosing and paying for medical care. Highly desirable as this may be, laymen generally are not enlightened consumers when it comes to evaluating the quality and worth of medical services. Moreover, many of them are still unable or unwilling to pay current prices for what are now generally acknowledged to be needed services.

Table 11-5. Subscription or Premium and Benefit Expense *Per Enrollee* in Private Health Insurance Organizations, by Type of Care, 1964

Type of Organization	Hospital Care Premiums (Dollars)	Hospital Care Benefits (Dollars)	Physicians' Services and Other Types of Care Premiums (Dollars)	Physicians' Services and Other Types of Care Benefits (Dollars)
Blue Cross-Blue Shield Plans	43.28	41.55	19.90	17.99
Insurance Companies				
Group policies	30.48	29.10	20.50	17.66
Individual policies	24.32	13.22	11.19	6.15
Independent Plans (generally comprehensive prepayment plans)	33.33	30.03	34.16	30.85

SOURCE: *Social Security Bulletin,* December 1965, p. 21.

In view of this and the outlook for medical-care costs, the problem of obtaining adequate medical care and making payment for it relatively painless may not be capable of an easy solution for some time to come.

Medicare

The 1965 amendments to the Social Security Act added two coordinated programs of health insurance for the aged—a basic hospital insurance plan and a voluntary supplementary medical insurance plan.

The hospital insurance program covers up to 90 days' in-patient hospital services in a spell of illness; the first 60 days are covered essentially in full after a deduction of $40. For each of the remaining 30 covered days in a "spell of illness," the patient pays $10 as coinsurance. In addition, each hospital insurance beneficiary will have a "lifetime reserve" of 60 additional days of in-patient hospital coverage. These additional days can be used at the patient's option, but only once, and are subject to $20 a day coinsurance. This hospital insurance also covers in-patient care for up to 100 days in a spell of illness for continued treatment in an extended-care facility after transfer from a hospital where the patient stayed three or more days. The first 20 days of extended care are covered in full. For each of the remaining days in a spell of illness the patient pays $5 coinsurance. Home-health services are covered up to 100 visits during the year for continued care following the patient's discharge from a hospital (after a stay of at least three days) or from an extended-care facility. The deductions will be adjusted from time to time as hospital costs rise.

Generally, the medical-insurance program pays 80 per cent of the reasonable charges for covered services, above a $50 annual deduction. The program covers physician's services regardless of where they are rendered, up to 100 home-health visits each year and a variety of other medical and health services, such as diagnostic X-ray and laboratory tests; X-ray, radium, and radioactive isotope therapy; prosthetic devices; and rental of durable medical equipment.

Enrollment in the medical insurance program is voluntary. The program is financed through a premium of $4 monthly paid by the beneficiary and an equal amount paid by the Federal Government out of general revenues.

Benefits from the hospital insurance program and the medical insurance program were first payable on July 1, 1966, except for services in extended-care facilities, which were first covered on January 1, 1967.

Eligibility. Although the program is not open to every person, most people will be eligible when they reach 65. People reaching 65 in 1968 and thereafter must accumulate the required amount of work credit under social security or the railroad retirement system to qualify for the basic plan. Wives, husbands, widows, and widowers, 65 or older, qualify on their own records or on the basis of their spouse's credits. No social security or railroad retirement credit is needed to join the supplementary plan.

One can enroll in the basic plan three months before his 65th birthday and any time afterward. One can enroll in the supplementary plan three months before the month he reaches 65 and up to three months thereafter. Those who miss that first seven-month period will be able to join in the next "general enrollment" period to be held October 1 to December 31 in each odd-numbered year starting with 1967. Also, the $4-a-month premium will be increased by 10 per cent for each 12 months in which one could have enrolled but did not.

Payments Procedures. The physician determines for his patients, as he always has, the nature of the services required. If these services require hospitalization or other institutional services, he makes the arrangements for his patient's admission and care. Every beneficiary must display his health insurance benefits card upon admission. At that time, the patient makes appropriate arrangements for the payment of the deduction and any coinsurance amount that he may be called on to pay to the hospital. The hospital is paid by the Social Security Administration or its agent, which most often is "Blue Cross," the agent for about 85 per cent of the hospitals in the United States.

Under the Medical Insurance Plan, the law requires the Secretary of Health, Education, and Welfare, to the extent possible, to contract with "carriers" to carry out the major administrative functions of the medical insurance program. A carrier is defined as a voluntary association, corporation, partnership, or other nongovernmental organization lawfully engaged in providing, paying for, or reimbursing the cost of health services under group-insurance policies or contracts, or similar arrangements, in consideration of premiums or other periodic charges payable to the carrier. The definition would specifically include a group-health organization or a health-benefits plan sponsored or underwritten by an employee organization. A State welfare agency may act as the carrier for its aged welfare recipients.

Institutional providers of service are reimbursed on the basis of reasonable costs. Payments for physicians' services are made on the basis of reasonable charges. The law provides that in determining the reasonable charge for a service, the customary charges of the physician and the prevailing charges in the community will be taken into account. The reasonable charge will not be higher than the charges generally paid for comparable services provided under comparable circumstances. Payment by carriers for physicians' services are made on the basis of a receipted bill or to a physician upon an assignment. Under either method, the carrier (after the deductible has been met) will pay 80 per cent of what it determines is the reasonable charge for the services rendered—to the patient if he has sent in the receipted bill or directly to the physician if he has accepted the patient's assignment. If the doctor has agreed to assignment, he must accept the reasonable charge as his full fee.

The provision in the income-tax law limiting medical-expense deductions to amounts in excess of 3 per cent of adjusted gross income for persons under age 65 has been reinstituted for persons aged 65 and over. Thus, partial or full recovery of the Government contribution will be made from enrolled persons with incomes high enough to require them to pay income taxes. A special deduction (for taxpayers who itemize deductions) of half the amount of premiums for insurance covering medical care has, however, been added. This deduction, applicable to taxpayers of all ages, cannot exceed $150 a year.

Premium rates for enrolled persons (and the matching Government contribution) will be increased from time to time if costs rise, but not more often than once every two years.

"Medicare" and "Medicaid" are undoubtedly the forerunners of coming programs to allay the costs of *adequate* medical care where they impose a financial burden.

QUESTIONS

1. Why are people in the United States spending as much as they are on medical care today?
2. What type of medical care are people demanding today for which their grandparents had no demand?

3. What is the relationship between the "miracles of modern medicine" and the high prices of medical goods and services?
4. What is the relationship between the supply of medical personnel and facilities and the current price of medical care?
5. What is the most-utilized type of medical service? The most expensive?
6. Why have doctors' fees risen no more rapidly than they have?
7. Why can groups charge lower prices for doctors' services?
8. What are the criticisms leveled against group practice? Are they valid?
9. How do doctors set their fees?
10. Why are drug prices at the levels where they are?
11. Donald Straus contends that "most American families simply are not able to pay for modern medical care." What is the basis of his contention?
12. What medical services should a family be able to have during any one year? How much will this list of services cost today?
13. How do families meet their medical expenses?
14. Which groups of the population in the United States receive aid from the government in meeting their medical expenses?
15. Why are prices of health insurance at the levels where they are?
16. About what proportion of the total personal medical bill in the United States is paid for by health insurance?
17. List the available types of health-insurance policies. What do each of these provide?
18. Why are group rates for health insurance lower than individual rates?
19. How do prepayment plans allay medical expense? Name three well-known prepayment plans. What are the "independents"? How do they compare with other prepayment plans?
20. What are three major objectives of any adequate system of medical care? Toward which form of organization does Dr. Howard Sprague think we are moving? Which system of medical care offers the most service for the lowest prices? Why? What are the objections to this system?

SELECTED READINGS

Commerce Clearing House, *Complete Guide to Medicare*, New York, 1957.
Dickerson, O. D., *Health Insurance*, Irwin, Homewood, Ill., 1959.
Evang, Karl, D. Stark Murray, Walter J. Lear, *Medical Care and Family Security*, Prentice-Hall, Englewood Cliffs, N. J., 1963 (Part III).
Harris, Seymour Edwin, *The Economics of American Medicine*, Macmillan, New York, 1964.
Somers, Herman Miles, and Anne Ramsay Somers, *Doctors, Patients and Health Insurance*, The Brookings Institution, Washington, D. C., 1961.
Weeks, Herbert Ashley, *Family Spending Patterns and Health Care*, Harvard University Press, Cambridge, Mass., 1961.
Your Health and Recreation Dollar, Household Finance Corp., Chicago, 1958.

NOTES

1. *Social Security Bulletin*, January 1966, Social Security Administration, U. S. Dept. of Health, Education, and Welfare, p. 15; and Bureau of the Census, *Statistical Abstract of the United States, 1967*, G.P.O., Washington, D. C., pages 69 and 71.

2. *Vital Statistics of the United States*, Public Health Service, U. S. Dept. of Health, Education, and Welfare, Washington, D. C., 1968, *passim*.
3. Walter J. McNerney, "Controls in the Medical Care Field," paper delivered at the annual meeting, Industrial Relations Research Assn., St. Louis, Mo., December 28, 1960, p. 16.
4. The Chase Manhattan Bank, "Financing Medical Care," *Business in Brief*, No. 29, November-December 1959, p. 6.
5. L. M. Abbe and A. M. Barney, *The Nation's Health Facilities*, Public Health Service Publication No. 616, Washington, D. C., 1958.
6. See *Physicians for a Growing America*, Report of the Surgeon General's Consultant Group on Medical Education, Frank Bane, Chairman, Washington, D. C., 1959; and "Medical Needs of 1970," *Scientific American*, September 1958, p. 86.
7. Herman M. and Anne R. Somers, *Private Health Insurance, Part I: Changing Patterns of Medical Care Demand and Supply in Relation to Health Insurance*, Institute of Industrial Relations, University of California, Berkeley, 1958, pp. 396–397.
8. In 1955, there were only 85,000 general practitioners in the United States, 22 per cent fewer than in 1940. Their number and relative percentage are both declining. However, a new hybrid who can deal with the whole person or family and coordinate the specialties as they apply to the individual is coming into being. See Somers, *op. cit.*, p. 398.
9. *Source Book of Health Insurance Data*, 1960, pp. 49 and 53; 1965, p. 55.
10. *Source Book of Health Insurance Data*, 1965, pp. 55–62.
11. Somers, *op. cit.*, pp. 403–405; and Howard B. Sprague, "Dear Grandchildren," *Parade*, January 29, 1961, p. 2. Dr. Sprague writes, "In Boston, for example, private rooms in the year 1970 may cost something like $65 a day."
12. *Source Book of Health Insurance Data*, 1965, p. 63.
13. Herman M. and Anne R. Somers, *Private Health Insurance, Part II: Problems, Pressures and Prospects*, Institute of Industrial Relations, University of California, Berkeley, 1958, p. 530.
14. *Location of Physicians*, Bulletin M-94, Bureau of Medical Economic Research, American Medical Assn., Chicago, January 1956, pp. 153–178; Seymour E. Harris, *The Economics of American Medicine*, Macmillan, New York, 1964, Chapter 6.
15. *Medical Economics*, November 1957, p. 141. Copyright 1957 by Medical Economics, Inc., Oradell, N. J. Reprinted by permission.
16. Selig Greenberg, "The Decline of the Healing Art," *Harper's*, October 1960, p. 136.
17. Dewhurst & Associates, *America's Needs and Resources*, Twentieth Century Fund, New York, 1955, p. 344.
18. See Paul T. Kinney, "Financing Medical Care," unpublished doctoral dissertation, University of Southern California, Los Angeles, 1957, pp. 99–101.
19. *Medical Economics*, January 20, 1958, p. 30.
20. *Source Book of Health Insurance Data*, 1965, p. 62.
21. "Financing Medical Care," *loc. cit.*
22. Donald B. Straus, "Can We Afford to Be Healthy?" *Harper's*, July 1960, p. 38.
23. *Ibid.*, p. 40.

24. *Source Book of Health Insurance Data,* 1965, p. 16; Louis S. Reed, "Private Health Insurance in the United States: An Overview," *Social Security Bulletin,* Social Security Administration, U. S. Dept. of Health, Education, and Welfare, December 1965, p. 15.
25. Straus, *op. cit.,* p. 41.
26. Louis S. Reed, *op. cit.,* p. 14; *Source Book of Health Insurance Data,* 1965, pp. 10–24.
27. *Social Security Bulletin,* December 1965, pp. 14 and 15.
28. *Source Book of Health Insurance Data,* 1965, p. 50.
29. *Accident and Sickness Review,* April 1960, p. 34.
30. *Source Book of Health Insurance Data,* 1965, *loc. cit.*
31. *Source Book of Health Insurance Data,* 1965, pp. 14, 16, and 18.
32. Reed, "An Overview," *Social Security Bulletin,* December 1965, pp. 6 and 15.
33. *Social Security Bulletin,* December 1965, p. 20.
34. Louis S. Reed, *Blue Cross and Medical Service Plans,* U. S. Public Health Service, Washington, D. C., 1947, p. 136.
35. Somers, *op. cit.,* Part II, p. 414.
36. *Social Security Bulletin,* December 1965, p. 9.
37. Louis S. Reed and Ruth S. Hauft, *Independent Health Insurance Plans,* 1964, Social Security Administration, Health, Education, and Welfare Dept., Washington, D. C., 1965.
38. *Ibid.*
39. Somers, *op. cit.,* Part II, p. 516.
40. McNerney, "Controls in the Medical Care Field," *op. cit.,* p. 12.
41. Eliot Friedsen and George A. Silver, "Social Science in Family Medical Care," *Public Health Reports,* June 1960, p. 489.
42. *Ibid.*
43. Sprague, *loc. cit.*
44. Eveline M. Burns, "Policy Decisions Facing the United States in Financing and Organizing Health Care," *Public Health Reports,* U. S. Dept. of Health, Education, and Welfare, Public Health Service, August 1966, p. 683.

PROBLEMS AND CASES

1. Consider your own needs for medical care. Which of the health-insurance policies described fills your needs best today? List the reasons why. Which one or ones will fill your probable needs ten years hence? List the reasons why.
2. Evaluate three systems of medical care in regard to how they meet Dr. Eliot Friedsen's and Dr. George Silver's criteria for any system of medical care. Why does controversy exist over the form of organization for our medical system in the United States? List the arguments presented on both sides. How do you think this controversy will be resolved? Why?
3. You are to undergo major surgery and be hospitalized for 14 days. Where in the United States will your surgeon's fees and hospital-room rates probably be least? Which of the health-insurance policies or plans described in this chapter would pay you the most in this instance if you had fulfilled all the eligibility requirements and were fully covered?
4. What is the current cost of the list of services Donald Straus contends each

Financing Medical Care

family should be able to get during any one year currently *in the city where you live*? How does this compare with the average cost of this list of services in the United States? Why is the sum higher or lower in your particular area?

5. Compare the premiums paid and the benefits received under three group health-insurance plans available to employees of three different firms in your area. How and why do they differ?

6. The Carrs are not covered under any form of health insurance and are considering the purchase of hospitalization insurance. They are both 35 years old. Their children are 10 and 12. Their only source of income is about $10,000 a year from the family business which they own and operate with the help of two employees. Which form of hospitalization insurance would you advise them to buy? Why? What will the premiums be? How do they compare with the premiums on other policies they might carry? What is the difference in coverage among the policies?

7. If the Carrs are also considering carrying insurance against the costs of medical care other than hospitalization, what type of policy or plan would you advise them to consider? What are the annual charges for each of these policies or plans? Exactly what does each of them offer?

8. The Boydens are 65. They have applied for and are eligible for Medicare, but they would like to purchase an insurance policy that will cover all costs of medical care excluded under Medicare. (The provisions of the current "Medicare" legislation are discussed on pages 482–484). Price three health-insurance policies available to them. What does each of these cover? What does it cost? Can they buy a "major medical" insurance policy? What does this type of insurance cover? What will a policy of this nature cost them?

12 EXPENDITURES FOR GOVERNMENT SERVICES

Taxes are what we pay for civilized society . . . .

OLIVER WENDELL HOLMES

In less than half a century the cost of government in the United States has risen fantastically. From the seemingly paltry 3 billion dollars spent by all governmental units in 1913[1] the sum has soared to approximately 200 billion dollars per year in the late 1960's. Even so, both the proportion of national income devoted to government expenditures and the average tax rate in the United States are less than they are in the United Kingdom, West Germany, France, or Canada.[2] Conversely, the governments of poorer, less advanced countries tax and spend less than those of more developed nations. Among the latter, interdependence is greater, and the proper performance of government's more demanding role requires greater outlays.

Of the three levels of government in the United States the states have always been the least important with respect to government expenditure. Prior to the First World War, the federal government expenditures were mainly for national defense, pensions and interest on prior wars, a few public buildings and public works, and the salaries of the relatively few government officials. Federal tax collections came mainly from liquor and tobacco excises and tariff duties on imports. Local government was responsible for most government functions and collected the greater share of tax revenue. The most important source of local government revenue was, and still is, the property tax.

Since the First World War, federal expenditures have risen sharply, and taxes have increased correspondingly. It may be noted from Table 12–1 that

Table 12-1. **Receipts and Expenditures of the Federal Government in 1967 (Estimates, in Millions of Dollars)**

Description	Receipts and Expenditures	Percentage of Total Receipts or Expenditures	
Payments			
National defense	61,404	42.3	
Space research and technology	5,300	3.7	
International affairs and finance	4,429	3.1	
Veterans' benefits and services	6,380	4.3	53.4
Agriculture and agricultural resources	3,645	2.5	
Natural resources	3,041	2.1	
Commerce and transportation	6,620	4.6	
Housing and community development	1,193	.1	
Health, labor, and welfare	39,331	27.1	
Education	2,774	1.9	38.3
Interest	10,152	7.0	
General government	2,523	1.7	
Other	1,744	− 1.2	
	145,048	100	
Receipts			
Individual income taxes	56,240	38.6	
Corporation income taxes	34,400	23.6	62.2
Excise taxes	13,257	9.1	
Employment taxes	24,339	16.7	
Estate and gift taxes	3,301	2.3	
Customs	1,845	1.3	29.4
Deposits by states, unemployment insurance	2,900	2.0	
Veterans' life insurance premiums	490	.3	
Other budget and trust receipts	8,766	6.0	
	145,539	100	

NOTE: Total of percentages not exactly 100 per cent because of rounding.
SOURCE: Bureau of the Budget.

53.4 per cent of the federal government's expenditures cover national defense, space research and technology, international affairs and finance, and veterans' services and benefits. If part of the interest on the national debt is added to this amount, it becomes apparent that about three-fifths of the federal expenditures are undertaken to allay the costs of past wars or to prevent future wars.

Perhaps 8 per cent of federal expenditures may be classified as welfare expenditures. These include *grants-in-aid* to states to pay a part of the amount distributed as aid to needy children, as pensions to those over 65, or as aid to the handicapped. Since the recipients receive these payments without having produced a good or a service, the payments, like unemployment insurance, pensions, and "social security," are known as *transfer* payments.

Nondefense federal spending has increased relatively less than the total of state and local government expenditures. As the population has increased, state and local government units have had to build schools, roads, hospitals, and sewers. In addition, they have had to provide an increased amount of welfare assistance, governmental machinery—courts, for one example—recreational facilities, and police and fire protection. In order to provide these services, state and local government units have had to raise their taxes again and again. Besides the property tax on which most of these units rely for revenue, they have imposed a host of newer levies wherever they could. These include sales taxes, income taxes, highway-user taxes, fees for the issue of licenses and permits, imposed taxes on gifts and estates, and miscellaneous taxes.

Most federal revenue, in contrast, derives from individual income taxes and, since the Second World War, from corporate income taxes as well, both excellent sources of revenue.

PRIVATE OR PUBLIC EXPENDITURES

Government expenditures are for goods and services produced for or on behalf of the citizens of the nation. Some of these goods and services are produced directly by governmental units—for example, national defense programs or police protection. However, most of them, such as missiles and roads, are produced for the government by private firms. In theory, the government produces these goods and services or has them produced. Private firms could not or would not produce them, since their production would not be possible or profitable. However, they are deemed important enough to the life and welfare of the nation not to chance any citizen's being without them.

To illustrate this point, no firm could afford to operate a lighthouse. If it should decide to do so, it would have some difficulty in stopping ships and collecting tolls. Besides, the problem would remain of how much to charge for its service. Since the elected representatives of the citizens of the United States have deemed the operation of lighthouses to be in the public interest, operating them is a governmental function. A problem arises because not every citizen benefits from the lighthouse directly. Nevertheless, everyone who pays taxes may be said to pay for some part of it.

In the case of private consumption, an individual or a family, for the most part, derives direct satisfaction from the goods and services chosen, bought, and paid for. In the case of goods and services bought by the government with taxpayers' money, which are consumed *socially* or *collectively*, one taxpayer may derive no direct benefit from them but a nontaxpayer or another taxpayer may. The individual or the family has not ordinarily made the choice on how the money shall be spent directly. In theory, both are paying for part of what is necessary for the public welfare, or to achieve the goals of our society. In practice, they may or may not have voted for the representative who supported a particular tax bill. They may or may not agree that a particular expenditure coincides with the public welfare, or that it will lead toward a desirable social goal.

In a democracy the will of the majority, insofar as it can be expressed, determines the pattern of government expenditures and the taxes that will be paid. In the United States, influential interest groups have been largely responsible for the pattern of expenditure and the pattern of taxation adopted.

Since taxes are used to buy goods and services, or the resources needed to produce them, they serve to diminish the supply of goods, services, and resources available to individuals and firms at a particular time for *private consumption*. Tax legislation allocates the national income for a particular period between the *private sector* and the *public sector* of the economy. The proportion that should be allocated to each is a matter of debate.[3] Tax legislation also serves to redistribute private incomes, since taxpayers are generally not recipients of government payments that equal their taxes. All in all, decisions on exactly what a desirable pattern of taxation should be are extremely difficult. Yet there are some existing principles that may serve as guides.

PRINCIPLES OF TAXATION

Adam Smith enumerated four maxims with regard to taxes in general. Reworded, they are: First, citizens are to be taxed according to their ability to pay, that is, in proportion to their incomes. This is his maxim of equality.

He has reference to equality of burden. Second, the tax that each individual is supposed to pay should be certain. It should not be arbitrary as to the amount to be paid and the time and place of payment. Third, every tax should be so levied as to be convenient for the taxpayer to pay it. Fourth, every tax should take as little as possible over and above what it brings into the public treasury.[4]

The last three maxims generally are agreed on. In the United States they have been heeded relatively well by most governmental units. Relatively few of these units still abide solely by the age-old principle of expediency, under which those who have money or goods and are *easiest to collect from* bear the heaviest burden of taxation.

The first maxim poses problems. Should a man who has ten times as much income pay ten times as much in taxes? In an effort to answer this and similar questions, the *benefit* and *sacrifice* principles come into play. According to those who advocate the benefit aspect, different people should be taxed in proportion to the "benefit" they may be expected to receive from government activity. Those who use the roads ten times as much as others, for example, should pay ten times as much in gasoline taxes, which then should be used to build roads.

Others have held that taxes should be levied so as to lead to an equitable pattern of income distribution or result in *equality of sacrifice*. With Adam Smith, they have held that the wealthy have greater ability to pay taxes. The wealthy sacrifice less when they give a dollar to the government than the poor who need the dollar more. Therefore, to achieve equality of sacrifice, proportionately more dollars should be taken away from those who have more than from those who have less. It is conceded, of course, that money may mean a great dealt to the man who has more and very little to the man who has less. Thus, the sacrifice each experiences cannot be equated.

In practice, the various forms of taxation commonly used in the United States cannot be said to conform too closely to either the benefit or sacrifice principles. Loosely, gasoline taxes, school taxes, taxes or assessments to build sewers, and the like, can be said to be paid by those who derive greatest benefit from the services provided. In contrast, the income tax may be said to rest on the principle of equality of sacrifice.

Economists now generally agree on an additional principle of taxation. The tax structure, they hold, should avoid interfering with attainment of the optimum allocation and use of resources within the economy. Ideally, it should, where possible, assist in the attainment of the optimum. However, there is some disagreement on the definition of the optimum as well as on the means for its attainment.

FORMS OF TAXATION

Taxes are usually termed progressive, regressive, or proportional, and direct or indirect.

Progressive taxes take a graduated proportion of higher incomes. A taxpayer with $4,000 a year of taxable income in 1968 paid a maximum of 17 per cent in federal income taxes; one with over $200,000 paid a maximum of 70 per cent. *Regressive* taxes take a greater proportion of lower incomes than of higher incomes. The sales tax is a typical regressive tax. Assume that it is set at 4 per cent and applies to everything bought by a consumer except food and shelter. The consumer with $3,000 a year in income may spend $2,000 on taxable purchases. He pays $80, or 2.6 per cent of his income, in sales taxes. The consumer with $500,000 a year in income may spend as much as $100,000 a year on taxable purchases. The sales tax on $100,000 is $4,000 or slightly less than 1 per cent of his total income. *Proportional* taxes take the same fraction or percentage from everyone's income. Some municipal income taxes are proportional. They are set at 1 per cent of every resident's income above a stipulated minimum.

Direct taxes are paid by the taxpayer on whom the burden of the tax falls. Income taxes, property taxes, and poll taxes are direct taxes. They cannot be "passed on." *Indirect* taxes are paid by the person to whom the tax can be *shifted*. Excise taxes on cigarettes are indirect taxes. The manufacturer pays the tax and affixes the stamp to the package to show that it is paid. Then he raises the price to the consumer as much as he can, considering the *elasticity of demand*,* so that it is the consumer who actually pays part or all of the tax. In some cases, as in local proportional payroll taxes, employers may find that they can pay less in wages and so shift the burden of the tax *backward* rather than *forward*. Often taxes are paid by firms and included in the price of a commodity, but the buyer is not aware of having paid them.

Federal taxes, as Table 12–1 shows, include individual income taxes, corporation income taxes, excise taxes, employment taxes, estate and gift taxes, customs, and a small group of miscellaneous levies. Each of these will be discussed in turn.

State and local taxes, as has been noted, include property taxes, sales taxes, highway-user taxes—mainly gasoline taxes—fees from licenses and permits, individual income taxes, corporate income taxes, estate and gift taxes, and a miscellaneous group of levies. Each of these also will be discussed in turn.

* Elasticity means the responsiveness of demand to price changes.

The Personal Income Tax

Foremost among the progressive forms of taxation is the personal income tax. Childless couples taking the two exemptions allowed, filing a joint return and taking 10 per cent in deductions, in 1966 would have paid the amount of income tax shown in Table 12–2. A childless couple would have paid no taxes if its income for the year did not exceed $1,333. ($1,333 less $1,200 for two exemptions leaves $133. Ten per cent of $1,333 is the remaining $133.)

How progressive is the personal income tax? As column 3 of Table 12–2 shows, as income increases, the average tax rate increases rapidly. The couple with an income of $100,000 a year pays an average *tax rate* more than four times that paid by the couple who receives an income of $5,000 a year; and the higher tax rate is applied to a larger base. Those with a joint income of $1,500,000 a year pay at an average rate that is more than six times that paid by the couple whose income was $5,000 for the year. Nonetheless, those in the higher-income brackets will still have more left after taxes than those in the lower-income brackets. The *marginal tax rate*, the tax rate on one extra dollar, or on that last dollar earned, may be the deciding factor as to whether to work and earn the additional dollar. In the highest tax brackets, the government may take 70 cents of that extra dollar.

Families with children have more exemptions, and often more deductions, as well; consequently, they pay less in taxes. Bachelors pay more. Couples with incomes over $50,000 a year find that they are taxed almost half of every extra

Table 12-2. **Taxes to be Paid at Different Income Levels by a Married Couple with No Children, at 1966 Rates**[a]

Income (Dollars) (1)	Personal Income Tax (Dollars) (2)	Average Tax Rate Per Cent (3) [(2) ÷ (1)]	Marginal Tax Rate (Per Cent) (4)	Disposable Income [Dollars (after Tax)] (5) [(1) − (2)]
1,200	0	0.0	0	1,200
3,000	215	7.2	15	2,785
5,000	501	10.0	17	4,499
10,000	1,342	13.4	19	8,658
20,000	3,484	17.4	28	16,516
50,000	13,964	27.9	48	36,036
100,000	43,860	43.9	60	56,140
200,000	108,772	54.3	69	91,228
500,000	316,640	63.3	70	183,360

[a] Two exemptions and 10 per cent in deductions have been taken.

Forms of Taxation

dollar they can earn near the *margin*. A bachelor experiences this when he earns in the vicinity of $20,000 a year.

Because of its progressive nature, the personal income tax obviously does make for greater equality in disposable incomes. However, taxpayers in the higher-tax brackets rarely pay as much as Table 12–2 would indicate. Very few taxpayers pay more than 50 per cent of their gross income in taxes. Those with high incomes buy municipal bonds, the income from which is tax-exempt; drill for oil, grow trees, or raise cattle so that they may take advantage of allowances to recover their costs; buy real estate which depreciates and so reduces taxable income; or attempt to derive their income from lightly taxed *capital gains.* Since capital gains come only from taking risks, and business losses from risky ventures may put a taxpayer in a lower-tax bracket, risk taking on the part of those in the higher-income brackets is encouraged rather than discouraged by the present tax structure. If a taxpayer in the highest-income bracket risks a marginal dollar and loses it, he can figure that 70 cents of it would have been taxed away in any case, and he has only lost thirty cents of his own.

However, those who profit inordinately in one year will be in a higher tax bracket that year and will pay more in taxes than the taxpayer with a steady income. To reduce this amount taxpayers may use "income averaging," which may reduce the tax considerably. For example, a single taxpayer earns $20,000 for the year but earned only $4,000, $5,000, $7,000 and $8,000 in the previous four years. He would determine his income for purposes of averaging by subtracting $8,000—33⅓ per cent of his total "base period" income (the income over the past four years)—from the $20,000 in taxable income he had this year. His income for averaging, the remainder, is $12,000. He then computes his tax as follows:

1. 33⅓ per cent of total base period income $ 8,000
2. ⅕ of income for averaging of $12,000   2,400
3.   Total $10,400
4. Tax on $10,400   2,318
5. Tax on $8,000 (from line 1)   1,630
6.   Difference $ 638
7. $638 x 4 $ 2,752
8. Line 4 plus line 7—total tax $ 5,070

Had he not used income averaging, his tax on his $20,000 income for the year would have been $6,070. Income from capital gains and income from property received as a gift or from wagers are also taken into consideration. However, in general (1) if income for averaging is over $3,000 (the required minimum for income averaging to be used), and (2) the current year's income is over 1⅓ times the average of the income of the preceding four years, income averaging should be tried. The lower tax payable when this method is appropriate results from the average of the income being taxed in a lower bracket than the higher-current income.

The Corporate Income Tax

In 1966, a corporation with no more than $25,000 a year in earnings over and above all its expenses paid 30 per cent of its net income in taxes to the federal government. If its net earnings were above $25,000 a year, it paid 30 per cent of its taxable income plus 18 per cent of the amount in excess of $25,000 in taxes. The national average rate for corporations was over 47 per cent, providing the government with its second largest source of revenue. Nonetheless, some individuals who own firms incorporate them so that their earnings from the enterprise may be left "in the firm" and taxed at a lower rate than they would as personal income. In small corporations, especially, if the principal stockholders are taxpayers in higher-income brackets, it may pay them not to withdraw earnings as dividends, but to leave them in the corporation.

Gift and Estate Taxes

The federal government collects a tax on gifts over $3,000 to any one donee. There is also a $30,000 tax exemption which may be subtracted from the total amount of gifts made during one's lifetime before computing the gift tax. Gift tax rates are progressive, like income-tax rates. Sample rates are shown in Table 12–3. *Recipients of gifts* pay no tax on the gift itself; they pay taxes only on any income received from a gift if the gift is in the form of rental property, securities, or any other income-producing asset.

Table 12-3. **Taxable Gifts**

From	To	Tax	Per Cent	Of Excess Over
(Dollars)	(Dollars)			(Dollars)
0	5,000	0.00	2.25	0
5,000	10,000	112.50	5.25	5,000
10,000	20,000	375.00	8.25	10,000
50,000	60,000	5,250.00	18.75	50,000
100,000	250,000	15,525.00	22.50	100,000
1,000,000	1,250,000	244,275.00	29.25	1,000,000

The gift tax ensures that when taxpayers in the higher-income brackets give away part of their assets in order to escape estate taxes at a later time, the government will still collect a tax on these assets. Nevertheless, it encourages the giving of gifts rather than the leaving of estates, since, especially in the higher brackets, the tax on gifts is lower than that on estates.

Estates are allowed a $60,000 exemption, after all funeral and administrative expenses, debts to be paid, and charitable bequests have been deducted from the total amount of the estate. However, there is no individual exception of $3,000 for each bequest, as there is in the case of gifts; and the tax rates on estates progress from 3 per cent to 77 per cent, whereas those on gifts range from 2.25 per cent to 57.75 per cent. Estate taxes are discussed further in the final chapter of this book.

Excise Taxes

Federal excise taxes are levied on tobacco, liquor, gasoline and diesel fuel, automobiles, trucks and trailers, truck accessories, tires and tubes, fishing equipment, firearms, telephone service, and air transportation. This is not a complete list.[5]

Some of these taxes are imposed on the articles when they are sold at retail, and the consumer pays the tax as an addition to the retail price. Automobiles fall into this category. They are subject to a tax that is 7 per cent of the sale price. Telephone service is subject to a 10 per cent tax. Air transportation charges are subject to a tax of 5 per cent, which is shifted to users of the service. The remainder of the taxes listed are paid by the manufacturers, or other producers or importers when they sell the products.

Even when they are not imposed directly on the consumer, most excise taxes still become part of the retail price of the taxed product. How much of the tax is included in the retail price will depend on the supply of the product and its elasticity, and on the demand for the product and its elasticity.

The question of who bears the burden of a tax, or its *incidence*, is often difficult to determine.[6]

Customs

The term customs is applied to any tax or duty paid to the government on a commodity that is brought into the country. Travelers returning to the United States now pay *duty* on that part of their total purchases made abroad that exceeds $100 in the dollar equivalent of the prices paid. There are some articles, antiques for example, that may still be brought in *duty-free*, but they are few.[7] However, tariffs on imports to the United States, as a whole, as is shown in Table 12–1, constitute one of the least important sources of federal revenue.

Other Federal Taxes

There are federal taxes on those engaged in any of the following occupations, trades, or businesses: amusement or gaming devices, bowling alleys, billiard and pool tables, wagering, liquor, narcotic drugs, marihuana, firearms, adulterated and processed or renovated butter, and filled cheese. The tax on gaming devices, wagering, liquor, narcotic drugs, marihuana, and firearms must be paid before carrying on a trade or business. This gives the responsible federal agencies information about who is carrying on the business legally. Those engaging in these businesses who have not paid the tax cannot display the stamp and are subject to federal prosecution.

There is a tax on motor vehicles over 26,000 pounds, that is, trucks and buses. There are the Social Security taxes which provide for Federal Old Age, Survivors' and Disability Insurance and Medicare, for most employees and many of the self-employed who elect to be covered.* All in all, there are federal taxes on numerous commodities that *Congress* has not considered as being the necessities of life. Yet there are many who consider some of the articles or services taxed, such as gasoline, highly necessary.

The Property Tax

About half of the revenue of state and local governmental units is derived from the property tax, and seemingly most property taxes are levied by cities and counties. As its name denotes, the property tax is a tax on land and buildings, or what is commonly called property. In many localities it is also a tax on personal property—furniture and jewelry, for example—and on savings accounts over a certain amount, on securities, or on other assets. Few localities delineate taxable property in exactly the same way. Then, too, rates among localities differ markedly. In Los Angeles County, they have varied from 5.33 per cent to 10.47 per cent of the assessed valuation of the taxable property, depending on which local community set the rate and collected the tax.[9]

But the variation in rates is only one of the many problems associated with this tax. Assessed valuations also vary from locality to locality. Property may be assessed at 20 per cent of its market value, at 40 per cent, at 50 per cent, or at whatever percentage the locality has decided on. It is to the taxpayer's advantage to pay an 8 per cent rate where property is assessed at 50 per cent of its market value—he pays 4 per cent of the market value—rather than a 5 per cent rate where property is assessed at full market value, which is rarely done. According to many property owners, assessors are notoriously inaccurate.

---

* For a discussion of Social Security taxes, see Chapter 16, pp. 471–476.

In any case, their judgment of value may not be infallible and, in consequence, personal assessment is being replaced by more accurate methods.

Assessments and rates normally do not change often enough to reflect changing property values or tax needs. When real estate values fall, the tax on real property tends to be burdensome; tax foreclosures become common. When real estate values increase, those who do not sell their property may not realize this increase. Nevertheless, their property valuations and tax rates ordinarily will increase.

Smaller parcels of property tend to be assessed at a higher percentage of their market value than larger parcels. All in all, the property tax is generally regressive.

Sales Taxes

State and local governments are deriving an increasing amount of revenue from retail sales taxes as time goes on. Taxes are imposed ordinarily on all retail purchases, except food, medicine, and other essentials, in some localities. Since there is a flat percentage of generally 3 to 4 per cent imposed on all commodities subject to the tax, this tax is regressive. It imposes a heavier burden on those with less income who usually of necessity spend a greater proportion of their incomes.

Highway-User Taxes

The two most commonly used forms of highway-user taxes are gasoline taxes and license fees on autos, trucks, and drivers. In some states, more revenue is collected from these levies than is spent for highway construction and maintenance. Theoretically, those who drive derive the benefit of having the highways for which their taxes pay. In practice, since automobiles and trucks are often necessities in our economy, these taxes tend to be regressive. Auto license fees constitute a partial exception; the more expensive the car, the higher its license fee.

Fees for Licenses and Permits

States charge license fees for the privilege of hunting, fishing, starting a business, acting as a corporation, operating a liquor store or a tavern, or engaging in whatever other endeavors have been made subject to licensing. Permits may be required for cutting timber or having slot machines that are available for public use. The activities for which permits are required vary from state to state.

Localities collect fees for the licensing of dogs and businesses, and whatever else they have made subject to licensing. Local permits often are required for hauling trash, burning waste materials, or whatever else the locality wishes to control. In theory, the fees collected for the issue of licenses and permits should pay for the administrative expense related to the control of restricted activities in the public interest.

Other State and Local Taxes

Many states and localities have followed the lead of the federal government in levying personal income and gift and inheritance taxes. As to the personal income tax, allowances for exemptions and deductions often differ markedly from those set by the federal government, and tax rates vary from state to state and from locality to locality. State and local rates are generally much lower than federal rates. Where the state collects an estate or inheritance tax, the amount paid is allowed as a credit against the federal estate or inheritance tax.

States collect a wage tax which may be as much as 3 per cent of payrolls in occupations covered by Social Security. Proceeds from this tax plus federal contributions go into funds from which unemployment compensation benefits or insurance may be paid to workers who become unemployed.

Some states collect poll taxes. Some tax corporate income. Some collect a severance tax when oil, gas, or other natural resources are removed from the earth. Some collect documentary stamp taxes.

This does not exhaust the list of state and local taxes. In addition, states and localities derive revenue from the operation of public utilities, from assessments on property owners who will benefit from specific improvements such as sewers, and from a miscellany of other sources. It is small wonder that for the individual taxpayer taxes often seem omnipresent.

THE FEDERAL INCOME TAX LAW

Since most citizens of the United States pay a tax on their incomes to the federal government, let us examine the provisions of the income tax law with which taxpayers should be familiar. Since 1943, the federal income tax law has stipulated that taxes could be withheld at the source of income or paid quarterly during the year in which the income to which they apply was earned. Employers have been required to withhold from the sum paid each employee each pay period for forwarding to the federal government monthly an amount that will enable the employee to accumulate the approximate total tax for which he will be liable at the end of the year. Income tax returns must be filed on or before April 15 of the year following the one in which the taxable income was earned. The tax returns must show how much the taxpayer owes in taxes for the preceding year and how much was overpaid or underpaid through withholding.

Taxpayers are required to compute their taxes and to submit any tax due with their returns. If the return shows that taxes were overpaid, the Director of Internal Revenue refunds the overpayment to the taxpayer. Overpayments earn no interest.

Self-employed individuals who expect to pay taxes of at least $40, unmarried persons who earn more than $5,000 a year, and married couples or heads of households who earn more than $10,000 must file estimates of their income for the year at the beginning of each year. They pay whatever part of the estimated tax will not be withheld at the source of the income in quarterly installments. Underpayments resulting from the fact that an estimate exceeded the permissible 30 per cent of error are subject to penalty. For farmers, the permissible margin of error is 33.3 per cent. The penalty is 6 per cent per year on the difference between 70 per cent, or 66.6 per cent for farmers, of the amount that should have been paid and the amount actually paid. Estimates may be revised quarterly.

Mandatory Income Tax Returns

Every citizen or resident of the United States under 65 years of age whose gross income during a taxable year is $600 or more must, according to law, file a federal income tax return. Those under 21 are *not* exempt from the requirement. Citizens or residents who earn less than $600 during the taxable year should file a return if any income tax is withheld, so that it may be returned. Those 65 or over on the last day of the taxable year are not required to file a return unless their gross income for the year exceeds $1,200.

Income Tax Forms

Persons subject to the federal income tax file their tax returns on forms 1040 or 1040A.

Form 1040A. The simplest income tax form is 1040A (see Figure 12–1). This form is a card on which the taxpayer answers a few questions, fills in his name, indicates whether he is single or married, and shows his income and exemptions for the year. If his income for the year has been less than $5,000 he may omit the tax computation. The government eventually will bill him for the tax due. The form may be used also by individuals or married couples who file a joint return if their income has not exceeded $10,000 before any deductions have been made and, if it consists entirely of wages or salary shown on

366   Expenditures for Government Services

Figure 12-1. Internal Revenue Service forms.

accompanying withholding statements, with no more than $200 from other sources, Form 1040A provides for a standard deduction of 10 per cent. Those whose legally authorized deductions from income tax computation purposes exceed 10 per cent are ill-advised to use this form.

Form 1040. Form 1040 may be used by anyone subject to the federal income tax. It must be used by those whose incomes do not derive essentially from wages or salary. If the total income of a taxpayer using this form is less than $5,000 for the taxable year, the taxpayer may elect not to itemize his allowable deductions from gross income and not to compute his tax himself. Instead he may use a table contained in the "Instruction Booklet" accompanying the tax form to ascertain the tax due. The table allows 10 per cent of gross income for deductions. Persons prohibited by law from using the shorter form have no choice other than to use this one.

(10) Form **1040** **U.S. Individual Income Tax Return** **1966**

for the year January 1–December 31, 1966, or other taxable year beginning ...., 1966, ending ...., 19...... U.S. Treasury Department—Internal Revenue Service

Please print or type

First name and initial (If joint return, use first names and middle initials of both)	Last name	Your social security number (Husband's, if joint return)
FRANK B. AND EVELYN H. (14)	JONES	516 04 1492
Home address (Number and street or rural route)		Your occupation
3700 MILL WAY		ELECTRICIAN (9)
City, town or post office, and State	ZIP code	Wife's number, if joint return
HOMETOWN NEW YORK	14202	575 10 1776

Enter the name and address used on your return for 1965 (if the same as above, write "Same"). If none filed, give reason. If changing from separate to joint or joint to separate returns, enter 1965 names and addresses.
FRANK B. AND EVELYN H. JONES 1150 ELM ROAD, HOMETOWN, N.Y. 14202 — Wife's occupation: CO-OWNER OF NURSERY SCHOOL

Your present employer and address ZERO POWER CO. HOMETOWN, N.Y.

Wife's present employer and address, if joint return SELF-EMPLOYED

Filing Status—check only one: (18)

- 1a ☐ Single
- (14) 1b ☑ Married filing joint return (even if only one had income)
- 1c ☐ Married filing separately. If your husband or wife is also filing a return give his or her first name and social security number.
- 1d ☐ Unmarried Head of Household (16)
- 1e ☐ Surviving widow(er) with dependent child

Exemptions Regular 65 or over Blind

- 2a Yourself . ☑ ☑ ☐ } Enter number of exemptions checked ▶▶▶ 3
- 2b Wife . . ☑ ☐ ☐
- 3a First names of your dependent children who lived with you MARIE (21) JAMES (22) .... Enter number ▶▶▶ 2
- 3b Number of other dependents (from page 2, Part I, line 3) 2
- 4 Total exemptions claimed . . . . . . ▶▶▶ 7

Attach Copy B of Form W-2 here

Income (30) If joint return, include all income of both husband and wife	5	Wages, salaries, tips, etc. If not shown on attached Forms W-2 attach explanation ▶	$ 7,814 65
(23)	6	Other income (from page 2, Part II, line 8) ▶	10,135 49
	7	Total (add lines 5 and 6) ▶	$ 17,950 14
(12)	8	Adjustments (from page 2, Part III, line 5) ▶	60 00
	9	Total income (subtract line 8 from line 7) ▶	$ 17,890 14
(11) Figure tax using either 10 or 11	10	Tax Table—If you do not itemize deductions and line 9 is less than $5,000, find your tax from tables in instructions. Do not use lines 11a, b, c, or d. Enter tax on line 12.	
(5)	11	Tax Rate Schedule—	
Tax Computation	11a	If you itemize deductions, enter total from page 2, Part IV . . . If you do not itemize deductions, and line 9 is $5,000 or more enter the larger of: (1) 10 percent of line 9 or; (2) $200 ($100 if married and filing separate return) plus $100 for each exemption claimed on line 4, above. Deduction under (1) or (2) limited to $1,000 ($500 if married and filing separately). ▶	4,703 15 (10)
	11b	Subtract line 11a from line 9	$13,186 99
	11c	Multiply total number of exemptions on line 4, above, by $600	4,200 00 (18)
	11d	Subtract line 11c from line 11b. Enter balance on this line. (Figure your tax on this amount by using tax rate schedule on page 11 of instructions.) Enter tax on line 12.	$ 8,986 99
	12	Tax (from either Tax Table, see line 10, or Tax Rate Schedule, see line 11) ▶	$ 1,597 14
	13	Total credits (from page 2, Part V, line 5) ▶	203 60
	14a	Income tax (subtract line 13 from line 12) ▶	$ 1,393 54
	14b	Tax from recomputing prior year investment credit (attach statement)	—0—
(9) **Tax Credits Payments**	15	Self-employment tax (Schedule C–3 or F–1) ▶	86 10
	16	Total tax (add lines 14a, 14b, and 15) ▶	$ 1,479 64
(140)	17	Total Federal income tax withheld (attach Forms W-2) ▶ $ 649 90	
	18	1966 Estimated tax payments (include 1965 overpayment allowed as a credit) ▶ 1,000 00	
	19	Excess F.I.C.A. Tax Withheld (two or more employers—see page 5 of inst.) ▶ —0—	
	20	Nonhighway Federal gasoline tax—Form 4136 (Reg. Inv)—Form 2439 (61) 24 00	
	21	Total (add lines 17, 18, 19, and 20)	1,673 90
(13) **Tax Due or Refund**	22	If payments (line 21) are less than tax (line 16), enter **Balance Due**. Pay in full with this return ▶	
	23	If payments (line 21) are larger than tax (line 16), enter **Overpayment** ▶▶▶	$ 194 26
	24	Amount of line 23 you wish credited to 1967 Estimated Tax	
	25	Subtract line 24 from 23. Apply to: ☑ U.S. Savings Bonds, with excess refunded or ☐ Refund only	$ 194 26

Attach Check or Money Order here

Under penalties of perjury, I declare that I have examined this return, including accompanying schedules and statements, and to the best of my knowledge and belief it is true, correct, and complete. If prepared by a person other than taxpayer, his declaration is based on all information of which he has any knowledge.

Sign here ▶ Frank B. Jones Evelyn H. Jones Date 3/24/67 (12)
If joint return, BOTH HUSBAND AND WIFE MUST SIGN (15) even if only one had income.

Sign here .... Signature of preparer other than taxpayer. Address Date ....

PAGE 1

Figure 12-1 (*continued*).

Joint Returns

When a husband and wife file a *joint return*, showing their combined income and their combined exemptions and deductions, the total combined taxable income shown is divided by two; the appropriate tax rate is applied to half of the total income so obtained, and the result is multiplied by two. Since

PART I. Exemptions Complete only for dependents claimed on line 3b, page 1 (22) (21) (19) Form 1040—1966—Page 2

(a) NAME (If more space is needed attach schedule)	(b) Relationship	(c) Months lived in your home. If born or died during year write "B" or "D"	(d) Did dependent have $600 or more income?	(e) Amount YOU furnished for dependent's support. If 100% write "ALL"	(f) Amount furnished by OTHERS including dependent.
(20) 1 Grace Smith	Mother	12	No	$ 815.00	$ 500.00
(21) Clara Jones (Forms 2120 Attached)	Sister	None	No	350.00	650.00

3 Total number of dependents listed above. Enter here and on page 1, line 3b ▶▶ 2

PART II. Income from sources other than wages, etc.

(57) 1a Dividends and other distributions on stock (Name of payer—write (H), (W), (J), for stock held by husband, wife, or jointly)
(114) Sh. of Jones Bro. Ptsp(H) $57.50; Acme Publishing Co. (H) $210; W & S Stockbrokers (W) $60; Optimist Fund (J) $136; So. American Development Co. (H) $40; Zepco, Inc (J) $86; Tiger Fund (H) $6; Zero Power Co. (H) $75; Country Investors (H) $55

Total line 1a ▶▶ $ 725.50
(61) 1b Exclusion (see instructions) $ 180.00
1c Capital gain distributions 102.00
1d Nontaxable distributions 161.00
1e Total lines 1b, 1c, and 1d 443.00
1f Taxable dividends (line 1a less line 1e—not less than zero) ▶▶ $ 282.50
(55) 2 Interest (name of payer)
2a Earnings from savings and loan assoc., mutual savings banks, credit unions, etc. Fidelity Bldg & Loan $16.75; State Savings Bank 18.42
Total line 2a $ 35.17
2b Interest on bank deposits (other than mutual savings)
Total line 2b
2c Other interest (bonds, etc.) U.S. Savings Bonds $75.00
Total line 2c $75.00
2d Total interest income (lines 2a, 2b, & 2c) ▶▶ $ 110.17
3 Pensions and annuities, rents and royalties, partnerships, estates or trusts, etc. (Sch. B) $ 7,827.82
4 Business income (Schedule C) —0—
(97) 5 Sale or exchange of property (Schedule D). 1,740.00
6 Farm income (Schedule F) —0—
(23) 7 Miscellaneous income (state nature) Prize won in contest $50
(46) Excess reimbursement of business expenses $125 Total line 7 ▶▶ 175.00
8 TOTAL (add lines 1f through 7. Enter here and on page 1, line 6) ▶▶ $10,135.49

PART III. Adjustments (39)

(37) 1 "Sick pay" if included in line 5, page 1 (attach Form 2440 or other required statement) $ 60.00
(52) 2 Moving expenses (attach Form 3903) —0—
(42) 3 Employee business expense (attach Form 2106 or other statement) —0—
4 Payments by self-employed persons to retirement plans, etc. (attach Form 2950SE) —0—
5 TOTAL ADJUSTMENTS (lines 1 through 4). Enter here and on page 1, line 8 $ 60.00
(47) EXPENSE ACCOUNT INFORMATION—If you had an expense allowance or charged expenses to your employer, check here ☑ and see page 7 of instructions.

PART IV. Itemized deductions—Use only if you do not use tax table or standard deduction. (124)

Medical and dental expense—not compensated by insurance or otherwise)—Attach itemized list. If 65 or over see instructions.
1 Total cost of medicine and drugs
2 Enter 1% of line 9, page 1
3 Subtract line 2 from line 1 — See Statement Attached
4 Other medical, dental expenses (include hospital insurance premiums)
5 Total (add lines 3 and 4)
6 Enter 3% of line 9, page 1
7 Subtract line 6 from line 5; see page 8 of instructions for maximum limitation ▶▶ $ 796.60 (127)
Contributions.—Cash—including checks, money orders, etc. (116) (itemize) First Church—$260; Community Fund—$200; Red Cross 7/6/66—$25; Boy Scouts 8/17/66—$2; General Hospital 10/17/66—$30; Share of Jones Bros. Partnership—$37.50 (114)
1 Total cash contributions $ 554.50
2 Other than cash (see instructions for required statement). Enter total of such items here.
3 Carryover from prior years (see page 8 of inst.).
4 Total contributions (add lines 1, 2, and 3—see instructions for limitation) ▶▶ $ 554.50 (87)
(122) Taxes.—Real estate $ 286.00
State and local gasoline 39.00
General sales (see page 15 of instructions) 106.00
State and local income 362.88
Personal property (119) Total taxes ▶▶ $ 793.88
Interest expense.—Home Mortgage (Old + New) $ 363.77 (87)
Other (itemize) Ace Building and Loan—Prepayment Penalty $60.00 (120)
City Finance Co. (Carrying Charges—See Statement Attached) 4.90 (121)
Total interest expense ▶▶ $ 428.67 (139)
Miscellaneous deductions.—(see page 9 of instructions)
Theft Loss (Movie Camera) $ 79.50 (134)
Alimony—J. Jones, New York, N.Y. 1,900.00 (137)
Union Dues (31) 150.00
Total Miscellaneous ▶▶ $2,129.50
TOTAL DEDUCTIONS (for page 1, line 11a) ▶ $4,703.15

PART V. Credits

1 Retirement income credit (Schedule B) $ 153.60 (74)
2 Investment credit (Form 3468) (63) 50.00 (114)
3 Foreign tax credit (Form 1116) (124) —0—
4 Tax-free covenant bonds credit —0—
5 TOTAL CREDITS (add lines 1 through 4). Enter here and on page 1, line 13 $ 203.60

PAGE 2

Figure 12-1 (*continued*).

the federal income tax is a progressive tax and each half of the combined income is subject to a lower tax rate than the combined total would be, they pay less in taxes than they would if they had to pay the rate applying to their combined total income. To illustrate, a single person with a taxable income of $20,000 for the year 1965 would have been liable for $6,070 in taxes for that year, but a couple with the same combined taxable income, filing jointly, would have been

The Federal Income Tax Law

SCHEDULE B (Form 1040) U.S. Treasury Department Internal Revenue Service	**Supplemental Schedule of Income and Retirement Income Credit** (From pensions and annuities, rents and royalties, partnerships, and estates or trusts) Attach this schedule to your income tax return, Form 1040	1966

Name and address as shown on page 1 of Form 1040

FRANK B. AND EVELYN H. JONES 3700 MILL WAY, HOMETOWN, NEW YORK 14202

PENSION AND ANNUITY INCOME

A.—General Rule (If you did not contribute to the cost of the pension or annuity, enter the total amount received on line 6 and omit lines 1 through 5.)   AMOUNT

1 Investment in contract . . . . . $7,500.00   4 Amount received this year . . . $1,000.00
2 Expected return . . . . 10,000.00   5 Amount excludable (line 4 multiplied by line 3) 750.00
3 Percentage of income to be excluded (line 1 divided by line 2) . . 75%   6 Taxable portion (excess of line 4 over line 5) . . . $250.00

B.—Special Rule—Where your employer has contributed part of the cost and your own contribution will be recovered tax-free within 3 years. If your cost was fully recovered in prior years, enter the total amount received on line 5 and omit lines 1 through 4.

1 Cost of annuity (amounts you paid) . $4,925.00   4 Amount received this year . . . $2,400.00
2 Cost received tax-free in past years . 4,600.00
3 Remainder of cost (line 1 less line 2) . $325.00   5 Taxable portion (excess, if any, of line 4 over line 3) . . . 2,075.00

Part II.—RENT AND ROYALTY INCOME

1. Kind and location of property	2. Total amount of rents	3. Total amount of royalties	4. Depreciation (explain in Part IV) or depletion (attach computation)	5. Repairs (attach itemized list)	6. Other expenses (attach itemized list)
BRICK STORE BUILDING HOMETOWN, N.Y.	$2,500.00		$240.00	$364.75	$910.42
ACME PUBLISHING CO. CLEVELAND, OHIO		$117.50			

1 Totals $2,500.00 $117.50 $240.00 $364.75 $910.42
2 Net income (or loss) from rents and royalties (column 2 plus column 3 less columns 4, 5, and 6) 1,102.33

Part III.—INCOME OR LOSSES FROM PARTNERSHIPS, ESTATES OR TRUSTS, ETC.

1 Partnerships (name, address, and nature of income) JONES BROS. TV REPAIR, HOMETOWN, N.Y.   2,642.50
   PLAYTIME NURSERY SCHOOL, HOMETOWN, N.Y.   1,400.00
2 Small business corporations (subchapter S—name and address) ....
3 Estates or trusts (name and address) J.B. JONES TRUST, NEW YORK, N.Y.   357.99
Total of Parts I, II, and III (Enter here and on page 2, Part II, line 3, Form 1040) . . .   7,827.82

Part IV.—SCHEDULE FOR DEPRECIATION CLAIMED IN PART II ABOVE—This schedule is designed for taxpayers using the alternative guidelines and administrative procedures described in Revenue Procedures 62-21 and 65-13 as well as for those taxpayers who wish to continue using practices authorized prior to these revenue procedures. Where double headings appear use the first heading for depreciation under Revenue Procedures 62-21 and 65-13 and the second heading for other authorized practices.

1. Group and guideline class —OR— Description of property	2. Cost or other basis at beginning of year —OR— Cost or other basis	3. Asset additions in year (amount) —OR— Date acquired	4. Asset retirements in year (amount) (applicable only to Rev. Proc. 62-21)	5. Depreciation allowed or allowable in prior years	6. Method of computing depreciation	7. Class life —OR— Rate (%) or life	8. Depreciation for this year B
1 Total additional first-year depreciation (do not include in items below)							
BRICK STORE BLDG	$12,000.00	1/1/57		$2,160.00	ST. LINE	50 YRS	$240.00

Total cost or other basis . . $12,000.00
2 Total depreciation (Enter here and in Part II, column 4 above) $240.00

SUMMARY OF DEPRECIATION

	Straight line	Declining balance	Sum of the years-digits	Units of production	Additional first year (section 179)	Other (specify)	Total
1 Under Rev. Proc. 62-21 .							
2 Other . . .							

PAGE 3

Figure 12-1 *(continued)*.

liable for only $4,380 in federal income tax.

Heads of Households

A person maintains a household, but does not live with a spouse. He or she supports a dependent, who qualifies as an exemption, and pays more than half the cost of maintaning a home. Such an individual is taxed at a rate about halfway between that paid by a taxpayer filing a separate return and that paid

Schedule B (Form 1040) 1966 — Page 2

(72) **Part V.—RETIREMENT INCOME CREDIT**

A.—General Rule

If separate return, use column B only. If joint return, use column A for wife and column B for husband→	A	B
Did you receive earned income in excess of $600 in each of any 10 calendar years before 1966? (Widows or widowers see instructions, page B–3)	☑ Yes ☐ No	☑ Yes ☐ No
If answer above is "Yes" in either column, furnish all information below in that column.		
1 Retirement income for taxable year:		
(a) **For taxpayers under 65 years of age:** Enter only income received from pensions and annuities under public retirement systems (e.g. Fed., State Govts., etc.) included on page 1, line 9, Form 1040 . . .	$2,075 00	
(b) **For taxpayers 65 years of age or older:** Enter total of pensions and annuities, interest, and dividends included on page 1, line 9, Form 1040, and gross rents from Part II, column 2 of this schedule . . .		$3,142 67
2 Maximum amount of retirement income for credit computation	1,524 00	1,524 00
3 Deduct: (a) Amounts received as pensions or annuities under the Social Security Act, the Railroad Retirement Acts, and certain other exclusions from gross income	—0—	—0—
(b) Earned income received (Does not apply to persons 72 years of age or over): (1) Taxpayers under 62 years of age, enter amount in excess of $900	$500 00	
(2) Taxpayers 62 or over but under 72, enter amount determined as follows: if $1,200 or less, enter zero; if over $1,200 but not over $1,700, enter ½ of amount over $1,200; or if over $1,700, enter excess over $1,450 . . .		7,332 40
4 Total of lines 3(a) and 3(b)	$500 00	$7,332 40
5 Balance (line 2 minus line 4)	1,024 00	—0—
6 Line 5 or line 1, whichever is smaller	$1,024 00	—0—

7 (a) Total (add amounts on line 6, columns A and B)	$1,024 00
If line 7(a) is less than $2,286 and this is a joint return and both husband and wife are age 65 or over, complete the Alternative Computation in B below which may result in a larger credit.	
(b) Amount from line 7 of part B below, if applicable	$1,024 00
8 Tentative credit. Enter 15% of line 7(a) or 15% of line 7(b), whichever is greater	153 60
LIMITATION ON RETIREMENT INCOME CREDIT	
9 Amount of tax shown on page 1, line 12, Form 1040	$1,597 14
10 Less: Total of any amounts shown on page 2, Part V, lines 3 and 4, Form 1040	—0—
11 Subtract line 10 from line 9	$1,597 14
12 Credit. Enter here and on page 2, Part V, line 1, Form 1040, the amount on line 11 or line 8, whichever is smaller . . . . (74)	$153 60

B.—Alternative Computation (after completing lines 1 through 7(a) above)

This method available if:
a. You are married and filing a joint return;
b. Both husband and wife are 65 or over, AND
c. Either one, or both received earned income in excess of $600 in each of any 10 calendar years before 1966.

Furnish the information called for below for both husband and wife even if only one answered "Yes" in column A or B above.	A—WIFE	B—HUSBAND	
1 Retirement income of both husband and wife from pensions and annuities, interest, and dividends included on page 1, line 9, Form 1040, and gross rents from Part II, column 2 of this schedule			
2 Maximum amount of retirement income for credit computation			2,286 00
3 Deduct: (a) Amounts received as pensions or annuities under the Social Security Act, the Railroad Retirement Acts, and certain other exclusions from gross income			
(b) Earned income received (Does not apply to persons 72 years of age or over): if $1,200 or less, enter zero; if over $1,200 but not over $1,700 enter ½ of amount over $1,200; or if over $1,700, enter excess over $1,450			
4 Total of lines 3(a) and 3(b)			
5 Total (add amounts on line 4, columns A and B)			
6 Balance (subtract line 5 from line 2)			
7 Enter here and on line 7(b) of part A above, the amount on line 6 or line 1, whichever is smaller			

PAGE 4

Figure 12-1 (*continued*).

by a taxpayer filing a joint return.

Reportable Income

All income received during the taxable year must be reported on the federal income tax form unless it is specifically exempted by law. Specific types of income that must be reported and exempted income are listed on the instructions that accompany Form 1040.

Dividends. All dividends distributed from the earnings of corporations or associations are taxable income. If a dividend is a return of principal or equity to an investor, it is not taxable. If a dividend is a return to an investor of a part of the principal or his equity, it is not taxable.

There are some who hold that dividends are taxed doubly. They are once under the corporate profits tax as earnings and again as income when they are received by the stockholder. As a partial remedy against this inequity, the law contains a *dividend exclusion* provision, which allows a taxpayer to exclude from his taxable dividends the first $100 received from domestic corporations. A husband and wife may each exclude $100 received in dividends even when they file a joint return.

Interest. All interest except that on municipal or state bonds is reportable income. Interest on federal government bonds is taxable income. Those owning Series E bonds may report their interest yearly or wait and report it when they cash in their bonds and receive it.

Rents and Royalties. Rents received from property and royalties received from property or literary or musical compositions are all to be reported. But all expenses incidental to the ownership and maintenance of the property or composition may be deducted in computing taxable income. The yearly depreciation allowance on income property is a deductible expense.

Income From Business or Profession. Profits from an unincorporated business or from a profession are taxable as individual income. The profit-and-loss statement for the business or the professional undertaking for the year must be shown to substantiate the amount of profit or earnings shown as taxable income.[10]

For those in business, all business expenses, including the expense incurred in entertaining customers, for attorney's fees, depreciation, contributions to pension, insurance and welfare funds, and any extraordinary expenses may be deducted from business income in determining profits. For those in the professions, dues, subscriptions to professional journals, and the expenses incidental to attending scientific meetings and conventions are deductible expenses.

Depreciation

Depreciation may be figured by any of three methods—straight-line, double-declining-balance, or the sum-of-the-year-digits—on any asset owned for more than a year for the purpose of making a profit from rents, royalties, a business, or a profession. Depreciation costs may be spread over the number of years that asset is expected to remain useful. If the straight-line method is used, the salvage value of the asset is deducted from the original cost; the amount to be depreciated is divided by the number of years the asset will last, and the answer is the amount of depreciation to be taken for the year. For example, an electric typewriter is used in connection with a business or profession. The original cost is $500, it has a salvage value of $100, and is expected to last ten years. The annual depreciation under this method is $40.

If the double-declining-balance method is used, the rate of depreciation may not exceed twice the straight-line rate. A uniform rate of twice the straight-line rate is allowed each year on the balance remaining after the previous year's depreciation has been subtracted from the original cost of the asset. No adjustment is made for any salvage value. The rate of depreciation in the previous example was 10 per cent per year, since the typewriter was depreciated in ten years. Under the double-declining-balance method, the rate could not exceed 20 per cent. The depreciation to be taken for the first year in this case would be 20 per cent of the unrecovered cost of $500, or $100. The second year, 20 per cent of the unrecovered cost of the $400 balance, or $80, may be taken. The third year, the allowance for depreciation would be 20 per cent of $320, or $64. When the depreciated value of the asset equals its salvage value, no further depreciation is allowed. This method has the advantage of allowing a higher amount of depreciation to be taken during the first years of the life of an asset, when its earnings may be highest.

When the sum-of-the-year-digits method is used, a fraction of the original cost less the salvage value gives the depreciation that may be taken for the year. The denominator of the fraction is the sum of the numbers representing the years of useful life of the asset. In the case cited, the denominator would be $10 + 9 + 8 + 7 + 6 + 5 + 4 + 3 + 2 + 1$, or 55. The numerator is the number of years of life remaining at the beginning of the relevant taxable year. For the first year, 10/55 of $500 less $100, or $72.73, would be allowed; for the second year, 9/55 of $400, or $65.45, and so on through the years. Again, the advantage of this method is that more depreciation is allowed during the earlier years of the life of the asset.

Certain depreciable tangible personal property, such as used property, may qualify for an additional 20 per cent of its cost in depreciation over and above the regular depreciation.

Household Expenses

If the taxpayer's business or profession is conducted from his home, he may treat that part of the rent or share of the house payments and utilities that is applicable to the business or profession as a business or professional expense.

If, for example, he uses one-sixth of the space in his home for his office, one-sixth of the house payments and utility payments for the year is to be treated as an expense of doing business or conducting his professional activities.

Capital Gains

Capital gains and losses arise from the sale of capital or fixed assets. Capital assets may be nonincome-producing or income-producing. A home or an automobile are nonincome-producing assets, and if they are sold at a profit, the excess of the sale price over the cost must be reported as a capital gain. However, if the cost is higher than the selling price, the resultant loss may not be deducted from taxable income. In the case of a home, unless it was rented, depreciation may not be taken into account. If a home from which no rental income was derived is sold at a profit, but the taxpayer in buying a new home pays as much or more than he received for his old home and moves in within a year, he need not report the profit on the sale. If he is building a home, he has to occupy it within eighteen months after sale if he is not to report any profit made on the sale of his old home. Should he profit on the sale of the new home, that profit would have to be reported as taxable income—unless he turned around and bought another home or reached the age of 65. Taxpayers over 65 who have occupied their principal residences over five years within eight years of its sale or exchange may exclude up to $20,000 of its sale price when computing taxable gains.

Stocks, bonds, and income property—unless one is in the real estate business, in which case the latter is a business asset—are examples of income-producing assets. Any profits made on the sale of assets of this nature are to be reported as capital gains and any losses resulting from their sale as capital losses.

Capital gains and losses may be short-term or long-term. Short-term capital gains or losses result from the sale of subject assets held six months or less. If the asset is held for more than six months before its sale, a long-term capital gain or loss results.

Reporting Capital Gains. A net long-term gain or loss is added to or subtracted from a net short-term gain or loss previously computed to determine the net capital gain or loss. Then 50 per cent of the long-term capital gain, or of the combined long and short-term capital gain if that amount is smaller, is subtracted from the combined short and long-term net capital gain. Thus, 50 per cent of long-term capital gains are not taxed.

If there was a net loss for the year, irrespective of whether it was short-term or long-term, up to $1,000 of the loss may be deducted from ordinary income. If the net loss exceeded $1,000, the excess may be carried forward indefinitely until absorbed, always retaining its original character as short-term or long-term. Furthermore, in any future years a capital loss deduction may be claimed to the extent that the carryover exceeds current capital gains in that year. However, this deduction may not be more than $1,000 of taxable income. To the extent that net capital losses are deducted from ordinary income, a net short-term capital loss must always be deducted first. Figure 12–2 may clarify these provisions.

When determining capital gains and losses, brokers' commissions should be added in computing the cost of the asset. Conversely, any commissions or transfer taxes should be subtracted when computing the selling price of the asset.

Reporting Capital Gains if Income is Over $26,000. Those whose taxable incomes are over $26,000 or who on a joint return report incomes in excess of $52,000 for the year ($38,000 if they file as head of a household) do well to use the alternative method, which they are permitted to choose in computing the tax on capital gains. For taxpayers who pay a rate of over 50 per cent in taxes, the levy on net long-term capital gains would be more than half the 50 per cent, or more than the 25 per cent that they pay, if they use the alternative method.

Since he pays less in taxes on long-term capital gains than on short-term gains, it behooves the taxpayer to take long-term rather than short-term capital gains insofar as possible. Holding an asset for over six months will result in only 50 per cent of the profits made on the sale being taxed. If the asset is held less than six months, all the profits on the sale would be subject to tax.

Stockholders who hold stock in order to profit from income received in dividends pay income tax on the total amount of dividends received less their dividend exclusion. The maximum tax paid on dividends may be 70 per cent. Those who hold stocks in order to profit from increases in their market prices are taxed on only 50 per cent of their gains, if they hold the stocks over six months, and pay no more than 25 per cent of these gains. As far as stockholders and other high-bracket taxpayers are concerned, the tax law as presently written encourages long-term risk taking. This practice may result in capital gains rather than the holding of stocks or other assets for their income-yielding propensities. If investors in their attempts to benefit from the lower tax rates on long-term capital gains invest in newly issued securities, the economy as a whole may grow at a faster rate than if tax laws were otherwise. Their investments add to the net capital of the economy by supplying funds for new buildings and equipment.

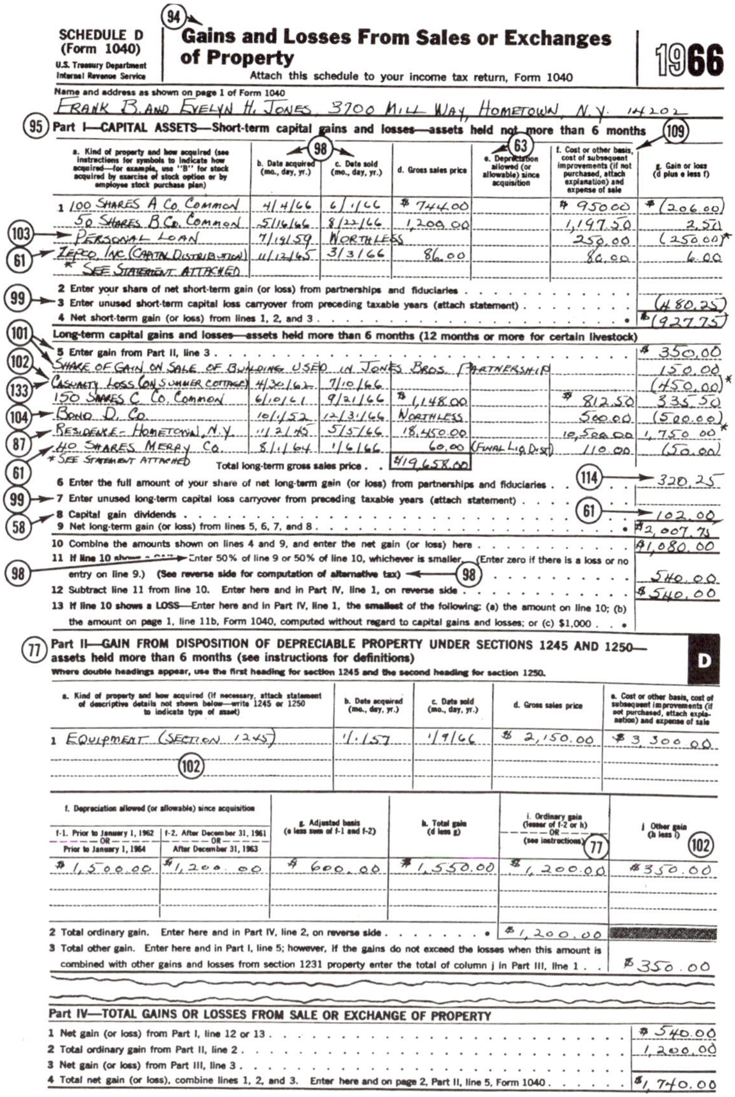

(94)

SCHEDULE D (Form 1040) U.S. Treasury Department Internal Revenue Service

Gains and Losses From Sales or Exchanges of Property

Attach this schedule to your income tax return, Form 1040

1966

Name and address as shown on page 1 of Form 1040

FRANK B. AND EVELYN H. JONES 3700 MILL WAY, HOMETOWN, N.Y. 14202

(95) **Part I—CAPITAL ASSETS—Short-term capital gains and losses—assets held not more than 6 months** (109)

a. Kind of property and how acquired (see instructions for symbols to indicate how acquired—for example, use "B" for stock acquired by exercise of stock option or by employee stock purchase plan)	b. Date acquired (mo., day, yr.) (98)	c. Date sold (mo., day, yr.)	d. Gross sales price	e. Depreciation allowed (or allowable) since acquisition (63)	f. Cost or other basis, cost of subsequent improvements (if not purchased, attach explanation) and expense of sale	g. Gain or loss (d plus e less f)
1 100 SHARES A CO. COMMON	4/4/66	6/1/66	$ 744.00		$ 950.00	$ (206.00)
50 SHARES B CO. COMMON	5/16/66	8/22/66	1,200.00		1,197.50	2.50
(103) PERSONAL LOAN	7/19/59	WORTHLESS			250.00	(250.00)*
(61) ZEPCO, INC (CAPITAL DISTRIBUTION)	11/12/65	3/3/66	86.00		80.00	6.00
* SEE STATEMENT ATTACHED						

(99)

2 Enter your share of net short-term gain (or loss) from partnerships and fiduciaries	
3 Enter unused short-term capital loss carryover from preceding taxable years (attach statement)	(480.25)
4 Net short-term gain (or loss) from lines 1, 2, and 3	$ (927.75)

(101) (102) (133) (104) (87) (61)

Long-term capital gains and losses—assets held more than 6 months (12 months or more for certain livestock)

a.	b.	c.	d.	e.	f.	g.
5 Enter gain from Part II, line 3						$ 350.00
SHARE OF GAIN ON SALE OF BUILDING USED IN JONES BROS. PARTNERSHIP						150.00
CASUALTY LOSS (ON SUMMER COTTAGE)	4/30/62	7/10/66				(450.00)*
150 SHARES C CO. COMMON	6/10/61	9/21/66	$ 1,148.00		$ 812.50	335.50
BOND D. CO.	10/1/52	12/31/66	WORTHLESS		500.00	(500.00)
RESIDENCE - HOMETOWN, N.Y.	11/2/45	5/5/66	18,450.00		10,500.00	1,750.00*
40 SHARES MERRY CO.	8/1/64	1/6/66	60.00	(FINAL LIQ. DIST.)	110.00	(50.00)
* SEE STATEMENT ATTACHED		Total long-term gross sales price	$19,658.00			

(114) (99) (61) (58) (98)

6 Enter the full amount of your share of net long-term gain (or loss) from partnerships and fiduciaries	320.25
7 Enter unused long-term capital loss carryover from preceding taxable years (attach statement)	
8 Capital gain dividends	102.00
9 Net long-term gain (or loss) from lines 5, 6, 7, and 8	$2,007.75
10 Combine the amounts shown on lines 4 and 9, and enter the net gain (or loss) here	$1,080.00
11 If line 10 shows a GAIN—Enter 50% of line 9 or 50% of line 10, whichever is smaller. (Enter zero if there is a loss or no entry on line 9.) (See reverse side for computation of alternative tax)	540.00
12 Subtract line 11 from line 10. Enter here and in Part IV, line 1, on reverse side	$ 540.00
13 If line 10 shows a LOSS—Enter here and in Part IV, line 1, the smallest of the following: (a) the amount on line 10; (b) the amount on page 1, line 11b, Form 1040, computed without regard to capital gains and losses; or (c) $1,000	

(77) **Part II—GAIN FROM DISPOSITION OF DEPRECIABLE PROPERTY UNDER SECTIONS 1245 AND 1250—assets held more than 6 months (see instructions for definitions)** D

Where double headings appear, use the first heading for section 1245 and the second heading for section 1250.

a. Kind of property and how acquired (If necessary, attach statement of descriptive details not shown below—write 1245 or 1250 to indicate type of asset)	b. Date acquired (mo., day, yr.)	c. Date sold (mo., day, yr.)	d. Gross sales price	e. Cost or other basis, cost of subsequent improvements (if not purchased, attach explanation) and expense of sale
1 EQUIPMENT (SECTION 1245) (102)	1/1/57	1/9/66	$ 2,150.00	$ 3,300.00

f-1. Prior to January 1, 1962 —OR— Prior to January 1, 1964 (f. Depreciation allowed (or allowable) since acquisition)	f-2. After December 31, 1961 —OR— After December 31, 1963	g. Adjusted basis (e less sum of f-1 and f-2)	h. Total gain (d less g)	i. Ordinary gain (lesser of f-2 or h) —OR— (see instructions) (77)	j Other gain (h less i) (102)
$ 1,500.00	$ 1,200.00	$ 600.00	$ 1,550.00	$ 1,200.00	$ 350.00

2 Total ordinary gain. Enter here and in Part IV, line 2, on reverse side	$ 1,200.00	
3 Total other gain. Enter here and in Part I, line 5; however, if the gains do not exceed the losses when this amount is combined with other gains and losses from section 1231 property enter the total of column j in Part III, line 1		$ 350.00

Part IV—TOTAL GAINS OR LOSSES FROM SALE OR EXCHANGE OF PROPERTY

1 Net gain (or loss) from Part I, line 12 or 13	$ 540.00
2 Total ordinary gain from Part II, line 2	1,200.00
3 Net gain (or loss) from Part III, line 3	
4 Total net gain (or loss), combine lines 1, 2, and 3. Enter here and on page 2, Part II, line 5, Form 1040	$ 1,740.00

Figure 12-2. **Internal Revenue Service form.**

Income from Annuities and Pensions

Veterans' pensions and social security payments are not taxable. Income from all other types of pensions and annuities, however, must be reported. The entire amount received each year as income from a *noncontributory* pension or annuity is taxable.

Since only the income received and not the paid-in principal is taxable in the case of annuities and pensions, any part of the principal that is returned is not taxable. If the person receiving the pension or annuity contributed to it and if his contributions will be recovered within three years from the date of the first pension payment, the payments are not to be reported as taxable income until the contributions have been fully recovered. After that time, all income from the pension or annuity becomes taxable.

The amount of taxable income on all other types of pensions and annuities is computed as follows:

$$\frac{\text{Principal}}{\text{Total Expected Return}} \times \text{annual payment received} = \text{amount nontaxable}$$

Annual payment received − amount nontaxable = taxable income

Thus, someone who invests $10,000 in an annuity contract, or contributes that amount to a retirement fund, and who expects to obtain $12,000 based on annuity tables,* receiving $1,200 a year, gets

$$\frac{\$10,000}{\$12,000} \times \$1,200, \text{ or } \$1,000, \text{ in nontaxable income}$$

each year. This is the return on his principal. ($10 \times \$1,000$, or $10,000, his invested principal, which in this case is returned to him in the ten years he is expected to live.) The remaining $200 of the $1,200 received is to be reported as taxable income.

Itemized Deductions

Deductions may be itemized or not at the discretion of the taxpayer. Items that may be deducted include eligible contributions, interest paid, taxes paid, certain medical and dental expenses, and sundry items. These deductions should be taken instead of the standard 10 per cent deduction when their total is greater.

Contributions. Contributions to religious, charitable, educational, scientific, literary, fraternal, and veterans' organizations; to organizations for the prevention of cruelty to children and animals; and to government agencies that use the gifts for public purposes may be deducted if the organizations have been formed under the laws of the United States. The organizations must not

---

* Tables that show, on the average, how long people of that age may expect to live and how much they will receive at the various rates of interest if they do live as long as expected. For a fuller discussion of the subject, see Chapter 16.

be operated for personal profit, must not propagandize, and must not attempt to influence legislation. Examples of organization gifts or donations that qualify as deductible contributions may be found in the instructions accompanying Form 1040.

In general, the total of the deductions for contributions should not exceed 20 per cent of the adjusted gross income, that is, gross income less business expenses. However, 10 per cent more may be added if the extra amount consists of contributions to churches or temples, religious associations, nonprofit educational institutions or hospitals, some medical research organizations, governmental units, or tax-exempt scientific, literary, religious, educational, charitable, or humane organizations that are supported by government or by contributions from the general public. If the taxpayer wishes, the entire 30 per cent deductible as contributions may be donated to groups in this last category. If charitable deductions to groups in the last category exceed 30 per cent in any year, the excess may be carried over and deducted over the following five years. Contributions may be made in money or property, but not in services. If a donation consists of property, it should be evaluated at a fair market price. How much old clothes or old books given to eligible organizations are worth is often a question to be settled with one's conscience. Dues unrelated to the earning of one's income, are not deductible. Neither is the price of tickets for which something of value is received, such as tickets for a dinner.

Interest. Interest paid may be listed as a deduction if it is paid or accrues during the taxable year as a result of loans, installment debt, mortgages, judgments, or delinquent taxes. Only the amount paid as interest on a mortgage, and not any repayment on the principal of the debt, is deductible. If the interest paid on an installment contract cannot be determined separately, 6 per cent of the average unpaid monthly balance may be deducted as interest for each payment made. The law lists many types of interest payments as nondeductible, such as interest paid on a debt incurred because of the purchase of tax-exempt securities. Individuals making interest payments not listed here may profit from further checks to determine whether their payments are deductible.

Taxes. State and local taxes are deductible. Federal taxes are not. To be deductible, a tax must be imposed only on the consumer. Therefore, state taxes on cigarettes collectible from the first person handling the cigarettes are not deductible. Taxes paid on alcoholic beverages in some states are deductible. Fees paid for hunting licenses or dog licenses and water taxes are not deductible. Since excise taxes and social security taxes are federal taxes, they are not deductible.

Medical or Dental Expenses. Medical or dental expenses for the taxpayer or any of his or her dependents. For example:

1. One-half of insurance premiums against the cost of medical expense ... $150.00
2. The cost of medicines and drugs in excess of 1 per cent of adjusted gross income. ... 50.00
3. Other medical and dental expenses for the year—all amounts paid for the prevention, cure, correction, or treatment of a physical or mental defect are deductible expenses; include remainder of premiums for insurance against the cost of medical expense. ... 700.00

   Total ... $900.00
4. Three per cent of adjusted income ... 450.00

   Subtracting the 3 per cent amount from the total medical outlays, the allowable deduction is ... $450.00

Itemized lists of medical and dental expenses must accompany the tax return and any expense compensated for by insurance or otherwise may not be listed or deducted. Premiums paid for insurance against medical, dental, or hospital expenses are deductible. Insurance premiums paid for policies that compensate for loss of earnings while incapacitated are not deductible. Traveling expenses incurred to visit a doctor, even if he is in another city, are deductible. So are expenses incurred traveling to a locality where a physical condition may be alleviated, such as prescribed trips to Arizona for asthma sufferers. Burial expenses are not considered medical expenses and are not deductible.

Before one reaches 65, one-half of the premiums paid for insurance covering medical care for one's self, one's spouse, or one's dependents in the years *after one reaches 65* are deductible up to a limit of $150, without regard to the 3 per cent limitation, if they are payable on a level payment basis for 10 years or more, or until one reaches 65. In the latter case they must have been payable for at least five years. The remainder of such premiums are deductible but subject to the 3 per cent limitation.

Other Deductions. Other deductions include losses resulting from casualties and theft that are not compensated for by insurance; payments for the care of children not exceeding a total of $900 to enable taxpayers in the lower-income brackets to be gainfully employed; expenses for education to better one's skills required by one's employment but not primarily for personal betterment; expenses necessary for obtaining income, such as the cost of investment advisory services or the safe deposit box in which to keep securities; and alimony.

Average Personal Deductions. For those itemizing deductions on taxable returns in 1964, personal deductions averaged 17 per cent of adjusted gross income for those in the $10,000–$15,000 income bracket; 16 per cent for those in the $15,000–$20,000 bracket; and 15 per cent for those in the $20,000–$100,000 income bracket.[11] These are average deductions. They cannot be used as a guide, since deductions are entirely an individual matter. However, it is interesting to note that personal deductions for those with incomes of more than $10,000 average more than 10 per cent of adjusted gross income, the standard deduction allowed lower-income bracket taxpayers.

The Internal Revenue Service permits the reduction of amounts subject to withholding by $700 for each $700 of itemized deductions above a set minimum averaging about 18 per cent of an annual salary. Since the highest withholding bracket is 30 per cent, each allowance for those in this category means $210 not withheld that may be used to earn interest until the federal income tax becomes due on April 15 of the year following the tax year.

Exemptions

The amount allowed for exemptions is subtracted after the total deductions to determine taxable income. The sum of $600 may be subtracted for each exemption claimed for the entire year. Each taxpayer may claim himself as an exemption. If he is over 65, he is entitled to claim two exemptions; if he is blind, he is entitled to an additional exemption. One exemption is allowed for the taxpayer's husband or wife, if the couple files a joint return. If separate returns are filed, a spouse may still qualify as an exemption if either has no income for the year and does not receive more than half of his or her support from another taxpayer. Again, if the taxpayer's spouse is over 65, the taxpayer is entitled to two exemptions on that account and, if a dependent or spouse is blind, an additional exemption.

Each of his children for which he contributes more than half support entitles the taxpayer to one exemption, even if the child receives over $600 in gross income, if the child is under 19 or a student. Scholarships may be disregarded when ascertaining if the taxpayer provides more than half of a student's support.

Any other dependent, for whom the taxpayer or his spouse pays more than half of the support, who receives less than $600 for the year in gross income, is closely related, does not file a joint return, and lives in the taxpayer's home also may be claimed as an exemption. The instructions accompanying Form 1040 list closely related dependents.

Retirement Income

Taxpayers who have retired, or are 65 or older, and have qualified by having earned more than $600 in each of any ten previous years may reduce their tax liability by a credit of 15 per cent of retirement income to a maximum of $1,524 for one person or $2,286 for a husband and wife who compute their retirement income credit jointly. For those under 65, such income consists of payments from pensions and annuities under a public retirement system. For those over 65, it includes pensions, annuities, interest, rents, and dividends. Limitations and types of income that must be subtracted from the $1,524 or $2,286 in computing the credit are listed on the instructions accompanying Form 1040.

Computing the Tax

A filled-in income tax return is shown in Figure 12–1. Form 1040 was used and some of the rates for married couples without children filing joint returns arc shown. Tax computation tables are included with the income tax forms mailed to taxpayers by the Internal Revenue Service.

Penalties and Appeals

Penalties are assessed by the government for failure to file income tax returns, for filing fraudulent returns, for not paying taxes when they are due, and for underestimating taxes by more than about one third. Interest at the rate of 6 per cent must be paid on delinquent taxes.

Where there is no fraud or serious error, the government has three years in which to examine an income tax return to determine whether a tax was accurately computed. Every return submitted is now audited by electronic computers. If the Internal Revenue Service finds more tax due than was paid, the taxpayer is notified, discusses the matter with a field officer of the Service and, in about 95 per cent of cases, there it ends. An agreement is reached as to the amount due, if any, and any additional tax is paid. If, however, the taxpayer wishes to appeal the matter, he may appeal to the tax court or the federal district court, circuit court, court of claims or, if all else fails, to the United States Supreme Court.

Minimizing Income Taxes

In order to minimize taxes, every taxpayer should avail himself of the most authoritative and complete courses of information on exemptions and deductions. Foremost among these is *Your Federal Income Tax—For Individuals*, Internal Revenue Service Publication No. 17, which is revised yearly and may be obtained from the U. S. Government Printing Office, Washington 25, D. C., for 50 cents. Most taxpayers who overpay their income tax do so because they are not aware of all of the exemptions and deductions to which they are entitled. Many others who do not keep accurate records consequently do not take all the exemptions and deductions for which they are eligible. When the amount of tax liability is deemed large enough, taxpayers whose business affairs are complex often consult a competent tax accountant or tax attorney.

For those in the higher-income brackets who buy tax-exempt municipal bonds, drill oil wells, raise beef cattle, cut timber, operate mines or quarries, buy older property that may be depreciated rapidly, and derive income from long-term capital gains, income taxes will be less than if their income came from other sources.[12] Where corporations pay for what otherwise would be an individual's personal expenses, such as insurance or vacations—and often these outlays are justifiable and allowed—the corporation's net cost may be only 52 cents for each dollar spent of dollars that would have been taxed under the corporate income tax.

Taxpayers with children may set up trusts from which their offspring each may receive up to $660 a year in income without incurring any tax liability. The children remain exemptions but, by putting the income from the assets in trust instead of keeping it for himself, the taxpayer reduces his taxes.

This list, of course, is not all-inclusive. The Internal Revenue Service is aware of the means used to minimize income taxes and expects that they will be used. To overpay may be foolish rather than virtuous.

QUESTIONS

1. Are taxes higher in the United States than they are elsewhere in the world? If so, why? If not, why not?
2. On which categories of expenditure does the federal government spend the most? How large a proportion of federal expenditure are welfare expenditures?
3. From which taxes does the federal government derive most of its revenue?
4. On which categories of expenditure do the states and localities spend the most? Why are state and local governmental expenditures increasing as rapidly as they are?
5. From which taxes do states and localities derive their revenue?
6. When and under what circumstances is government justified in undertaking an activity and levying taxes in order to do so?
7. Why is there opposition to the extension of governmental activities? Do you think this opposition is justified or do you not? Give the reasons that you think justify your opinion.
8. What are Adam Smith's four *maxims of taxation*? On which one is the income tax based?

9. Explain the *benefit* and *sacrifice* principles of taxation. Give examples of taxes based on each of these principles.
10. What is a progressive tax? A regressive tax? Why are we concerned with whether a tax is progressive or regressive? Give examples of both types of taxes.
11. Define direct taxes; indirect taxes. Give examples of each. When can a tax be shifted? What will determine to what extent a tax can be shifted?
12. Define marginal tax rate. Why are we concerned with the marginal tax rate?
13. List five "tax shelters" commonly used by higher-income bracket taxpayers to minimize the income tax paid over the five-year peroid?
    now in effect, should one have a high income one year and a relatively low income for the next four years or spread the total income over the five years so that the income level every year will be as low as possible in order to minimize the income tax paid over the five-year period?
14. Why do higher-income bracket taxpayers who control corporations and wish to minimize their personal income tax liability often refrain from the declaration of dividends?
15. Is there a federal tax on all gifts? List the major provisions of the gift tax. Does the donee of a block of stock have to pay a gift tax on that stock?
16. Are estate taxes higher or lower than gift taxes?
17. List eight federal excise taxes. What type of tax is an excise tax? What determines the *incidence* of an excise tax?
18. Can you justify the federal taxes on selected occupations? Give the reasons as you see them to explain why these taxes were passed or are retained.
19. What are the objections to the property tax? Are any of them justified? Explain.
20. What are the objections to the sales tax? Are any of them justified? Explain.
21. What other taxes do states and localities impose in order to gain revenue? Describe each tax named.
22. Who in the United States must pay the federal income tax? When are tax payments due?
23. Referring to the federal income tax, define: short-form; long-form; standard deduction; joint return; reportable income; capital gains; exemption.
24. Differentiate between a long-term capital gain and a short-term capital gain.

SELECTED READINGS

Buchanan, James M., *The Public Finances*, rev. ed., Irwin, Homewood, Ill., 1965.
Dickerson, William E., and Leo D. Stone, *Federal Income Tax Fundamentals*, 2d ed., Wadsworth, San Francisco, 1966.
Due, John F., *Government Finance*, Irwin, Homewood, Ill., 1963.
Eisenstein, Louis, *The Ideologies of Taxation*, Ronald Press, New York, 1961.
Farmer's Tax Guide, Internal Revenue Service Publication No. 225, U. S. Dept. of Treasury, Washington, D. C., free.
Federal Tax Course, Prentice-Hall, Englewood Cliffs, N. J., published annually.
Federal Taxes, Prentice-Hall, Englewood Cliffs, N. J., published annually.
How to Prepare Your Personal Income Tax Return, Prentice-Hall, Englewood Cliffs, N. J., published annually.
How to Reduce Taxes by Dividing Income among the Family, Prentice-Hall, Englewood Cliffs, N. J., 1956.

Investor's Tax Guide, Merrill Lynch, Pierce, Fenner & Smith, New York, published annually.
J. K. Lasser's Your Income Tax, Simon & Schuster, New York, published annually.
Olson, R. L., and R. L. Gradishar, *Saving Income Taxes by Short-Term Trusts*, Prentice-Hall, Englewood Cliffs, N. J., 1956.
Poole, Kenyon E., *Public Finance and Economic Welfare*, Rinehart, New York, 1956.
Public Finance, Needs, Sources and Utilization, National Bureau of Economic Research, Princeton University Press, Princeton, N. J., 1961.
Shultz, William J., and C. Lowell Harriss, *American Public Finance*, 8th ed., Prentice-Hall, Englewood Cliffs, N. J., 1965.
Standard Federal Tax Reporter, Commerce Clearing House, New York, published annually.
State and Local Taxes, AFL-CIO, Washington, D. C., 1959.
Tax Guide for Small Business, Internal Revenue Service Publication No. 334, U. S. Dept. of Treasury, Washington, D. C., published annually.
Tax Ideas, Prentice-Hall, Englewood Cliffs, N. J., latest year.
Teaching Federal Income Taxes, Internal Revenue Service Publication No. 19, U. S. Dept. of Treasury, Washington, D. C.
U. S. Master Tax Guide, Commerce Clearing House, New York, published annually.
Your Federal Income Tax, Internal Revenue Service Publication No. 17, U. S. Dept. of Treasury, Washington, D. C., published annually.

NOTES

1. Bureau of the Census, *Government Finances in 1960*, G-GF60 No. 2, September 16, 1960.
2. Harry T. Oshima, "Share of Government in Gross National Product for Various Countries," *American Economic Review*, June 1957, pp. 382–383.
3. See Henry E. Wallich, "Private vs. Public," *Harper's Magazine*, October 1961, pp. 12, 14, 16, 22, 25; and John Kenneth Galbraith, *The Affluent Society*, Houghton-Mifflin, Boston, 1958.
4. Adam Smith, *The Wealth of Nations*, Cannan ed., Modern Library, New York, 1937, pp. 777–778.
5. For a complete list, refer to *Tax Guide for Small Business, Individuals, Corporations, Partnerships, Income, Excise & Employment Taxes*, issued annually as Publication No. 334 by the Internal Revenue Service, and obtainable from the U. S. Government Printing Office or District Director of Internal Revenue for 50 cents.
6. See Richard A. Musgrave et al., in *Compendium of Joint Committee on the Economic Report, November 9, 1957*, U. S. Government Printing Office, Washington, D. C., 1957; and Richard A. Musgrave, *The Theory of Public Finance*, McGraw-Hill, New York, 1959.
7. For a complete list of customs regulations refer to U. S. Treasury Dept., Bureau of Customs, *Customs Regulations of the U. S.*, U. S. Government Printing Office, Washington, D. C., latest year.
8. See *Tax Guide for Small Business*, etc., *loc. cit.*
9. *Los Angeles Times*, October 31, 1961, Part III, p. 1.

10. It would be well to be guided by the *Tax Guide for Small Business, loc. cit.*, in preparing this schedule.
11. U. S. Treasury Department, Internal Revenue Service, *Statistics of Income 1964, Individual Income Tax Returns*, U. S. Government Printing Office, Washington, D. C., 1965, pp. 50–51.
12. Refer to the "Tax Report," which appears in the *Wall Street Journal* every Wednesday. *Changing Times* has helpful articles from time to time. *Tax Ideas*, published annually by Prentice-Hall, Englewood Cliffs, N. J., also may prove helpful.

PROBLEMS AND CASES

1. Figure your own or your parents' federal income tax for the year, using the long form. If for any reason the actual figures needed are not matters of open knowledge or available, or there are none applicable, you may use hypothetical figures; but fill in each line and each schedule and compute the hypothetical tax. The forms are available from the local office of the Internal Revenue Service.

   (Refer to the instructions accompanying Form 1040 when necessary in the following problems.)

2. Indicate whether or not a declaration of estimated tax is to be filled in each of the following cases:
   (a) A person whose total expected tax exceeds the amount withheld for the payment of income taxes by $65.
   (b) A head of a household—widow in this case—with an income for the year of $75,000.
   (c) A married couple whose joint income is $9,200 for the year—except for $150 their entire income was derived from wages subject to withholding.
   (d) A single person with an income of $4,800 for the year, all from wages subject to withholding.
   (e) A married person who is not entitled to file a joint declaration and whose income for the year, all from wages subject to withholding, amounts to $7,700.
   (f) A retired single person who receives no wages and whose income from his investments amounts to $5,200 for the year.

3. A woman receives $80 a week during the period that she is hospitalized and then is recovering at home from injuries incurred in an automobile accident. The firm where she works has a plan under which employees contribute $5 a month and the employer as much more as is necessary so that there will be a large enough fund to enable employees to receive two-thirds of their regular pay for as many as 90 days if they cannot work because of illness or injury. Is the $80 a week the employee received while away from work because of her injuries to be included in her taxable income for the year?

4. A married couple with a son still living at home are both employed. The husband's income is $9,200 for the year; the wife's $7,640. In addition they have $450 in joint income from interest and dividends. The son is a full-time college student but earns $890 during the year working. Should the couple file joint or separate returns? May their son be included as an exemption on a joint

return if they choose to file one? May he be included as an exemption on one or both returns if they file separate returns? Must he file his own return? If so, if he takes a standard deduction, how much tax must he pay?

5. A bachelor who is the sole support of his widowed mother finds his expenses for the year were as follows:

Food	$1,200
Clothing	350
Housing	
Payments on principal of mortgage	600
Interest on mortgage loan	360
Utilities (excise tax on telephone $12 included in utility total)	480
Household supplies, etc.	60
Property taxes	220
Property insurance	60
Automobile	
Car payments (including $240 in interest)	720
Car depreciation	600
License fees	28
Gasoline and oil (including $32 tax)	322
Car repairs	56
Life insurance premiums	120
Health insurance premiums	60
Charitable contributions	40
Medical expense and drugs (for mother) not covered by insurance	80
Recreation	360
Personal expense (toiletries, etc., dues, haircuts, cleaning, cigarettes)	254
Sales taxes	24
Miscellaneous (furnishings, vacation, etc.)	120
Withholding tax	1,205

If his income for the year was $8,050 of which $8,000 was from his salary and $50 from interest on shares in a savings and loan association, show how he should complete his income tax form so as to minimize the tax. Should he use a standard deduction? Why or why not? If he were self-employed as a real estate appraiser and needed his automobile in order to do his work, would his allowable deductions be different? Complete his income tax form and compute his tax for the year under this supposition.

6. On April 19 you purchased 100 shares of the X Corporation's stock and paid $4,792 for it. This sum included the broker's fees and all other expenses incidental to the purchase. On July 22 you purchased 100 shares of the Y Corporation's stock and paid $9,308 for it, including all the expenses involved in this transaction. On October 30 you sold the 100 shares of the Y Corporation's stock for $8,500. On December 12 you sold the X Corporation's stock for $6,300. How much is your short-term capital gain or loss? How much is your long-term capital gain or loss for the year? How much is your tax on your capital gains or losses for the year? Would it be different if, although your capital gains or losses remained the same, you were in a much higher income bracket?

7. A widow of 74 is still in the real estate business and derives a net profit of

$12,400 from the business for the year. Her income, as has been the case for the past 10 years has been over $20,000 for the year and stemmed from the following sources:

Income from business	$12,400.00
Interest income (taxable)	2,612.40
Dividends (after $50 exclusion)	3,905.80
Rent income (gross)	1,440.60
Income from annuity (taxable)	2,400.00
Social Security retirement benefits	1,321.20
Total	$24,080.00

Is she entitled to a retirement income credit, and if so, what is the amount of this credit?

8. Dorsey, who is 22 years old, is a full-time college student. He earns $2,040 on his part-time job during the year. Do his parents have to pay federal personal income tax on the amount of his earnings? If he files his own form 1040A and takes the standard deduction, how much tax will he pay? Fill out the son's income tax form.

9. The Bronsons are a young married couple with two young children. The family's income, entirely from the father's salary, is $7,800 for the year. If they do not own their home, pay little or no interest, donate less than $100 a year to charity, have no work-connected deductions, and have not suffered any large casualty losses or incurred more than $250 for the year in medical expenses, would you advise them to choose a long or short form when they file their federal personal income tax return for the year? If during the next year they are in an automobile accident and incur over $1,500 in deductible medical expenses and a $250 uncompensated casualty loss, would your advice be the same? Why? In the year following the accident they buy a home and a new car and therefore their property and sales taxes amount to $520, and the interest on their mortgage loan amounts to $188. Should they file a long or short form when they file their personal income tax return for that year? Why?

10. Your grandparents, both in good health, are 72 years old. Their income is derived from Social Security, $190.50 a month; payments they receive on property they sold, $300 a month on the principal and $50 a month in interest; and an annuity for which they paid entirely and which now pays them $125 a month. Are they required to file a federal income tax return each year? If so, fill it out for them. Their expense on medical bills and drugs was $185 for the year. They paid $240 in property taxes on their home. (Remember they pay a sales tax.) Their contributions to charitable organizations amounted to $75.

13 PROPERTY AND CASUALTY INSURANCE

Nobody can afford all the insurance he needs.

LIFE

An individual who buys insurance on his life, his house, or his car is choosing certainty in preference to uncertainty. He is accepting the certain loss of the small sum spent on the insurance premium in place of a small chance of large loss or a large chance of no loss at all.[1] The average American spends approximately 4 per cent of his income on insurance premiums, which provide sizable sums for the few persons who suffer financial losses resulting from fire, floods, storms, accidents, major illness, and premature death. This *spreading of risks* is especially important to people with inadequate resources, since they can seldom afford the financial losses that might occur if they assumed their own risks.

HAZARDS AND RISKS

The average family faces many hazards and assumes many risks. The family home and its furnishings may be destroyed by fire, flood, windstorm, earthquake, or by other catastrophes. The family's car or cars may be destroyed, stolen, or burned. Most families spend more than $100 a year to transfer these risks to one or more insurance companies.

Many of the family's possessions threaten the health and safety of other persons. The family car may maim and kill. Childrens velocipedes and bicycles may incapacitate aged persons. Carelessly driven golf balls or motorboats are increasingly hazardous. A broken step or roller skates left on the walk at night may lead injured parties to file damage suits, which endanger the family's savings and other assets. The family dog may prove costly to the head of the household and require several unpleasant days in court if it attacks a deliveryman. Most families spend more than $100 a year on automobile liability insurance, but many carry no insurance on the remainder of these risks.

The aforementioned hazards and risks account for the existence of property and casualty insurance—the subject of this chapter. The following chapter will be devoted to the risk of premature death and the fact that the typical family needs to spend several hundred dollars a year on life insurance. The risks of ill health, accident, and disability were explored earlier in the book. As we saw, a typical family may find it expedient to spend more than $300 a year for insurance protection or a health plan to obtain partial coverage of these risks. According to one estimate, partial but adequate insurance coverage for all of the typical family's risks would cost $1,470.60 a year. This estimate was based on a young family of four with a $7,500 income and a $20,000 home; it leads to the conclusion that "nobody can afford all the insurance he needs."[2] Consequently, risks should be examined carefully and insurance bought selectively.

Insurable Interest

Several hundred years ago, when insurance was a novelty, frauds were sometimes perpetrated by persons who bought insurance on the lives and property of others in whom they had no insurable interest. Thus, Sam Jones might have carried insurance on Bill Brown's life or on his home. If Jones lacked conscience, he might have murdered Brown, burned his house, or both, because he had nothing to lose—he had no insurable interest in Brown's continued existence. Nowadays, an individual goes to prison if he takes out a flight insurance policy on his financially self-sufficient mother-in-law without

Hazards and Risks

her knowledge, and places her and a bomb aboard her departing plane. Instances of this sort are rare and newsworthy now. A person may insure his own life and property or the lives of those in whom he holds an insurable interest. A man with a $20,000 home would be foolish to carry an excess of insurance because insurance companies compare claims in a central bureau and would indemnify him for no more than the true value of the property or the actual amount of loss sustained. A man whose income is $1,000 a month will be questioned if he seeks to buy health, accident, or disability insurance that would pay more than medical costs plus this monthly sum.

Coinsurance

A person who underinsures must recognize that he coinsures or shares some of the risk with an insurance company. A business building worth $50,000 should be insured for the full combustible value minus possible salvage—or approximately $40,000. Thus, if the owner carries that amount of insurance on the building, his losses up to the amount of his insurance will be paid in full. However, if he carries only $30,000 on this building, a $2,000 fire loss would yield him only $1,500 because he has shifted only three-fourths of the risk to the insurance company. Most losses are partial losses; therefore, most insurance agents encourage the carrying of insurance up to the coinsurance requirement.

Order of Significance of Risks

An individual must try to avoid the wastefulness of overinsurance and the perils of underinsurance. This objective requires a careful evaluation of the assets whose losses may be so catastrophic that insurance coverage seems urgent. On the contrary, an old car whose total loss may amount to $400 might not be worth a yearly premium of $50 for collision insurance. If the car is damaged extensively, it would not be worth the cost of labor and new parts. If the other driver should be judged responsible for the old car's destruction, his liability insurance would be used to replace the car. If the old car's owner were responsible for the accident, the loss of the $400 car would be disappointing, but not catastrophic.

Insurable Risks

A person may insure against almost any hazard. If the frequency and intensity of a risk or hazard can be predicted, an insurer can set a premium and assume the risk. Insurers who hesitate to assume risks may act as a group or *insurance syndicate* such as Lloyds of London. They may also *reinsure* by selling part of the risk to other insurers who *underwrite* the policy. Insurance is being written to cover losses resulting from anything. It covers losses arising from earthquakes, sonic booms, abnormal weather, and virtually everything where the moral hazard may be controlled within reason, or anything that may not be described as an act of war or civil insurrection. A few examples of the insuring of unusual risks and hazards may illustrate several of the basic principles of insurability of risks.

Most major league baseball teams carry flight insurance to cover their financial loss in case an entire team should be lost in a single air tragedy. Each league has an agreement whereby the remaining teams would option players to the stricken team, which could be rejuvenated at the cost of several million dollars. In the early 1960's, American League teams were insured for $52 million; National League teams carried $34 million of flight insurance.

Many carnivals, track meets, and other outdoor summer events are insured against inclement weather. Hurricane insurance is so common that hurricane Carla cost insurance companies nearly $100 million in 1961. Windstorm insurance covers many properties in the so called tornado belt in the Midwest.

Fire and storm insurance premiums can be set at levels that are appropriate for each region if data have been accumulated in recent years on the frequency of these occurrences and the amount of damages suffered. Thus a city's fire loss ratio may be well known and fire insurance premiums will reflect that fact. The probability of a crop-destroying hailstorm may be statistically predictable in certain farming areas. Farmers in the Midwest frequently pay small hail-insurance premiums, which provide sizable sums for the relief of those stricken by a local storm. Earthquakes cause extensive damage over large areas. However, earthquake insurance is so costly that few persons outside the quake-prone area carry it. Thus the risk is not well distributed, and the rates must be very high.

Until recently, most American insurance companies have been content to let unusual insurance groups such as Lloyds of London experiment with unique risks and hazards. Insurance companies in this country are now very competitive, however, and the insurance business is branching into new fields.

Classified Insurers

For years, it seemed prudent to encourage individual insurers to concentrate on special kinds of insurance designed to cover specific risks and hazards. Some insurers specialized in life insurance; others concentrated on fire and marine insurance, personal property insurance, or casualty insurance. It was believed that these classified insurers might develop unusual proficiency and insight as a result of this specialization. It was presumed, also, that insurers could be regulated more effectively if their risks, reserve requirements, and safety precautions were subject to precise calculation and review. The state of New York insisted that insurers doing business in the state submit to regulation in the specialized classifications. These classifications were generally accepted in other states.

Triumph of the Muliple-Line Principle

Then this approach changed. New York led the way in 1949, whereupon every state has permitted an insurer to operate in the entire field of insurance, except life insurance. Once the barriers were down, insurance companies broadened their lines and competition increased as established companies invaded new territories. Insurers added *policy endorsements* to give their customers increased coverage. Sometimes the customers were confused by the claims and counterclaims of agents who offered new coverage and revised rates. Some company officials and many government officials viewed the trend with alarm. They feared that insurers might reduce rates for hazards for which they lacked experience and thereby spoil the market for stable companies in possession of experience tables. It was thought that the public interest would not be served if competition leaped the bounds to which it had been confined by the American plan of classified insurance.[3]

As a result of the newer approach certain standard definitions and standard insurance policies have come into common usage. In discussing these policies, it should be remembered that variations and other definitions may be found.

PROPERTY INSURANCE

A homeowner who seeks insurance coverage on his property will find two types of standard policies on the market, each with several variations. The first of these policies is basically a fire-insurance policy with various extensions or endorsements. The second is a multiple-peril policy, which appears in several forms.

Fire Inurance with Extended Coverage Variations

Prior to 1925, fire insurance was available but it did not cover additional perils. The owner bought additional policies from insurers operating under other classifications if he wished to be covered from damage caused by tornados, explosions, and other perils. About 1925, several midwestern companies added supplemental *endorsements* to their fire-insurance policies covering losses caused by explosion, tornado, and falling aircraft. A few years later, these endorsements evolved into the so-called *extended coverage endorsement*,

Figure 13-1. Property-insurance policy showing extensions of coverage.

Limitations of Coverage

9 1. **LOSS DEDUCTIBLE CLAUSE NO. 1** — **Applicable to loss by windstorm or hail only if so stated on the Declarations Page:** With respect to buildings or structures, this Company shall be liable only when such loss in each occurrence exceeds the amount of the deductible stated on the Declarations Page and then only for its proportion of the loss in excess of the deductible amount. This Loss Deductible Clause shall apply to Residence Glass but shall not apply to Rental Value nor Additional Living Expense claims.

No more than one deductible amount shall apply in event of loss by the same peril insured against under both Coverage A—Dwelling and Coverage B—Personal Property arising out of any one occurrence. The highest deductible will always apply in the event that the deductible amounts are not the same.

10 2. **LOSS DEDUCTIBLE CLAUSE NO. 2**—**Applicable to loss by certain perils other than windstorm or hail only if so stated on the Declarations Page:** With respect to buildings or structures, this Company shall be liable only when such loss in each occurrence exceeds the amount of the deductible stated on the Declarations Page and then only for its proportion of the loss in excess of the deductible amount. This Loss Deductible Clause, however, shall not apply to loss by: fire; lightning; explosion; riot; riot attending a strike; civil commotion; aircraft; vehicles; smoke; vandalism and malicious mischief; theft or attempted theft; sudden or accidental tearing asunder, cracking, burning or bulging of steam or hot water heating systems (except appliances for heating water for domestic consumption). This Loss Deductible Clause shall apply to Residence Glass but shall not apply to Rental Value nor Additional Living Expense Claims.

No more than one deductible amount shall apply in event of loss by the same peril insured against under both Coverage A—Dwelling and Coverage B—Personal Property arising out of any one occurrence. The highest deductible will always apply in the event that the deductible amounts are not the same.

Exclusions

This policy does not insure against loss under Coverage A—Dwelling:

11 1. By termites or other insects; wear and tear, deterioration; smog; smoke from agricultural smudging or industrial operations; rust; wet or dry rot; mould; mechanical breakdown; settling, cracking, shrinkage, bulging or expansion of sidewalks, driveways, pavements, foundations, roofs, walls, floors or ceilings. If loss by fire, smoke (other than smoke from agricultural smudging or industrial operations), explosion, collapse, water, or glass breakage ensues, and if such ensuing loss is not otherwise excluded elsewhere in this policy, this Company shall then be liable only for such ensuing loss;

12 2. Occasioned by enforcement of any local or state ordinance or law regulating the construction, repair, or demolition of building(s) or structure(s) unless such liability is otherwise specifically assumed by endorsement hereon;

13 3. To retaining walls not constituting a part of a building when such loss is caused by pressure of ice or water;

14 4. By contamination.

(See Definitions, Exclusions, and Conditions Applicable to Both Coverages A and B on pages 5, 6 and 7 as well as General Conditions Applicable to the Entire Policy on pages 9, 10 and 11).

Coverage B—Personal Property
Perils Insured Against

15 **Coverage B insures against direct loss or damage to unscheduled personal property** (as defined on page 5) **by the perils given below,** except as hereinafter provided.

A—FIRE, LIGHTNING, and MEASURES USED BY CIVIL AUTHORITIES TO COMBAT FIRE;

†B—WINDSTORM or HAIL;

C—EXPLOSION, RIOT, RIOT ATTENDING A STRIKE, CIVIL COMMOTION;

D—VEHICLES or AIRCRAFT;

E—Sudden and accidental damage from SMOKE, other than smoke from agricultural smudging or industrial operations;

F—VANDALISM and MALICIOUS MISCHIEF meaning only the wilful and malicious damage to or destruction of the property covered;

G—BURGLARY from within a building or room (of which there must be visible evidence of forceful entry), HOLD-UP or ROBBERY;

*H—FALLING OBJECTS, but excluding loss to the interior of the building(s) or the property covered therein, caused by falling objects unless the building(s) containing the property covered shall first sustain an actual damage to the exterior of the roof or walls by the falling object;

*I—COLLAPSE of building(s) or any part thereof;

*J—WEIGHT OF ICE, SNOW or SLEET;

*K—FREEZING of plumbing, heating and air conditioning systems and domestic appliances;

*L—Accidental discharge, leakage or overflow of WATER or STEAM from within a plumbing, heating or air conditioning system or domestic appliance, as well as the cost of tearing out and replacing any part of the building(s) covered required to effect repairs to the system or appliance from which the water or steam escapes, but excluding the cost of repairing or replacing the system or appliance from which the water or steam escapes;

*M—Sudden and accidental injury to ELECTRICAL APPLIANCES, devices, fixtures and wiring, except television picture tubes, resulting from electrical currents artificially generated;

*N—THEFT or LARCENY (mysterious disappearance of any insured property shall be presumed to be due to theft, provided that it occurred under circumstances which would justify the inference that the property was stolen);

*O—COLLISION, DERAILMENT or OVERTURNING of any conveyance in or on which the insured property is contained, but excluding loss to the equipment, furnishings or appurtenances of any boat, including outboard motors, while the boat is afloat;

*P—EARTHQUAKE.

†Subject to Loss Deductible Clause No. 1 as stated under Limitations of Coverage applicable to Coverage B—Personal Property.

*Subject to Loss Deductible Clause No. 2 as stated under Limitations of Coverage applicable to Coverage B—Personal Property.

Extensions of Coverage

16 1. **PERSONAL PROPERTY OF GUESTS AND SERVANTS:**

At the sole option of the insured, coverage shall also apply:

(a) To personal property not otherwise insured belonging to guests while the property is on the described premises or while in a temporary residence of, and occupied by an insured;

(b) To personal property not otherwise insured belonging to servants of the insured who live on the described premises, while such property is on the said premises, and also while away from said premises when the servants are actually engaged in the service of the insured.

17 2. **IMPROVEMENTS, ALTERATIONS OR ADDITIONS AND ADDITIONAL LIVING EXPENSE:**

At the sole option of the insured (if not the owner of the described premises), coverage shall also apply:

(a) Up to ten per cent **(10%)** of the limit of insurance under Coverage B, as an additional amount of insurance, to cover improvements, alterations or additions to the described building and private structures appertaining thereto;

(b) Up to twenty per cent **(20%)** of the limit of insurance under Coverage B, as an additional amount of insurance, to cover loss (where such loss is by any peril insured hereunder) of Additional Living Expense (as defined on page 5).

18 3. **AUTOMATIC INSURANCE AT NEWLY ACQUIRED PREMISES:**

The insurance afforded by Coverage B with respect to the described premises shall apply to any other premises of which the named insured acquires ownership or control, if it replaces the described premises, provided that notice of the newly acquired premises be given to the Company within the following time limits: (a) within the policy term then current, or (b) if acquisition is within 30 days before the end of such term, then within 30 days after the date of such acquisition. The named insured shall pay any additional premium required.

Page 4

Property Insurance

Figure 13-1 (*continued*).

Limitations of Coverage

19 **1. LOSS DEDUCTIBLE CLAUSE NO. 1: Applicable to loss by windstorm or hail only if so stated on the Declarations Page:** With respect to personal property in the open, this Company shall be liable only when such loss in each occurrence exceeds the amount of the deductible stated on the Declarations Page and then only for its proportion of the loss in excess of the deductible amount. This loss deductible clause shall not apply to Additional Living Expense.
No more than one deductible amount shall apply in event of loss by the same peril insured against under both Coverage A—Dwelling and Coverage B—Personal Property arising out of any one occurrence. The highest deductible will always apply in the event that the deductible amounts are not the same.

20 **2. LOSS DEDUCTIBLE CLAUSE NO. 2—Applicable to loss by certain perils other than windstorm or hail only if so stated on the Declarations Page:** Each claim for loss or damage (separately occurring) caused by perils H, I, J, K, L, M, N, O and P, to unscheduled personal property, shall be adjusted separately and from the amount of each such adjusted claim or the applicable limit of liability, whichever is less, the amount indicated on the Declarations Page shall be deducted. This Loss Deductible Clause does not apply to Additional Living Expense.
No more than one deductible amount shall apply in event of loss by the same peril insured against under both Coverage A—Dwelling and Coverage B—Personal Property arising out of any one occurrence. The highest deductible will always apply in the event that the deductible amounts are not the same.

21 **3. JEWELRY, WATCHES, STERLING SILVER AND FURS:**
The coverage on unscheduled jewelry, watches, sterling silver and furs, is limited to twenty-five per cent (25%) of the limit of insurance under Coverage B. This limitation shall apply only to loss caused by burglary, hold-up, robbery, theft, larceny, vandalism or malicious mischief.

22 **4. MONEY, SECURITIES, ACCOUNTS, BILLS, MANUSCRIPTS, ETC.:**
The coverage on money, securities, accounts, bills, manuscripts, etc., in any one loss is limited to:
(a) One Hundred Dollars ($100) to money, bullion and bank notes;
(b) Five Hundred Dollars ($500) to accounts, bills, deeds, evidences of debt, letters of credit, notes other than bank notes, passports, railroad and other tickets, and securities;
(c) One Thousand Dollars ($1000) to manuscripts.

23 **5. STAMP AND COIN COLLECTIONS:**
The coverage on unscheduled stamp and coin collections in any one loss is limited to:
(a) One Hundred Dollars ($100) to unscheduled coin collections;
(b) Five Hundred Dollars ($500) to unscheduled stamp collections.

24 **6. SPECIFICALLY INSURED PROPERTY:**
No insurance under Coverage B shall apply to any property scheduled or specifically insured under any other portion of this or any other policy.

25 **7. ANIMALS, BIRDS, PETS:**
Animals, birds and pets are covered only while on the premises of the principal residence of the insured and shall not be covered for loss or damage caused by burglary, hold-up, robbery, theft, larceny, vandalism or malicious mischief.

26 **8. PROPERTY ORDINARILY SITUATED ELSEWHERE:**
Unscheduled personal property away from the described premises while in any dwelling or premises thereof, owned, rented or occupied by an insured, or while kept at a place of storage, is not covered against loss or damage caused by burglary, hold-up, robbery, theft, larceny, vandalism or malicious mischief, except while an insured is temporarily residing therein. The coverage for loss or damage to such property caused by other perils insured hereunder is limited to ten per cent (10%) of the amount of Coverage B.

Exclusions

This policy does not insure against loss under Coverage B—Personal Property:
27 1. To farm equipment, implements or supplies; poultry; crops, grain, seed, feed or hay;
28 2. To automobiles, vehicles licensed for road use, motorcycles, inboard motor boats, sailboats, aircraft; nor their equipment, furnishings and appurtenances. This exclusion does not apply to outboard motor boats, including their trailers, equipment, furnishings and appurtenances;
29 3. To property pertaining to a business, which includes trade, profession or occupation, away from the described premises, nor to articles carried or held as samples or for sale or for delivery after sale or rental to others;
30 4. To any property owned, used or worn by military personnel while such property is situated on a military installation;
31 5. To property on exhibition at fair grounds, or on the premises of any National or International Exposition;
32 6. To furniture, floor coverings, or other personal property rented to the insured, or to members of the insured's family, as part of the furnishings and equipment of any hotel room, furnished apartment or dwelling;
33 7. As respects the perils of Windstorm or Hail: (a) Loss caused directly or indirectly by frost or cold weather or ice (other than hail), sleet or snowstorm all whether driven by wind or not; (b) Loss to the interior of the building(s) or the property covered therein caused by rain, snow, sand, or dust, all whether driven by wind or not, unless the building(s) covered or containing the propeqy covered shall first sustain an actual damage to roof or walls by the direct force of wind or hail and then this Company shall be liable for loss to the interior of the building(s) or the property covered therein as may be caused by rain, snow, sand, or dust entering the building(s) through openings in the roof or walls made by direct action of wind or hail;
34 8. As respects the peril of Weight of ice, snow or sleet: Loss to the interior of the building(s) or the property covered therein, caused by weight of ice, snow or sleet unless the building(s) containing the property covered shall first sustain an actual damage to the exterior of the roof or walls by weight of ice, snow or sleet;
35 9. As respects the peril of Collapse of building(s) or any part thereof or the peril of Weight of ice, snow or sleet: Loss to outdoor equipment except as the direct result of the collapse of a building.
(See Definitions, Exclusions and Conditions Applicable to Both Coverages A and B on pages 5, 6 and 7 as well as General Conditions Applicable to the Entire Policy on pages 9, 10 and 11.)

Definitions, Exclusions and Conditions Applicable to Both Coverages A and B

Definitions

36 **1. DWELLING:**
The word "dwelling" shall mean the described dwelling building, including additions in contact therewith, occupied principally for dwelling purposes, and shall also include:
(a) Building equipment, fixtures and outdoor equipment all pertaining to the service of the premises (if the property of the owner of the dwelling and when not otherwise covered under this or any other policy), while located on the described premises or temporarily elsewhere;
(b) Materials and supplies intended for use in construction, alterations or repairs of the structures covered hereunder, while located on the described premises or adjacent thereto;
(c) Wall-to-wall carpeting only when installed in lieu of a finished floor.

37 **2. PERSONAL PROPERTY:**
The words "personal property" shall mean all unscheduled household and personal property usual or incidental to the occupancy of the premises as a dwelling, owned, used or worn by the insured and members of the insured's family of the same household, while in all situations anywhere in the world, except as provided herein.

38 **3. RENTAL VALUE:**
The term "Rental Value" shall mean the fair rental value of the building and private structures or parts thereof described in Coverage A, as furnished or equipped by the owner or lessor, whether rented or not. Loss shall be computed for the period of time, following loss, which would be required with the exercise of due diligence and dispatch to restore the property to a tenantable condition, less such charges and expenses as do not continue. Coverage hereunder shall also extend to include actual loss, during the period of time, not exceeding two weeks, while access to the premises described is prohibited by order of civil authority, but only when such order is given as a direct result of damage to neighboring premises by a peril insured against.

39 **4. ADDITIONAL LIVING EXPENSE:**
The term "Additional Living Expense" shall mean the necessary increase in living expense incurred by the insured, in event of damage or destruction of the building or of the personal property by a peril insured against, in order to continue as nearly as practicable the normal standard of living of the insured's household for the applicable period described in (a) or (b) below: (a) the time required, with the exercise of due diligence and dispatch, to repair or replace the damaged or destroyed property; (b) the time required for the insured's household to become settled in any permanent quarters. Coverage hereunder shall also extend to include the necessary increase in living expense, during the period of time, not exceeding two weeks, while access to the premises described is prohibited by order of civil authority, but only when such order is given as a direct result of damage to neighboring premises by a peril insured against. This Company shall not be liable for additional living expense due to the cancellation of any lease, or any written or oral agreement.

Page 5

which made provision for these additional perils. Soon thereafter, an *additional extended coverage endorsement* was available for an added fee (see Figure 13–1). The latter policy supplement covered ten additional perils, including damage caused by bursting water pipes and losses of personal property away from the premises. These policies became standard in the 1950's with Homeowners A, B, and C designations corresponding to the former fire-insurance policies supplemented with extended coverage and additional extended coverage endorsements. The policyholder should recognize that the common use of the terms "all risk" or "all perils" in these policies does not mean what he may wishfully think. Certain perils are subject to limitations and exclusions, which are to be found in the policy's fine print. For example, persons who live in an earthquake belt will find that their dwellings are not covered against this peril in one of these additional extended coverage policies unless the property suffers damage from fire caused by a quake.

Homeowners' Policies H-1 to H-5

By 1962, the homeowners' A, B, and C policies were being replaced in most of the states by a new series of policies designated as H-1, H-2, H-3, H-4, and H-5. These newer policies are basically multiperil policies. They cover a dwelling, its contents, additional living expense associated with the destruction of one's property, comprehensive personal liability, medical payments, and physical damage to the property of others. In most instances this insurance unit is important to all homeowners, some of whom might neglect certain of the items if they were not included. This assembled coverage can be offered for a lower premium than the cost of a number of separate policies covering the same perils. The H-1 to H-5 series of homeowners' policies is also more flexible and adaptable to a variety of homeowner requirements than the A, B, and C series.

The homeowners' policy H-1, often called the standard form policy, is comparable but superior to the former homeowners' A policy. It covers fire, vandalism, malicious mischief, theft of personal property, a 10 per cent allocation for living expenses, personal liability, medical payments, and payments for physical damage to the property of others. The H-2 policy includes the same coverage as the H-1 policy plus insurance against damage caused by explosions, leakage of steam boilers, or both; hot-water heaters and plumbing; certain types of damage to lawns, fences, and driveways; smoke damage from fireplaces; glass breakage, building collapse, some damage to electrical appliances and fixtures; damage from falling objects; and twice as much living allowance as is included in the H-1 policy. This H-2 policy is sometimes called an "all-risk" or *broad form policy*. Policy H-3 includes the all-risk coverage and for homeowners it includes a 40 per cent allocation for coverage of personal effects both on and off the premises. The H-4 policy is for tenants who wish to insure the contents of a building but not the building itself. The H-5 policy allocates up to 50 per cent of the coverage for the building's contents. This so-called *comprehensive policy* is designed to meet the needs of high-income families whose homes contain antiques, works of art, and costly furnishings.

Insurance buyers usually will find one of these H-1 to H-5 policies suitable and adequate for their needs. Actually, many of these policies contain an excess of coverage on certain items. The homeowner who has decided which of the policies he needs may be able to shop among companies for low rates, since the terms of the policies have been standardized. In some instances, moreover, the policy's costs may be reduced by scaling down certain coverages or by accepting a *deductible clause*, which requires the homeowner to assume the first few dollars of loss on specified perils.

AUTOMOBILE INSURANCE

A typical American family spends more on insurance for its automobile than for its home, because a moving car encounters scores of opportunities for its own destruction and for damage to other cars, property, and persons. The peril is great, the rates are high. In most states the law requires drivers and owners of cars to satisfy all claims that may be brought against them.

Automobile insurance is increasingly important in this country with 80 million cars, congested streets and highways, crowded courts, and sharply increasing repair costs. Automobile-insurance premiums paid by Americans have quintupled since the end of the Second World War, totaling $9 billion by 1966. Court awards to persons injured by automobiles have risen at a fantastic rate. Competition is keen among the 700 companies in the automobile-insurance field. New types of policies and new rate schedules have been launched so rapidly that many of the customers have been confused and the industry seems to be in transition.

Types of Coverage Available

Automobile insurance may be divided into five categories: personal and property liability insurance; fire, theft, and comprehensive damage insurance; collision insurance; medical coverage; and miscellaneous coverage. The coverage included in any policy and the claims-settlement record of insurance companies should be studied carefully before comparing rates.

The most important type of automobile insurance to carry is liability insurance. The next most important, according to the statistics on frequency of loss, is comprehensive. Beyond this, collision insurance should be carried by persons with reasonably good cars.

Liability Insurance. The owner of a car needs liability insurance, which protects him against claims for personal injuries or property damage caused by his car or by himself while driving another car. There are two types of liability insurance, bodily-injury liability and property-damage liability. In the former, the insurance company agrees, in consideration of the premium, to pay all sums up to the limit of the company's liability for which the insured becomes legally obligated as a result of injury, illness or death of a pedestrian, or of the driver or passengers of another car. The insurer pays the expenses of defending any lawsuit brought against the owner as a result of an automobile accident, and the expenses of providing bail or posting bonds. Members of the insured's family using an automobile with the insured owner's permission also may be covered. Property-damage insurance provides similar protection to the owner of a car against damage that he may cause to another's car or other property as the result of an automobile accident.

Claims for bodily injury or property damage may total tens of thousands of dollars. Most states have Motor Vehicle Safety or *Financial Responsibility Laws*, which hold owners and drivers of motor vehicles responsible for any expenses resulting from an accident caused by them. If the car's owner or driver is responsible for an accident and carries no insurance or inadequate insurance, and cannot settle or deposit security within 60 days for damages resulting from the accident, he automatically loses his car registration, driver's license, or both.

Liability insurance policies are commonly referred to as $10,000/$20,000 or $100,000/$300,000, or simply as 10/20 or 100/300. The first figure is the maximum amount the insurance company will pay for personal injury to any one person. The second is the maximum amount it will pay because of any one accident.

Since the insured has to pay any damages assessed against him above the amount for which he is insured, and juries often award sizable sums to those who have been injured, it is expedient to carry a relatively large amount of liability insurance. The amount of coverage provided increases at a faster rate than premiums for this type of policy. For example, in Los Angeles, drivers over 25 who do not use their cars for business and drive less than ten miles to work paid in 1967 the amounts shown in Table 13–1 for personal and property liability insurance.

Comprehensive Insurance. Fire, theft, and comprehensive insurance reimburses the insured for direct or accidental loss of or damage to his own car for any cause other than mechanical breakdown, wear and tear, freezing, col-

Table 13-1 Liability Insurance Costs, Los Angeles, 1968.

Premium (Dollars)	Coverage	Increase in Coverage (Per Cent)	Increase in Cost (Per Cent)
42.20	10/20	—	—
47.30	25/50	150	12
49.80	50/100	400	18
52.80	100/300	900	25

lision, or upset. The protection may include loss or damage due to fire and theft, glass breakage, vandalism, windstorm, hail, flood, smoke, falling objects, and any other causes listed in the policy. Separate policies are available for only fire or for fire and theft. If an automobile is financed, the financing agency ordinarily requires that the car buyer carry comprehensive insurance and collision insurance so that the lender's investment may be protected.

Sometimes a comprehensive policy contains a *deductible clause*, which provides that the policyholder will pay the first few dollars of any loss. Some of these policies are known as 70–30 or 80–20, which indicates the company's and the policyholder's share of the costs of certain minor repairs, replacement, or spot painting.

Collision Insurance. So-called collision insurance reimburses the insured if his car strikes or is struck by an object or another car, or if the car is upset. Reimbursement is made to the insured, regardless of who was at fault in the accident. A collision-insurance policy usually includes an *uninsured motorist endorsement*, which offers protection against damages that may be caused by an irresponsible driver with no insurance. In practice, the insurance company will pay the damages of the insured in any case and then will sue the other driver involved if he was thought to be at fault and if it is worthwhile. The suit is brought in the insured's name.

Most collision insurance policies are written with a *deductible clause* in which the insured pays the first $50 or $100 of the loss. Any sum above the deductible amount is paid by the insurance company. A deductible clause makes it possible for the insurance company to offer collision insurance at a lower rate than would be possible if it had to investigate and pay the additional small losses. Therefore, the higher the deductible amount, the lower the premium on this segment of an automobile insurance policy.

Medical Coverage. Car owners may buy optional coverage for medical payments. In case of an accident, this coverage will compensate persons riding in or driving the insured's car for medical, dental, surgical, hospital, nursing, or funeral expenses resulting from an accident, regardless of who may have been at fault. This policy also will compensate the policyholder and his family for specified medical expenses listed in the policy incurred as a result of an accident involving a vehicle that they do not own but in which they were riding, or as a result of being hit while a pedestrian. The additional cost for this coverage is relatively low. In 1966, for a preferred risk, the charge for $250 coverage per person was less than $8 per year.

Miscellaneous Coverage. Many policyholders choose to buy additional features with their car-insurance policies. Such features may include the company's obligation to provide tow-in service for a stalled car, make provision for car rental following damage to the policyholder's car, or insure the policyholder in case he suffers injury or loss caused by an uninsured driver. Some companies include the latter feature as an integral part of their policies. Several states, led by New York, have required that this feature be incorporated into all policies sold within the state. Many insurance representatives also serve as agents for automobile clubs that provide tow-in service and other services for their members.

Types of Automobile-Insurance Companies

More than 700 companies write automobile insurance in the United States, but not all of them write policies in all states. Some are specialty companies selling only automobile insurance. Others sell other types of insurance as well. Most insurance companies are stock companies, mutual companies, or so-called reciprocals.

Stock Companies. Stock companies are corporations that are trying to make a profit for their stockholders. These companies charge rates based on experience tables. Until a few years ago, their rates were rigid and often a bit high, although they were differentiated according to area and degree of personal risk. Stock companies tend to be old and well supported with reserves that have been set aside over the years.

Mutual Companies. Mutual insurance companies are owned by their policyholders, who share the profits or losses of the companies. Mutual policies vary in cost depending on the total amount of losses suffered by the company. The policyholder's net cost of these policies—that is, the premium minus dividend refund—tends to be relatively low compared to the cost of policies in other types of companies. Some of these companies offer nonassessable policies, which are sold at a rate that cannot vary regardless of profits or losses.

Mutual companies outnumber other types of automobile-insurance companies, and many of them are among the largest insurers in the country. Most of the mutuals are required to accumulate sizable reserves; hence their solvency is assured.

Reciprocal Companies. The so-called reciprocals include organizations such as automobile clubs that are formed to spread the risks that may be incurred by members of the group. Many reciprocals are nonprifit organizations. Their rates are neither the highest nor the lowest charged for automobile insurance. Free tow-in service, low automobile-financing rates, free highway information, and some other services provided by the reciprocals have endeared them to their clientele.

The American Agency System. Until a few decades ago, almost every car driver bought his insurance from an agent or broker who was free to offer the policies of a number of companies. The agent played a dual role, representing insurance companies at the same time that he actually represented his client personally as the client shopped among insurers for the best coverage and the lowest rates. Many of these agents served the customer's needs. They gained their loyalty, sold them several types of insurance, and reaped additional commissions as they renewed policies year after year. Commissions for new policies and policy renewals constituted a major cost of automobile insurance. Rates were held rather high by *rating bureaus*, which gathered experience tables and established rates that member insurance companies filed in each state.

Independent Insurance Companies. Since 1940, several independent insurance companies have revolutionized the automobile-insurance business. These companies hire their own agents and adopt central billing systems. Agents' commissions are reduced, especially on policy renewals that are solicited and billed from central billing offices. With these economies, the independent companies have been able to reduce their rates. With this advantage, they claim that they have been able to screen out the poor-risk customers and reduce their rates still further. Rival agents and some of the customers infer that the claims-settlement record of the independent companies is less than satisfactory. They allege that this alone may account for the ability of these companies to offer reduced rates.[4]

Automobile Insurance: Risks and Rates

Insurance rates vary from company to company and depend largely on the *risk category* assigned to the driver or drivers of the car. Most companies have at least six risk categories governed by the driver's age, his past record as a driver, the use of the automobile, and the type of car being insured. Very young and very old drivers are categorized as greater risks. Persons driving sports cars are considered to be high risks. Premium rates on collision insurance are higher if any male person under 25 will be driving the car. However, in many states, if all male drivers in the household have successfully completed a recognized driver-education course, and this fact can be verified by the insurance company, the automobile casualty and collision premiums for the car will be reduced by 10 per cent. Young men who make high grades in school are sometimes assigned to a *preferred risk* category at lower rates.

The original factory-advertised price of the car is a factor in the premium charged for collision insurance. Higher-priced cars cost more to replace if they are demolished in an accident. A car with relatively high repair costs necessitates high rates. The rate charged for automobile insurance also depends on insurance statistics for the state and community in which the insured lives. Since accidents are more frequent in metropolitan areas, it behooves drivers in these areas to carry more insurance.

In shopping for insurance, it is necessary to do more than compare rates. A poor or inadequate policy may result in an unnecessary loss. Household Finance Corporation recommends:

Compare coverages—some are more liberal than others.
Read every policy submitted to you and ask for an explanation of any clauses or restrictions you don't understand.
Pay particularly close attention to any provisions which may cancel the policy.
Know all the details of coverage and be sure you understand the provisions for settling claims.
Check into the company's reputation for paying losses and for cancellation of contracts.
Check services rendered by company or agency.
Be sure the company you choose is licensed to do business in your state.[5]

Settlement of Claims

An automobile-insurance company should be judged by its rates, by the risks it assumes contractually, and also by the promptness and the adequacy with which it settles legitimate claims. Most customer complaints arise from the alleged mistreatment of persons filing claims for damages against automobile insurers. These complaints range from allegations of delayed and inadequate settlements to overgenerous settlements that are offered as an excuse for charging high rates.

The Reason and Necessity for Contesting Claims. During the 1950's and early 1960's, losses paid on claims against automobile insurance companies have increased approximately 7 per cent each year. Deaths have been declining, but the number of injuries has increased, and claims have soared astronomically.[6] Automobiles maim increasing numbers of pedestrians on crowded streets and highways. Occupants are injured within their cars in collisions or suffer injury when their car is bumped from the rear.

Police and insurance-company investigators occasionally find persons who fake an accident hoping to receive a settlement from an insurance company. The ambulance-chasing lawyer is also well known to insurance company investigators. Each of these costs insurance companies and their policyholders large sums each year.

Injured persons file suit for damages; lawyers often handle cases on a *contingent fee* basis, which allocates to them a percentage of the settlement. In many areas the court cases require a delay of from one to three years in spite of the fact that the courts devote approximately two-thirds of their time to suits involving automobile accidents.

Much automobile litigation is settled out of court, however, with the insurance company paying somewhat less than the amount originally sought by the plaintiff. It is alleged that many of these cases have nuisance value, which forces the insurer to offer a compromise settlement.

Of the claimants who go to trial, many obviously press their claims in the expectation that judges, juries, or both will award sizable damages. This arrangement is very unsatisfactory. It is slow; there is uncertainty and hardship for injured persons; the court costs and lawyers' fees impart nuisance value to many cases and raise awards in other instances. The claimant gets so much less than the insurance company pays that insurance companies feel that they are being bilked; the customers, on the other hand, feel that the insurance rates are too high, and claimants are frequently dissatisfied. This means of settlement, incidentally, is under attack by persons who favor the universal adoption of Pennsylvania's plan of handling automobile cases. Under this plan referees are authorized to grant immediate awards based on actual damages sustained with little need for assessing responsibility for the accident.[7] It is suggested, also, that everyone should carry collision insurance with perhaps $200 deductible. Litigation over the cause of the accident would then cease and insurers would bear all repair and replacement costs in excess of $200.

Many owners of cars are also directly responsible for high insurance rates. These persons, sometimes called *premium retrievers* by insurance company agents and officials, file doubtful or exaggerated claims for paint scratches, pitted windshields, and hubcap losses. Obviously, if a company must return premiums to its customers for small claims of this sort, it has little or nothing left for the big, valid claims filed by a few of the insured.

Alleged Inadequacy of Claims Settlement. Insurance buyers like to assume that a company that offers coverage for ten or twenty dollars less than competing companies has found ways of reducing costs. The buyers hope that this may have been possible because of the company's policy of selling only to preferred-risk customers. They feel betrayed when and if they discover that the company is noticeably stingy in settling claims.

Most companies make adequate settlements of *first party claims* filed by their own policyholders. Some of these claims, including broken and pitted windshields, stolen accessories, and scratched paint, are an obligation of the insurer under the terms of the comprehensive coverage. Fire, theft, and collision also are included in first party claims. Some companies may be slow in handling these claims, or may take too much of the customer's time. However, the settlements usually are adequate, even though the company may insist on its right to replace a stolen automobile with an equivalent car of comparable market value.

A perpetual controversy rages around the settlement of *third party claims*, in which other persons file claims against the policyholder's insurance company for damages suffered or imagined. Personal injury cases are usually settled quickly to prevent them from "mushrooming." In contrast, the owner or driver of a car usually has difficulty in collecting for his own car repairs from the owner or driver of the other car following an accident. First the offended party must prove the other party's guilt or negligence; then he must establish the amount of his own damages and be prepared to sustain his argument in court. If the accused policyholder denies guilt or negligence, his company is likely to contest a settlement. Many policyholders sincerely believe that they were not responsible for the accident; others deny responsibility for fear that an admission of guilt or negligence will endanger their policy renewal. In either case, the third party's opportunity for a quick, amicable, adequate settlement of his claims is limited.

Threat of Policy Cancellation

An insurance company has cause to discipline those of its policyholders who file too many claims or appear to have too many accidents or moving traffic violations that indicate the probability of accidents. An insurance company can pull the rug out from under a car owner by canceling or threatening to cancel his automobile-insurance policy. Most companies promise five or ten days' notice prior to policy cancellation. A few companies promise no cancellations, but they cannot guarantee renewal at normal rates if the policyholder becomes a poor risk. The customer, once spurned by an insurer, will have difficulty finding another that is willing to assume his risks. Most certainly, he will be rejected by the companies selling at low rates to selected customers.

Assigned Risks. The owner of a car who cannot find an insurer may be compelled to utilize an assigned-risk category. In this instance, he will be assigned to an insurance company that must take its quota of assigned risks. Automobile-insurance companies must sell insurance to assigned-risk customers, but they are permitted to categorize the risk involved and to charge a high premium accordingly. Customers who feel that they have been mistreated by the company may appeal to an insurance commissioner in many states.[8]

Classified Ratings. The rating of customers by automobile insurance companies places many car owners on the defensive. The arbitrary classification of young males and aged persons seems unfair to many within these groups, whose driving records are spotless. The upward reclassification of young males when they marry or if they make good grades in school may be justified by certain statistics, but some persons feel that group classifications of this sort are too generalized to be accurate. Drivers who think that their classifications have been downgraded unjustly because of moving traffic violations that they consider to have been unfair, naturally will deny the validity of the classified-rating system. Perhaps the reclassifications may be improved over the years until they approximate the actual potential risk of most drivers.

Many automobile-insurance customers have lost their bargaining power. They are not sought out by insurance agents; some of them must search for a company to cover their risks. Insurance commissioners are aware of the customer's waning bargaining power. The extension of noncancellation clauses in automobile-insurance policies, supported by adequate state supervision of assigned-risk premium rates, offers the hope that the balance may be redressed.

QUESTIONS

1. Describe a number of hazards that confront typical homeowners and automobile owners. Are all risks insurable? Why?
2. Why must a person have an insurable interest in a risk before he should be allowed to carry insurance on it?
3. Explain and illustrate the principle of coinsurance. Why must one be selective in determining which risks to insure and for how much?
4. What are the chief arguments for and against (*a*) the American system of classified insurance; (*b*) the agency system; and (*c*) independent insurers?
5. How has homeowners' insurance evolved in the last half-century? Explain the type of coverage in H-1 to H-5 policies.
6. List and explain the five chief segments of an automobile-insurance policy.
7. Explain the three chief types of automobile-insurance companies.
8. What explains the rapid gains made by independent automobile-insurance companies compared with companies operating under the American agency system?
9. Explain the interrelationship between automobile risks, insurance premium rates, and claims settlement.

10. Why, for whom, and in what ways is the settlement of automobile accident claims so unsatisfactory?
11. What is the relationship between classified ratings, policy cancellation, and assigned risks? Do you believe that automobile-insurance companies must have the right to classify their policyholders? Does this right need supervision?
12. Note carefully the key terms in this chapter and be prepared to identify them.

SELECTED READINGS

Best's Insurance Reports, Fire and Casualty edition, Best, New York, issued annually.
Greene, Mark R., *Risk and Insurance*, Southwestern Publishing Company, Cincinnati, 1962.
Insurance Information Institute, *Insurance Facts*, issued annually, New York.
Kulp, C. A., *Casualty Insurance*, 3rd ed., Ronald Press, New York, 1956.
Magee, John Henry, *Property Insurance*, 3rd ed., Irwin, Homewood, Ill., 1955.
Mayerson, Allen L., *Introduction to Insurance*, The Free Press, Macmillan, 1962.
Michelbacher, G. F., *Multiple-Line Insurance*, McGraw-Hill, New York, 1957.
Snider, H. Wayne, *Readings in Property and Casualty Insurance*, Irwin, Homewood, Ill., 1959.

NOTES

1. Milton Friedman and L. J. Savage, "The Utility Analysis of Choices Involving Risk," *Journal of Political Economy*, Vol. LVI, 1948, pp. 279–304, as found in George J. Stigler and Kenneth E. Boulding, *Readings in Price Theory*, Irwin, Homewood, Illinois, 1952, p. 57.
2. Ernest Havemann, "High Cost of Playing Safe," *Life*, March 31, 1961, p. 78.
3. See G. F. Michelbacher, *Multiple-Line Insurance*, McGraw-Hill, New York, 1957, pp. 1–25.
4. Perrin Stryker, "Auto Insurance Battered by Its Own Boom," *Fortune*, October, 1960, p. 143.
5. Household Finance Corp., *Money Management, Your Automobile Dollar*, Chicago, 1956, p. 23.
6. Stryker, *op. cit.*, p. 145.
7. Paul Friggens, "Here's Hope for Speedier Justice," *Reader's Digest*, April 1960, pp. 197–201.
8. "How Good Is Your Insurance?" *Consumer Reports*, April 1962, pp. 204–210.

PROBLEMS AND CASES

1. List the types and amounts of property and casualty insurance coverage your household should be carrying currently, in view of the hazards and risks against which it should and could be insured. Determine from an insurance broker how much such coverage would cost. What percentage of your budget would be required for this purpose? What are the arguments for and against spending this much of your budget on insurance?
2. Why was it found inappropriate a century ago for one man to carry insurance on another man's life? Why is it appropriate now for a corporation to carry insurance (payable to the corporation) on the lives of its chief officers?
3. Would many persons be tempted to underinsure their buildings if it were not

for the coinsurance requirement? If underinsurance became general, how would claims for fire losses be covered? Wouldn't this be inequitable for those who carried the highest percentage of coverage on their buildings?

4. Earthquake insurance on the west coast costs about as much as fire insurance and associated coverage under a Homeowner's Policy. According to the basic insurance principle, why must this insurance cost so much? What are the prospects for reducing its price by spreading the risk to other areas?
5. Which Homeowner's Policy would best cover (1) an affluent family with many treasured items and art objects, (2) a tenant, (3) a family that takes frequent trips in a house trailer?
6. Would a two-carat diamond ring be covered by an average-priced Homeowner's Policy? What precautions would be advisable? Should it be covered in a separate policy?
7. List the types and amounts of automobile insurance you should be carrying in view of the hazards and risks against which you could and should be insured. Determine the cost of this much insurance. Where can it be obtained most economically? (Inquire about rates from several sources and compare their rates.)
8. Which part of an automobile-insurance policy is designed for the benefit of the car's owner? Which parts are designed for the benefit of his family or his invited guests? Which are for the protection of the owner and passengers in "the other car?"
9. Why should motorists carry unusually large amounts of insurance today? Do the added amounts increase the cost proportionally? Why?
10. Why are deductible clauses increasingly used in property and casualty insurance? What are the alternatives?
11. If a little known mutual insurance company from a distant state defaults on its obligations, would the insured still be liable for personal or property damage for which he had been charged? Why?
12. Distinguish between first-party claims and third-party claims against an automobile insurance company. Why are the latter so difficult to settle? What remedies for crowded courts and settlement delays have been suggested?
13. If the Browns' teen-age son has a poor driving record followed by several accidents, what measures may the company take against Mr. Brown? Why is it unlikely that Brown can change his policy to another company to avoid higher rates?
14. In most states, can an automobile-insurance company arbitrarily cancel a policy? Has the threat of cancellation been abused? To whom would the policyholder appeal? Are no-cancellation guarantees frequently advertised and offered by some companies? What other recourse against an accident-prone client would such a company have?

14 LIFE INSURANCE

You've got to be a nut to buy life insurance,
Here's a guy betting you're going to live
And you're betting him you're going to die
And you hope he wins
And they charge you for thinking that way.

READER'S DIGEST

The face value of all life insurance in the United States exceeds $1.0 trillion. This is more insurance per capita than in any other country in the world, yet it would provide the average American policyholder with much less than two years of his family's normal income.[1]

Actually, life-insurance coverage is not spread evenly enough to offset the risks confronting young families and low-income groups throughout the country. Young people are too busy with living to think of death. However, it is imperative that they turn their attention to the use of life insurance as a means of assuring continuity of the income that makes the good life possible.

NEED FOR LIFE INSURANCE

All men are mortal. Each must die sometime. Normally, a man or woman survives the perils of childhood, lives to raise and support a family, and retains good health and a satisfactory income long enough to accumulate savings for the years of retirement when income is minimal. When someone dies before completing his full life cycle, he leaves distraught relatives and friends behind. Sometimes he leaves dependents financially stranded—persons for whom he would have provided support had his life been spared.

Probability of Premature Death

For any age group there are *mortality tables*, which may be used to predict the number of deaths that may be anticipated. For example, the 1959–1961 total population data in the mortality tables, as shown in the right-hand columns of Table 14–1, would indicate that a twenty-year-old American may expect to live 52.58 more years and that 1.15 persons in a thousand will die at the age of 20. The same table reveals that 30-year-olds may expect 43.18 years of additional life and that 1.43 persons in a thousand will die at the age of 30.

The mortality table indicates that individuals face an increasing risk of premature death within any one year after their tenth birthday. It should be obvious, also, that as the risk of premature death increases, the rates charged for insurance must be increased to provide funds for the mounting death claims that surely will be filed.

Financial Consequences of Premature Death

Even though death does not strike young and middle-aged adults very often, the few instances in which it does occur may leave relatives and dependents in emotional shock and financial difficulty. The grief that relatives and close friends must suffer is only part of their loss. It is the financial loss associated with a premature death that must be considered here.

Unpaid Bills. It is quite common, nowadays, for a person to owe several bills contracted in the course of routine expenditures and durable goods accumulation. Nearly everyone meets his bills promptly when they are due; however, a few are concerned with the fact that their solvency depends on the receipt of their next paycheck. Some individuals may use credit so extensively that their earnings are committed for several months in the future. A typical family may need a clean-up fund of approximately a thousand dollars to pay

Table 14-1. Mortality Tables (Percentages)

Age	American Experience (1843–1858) Deaths Per 1,000	Expectation of Life (Years)	Commissioners 1941 Standard Ordinary (1930–1940) Deaths Per 1,000	Expectation of Life (Years)	Commissioners 1958 Standard Ordinary (1950–1954) Deaths Per 1,000	Expectation of Life (Years)	Annuity Table for 1949—Male (1939–1949) Deaths Per 1,000	Expectation of Life (Years)	United States Total Population (1959–1961) Deaths Per 1,000	Expectation of Life (Years)
0	154.70	41.45	22.58	62.33	7.08	68.30	4.04	73.18	25.93	69.89
1	63.49	47.94	5.77	62.76	1.76	67.78	1.58	72.48	1.70	70.75
2	35.50	50.16	4.14	62.12	1.52	66.90	.89	71.59	1.04	69.87
3	23.91	50.98	3.38	61.37	1.46	66.00	.72	70.65	.80	68.94
4	17.70	51.22	2.99	60.58	1.40	65.10	.63	69.70	.67	67.99
5	13.60	51.13	2.76	59.76	1.35	64.19	.57	68.75	.59	67.04
6	11.37	50.83	2.61	58.92	1.30	63.27	.53	67.78	.52	66.08
7	9.75	50.41	2.47	58.08	1.26	62.35	.50	66.82	.47	65.11
8	8.63	49.90	2.31	57.22	1.23	61.43	.49	65.85	.43	64.14
9	7.90	49.33	2.12	56.35	1.21	60.51	.48	64.89	.39	63.17
10	7.49	48.72	1.97	55.47	1.21	59.58	.48	63.92	.37	62.19
11	7.52	48.08	1.91	54.58	1.23	58.65	.49	62.95	.37	61.22
12	7.54	47.45	1.92	53.68	1.26	57.72	.50	61.98	.40	60.24
13	7.57	46.80	1.98	52.78	1.32	56.80	.51	61.01	.48	59.26
14	7.60	46.16	2.07	51.89	1.39	55.87	.52	60.04	.59	58.29
15	7.63	45.50	2.15	50.99	1.46	54.95	.54	59.07	.71	57.33
16	7.66	44.85	2.19	50.10	1.54	54.03	.55	58.10	.82	56.37
17	7.69	44.19	2.25	49.21	1.62	53.11	.57	57.13	.93	55.41
18	7.73	43.53	2.30	48.32	1.69	52.19	.58	56.17	1.02	54.46
19	7.77	42.87	2.37	47.43	1.74	51.28	.60	55.20	1.08	53.52
20	7.80	42.20	2.43	46.54	1.79	50.37	.62	54.23	1.15	52.58
21	7.86	41.53	2.51	45.66	1.83	49.46	.65	53.27	1.22	51.64
22	7.91	40.85	2.59	44.77	1.86	48.55	.67	52.30	1.27	50.70
23	7.96	40.17	2.68	43.88	1.89	47.64	.70	51.33	1.28	49.76
24	8.01	39.49	2.77	43.00	1.91	46.73	.73	50.37	1.27	48.83
25	8.06	38.81	2.88	42.12	1.93	45.82	.77	49.41	1.26	47.89
26	8.13	38.12	2.99	41.24	1.96	44.90	.81	48.44	1.25	46.95
27	8.20	37.43	3.11	40.36	1.99	43.99	.85	47.48	1.26	46.00
28	8.26	36.73	3.25	39.49	2.03	43.08	.90	46.52	1.30	45.06
29	8.34	36.03	3.40	38.61	2.08	42.16	.95	45.56	1.36	44.12
30	8.43	35.33	3.56	37.74	2.13	41.25	1.00	44.61	1.43	43.18
31	8.51	34.63	3.73	36.88	2.19	40.34	1.07	43.65	1.51	42.24
32	8.61	33.92	3.92	36.01	2.25	39.43	1.14	42.70	1.60	41.30
33	8.72	33.21	4.12	35.15	2.32	38.51	1.21	41.75	1.70	40.37
34	8.83	32.50	4.35	34.29	2.40	37.60	1.30	40.80	1.81	39.44
35	8.95	31.78	4.59	33.44	2.51	36.69	1.39	39.85	1.94	38.51
36	9.09	31.07	4.86	32.59	2.64	35.78	1.49	38.90	2.09	37.58
37	9.23	30.35	5.15	31.75	2.80	34.88	1.61	37.96	2.28	36.66
38	9.41	29.62	5.46	30.91	3.01	33.97	1.73	37.02	2.49	35.74
39	9.59	28.90	5.81	30.08	3.25	33.07	1.87	36.08	2.73	34.83
40	9.79	28.18	6.18	29.25	3.53	32.18	2.03	35.15	3.00	33.92
41	10.01	27.45	6.59	28.43	3.84	31.29	2.22	34.22	3.30	33.02
42	10.25	26.72	7.03	27.62	4.17	30.41	2.48	33.30	3.62	32.13
43	10.52	26.00	7.51	26.81	4.53	29.54	2.80	32.38	3.97	31.25
44	10.83	25.27	8.04	26.01	4.92	28.67	3.19	31.47	4.35	30.37
45	11.16	24.54	8.61	25.21	5.35	27.81	3.63	30.57	4.76	29.50
46	11.56	23.81	9.23	24.43	5.83	26.95	4.12	29.68	5.21	28.64
47	12.00	23.08	9.91	23.65	6.36	26.11	4.66	28.80	5.73	27.79
48	12.51	22.36	10.64	22.88	6.95	25.27	5.25	27.93	6.33	26.94
49	13.11	21.63	11.45	22.12	7.60	24.45	5.88	27.07	7.00	26.11
50	13.78	20.91	12.32	21.37	8.32	23.63	6.56	26.23	7.74	25.29
51	14.54	20.20	13.27	20.64	9.11	22.82	7.28	25.40	8.52	24.49
52	15.39	19.49	14.30	19.91	9.96	22.03	8.04	24.58	9.29	23.69
53	16.33	18.79	15.43	19.19	10.89	21.25	8.84	23.78	10.05	22.91
54	17.40	18.09	16.65	18.48	11.90	20.47	9.68	22.99	10.82	22.14
55	18.57	17.40	17.98	17.78	13.00	19.71	10.56	22.20	11.61	21.37

Table 14-1 (Continued)

Age	American Experience (1843–1858) Deaths Per 1,000	Expectation of Life (Years)	Commissioners 1941 Standard Ordinary (1930–1940) Deaths Per 1,000	Expectation of Life (Years)	Commissioners 1958 Standard Ordinary (1950–1954) Deaths Per 1,000	Expectation of Life (Years)	Annuity Table for 1949—Male (1939–1949) Deaths Per 1,000	Expectation of Life (Years)	United States Total Population (1959–1961) Deaths Per 1,000	Expectation of Life (Years)
56	19.89	16.72	19.43	17.10	14.21	18.97	11.49	21.44	12.49	20.62
57	21.34	16.05	21.00	16.43	15.54	18.23	12.46	20.68	13.52	19.87
58	22.94	15.39	22.71	15.77	17.00	17.51	13.48	19.93	14.73	19.14
59	24.72	14.74	24.57	15.13	18.59	16.81	14.54	19.20	16.11	18.42
60	26.69	14.10	26.59	14.50	20.34	16.12	15.66	18.48	17.61	17.71
61	28.88	13.47	28.78	13.88	22.24	15.44	16.87	17.76	19.17	17.02
62	31.29	12.86	31.18	13.27	24.31	14.78	18.20	17.06	20.82	16.34
63	33.94	12.26	33.76	12.69	26.57	14.14	19.67	16.37	22.52	15.68
64	36.87	11.67	36.58	12.11	29.04	13.51	21.28	15.68	24.31	15.03
65	40.13	11.10	39.64	11.55	31.75	12.90	23.07	15.01	26.22	14.39
66	43.71	10.54	42.96	11.01	34.74	12.31	25.03	14.36	28.28	13.76
67	47.65	10.00	46.56	10.48	38.04	11.73	27.19	13.71	30.53	13.15
68	52.00	9.47	50.46	9.97	41.68	11.17	29.58	13.08	33.01	12.55
69	56.76	8.97	54.70	9.47	45.61	10.64	32.20	12.46	35.73	11.96
70	61.99	8.48	59.30	8.99	49.79	10.12	35.09	11.86	38.66	11.38
71	67.67	8.00	64.27	8.52	54.15	9.63	38.27	11.28	41.82	10.82
72	73.73	7.55	69.66	8.08	58.65	9.15	41.77	10.71	45.30	10.27
73	80.18	7.11	75.50	7.64	63.26	8.69	45.62	10.15	49.15	9.74
74	87.03	6.68	81.81	7.23	68.12	8.24	49.85	9.61	53.42	9.21
75	94.37	6.27	88.64	6.82	73.37	7.81	54.50	9.09	57.99	8.71
76	102.31	5.88	96.02	6.44	79.18	7.39	59.61	8.58	62.96	8.21
77	111.06	5.49	103.99	6.07	85.70	6.98	65.22	8.10	68.67	7.73
78	120.83	5.11	112.59	5.72	93.06	6.59	71.37	7.63	75.35	7.26
79	131.73	4.74	121.86	5.38	101.19	6.21	78.11	7.17	83.02	6.81
80	144.47	4.39	131.85	5.06	109.98	5.85	85.50	6.74	92.08	6.39
81	158.60	4.05	142.60	4.75	119.35	5.51	93.59	6.32	102.19	5.98
82	174.30	3.71	154.16	4.46	129.17	5.19	102.44	5.92	112.44	5.61
83	191.56	3.39	166.57	4.18	139.38	4.89	112.11	5.54	121.95	5.25
84	211.36	3.08	179.88	3.91	150.01	4.60	122.67	5.18	130.67	4.91
85	235.55	2.77	194.13	3.66	161.14	4.32	134.18	4.84	143.80	4.58
86	265.68	2.47	209.37	3.42	172.82	4.06	146.71	4.51	158.16	4.26
87	303.02	2.18	225.63	3.19	185.13	3.80	160.33	4.20	173.55	3.97
88	346.69	1.91	243.00	2.98	198.25	3.55	175.12	3.90	190.32	3.70
89	395.86	1.66	261.44	2.77	212.46	3.31	191.15	3.62	208.35	3.45
90	454.55	1.42	280.99	2.58	228.14	3.06	208.49	3.36	227.09	3.22
91	532.47	1.19	301.73	2.39	245.77	2.82	227.19	3.12	245.98	3.02
92	634.26	.98	323.64	2.21	265.93	2.58	247.33	2.88	264.77	2.85
93	734.18	.80	346.66	2.03	289.30	2.33	268.96	2.67	282.84	2.69
94	857.14	.64	371.00	1.84	316.66	2.07	292.12	2.47	299.52	2.55
95	1,000.00	.50	396.21	1.63	351.24	1.80	316.83	2.28	314.16	2.43
96			447.19	1.37	400.56	1.51	343.12	2.10	329.15	2.32
97			548.26	1.08	488.42	1.18	370.97	1.94	344.50	2.21
98			724.67	.78	668.15	.83	400.35	1.79	360.18	2.10
99			1,000.00	.50	1,000.00	.50	431.20	1.65	376.16	2.01
100							463.41	1.52	392.42	1.91
101							496.87	1.40	408.91	1.83
102							531.39	1.29	425.62	1.75
103							566.76	1.20	442.50	1.67
104							602.71	1.10	459.51	1.60
105							638.96	1.02	476.62	1.53
106							675.14	.94	493.78	1.46
107							710.90	.86	510.95	1.40
108							745.82	.75	528.10	1.35
109							1,000.00	.50	545.19	1.29

SOURCE: Institute of Life Insurance, *Life Insurance Fact Book*, 1966, pp. 110, 111.

off miscellaneous obligations that are due and payable if the death of the family's chief provider terminates the source of income. Without the benefit of insurance, the payments that are due and past due can leave bereaved dependents financially destitute.

Cost of Accident or Last Illness. Five hundred dollars a week is not an unusual amount to pay when a serious illness requires hospitalization or unusual services. A family that undertakes this expense to save one of its members may have spent its savings, entered into debt, or both. If the hospitalized patient happens to be a family's chief provider, the financial loss may be severe. Then, if death follows, the survivors are left with a legacy of debt. If a mother with children dies, the surviving husband may be saddled with debt, distraught over the loss of his wife, and financially pressed because he must employ some disinterested person to care for his children. Without the aid that insurance can provide, these financial burdens may be catastrophic.

If a father or a mother is killed instantly in an accident, the survivors will be spared the costs of the last illness. But accidents cost money too. A car may have been wrecked, causing some financial loss. Damage suits against other drivers and their insurance companies seldom are settled in less than a year. The deceased's dependents may be subjected to litigation because of damage to the persons or property of others involved in the accident, and a financial settlement may diminish the remaining assets of the survivors. In this instance, there is an urgent need for adequate amounts of automobile liability insurance —or else an adequate amount of life insurance.

Funeral Costs. The demise of anyone entails funeral costs. Most families select funeral services and caskets that cost approximately a thousand dollars. This unusual expense would ruin nearly any family's budget. If it is associated with the loss of the family's chief source of income, it may be unduly burdensome. If a mother must be buried and the care of her children must entail additional financial outlays, the financial plight of the surviving father could become unbearable, if not hopeless.

Loss of Anticipated Income and Services. When the husband and father of a young family dies prematurely, the loss of income becomes greater over the years. The children's needs would have been met by their father who normally would have been earning more as the children emerged into their teen-age years. For lack of this increase in income, these children are likely to be deprived of such extras as dancing lessons, music lessons, orthodontia, and several forms of recreation, entertainment, and specialized clothing, which seem so important to teen-agers. Most young people would feel rejected without these things; their personalities may be dwarfed; and their futures could be endangered. Most likely, the father would have provided his children with these advantages. In his absence, substitute income, probably in the form of life insurance benefits, proves most helpful.

Financial Loss Resulting from Untimely Death of the Breadwinner

If a child dies, the family suffers a great sentimental loss, but the financial loss is limited to funeral costs and costs of the last illness. The financial loss may be no greater following the early death of certain childless wives who are not gainfully employed.

The financial loss associated with the early death of a mother may be estimated in terms of the cost of replacing her motherly services and evaluating her worth as a stimulus to her husband's success in his career. Actually, neither of these contributions can be evaluated, but an estimate of $200 a month until the children are of age may be reasonable. On this basis, the family's financial loss might be said to be $24,000 if a suitable housekeeper must be employed for ten years at $2,400 annually. This $24,000 will be an additional financial burden for the bereaved husband unless he remarries, or unless the deceased wife leaves a legacy or insurance, or unless in-laws, a charitable agency, or a governmental agency intervenes with financial or other assistance.

The financial loss from the early death of a young father may be estimated in terms of the amount necessary to replace his income and expected future salary increases. If the remaining family members hope to maintain their level of living, they will need at least three-fourths of the deceased father's salary. This amount will have to be increased when the children are in high school and college, but it may be diminished when the children become self-supporting. According to this estimate, the family of an $8,000-a-year man would need at least $6,000 a year to continue its mode of living. Approximately half of this amount will be provided for some years by Social Security benefits, so this family would need additional income of at least $3,000 a year from insurance or from some other source. The family's net loss might be calculated at the rate of $3,000 a year for the number of years until the children come of age, plus a continuation of the same sum for the widow as long as she may live. The latter may be especially urgent because the widow will receive no Social Security benefits until her sixtieth birthday unless she is totally disabled. The Social Security payments are directed for the support of the children until each reaches eighteen or age twenty-two if he is a full-time student.[2]

The total financial net loss resulting from a father's premature death may be estimated at $3,000 a year times the remaining life expectancy of his widow.

If she were 28 years of age at the time of his death, for example, the minimum financial loss would be $3,000 multiplied by 45 years, or $135,000. Another way to estimate this loss would be to find the size of the principal sum that would be necessary to invest in an annuity or some similar investment to provide $3,000 a year as long as the widow might live. It would take approximately $80,000 at interest with a slow attrition of the principal to provide the required $3,000 each year. This sum would represent the family's financial loss resulting from the premature death, and this assumes a very meager level of living for the family's remaining years.

Upon review of these financial net losses, it would seem that a family with an income of $8,000 a year should carry at least $80,000 of insurance on the father, approximately $24,000 on the mother, and perhaps a thousand or two on each dependent child. This total would amount to at least $100,000 and should be compared to the $17,000 average of life insurance carried currently by American families with $8,000-a-year incomes. The coverage on fathers and mothers nowadays is less than 20 per cent of the insurance that might be needed in the event of the untimely death of either. By comparison, life insurance on children is more than adequate. The catastrophic consequences of inadequate insurance coverage suggests the need for careful analysis of insurance needs and their proper coverage. Perhaps a family can be insured adequately by combining two or more of the types of life insurance discussed under the next headings.

TYPES OF LIFE-INSURANCE POLICIES

The family that is unwilling or unable to pay for enough life insurance to cover its possible needs may find that dollars go farther when spent on insurance policies specifically designed to cover the most urgent needs. An examination of the predominant types of life-insurance policies may indicate the circumstances under which one type of policy should be favored over another.

The types of life insurance that will be examined here include term insurance, whole, ordinary, or straight life insurance, limited-payment life insurance, endowment insurance, and combinations of these four. Miscellaneous policy features and details also will be discussed in an attempt to correlate specific insurance policies with personal needs. In this way, the answers to questions concerning personal needs for insurance may become apparent.

Term Insurance

Persons in urgent need of additional life-insurance coverage for a specified period of years should consider the purchase of term insurance. Most term insurance is five-year term or ten-year term, which means that a 25-year-old person pays a stipulated rate such as $5 a year for each thousand dollars of term-insurance coverage. This rate would remain constant throughout the five- or ten-year period of the term.

Renewable Term Insurance. If a policy is designated as renewable term insurance, the insured can continue the policy for an additional term of years. The right to renew is especially important to some persons because it guarantees the right to continue the policy without a new physical examination.

Step-Rate Premiums. A term-insurance policy provides its owner with financial protection at minimum rates, which are correlated with the life-expectancy data found in mortality tables. At age 25, for example, a five-year term policy may be bought by someone who can pass the physical examination, for approximately $5 per thousand per year. This low premium rate, which would be paid each year for five years, correlates with the low probability of death between the ages of 25 and 30. At age 30, however, persons who buy this policy, or persons who renew from a previously held term policy, would have to pay a premium of approximately $5.50 per thousand per year, as may be seen from Table 14-2. At age 35 the premium would be approximately $6, and the rate would increase astronomically until it reached $75 per thousand per year for any 70-year-old policyholder with renewable term insurance who wishes to renew at this rate.

Advantages of Term Insurance. As Table 14-2 indicates, term insurance is priced in accordance with the probability of death for each age group. Term insurance is the lowest-priced insurance that can be bought in one's early years. It provides protection; it contains no frills; it should be considered as a temporary solution for the insurance needs of young fathers.

Many persons who consider term insurance as a temporary expedient for their insurance needs will be especially interested in *convertible-term insurance*. The element of convertibility guarantees the right to exchange or convert a term policy into some other type of insurance policy at a later date without the requirement of another physical examination. The premium rate for the new policy will depend on the age of the policyholder at the time of conversion, unless he wishes to convert to the original date of issue by paying up the difference in back premiums and the interest. Term insurance appeals to many persons who appreciate both its low initial rates and the right to convert it later to other types of so-called permanent life insurance.

Unfavorable Features of Term Insurance. Many life-insurance companies do not sell term insurance. Many potential buyers dislike term insurance because it provides minimum protection with no guaranteed loan values and no cash-surrender value. Once a policyholder has survived the term of years covered by the policy, he may feel cheated because neither he nor his beneficiary has collected anything from the company. Such a policyholder should remember that this merely represents the basic principle of insurance: many persons pay small premiums into a pool or fund from which large sums may be paid to the beneficiaries of those few who suffer loss.

Table 14-2. **Step-Rate Premiums—Term Insurance**

Age	\multicolumn{10}{c}{Rates Are for $1,000 of Insurance for Each Year (in Dollars)}
	25	30	35	40	45	50	55	60	65	70
										75
									47	
								31		
							21			
						15				
					10					
				8						
			6							
		5.50								
	5									

SOURCE: These rates approximate the quoted premiums of several companies.

The most unfavorable feature of term insurance is that the premium must be very high in the policyholder's later years. As indicated by Table 14–2, these rates are virtually prohibitive by the time the insured reaches the age of retirement. Many persons feel especially resentful about the fact that they pay throughout their lives and then feel compelled to drop the policy in later years when death is imminent and probable. This attitude toward term insurance has diminished its acceptance and discouraged companies and salesmen who might otherwise promote its sale.

It should be noted, however, that this view is unfair because term insurance is priced in correlation with the probability of death for each age group. The young policyholders gain; the older policyholders pay in accordance with the risks involved. Ideally, a prospective insurer and his agent should set up an insurance program that appropriately might include term insurance to be replaced with other types of insurance in later years.

Whole- or Straight-Life Insurance

Persons who want life insurance with a *level premium*, which remains constant throughout a lifetime, will find that whole-life insurance or straight-life insurance may be designed for their needs. Sometimes these policies as well as the limited-payment life-insurance policies to be described presently are known as *ordinary life insurance*. The significant fact is that whole-life or straight-life insurance is not divided into terms of years with step-rate premiums. Rather, it continues for the whole life of the insured; it is bought for a time period that is expected to endure throughout the life of the policyholder. Like term insurance, straight-life insurance is paid only to a beneficiary upon the death of the insured.

Policy Reserves. Straight-life insurance premiums are higher than term-insurance premiums in the early years. A 25-year-old policyholder would pay a rate of approximately $13 per thousand per year compared to $5 per thousand for term insurance, for example. This extra premium permits the insurance company to accumulate reserves, which may be credited to the straight-life policies. After some years, the policyholder may borrow against his policy up to the amount of these reserves. If he decides to drop the policy, he will receive the so-called cash-surrender value of the policy, which is approximately the value of the reserve that has accumulated.

Permanent Insurance. Although the premium on a level-premium policy will be higher in the early years than the premium on a term-insurance policy, it will be lower in the later years. For this reason, a straight-life policy is regarded as permanent insurance. The premiums do not rise to prohibitive rates in the insured's last years, perhaps making it necessary for him to drop the policy.

Some of the advantages of straight-life insurance will not become apparent until limited-payment life insurance and endowment insurance are discussed. Let it be said, however, that straight-life insurance is the lowest-priced, permanent life insurance that can be bought.

Several companies make an attractive presentation for straight-life insurance by advertising it as "zero cost" insurance. As the story goes, a man at, say, 37 years of age could take a $15,000 policy, pay in $10,342 in premiums to age 65, leave the dividends with the company, and have a cash value of $13,545 at the time of his retirement. This, it will be noted, represents zero cost for insurance protection to age 65 plus the return of all premiums along with an additional $3,203 if the company's earnings and dividends continued at their current rate. Actually, an insured man who died before attaining his sixty-fifth birthday would have paid annual premiums to the time of his death. Thus the term zero cost insurance is inaccurate. As for the man who lives to age sixty-five and collects $13,545, it may be said that the annual premiums for 28 years might have bought insurance protection plus a still larger investment return. However, since this investment return would have been reduced by high-income and capital-gains taxes, persons in high-tax brackets might have been wise to buy the insurance.

Chief Disadvantage of Straight-Life Insurance. The attempt to set insurance premiums at level rates throughout the policyholder's lifetime requires that these premiums be substantially higher in early years than the low rates charged for term insurance. A 30-year-old man buying a straight-life policy would pay approximately $15.50 per thousand per year throughout his lifetime; a man who delayed the purchase of this policy until his thirty-fifth year would pay a level premium of approximately $19 per thousand. At these rates, the younger customers buy less protection with their insurance dollars than the amount of term insurance they could buy for the same number of dollars.

This is especially unfortunate, since it is these younger men in their twenties and thirties who need so much protection. They usually have several young children, and their wives would be too busy raising the youngsters to earn a living if the husbands died prematurely. Most companies, however, at small extra cost provide additional income on an ordinary life policy for the years in which the young children are growing up. The companies call this a *family-income rider.* It regains some of the advantages of low-cost term insurance.

The built-in reserve in the straight-life insurance policies may or may not be an asset to these policies. Actually, it is doubtful whether young, underinsured policyholders should be asked to contribute to this reserve when more insurance coverage without it might serve their objectives much better. This conclusion may be substantiated by the fact that the interest return on these reserves is usually only about 4 per cent.

Limited-Payment Life Insurance

Life insurance is called limited-payment life when the premiums are payable only for a specified number of years or until the policyholder's death, if prior to the end of the designated period. Limited-payment life insurance policies normally are written as 20- or 30-year payment plans. Thus, if a 25-year-old man buys a 30-year payment policy, he would pay annual premiums of approximately $20 per thousand until his fifty-fifth year. Thereafter the policy would be *paid up*. Its reserves would draw interest and the policy would *mature* or increase in value so that it would be worth its face value by the expected date of the policyholder's demise.

Advantages of Limited-Payment Life Insurance. The chief advantage of limited-payment life insurance lies in the fact that the insured is no longer burdened with insurance premiums after a specified time. A secondary advantage is that the higher premiums in the early years build up reserves and constitute a forced savings plan to which the policyholder is likely to adhere. The policy is also identifiable as a savings plan because the accumulated reserves are available for policy loans and the policy has a sizable cash-surrender value. A professional athlete with a few years of high income followed by an early retirement would find limited-payment life insurance tailored to his needs.

Disadvantages of Limited-Payment Life Insurance. The very fact that limited-payment life insurance includes savings features and high costs, implies that insurance protection is likely to be minimized by young families who need the most protection. A young married man with a wife and several children is gambling with the security of his family if he spends approximately $200 a year on a 30-payment life policy instead of spending the same sum annually on term or whole-life insurance. Presumably, if he carries limited-payment insurance and survives these years, he will have accumulated some savings. Meanwhile, the lack of adequate insurance protection for his family would have proved catastrophic had he died during the interval. Young business and professional people are usually in need of thousands of dollars of insurance protection in their early years. Seldom do they have an urgent need for ending their premiums at age 55 or thereabouts. Since the primary purpose of life insurance is the protection it provides, built-in savings constitute only a secondary objective. The savings should not be considered important until and unless arrangements have been made for adequate amounts of protection.

If a family has sufficient assets or income, so that it is adequately protected against the financial losses ordinarily covered by life insurance, then one might advocate limited-payment life insurance. In that case its income, estate, and inheritance-tax advantages, its creditors' advantages, and its built-in savings features enhance its value. Many persons buy limited-payment life policies with the flattering thought that they are building an estate along with their purchase of insurance protection. But insurance companies seldom offer attractive savings opportunities. Their reserves must be invested so conservatively that their average earnings are low and so are the built-in earnings paid on their policies. By statutory law the insurance companies are compelled to make conservative investments, which usually limit their earnings on reserves to 4 or 5 per cent.

American families spent 12.6 per cent of their life-insurance dollars on limited-payment life policies in 1962. This had been reduced from 25.3 per cent a dozen years earlier.[3]

Endowment Insurance

An endowment policy provides insurance coverage for a specified number of years (see Figure 14–1). At the end of that period, the full face value of the policy becomes payable to the insured if he is still living. Endowment policies accounted for 7 per cent of American insurance dollars in 1962, compared to 15 per cent a decade earlier. The dire need for more savings and for more retirement income is generally recognized in the United States today.

Advantages of Endowment Insurance. The obvious purpose of endowment insurance is to provide a small estate for the policyholder at some future date. This use of insurance for estate building is highly commendable for persons who can afford it without neglecting their basic need for insurance protection.

Matured endowment payments amounted to approximately one billion dollars annually and have been increasing at a rate of 6 per cent a year.[4] They aid young people in college programs and help the aged to cope with their financial problems.

The Case Against Endowment Insurance. Parents are told that they may buy an endowment-at-age-twenty policy for a newborn child to provide for the child's college education and insure its life in the meantime. Usually the endowment falls far short of the amount required for a college education. In most instances, the family would be wiser to add to the father's insurance holdings in the hope that the child's education would thus be provided for whether the father lives or dies prematurely.

Another objection to endowment insurance is the fact that its benefits are subject to the effects of inflation, since the benefits are not derived until years after the saving has occurred. A person who saves and invests in the stock market or in variable annuities—to be considered in Chapter 16—usually can offset the effects of inflation. In recent years, savings have been so eroded by inflationary price increases that the endowment-at-age-twenty policies have fallen far short of their objective. Endowment-at-age-sixty-five policies have been helpful, but the plight of aged people has been aggravated by increased costs of all kinds, and endowment payments seldom have provided enough assistance.

Miscellaneous Policies and Policy Combinations

Most of the life-insurance policies written represent the four types previously discussed. In recent years, however, insurance companies have offered new kinds of policies that represent more than one of these types of insurance. Let us consider some of these policies, since they have become increasingly popular. First, there is declining term insurance as used in a mortgage retirement policy because it is so often found in policies nowadays.

Mortgage-Retirement Policies. A family that exchanges its savings for the down payment on a home is financially vulnerable for a few years. This is especially true because most buyers of homes acquire better dwellings than they had previously owned or rented. Normally, they also spend additional sums on household furnishings, landscaping, and the other accoutrements of homeownership. In view of this extensive program of expenditures, the family certainly cannot risk the loss of its chief provider's income. Nor can the family bear to lose the new home. Into this breach has come mortgage-retirement insurance, which is designed to protect the family's home, even if the income of the father should be terminated by his untimely death.

Mortgage insurance is sold as a rule as a separate *declining-term* insurance policy. The amount of term insurance purchased would correspond to the amount owed on the mortgage. This amount would be carried in the mortgage insurance policy the first year and would retire the mortgage if the family's breadwinner dies during that time. Each succeeding year, the amount of term insurance would diminish by the same sum as retired on the mortgage. The declining-term policy can be offered at an attractively low constant rate or at a low and declining rate.

Family-Income Policy. Sometimes declining-term insurance is included in combination with straight-life insurance. This is known as a family-income policy. An underinsured father, for example, might buy a $20,000 straight-life policy and perhaps $15,000 of declining-term insurance. Thus, in the event of the father's death the following year, his family would receive the basic $20,000 plus $15,000. This would provide the family with an income of nearly $200 a month for 15 years—the years in which the children were growing—if the term insurance received by the family were used for living expenses at the rate of $1,000 a year and the interest from investment of the straight-life insurance proceeds also were available for living expenses. The sum of these two benefits would provide nearly $200 a month of insurance to the bereaved family. In subsequent years, the term insurance would decrease at a rate of $1,000 a year as the time when the children would be able to fend for themselves drew nearer.

420   Life Insurance

Figure 14-1. Sample life-insurance policy.

METROPOLITAN LIFE INSURANCE COMPANY

A MUTUAL LIFE INSURANCE COMPANY — INCORPORATED BY THE STATE OF NEW YORK

HOME OFFICE   NEW YORK

HEREBY INSURES THE LIFE OF
ALISON E FLOHN

herein called the Insured, in accordance with the terms of this Policy, No. 21 082 452 A, and

Promises to Pay at Its Home Office in the City of New York,

if the Insured is living on the 13TH day of NOVEMBER 1973, upon surrender of this Policy,
(MATURITY DATE)

ONE THOUSAND DOLLARS
GEORGE S FLOHN FATHER

to... Owner of
and Applicant for this Policy, or if the Owner is not living on the Maturity Date, then
to RUTH C FLOHN MOTHER .... Contingent Owner,
subject to Provisions 1 and 2 hereof, and FURTHER PROMISES TO PAY to the Owner, if living, otherwise to the Contingent Owner, subject to Provisions 1 and 2 hereof, upon receipt of due proof that the death of the Insured occurred prior to the Maturity Date and upon surrender of this Policy, the amount of insurance determined in accordance with the schedule below for the period in which such death occurs.

Schedule of Amount of Insurance Herein Referred to

Age at Issue	Amount Payable Provided Death Occurs After the Policy Has Been in Force From the Date of Issue For the Following Periods					
	Under 1 Year	1 Year	2 Years	3 Years	4 Years	5 or more Years
0	$100	$200	$300	$400	$400	$1,000*
1	200	300	400	400	1,000*	
2	300	400	400	1,000*		
3	400	400	1,000*			
4	400	1,000*				

*The amount of insurance in each succeeding year will be $1,000 (Ultimate Amount).

NOTE: If death occurs after the Insured reaches age 4 years and 6 months, and if $400 is payable under the Schedule above, such amount will be increased to $1,000.

This Policy is issued on the basis of the Insured's age being 3 years and the Applicant's age being 37 years, and in consideration of the Application therefor, copy of which Application is attached hereto and made part hereof, and of the payment of the premiums as hereinafter provided. A premium of $ 53.71 is payable as of the date of issue and maintains this Policy in force for a period of 12 months from its date of issue as set forth below. Subsequent ANNUAL premiums in the amounts shown below are payable on the 13TH day of each NOVEMBER (herein called the due date) until premiums, including the first premium, shall have been paid for the number of full years shown below or until the prior death of the Insured, except as any such premium may be waived in accordance with the provisions of this Policy entitled "Total and Permanent Disability Benefit" and "Applicant's Waiver of Premium Benefit."

	AMOUNT	NUMBER OF FULL YEARS PAYABLE
Premium for the Life Insurance (including the cost of the Total and Permanent Disability Benefit)	$ 50.13	20
Premium for the Applicant's Waiver of Premium Benefit	$ 3.58	18
Total ANNUAL Premium under this Policy	$ 53.71	

The Provisions and Benefits printed or written by the Company on the following pages are a part of this Policy as fully as if recited over the signatures hereto affixed.

In Witness Whereof, the Metropolitan Life Insurance Company has caused this Policy to be executed this 13TH day of NOVEMBER 1953 which is the date of issue of this Policy.

W. J. Barrett
Secretary.

Policy Registrar.

President.

20 YEAR ENDOWMENT POLICY
With premiums payable until the Maturity Date or until prior death of Insured.
Graded Amount of Insurance.
Total and Permanent Disability Benefit after age 15.
Applicant's Waiver of Premium Benefit—Limited. Annual Distribution of Divisible Surplus.

Figure 14-1 (*continued*).

GENERAL PROVISIONS

The Contract—This contract is made in consideration of the payment of premiums as specified in this policy. This policy and the application, a copy of which is attached to and made a part of the policy, constitute the entire contract.

All statements in the application shall be deemed representations and not warranties. No statement shall be used to void this policy, or shall be used in defense of a claim, unless it is contained in the application.

Agent's Authority—None of the provisions of this policy can be waived by any agent, nor can any provisions be changed except by endorsement on or a rider attached to this policy signed by the President or Secretary.

Incontestability—This policy will be incontestable, except for nonpayment of premiums, after it has been in force for two years from its date of issue, provided the Insured is alive at the end of such two-year period. However, any Waiver of Premiums Disability Benefit included in this policy will be incontestable after it has been in force for two years from its date of issue only if Total Disability of the Insured has not occurred during such two-year period.

Assignment—This policy may be assigned. If the assignment is absolute, all rights of the Owner, any Contingent Owner, any Beneficiary, and any Contingent Beneficiary will be automatically transferred to the assignee. If the assignment is collateral, such rights will be transferred only to the extent of the assignee's interest.

However, an assignment will not be binding upon the Company unless made in writing and until filed at the Home Office, nor will it apply to any payment made by the Company before the assignment was filed. The Company assumes no responsibility for the validity of any assignment.

Policy Payment—All payments by the Company under this policy are payable at the Home Office. The Company reserves the right to require surrender of this policy upon its termination.

Change of Plan—If no premium is in default beyond the grace period, this policy may be changed to another plan of insurance, subject to the Company's approval and to such conditions and payment, if any, as the Company shall determine.

Suicide—If, within two years from the date of issue, the Insured dies as a result of suicide, while sane or insane, the liability of the Company will be limited to an amount equal to the premiums paid, without interest.

Age—This policy is issued at the age shown on page 3, which is the Insured's age last birthday on the date of issue, based on the date of birth as given in the application. If the date of issue falls on a birthday of the Insured, the age last birthday will be deemed to be the age attained by the Insured on such date of issue.

If the age of the Insured has been misstated, the amount payable and every benefit accruing under this policy will be such as the premium paid would have purchased at the correct age.

The age of the Insured may be established at any time upon production of evidence satisfactory to the Company of the Insured's date of birth.

Basis of Values—The Guaranteed Cash Values, insurance benefits, and reserves provided by this policy, including all nonforfeiture factors and net premiums referred to in the policy, are computed taking into account that the policy is issued on the basis of age last birthday and providing for immediate payment of death benefits. All values, benefits, and reserves are based on the Commissioners 1958 Standard Ordinary Mortality Table, except that values, benefits, and reserves for nonparticipating Extended Term insurance are based on the Commissioners 1958 Extended Term Insurance Table. The computations are made using interest at the rate of 3% per year during the first 20 policy years, and at the rate of 2½% per year thereafter.

The Guaranteed Cash Values and the values of the insurance benefits shown in the Table on page 8, as well as corresponding values for years beyond those consecutively shown, are computed by the Standard Nonforfeiture Value Method, using the nonforfeiture factor shown in the Table for the indicated number of years and using the net level premium, if any, as the nonforfeiture factor thereafter; but such values are not less than those necessary to provide Extended Term insurance for a period of 60 days.

Any additional benefits which may be included in this policy, as set forth in that portion of this policy which follows page 12, do not affect the Guaranteed Cash Values, nor the values of the insurance benefits specified in the policy provision entitled "Insurance Options on Nonpayment of Premiums".

As used in the policy provision entitled "Insurance Options on Nonpayment of Premiums", attained age means the Insured's age at issue (as shown on page 3) plus the number of years and completed months from the date of issue.

The values under this policy are, in all cases, equal to or greater than those required by the law of the State in which this policy is delivered.

103-65

Family-income policies represent an attempt to meet a family's insurance needs at the lowest possible cost. This combination of two types of insurance is usually available at less commission and sales cost per dollar of premium than the same insurance would cost as two separate policies.

A Family-Maintenance Policy. A combination of a fixed amount of term insurance and a fixed amount of straight- or whole-life insurance is known as a family-maintenance policy. The proceeds of these two kinds of insurance potentially can maintain a family's standard of living if the policyholder dies prematurely. The term insurance is carried temporarily during the period of the young family's greatest need. Then it may be reduced in amount or even discontinued if and when the family's chief wage earner has survived some of these years. Typically, a family-maintenance policy might include at least $10,000 of straight- or whole-life insurance and $15,000 of term insurance, which might be reduced to $10,000 in five years and to $5,000 after ten years. In this way, the cost declines in accordance with the need for insurance. Of course, the $15,000 of term insurance might be kept longer, if the policyholder chooses to continue carrying it at increasingly high term-insurance rates.

The Family Policy. A recently devised single insurance policy that provides protection for every member of a family is known as a family policy or family-protection policy. Family policies, which have been very popular in recent years, usually are available to husbands up to 50 years of age, to wives in their early and middle adult years, and to children to age 18. Newly born children are included automatically and the rates charged by many companies do not vary with the number of children in the family. Many family policies include whole-life insurance on the head of the household, supplemented by convertible term insurance for the wife and children. A family policy including $10,000 on the father's life usually provides $2,000 on the lives of the wife and each of the children. Family policies are popular because of their automatic inclusion of family members, because they require a single premium for a combination policy, and because, frequently, they include double indemnity, conversion, waiver of premium, and other clauses that are attractive to prospective insurers.

The Modified-Life Policy. Young men who are reluctant to buy life insurance may be induced to purchase a modified-life policy. These policies have unusual appeal because they begin with low-priced term insurance, which continues for three or five years at which time the policy automatically converts into straight-life insurance. Prospective customers are told that the rate increase after the third or fifth year can be met by devoting the policy's dividends to cover the higher premium. In many years, this has been possible with "modified-three" policies issued by several companies.

A young man who is willing to start his insurance program early will find the modified-three policy as low priced as any for the first three years. Thereafter his straight- or whole-life policy will be priced at rates commensurate with his age. Once the policy is in its second stage, a permanent insurance program is in effect. The policy serves as insurance coverage throughout the policyholder's life. It has reserves that permit policy loans and provide a cash-surrender value. At age 65, it may be surrendered for about three-fifths of its face value if the policyholder wishes to use it at the time of his retirement.

A Jumping-Juvenile Policy. A new type of straight-life, juvenile insurance, which parents often carry on the lives of their children, is called the Jumping-Juvenile Policy because the face of each $1,000 policy jumps up to $5,000 when the child reaches his twenty-first birthday. This policy costs more than a $1,000 policy would normally cost, but the child is certain of the $5,000 policy without the necessity of passing another physical examination. In addition, the relatively high cost of each $1,000 of insurance in the low-risk childhood years means that reserves are being accumulated that can be borrowed to finance a college education. Most companies limit each policy to an original face value of $5,000. With a policy in this amount, the insured child holds a low-premium $25,000 straight-life policy on his twenty-first birthday.

Other Variations of Life-Insurance Coverage. There are dozens of other life-insurance policy combinations and variations. Many of these are covered elsewhere where they supplement the subject at hand. For example, credit life insurance, which will be discussed here, was mentioned in Chapter 3; health insurance and major medical insurance were considered in Chapter 11, and annuities will be discussed in Chapter 16. Many of these insurance variations are relatively new; they encompass specialties that need the pioneering effort of vigorous companies. Life-insurance companies have moved into these borderline areas; hence, the passing reference to them in this chapter.

Industrial Insurance

A few insurance companies offer weekly or monthly collections of premiums in a plan that is called industrial insurance. This requires frequent small premiums for those who are unable or unwilling to pay larger premiums less often. Unfortunately, the expense involved in frequent collections increases the cost of industrial insurance. Most of the policyholders pay nearly double the usual rate and carry a mere $500 or $1,000 of insurance coverage. Moreover, two-thirds of industrial insurance is in the form of high-cost limited-payment life insurance or endowment insurance. This is particularly tragic, since the industrial insurance customers are often without other insurance protection and they have few assets of any other kind. Under these circumstances, industrial insurance is often characterized as burial insurance. With the rapid rise of workingmen's incomes, industrial life-insurance sales have increased less rapidly than the sales of other types of life insurance in this country.

Group Insurance

In 1965, there were 61 million group-insurance certificates held by people in the United States as evidence of membership in group-insurance plans. Almost all of this was renewable term insurance, and its volume has been increasing at a phenomenal rate.[5] In most instances, this insurance is issued to groups of workers in the employ of a single company; a single insurance contract applies to an entire group of employees. Sometimes a *multiple-employer group* or an entire industry arranges for group insurance, which may be administered by trustees representing various units or factions within the associated groups. Some labor unions arrange for group insurance for their members.

Many group-insurance contracts have to be negotiated because the group to be covered may include a disproportionate number of middle-aged or aged persons whose physical conditions may not be encouraging. When the contract terms have been settled, all members of the group and those who become associated with it later are invited to join. Usually no medical examination is required of those who join a group-insurance plan.

The premiums on group insurance are relatively low because of the lower selling and administrative costs to service a group. Sometimes each employee pays his share of the premium directly to the employer; sometimes the money is deducted from the employee's paycheck; sometimes the employer pays the premium and charges it as a business expense. Most states limit an employee's contribution to group insurance to 60 cents per thousand per month. In many instances, the employer's contribution has been won as a fringe benefit by a group of employees or by their union. In nearly every instance, group insurance is a bargain for those whom it covers. This form of insurance coverage accounts for 34 per cent of all life insurance in the United States, and it is likely to increase rapidly in the near future.

Credit-Life Insurance

Credit-life insurance is written in favor of a lender or a sales finance company and is used to repay a debt in case the borrower should die. Actually, it is declining-term insurance designed to serve the same purpose as a mortgage-retirement policy. In 1965, a total of $57 billion of credit-life insurance was in force, having increased by 14 per cent over the previous year.[6] It is anticipated that increasing numbers of college students will use these policies in the future to provide security for lenders who advance funds for a college education.

Miscellaneous Life-Insurance Policy Features

A life-insurance policy is a comprehensive document filled with carefully worded clauses. In many states where standard forms are used, the insurance buyer is protected by the supervision of these forms by the State Insurance Commissioner. Ideally, however, each policyholder should want to know more about the precise phraseology employed. Some of the principal features of life-insurance policies are described below.

Grace Period. Life-insurance policies commonly include a clause permitting a 30- or 31-day delay in the payment of premiums. The policy remains in force throughout the grace period.

Nonforfeiture Clause. A policyholder who cannot pay an insurance premium has an option, usually called the nonforfeiture clause, to request the company to pay the surrender value in cash, make a policy loan, or provide additional insurance, for a specified extension of time according to the terms of the policy. These amounts or values correspond to the reserve built into a straight-life, limited-payment life, or endowment policy.

Cash-Surrender Value. In accordance with the nonforfeiture clause, life-insurance policies, excluding term insurance, have a specified cash-surrender value, which the policyholder may collect at any time he wishes to cease premium payments and surrender his rights under the policy. Most policies have no cash-surrender value during the first two or three years of the life of the policy.

Policy Loans. Except for term insurance, life-insurance policies have specified policy loan values that enable policyholders to borrow on them at an interest rate of approximately 5 per cent. In effect, a policyholder borrows the reserves built into his own policy. Insurance companies lend policyholders, holding the policy as collateral for the loan.* If the loan is not repaid, its

---

* Insurance companies were forced to borrow at high rates in short-term markets to meet policyholder demands for loans in the tight money period of 1966.

amount will be subtracted with interest from the company's payment to a beneficiary, someday. Loans on policies are convenient and unembarrassing, and may be made at relatively low-interest rates, but there is too little compulsion to repay them. Many policies have little value because their owners neglect to repay their loans. Most policies have no loan value during the first two or three years of their life.

Extended-Term Insurance. When the insured fails to pay a premium on a life-insurance policy that has accumulated reserves, the company automatically will provide additional insurance at the policy's face value until the reserves are decimated at term-insurance rates. If the owner of the policy wishes to receive his built-in reserves in the form of cash or if he wishes to borrow on the policy to reinstate it, he must reply to the company's query and specifically state this preference; otherwise he will receive extended-term insurance.

Policy Reinstatement. A life-insurance policy is certain to contain a clause pertaining to the reinstatement or revival of a lapsed policy. Usually the policyholder must pay the past due premiums and prove that he is currently insurable. Many persons would prefer to buy a new policy if they can meet these two requirements, but there are instances in which the lower rates and special conditions of the lapsed policy may justify its reinstatement.

Waiver of Premiums. If the insured becomes totally disabled, most life-insurance policies will permit the omission or waiver of premiums during the period of such disability. Insurance companies differ in the degree of disability that they require. Some of them stipulate that disability must be total for a specified period of time, such as six months, before they invoke the waiver-of-premiums clause. A policyholder who is totally and permanently disabled may enjoy the full benefits and coverage of his life-insurance policy without further premium payments by virtue of the waiver-of-premiums clause.

Disability Benefit. Some life-insurance policies have *an endorsement* or added provision that states that the insured will receive a monthly disability benefit if he becomes totally and permanently disabled. This disability benefit is used increasingly in conjunction with health, accident, and medical-insurance policies.

Double-Indemnity Insurance. A double-indemnity clause or policy endorsement stipulates that the insurance company will pay double the face value of the policy if the policyholder dies as the result of an accident. A few deadly diseases are sometimes included in the terms of this provision. Healthy young persons who are not supposed to die from natural causes may be wise to purchase this double-indemnity clause for approximately two additional dollars a year for each $1,000 of insurance. A few people even buy treble-indemnity insurance. Actually, this additional coverage is priced in accordance with data from mortality tables, and it is probably worth neither more nor less than its cost.

Double-indemnity insurance seldom is offered where unusual risk or violence may be present. For example, an insurance company that pays the face value of its policies on suicides after the policy's second or third year never will pay double or treble indemnity where suicide is involved. Companies that pay the face value of a policy for deaths occurring in insurrections, military combat, or accidents on unscheduled airlines will not pay double indemnity where these are the cause of death.

Extra-Premium Insurance. A person who flies his own plane, works in a hazardous occupation, is likely to be in military combat, or suffers from some physical impairment may not be able to purchase life insurance at the standard rates. He may be classified as a substandard risk whose insurance will cost more on a flat-rate basis, a percentage basis, or on a *rated-up age plan* in which he pays at the same rate as those who are older than he. Thus, a 30-year-old individual with a moderate heart ailment might be able to buy life insurance if he were willing to pay the rate required of 40-year-old prospects. A professional soldier would be asked to pay an additional premium or submit to a war clause in his policy that might negate his insurance benefits if he were killed in combat. Because of this possibility and because insurance companies avoid selling to men of military age in wartime, the United States government instituted its so-called GI insurance during the First World War and during military engagements since that time.

Policy-Settlement Options. An insured person may surrender his permanent life-insurance policy and convert its reserves into cash, paid-up insurance, or an annuity which directs the company to commence sending him regular payments. Sometimes the policy has accumulated so little in reserves that a cash settlement is the only one of these courses that the policyholder would be likely to take. If the policy includes sizable reserves and is an endowment at age 65, the policyholder might consider paid-up insurance, or an annuity, instead of taking a cash settlement.

If the policyholder dies, his beneficiary usually has a choice among the three aforementioned options. Sometimes while still living, a husband elects an annuity-type settlement because he lacks faith in the ability of his wife, his children, or both, to handle large sums of money. If the insured exercises this option, he should be certain that his family will have an adequate sum of money available for the settlement of debts, medical and hospital bills, and funeral expenses. Actually, the settlement options probably should be left to the judgment of the beneficiary; ideally the beneficiary should have acquired experience and judgment in the use of large sums of money.

Supplementary Contracts. If either the insured or the beneficiary elects to leave the insurance money with the company, he or she enters into a supplementary contract to assure future payments by the company as stipulated in the agreement. These settlements usually take the form of an annuity contract, which may call for monthly payments to the annuitant for a certain number of years, monthly payments as long as the annuitant may live, or monthly payments to the annuitant and a designated beneficiary until the face value of the annuity has been paid out. These choices, stated briefly here, represent the options that are open to an insured person or his beneficiary. This subject will be explored more extensively in Chapter 16.

Designation of the Beneficiary. A policyholder may name the person who, as beneficiary of the policy, will receive payment of the policy when the policyholder dies. Actually, the policyholder himself collects only on a policy loan, a surrendered policy, or an endowment policy. A beneficiary collects in all other instances.

A policyholder who wishes to designate a different beneficiary should notify the company and complete the change of beneficiary forms as required. Failure to do so might create a chaotic and tragic situation that would deprive his newly acquired bride or his latest child of rightful funds. It is also wise to designate a *primary beneficiary* who will presumably receive the insurance payment, and a *contingent beneficiary* who will receive payment in the event of the death of both the insured and the primary beneficiary. If one of the designated beneficiaries is not of legal age, a guardian will have to be appointed to serve on his behalf. Trusts, guardianship, and trustee arrangements will be discussed more completely in Chapter 17.

LIFE-INSURANCE COMPANIES

Insurance prospects may wish to learn something about the company on which the financial destiny of their dependents may depend. To judge one company or type of company, it may be necessary to study others.

Actually, few people search out information about insurance or insurance companies. Usually, a person is solicited by one company's agent who arouses interest in one or more of the policies offered by his company. Seldom does the prospective customer invite other companies to counter these suggestions and offer their own wares. It seems appropriate, therefore, to discuss insurance companies in a general way so that a reader can compare any one of them with this generalized description of the others.

Types of Life-Insurance Companies

There are several ways in which life-insurance companies may be categorized. Usually, they are classified according to their form of organization—whether they are stock companies, mutual companies, mixed companies, fraternal companies, government-insurance operations, of miscellaneously owned insurance operations. In surveying companies under these classifications, we also shall examine their agency systems, their reserves, their investment policies, and their regulation. These facets of the business are common to most life-insurance companies. Therefore each of them will be dealt with independently.

Stock Life-Insurance Companies. An insurance company that is owned and controlled by its stockholders is known as a stock company. The stockholders obviously seek dividends from the company's earnings; hence the policyholders do not normally participate in the earnings. In a few instances, *participating policies* are sold at slightly higher rates and *policyholders' dividends* may be paid in addition to stockholders' dividends. Most stock companies, however, limit their offerings to *nonparticipating policies* at lower rates and pay no policyholder dividends.

Stock companies are among the oldest and largest of the life-insurance companies. These companies, sometimes known as *old-line companies*, usually have accumulated huge reserves, and generally they are recognizable for their strong financial position. These companies, like the mutual companies, also are known as *legal-reserve companies* because they maintain reserves equal to or in excess of the legal requirement.

Mutual Life-Insurance Companies. Since early in the century, mutual companies, owned by their policyholders, have been on the ascendancy in this country. Today the mutuals lead other life-insurance companies both in volume and in assets. Mutual policyholders elect directors who control the company. There are no stockholders. Earnings are paid as dividends to policyholders or are accumulated as reserves. Mutual companies are required to maintain reserves in proportion to the volume of their obligations; hence the term legal-reserve company is applicable to them.

When the mutual companies paid their first dividends, their impact on policyholders was immediate. Unfortunately, some of the mutuals were without adequate reserves. Some of them went into bankruptcy, and sometimes they had to levy special assessments on their member policyholders in order to remain solvent. In recent years, the mutuals have been managed more conservatively, and reserve requirements have been scrutinized more effectively by supervisory authorities. Mutual companies are now thoroughly respectable; they are usually well managed; their reserves are ample and well invested; their policies are competitively priced; and their policy dividends are usually moderate.

Mixed Companies. Because of the impact of the mutual companies, a compromise between the mutual and the stock company has evolved—the mixed company. These companies have stockholders, but they permit policyholders to share in selecting the company's directors. With this compromise, and a ceiling limit on the voting power of any one stockholder, both the stockholders' interests and the policyholders' interests find expression in the company's board of directors.

Life-insurance companies that issue both participating and nonparticipating policies are sometimes called mixed companies because the dual interests of both the stockholders and the policyholders are represented by the payment of stockholder and policyholder dividends. Insurance buyers are attracted by the hope of policyholder dividends.

Fraternal-Insurance Companies. Fraternal-insurance companies write less than 3 per cent of the life insurance in force in the United States and Canada, and their share of the business has not been increasing. The reason for this poor record probably may be attributed to the unhappiness of many of the older lodge brothers over the high cost of the term insurance that is usually promoted by these fraternal orders.

Government-Insurance Operations. The United States Government offers (1) veterans' insurance and (2) Old-Age and Survivors' Disability Insurance (OASDI), which is an important part of our Social Security system.

Veterans' insurance, commonly known as GI insurance, is offered to eligible ex-service men and women (1) of the First or Second World Wars, who pay modest rates and receive an annual refund, or (2) of later military engagements, who pay very low rates and receive no refund. In either case, the Government's low rates are subsidized by the payment of combat deaths from noninsurance funds and the payment of administrative costs of the insurance operation from Veterans' Administration appropriations.

The Old-Age and Survivors' Disability Insurance (OASDI) operation of the Social Security Administration is well known and will be discussed at length in Chapter 16. Suffice it to say that OASDI provides death benefits for qualified covered persons and endowment-at-age-65 insurance for those who are eligible. Details are subject to change, but it can be said that OASDI has become the pillar of many a family's financial program to which another life-insurance program should be added.

Insurance-Company Earnings and Costs

Understandably, life-insurance companies and their agents are torn between the desire to write more insurance and the necessity for careful selection of the risks they assume. An individual whose good health merits his inclusion with a group of healthy policyholders will contribute to his company's prosperity and to his own financial security.

Basically, a life-insurance policy is safeguarded by three things. First, it is protected by the fact that the company's inflow of funds equals and exceeds its outflow of funds designated for policy settlements, additions to reserves, operating costs, etc. Second, the accumulated reserves are invested in government and corporate bonds, limited stockholdings, and real estate. Third, insurance-company regulation is highly effective.

Among all life-insurance companies in the United States, the inflow of funds is sufficient to pay out 53 per cent of the income for policyholder claims, to set aside 22.6 per cent for additions to reserves, to provide for taxes and operating costs, and to distribute eight-tenths of one per cent as dividends for stockholders.[7] By 1965 these companies had accumulated $158.9 billion in assets, which they invested in government and corporate bonds, stocks, and real estate. In fact, their impact upon the financial market as institutional investors is enormous.

The reserves of these companies, their investment policies, and their treatment of the customers are carefully scrutinized by insurance commissioners in the states. Certain states maintain very high standards in their regulation of life-insurance companies. There is also a possibility that the federal government will become more active in this sphere. The companies must submit to financial audits and to investigation of their reserves, surplus account, and investment policies. Policy forms are scrutinized and standardized. Advertising is examined for fraudulent or excessive claims. Agents are examined, licensed, and sometimes subject to dismissal from the profession. These rules raise professional standards. The policyholders' interests are protected. Confidence is engendered so that the public may seek the insurance protection it needs, free from the fear of entrusting its funds to unscrupulous hands.

QUESTIONS

1. List and explain the elements of financial loss which a family will suffer in case of the premature death of (a) the father, (b) the mother, (c) one of the children.
2. How much life insurance should a typical family have? How much life insurance does the average family carry?
3. Under what circumstances may straight or whole life insurance seem to solve a family's insurance needs? What is so-called zero cost insurance?
4. What are the arguments for and against 30-payment life insurance? Explain.
5. Evaluate (a) endowment-at-age-20 insurance, and (b) endowment-at-age-65 insurance. Would other types of insurance and/or savings be better? Why?
6. Name and explain several types of life insurance which are found often in combination policies. Why are they combined in this way?
7. What are the advantages and disadvantages of (a) industrial insurance, (b) group insurance?
8. Name and explain several items which are included in the nonforfeiture clause in a life-insurance policy.
9. What policy-settlement options usually are available to (a) a wife who has been recently widowed, (b) an insured man whose endowment-at-age-65 policy has just matured?
10. What are the advantages and disadvantages of (a) stock, (b) mutual, and (c) mixed life-insurance companies?
11. Approximately what percentage of life-insurance premiums are needed for (a) the satisfaction of claims settlement, (b) addition to reserve, (c) dividends for stockholders?
12. Which aspects of life-insurance company operations are of greatest concern to regulatory bodies? Why?
13. Note carefully the key terms in this chapter and be prepared to identify them.

SELECTED READINGS

Cohen, Jerome B., *Decade of Decision*, Health Insurance Institute, New York, 1961.

Huebner, Solomon S., and Kenneth Black, Jr., *Life Insurance*, 5th ed., Appleton-Century-Crofts, New York, 1958.

Larson, Robert E., and Erwin A. Gaumnitz, *Life Insurance Mathematics*, Wiley, New York, 1951.

Institute of Life Insurance, *Life Insurance Fact Book, 1966*, New York, published annually.

Maclean, Joseph B., *Life Insurance*, 9th ed., McGraw-Hill, New York, 1961.

Mehr, Robert I., and Robert W. Osler, *Modern Life Insurance*, Macmillan, New York, 1961.

Menge, Walter O., and Carl H. Fischer, *The Mathematics of Life Insurance*, Macmillan, New York, 1965.

Redeker, Harry S., and Charles K. Reid, II, *Life Insurance Settlement Options*, Little, Brown, Boston, 1957.

NOTES

1. *Life Insurance Fact Book*, Institute of Life Insurance, New York, 1966, pp. 5–10.
2. Social Security regulations currently provide approximately $3,000 a year for

a widow and two children. These regulations are subject to frequent revision. See Chapter 16.
3. *Life Insurance Fact Book, op. cit.,* p. 25.
4. *Ibid.,* p. 43.
5. *Ibid.,* p. 26.
6. *Ibid.,* p. 30.
7. *Ibid.,* pp. 52 and 61.

PROBLEMS AND CASES

1. If the male head of your family should die, what would be the financial loss to other family members (1) immediately, and (2) in the long run?
2. Check the mortality table to determine the number of years of expected life remaining for an average person of your age. Note the improvement in life expectancy as represented in the first four columns of Table 14–1.
3. Under what circumstances may term insurance seem to solve a family's insurance needs? Why?
4. Analyze your own insurance needs (1) now, (2) ten years from now, and (3) thirty years from now. What types of insurance should you probably carry? Why? Investigate the rates and policy provisions of several companies. Which of these offer the lowest rates and the greatest benefits?
5. What are the advantages and disadvantages of term insurance? To what extent are the disadvantages offset by whole-life insurance? Explain.
6. At your present age, calculated to the nearest birthday, how much more would you pay per thousand for a straight-life policy than for a term-insurance policy? How much more would either one cost if you live to age 50? 65? 75? 90? Which should you buy? If the savings of the difference in annual premiums were invested wisely, would the sum accumulated change your decision? Are there any other policy features that might affect that decision?
7. Jim Stevens is a professional ballplayer who may expect to receive an excellent income for about twenty years. What type of life insurance should he consider buying? Why?
8. Explain how it is possible for someone to buy zero cost insurance by paying for years and then get his money back at age sixty-five? Since he didn't die during that time what did he receive for his zero cost insurance? If he had died in the interval would the insurance have been at zero cost?
9. Explain endowment at age 65 insurance as if it were zero cost insurance followed at age sixty-five by an annuity policy.
10. When an infant is born, should the father (1) buy more insurance on his own life or (2) buy the child an endowment-at-age-twenty policy? Why?
11. Explain the applicability of declining-term insurance for (1) insurance-during-mortgage retirement, (2) coverage of a family's needs in the first years after the death of a breadwinner.
12. Explain credit life insurance as declining-term insurance. Why do most finance companies promote it? Why do some lenders provide it without cost?
13. What are the financial advantages of group insurance that account for its ready acceptance? Why is so much of it paid for by employers?
14. You cannot pay the next premium on your twenty-year-old whole-life policy. What are your options?

15. Mr. Brown dies at age 40. He has left all policy options open for his wife's decision. What are her choices?
16. When, if ever, does a policyholder, himself, ever collect from the insurance company?
17. Ben Smith, age 30, has high blood pressure and an insurance company will sell him a policy only if they can *rate up* his age by ten years. Explain the rationale of this plan and state whether you think Smith, with a large family and little insurance, should buy the policy. Why?
18. Jones is about to embark on a 5,000-mile business trip. What are the odds of an airline crash that would result in Jones' death? Should he pay five dollars for a $160,000 "trip policy"? Why are the airline pilots opposed to the sale of these policies in large denominations?
19. Are life-insurance companies regarded as safe because they (1) set aside reserves every year; (2) add the interest derived from their reserves to current revenue from premiums; and (3) pay current claims from current revenues that are backed by reserves? Does this explain how Prudential Insurance Company's assets of $23.6 billion were deemed very adequate to support $121.7 billion of life insurance in 1967? How does the fact that Prudential has a very high rate of new business growth improve the company's position?

PART IV

LIFETIME FINANCIAL SECURITY

15 INCOME-MANAGEMENT STRATEGY

Seems like every time history repeats itself, the price goes up.

CHANGING TIMES

Most people save; they buy homes, life insurance, and securities. However, they may still fail to manage their personal finance effectively unless they learn to cope with unusual situations that arise during inflationary periods, deflationary periods, and wartime periods of price controls, credit controls, and wage controls. This chapter will discuss the causes and effects of inflation and deflation, and government policy for dealing with them. This presentation will suggest the proper income-management strategy that people with foresight should strive to pursue.

BUSINESS-CYCLE IRREGULARITIES

The recurring sequence of periods of prosperity and recession, known as the business cycle, affects employment, the prosperity of business firms, personal incomes, and personal expenditure patterns. Virtually no one is untouched by this phenomenon. Thousands of economists, bankers, investment specialists, and other experts devote a major portion of their time to a study of the business cycle. Sound and unsound predictions are available to anyone who reads the financial section of a weekly newsmagazine or one of the better daily newspapers. Some experts attribute business-cycle irregularities to the uneven flow of money and credit, the changing rates of saving and the investment of savings, and the shift of business and consumer confidence from overoptimism to pessimism and back to overoptimism again. A few theorists have attributed recurring prosperity and recessions to other causes. Some of their theories are as extreme as the varying intensity of the sun's rays, which they explain as the basis for abundant or inadequate harvests. Whatever the cause or causes of business-cycle irregularities, the change from a period of business expansion to a period of business contraction and back to expansion again occurs repeatedly. Until these cyclical changes can be eliminated, everyone must learn to live within a framework of recurring prosperity and threatened adversity.

Twin Disasters—Inflation and Deflation

If price levels and the value of the dollar remained constant at all times, the planning of future saving, buying, and investing would be relatively simple. A person could plan to spend something like 90 per cent of his current income and, knowing the amount of his savings, he could project the value of his future purchasing power. He could estimate precisely the value of his investments. He could retire with the assurance that his standard of living would not fall below a projected level. An individual's plans and calculations, however, are threatened continually with unpredictable visitations of the twin disasters, inflation and deflation.

Income Irregularity. One of the most obvious symptoms of the business cycle is the change in personal income, business earnings, and governmental revenues. Personal income in the United States tends to increase at a rate of approximately 6 per cent a year because of population and productivity increases. In some prosperous years, the increase amounts to an additional 10 per cent; most of the working force is fully employed and paychecks reflect some overtime employment. In periods of business recession, unemployment may affect 6 per cent of the labor force and paychecks may exhibit a lack of overtime work. Statistics indicate that average personal incomes decline about 5 per cent during a mild recession. Incomes declined 50 per cent during the depression of the 1930's. Once confidence is restored, however, personal incomes move upward again, business firms prosper, and government revenues from sales and income taxes increase reassuringly.

Price-Level Irregularities. When labor is fully employed and business is good, prices tend to rise. During recessions, prices level off and business volume declines. Half a century ago, prices usually declined during depressions, but nowadays businessmen try to hold the price line. Some economists who compare price-level data with personal-income data have concluded that in the long run personal incomes provide increasing purchasing power, even though in recession years the increase is not apparent to many persons, a few of whom actually suffer a loss of purchasing power.

Asset-Valuation Irregularities. Property values, common-stock prices, and the prices of many consumer-durable goods reflect the fluctuations of the business cycle. During recessions, homes, automobiles, and appliances sell slowly and at discounts. In prosperous years the prices of these items hold firm and tend to rise. Often the stock market rises and falls with the business cycle, if not in anticipation of cyclical changes. Bond prices and many fixed-dollar assets lose value during boom years in contrast with the skyrocketing prices of common stocks and some real estate. The uncertain and irregular movement of these prices casts a shadow of doubt on the current value of any one individual's assets. It complicates the problems of durable-goods purchases, of asset accumulation, and of estate building.

Personal Finance Throughout the Business Cycle

Apparently, many optimistic people try to buy too many things during the boom phase of the business cycle. In doing so, they contribute to the unusual demand that supports high and rising prices. When recession sets in, these people, fearful of unemployment and burdened with personal debt contracted in the previous period of prosperity, are inclined to buy so sparingly that they contribute to the underemployment of labor, raw materials, and management facilities. A reversal of this pattern of personal expenditures would assist in leveling out the business cycle. Moreover, it would enable those willing to forego the temptation to spend in boom times to buy more goods with a given number of dollars in periods of recession.

INFLATION

Inflation may be defined as ". . . a disproportionately large and relatively sudden increase in the general price level."[1] This brief definition does not suggest that inflation causes hardship and uncertainty. Neither does it analyze the causes of the price changes nor suggest a remedy. Let us consider these aspects of inflation along with some observations relative to the conduct of one's personal finances during an inflationary period.

Causes and Apparent Remedies

Inflation seems to have many causes, and a controversy still rages on this subject. Some of the causes seem to stem from the periodic overoptimism of individuals; this leads to excessive spending at times and to underspending at other times. Some causes seem to be associated with a government's handling of the money and credit supply, its revenues, and expenditures; some seem to be related to the changing rate of optimism and expansion planning by businessmen. The tendency to build and expand too much at some times and too little at others leads to spasmodic changes in employment, personal incomes, profits, and utilization of available savings. These, in turn, affect public optimism and spending habits. This spending and investing or failure to spend and invest, is itself a cause of the boom-or-bust phases of the business cycle.

Cost-Push Inflation. When high-level production calls for the full employment of labor, plant facilities, and raw materials, some of these components become scarce. Labor is employed at time-and-a-half overtime rates. New employees are hired in spite of the training costs necessitated by their employment. Stand-by plant facilities are utilized, even though they may be submarginal or less efficient. Costs often rise faster than the rate of productivity increases, and prices tend to rise along with costs.

Any other cause of a sharp price rise also may be regarded as a contribution to inflation. For example, higher taxes may force prices upward; management may raise prices unjustifiably; stockholders may insist on exorbitant earnings to sustain the high market levels of their holdings. Indeed, the untoward demands of any of the *factors of production*—that is, land and resources, labor, capital, and enterprise—can be met only from (1) increased productivity at lower costs, (2) at the expense of one or more of the other factors of production, or (3) by a rise in prices. In prosperous years there is little resistance to price increases; hence, prices tend to rise in accordance with costs.

Certain price increases, however, push up the cost of producing other products or the cost of living. This phenomenon is known as the *price spiral*, and it may become dangerous if the increase is not enjoyed by all segments of the population or if the spiral drives certain products out of the market. For example, many American-made products have difficulty competing in foreign markets with similar products. They might have no such difficulty if their prices were lower.

Demand-Pull Inflation. An abnormally strong demand for various products tends to cause their prices to become firm and then to increase. The abnormal demand may be caused by full employment and increased personal incomes, or it may reflect a newly acquired consumer preference. For example, the relatively high price of beef since the Second World War may be attributed to the unusual propensity that Americans have demonstrated for some of the more expensive cuts of beef. If this preference for beef were not so strong, Americans would eat more pork, fish, or fowl. Then the price of beef would decline until demand and supply reached a new equilibrium. Those who persist in buying unusual amounts of certain commodities under these circumstances are the victims of high prices caused by demand-pull inflation.

Money and Credit Inflation. A hundred years ago, governmental treasuries and certain banks issued excessive amounts of paper money. A few people knew that the money supply was being diluted. Others found that it took more of the "cheap" dollars to buy a given amount of goods. To both, the situation was known as monetary inflation. For years, some people valued coins in terms of their gold or silver content or because of the reserves held in support of their value. As paper money and other money substitutes became prevalent, many experts maintained that a form of money must be (1) the accepted medium of exchange, (2) the standard of value, and (3) sufficiently scarce, if it were to serve its purpose. If too many dollars are chasing too few goods, prices rise and inflation sets in.

Banks with reserves of approximately 16 per cent of their deposits can create *bank credit* and extend it in the form of checking accounts to responsible businessmen or to the government. The creation of *bank credit* in this manner may lead to inflation when and if the resulting deposits raise prices by commanding the employment of excessive amounts of labor, resources, and plant facilities. The additional purchasing power may create excess demand, in a period of full employment, because it has not been withdrawn from the stream of savings, or of spending for other items.

Consequences

Inflation may be planned and utilized as a stimulant to an underdeveloped economy or as a means of increasing the growth rate of one that is already mature. When planned and utilized in this way, it is often called *controlled inflation*. This distinguishes it from unplanned, mild, *creeping inflation* or from dangerous, uncontrolled, *runaway inflation,* or *hyperinflation* any inflation has harmful side effects, which are especially distressing to certain segments of the population and which contribute to their financial problems.

Fixed-Income Recipients in Inflationary Times. People whose wages, interest, receipts, or other incomes do not rise as rapidly as the rate of price increases will be the principal losers in an inflationary period. Aged persons on fixed-retirement incomes are conspicuous victims of inflation. A few wage earners suffer because their wage contract cannot be changed. Quite often, this category includes certain civil service workers whose incomes are frozen by a salary schedule unless a legislative body decrees otherwise. In fact, any group whose incomes are fixed may endure a loss in purchasing power during a period of inflation. As the economist would say, the *real incomes* of these people decline.

Inflation, on the other hand, creates only an illusion for those whose incomes increase as fast as prices rise. These people have more money. They live in a false prosperity known as an *inflationary illusion*. Their purchasing power, or real income, seldom is enhanced by inflation. As prices rise, they are compelled to run on a treadmill in order to maintain their former standard of living. Because mild or creeping inflation gives the masses an illusory feeling of prosperity, the few inflation victims on fixed incomes are powerless to inveigh against it.

Individuals who thrive on inflation because their wages, profits, dividends, or capital gains increase faster than prices may be happy about the turn of events. However, they should not be deluded; their savings and many of their accumulated assets eventually may suffer an erosion in value. The temporary gains of these people may be the cause of increasing costs for others and the basis for further price spiraling.

Incentives Distorted by Inflation. Saving and the holding of property or investments, as well as some forms of labor and business enterprise, are inadequately rewarded during periods of inflation. Savings erode because saved money plus interest often buys less than the money without interest would have bought at the time it was saved. This is especially true when low-interest bonds are involved; there were years soon after the Second World War, for example, when bank savings accounts and United States Savings Bonds paying 3 per cent interest were yielding less each year than their rate of erosion by inflation. Many bond issues suffer price declines in years of prosperity because their yield is low and because their fixed-dollar redemption price suffers in a period of rising prices.

The best rewards are enjoyed in such times by those who invest in speculative real estate and in speculative common stocks. Sometimes they divert money and effort from legitimate enterprise, which may wither for lack of the promise of high rewards. Routine saving and cautious investment give way to ingenious attempts to make a "fast buck." This distortion of incentives is not commendable.

Inflationary periods also distort the incentives of ordinary workers and small merchants. During the hyperinflation in Germany in 1922, workers received and spent their week's pay in advance of the work week, for it would have bought little at the end of the week. They spent the money for all sorts of bizarre things, for it would have been folly to have saved it. Small merchants were not anxious to sell from inventory because the same items would bring much more a few days later. Routine production and distribution were relatively unprofitable. Nearly everyone looked forward to see what he would have to pay for the next inventory or replenishment of raw materials before he decided to sell his current stock of goods. Forward planning and contracts involving future prices were virtually nonexistent. Finally, business reached a stalemate until the German money system was overhauled and confidence was restored.

In an inflationary period, people convert their incomes and assets to items of recognizable value such as gold, diamonds, works of art, and other movable, precious articles. In fact, the desire and demand for these things reaches such proportions that their price rises to unjustifiable levels. Many a so-called *inflationary bubble* has thrived for a time, then burst in the faces of those who had sacrificed to hoard the overpriced gems, or black tulip bulbs, or Florida real estate. In the meantime, many a legitimate enterprise has starved for lack of investment funds; the economy has floundered, and unemployment, relief, and taxes have risen. Nothing short of a political unheaval, drastic revision of the money system, or an unprecedented restoration of confidence and recovery could release such a nation from the inflationary spiral that has menaced it.

The Individual's Financial Survival in Inflationary Periods. Nevertheless, there are certain ways in which an individual may survive or even thrive in an inflationary period. He may thrive by placing his savings and surplus income immediately into certain speculative investments. However, his gain is apt to be short-lived; his very actions merely may extend the price spiral in speculative and luxury-type areas. Funds will flow into those activities that offer the highest return.

Persons with vision, foresight, and prudence will see immediately that inflation must be starved; it must not be fed. This means that wages and other costs must not rise faster than the rate of productivity increase. Such a course may lead to austerity, but holding the line on wages, prices, and other costs may be the only way to avert financial disaster. By understanding the situation, by reacting unselfishly, and by exercising influence in behalf of efforts designed to stem the tide of inflation, once it has been recognized, the enlightened individual may perform a valuable service to his fellow man.

DEFLATION

There have been no serious depressions since the 1930's in the United States. Moreover, many economists now hold the view that there will be no more of them in the United States. They cite two reasons for their opinions. First, the nation now has more knowledge than ever before, and violent swings in the business cycle can be prevented. Second, a series of safeguards, known as built-in stabilizers, are now part of the economic institutional structure. When a recession occurs, these counterforces are put to work.

The United States experienced four recessions between 1947 and 1966. If present patterns continue, it is likely that the economy will experience a mild recession about once every three years. Recessions differ from depressions to the extent that recessions are not as serious or as widespread, but both terms describe periods during which the economy contracts. The result of the contraction is that the national income declines, investment declines, sales decline, spending declines, and the employment of resources declines. For most families, a working member's unemployment results in a drastic curtailment of income. Prices may or may not fall. Since the beginning of the Second World War, except for short periods, they have not.

Maintaining Income

Maintaining income, or increasing real income—that is, the commodities that can be bought by the income—during a period of economic contraction poses a different problem for recipients of different types of income. The fixed-income recipient, the wage earner, the businessman, and the investor, therefore, have to pursue separate courses of action.

The Fixed-Income Recipients. This is the group that is singled out most often as the one that profits from a recession. It is argued that, *if prices fall,* the incomes of its members buy more. Their real incomes increase and, therefore, they are better off. But, as previously indicated, prices have not fallen consistently during recessions since the 1940's. This group is better off only in a relative sense because its members have income when others may have none.

Wage Earners. For wage earners, the problem of maintaining real income during periods of economic contraction is first a problem of remaining employed. If jobs are lost, it becomes a problem of supplementing unemployment compensation for those eligible for its benefits or of having income from other sources for those not eligible. Some union contracts now provide for a *guaranteed annual wage*. Recipients receive the set amount during the year, whether they work all year or not. Many firms pay workers two, three, or four weeks' wages when they are laid off or terminated. However, the best insurance against loss of income due to unemployment is a savings account or some other store of liquid assets. If these assets earn a good return, so much the better.

Under some union contracts, if prices rise, wages rise; but if prices decline, wages decline. The determinant is the Bureau of Labor Statistics Cost of Living Index. Real income is thus automatically adjusted to remain at approximately its previous level. In most cases, however, wages remain at their previous level, recession or not. Therefore, even if some prices fall, wage earners who remain employed may be better off.

Businessmen. Many a firm profits during a period of economic contraction. Producers and distributors of *inferior products*—inferior in the sense that people would prefer to buy other, more expensive products—sell in greater volume. Such products include margarine, for example, as opposed to butter, and less expensive versions of a myriad of products. The "poor man's" products cost less. Those who can no longer afford the higher-priced products shift to the lower-priced items.

Repair services prosper. People repair products rather than buy new ones. Consequently, repair-parts vendors' sales increase. Used automobiles and appliances and other used products sell in increased quantities. Sales of necessities—and food is the foremost example—do not fall off materially. And sales of materials and tools needed for do-it-yourself projects increase.

Businessmen may suffer, however, not only from the decrease in sales in affected lines, but from the drop in prices, especially if they have sizable inventories. Moreover, those who sell on credit—almost the entire business community—usually find debtors paying more slowly. Consumers tend to keep up their payments as long as they can, but repossessions and foreclosures do increase during periods of recession. Insurance policies are allowed to lapse in a relatively few instances, but loans against policies increase.

Investors. Customarily it has been argued that in times of recession, investors should hold fixed-income securities for, as prices fall, their yields constitute a higher real income. If a bond continues to pay $4 a year and prices are falling, the investor receives a higher real return as time goes on. But prices have not really fallen in recent years. On the contrary, investors have found bond prices rising during periods of contraction, equalizing their real rates of return—that is, what they could buy with the $4 of interest or with the receipts from the bond sale if the bonds were sold at the time.

To protect themselves against loss of income during recessions, investors have found it advisable to invest in the stocks of recession-proof industries. They have also found it advantageous to hold mortgages on higher-priced homes—where the owner's income is not particularly affected—or lower-priced rental units that may be considered inferior goods, or they may buy state and municipal bonds that can be sold to persons who are concerned about assured tax-exempt income.

Moreover, even though prices as a whole do not fall, some prices may fall during a recession. Investors in a relatively liquid position can take advantage of bargains. They can also acquire "distressed" merchandise, securities, and property that must be liquidated by those who find themselves in need of cash. If the seller needs cash immediately, he may sell for much less than the market price. In a recession, persons with ready cash and business acumen generally profit.

If stock quotations are declining, the investor may "sell short" judiciously.* Since the sales of luxuries decline first, stocks in luxury-goods industries offer likely prospects for gain through "selling short," especially where the luxury is one ordinarily bought by wage-earner and middle-income groups.

COUNTER-CYCLICAL MONETARY AND FISCAL POLICIES

Since the creation of the Federal Reserve System in 1914, it has been expected that coordinated action by the banks might be used to alleviate the extremes of the business cycle. Such action could very well ease the personal distress which is prevalent during recessions and depressions. As early as 1919, the Federal Reserve Board tried to offset a depression by using *monetary policy*, that is, by increasing or decreasing the money supply. For reasons much too complex to cover in this brief account, monetary policy failed to stem the tide in 1929, and the country was plunged into the great depression which endured for nearly a decade. From this painful and costly experience, *fiscal policy* was developed; this policy increases or decreases the Federal Government's taxing and spending. The Employment Act of 1946 affirmed the will of Congress and allayed the anxieties of masses of persons who feared a postwar depression. The Act set up the Council of Economic Advisers who were to interpret national income statistics and urge counter-cyclical policies to offset the effects of inflation and deflation.

* See Chapter 7.

Monetary Policy

When banks create *bank credit* by lending and thus adding to the checking accounts of responsible businessmen, they stimulate the employment of labor, resources, and plant facilities. The United States Government and the Federal Reserve System frequently have acted to stimulate and revive the economy during depressions and recessions by using this device. The same techniques have been utilized in wartime as a device for financing and encouraging the production of military hardware. The use of this device, however, tends to increase prices if an economy is already operating at full capacity.

Bank credit has been used cautiously to speed up the rate of growth of the highly developed economy in the United States. Certain experts, however, fear that inflation may accompany this experiment; others of a more liberal persuasion believe that the use of bank credit in an economy with 4 per cent of unemployment, or more, merely will nudge the economy along at a faster pace without inflationary results.

Individuals also should understand why a government may sometimes wish to decrease the amount of available bank credit as a means of combating inflation. To the individual, this may mean less overtime employment because fewer dollars have been loaned to the government or to enterprises that might wish to expand their businesses. It may mean fewer new appliances or automobiles in a boom year because (1) the Federal Reserve wishes to tighten the controls on credit, (2) bankers create less credit for finance companies to borrow, and (3) finance companies find it expedient to increase the required down payment or reduce the number of months in which loans must be repaid.

A few people, of course, must be denied new cars, new homes, and appliances when too many of them purchase with income to be earned at some future date. This would overload the economy's productive capacity and cause inflationary price increases. Actually, the public might be wise enough to know that it can have only those new cars, appliances, and homes that the nation's enterprisers and laborers can produce. The use of excessive amounts of credit creates *an inflationary illusion* by putting more money in people's pockets. It may create a price spiral; it usually cannot produce more goods for immediate availability.

Fiscal Policy

As fiscal policy evolved during the 1930's, it was based upon such *built-in stabilizers* as unemployment insurance and expenditures for various types of relief. Later, however, it featured *discretionary stabilizers*, namely, administrative decisions and special legislation designed to assist monetary policy in the attack upon deflation and inflation. Each of these types of stabilizers will be considered in turn.

Built-in Stabilizers

The built-in stabilizers operate to keep national income and spending from falling. If high-level prosperity can be sustained, sales will be high; firms will continue to produce and to employ labor, land, and capital.

The built-in stabilizers which are already available include:

1. Economic incentives and inducements to encourage plant utilization, full employment, and business expansion by private enterprise.

2. Social Security, which employs fixed payments that continue at the same level, whether the economy is expanding or contracting. During recessions they sustain the rate of spending.

3. The increased number of people living on fixed-retirement incomes. Their spending continues at the same level, no matter what the state of the economy.

4. Unemployment compensation. There is a tendency for the amounts collected by the unemployed to increase and the periods for which they may receive unemployment compensation to lengthen, during recessions.

5. The increased level of transfer payments other than unemployment compensation. These now include veterans' pensions and various aid-program payments, such as aid to needy children and aid to the handicapped, in which the state and federal governments participate. These include agricultural and other subsidies as well.

6. The federal-tax structure. As incomes decline, so does the income tax, leaving a higher proportion of income to be spent by individuals.

7. The tendency for wages to stabilize, even if the economy as a whole contracts. This is due in part to union contracts and in part to minimum-wage laws.

8. The tendency for prices to stabilize when the economy contracts. This results from an increased number of larger firms that have the resources to maintain prices while they "wait out" a recession.

9. The tendency for profits and rents to stabilize for the increasing number of firms and resource owners or landowners who have diversified their holdings. As a result there are many products and resources whose sales and prices are not particularly affected in a recession.

10. Increased-margin requirements. Investors bought stocks with as little as 10 per cent down payment before 1933; they used the stock as collateral for loans and borrowed the other 90 per cent. However, when stock prices fell, the collateral was worth less, and they had to pledge more collateral or pay off the loans. When they could not, they defaulted; this affected a bank that could not meet its obligations. Higher-margin requirements diminish this practice. With

higher-margin requirements, nowadays, margin calls and the dumping of stocks are less frequent.

11. Government savings and deposit insurance now safeguard individuals' accounts up to $15,000. Banks, savings and loan associations, and individuals, therefore, are both more secure.

12. The fact that government-insured mortgages and conventional mortgages all now have level monthly payments for home buyers. There is no longer the problem of a mortgage not being renewed, and the percentage of foreclosures has been reduced to an almost insignificant figure. In most cases, lenders will extend a mortgage rather than foreclose. In addition, the payments coming in regularly at the same level stabilize the income of the financial institutions holding the mortgages.

13. The tendency for families to attempt to continue to live as they have, even when incomes decline. They may use up savings or go into debt, but they keep up fixed payments as long as possible, only decreasing "unessentials," which differ for each family. The fact that fixed payments take an increasing part of family incomes is in itself a stabilizer.

Discretionary Fiscal Policy

The federal government's utilization of its taxing and spending policies to offset the high and low phases of the business cycle is known as fiscal policy. Thus, if government spending is increased while taxes are held constant or even decreased, more government dollars flow into the hands of contractors, laborers, and suppliers with the expectation that business will improve. In this instance, the government is operating on an antideflationary deficit; it increases its debt, and its spending encourages business recovery. Conversely, if government should tax more and spend the same amount or even less, then money would be siphoned off from the economy. Personal and business spending would decline, and a business expansion would level out.

The *national income accounting* concept, which has been developed since 1929, is generally used by economists in their explanations of the interrelationships among *income, consumption expenditures, saving,* and *investment*. National income accounting deals with aggregative data. The foremost of its categories is the *Gross National Product (GNP)*, the aggregate retail value of all the goods and services produced within a given time period, usually a year. The rise or fall of *GNP* is under constant scrutiny by the President's Council of Economic Advisors in Washington. The Council regards the GNP as one of the most important indicators of the trend of economic activity and the resultant level of employment. Income derives from the employment of labor, resources, and production facilities. Personal consumption expenditures, saving, and investment depend upon income. A brief explanation of the circular flow may clarify the relationship of income to consumption expenditures, saving, and investment.

The Circular Flow. Goods and services are produced by firms employing members of *households*. The finished goods and services flow from the firms to the households as indicated in the circular flow chart of Figure 15-1. Actually the households which provide labor and other productive services are paid

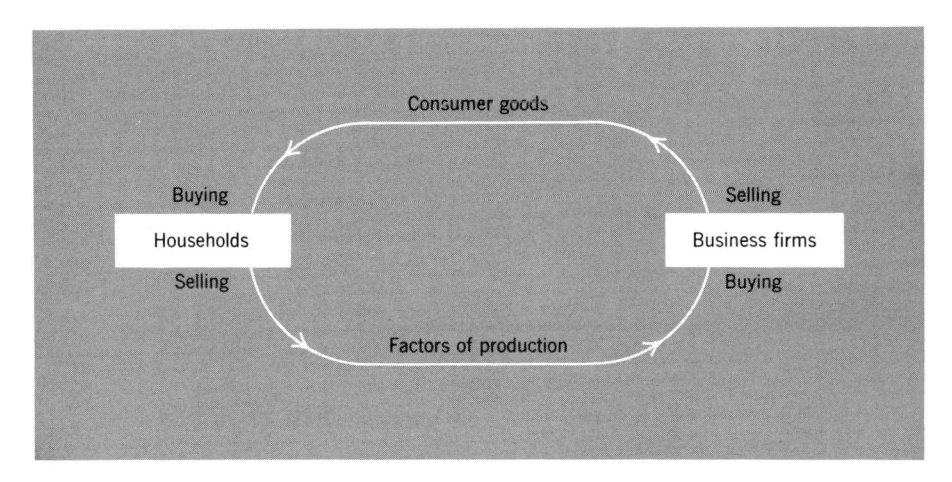

Figure 15-1. Circular flow. (*Source*. Taken from Haveman and Knopf's *The Market System*, Wiley, Figure 2-1, p. 32.)

wages, interest, rents, and profits, which they spend for the finished goods and services as indicated in the circular flow chart represented in Figure 15–2. Normally the flow of money corresponds with the flow of finished goods and services. Sometimes additional sums are available for wages, interest, rent, and profits. Thus an increase in total wages caused by businessmen's decisions to build new factories, stores, or office buildings will increase the money flow to laborers and contractors. The latter, in turn, seek to buy more finished goods and services than the business firms are prepared to sell immediately. If production had been at the full-employment level, employment could not expand. Firms would simply raise their prices. Money income would increase as wages, interest, rent, and profit increased, but *real income*—the goods and services that the income would buy would not increase. If the economy had been operating at a level below full employment, firms would increase their production. Then employment, income, and the flow of funds within the system would increase.

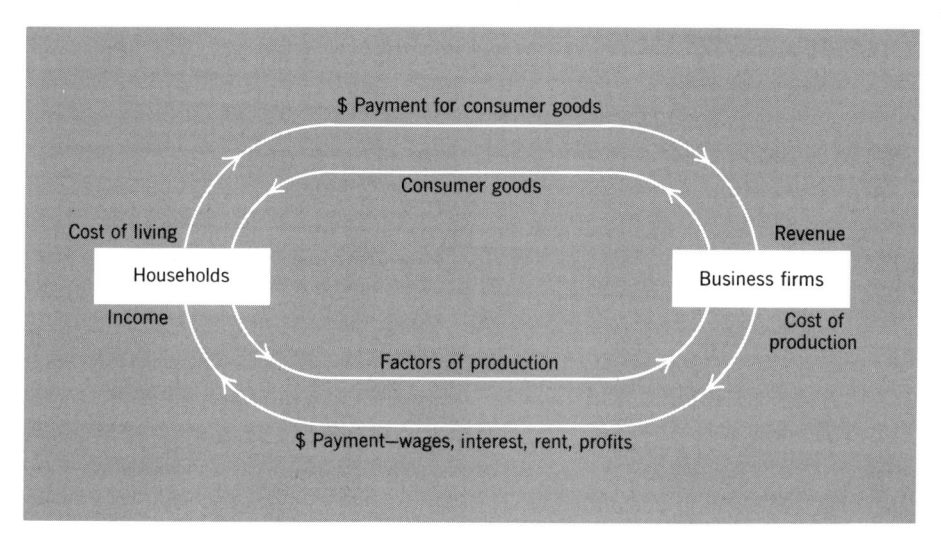

Figure 15-2. Circular flow. (*Source.* Taken from Haveman and Knopf's *The Market System*, Wiley, Figure 2-2, p. 33.)

Overly simplified though it is, Figure 15-2 illustrates the existing interdependence of production, employment, income, and money flows. If population increases or households decide to ascend to higher levels of living, consumption should increase, although partially on credit. Firms will hire more of the factors of production—land, labor, capital, and management—in order to produce more, and they will pay out more in rent, wages, interest, and profits. Income will increase, and the quantity of funds flowing through the system will be greater.

Income Versus Savings Interrelationships

Personal income after taxes leaves disposable income (DI), which is saved (S) or used for consumption expenditure (C). Thus ($DI - S = C$). In fact, consumption-expenditures data, which would be most difficult to gather, are formulated by subtracting obtainable data on savings from available data on disposable-personal income.

Obviously, income is a determinant of the amount that can and will be saved. Low-income families save little or nothing. Nearly all personal savings come from above-average income families. Normally, saving increases in prosperous years, since consumption spending lags behind increases in income. However, in a period of sustained prosperity, as in the mid-1960's, consumer levels of aspiration may rise, and the percentage of disposable income devoted to savings may decline. Unfortunately, this change in consumer spending and saving habits may occur in the midst of a period of economic expansion when the economy is already becoming "overheated" with excessive demand. Thus a threat of demand-pull inflation brought higher-interest rates in 1966. The Federal Reserve System sought to "dampen the boom" by tightening the money supply to offset demand-pull inflation. The higher-interest rates, designed to increase savings and to discourage borrowing for business expansion and housing construction, affected new housing starts adversely. When the high-interest rates failed to curb consumption spending generally, the government was forced to increase business and personal taxes. Such action was designed to "soak up" purchasing power and reduce consumer demand to the level of the economy's full-employment potential.

At some other time, too much personal disposable income may be saved. When this happens, personal savings will exceed the amount needed for investment, and business and personal incomes will suffer. The idle savings are not being returned to the circular flow at the same moment that consumption expenditures are low. Individuals may enhance their own financial position by saving a large percentage of their disposable income, but total personal incomes will decline if society *en masse* saves more than is needed for investment purposes. This is true because a decline in investment, followed by a decline in personal income of the masses, will provide less available income for saving in a later period. This phenomenon is known as the *paradox of thrift*.

Ideally, savings should equal investment ($S = I$). Thus saved money may be invested in new productive facilities and the savings, being promptly invested and expended, will be returned to the circular flow.

Savings Versus Investment Interrelationships

Desirably savings (S) should be invested (I) promptly and returned to the circular flow in the form of wages, interest, rent, and profit derived from the production of machines, buildings, and inventories. Thus if $S = I$ (savings equal investment) consumption spending plus new investment equals consumption spending plus savings, and the economy represents a balance of economic forces. The following is a more formal statement of the situation:

By definition: DI (disposable income) $= C + S$ (consumption spending plus savings)

If: $S = I$ (savings equal investment)

Then: $C + I = NNP$ (consumption spending plus investment equals net national product) [NNP + depreciation allowances $= GNP$]

The circular flow is maintained at equilibrium NNP.

Thus, the stability of NNP equilibrium is dependent upon $S = I$.

The circular flow would be broken if $S > I$ (S were greater than I), because savings are being hoarded. The circular flow of income will decrease and the volume of goods, services, and income are destined to decline. If $S < I$ (S is less than I), there is a shortage of investable funds compared with the desire for new plant facilities and inventory. This imbalance may be redressed by borrowing from banks, from another country, or from government. As a result of borrowing, the circular flow will increase. The new input of investable funds creates (1) additional wages, interest, rent, and profits while new production facilities are under construction, and (2) more goods and incomes when the new facilities are placed in production.

The Multiplier

When successful businessmen borrow from banks to build new production facilities, the banks may sometimes lend more than the saved funds that have been placed at their disposal. This creation of bank credit in the form of deposits is thus available for loans and for paying the contractors, laborers, and suppliers who provide the new buildings, machines, and inventory for the business expansion. Thus every cent invested by the businessmen becomes another person's income. Approximately two-thirds of this income is spent by laborers, suppliers, and contractors for food, car expense, insurance, etc.; the recipients of these funds spend approximately two-thirds; and so on until the infusion of a businessman's dollar of borrowed credit from the bank multiplies to approximately three dollars of additional national income by the time it has changed hands many times, that is, $1 + \frac{2}{3} + \frac{4}{9} + $ etc., etc., to infinity $= 3$. Thus if people spend approximately two-thirds of their after tax personal incomes—or 92–94 per cent of their disposable personal incomes—the transfer of consumption expenditures into income and into consumption expenditures again and again will yield a multiplier of approximately three.

If businessmen and bankers lack confidence in the future, their failure to continue business expansion may bring on a recession. If they are unusually optimistic, their rapid credit creation and business expansion will be a major cause of an expansion that may overstrain the country's skilled labor and production facilities. Such action would result in rising wages and costs—known as cost-push inflation. If more of the invested money that supports the business expansion had been previously saved, the savings itself would constitute a denial of spending, and the boom would be dampened to that extent.

Obviously, savings performs an important and necessary function in providing investable funds. Thus once more it can be concluded that, ideally, savings should equal investment. It must be conceded, however, that expansion, economic growth, and prosperity may be hastened by an infusion of bank credit into the economy. Preferably, the infusion of credit should not be excessive in some years and sparse in other years lest the economy's stability be endangered.

During recessions, when successful businessmen and bankers lack enough confidence to expand bank credit and business investment, the economy suffers and personal incomes decline unless (1) business investment can be revived, or (2) government increases spending or spurs consumption by reducing personal-income taxes. These choices, formulated and advocated by the renowned English economist John Maynard Keynes during the great depression of the 1930's, have guided government policy in recent years.

Graphic Presentation of National Income Accounting

A major objective of the federal government, since the passage of the Employment Act of 1946, is the maintenance of high-level prosperity in the form of a high and rising Gross National Product (*GNP*). The term, Net National Product (*NNP*) which includes *GNP* less capital consumption or the replacement cost of productive facilities (*GNP* − depreciation = *NNP*) is used frequently in this presentation. In the graphic illustration of the determination of national income—right angle *ABD* in Figure 15–3—the line

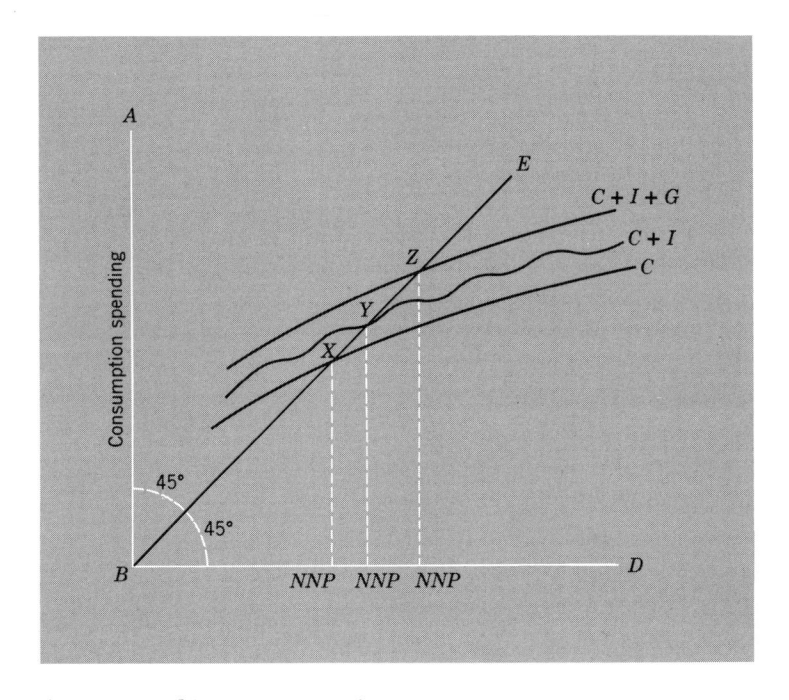

Figure 15.3   National income accounting.

BE is a guideline formed by a 45-degree angle so that any point on BE lies equidistant from AB, which presents the measurement of consumption spending and BD which represents the measurement of Net National Product (NNP). The line C joins a number of points or examples of consumption spending within an economy. For example, a low-income economy's spending will appear as a point to the left of X on the C line. These expenditures will tend to be relatively low and probably above the guideline BE, thus indicating that the economy may be spending beyond its current income. As more income is acquired, spending will be represented by points farther to the right of X, which indicate more spending and some saving. Points to the left of X on the C line represent negative savings in a low-income economy. Points to the right of X represent increased savings in a prosperous economy. A dotted line from X to the BD line measures the Net National Product (NNP), which in this instance is quite low. For lack of savings and new investment, the health of the economy as measured by NNP (or by NNP + depreciation allowances = GNP) would be in a very unsatisfactory condition.

The $C + I$ (consumption expenditures plus business investment) line in Figure 15–3 represents consumption expenditures plus the addition of business investment. This line is irregular and wavering to reflect the fact that the area between C and $C + I$ represents alternating high and low business confidence and investment. When businessmen are confident, they borrow and invest heavily in new plant facilities. This investment, followed by the aforementioned multiplier, is represented on the graph with the line $C + I$, which intersects the guideline BE at Y. A dotted line from Y to the base line BD indicates that the nation's NNP has increased substantially because of added business investment and the expenditures it generates. The irregularity of I, however, causes NNP to increase disappointingly in some years. According to the Keynesian theory, at such times government should (1) encourage businessmen to stabilize their investment or (2) instigate a *compensating fiscal policy* by deficit-spending additional billions of dollars in order that national income will rise to keep pace with population increase and with the desired increase in the standard of living. Thus, the G in the $C + I + G$ line represents additional government spending (or continued spending with lower taxes). With the assistance of the aforementioned multiplier, this action not only offsets the irregularity of business investment (I) but also increases the NNP as measured by the dotted line from the new equilibrium point Z to the line BD.

Since the 1930's the United States Government has been utilizing fiscal policy and antideflationary budgets to increase NNP and personal income. This action has been a matter of national policy since 1946. The successful use of fiscal policy depends upon accurate timing. The president's request for several billions of deficit spending may be delayed in Congress and spent, finally, during a subsequent boom period. This would cause great harm to the economy since the added expenditures might threaten the nation with (1) an overheated expansion, that is, overemployment of skilled labor and plant facilities, and (2) price and wage spirals, which could bring about inflation. Also it should be noted that fiscal policy may work both ways. Sometimes, we need a tax increase and a budgetary surplus during periods of overly full employment. Both of these can dampen inflationary pressures resulting from the rising prices of resources that are not available in sufficient quantities to satisfy all demands from households, firms, and governments.

Some interesting, recent examples of the use of these policies were evident in the "tight money" policy of 1966. Tight money dampened the overexpansion and the threatened inflation of that year—with adverse effects upon housing starts, automobile sales, and stock market quotations. Early in 1967, the government seemed to reverse this policy with (1) efforts to make housing loans available at lower rates, (2) reintroduction of the 7 per cent business-investment tax credit to encourage businessmen's expansionary investments, (3) reduction of discount rates by the Federal Reserve, and (4) increased government spending in certain budget categories. Incidentally, the first hint of this change in policy brought a 14.9 million share day—the second highest on record—to the New York Stock Exchange, with Dow-Jones averages rising 13.7 points in the first hour of trading following the announcement of the Federal Reserve's reduction of its discount rate. Further evidence of the use of fiscal policy can be seen in its effect upon the nation's economy in 1968 and for some months following the addition of a 10% sur tax for personal and corporate income taxpayers.

Personal Finance in an Era of Affluence

Since the Second World War, Americans have been protected by Social Security, millions of them have not experienced unemployment, and most of them cannot recall a year in which their incomes have not increased. These bountiful years reflect improved technology, good business judgments, and monetary and fiscal policies that were designed to achieve high-level prosperity.

The confidence of new investors was one of the major factors that accounted for the bull market in stocks in the early 1960's. Middle-aged investors in this era were too young to remember the fear and constraints that were prevalent during the Great Depression. Many of these new investors were in the age group that had been in military service. They had been educated under the GI Bill, and their homes had been financed with GI loans. Most of them enjoyed an increase in the value of their assets in every year of their adult lives. Naturally, they were confident.[2] They were the product of their environment. They and the country's newly formed institutional investors joined in raising market quotations to an all time Dow-Jones high of 997. Eventually of course, the market leveled off in 1963, but who can predict that such confidence and the country's planned prosperity program will not push the market up again?

PERSONAL FINANCE IN WARTIME

A dark cloud on the economic horizon in the late 1960's was the ever-present threat of a major war. Outbreak of war would disturb the nation's economy and upset the financial aplomb of individual citizens. Recent major wars have been massive military and economic engagements in which two or more antagonists have struggled until one or more have been utterly exhausted or destroyed.

In an effort to overcome an enemy, each nation diverts large segments of its civilian economy to the war effort. Individuals must be deprived of luxuries, leisure, and some necessities so that approximately half the total national productivity may be used to support the military action. No sacrifice, no risk, is considered too great. Defeat would be followed by unimaginable financial loss, personal suffering, humiliation, and subjugation.

The United States is a democracy, and the country's leaders have guided three wartime generations through wartime controls. Some people have to be persuaded of the necessity for the war effort; some have to be convinced that the controls are imperative. The leaders' doubts and the necessity for political expediency cause delay, ineffectiveness, and failure. After several years, the controls are generally unpopular; usually they are overthrown at the first sign of victory. Whether popular or not, wartime controls seem to be necessary in a major war. Their consideration here seems to be warranted because they affect the financial plans and aspirations of individuals.

Need for Wartime Controls

A nation engaged in a major war may have to increase its productive and economic activity by 50 per cent, while reducing the volume of the facilities devoted to civilian goods production by a third. This transition must be accomplished within a year or two. Several dictatorial countries are virtually *arsenal economies* in a state of war readiness that cannot be matched by the democracies. In a free-enterprise economy such as that of the United States, the dislocations and growing pains are too great to be absorbed readily. The pricing mechanism in a free-market economy seems to be unable to adjust to demand

and supply changes of the magnitude required by a transition to a wartime economy. This is demonstrated by the five graphs in Figure 15-4.

Graph 1 represents a theoretical prewar or peacetime situation by showing a $d \ldots d$ demand curve and an $s \ldots s$ supply curve. The point of intersection of the two curves represents a position of equilibrium between supply and demand. This equilibrium point when lined up on the vertical or price axis of the right angle shows the price level at which this equilibrium between demand and supply will occur.

Graph 2 represents the first stage in a wartime civilian economy. Added to the $d \ldots d$ and $s \ldots s$ curves is a $d' \ldots d'$ curve, which represents an increase in civilian demand resulting from full employment, overtime pay, and bulging profits in the civilian economy in the first stages of the war. A new higher-price level results from the intersection of the increased demand $d' \ldots d'$ and the unchanged supply $s \ldots s$ curve.

Graph 3 indicates that in peacetime high prices would be followed by an addition to supply. This addition is represented by the secondary supply curve $s' \ldots s'$, which would reduce the price level to approximately its first position. It represents the self-operating market economy in which price adjustments are capable of bringing supply and demand into a stable, peacetime equilibrium. In this case, demand increases first, price levels increase and induce a greater supply to enter the market, and then prices decline to the new point of supply-demand equilibrium.

Graph 4 represents a typical wartime situation in the civilian economy. Civilian demand $d' \ldots d'$ has increased, but civilian supply $s' \ldots s'$ has been forceably decreased because of plant, labor, and materials conversion to the war effort. As a result of these changes, the wartime price is very high and there is no way to force its reduction because civilian supply cannot be permitted to increase in this wartime situation. With high prices, strong demand, and inadequate supplies, an *inflationary gap* exists because too many dollars are chasing too few goods. The inflation is likely to intensify itself with higher and higher prices, a distortion of incentives, a disturbance of the war effort, and a legacy of debt in the postwar years. Obviously, since the high prices cannot be permitted to bring about an increase in civilian goods and services, there is no reason for permitting them to be so high. Upon this line of reasoning, the case for price controls rests.

Graph 5 illustrates the fact that price levels cannot be rolled back if the controlled prices are established after prices have risen to a point in line with the intersection with curves $d' \ldots d'$ and $s' \ldots s'$. Actually, the only stable, controlled prices would have to be in line with that point of intersection. If, however, a price rollback sets the prices at a point in line with the prewar $d \ldots d$

Personal Finance in Wartime

Graph 1 — Prewar price determination

Graph 2 — Wartime prices first stage

Graph 3 — Normal peacetime price adjustment

Graph 4 — Typical wartime prices situation

Graph 5 — Attempted price roll-back

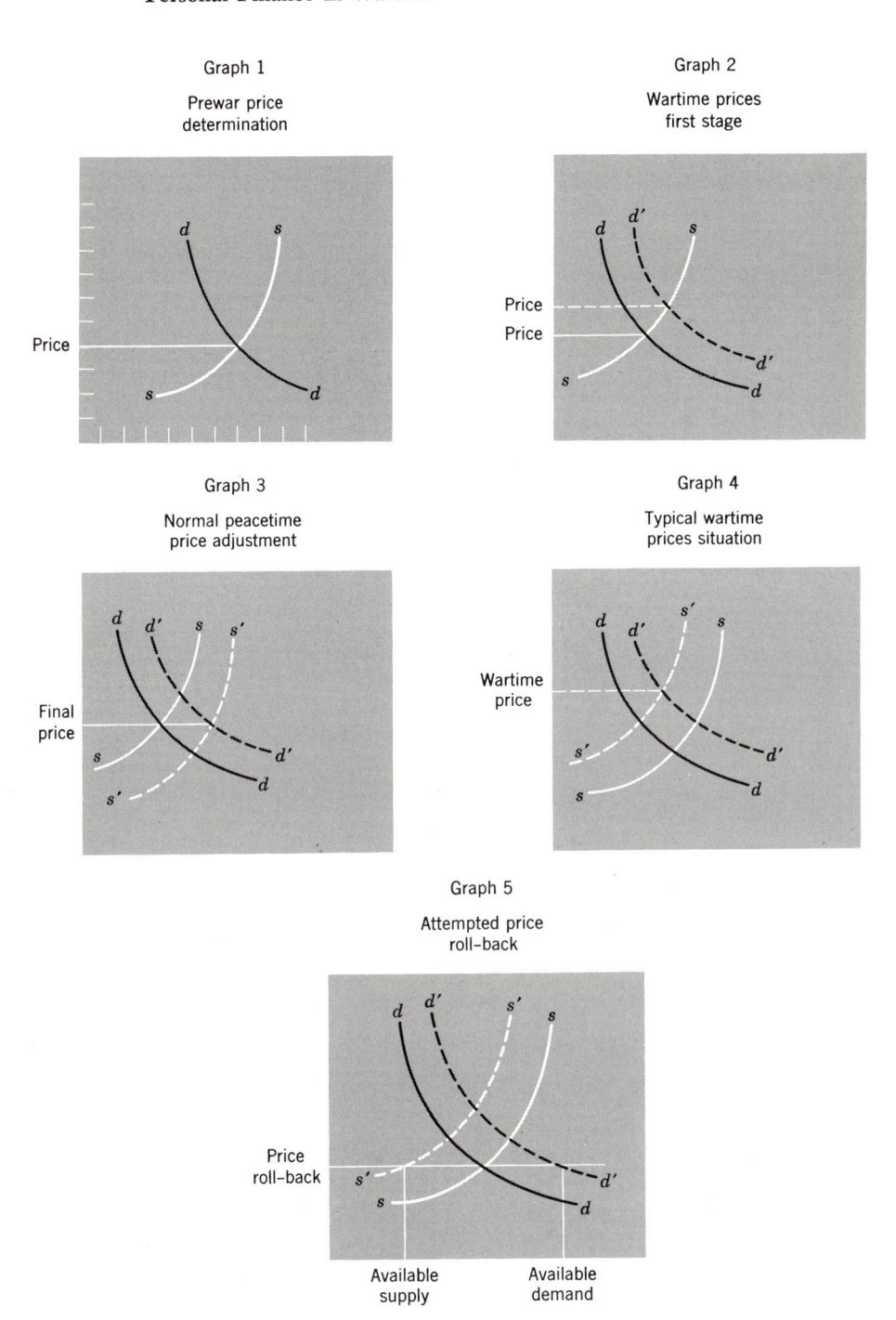

Figure 15-4. **Wartime civilian economy; supply-demand-price relationships.**

and $s \ldots s$ intersection, then the available supply at that price would be far short of the available demand at that price. Black markets would then result because people would be willing to pay "under-the-table" for scarce items or luxuries that they desire very much. This illustration demonstrates the fact that prices must be controlled early in the war period because an attempt to roll them back later is likely to be ineffective. Basically, price controls seek to "hold the line" on wartime prices so that they cannot spiral upward any further, with detrimental effects upon civilian life and the war effort.

Types of Wartime Controls

In several major wars in which the United States has been engaged, a wide variety of wartime controls have evolved. A few of them emerged during the First World War. These reemerged and were supplemented by others in the Second World War. The Korean War, which appeared to be the beginning of a third world war, saw a reintroduction of most of the controls in use during the Second World War. It seems likely that many of these controls will be used again if a major war must be fought. Since this is a distinct possibility, it is appropriate that these controls be examined because they affect the personal finances of every individual in wartime.

Credit Controls. In the Second World War and the Korean War, the Board of Governors of the Federal Reserve System instituted credit controls. These controls fixed the minimum down payment on automobiles and appliances at one-third of the selling price of these items. As the war evolved, the rule required that monthly credit terms be raised so that payments would be completed within fifteen months. These requirements, it will be noted, were designed to discourage the purchase of appliances and cars on credit. People had to make the old car last longer, unless they were willing to make substantial cash and monthly payments. The sale of new and used cars declined, and materials and manpower were diverted to the war effort in accordance with the government's desires.

Fiscal Policy. The United States government has increased taxes and sold war bonds in wartime in an effort to take civilians out of the market for scarce goods and services. Nearly everyone has been encouraged to use the payroll-deduction plan for buying bonds, and tax increases have been legislated immediately in each war. The government's fiscal policy is not one of the wartime controls *per se*, but it is a very important supplement to the controls. Civilians have not always understood that wars are not prosperous years during which one may work and spend as one wishes. Men and women in uniform are resentful when they compare their lot with that of civilians back home. The government's controls and its fiscal policy tend to rectify this inequity. Some experts have proposed the freezing of checking accounts and other expendable income in any future war when no one may spend more than he did in prewar years. This suggestion, known as the *consumer expenditure-rationing proposal*, would hold the line on prices and wages and place everyone in a financial straightjacket.[3] Nonetheless, this drastic proposal may be necessary if a major war must be fought.

Wage and Price Controls. Midway in the Second World War and immediately in the Korean War, the United States government instituted wage controls and price controls. In each instance, wages were frozen as of a certain prior date, and their increase was permitted only after hearings were held or in accordance with a prescribed formula. Scarce labor would have forced wages much higher without the controls, but high wages could not have provided ample supplies of labor, so the controls were justified and necessary. Organized labor cooperated but insisted that the government must hold the line on prices and that no one should gain exorbitant profits from the war effort.

Price controls began in the First World War with an attempt to control the price of sugar and a few other items. In the following wars, an attempt was made to decree certain prices. This was supplemented with a *price freeze* in which certain prices were to remain as they had been on a particular previous date, unless changed by price boards or by formulas decreed by the price-control authorities. So many appeals for price increases reached the price boards that a system of *formula pricing* was instigated. This system permitted retailers to add their normal markups to wholesale or raw-product prices, which were controlled at the factory, the farm, or the port of entry. It should be noted that formula pricing was overly generous for merchants when their volume was high in the early stages of the war. It was less than generous when inventories were virtually unobtainable and when taxes and other costs had increased. Finally, the price authorities in 1943 and 1950 designed a *cost-absorption formula*. A manufacturer or retailer had to absorb additional costs and hold the line on prices if his earnings were high enough to be regarded as excess profits according to the definition used for the excess-profits tax. If earnings were not that high, the businessman might receive permission to raise prices. There can be no doubt that prices were held at lower levels than the wartime supply-demand situation would have decreed. This became evident with the removal of price controls and the rapid price-level increase in 1946.

Rationing. After several years of war, certain civilian goods are usually in such short supply that they must be allocated or rationed to consumers. Price controls alone have not been able to equate supply with demand. Early in each major war, *voluntary rationing* has been implemented by retailers on a one-to-a-customer basis. In practice, the retailers usually allocated available merchandise to their charge-account customers only and gained the ill will of others. Moreover, the customers, as a rule, rushed to get their allotment, whether or not it was needed. Thus voluntary rationing has given way always to other rationing arrangements administered by governmental rationing boards.

In major wars, the United States government has issued ration books with certain stamps in the book designated for the purchase of specific items. Thus, for example, orange stamp number 10 might permit the purchase of one pair of shoes within a specified time period. This *quantitative rationing* usually kept demand in line with supply, but it may have failed to provide shoes enough for families with many children, families who entered the war with too few shoes or families who bought shoes of inferior quality. Under this form of rationing, the shoe-buyer's attention was diverted from his quest for a bargain to his desire for long-lasting shoes, whatever the cost.

The government has also used *differential rationing*, especially in its gasoline rationing program during the Second World War. In this instance, the owner of a car was provided with an A ration book that provided the right to buy a limited amount of gasoline, or a B book that permitted more gasoline purchase if he accepted passengers in a car pool, or a C book if he happened to be a doctor or other important person whose gasoline needs were much greater. In this instance, it should be noted, the customer's attention was diverted away from the cost of the gasoline. In fact, the customer probably spent unusual sums on car repairs and tune-ups in his effort to increase mileage per gallon. It is one of the costs of wartime that controls deter the people from their normal vigilance in financial matters. Moreover, it was rubber, not gasoline, that was in short supply in the United States during the Second World War.

A *point-system rationing* scheme used in the Second World War permitted customers to spend their ration points along with money for items within a group of commodities. One might have used blue stamps for cheese or for butter, cream, or canned meat, for example. This plan did not ration perfectly, however; the demand for cheese, in this case, might have exceeded the supply. Also, the plan had the fault of all ration plans. The customer found ration coupons scarcer than money in a wartime civilian economy; hence he ceased to be as frugal with his money as he should have been.

In England, during the Second World War, meat and a few other products were allocated by *value rationing*. The customer's attention was on the shilling cost of items; his purchases of certain items were limited to so many shillings worth a week. This plan merits the attention of students of this subject who might hope to find a union between the necessity for rationing and the continued practice of alert shopping and financial prudence when one is making a purchase.

Decontrol. Price controls, rationing, and wage controls usually have been unpopular. In the words of John Kenneth Galbraith, an experienced price controller, "Price-fixing by authority . . . is clearly a case of government without the consent of the governed. . . ."[4] The populace always has found politicians who were ready to overturn wartime controls at the first moment of victory. This action usually has been premature. Ordinarily, supply has been far behind demand, and postwar prices have risen sharply until a new supply-demand balance could be reached. Apparently the controls should have been terminated, but the timing was poor. Also, it is obvious that politicians and ordinary citizens need foresight and vision in these matters.

Personal finance should retain its individual and personal objectives. Nevertheless, these should be tempered in wartime and during the immediate postwar period by recognition of social and national needs. Sound economic conduct necessitates the avoidance of inflationary wages and prices, and the maintenance of a reasonable equilibrium between supply and demand.

Recapitulation

The spending, saving, and investing programs of individuals are determined in large degree by the level of their personal incomes. These, in turn, are subject to the vagaries of the business cycle, to threats of inflation, and to wartime price and wage controls. In spite of the government's valiant efforts to stabilize the economy, business-cycle humps and troughs will continue to provide external disturbances in which spending and saving incentives will be intensified or diminished. Certain investments will be attractive only at certain times. The preference for investment instruments will shift from stocks to bonds or to something between. We live in an exhilarating, dynamic world in which individuals formulate their saving and investment goals, objectives, and aspirations. Then, in the face of rapidly changing conditions, they have to remain flexible because identical situations do not reappear very often. It seems that everytime history repeats itself, the price goes up.

QUESTIONS

1. In what ways would income management be simplified if business-cycle fluctuations and wartime situations could be eliminated?
2. Why are inflation and deflation called "twin disasters"? Is one more disastrous than the other? Is there a cause-effect relationship between them?
3. How are (*a*) income, (*b*) price levels, and (*c*) asset values affected by inflation

and by deflation? How can individuals cope with these situations? What can be done by businessmen? By the national government?
4. Explain three or more causes of inflation and the remedies that are apparent.
5. What can businessmen do to cope with deflation? List and explain the government policies in a deflationary period.
6. How does deflation affect (a) fixed-income recipients, (b) wage earners, (c) businessmen, and (d) investors? How can each of these groups cope with the situations most advantageously?
7. Use a circular flow graph to indicate the interrelationships between the production and consumption of physical goods. How does the flow of money from households to firms and back again illustrate the same interrelationship? What is the effect if the money flows are temporarily out of line with the goods flow? How or why can the money flows be temporarily increased or decreased?
8. Refer to a national income accounting graph and explain why the consumption line (C) tends to bend downward to the right. Why does the C + I line waver at times and with what effects upon personal income, savings, and investment? What is the objective of government as illustrated by the addition of G to the C + I + G line? Explain the effect of the so-called multiplier.
9. Why does a major war create an inflationary gap in the civilian economy? How would the free-market price system correct this situation in peacetime? Why can the price system not perform the same service in wartime?
10. Study the graphs in Figure 15–4 and be prepared to use them in explaining the need for price controls in wartime.
11. Why are wartime controls used cautiously and somewhat belatedly? Do you agree with this policy? Why?
12. What are the effects of (a) credit controls and (b) fiscal policy? Why do people oppose each of these? Should they?
13. Why are wage controls necessary? Should they be instituted without price controls? Why?
14. Name and explain four types of price controls. What are the strong and weak points of each? What is their effect on the individual and his income-management strategy? Should they be opposed? Why?
15. Why is rationing necessary as a supplement for price controls? Name and describe several types of rationing.
16. What should be the individual's reaction to wage controls, price controls, and rationing in wartime? When should these controls be removed? Why?
17. Note carefully the key terms in this chapter and be prepared to identify each of them.

SELECTED READINGS

Abramson, Adolph G., and Russell H. Mack, *Business Forecasting in Practice: Principles and Cases*, Wiley, New York, 1956.

Backman, Jules, *The Economics of Armament Inflation*, Rinehart, New York, 1951.

Bolton, Roger E., *Defense and Disarmament: The Economics of Tradition*, Prentice-Hall, Englewood Cliffs, N. J., 1966.

Chandler, Lester V., and Donald H. Wallace, *Economic Mobilization and Stabilization*, Holt, New York, 1951.

Collery, Arnold, *National Income and Employment Analysis*, Wiley, New York, 1966.

Dauten, Carl A., *Business Cycles and Forecasting*, South-Western, Cincinnati, 1961.
Duesenberry, James S., *Business Cycles and Economic Growth*, McGraw-Hill, New York, 1958.
Enke, Stephen, *Economics for Development*, Prentice-Hall, Englewood Cliffs, N. J., 1963.
Galbraith, John Kenneth, *The Great Crash 1929*, Houghton Mifflin, Boston, 1961.
———, *The Theory of Price Control*, Harvard University Press, Cambridge, Mass., 1952.
Hart, Albert G., *Defense without Inflation*, The Twentieth Century Fund, New York, 1951.
Klein, Lawrence R., *The Keynesian Revolution*, Second Edition, Macmillan, New York, 1966.

NOTES

1. Harold S. Sloan and Arnold J. Zurcher, *A Dictionary of Economics*, Barnes & Noble, New York, 1953, p. 166.
2. Kenneth Trefftzs, "What Put the Stock Market Where It Is?" *Report to Management, No. 3*, Graduate School of Business Administration, University of Southern California, January, 1962.
3. Tibor Scitovsky, Edward Shaw, and Lorie Tarshis, *Mobilizing Resources for War*, McGraw-Hill, New York, 1951, pp. 147–148.
4. John Kenneth Galbraith, *The Theory of Price Control*, Harvard University Press, Cambridge, Mass., 1952, p. 4.

PROBLEMS AND CASES

1. If we anticipate that prices will rise 3 per cent a year over the next 20 years, should we buy at face value a debenture paying 5 per cent interest maturing in 20 years or should we buy a share of common stock, also selling at par value paying annual dividends equivalent to 2 per cent of its current value, which has been appreciating 2 per cent per year over a period of years and may be expected to continue to do so? Why?
2. If your income were reduced by 25 per cent because of partial unemployment, show your revised plan of monthly expenditures and explain why you made the adjustments that you did.
3. If your income were increased by 25 per cent because of full employment, bonuses, etc., show your revised plan of monthly expenditures and explain why you made the adjustments that you did.
4. Use a circular flow graph to indicate the interrelationships between the production and consumption of physical goods. How does the flow of money from households to firms and back again illustrate the same interrelationship? What is the effect if the money flows are temporarily out of line with the goods flow? How or why can the money flows be temporarily increased or decreased?
5. If Brown's consumption expenditures are other men's income, how can Brown's savings also become other men's income? If Brown's savings are extensive and are promptly invested, would the incomes of others benefit accordingly? If Brown and nearly everyone else saved extensively, would total national income increase accordingly? What is meant by the paradox of thrift?
6. Is the ability of individuals and the masses to save influenced or determined by

their incomes? Do savings increase more rapidly than the GNP? When? Why? What increases the GNP besides the ability of individuals to produce more and earn higher incomes?

7. If one man's expenditure is another man's income, can it be said that the economy could be lifted by raising the productivity of people who are underachievers?

8. When people save, they deny themselves certain purchases that would have yielded pleasure and satisfaction. Does this saving remove part of their income from the circular flow and does it deny someone else his income? If savings are invested promptly, is the circular flow maintained? If investment is financed from unsaved funds, explain how the multiplier increases the NNP or the GNP. Is this always beneficial to the economy? Explain.

9. If businessmen borrow and spend ten extra billions on new plants and equipment, how much will the GNP probably rise because of this expenditure? Explain how and why. Does the multiplier work in reverse in a period of declining GNP?

10. Preliminary figures for the first half of 1967 indicated that federal spending had risen 19.3 per cent in a year and a half, consumer prices had risen 3.6 per cent in the same period, and industrial production seems to have declined. Does this indicate the economy's need for very much government spending? Does this suggest that inflationary pressures were uppermost? Could this threat have been met by raising taxes to curb consumer expenditures? Would an early termination of the Viet Nam War have helped to stem the inflationary tide?

11. If you had bought common stocks as an inflationary hedge in 1967, should you have anticipated the possibility of tight money policy or of new federal taxes and the effect of these actions upon your investment? If these strong antiinflationary remedies had proved too strong and brought on a recession a year later, what built-in stabilizers and other government action might be expected to prevent a sharp recession—especially in an election year? What, then, might have been your 1967 estimate of external factors, and what might have been your decision about buying common stocks at that time? Compare your decision with the actual situation as you find it in 1968–1972 when this analysis is subject to realistic verification.

12. Refer to a national income accounting graph and explain why the consumption line (C) tends to bend downward toward the right. Why does the $C + I$ line waver at times and with what effects upon personal income, saving, and investment? What is the objective of government as illustrated by the addition of G to the $C + I + G$ line? Explain the effect of the so-called multiplier as government introduces additional funds obtained by deficit financing. With what success or lack of success has this been done in the last 5 years? The last 10 years?

13. Why and how is a major war such a major disturbance in the economy that it upsets spending, saving, and investment programs? Why can't the free market pricing system achieve a stable wartime equilibrium by adjusting prices, wages, interest, and government spending?

14. Explain with a graph the wartime inflationary gap and the need for wartime price and wage controls.

15. With high wages, high prices, high taxes, and payroll withholding for war-bond purchases, could many persons have traded their car for a better used car (no new cars were available) in 1945 when all installment payment plans had to be completed within fifteen months? Explain.
16. Why might the impoverished Smiths with a large family have declared that price controls without rationing were inequitable?
17. How did Britain's "value rationing" return the consumer's attention to the amount and value of a product he would receive for each shilling of expenditure?
18. Consider the possibility of the proposed consumer expenditure rationing proposal which might be imposed on a "cashless, checkless society" in a major war—with payrolls transferred from factory to bank on a computer tape, and store credit paid by transferring sales slips directly to one's checking account. Add to this, withholding for taxes, social security, and bond purchases. Would this arrangement limit the threat of demand-pull inflation? What other inflation causes might still exist?
19. Are you convinced that inflation and deflation are major disturbances in the economy and that there is danger if either is allowed to run unchecked? Which is the greater threat currently? Is the federal government "playing with fire" when it attempts to offset one with the other? How successful has this policy been in the last 5 years? The last 10 years?

16 RETIREMENT PROGRAMS

Those who do not wish to grow old should die young.

SPANISH PROVERB

The average life expectancy of a child born in the United States these days is more than 70 years. Those who reach 65 may anticipate another 15 years or more. Those who reach 70 may expect at least another 12.[1]

The most common retirement age is still 65, yet relatively few families have enough to enable them to live more than 15 years without income. In 1962, the median of the liquid-asset holdings of those over 65 was approximately $1,500; but almost half of them had less than $500 in liquid assets.[2] The median income of persons 65 and over in the United States in March of 1966 was $1,387.[3] It is true that living costs decrease when children have gone and activities are curtailed. Nevertheless, $1,387 a year is hardly an adequate income for anyone in the United States by any set of standards. Furthermore, 1.8 million of those over 65 in 1964 were indigent, that is, nonself-supporting, with presumably little or no assets, and no income.[4]

Four facts have now been widely recognized: first, many do not or cannot practicably save enough for their old age, nor can they afford insurance against contingencies such as catastrophic illness, which might deprive them of their savings; second, the means test applied to those who are in need of assistance leaves most people shorn of dignity; third, the number past 65 is growing and will continue to grow as longevity increases; and fourth, many younger people cannot or will not support their parents, and the older people, in turn, do not want to depend on their children. Consequently, social insurance or *social security* has been generally accepted as one of the main bulwarks against privation for those over 65. More than seven out of every ten aged persons now receive some sort of social security payment.[5]

Besides, about 28 million persons were covered by private pension plans in 1965, including about two million over 65 who had already retired.[6] Many of these pensions were paid for, in whole or in part, by employers. However, social security and pensions ordinarily are not enough if one plans to do much more than subsist; intelligent planning must provide for more than subsistence. Everyone has to plan in order to have whatever each may consider to be an adequate income for retirement years.

Retirement incomes also may derive in part from individual or group annuities—employers often contribute to group annuities under employee retirement plans—and from the income from savings and investments. In some cases, they may be supplemented by earnings from part-time employment. Each of these means of accumulating retirement income will be reviewed in this chapter.

PLANNING FOR RETIREMENT

Retirement always entails major adjustments for every individual. However, most people in the United States can look forward to a number of happy and productive years after they retire if they plan properly for this period. This planning must start years before retirement and must take into consideration that good health during these later years may become more difficult and, consequently, more expensive to maintain. Moreover, away from one's work, customary routine, and social activities, it is easier to become isolated and disorganized. One's feeling of usefulness and prestige may be endangered. Society still fails to make adequate use of retired people and their accumulated wisdom and experience. Then, too, it is often difficult to find housing that is inexpensive and yet fits changed and changing needs. Furthermore, income may be reduced.

Consequently, it pays when young to purchase noncancelable health insurance that will remain in force after one reaches 65 and will provide benefits needed to supplement government health plans when the costs of medical care are highest. It is also well to recognize that the pursuit of activities that will replace work and allow one to make use of one's wisdom and experience may be expensive. For this reason, experience in wise financial management may be used in good stead at any time to cope with the problem of how to meet changing needs with an unchanged or reduced income.

Sources of Retirement Income

Those over 65 receive less than a proportionate share of the national income. The median income of a man over 65 in 1963 was $1,993. The median income of all male income recipients in the United States in that same year was $4,551. The median for women over 65 was $920; for all women $1,372. A total of 50.2 per cent of the men and 86.1 per cent of the women received less than $2,000 for that year.[7] In many cases the planning was manifestly inadequate. Table 16-1 shows the sources from which the retirement income derived. Employment, Social Security, and investment income are by far the most important sources of income for this group.

Planning for Retirement Income

The almost minimal cost of living for a retired couple in Los Angeles in 1965 was estimated at $1,500.[8] The average monthly benefit for approximately 75 per cent of those 65 and over who received Social Security in 1964 was $137.70 [9] a month for an aged couple, or $1,652.40 a year, which was intended to give them enough to maintain a very modest level of living. As they need more for even this standard of living, Congress will probably amend the Social Security Act, as it did in 1967, so that, on the average, they can continue to live in this fashion as prices increase.

Since most people want more than this level of living when they retire, they must plan to supplement their social security benefit income. The young employee choosing among firms offering various pension plans should consider how much he will receive in social security and pension payments when making his choice. He also must realize that, although social security benefits probably will be adjusted to keep pace with price increases, other payments, unless they are variable annuities—to be discussed shortly—may not keep pace with price increases. Investing under a systematic plan in common stocks, mutual funds, or real estate that will appreciate enough to permit maintenance of the desired standard of living probably will be necessary for anyone who wishes to enjoy a retirement level of income that approximates what he receives while employed. But potential retirees also should prepare themselves for whatever

Table 16-1. **Sources of Income Received by Persons Aged 65 and Over in 1962**

Source	Married[a] Couples	Nonmarried Men	Women
Number reporting	5,443	2,345	6,267
Per cent reporting			
Earnings	55	28	23
Retirement benefits	84	72	64
OASDI	79	68	60
Other public	12	8	7
Private group pensions	16	10	3
Veterans benefits	14	11	6
Interest, dividends and rents	63	45	50
Public assistance	8	18	17
Other[b]	10	3	10

[a] With at least one member aged 65 or over.
[b] Private individual annuities, unemployment insurance, and contributions from relatives and friends not in household.
SOURCE: U. S. Department of Health, Education, and Welfare, Social Security Administration, *Social Security Bulletin*, March 1964, p. 6.

type of part-time employment is a part of their planned-retirement program. This may involve training for a trade or profession that was not pursued during preretirement years. For the fortunate few who plan well and fare well, retirement years can be both high-income and generously rewarding years.

SOCIAL SECURITY

The Social Security Act has been in effect since 1937. It now provides for five types of benefits: first, contributory old-age, survivors', and disability insurance benefits; second, hospital-insurance benefits; third, medical-insurance benefits; fourth, unemployment compensation insurance benefits; and fifth, old-age assistance and public welfare. Only the first of these concerns this discussion.

Under the old-age, survivors', and disability insurance program, employees, employers, and the self-employed pay social security taxes, which go into special trust funds. When earnings stop because the insured has retired, died, or become disabled, benefit payments may be made from the funds. One difference between social security and private insurance is that a person who qualifies may receive more in benefits under the social security program than he is mathematically or actuarially entitled to on the basis of his contributions or payments.

The social security system is mainly on a self-supporting "pay-as-you-go" basis; thus there is no need of having large reserves. As more people become eligible for old-age, survivors', and disability insurance benefits, as well as hospital-insurance benefits, the tax rates will increase. According to present laws, they will be raised to 4.8 per cent for both employee and employer in 1969; and to 5.9 per cent by 1987. Rates for the self-employed will be 6.9 per cent in 1969 and 7.9 per cent by 1987. Social Security taxes are paid only on the first $7,800 of earnings in any one year.

Eligibility for Benefits

Virtually all of those working in the United States are covered by Social Security. The exceptions are federal employees covered by federal retirement systems, persons covered under the railroad retirement system, and minor children working for parents, a wife employed by her husband, or parents doing household work for their children.

To be *fully insured*, a worker who reached 65 (62 if a woman) or who died in 1967 would need credit for 4 years of work; in 1968 he would need 4¼ years, and then one quarter more for each additional year until 1991, when 10 years' work will be required as the maximum. Those who have credit for at least 1½ years' work within the 3 years before they die or become entitled to retirement benefits are said to be *currently insured*.

To receive retirement, survivors', or disability benefits, the insured, his dependents, or both *must apply* for them and, as Table 16–2 shows, must be fully or currently insured, or both, depending on the requirements. When an insured individual receives old-age or disability benefits, or dies, payments also can be made to certain of his dependents. These include unmarried children under 18 years of age or between 18 and 22 if they are full-time students; unmarried children 18 or over who were severely disabled before they reached 18 and have remained so since; a wife or widow, regardless of her age, if she is caring for a child who is receiving payments based on the insured's social security account; a wife 62 or widow 60 or older, even if there are no children entitled to payments; a disabled widow, widower, or divorced wife over 50; a dependent husband or widower 62 or over; and a divorced wife at 62 or a surviving divorced wife entitled to support by the insured under specified conditions. Additional survivors' benefits may be paid to dependent parents.

Besides this, a lump-sum death payment may be made to the widow or widower of the deceased or be applied to his burial expenses. The lump sum is three times the amount of his monthly retirement benefit, but it cannot exceed $255.

Any individual can receive benefits only under one social security account. For example, a woman who is eligible for benefits based on her own earnings

Table 16-2. **Retirement, Survivors', or Disability Benefits**

Retirement Payments

Monthly payments to:	If you are:
You as a retired worker and your wife and child	Fully insured[a]
Your dependent husband 62 or over	Both fully and currently insured

Survivors' Payments

Monthly payments to your:	If at death you are:
Widow 60 or over	Fully insured
Widow, regardless of age, if caring for your child who is entitled to benefits	Either fully or currently insured
Dependent child	Either fully or currently insured
Dependent widower 62 or over	*Both* fully and currently insured
Dependent parent at 62	Fully insured
Dependent divorced wife, regardless of age, if caring for your child who is under 18 or disabled and is entitled to benefits	Either fully or currently insured
Lump-sum death payment	Either fully or currently insured

Disability Payments

Monthly payments to:	
You and your dependents if you are totally disabled for work	*If you are fully insured and meet work requirements*

[a] Except for certain persons over 72 who are subject to much lower eligibility requirements.
SOURCE: *Your Social Security.* U. S. Department of Health, Education, and Welfare, Social Security Administration, October 1965, p. 8.

and also for a wife's benefits based on the earnings of her husband will receive the amount that is the larger of the two.

To check on an account—and it is wise to do so every three years—one should write to the Social Security Administration, Baltimore, Maryland 21235, and include one's Social Security number. To be sure to receive benefits for which one is eligible, one should visit the nearest Social Security office (1) upon starting to work, since no contributions can be credited to an account until one has acquired a Social Security number; (2) if an insured individual in the family dies or becomes permanently disabled; or (3) if the inquiring individual is approaching age 62 or 72.

Estimating Payments

Benefits are based on average earnings. The higher the average earnings, the larger the benefit payments.

Old-Age and Survivors' Insurance Benefits. Most people may estimate their average yearly earnings on which the retirement or survivors' benefit payment will be based in three steps. First, they count the number of years after 1950 and up to but not including the year they reach 65, or 62 if they choose to retire at that age. If the result is less than five, they increase it to five. Next, they select an equal number of years after 1950 in which their earnings were highest. Then, they average their earnings in the selected years. For example, if someone worked five years after 1955 before reaching 65, and earned $4,200, that is, the maximum for social security computation, in each of his highest earnings years after 1950,* the average yearly earnings on which the amount of his benefit payments would be based is $4,200. This is an approximate method. The exact number of years to be averaged ranges from five for those born in 1896 or earlier to 35 for women and 38 for men born in 1929 or later. Table 16–3 may be used to find estimated benefit payments.

As Table 16–3 indicates, men and women who are eligible may choose to start receiving benefits when they are 62 or older. Widows may choose to start receiving benefits at 60. Benefit payment amounts are based on the sum payable at 65, in any case. Consequently, those who choose to begin benefits before they reach 65—and this applies to wives who also may choose to receive their benefits before 65 if their husbands are already in retirement—receive a lesser amount. However, their payments spread over a longer period of time. Actually, they can be ahead for as many as 15 years. If they receive benefits for more than 15 years, the chances are that they will get less over the long run than if they had held off taking them until they were 65.

Benefits for the insured range from $55 a month for those who retire at 62 with credit for average yearly earnings of $899 or less, to $434.30 a month, the maximum payment that may be made to a family. The average monthly benefit for a retired worker and his aged wife in 1964 was $137.70.[10]

A man retiring at 65, having earned $5,400 or more a year in qualifying for social security, would receive $165 a month. If his wife were 65, too, her benefit would be $82.50, giving them a total of $247.50. They would have had to invest $74,250 at 4 per cent in order to have the same monthly income. The sum of $130,320 would have had to be invested at 4 per cent to earn the $434.40 a month maximum family benefit payment.

To illustrate the family protection provided, take the case of a husband and wife, both 35, who have three children, aged 1, 6, and 11. Assume that the husband had maximum coverage under Social Security. In the event of his death, his family would receive a $255 lump-sum death benefit; it would then

---

* Earnings of $4,800 may be counted from 1966; $7,800 from 1968.

Table 16-3. Examples of Monthly Cash Payments

Average Yearly Earnings after 1950[a]	$899 or Less	$1800	$3000	$4200	$5400	$6600	$7800
Retired worker—65 or older / Disabled worker—under 65	55.00	88.40	115.00	140.40	165.00	189.90	218.00
Wife 65 or older	27.50	44.20	57.50	70.20	82.50	95.00	105.00
Retired worker at 62	44.00	70.80	92.00	112.40	132.00	152.00	174.40
Wife at 62, no child	20.70	33.20	43.20	52.70	61.90	71.30	78.80
Widow at 62 or older	55.00	73.00	94.90	115.90	136.20	156.70	179.90
Widow at 60, no child	47.70	63.30	82.30	100.50	118.10	135.90	156.00
Disabled widow at 50, no child	33.40	44.30	57.60	70.30	82.70	95.10	109.20
Wife under 65 and one child	27.50	44.20	87.40	140.40	165.00	190.00	214.00
Widow under 62 and one child	82.50	132.60	172.60	210.60	247.60	285.00	327.00
Widow under 62 and two children	82.50	132.60	202.40	280.80	354.40	395.60	434.40
One child of retired or disabled worker	27.50	44.20	57.50	70.20	82.50	95.00	109.00
One surviving child	55.00	66.30	86.30	105.30	123.80	142.50	163.50
Maximum family payment	82.50	132.60	202.40	280.80	354.40	395.60	434.40

[a] Generally, average earnings are figured over the period from 1950 until the worker reaches retirement age, becomes disabled, or dies. Up to five years of low earnings can be excluded. The maximum earnings creditable for social security are $3,600 for 1951–1954; $4,200 for 1955–1958; $4,800 for 1959–1965; and $6,600 for 1966–1967. The maximum creditable in 1968 is $7,800, but average earnings cannot reach this amount until later. Because of this, the benefits shown in the last two columns on the right generally will not be payable until later. When a person is entitled to more than one benefit, the amount actually payable is limited to the largest of the benefits.

SOURCE: *Your Social Security*, U. S. Department of Health, Education, and Welfare, Social Security Administration, January 1968, pp. 4 and 5.

receive $438.40 a month for 12 years, until the second child reached 18; $327 a month for five more years, until the youngest child was 18; no benefit for 8 years until the widow reached 60, and then $156 a month until she died. If the widow lived to be 72, total family and death benefits would be $105,213.60. Even if the widow remarried or earned too much to receive benefits before 60, the children alone would still be entitled to payments totaling $82,749.60. In 1968, $85,500 in life insurance would have cost the husband, on the average, $1,423 a year.[11] Under Social Security, he contributed a maximum of $343.20 a year.

Those who retire but continue working to some extent may earn up to $1,680 a year—or $140 a month, irrespective of earnings for the year—without curtailing the amount of their own or their family's benefits. Above that, $1 in benefits is withheld for each $2 earned from $1,680 to $2,880, and for every $1 earned above $2,880. The person who receives benefits and earns $2,000 a year would lose $160 in benefits that year, if he earned over $140 every month. If he earns $3,000, he will lose $720: one-half of the $1,200 between $1,680 and $2,880, plus $120, the amount over $2,880.

Income from investments, royalties, pensions, or annuities does not curtail benefits. Nor is there any deduction from benefits because of earnings from employment if one is over 72.

Disability-Insurance Benefits. Those under 65 who are insured under Social Security and who acquire a mental or physical disability that is medically verifiable, that is expected to last or have lasted for at least 12 months or is expected to result in death, and that prevents them from engaging in "any substantial gainful activity," qualify for monthly disability benefits. But they must have had social security credit for at least five years of work in the ten-year period preceding the disablement. Disability-benefit payments are equal to the retirement-benefit payments paid to those over 65 and, therefore, range from $55 to $218 a month, depending on past earnings. The dependents of the disabled receive the same benefits they would have received had he retired at 65.

The Social Security Act has been amended several times since its passage, and it must be anticipated that it will be amended again from time to time. There will be changes in the types of benefits available, the eligibility requirements, the amounts to be received in benefits, and the amounts to be contributed. Both benefits and contributions may be expected to increase.

ANNUITIES

Annuities are intended to provide income for as long as one lives. They are, therefore, the opposite of life insurance, which provides payments for beneficiaries when the insured is no longer alive.

Annuitants pay a fixed sum, all at once or in installments over a period of years. The contract they purchase specifies that they and their designated survivors shall receive payments in the future, usually at periodic intervals over a number of years or for as many years as they may live. Generally, annuities are bought because they will provide more income than the recipient would derive from investing the money otherwise. Moreover, they protect the annuitant from exhausting his principal if he lives longer than he planned.

Types of Annuities

Annuities are known by designations that indicate how the annuity is to be paid for, when the income is to be received, and how the income from the annuity is to be collected. If, for example, annuities are to be paid for in one lump sum, they are known as *single-premium* annuities; if in yearly installments, as *annual premium*. If income from the annuity is to start at once, it is known as *immediate* annuity; if it is to start at a later date, it is known as a *deferred* annuity. A *temporary* annuity provides a specified income for a specified period of time. A *straight-life* annuity provides income during the life of the annuitant. All payments under the contract stop when he dies. An *installments-certain* annuity provides a specified income per year for the number of years specified, usually 10 or 20. If the annuitant does not live that long, his designated survivors receive the payments. This type often is described as having a guaranteed number of payments. An *installment-refund* annuity provides that the annuitant shall receive the specified payments during his life and that the remainder of what was paid for the annuity shall be remitted to his heirs in installments. A *cash-refund* annuity provides that the annuitant shall receive the specified payments as long as he lives and that the balance remaining shall be paid to his heirs in cash. A *joint* and *survivorship* type of annuity contract stipulates that the specified payments continue as long as any of those designated in the contract are alive. Married couples frequently buy these so that when one of the two dies, the surviving spouse will continue to receive income from the annuity.

A *variable annuity* is one from which the annuitant derives an income based on how much the funds that he paid for it have earned while invested by the insurance company, generally in common stocks. Variable annuity funds generally are divided into units. The value of a unit is computed by dividing the total market value of an annuity fund at a particular time by the number of units outstanding. If a fund is valued at 2 million dollars, for example, and there are 20,000 units outstanding, each unit is worth $100.

Some insurance companies offer combinations of the various types of annuities. Therefore, one may buy a quarterly premium, deferred, installment-certain, joint, fixed, and variable annuity. The fixed annuity, in distinction to the variable annuity, does not change in value as investment earnings rise or fall. On fixed and variable annuities, some portion of the premiums are used to purchase a fixed-value annuity and the remainder a variable annuity.

It may be noted that so-called retirement or elective annuities are deferred annuities. So-called "tax-sheltered" annuities are generally deferred annuities. They are bought by qualifying employee groups of five or more and the periodic payments are deducted by employers from wages and salaries. Self-employed persons may set aside up to 10 per cent of their annual income, to a maximum of $2,500 a year, in a retirement fund under the "Keogh" plan. (Keogh was the Congressman who sponsored the permissive legislation.) Payroll deductions and the self-employed contributions are not considered current income, and no federal personal income tax is paid on them. A federal income tax is paid on the proceeds from the annuity when they are received, but by then the annuitant may be over 65 and in a lower tax bracket.

If this is a deferred straight-life annuity, to be explained presently, the annuitant may avoid all taxes on this income, but only because, having died, he never receives the proceeds. Many who buy them never do. On the other hand, tax-sheltered annuities provide higher retirement incomes than would have been available from the investment of the same monies without the additional "tax dollars." Tax-sheltered variable annuities provide the advantages of both the deferred tax payments and the possible appreciation in market value of the common stocks in which the annuitant's funds are invested.

Annuity contracts may provide also for *participation*. Annuitants participate in the earnings of the company by receiving dividends, which are sometimes paid in cash, which may be applied toward premium payments, or which may be left with the company to accumulate interest at a specified rate and later be added to the annuity. They may allow a *cash value* whereby the contract may be surrendered for a specified percentage of its face value in cash after a certain number of premiums have been paid. They may include *loan privileges*, in which a specified percentage of the face value may be lent to the annuitant with the value of the annuity reduced by any portion of the loan that remains unpaid; and they may stipulate that *death benefits* be paid to a designated beneficiary if the annuitant should die before receiving any annuity income. All these aspects make annuities resemble life insurance more closely and, incidentally, add to the cost. Increasingly, contracts are being written to combine life insurance and annuities.

Cost of Annuities

The cost of annuities varies with the age and sex of the purchaser, the designated recipients, or both; with the type of annuity purchased, and the company from which it is bought. In general, the more that is to be paid out, the higher the expense connected with the annuity, the shorter the period during which the insurance company may derive earnings from the amount paid in, the costlier the annuity.

The Straight-Life Annuity. The straight-life annuity, or *life annuity*, as it is commonly known, is the oldest form of annuity and still the least expensive. Since disbursements under this type of annuity cease as soon as the annuitant dies, he pays in only enough to enable the insurance company to meet the installments as long as he lives and to cover its expenses. By using actuarial tables, the insurance company can predict how many annuitants it will have to pay and for how long. Prices of these annuities are predicated on the company's ability to use the residue from the amount paid in by those who die before collecting as much as they have contributed, plus the earnings from the investment of these funds. Consequently, payments *to the purchaser* under this type of annuity are higher than under any other type acquired for the same price. The chances, however, that he will not receive as much as he paid in also are high.

If purchased from a reputable company, the straight-life annuity is a safe way to pay for security of income and, in some cases, a lessening of anxiety. Since an older person probably will not receive as many payments, especially if he buys an *immediate* annuity, the older the purchaser, the lower the price. Contrarily, the income from investing his money until the annuity is to be paid makes the price to the younger purchaser of a *deferred* annuity less than otherwise. Women tend to outlive men; therefore, they pay a higher price for such annuities.

The Installments-Certain Annuity. The installments-certain guaranteed payment, or guaranteed-income annuity, costs more than a life annuity. The reason is that the insurance company will not be able to use the residual funds in the accounts of annuitants who die before receiving the stipulated number of disbursements to pay other annuitants. However, it insures that the purchaser or his beneficiaries will receive as much as was paid in.

Refund Annuities. Refund annuities cost more than life annuities or guaranteed-payment annuities because the remainder of the purchase price must be returned to the annuitant's estate when he dies. The refund may be in cash or in installments. If it is cash, the company no longer has that amount available from which to derive offsetting earnings. If the refund is to be paid in installments, the price of the annuity may be a little lower, since the company has the use of the funds for a longer time.

Costs of different contracts vary from one insurance company to another. A man of 40 who agrees to pay an annual premium of $100 will receive *each month*, according to one company's plan, the choices shown in Table 16–4. If he saved instead the $100 a year for the 20 years until he was 60 without accumulating interest, he would have saved $2,000. With interest at 4 per cent compounded, he would have saved $2,978. At the age of 60, to obtain the income he would receive from any of these annuities, he would have to realize

Table 16-4

If He Starts Collecting at the Age of	Under a Straight-Life Annuity (Dollars)	Under an Installment-Refund Annuity (Dollars)	Under an Installments-Certain-for-10-Years Annuity (Dollars)
60	13.78	11.72	12.77
65	21.58	17.65	19.06
70	33.17	25.84	27.27

an annual return of 7 or 8 per cent on the $2,000 he had saved; of 9 to 12 per cent for the return he would receive at 65; and of 12 to 17 per cent for the return he would receive at 70.

Variable Annuities. Prices of *units* under variable annuities often are established so that an annual premium of $100 will buy one unit. But premiums also are quoted in terms of how much must be paid to buy an annuity of $10 a month if appreciation of the funds is estimated correctly. Since funds of annuitants are invested in common stocks, the annuity income received will depend on how much the stocks appreciate. If the funds invested are well managed, variable annuities provide a hedge against inflation; over the years, as prices increase, the value of the stocks in which the annuitants' funds are invested also should rise, and the income from the annuity should increase accordingly.

Whether to Buy an Annuity

The question of whether to buy an annuity can be answered only by each individual. First, he must take into consideration how much income per month he needs or wants after he has retired or is no longer deriving sufficient income from current endeavors. Then he must know how much he will have from other sources of income, such as social security, pensions, investments, employment, and contributions by children or relatives; how much an annuity of the type that he wants costs,[12] and how much financial or psychological advantage he will derive from buying an annuity rather than from managing his own investments.

He should also consider his estate. If, for example, a person were 65 and considering buying an immediate straight-life annuity to pay $3,000 a year, its cost in 1968 would have been about $33,000. This sum invested at 5 per cent could yield only $1,650 a year but the $33,000 would be there, as an estate, when the annuitant died. Thus the choice is between receiving a 9.1 per cent return while alive, if one buys the annuity $\left(\frac{3{,}000}{33{,}000}=.0909\right)$—and a 9 per cent return generally involves high risk—and preserving the principal for one's estate.

The computations, in each case, have to be made in terms of individual circumstances and individual desires. It is well to have them done by an expert on insurance and annuities if any considerable sum is involved. One other factor might be taken into account when making the decision on whether to buy an annuity. Statistics have indicated that older people who have annuities and do not have to worry about having income for as long as they live tend to live longer.

PENSION PLANS

Although well over one-third of those employed in the United States are eligible for pensions upon retirement and, although pensions account for an increasing part of retirement income, in most cases the income from pensions alone usually will not be enough for full support during the retirement years.[13] Ordinarily pension income does not average one-third of annual earnings before retirement. It is anticipated that 45 to 55 per cent of employees, not taking into account government and railroad employees who are covered under their own retirement plans, and agricultural and domestic workers who have no coverage, will be affected by private pension plans before 1970.[14] Benefit levels under the various plans are increasing.

Pension plans are more likely to be found in large firms than in smaller companies. Coverage varies from a very small proportion of employees in construction and service industries in most areas to very high proportions in public utilities and finance. Office workers are more likely to be covered than are plant workers.[15]

In 1962, 90 per cent of the welfare or pension funds were administered by the management of firms, 6.5 per cent jointly by management and labor, and 2.5 per cent by unions.[16]

Rationale of Pension Plans

Since 1950, an increasing number of employers and employees have accepted the idea that deductions from employees' paychecks and contributions from employers to a pension fund from which employees would derive retirement income are advantageous. For the employee, a pension plan usually insures that he will have more income at retirement than if he had received the additional compensation—even if, as is most unlikely, he had saved a like amount at the maximum rate of interest under safe investment conditions.

The employer derives several advantages from contributing to a pension plan. For one thing, employees with a personal interest in a pension plan tend to stay with the company. As a result, there is less employee turnover and less expense from loss of experienced personnel and for the training of new personnel. Second, employees who are satisfied with a pension plan may be more loyal, more secure, and more productive. Third, most contributions to pension plans may be deducted from income as a business expense and, consequently, reduce taxable income and taxes. Fourth, the employer is in a better position to compete for desirable employees, since he offers additional fringe benefits.

It is interesting to note that the employer may be contributing dollars that otherwise would have been paid in taxes; that the employee will have income that otherwise he probably would not have when his needs become greater; and that when the employee is over 65, he will be entitled to a 15 per cent retirement-income credit against his income tax and, in consequence, will derive a still larger benefit from pension dollars. However, many employees who have contributed under pension plans will not qualify for benefits when they retire. Moreover, under some plans there is a risk that funds from which benefits would be paid will not be there when the employee retires.

Types of Pension Plans

Pension plans may be insured or uninsured. There were 66,260 insured pension plans covering 7 million persons in the United States in 1965.[17] In contrast, 21 million were under noninsured plans.[18] Insured plans are under insurance-company contracts which provide for either *deferred annuities, deposit-administration plans, individual-policy pension trusts*, or variations to meet specific problems.

Deferred group annuities have been the most popular types of insured-pension plan, but this plan is declining in relative importance. Under deferred group-annuity plans, a paid-up annuity benefit is purchased each year for each eligible employee who, upon retirement, begins to receive income from the total annuity benefits he has accumulated throughout the years of his employment.

In recent years, the *deposit-administration* type of group annuity has been the most popular. Under this plan, a single fund is set up for all employees in an insured group. As each employee retires, money is withdrawn from the fund to purchase an annuity for him.

Under *individual-policy pension trusts*, in most cases, a life-insurance policy that is an endowment policy or a whole-life policy is purchased for each eligible employee. When the employee retires, the policy provides an annuity for him.

The deposit-administration type of plan is generally the least expensive and provides the most income in relation to contributions. The reasons for this are that the insurance company can average out the risks over the group, since not all will survive to collect the annuity, and that during the years in which funds are not being used, they can be invested.

Pension plans also are referred to sometimes as *conventional* or *pattern*. Under a conventional plan, the employee usually contributes as well as the employer. Under a pattern plan, in most instances, only the employer contributes. Under conventional plans, benefits vary both with years of service and rates of compensation. Under pattern plans, the pension provided is a flat-dollar amount that may vary with years of service, but not with the compensation rate of the employee. The pattern plans are the ones that have been worked out by certain unions and that have been adopted by many companies as a result of negotiations with the unions. Many of the plans also permit retirement in case of disability and provide for disability pensions and death benefits.

Noninsured pension funds, whether union managed, employer managed, or employer-group managed, are subject to the provisions of the federal Welfare and Pension Plans Disclosure Act. The amount in the fund always will depend to some degree on how well the fund is administered.

Some plans now provide for *variable* pensions. These are like variable annuities. The amount of the pension will depend on how well the pension fund was invested and how much its assets are worth at the time the pensioner starts to collect his pension.

Other Financial Arrangements for Retirement

Eligibility requirements, contributions, retirement qualifications, and benefits vary from one plan to the next, as do vesting privileges;* but retirement eligibility at 65 or at the end of 15 years' service is a common provision, and benefits are increasing steadily. Increasingly, they may be expected to form a more important component of retirement income.

Retirement years can be happy years if they are planned for and if planning starts early. The planning must take into consideration the greater problems that will be involved and the higher costs of maintaining mental and physical health, the changed needs, and the income that will be wanted. Social

---

* Vesting privileges allow an employee to quit his job prior to normal retirement age without forfeiting his accrued pension credits.

Security and pensions ordinarily will not provide as much income as is wanted if retirees are not to curtail activities. Consequently, potential retirees, and that includes all those who start to work, should start a systematic investment program that will provide retirement income. Then, when one retires the accumulated assets may be liquidated at the proper rate to yield the desired monthly income. Mutual funds offer such arrangements. Banks, in many cases, through their trust departments, also offer such arrangements. With proper planning, *disinvesting* during retirement years can be effortless if not entirely painless.

Operating as a mature individual in our society involves assuming economic responsibility for one's self and one's dependents. This obligation may necessitate making many a painful decision; but these decisions offer a sense of accomplishment. In addition, assuming one's responsibility as a citizen and contributing member of the societal body may require many decisions regarding how much of what one receives should be retained and accumulated for one's lifetime and how much returned for the common weal. When groups had closer ties, many older people were taken care of by the younger members as a matter of custom. In most European countries and the United States the government, that is, the citizens through their representatives, is now doing, to some extent, what individuals have not been able to do or, in some cases, perhaps would not do for themselves. Many of the impoverished groups over 65 in the United States lost jobs, property, and savings during the 1930's and never rose from the lower-income groups thereafter. Many are women who have never been employed outside of the home. Many are men and women who no longer have employable skills or are no longer employable because of their physical or mental condition. Old-age, survivors', and disability insurance, private pensions, and annuities make living for these groups possible and, if they are sufficient, enjoyable. But, on the whole, the groups who have the higher incomes during retirement years receive income from their investments. If this was the result of their own efforts and judgment, they have acquired so-called psychic income—satisfaction—as well.

QUESTIONS

1. On what grounds can a system of "social security" be justified?
2. What types of benefits are provided for under the Social Security Act?
3. How do "social insurance" and "private insurance" differ?
4. Who in the United States is eligible to receive Old-Age, Survivors', and Disability Insurance benefits under the present law? Explain the requirements that have to be met in order to collect each of these benefits in detail.
5. How do annuities differ from life insurance?
6. Why do people buy annuities? List the advantages and disadvantages of investing in annuities. Would your list be different if you were 60?

7. Identify the various types of annuities that may be purchased. List the advantages and disadvantages of buying each one for the man of 25; for the man of 55.
8. If one assumes that prices will continue to increase at the rate they have, which type of annuity should one purchase? Why can this type of annuity pay more than the others?
9. Why are private pension plans more likely to be found in larger companies than in smaller ones? When is it to an employer's advantage to institute a pension plan? When is it to an employee's advantage to take somewhat less in take-home pay in order to be covered by a pension plan?
10. What are the three most common forms of insured pension plans? Distinguish among them, and point out the possible advantages and disadvantages of each.
11. How do *conventional* and *pattern* pension plans differ?
12. Define *vesting*. What questions about pension plans should an employee ask if he has his choice of two equally desirable jobs with the same wage but different pension plans. He is 25 at the time.
13. Under what act were pension funds safeguarded?
14. What factors should be taken into account in preretirement planning? When should preretirement planning begin?
15. Which expenses are lower and which higher during retirement years for most people? Why?
16. What types of income do not reduce OASDI benefits?
17. What are the most important sources of income for those over 65? Will these sources remain the most important ones in the future? Why, or why not?

SELECTED READINGS

Rights and Responsibilities of Those Who Receive Social Security, Retirement or Survivors Benefits, Social Security Administration, U. S. Dept. of Health, Education, and Welfare, Washington, D. C., 1965.

Burns, Eveline, *Social Security and Public Policy*, McGraw-Hill, New York, 1956.

Carson, John J., and John W. McConnell, *Economic Needs of Older People*, Twentieth Century Fund, New York, 1956.

Close, Kathryn, *Getting Ready to Retire*, Pamphlet No. 182, Public Affairs Committee, New York, latest edition.

What Medicare and the New Social Security Changes Mean To You, Prentice-Hall, Englewood Cliffs, N. J., 1966.

Friedmann, Eugene A., *The Meaning of Work and Retirement*, University of Chicago Press, Chicago, 1954.

"How Annuities Provide Security," *Handbook of Life Insurance*, Chap. 3, Institute of Life Insurance, New York, latest edition.

J. K. Lasser's Your Social Security and Medicare Guide, Simon & Schuster, New York, 1966.

J. K. Lasser Tax Institute, and Sam Shulsky, *Investing for Retirement*, Business Reports, Inc., Larchmont, N. Y., 1957.

Magee, John H., *Life Insurance*, rev. ed., Irwin, Homewood, Ill., Chap. 8.

Matteson, William J., and E. C. Harwood, *Life Insurance and Annuities from the Buyer's Point of View*, American Institute for Economic Research, Great Barrington, Mass., latest edition.

McGill, D. M., *Fundamentals of Private Pensions*, Irwin, Homewood, Ill., 1965.
Moore, Elon H., *The Nature of Retirement*, Macmillan, New York, 1959.
Pension Guide Plan, Commerce Clearing House, New York, 1965.
Pollak, Otto, *The Social Aspects of Retirement*, Irwin, Homewood, Ill., 1956.
Prentice-Hall Social Security Tax Service, Prentice-Hall, Englewood Cliffs, N. J., continuously updated.
Social Security Administration, U. S. Dept. of Health, Education, and Welfare, Washington, D. C., OASDI booklets.
  Social Security and Your Household Employee, No. 21.
  Self-Employment and Social Security, No. 22.
  If You Work after You Start Getting Social Security Benefit Payments, No. 23.
  Good News for Household Workers, No. 24.
  How Does Social Security Affect Farm Families? No. 25d.
  The Social Security Retirement Test for Farm People, No. 25e.
  What If You're Disabled? No. 29a.
  How to Estimate Your Social Security Payments, No. 30.
  Old-Age, Survivors, and Disability Insurance for Employees of State and Local Governments, No. 32.
  Social Security for Clergymen, No. 33h.
  Facts about the Old-Age and Survivors Insurance Trust Fund and the Disability Insurance Trust Fund, No. 36.
  Social Security Amendments of 1960, No. 1960-1.
  Your Social Security, No. 35.
  Free copies of these booklets may be obtained from local Social Security offices or from Washington, D. C.
Turnbull, John G., C. Arthur William, Jr., and Earl F. Cheit, *Economic and Social Security—Public and Private Measures Against Economic Insecurity*, Ronald Press, New York, 1957.

NOTES

1. *Life Insurance Fact Book, 1961*, Institute of Life Insurance, New York, 1962, p. 109.
2. *Social Security Bulletin*, November 1964, pp. 6 and 7.
3. *Statistical Abstract of the United States*, 1966, p. 285.
4. *Ibid.*, p. 343.
5. *Extending Private Pension Coverage*, Hearings before the Subcommittee on Employment and Retirement Incomes of the Special Committee on Aging, U. S. Senate, 89th Congress, First Session, March 4, 1965, Part I, U. S. Government Printing Office, Washington, D. C., 1965, p. 5.
6. *Ibid.*
7. U. S. Bureau of the Census, *Statistical Abstract of the United States: 1965*, Washington, D. C., 1965, p. 347.
8. *Retirement Income of the Aging*, Hearings before the Subcommittee on Retirement Income, Special Committee on Aging, U. S. Senate, July 1961, p. 16, revised to 1965 using Consumer Price Index of the Bureau of Labor Statistics.
9. *Social Security Bulletin*, Statistical Supplement, 1964, p. 76.
10. *Retirement Income of the Aging, op. cit.*, p. 18.

11. *Life Insurance Fact Book, op. cit.,* p. 53.
12. To figure whether the price being paid for an annuity is equitable, (a) find the current rate of interest that can be obtained on relatively riskless investments or savings—assume that it is 5 per cent compounded annually in this case; (b) find the number of years that the annuity income will be needed by consulting an actuarial table on life expectancies—assume that it is 15 years in this instance; and (c) using the formula for computing the present value of a deferred annuity (which is the sum of the present values of each of the annuity payments)

$$m \mid a_{\overline{n}|}$$

where the annuity is payable for n years but deferred m years and a is the present value of an annuity of 1, and an annuity table, compute the present value of the annuity being considered. If what is wanted is $1,200 a year for 15 years, 20 years from now, then

$$20|a_{\overline{15}|}$$
$$= a_{\overline{35}|} - a_{\overline{20}|}$$
$$= 3.91 \times 1200$$

Amazingly, less than $4,800 will buy this annuity which will amount to $18,000 paid in full. Compounding interest causes a sizable accretion.

13. Robert Tilove, *Pension Funds and Economic Freedom,* The Fund for the Republic, 1959, p. 17; and Margaret S. Gordon, *Work and Patterns for Retirement,* University of California, Berkeley, 1961, p. 36.
14. Tilove, *op. cit.,* p. 19.
15. Gordon, *loc. cit.*
16. *Wall Street Journal,* March 21, 1962, p. 26.
17. *Life Insurance Fact Book, op. cit.,* p. 35.
18. *Ibid.,* p. 37.

PROBLEMS AND CASES

1. Assume that a man who has just reached 65 has worked 34 years in "covered" employment and earned more than the maximum amount to which deductions are applicable in all of these years. He retires today. How much will he receive in monthly retirement benefits? If he is married, how much will he and his wife receive? If he dies three years hence, how much will his widow receive in death benefits? Will her benefit payments continue? For how long?
2. Assume that a man of 38 dies. He had maximum coverage under Social Security. How much in Social Security benefits will his wife, who is 32, and his children, who are 10, 7, and 3 years old, receive in all?
3. A man has to decide whether to start receiving his Social Security benefits at 62 or at 65. He has worked seven years in "covered" employment and his wages in his five highest earning years were $4,920, $3,880, $4,800, $4,730, and $4,670. How much will he receive in monthly retirement benefits if he retires

at 62? How much if he retires at 65? If he lives to be 82, which would have been the more profitable course? If he lives to be 69, which choice would have been the more profitable?

4. A woman who has been self-employed and covered by Social Security for ten years becomes disabled by illness and unable to continue working. While employed she contributed the maximum allowable amount each year. How much will she collect in monthly disability benefits? How much will her mother, who is entirely dependent on her, collect?

5. A man of 67 who is collecting retirement benefits earns $120 in two successive months and $1,600 for the year. How will this be deducted from his retirement benefits?

6. A man of 40 decides to buy an annuity. He can pay $100 a month until he is 60 and then he wants to start receiving annuity payments. In view of the fact that he wants to receive maximum income, which type of annuity should he buy? Using Table 16–3, how much will he receive if he buys this type of annuity? If he wants whatever is left in his annuity fund to be paid to his heirs in one lump sum, which type of annuity should he buy? How much will he receive if he buys this type of annuity?

7. A man of 40 is considering changing employment. He is presently under a fixed pension plan, which provides that he may retire at 60 with one-third of his present salary. It is an insured deposit-administration type of plan with vesting privileges. His contemplated employment will pay him $300 a year more in salary at first and will give him a better chance for advancement. The company also has a pension plan. It is not insured, has no vesting privileges, but it provides for variable pensions payable at 65. List all of the factors that he should take into consideration in making his decision. Should he change employment?

8. John Warren is 75. He is entitled to the maximum Social Security payment each month. How much is he receiving a month? If his wife is 72, how much, in total, are they both receiving?

9. Warren is offered a part-time job that pays $200 a month. By how much will his Social Security payment be reduced if he accepts it? Should he?

10. Mrs. Warren falls ill. She is eligible for Medicare, including the medical-insurance benefits. If she is in the hospital for four weeks, incurring hospitalization charges amounting to $1,200 and, in addition, her physician's charges are $238, how much of both sets of charges will be paid for under Medicare? If she enters a convalescent home (an eligible extended-care facility) for three additional weeks, incurring $540 in charges, will these be paid for under Medicare? To what extent?

11. Her doctor visits Mrs. Warren at home, after her return. Is his fee covered under Medicare? Are four subsequent home visits by a nurse, as directed by the doctor, covered? Prescribed diagnostic laboratory tests?

17 ESTATE PLANNING

If a man leaves his estate in an uncertain condition, the lawyers become his heirs.

EDGAR W. HOWE

The ultimate objective of any personal finance program is the planning of one's estate. In planning an estate an individual seeks many things.[1] First, he endeavors to maximize the enjoyment derived from his property during his own lifetime. In the process, he accumulates the estate he wants to leave behind. He then arranges for the disposition of his property in accordance with his wishes and attempts to achieve a minimization of estate taxes and estate shrinkage.

Asset accumulation for the purpose of maximizing one's estate is no longer widely fashionable. It tends to be a secondary goal, at best, in our society. In fact, estate planning has become largely the concern of those who are wealthy and then in their later years. In actuality, in view of the present schedule of estate taxes, it should be the concern of every family with a potential net estate of more than $5,000. For that matter, it should concern everyone who wishes to bequeath his possessions according to his own particular set of preferences.

Estate taxes were designed to prevent an undue concentration of wealth. There is still a prevailing fear in some quarters that families who hold relatively large amounts of wealth can, by passing it on to the younger members, eventually become dynastic. They would thus make the distribution of income in our society more unequal. Therefore, it is likely that estate taxes will increase rather than decrease in the future, rendering estate planning all the more imperative.

BUILDING AN ESTATE

The building of an estate for eventual gift or bequeathal ideally necessitates the consideration of who one's heirs are to be; how much income they will need or want; and how much of the proper assets are required to provide this income. Relatively few estates are built with all these considerations in mind. In most cases, the person acquiring wealth simply follows his chosen or unchosen pattern of accumulation. He gives little or no thought to how his estate or his heirs will be affected.

In addition to the estate one wishes to give away or leave, one has to plan a "living estate." Otherwise one cannot provide for uncommonly large expenditures that cannot be met out of current income while one is alive, such as children's education, weddings, or expensive vacations, and for retirement income. Since retirement planning was discussed thoroughly in the preceding chapter, it is only mentioned here. However, it should be remembered that a bequeathable estate must be built from income and assets that are over and above the sum consumed during one's lifetime.

Objectives

The first objective when building a bequeathable estate should be to make certain that death benefits plus income from accumulated assets will be sufficient to care for the needs of one's dependents. This ordinarily means providing for one's wife during her lifetime and for children until they have completed their full-time schooling and are employed or, in the case of a young woman, married. The assets may be life insurance, savings accounts, annuities, securities, real estate, personal property intended for liquidation, such as art collections, or a business that will continue to have earnings after one dies.

Building an Estate

The second objective—but this is only for the farsighted—involves planning and accumulating so that one's heirs will, in turn, have estates to pass on to their heirs.

Both objectives can be realized only after careful analysis and many exacting decisions. An individual can plan his employment so that he and his surviving dependents will be eligible for maximum benefits under Social Security. He can buy enough of the proper kinds of life insurance to meet his objectives. He can seek employment with firms having the most generous pension and profit-sharing plans, other factors being equal. He can join organizations that offer the benefits desired. He can accumulate the savings accounts, the annuities, and the investments in equities and property that will best serve as a "living estate" and a bequeathable estate. He can go into a successful business that will be there for his heirs. He can consider these possibilities, of course, only if he has the means, the foresight, and the opportunity. However, if he plans and, in each case, knows what and how much is wanted, the means and the opportunity often turn up.

Advisors in Building an Estate

The two advisors most often needed when planning the building of an estate are the life-insurance agent and the investment counselor. The initial plan may be very simple. The young man who takes out a life-insurance policy with a supplementary annuity provision to provide for his wife and children for as long as they will need income is planning and building a substantial estate. If he chooses his advisors well, he may have the maximum amount of insurance and the largest annuity he can afford for the lowest possible cost.

Once life insurance no longer suffices in achieving the particular objectives of the estate planner, investments must be selected. If the proper investments are chosen, they may double or treble in value in 15 to 25 years. For example, any investment that earns 5 per cent compound interest will double in value in slightly less than 15 years. An investment earning 6 per cent compounded will double in value in less than 12 years. The risk must be considered, however, as well as the yield and appreciation.* What is needed is a skilled and completely honest investment counselor who can analyze particular securities and other types of investments intelligently. Considering the amount that can be invested, he can choose those that will yield the maximum amount of income when it is wanted, involve the minimum of risk, and appreciate faster than any competing investments. In the absence of a capable candidate, a mutual fund may be the answer.

* See Chapters 4–8.

DISPOSITION OF AN ESTATE

Once an estate has been accumulated and it is time for its disposition—before or after death—one should, if one has not already done so, make a will. One should also provide for the minimization of estate taxes and take steps to assure that as large an estate as possible will be passed on to future generations. These considerations will be discussed in detail in consecutive order.

The Importance of a Will

If an individual dies intestate, that is, without making a will, his or her property will go to those whom state law designates. Often these will not be the persons one would have chosen as heirs. That is why a will is essential if property not previously disposed of is to be bequeathed after death in accordance with one's wishes.

Statutes of Descent and Distribution

State laws vary, but most of them contain stipulations of the following kind. If there is no will and an unmarried man or woman or widower dies:

1. Property generally is divided between the parents. If one of the parents is dead, the surviving parent inherits the entire estate.
2. If there are no surviving parents, the property is divided among the brothers and sisters. If one of them has died, his or her share is divided equally among his or her children.
3. Where there are no parents or brothers or sisters or their offspring, property will go to the closest relative.
4. If there are no relatives, the property goes to the state.

If a married man or woman dies intestate:

1. If there are no children or grandchildren, a specified amount (often $5,000), plus half of what is left after this amount is deducted from the estate goes to the surviving spouse. The remainder goes to the parents of the deceased. If the parents are not alive, the surviving spouse may inherit the entire estate.
2. If there are children, one third or one half goes to the surviving spouse, the remainder to the children. In addition, in some states where homestead or dower or curtesy laws exist, the real property will remain the surviving spouse's to the extent prescribed.
3. If the surviving parent dies, the property is divided equally among

the children. Descendants of deceased children divide their parents' share equally.

Not leaving a will ordinarily is very disadvantageous. It may result in property going to someone who does not need it. Wealthy parents have received estates, while second wives and their children have been left penniless. If children under 21 inherit property, a guardian will have to be appointed. This involves the expense of a bond for the guardian and an annual accounting to the probate court. Consequently, the surviving parent, even if he or she is appointed the guardian, will have less to spend on the children. In addition, if persons appear who claim to be heirs, there may be long and costly legal proceedings which diminish the estate of the genuine heirs. Finally, without a will, taxes on an estate rarely can be minimized—an important consideration.

Drawing up the Will

Each state stipulates the minimum age at which one may draw up a will. The minima are generally 18 or 21. In every state, the person making the will must be of sound mind insofar as the court can ascertain.

A will cannot be too precise, and there are many legal formalities that should be observed to prevent misunderstandings and contests later when the will is being probated. Most important, though, to its legal validity, a will must be signed and witnessed—in some states by two and in others by three witnesses. A handwritten or *holographic* will that is signed but unwitnessed may be held valid, however, and may be sufficient if no significant amounts of property are involved. A form of will that serves most purposes is shown in Figure 17–1.

Wills are written in a language that is entirely their own. The following are the ordinarily unfamiliar terms often used in them.

Administrator: The person or institution that the court will appoint to manage and distribute the estate of a person who does not leave a will.

Beneficiary: One who is willed property.

Bequeath: To give personal property.

Codicil: A provision added to a will after it is first written. It makes a change. Any change should be made in a codicil, since alterations are not permitted.

Decedent: One who died.

Devise: To give real property. A devisee receives real property.

Executor: The person or institution named in the will to carry out the provisions of the will. A woman is an executrix.

Legatee: One who receives personal property under a will.

Figure 17-1. **Example of a will.**

LAST WILL AND TESTAMENT

I, ..., a resident of
...., State,
declare this to be my last Will and revoke all other Wills previously made by me:

FIRST: I direct that my legal debts be paid as soon as they can be practicably after my death.

Second: I give and bequeath to (relationship) (name) the sum of ...

.... (Additional bequests)

Sixth: The remainder of my estate I give, devise and bequeath to ...

........................: I appoint ....

as Execut............ of this Will ....

This Will was signed by me on the .... day of ...., 19......,
at ...., State.

THE FOREGOING INSTRUMENT was, on the date thereof, signed by the test........................,
...., in our presence, we being present at the same time, and ....he then declared to us that the said instrument was h........ last Will; and we, at the request of said ...., and in h........ presence, and in the presence of each other, have signed the same as witnesses. We further declare that at the time of signing this will the said .... appeared to be of sound and disposing mind and memory and not acting under duress, menace, fraud or the undue influence of any person whomsoever.

.... residing at ....
    Signature of Witness
.... residing at ....
    Signature of Witness
.... residing at ....
    Signature of Witness

Noncupative will: An oral will uttered by someone who is dying, or by a soldier or sailor during combat. The witness is required to write what was said and present the will for *probate*—proof of validity—before a designated period of time has expired.

Probate: The court that has jurisdiction over Wills and Estates. It is known as the Surrogate court in some areas.

Real property: Immovable property, that is, land and buildings.

Testate: Having left a will.

Testator: One who makes a will. A woman is a testatrix.

It is recommended as a matter of custom that every will include a directive that debts and funeral expenses be paid; instructions concerning the disposition of one's remains; detailed specifications on how and to whom real and personal property is to be distributed; stipulations as to charitable bequests; designation of an executor and a guardian of minor children, if there are any; detailed instructions on the setting up of trusts and foundations where applicable; and whatever final word one wishes to have others hear. In a sense, it is one's last chance to tell anyone anything. When a significant amount of property is involved and especially when trusts and foundations are being established, the advice of an attorney who is a specialist in wills and estates should be sought.

Changing or Revoking a Will

It is important to revise a will whenever one marries, when a child is born or adopted, when one's spouse dies or one is divorced, or when one has any other good reason for changing bequests and devises. A child born after a will is made and not mentioned in the will receives nothing. Changes or additions may be made in a *codicil,* or the entire will may be rewritten. If the earlier will is revoked, a statement to that effect should appear in the later will. Any will bearing a later date and differing materially from an earlier one usually will be held to be the "last will" in court. If a testator destroys a will or it is found in such condition that it would seem he intended to destroy it, it is deemed to have been revoked.

Safeguarding a Will

Much may depend on a will. Consequently, it should be carefully safeguarded. Yet it should not be kept in a safe-deposit box, since in most states the box will be sealed upon the death of the testator and remain sealed until such time as it is opened in the presence of a state-tax official. It is not even a good idea for a husband and a wife to keep their wills in each other's safe-deposit boxes. Both may die within a relatively short time. The safest procedure is to file the will with an attorney, with the trust department of a bank, or to keep it in a strongbox at one's home or office—provided that one has left a letter of instructions with an attorney giving the whereabouts of the will.

Letter of Instructions

Few persons expect to die when they do and, therefore, relatively few leave their affairs in perfect order. Those who have to administer an estate or take care of what is left often find themselves without the necessary information on which to proceed. To facilitate their job, it is advisable to leave a letter of instructions that contains the following information:

1. Names and addresses of those to be notified at death, and relationship of members of family and relatives.
2. Location of the will.
3. Names and addresses of physician, attorney, insurance broker, accountant, investment counselor, stockbroker, employer, and all business associates.
4. Location of safe-deposit boxes and keys to them.
5. List of bank accounts and location of passbooks.
6. List of all savings accounts, other than bank accounts, and passbook locations.
7. Location of cash not deposited.
8. List of stocks and bonds owned and location, if not in safe-deposit box.
9. Location of deeds, mortgages, abstracts, and insurance policies for real property owned, if not in safe-deposit box.
10. List of insurance policies, especially life, and location of policies.
11. Locations of any trusts and retirement systems in which one has an interest.
12. Location of birth certificate or other evidence of birth; marriage license or licenses, and other personal papers; Social Security number and card; certificates of automobile ownership; and other proofs of ownership.
13. Location of all personal property.
14. Location of copies of income tax returns for the previous five years.
15. Location of receipted bills and canceled checks for the previous five years.
16. List of debts, and names and addresses of all creditors.
17. Additional names and addresses that may be needed—relatives not to be notified upon death, but who may appear when the will is probated; former spouses, and others.
18. List of any gifts made, information concerning which will be needed to file the estate-tax return.

19. A list of any prepayments that may have been made, especially for funeral arrangements.

20. Any instructions that concern the disposal of the remains. This is often a better place for these instructions than the will.

Birth certificates are important documents when one dies. Life-insurance companies require them as evidence that one was born when the policy stated, and the collection of death benefits may be delayed until the beneficiary can furnish evidence of the birth of the insured. For that matter, every document referred to in the letter of instructions is important to the administrator of an estate. Therefore, the letter should be left with one's spouse, and copies of it filed with one's attorney and the person designated as the executor of one's estate.

The above list is not all-inclusive. Some may wish to add the groups to which they belong. Almost everyone will find an omission if he carefully considers his own personal affairs. These items should be included. Even with all of the necessary information, an executor may have a trying ordeal in settling an estate. In fact, there have been instances of securities or jewelry known to exist and to be part of the estate never being found.

Probate

The official process of proving a will genuine is known as probating the will. Until a will is accepted as genuine, an estate is "in probate." Special probate courts, which have jurisdiction over wills and take proof of their validity, exist in each state.

Duties of an Executor or Administrator

An executor, the person so designated in a will, or the administrator, who is appointed if there is no will, is expected to act as if he were the person who died and "wind up" his affairs in responsible fashion. He is entirely accountable for carrying out the deceased person's plans for the disposition and distribution of the estate. Should the person designated as executor be unable or unwilling to take on the responsibility, the *alternate executor*, if one has been named in the will, inherits the obligation. If there is no alternate, the probate court will appoint an "Administrator with Will Annexed" to dispose of the estate under the terms of the will.

An executor or an administrator may be an individual, a bank, or a trust company. In some cases, coexecutors are named. If there are several, and coordinating their activities and decisions gives rise to problems, a bank may be appointed to act as agent for the coexecutors.

Fees for Services. Executors and administrators are paid for their services. Fees vary from state to state, but normally they are higher for smaller estates and lower for larger ones. In many states they are set at 7 per cent of the first $1,000 of an estate; 4 per cent of the next $9,000; and then progressively less until, for estates of over $500,000, they are only 1 per cent per $1,000. In addition, the probate court may allow "reasonable" fees for any "extraordinary" services; and in many states there is an appraiser's fee to be paid to a court-appointed appraiser who estimates the value of the assets in the estate. Some of the additional fees may seem unduly high at times. They will always cause some shrinkage in the assets of the estate.

Duties. If he has done his job conscientiously, there is little doubt that an executor has earned his fee, for his duties include:

1. Assembling all of the estate's assets and preparing an accurate inventory of them.

2. Having the assets of the estate properly appraised. Where not required by state law and where the bulk of the assets consists of marketable securities on which quotations can be obtained without charge from any reputable brokerage firm, or of any other assets whose value can be estimated accurately by the executor, a proper appraisal need not require an outside appraiser.

3. Preparing and filing, at the proper times, of estate, inheritance, and income tax returns; paying the taxes required by such returns; and obtaining the proper clearance of all tax matters.

4. Giving adequate protection to all of the assets of the estate.

5. Approving or rejecting claims filed against the estate, obtaining court approval, where necessary, of claims and paying the amounts approved.

6. Defending actions on rejected claims.

7. Maintaining adequate insurance in insurable estate property.

8. Keeping all improved real property rented and repaired.

9. Paying all real and personal property taxes when due.

10. Collecting income due and managing the investments of the estate prudently.

11. Selling property when necessary to pay taxes, claims, expenses, and bequests.

12. Operating, liquidating, or both, any business belonging to the estate.

13. Keeping an accurate record of receipts and disbursements and, when the estate is ready to close, submitting to the court a detailed statement on these matters, together wih a complete account of all acts performed as executor or administrator.

14. Distributing the estate in accordance with the court's orders.

If the executor or the administrator is not an attorney or an accountant, and the estate is at all complex, he will require the services of one or both. If he is not experienced, he may turn the task over to a bank or trust company that handles estates routinely. However, it should be remembered that, if the executor or administrator or his agent fails to perform the duties for which he is responsible in a proper manner, he may be held personally liable.

Duties of a Guardian

A *guardian* should not be confused with an executor or an administrator. Guardians of estates are appointed by the court of jurisdiction to deal with and manage the property of minors and of persons who, by reason of old age, physical handicap, or mental illness, are unable to deal properly with their own property. Because such persons are said to be under "legal disability," their interests and rights are guarded by the courts. Strict accounting is required of guardians. Approval of the court must be granted before they may purchase or sell property under their guardianship or spend any of the guardianship funds.

Guardians post bonds in an amount fixed by the court. They are paid fees fixed by the court as reasonable compensation for the duties performed and the responsibilities assumed. Banks and trust companies may be appointed guardians. In view of their experience, it often may be advisable to use them.

MINIMIZING ESTATE TAXES

Proper planning can result in estate taxes being materially reduced. Estates are subject to the federal-estate tax and to state-estate and inheritance taxes. An estate tax is a tax on the estate. An inheritance tax is a tax on the beneficiaries or heirs who receive bequests.

Federal-Estate Tax

The federal-estate tax is a tax on the right to transfer the estate. It applies to the *net estate* of the deceased.

The Gross Estate. All property of the deceased person, real and personal, tangible and intangible, is included in his *gross estate*. Insofar as life insurance is concerned, if he retained any of the incidents of ownership in the policy,* it, too, is included in the gross estate. His or her share of any property owned jointly is included. Property in *revocable trusts*,** *testamentary trusts*, and

---

* Incidents of ownership in a life-insurance policy include the rights to dispose of its proceeds.
** Trusts are explained later in this chapter.

even in *irrevocable trusts* is included, if the deceased retained the right to alter the terms of the trust or received any benefit from it. Gifts made within three years of death, unless it can be proven that they were not made in contemplation of death, are included.

The Net Estate. To compute the amount of the *net estate* that is subject to the federal-estate tax, there may be deducted from the gross estate: the expenses of the last illness of the decedent, the funeral expenses, the debts of the decedent, and all probate and administrative expenses connected with the estate, including all legal fees. The remainder is the *adjusted-gross estate.*

If the decedent was married, a *marital deduction,* amounting to one-half of the adjusted gross estate, provided that the decedent willed one-half or more of the estate to the surviving spouse, also may be taken. The assumption underlying the marital deduction is that each member of a married couple owns half of the jointly owned property. If a surviving spouse is willed *less* than one-half of the estate, the marital deduction will be *one-half of the willed amount.*

Deductions may then be made for any bequests to qualified charitable and other religious, educational, health, or welfare groups or organizations to which gifts may be presented tax-free. Trusts and foundations will be discussed presently.

Credit on Previous Bequests. If property has been part of an estate on which the federal-estate tax has been paid within the preceding ten years, a credit will be allowed against the federal-estate tax otherwise due on the property. If the estate tax had been levied within the preceding two to four years, the credit allowed is 80 per cent; four to six years, 60 per cent; six to eight years, 40 per cent; and eight to ten years, 20 per cent.

Credit for State Taxes. Estate or inheritance taxes paid to states may be deducted from the amount due as federal-estate tax, up to the limits shown in Table 17–1. The table does not include all tax brackets. Furthermore, estates of certain specified servicemen are subject to different credits. In computing their taxes, executors should refer to Sections 2011(d) and 2201 of the Internal Revenue Code. The complete table from which Table 17–1 was abstracted is contained in Section 2011 of the Internal Revenue Code.

The rate of tax credit graduates progressively to offset the ascent of state-estate and inheritance taxes. The credit shown in the table is the maximum amount deductible. The actual amount to be deducted is what has been paid as a state-inheritance or estate tax, or the amount shown in the table, whichever may be smaller.

Table 17-1. **State Death Tax Credit**

Taxable Estate (after Deducting the $60,000 Exemption) From	To	Tax Credit Equals	Plus Per Cent	Of Excess Over
0	$ 40,000	0	0.0	0
40,000	90,000	0	0.8	40,000
90,000	140,000	400	1.6	90,000
140,000	240,000	1,200	2.4	140,000
440,000	640,000	10,000	4.0	440,000
840,000	1,040,000	27,600	5.6	840,000
1,540,000	2,040,000	70,800	7.2	1,540,000
4,040,000	5,040,000	290,800	11.2	4,040,000
10,040,000	—	1,082,800	16.0	10,040,000

Federal-Estate Tax Rates. The federal-estate tax is sharply progressive. Tax rates vary from 3 per cent on estates of less than $5,000 to 77 per cent on estates over $10,000,000 as Table 17–2 indicates.

Table 17-2. **Federal Estate Tax Rates**

Taxable Estate (after Deducting the $60,000 Exemption) From	To	Tax Equals	Plus Per Cent	Of Excess Over
0	$ 5,000	0	3	0
5,000	10,000	150	7	5,000
10,000	20,000	500	11	10,000
20,000	30,000	1,600	14	20,000
30,000	40,000	3,000	18	30,000
40,000	50,000	4,800	22	40,000
50,000	60,000	7,000	25	50,000
60,000	100,000	9,500	28	60,000
100,000	250,000	20,700	30	100,000
250,000	500,000	65,700	32	250,000
500,000	750,000	145,500	35	500,000
1,000,000	1,250,000	325,700	39	1,000,000
2,000,000	2,500,000	753,200	49	2,000,000
5,000,000	6,000,000	2,468,200	67	5,000,000
10,000,000	—	6,088,200	77	10,000,000

The complete table from which Table 17-2 was abstracted is contained in Section 2001 of the 1954 Internal Revenue Code. In computing taxes, reference should be made to the Code.

Estate Tax Computation. The federal estate tax on the estate of a single decedent with a gross estate of $235,000 would be computed as shown in Table 17-3.

Table 17-3

Gross amount of estate		$235,000
Deduct:		
Exemption	$60,000	
Funeral, probate, administrative expenses, etc.	30,000	
Charitable bequests	10,000	
Total deductions and exemption		100,000
Taxable estate or net estate		$135,000
Tax rates:[a]		
Tax on $100,000		$ 20,700
Tax on additional $35,000		10,500
Total tax		$ 31,200
Less credit for state death taxes:[b]		
Credit on $90,000	$ 400	
Credit on additional $45,000	720	
Total credit		$ 1,120
Net tax		$ 30,080

[a] From Table 17-2.
[b] From Table 17-1.

If the deceased person had been married, and his wife had survived him, the federal-estate tax would have been computed as shown in Table 17-4. The difference is explained by the allowable marital deduction. In this case, the *adjusted gross estate* was $235,000 less $30,000 paid on debts and allowable expenses, or $205,000. One-half of $205,000, or $102,500, was the allowable marital deduction. Obviously, taxes on a net or taxable estate of $32,500 are far less than on a taxable estate of $135,000, since the estate is in a much lower tax bracket. Since the rates progress so sharply, the drop in the tax in the latter instance is more than proportional.

STATE-INHERITANCE AND ESTATE TAXES

There is an inheritance or estate tax in every state in the United States except Nevada. However, those who move to Nevada to escape estate or inheri-

Table 17-4

Gross amount of estate		$235,000
Deduct:		
Exemption	$60,000	
Funeral, probate, administrative expenses, allowed claims, debts	30,000	
Charitable bequests	10,000	
Transfers to surviving spouse	102,500 (marital deductions)	
Total deductions and exemption		$202,500
Taxable estate		$ 32,500
Tax rates:[a]		
Tax on $30,000	$ 3,000	
Tax on additional $2,500	450	
Total tax		$ 3,450
Less credit for state death taxes:[b]		
Credit on amounts under $40,000		none
Net tax		$ 3,450

[a] From Table 17–2.
[b] From Table 17–1.

tance taxes should remember that there will be no state death-tax credit to offset federal-estate taxes. Consequently, taxes against estates will be almost as high as if they lived in another state because they will be taxed at a higher rate in a higher bracket.

The Inheritance Tax. Inheritance taxes vary from state to state. Allowable deductions from the gross estate also vary. However, expenses involved in the settlement of the estate and whatever was paid to clear debts are deductible under any of the state laws.

Both the allowable exemptions and the tax rates tend to vary according to the closeness of the relationship of the heirs and beneficiaries. In all cases, the tax rates mount progressively. In some states they may be as high as 20 per cent of the net estate after the exemption has been deducted. Table 17–5 shows a typical inheritance tax-rate schedule.

All of the property in the estate that was owned by the deceased and that was over the amount of the exemption ordinarily is subject to tax except for the proceeds of life-insurance policies. These are exempted to a greater or lesser extent, according to the state. Real property and tangible personal property usually are taxed in the state where they are located. Securities and other intangible personal property are taxed as a rule by the state in which

Table 17-5. Typical State-Inheritance Tax Rates

Relationship to Decedent	Exemption (Dollars)	Tax Rates on Net Estate under $25,000	$25,000 to $50,000	$50,000 to $100,000	$100,000 to $200,000	$200,000 and Over
Widow	24,000	2%	3%	4%	7%	10%
Minor children	12,000	2	3	4	7	10
Husband, parents, grandparents, other children	5,000	2	3	4	7	10
Brother, sister, niece, nephew, son-in-law, daughter-in-law	2,000	5	7	10	12	15
Uncle, aunt, cousin	500	6	9	12	12	15
Other	50	7	10	12	12	16

NOTE: Maximum rates vary from about 10 to 20 per cent. Property that has been taxed by the same state under the provisions of the inheritance tax within the previous five years ordinarily will not be taxed a second time.

the deceased resided. Where he had homes in more than one state, his estate may be subject to tax in each.

The Estate Tax. In states where there is an estate tax, in addition to an inheritance tax, the purpose of the estate tax is to bring the *total* state taxes on an estate up to the amount of the *maximum credit* allowable under the federal estate-tax law. Rates vary, but they generally succeed in their purpose. Property that has been given away within the two or three years preceding death generally is held to have been given away in anticipation of death. Such property usually is subject to the inheritance tax, and where they exist, to estate taxes.

Trusts

Assets in personal trusts at banks and trust companies totaled over 62 billion dollars at the end of 1960.[2] This was about three times the total assets of this country's mutual investment funds.

A trust is a contract under which the *settlor, grantor,* or *trustor,* that is, the one who establishes a trust, places assets that he owns under the control of a *trustee* for the benefit of a beneficiary or beneficiaries. Trustees may be individuals or institutions such as banks and trust companies. Designation of a bank or trust company as trustee assures greater permanency of the trust. Normally it provides better facilities for and more experience in the handling of trusts.

Beneficiaries who receive income from trust funds during their lifetime are known as *life tenants* or *income beneficiaries*. Those who are designated to receive the principal when the trust terminates are known as *remaindermen*.

Trustees are required to invest trust funds so that income will be at *a maximum consistent with the safety of the principal*. The trustor may stipulate the types of securities or property in which trust funds may be invested. Otherwise the trustee is limited to those investments permitted by the laws and regulations of the state having jurisdiction, and state laws tend to be conservative; most states do not permit investment in common stocks. Consequently, income earned may be lower. Trustees are responsible for trust funds. Nevertheless, they are not personally liable for losses sustained if they act as a prudent man would under the circumstances and not in a fraudulent or careless manner.

The laws of the various states stipulate how trustees are to be paid and in what amounts. The rates vary among the states, but generally they are based on a sliding scale, so that the larger the trust fund, the higher the fee. A typical fee for the average trust fund is 0.6 per cent of the value of personal property other than obligations secured by real estate, and 0.75 per cent of the value of such obligations and of real property held in the trust.

In most states, trusts cannot exist more than 21 years and 9 months after the death of the last survivor among the beneficiaries mentioned in the trust agreement. In some states, they must be terminated sooner. Those who will benefit from *revocable living* trusts must be alive when the trust agreement is drawn and those who will benefit from *irrevocable* and *testamentary* trusts, when the trustor dies.

The three types of trusts of major concern in estate planning are living trusts, testamentary trusts, and life-insurance trusts.

Living Trusts. The living trust becomes effective as soon as it is established by the trustor or donor. The beneficiary may start to receive income from the trust immediately thereafter. Establishing a living trust involves only a simple agreement among donor, trustee, and beneficiary. It may be used when the trustor wishes someone else to manage his financial affairs because he is too busy or does not feel competent to do so. This applies to many a high-income recipient. Or it may be used to minimize income taxes and estate taxes.

Property that is part of a living trust is not subject to the laws of descent and distribution upon death of the donor. If the trust agreement so provides, it will remain the beneficiary's. Ofter he or she is not the one who would receive it under the law.

In addition, trust agreements are not a matter of public record. Wills are. If the trustor wishes to be discreet, property should be transferred by means of a living trust—not willed. And, since property transferred to a living trust established for a beneficiary or beneficiaries may not be part of a trustor's estate, ultimately there may be less in probate fees to be paid.

Living trusts may be revocable or irrevocable. A revocable trust may be nullified at any time. The high-income recipient probably would be prudent to establish a revocable trust, since most likely he would want to retain the right to reclaim his property when and if he should desire to do so. However, there are few tax benefits to be derived from establishing a revocable trust. Since the property still would be his, the trustor may pay income tax on all trust income, even that paid to the beneficiaries. The income paid to beneficiaries will be considered gifts subject to gift taxes.

The principal of the revocable trust, or what remains of it, becomes part of the donor's estate and is subject to the estate tax. Subsequently, if the original beneficiary or beneficiaries die, but the trust continues for the benefit of other beneficiaries, no estate taxes will be paid by the original beneficiaries' estates. Nor will any be paid by succeeding beneficiaries as long as the trust continues in effect.

Irrevocable trusts may be short-term or long-term. Property in a short-term irrevocable trust, if the beneficiary is a person, must not revert to the trustor for ten years if he is to take advantage of the tax law which holds that *income from irrevocable trusts is not taxable as part of the trustor's income.* If the beneficiary is a religious, educational, research, or welfare organization, or a hospital, the income will not be taxed as part of the grantor's income unless the reversion takes effect within two years. Long-term irrevocable trusts are those that remain in effect for more than ten years.

Generally speaking, if the trustor derives direct benefits from the trust or retains the power to administer its assets as though it were still his own property, he will lose his tax benefits. However, he may withhold income from a beneficiary temporarily if it will be paid later. He may also borrow from the trust if he pays competitive rates of interest and gives adequate security for the loan.

Several well-known *college-investment plans* are living irrevocable-trust arrangements. Under these, the donor transfers property to the college for a period exceeding two years. There is no tax on the transfer, since it is being placed in trust for an educational institution. Should he die, if he has not reclaimed the property, it becomes an addition to the college's endowment fund, and it will be no part of his estate. In fact, the amount of the "contribution" will be deducted from the remainder of his estate in computing the amount of his taxable estate. The college or its agent under this plan acts as trustee and pays the donor during his lifetime whatever percentage of the income earned from this property he may specify, up to 100 per cent. Normally he will specify an amount that will enable him to live as he wishes but not put him in too high a tax bracket. Thus he may have a relatively well-assured retirement income without having to manage his own investments and also minimize his estate taxes.

Many families use irrevocable living trusts to minimize taxes. For example, assume that the parents filing joint income tax returns are in the 50 per cent tax bracket and want to set aside funds for a son's college education. If they invest $10,000 at 5 per cent, they would owe $250 a year, approximately, in income tax—50 per cent of $500. In ten years, the college fund, not considering the $10,000 principal, would amount to $2,500.

An estate or trust is a separate taxable entity and pays taxes as though it were an individual in the applicable income-tax bracket. If the $10,000 were transferred to an irrevocable living trust, it would have the same $500 yearly income at 5 per cent, but only $400 would be taxable. The trust has a $100 trust exemption. At the 20 per cent tax rate, the trust pays $80 a year in federal taxes. Thus the trust's $500 income produces $420 of income after taxes. In ten years, the college fund would be $4,200 instead of $2,500.

Many parents buy property or other investments and place them in irrevocable living trusts for their children. The income from the investments then belongs to the children who pay income taxes in their own lower-tax brackets. The parents do not lose the $600 income-tax exemption if they continue to contribute more than half of the children's support each year.

Say a family in the 50 per cent income-tax bracket also has an aged relative and has set aside a stock fund to contribute to his support. If the investment income from this fund were $2,600 a year, with the 50 per cent tax rate and a $200 dividend exclusion (if both husband and wife received dividends and took the $100 exclusion), and no other deductions and exemptions are considered, there would be $1,200 a year left. Instead, suppose that they set up an irrevocable living trust for the relative, using enough money to produce $1,200 a year for his support—the same amount as invested before. If he has $600 in other dividend income and Social Security, which is tax exempt, his total taxable income will be $1,800 a year. On this he will pay a tax of about $63 a year, or $630 in ten years.

This leaves a trust income of $1,400—$2,600 less $1,200—since *income paid out to beneficiaries is not part of taxable trust income.* On this, the trust pays about $480 in taxes, or $4,800 in ten years. The total taxes paid by the trust and the relative in ten years is $5,430, that is, $4,800 plus $630. This should be compared with the $12,000 or so that would have been paid in income tax had there been no trust.

Living trusts are flexible. They can be used to transfer property for a period of years, have income paid to another person or institution for a period of years, and then have the property or the income revert to the trustor. Or they can be used to arrange for the disposition of property at whatever time the donor specifies. This may occur, for example, when beneficiaries marry, have children, die, or when the trustor dies. *The trustor may also be the trustee*, or his wife may be made trustee when he dies.

The living trust remains in effect upon the donor's death. It thus avoids the probate delays of a testamentary trust. If the amount put in trust when the trust is established is above the gift-tax exemption, the gift tax will have to be paid, but gift taxes are lower than estate taxes. If the living irrevocable trust is in effect upon the death of the trustor, as previously indicated, his taxable estate is less by the amount of the trust, and thus the estate tax is lower.

Testamentary Trusts. Testamentary trusts are provided for in a will and are not established until after the death of the trustor. In many instances, the executor of the will also will be the trustee, but this is not always the case.

The testamentary trust is part of the estate. There is no immediate estate-tax advantage in leaving the property in trust. Ordinarily, the trust is established because the trustor deems the trustee more capable of managing financial affairs than his beneficiary or beneficiaries. Or he may want to preserve a greater portion of the estate for future generations.

If a testamentary trust is established for the benefit of a minor child, no guardian need be appointed. A saving results because the trustee's fee usually will be less than a guardian's fee. In addition, trustees have wider latitude in managing property. They do not have to account to a probate court.

A testamentary trust does result in an estate-tax advantage when heirs and beneficiaries die in subsequent years. For example, if the original trustor establishes a testamentary trust from which his wife will receive the entire income during her lifetime, then their children during their lifetime, and thereafter their grandchildren during their lifetime, no further estate tax would be paid on the property in trust until the grandchildren died. There would be only one transfer of property—when the trustor died—upon which estate taxes had to be paid.

Life-Insurance Trusts. Life-insurance trusts are actually one specific form of testamentary trust. This type provides that upon the death of the insured, the proceeds from insurance policies will be left with the insurance company. Only the interest income or specified periodic payment from the proceeds plus interest will be paid to the beneficiary or beneficiaries. Or the proceeds will be turned over to a bank, trust company, or individual trustee to invest for the benefit of the beneficiary or beneficiaries. This type of trust is advantageous when the beneficiary is not adept at financial management.

There is little or no advantage in establishing this type of trust when policies are small. The income that could be earned on the principal sum would be insufficient to contribute substantially to the support of the beneficiaries. In the case of larger policies, whether the proceeds are to be left with the insurance company or placed in trust with a bank or trust company poses a problem.

If left with an insurance company, the funds will be segregated from the other assets of the company. Since establishing a life-insurance trust in many respects resembles buying an annuity for beneficiaries, the insured should consider the proceeds as being used to acquire an annuity in the event of his death. If the proceeds of the policy plus interest were simply paid out to beneficiaries for as long as they lasted, the interest paid by the insurance company rarely would exceed 4 per cent. The proceeds would be paid for only as long as they lasted after the insured's death, not necessarily when or as long as they were needed. Providing for use of the proceeds to acquire an annuity that will provide income until children are 21, for example, or during the years when they are in college, ordinarily is better practice. An increasing number of life-insurance policies do precisely this. But, unless a *variable annuity* were acquired, returns may be lower than if the proceeds were left in trust with a professional trustee. Life-insurance companies are even more severely limited under the law than trustees in the type of investments they can make.

Custodian Accounts

A custodian account permits the donor of securities, a member of his family or, in most states, an agent of the donor outside the family, such as a bank or trust company, to serve as a custodian of stocks owned by a child. The custodian may sell the stocks, and reinvest the proceeds and the income received on stocks owned from year to year.

The various states have placed some limitations on the activities of custodians. A custodian cannot legally use a child's money to buy stocks on margin, for example. However, these limitations are few and reasonable.

If a parent uses his own money and not custodial-account money to support the child who owns the stock, the annual income from the securities in the custodial account are taxed as the child's. He files his own return each April, no matter how young he may be, and pays an income tax in his own bracket. This may mean a very low income tax or none at all. Since he is allowed one exemption for himself and the customary dividend exclusions, where the custodial account is composed of stocks in United States corporations, no federal tax is due on the first $770 of income. In addition, even though a parent may serve as a custodian for a child's income-producing account, he will still retain his $600 tax exemption for the child as long as he continued to provide over half of the child's support and the child is under 19 or is a full-time student.

When the child reaches 21, the property in the custodial account becomes his. No formal accounting is required. However, if more than $3,000 is placed by each parent in a single year in the child's account, and if the parents have exceeded the total of $30,000 that may be given away by each person during his lifetime without being subject to a gift tax, then the gift tax will apply to the amount transferred to the custodial account in excess of the exclusions.

Should the donor die, the securities in the child's account are not part of his estate. Estate taxes consequently will be less. And, since setting up a custodial account avoids the costs of selecting and appointing trustees, of drafting formal trust agreements, of periodic accountings required of trusts, and of trustees' fees, the estate will be larger.

Foundations

One of the means of minimizing federal-estate taxes is the establishment of a foundation. A foundation is a nonprofit organization with its own capital fund that is supposed to use its resources solely for public welfare. It may be a state-chartered corporation, a trust, or an unincorporated association. If it is properly set up, with a special Treasury-approved tax status, it pays no federal taxes at all.

The motive behind the establishment of most private foundations is the retention of control over wealth. In a typical case, there may be a family-owned business worth so much that upon the owner's death it normally would be subject to an estate tax of 35 per cent or more. The estate tax could cause a forced sale of part or even all of the business. Heirs might lose control of the firm and might have to sell their shares at a poor price. The owner, anticipating these contingencies, may establish a foundation. The foundation may use its income for any purpose "in the public interest" as authorized under Section 501(a) of the Internal Revenue Code. Year by year, the owner may make gifts of the company stock to the foundation, and these qualify as charitable bequests. Ordinarily, he will continue this practice until the value of his remaining holdings are down to the point where eventual estate taxes could be paid without undue strain or at which the foundation's holdings constituted firm control of the company. He and those he has designated control the foundation and direct its activities. Thus he still controls the shares he has donated. When he dies, control of the foundation passes to those he has named, and they, in turn, also continue to control the business. In addition, since whatever he leaves to the foundation qualifies as a charitable bequest, it will be deducted from his gross estate when calculating the amount of his taxable estate.

When Henry Ford died in 1947, he left 1,805,000 shares of nonvoting Ford Motor Company stock to the Ford Foundation. There was no tax on this bequest, and it was deducted from his gross estate and consequently was not included in his net or taxable estate. Some 95,000 shares of voting stock were left to his heirs. Thus the family has retained control of the business; and, since the directors of the foundation reflect the family's philanthropic philosophy to some extent, the uses to which the family's money have been put are probably in accordance with its preferences.

There are a few additional advantages in establishing a foundation. A foundation usually can handle charitable bequests more efficiently than an individual who may not give them his full attention. And, if donations to the foundation are made in more prosperous high-income years, they will result in higher contributions when they are needed as tax deductions. Furthermore, distributing this money to charities in less prosperous years may result in adding to the philanthropic effectiveness of the donations.

Second, foundations may be established for the benefit of employees of the founder's firm and thus result in an improvement of employees' morale and productivity.

Third, the founder or members of his family may deal privately with a foundation, provided that the transactions can be considered to improve the income or asset position of the foundation. For example, if any of them borrows money from the foundation, adequate security must be provided and reasonable rates of interest must be paid, just as though the borrower were dealing with an appropriate financial institution. The foundation may employ the founder and members of his family and pay them "reasonable" compensation. However, if the foundation is found to have been established simply for private benefit and its income is not being used solely for the public welfare, it may lose its tax-exempt status or even its charter.

Since the tax advantages enjoyed are approximately the same as if the amount donated to a foundation had been contributed directly to charity, high-income families often consider the establishment of foundations when planning to minimize estate taxes.

Accumulating Treasury Bonds

Certain Treasury bonds and certificates will be redeemed by the government at par for payment of estate taxes. From time to time, these may be purchased at a discount. The series of bonds or certificates available, the interest rate paid, and the discounts will, of course, vary from one period to another. Securities must be owned by the decedent at the time of his death if they are to be used for payment of estate taxes at par. Therefore, if an individual anticipates having to pay an estate tax in the not too distant future, he might investigate the market for these Treasury obligations.

Gifts

The most effective method of minimizing estate taxes is to give away one's property while one is alive. Gifts and gift-tax rates and exemptions have been mentioned before, but the main points to consider when making gifts in order to minimize estate taxes are reiterated here.

First, the $3,000 annual gift allowances permitted for each recipient under the law—$6,000 when a couple makes the gift—are unlimited in number. They may apply to any number of recipients each year.

Second, the $30,000 additional lifetime-gift allowance—$60,000 for a couple giving jointly—may be used at any time. It is entirely separate from and in addition to the annual allowances.

Third, half of any gift from a husband to a wife or from a wife to a husband is tax-free under the marital deduction.

There are some restrictive rulings regarding tax-free gifts. A gift made within three years of the taxpayer's death may and is likely to be ruled an action "in contemplation of death" and consequently taxed as part of the estate. It is well to check the other restrictive rulings before embarking on a program of systematic giving.

Nonetheless, in spite of graduated gift taxes—they range from 2.25 per cent to 57.75 per cent—almost any person can save on taxes by making gifts and paying the gift tax rather than the estate tax. Rates of the gift tax are one-fourth lower than estate-tax rates, which graduate from 3 per cent to 77 per cent. In addition, the higher-bracket rates of the gift tax do not apply until the donor has given away sizable sums over and above the exemptions. Therefore, the first gifts to be taxed will be in the lower brackets to which lower rates apply. Yet they take away from the total of the taxpayer's estate, bringing it down from the higher-bracket estate-tax rates. Thus they effect a more than proportional saving. Beyond this, payment of the gift tax itself reduces the estate and therefore pares the estate tax even more.

An example may make clearer the savings to be effected by gifts. A taxpayer with $310,000 in assets gives $66,000 to his wife and $6,000 to each of his two children one year, a total of $78,000; in the next six years he gives $6,000 each to his wife and children, a total of $108,000. This is the maximum allowed to this couple giving jointly in these years plus its lifetime tax-free allowance. Some years later he dies, leaving half of the remaining estate of $124,000 or $62,000, to his wife, and half to the children. After expenses and bequests of $4,000, his wife is left with $60,000 on which there is no estate tax—and no gift tax; and the children are left with $60,000 on which there is no tax. One-half of the $124,000 less $4,000, or $60,000, was deducted as a marital deduction.

To cite one example, the type of asset to be given away is an important consideration. Giving away life-insurance policies may be more advantageous than giving away stocks. Let us assume that a taxpayer gives away $50,000 in securities that pay $2,000 in dividends a year to his three children. Each child can then file his own separate income-tax return, take his exemption, standard deduction, and dividend exclusion, and pay no tax. And by not having the dividends as taxable income, the taxpayer reduces his income tax. He has also reduced his estate by $50,000 plus the income that would have been accumulated. Estate taxes, if he left a taxable estate of $100,000 or more, would have been reduced by as much as $15,000 or more. Gift taxes may be avoided by him and his wife each giving away less than $30,000 worth of the stocks.

If, instead, he assigned a $100,000 life-insurance policy to his three children, his eventual estate is reduced by the $100,000 that would have been collected on his demise. If the remaining taxable estate amounts to $100,000, his estate taxes will be lessened by about $30,000.

As to how much he is giving away at the time of assignment, if he is 50 and has been paying premiums for 10 years, the cash value of the policy was probably between $16,700 and $17,800, depending on whether the policy paid dividends. For tax purposes, this gift is valued at about $20,500 (the present discounted value of the future benefits assuming he will live as long as the actuarial table predicts). The amount is well below the $30,000 lifetime-gift exemption. It is also apart from the annual $30,000 per person gift-tax exclusion.

The result: his securities remain intact; the current gift tax is avoided (about $2,000 if $100,000 in securities had been given to the children jointly by him and his wife); and since the children would have had to assume the securities at their original cost to the taxpayer, they would have had to pay a capital-gains tax on any gain since that time when they sold them. If he held the securities until his death and the children inherited them then, their tax base would be the current value of the securities at that time.

Planning to minimize estate taxes through gifts should start as soon as one has an estate. Gifts are not used nearly to the extent that they might be. One study reported more than half of the people leaving estates between $1 million and $1¼ million in 1957 and 1959 had reported no lifetime gifts at all.[3] If they had children, the opportunity of having the children assume responsibility for and come to understand the proper management of their funds during the parents' lifetime was also forgone.

MINIMIZING ESTATE SHRINKAGE

In order that an estate may be preserved and may appreciate in value, it is ordinarily necessary to establish trusts. Trusts were discussed previously. In addition to their other advantages, if properly set up they may save postdeath estate administrative expenses of as much as 10 per cent. Moreover, the more responsible the management of the trust, the better are the chances of the principal of the estate appreciating rather than shrinking.

But other considerations also are pertinent. If an estate is composed in any major part of assets that have risen sharply in value since they were acquired, it may be advantageous to hold them until death. In that case, neither the estate nor the heirs will ever have to pay a capital-gains tax on the rise that occurred in their value to that time. If they are given away, even to a trust, a capital-gains tax of no more than 25 per cent probably would be paid sooner or later on the rise in value. It must be paid if they are sold. It need not be paid if they are inherited, for they are thus acquired without a sale having taken place.

Title holdings should be arranged advantageously when possible. Property held jointly becomes the surviving owner's if the title so stipulates, and probate costs are thus lessened, but the decedent's interest is still part of his estate. However, if the title to property is in children's names, that property will not be part of the estate.

Business organizational structures may or may not be advantageous insofar as maximizing assets in an estate are concerned. A partnership has to be liquidated upon the death of one of the partners, and a new partnership then must be formed to carry on the business—if it can be carried on. Even at best, there is some legal expense involved that will reduce the estate. A corporation goes on as long as its charter says it may—and some charters give no time limit—or as long as it is a going concern. A sole proprietorship often ends with the death of the proprietor.

Consideration should be given to training understudies or appointing substitutes for essential roles in one's home or business. Then there will be no unnecessary expense to be borne by the estate or one's heirs, and the business may continue operating profitably and producing income. Contracts always should contain a clause stipulating who retains rights under the contract in case one of the principals dies. This is insurance against unnecessary legal fees.

Assets should be evaluated periodically to determine whether they fit estate plans; assets that heirs might have to liquidate at a loss do not.

In formulating estate-disposition plans, if an appreciable amount is involved, one's family attorney, accountant, banker, trust officer of a trust institution, life-insurance broker, investment counselor, family members, and business associates should all be consulted. If they are concerned, they should be part of the "planning group." For, after all, the best safeguard against estate shrinkage is intelligent planning that will result in leaving one's affairs in order. If wills are ambiguous, probate may be lengthy and *costly*. If the heirs disagree, the attorneys may "inherit the estate." If tax planning was inadequate, the estate may vanish. Marilyn Monroe's did.[4] Under our economic system one may and should plan for a lifetime and beyond.

QUESTIONS

1. What considerations should be paramount when planning the accumulation of a bequeathable estate? A living estate? How do the two differ?
2. Why is it essential for most people to make a will? What are the essential parts of a will?
3. Define the following terms: holographic will; beneficiary; codicil; probate; testator.
4. When should one change or revoke a will? How should this be done?
5. Where should a will be filed for safekeeping? Why not keep it in your safe-deposit box?
6. What should be contained in a decedent's letter of instructions?
7. What are the qualifications for an executor? What are his duties? How is he compensated?
8. What are the qualifications of a guardian? What are his duties? How is he compensated?
9. The federal estate tax is a tax on what right? Exactly, to what does it apply?
10. Exactly what may one deduct from the gross estate to arrive at the amount of the net estate?
11. Explain the allowable "marital deduction" and what effect it has on the taxable estate and estate taxes.
12. How much exemption from the federal estate tax is every estate allowed?
13. Explain the credit for previous bequests and the credit for state taxes paid. What effect do they have on the estate tax?
14. Differentiate between state inheritance taxes and state estate taxes. Under state inheritance-tax laws, what determines the allowable exemption and the applicable rates to be paid?
15. What is a trust? Differentiate between living trusts and testamentary trusts.
16. Define trustor; beneficiary; trustee; life tenant; remainderman.
17. What are the duties of trustees? How are they compensated for their work?
18. How long may trusts last?
19. Differentiate between a revocable and an irrevocable trust. When is one advantageous and when is the other?

20. How may families use living trusts to minimize taxes?
21. When should a testamentary trust be established? What advantages may accrue from the creation of testamentary trusts?
22. What is a life-insurance trust? When should such a trust be established and what advantages may accrue from its use?
23. What is a custodian account? When should such an account be set up and what advantages may accrue from its use?
24. What is a foundation? When is it advantageous to establish a foundation and what advantages may accrue from its judicious use?
25. What means should one consider when one is attempting to minimize estate taxes? What is usually the most effective method? Why?
26. What additional considerations should be kept in mind if one is attempting to prevent estate shrinkage?

SELECTED READINGS

A Guide to Federal Estate and Gift Taxation, Internal Revenue Service Publication No. 448, U. S. Dept. of Treasury, Washington, D. C., 1961.

Brosterman, Robert, *The Complete Estate Planning Guide*, McGraw-Hill, New York, 1964.

Callahan, Parnell, *How to Make a Will*, Oceana Publications, New York, latest edition.

Casey, William J., *Estate Plans*, Institute for Business Planning, New York, latest edition.

Casey, William J., and J. K. Lasser, *Tax Shelter for the Family*, Business Reports, New York, 1953.

Cosner, Andrew James, *Estate Planning*, Little, Brown, Boston, 1956.

Federal Estate and Gift Taxes Explained, Commerce Clearing House, Chicago, latest edition.

J. K. Lasser Tax Institute, *Estate Tax Techniques*, M. Bender, Albany, 1955.

J. K. Lasser Tax Institute and Ralph Wallace, *How to Save Estate and Gift Taxes*, American Research Council, Larchmont, N. Y., latest edition; other publications from this institute on this topic appear periodically.

MacNeill, Earl S., *Making the Most of Your Estate*, Harper, New York, 1957.

Masteller, Kenneth C., *How to Avoid Financial Tangles*, American Institute for Economic Research, Great Barrington, Mass., latest edition.

Prentice-Hall Trust Course, Prentice-Hall, Englewood Cliffs, N. J., latest year.

Regulations Relating to Estates, Trusts, Beneficiaries and Decedents, Internal Revenue Service Publication No. 414, U. S. Dept. of Treasury, Washington, D. C., 1958.

Rogers, Donald E., *Teach Your Wife to Be a Widow*, Holt, New York, 1953.

Spinney, William R., *Estate Planning*, Commerce Clearing House, New York, latest edition.

Stephenson, Gilbert T., *Estates and Trusts*, 4th ed., Appleton-Century-Crofts, New York, 1965.

Tractman, Joseph, *Estate Planning*, Practicing Law Institute, New York, 1958.

Wills Course, Prentice-Hall, Englewood Cliffs, N. J., latest year.

Wormser, René A., *Personal Estate Planning in a Changing World*, Simon and Schuster, New York, latest edition.

NOTES

1. Some references that will be helpful in estate planning may be found in the list of selected readings. Also see Irving Pfeffer, "The Nature and Scope of Estate Planning," *California Management Review*, Fall, 1966, pp. 23–32.
2. *U. S. News & World Report*, October 16, 1961, p. 123.
3. Carl S. Shoup, *Federal Estate and Gift Taxes*, the Brookings Institution, Washington, D. C., 1966.
4. Articles in *Los Angeles Times*, June 2, 1965.

PROBLEMS AND CASES

1. Paul Smith has assets worth $500,000. He is 40 years old, married, and has three children, two boys aged 10 and 14, and a girl of 7. His wife is 35. He wants to plan to build a living estate and a bequeathable estate sufficient to pay his children's college expenses; provide income of $400 a month for each of them until they are through school; provide income for his wife throughout her lifetime at the rate of $1,000 a month; effect a minimization of estate taxes, and leave as much as possible to be passed on for as long as possible. What would you advise him to do? Be detailed in your suggestions. Give the reasons why you make the suggestions and recommendations that you do.
2. The head of a family died intestate. His estate, after taxes and administrative expenses were paid, amounted to $50,000. Under the laws of the state in which you live, how much of his estate will his mother, who is still alive, receive? If he and his wife are both involved in an accident and his wife died before he did, how much would the children receive?
3. Draw up a sample will for the Mr. Smith referred to in Problem 1. Among his assets were $100,000 in life insurance valued at its present cash value of $50,000 and a $40,000 house with a mortgage outstanding against it of $10,000.
4. A reputable trust company is trustee for an estate of $250,000. The two remaindermen believe that the trustee is too conservative and that they should be earning and receiving a higher return on their principal. What are they legally empowered to do under the laws of the state in which you live? Is the trustee allowed to invest the entire principal in common stocks if this is what they wish him to do? If one of the remaindermen dies, will the other find the amount in trust augmented by the sum originally bequeathed to his co-legatee? If not, by how much will the trust be augmented?
5. How much in federal-estate taxes will the estate of Mr. Smith of Problem 1 ultimately have to pay under your plan in state inheritance and estate taxes in the state in which you live?
6. Compute the federal-estate tax in the case of an adjusted-gross estate of $600,000 where there are $10,000 in charitable bequests and a $16,400 credit for state-death taxes. The decedent was single. What would the tax be if the decedent was married? Assume his wife survived him.
7. Compute the amount of the federal gift tax in the following cases (unless otherwise indicated, none of the donors has previously made a gift subject to the provisions of the tax laws).

(a) A single person's gift of $5,000 to a parent.

(b) A married person's gift of $5,000 to a parent (if the spouse agrees and wishes to maximize the tax advantage).

(c) A married couple's joint gift of $10,000 worth of common stock given to each of its four children for each of five years in a row.

(d) If the couple referred to in (c) had previously used up its gift-tax exclusion.

(e) If the couple referred to in (c) before using up any of its gift-tax exclusion made the gift to a foundation instead of to its children.

(f) If the couple referred to in (c) remained co-owners of the stock with each of its four children.

8. Robert Stanley is the sole owner of a large and profitable concern. He is 60 and can live as he wishes for the remainder of his life on the income from his investments, even if he draws nothing from the firm. His attorney has suggested he incorporate the firm, then establish a foundation, and give the stock to the foundation over a period of years. Why might he want to do this? Why not? If the foundation is established what will determine how much stock he should give the foundation in any one year?

9. Mrs. McKee, a widow, has three children, 19, 24, and 27 and two grandchildren. Her assets consist of a paid-up life insurance policy with a face value of $75,000; $185,000 (market value) in common stocks, mainly dividend paying and the unmortgaged home (appraised at $40,000) in which she lives alone. How would you advise she rearrange her asset holdings so as to (1) maximize the estate her heirs will receive (the children and grandchildren will all share equally) after taxes; (2) provide $12,000 in income for herself as long as she lives and thereafter maximize the after-tax estate her heirs will inherit; (3) provide for an income for herself of $12,000 a year as long as she lives, an income for her children (all three to receive $4,000 a year during their lifetime), and for the passing on of the "corpus" of the estate without tax liability to her grandchildren. Should she consider turning over her assets to a college or university under one of the trust or endowment plans that will arrange for her to receive an income for life? Would this fit any of her objectives if they are as given in (1), (2), or (3) above? Why or why not? What estate objectives would those rationally choosing such a plan probably have? Would they be likely to have children, grandchildren, or other favored heirs? To whom or which type of institution would you advise she go for the implementation of her estate plan?

APPENDIX
Checklist for Evaluating a House

Scale:

Minor defect	1 demerit
Fairly important defect	2 demerits
Serious defect	4 demerits
Disqualifying defect	4+ demerits or disqualification

The Defect	*Demerits*

Inside the House

Floor plan, size of room or enclosed area, traffic flow
Small house, 2 stories (stairs tend to waste space)	2
Unavoidable traffic through living areas	2
Must pass through one bedroom to reach another	2
Generally poor layout (many, many forms)	4+
Low ceilings (under 8 feet)	2

The Defect	Demerits
Inside the House (continued)	
Small rooms (small for their purpose and the number of people who will use them at one time)	4
Any feeling of being cramped or closed in in enclosed areas	Dis.
Closets and storage space	
No coat closet, or inconveniently located relative to social area	2
Inadequate storage space, for each area where storage space is needed[a]	4
Interior walls, trim, and decoration	
Deep, extensive plaster cracking, if structural	Dis.
Extensive plaster cracking, nonstructural	4+
Wavy corners and surfaces, with breakage of outside corners	4
Extensive rough patching	4
Conspicuous dry-wall joints	2–4
Needs repainting or repapering (for each area)	2–4
Mildew (inspection made under pictures, rugs; behind hangings; in closets)	2–4
Rain-leakage stains	4
Badly fitting wood trim with open joints	2–4
Fireplace and chimney	
Poor fireplace draft (test with strip of newspaper or cigarette smoke)	2–4
Absence of damper	2
Absence of wood closet	2
Fireplace on short wall of room	2
Lack of chimney lining (use flashlight)	4
Doors and windows	
No weatherstripping	2
General sticking, if nonstructural	4
Rotted window sills (many)	2–4
Rattling windows	2
Floors and stairs	
Conspicuous cracks in wideboard floors, but otherwise in good shape	2
Badly worn floors	4
Sagging and spongy floors	4
Firm but creaky floors	1

The Defect	Demerits
Inside the House (continued)	
Stair treads under 9 in., or risers over 8 in.	2
Triangular treads at turns	1
Absence of handrail	1
Stairs under 31 in. wide	2
Inadequate head room on stairs	2
Kitchen	
Poor arrangement (many forms)	4+
Inadequate counter space (20 sq. ft. minimum)	4
Inadequate cupboard and drawer space (90 sq. ft. minimum)	4
Inadequate window space	2–4
No room for breakfast table and chairs	2
No exhaust fan close to range	1
Inadequate space for newer appliances	4+
Bathrooms and lavatories	
Only one bathroom (except in a small house)	4+
Absence of effective exhaust fan in windowless bathroom	2
Light switch or electric outlet near tub or stall shower (to be taken out)	1
Leg-type tub	1
Absence of shower (circular shower rod over tub does not qualify)	1
Basin under 17 x 19 in.	1
Poorly joined floor tile	2
Absorbent wallboard	2
Permanent fixtures in poor condition	2–4
Poor layout including radiator locations	2
No special bathroom heater or infra-red heat lamp unless small steamheated bathroom)	2
Poor lighting over mirror	1
No electric outlet for shaver	2
Attic: utility and ventilation	
Reached only by stepladder or fixed vertical ladder	2
Absence of floor	2
Absence of windows or louvers (2 at least 2 sq. ft. each)	2
Moist insulation (in winter with house heated)	4
Inadequate head room	2

The Defect	Demerits
Structure of House	
Attic: structural analysis	
Sloping roof with rafters less than 2 x 6	4
Sloping roof with appreciable ridge sag	4
General decay of roof framing (but, if there are special reasons and the rest of the house is sound, bids should be obtained on reframing or complete reroofing)	Dis.
Inadequate nailing (at least two nails should be visible where each rafter joins horizontal members)	4
No building paper in walls (if this can be determined)	4
No sheathing in walls (if this can be determined)	4
Heavy moisture deposit on underside of roof or on wall surfaces (in winter, with house heated)	4
Heavy moisture deposit on underside of roof or on wall surfaces (when house is not heated)	4
Wood in contact with chimney	4
Loose mortar in chimney joints	2
Rain-leakage stains	4
Insulation	
None[b]	4+
Attic insulated, but not walls[c]	4
Walls insulated, but not attic[c]	2
Wall or roof insulation without a vapor barrier[d]	4
Basement: utility and dryness	
Unpaved or broken floor	2
No entrance except through house	2
Absence of floor drain or sump	1
Severe flooding (water marks on walls)	4+ or Dis.
Moderate flow across floor after heavy rain (if you plan to finish the basement)	2–4 Dis.
Low ceiling (precludes walking)	2
Windows below ground level	1
Basement: structural analysis	
Foundation wall thickness under 8 in.	4
Severe cracks in foundation walls	Dis.
Loose mortar in chimney joints	2

The Defect	Demerits
Structure of House (continued)	
Extensive sill rotting	4+
Sills not bolted to foundation walls (in earthquake regions)	2–4
Wood posts set in concrete	2
Absence of bridging between floor joists (except under 10-ft. span)	4
Joints in built-up girders other than at points of support	4
Absence of fire stops	2
Support added to joists or girders after house was built	2–4
Absence of subfloor	4
General decay of cellar framing	Dis.
Crawl spaces	
Low (under 18 in.), unventilated, blocked with boulders or heating ducts, littered	4+
Protection against rot and termites	
Less than 6 in. of masonry between ground and wooden members	4
Wooden porch in contact with earth	2
Termite infestation	Dis.[e]
Utilities	
Heating plant	
High fuel bills (past bills should be checked, if possible)	4+
Inadequate heating capacity	4+
Warm-air registers in floor rather than wall	2
Inadequate draft (accumulation of soot on cellar walls and ceiling and around automatic draft regulator; heavy pulsation as oil burner starts)	2
Dirty warm-air system (heavy smudging on and above registers)	4
Dilapidated furnace or boiler	4+
Rusted warm-air ducts	4
Rusted smoke pipe	1
Lack of thermostat	2
Plumbing	
Water heater under 50-gal. capacity	2
Water hammer	2

The Defect	Demerits
Utilities (continued)	
Clogged or undersized pipes (low pressure at faucets)	4+
Low municipal water pressure	4+
Inadequate water supply (private system)	4+ to Dis.
Sluggish drains	2
Very hard water and no water-softening system	2
Electrical	
Inadequate outlets and switches	2
Less than 100-ampere service	4
No 20-ampere outlet available in kitchen	2
Badly rusted armored cable (general condition in cellar)	4

Outside the House

The Defect	Demerits
Exterior walls and corners	
Moderately deteriorated siding	2–4
Severely deteriorated siding	4+ to Dis.
Framing failure (severe bulging of wall or walls)	Dis.
Walls or corners out of plumb	Dis.
Outside chimney leaning away from house	Usually Dis.
Open joints in outside chimney	2
Crumbling putty on windows	1–2
Caulking needed in general	2
Pointing needed for brick walls and chimneys	2–4
Deteriorated flashing around windows	2–4
Exterior paint	
General blistering and peeling of new paint, if caused by condensation in walls	Usually Dis.
Normal paint failure (chalking or powdering with age)	2
Roof	
Failing shingle roof (many broken, warped, and upturned shingles)	4
Complex roof design (many valleys, peaks, dormers)	4
Deteriorated flashing	2–4
Gutters and leaders	
Rusted gutters	2
Rotted wooden gutters	4

The Defect	Demerits
Outside the House (continued)	
Sound wooden gutters but not metal lined	2
Absence of tile drains to lead-off water from rain spouts	1
Screens, storm windows, doors	
Absence of screens, or screens in poor condition	2
Absence of storm windows and doors where required by climate	4
Garage	
Two-car garage less than 22 x 20 feet	4
One-car garage less than 20 x 12 feet	2
Attached garage without fire door between garage and house	2
Inconvenient door	2
Lot and land	
Landscaping poorly maintained	4
Frontage under standard for neighborhood	4+
House on inadequately compacted fill	4+ or Dis.
House near water course subject to flooding	4+ or Dis.
Hillside lot subject to erosion (no terracing)	4
Collapsing retaining walls	Dis.
Absence of mature trees, except where generally unavailable	4
Driveway, walks, patio in need of repairs (cracked cement)	4

[a] Each bedroom lacking a closet at least 60 inches wide and 20 inches deep rates two demerits, if closet is still usable though inadequate.

[b] In a few spots in the United States where the temperature rarely is below 55° or above 85° (some areas on the coast in Southern California, for example), insulation may not be necessary.

[c] At least three inches of soft insulation, with an effective vapor barrier, or equivalent reflective insulation (three or four layers of foil).

[d] Except where outside temperature seldom drops below freezing.

[e] Often but not necessarily disqualifying. Consult architect.

SOURCE: Adapted from *Consumer Reports, 1961 Buying Guide Issue*, pp. 191–199.

AUTHOR INDEX

Black, Hillel, 58n
Bullock, Hugh, 226n, 234, 235
Burk, Marguerite C., 114n

Campbell, Persia, 80n
Cave, Roy C., 67n
Chapman, John M., 80n
Churchill, Betty C., 127n, 130n
Clendenin, John C., 118, 125n, 137n, 182n, 218, 228
Comer, Mary E., 78n
Corey, Lewis, 191n

Disraeli, Benjamin, 245

Feldman, Frances Lomas, 26n
Friedman, Milton, 12, 27, 387
Friggins, Paul, 401n

Galbraith, J. Kenneth, 58n, 463
Goldsmith, Raymond W., 88n
Goldstein, Sidney, 127n
Gordon, Margaret S., 481n

Havemann, Ernest, 388n
Hollingshead, August B., 26n
Huntington, Emily H., 43n

Katona, George, 7, 29n
Keats, John, 58n
Kinney, Paul T., 328n
Kuznets, Simon, 12

Lamale, Helen Humes, 7n
Lane, Sylvia, 80n
Lee, Russel, 328
Lipsey, Robert E., 88n

Maisel, Sherman, 248
Mayer, Kurt B., 127n
Michelbacher, G. F., 391n
Miller, Herman P., 11, 12, 27n
Morse, Richard L. D., 67n
Musgrave, Richard A., 361n
Myers, James H., 80n

Neal, Charles, Jr., 30n

Packard, Vance, 58n
Phelan, Vincent B., 263n
Phelps, Clyde W., 80n, 81n, 130n, 314
Phillips, E. Bryant, 36n
Pollard, Spencer D., 83n
Porter, Sylvia, 58n, 80n

Rose, Billy, 145

Savage, L. J., 387
Schiller, Maurece, 161
Scitovsky, Tibor, 461n
Shaw, Edward, 461n
Shay, Robert P., 80n
Shockett, Sol, 78n
Shoup, Carl S., 513n
Straus, Donald B., 330
Stryker, Perrin, 399n

Tarshis, Lorie, 461n
Trefftzs, Kenneth, 456n

Whyte, William H. Jr., 37n
Winnick, Louis, 251n
Wise, T. W., 191n, 192n

Zwick, Jack, 131n

527

SUBJECT INDEX

Accounting, a management tool, 131-133
   balance sheet, 131
   profit and loss statement, 132
      addition to surplus, 132
      depreciation, 132
Actuarial tables, mortality tables, 408, 409
Additional extended coverage endorsement, 393, 394
Airline stocks, 159
American Public Health Association, 251
American Stock Exchange, 188
Analysis of corporate securities, 145-174
   fundamental approach, 156
   portfolio management, 171
   technical approach, 169
   types of securities, 146
Annuities, 476-481
   cost of, 478
   installment refund, 479
   installments certain, 479
   Keogh Plan, 478
   straight life, 478
   tax shelter, 477
   variable, 477, 480
   whether to buy, 480
Assigned risks, automobile insurance, 403
Automobile insurance, 395-403
   assigned risks, 403
   claims settlement, 400
   classified ratings, 403
   collision, 397
   comprehensive, 396
   deductible clause, 397
   liability, 396
   medical coverage, 397
   miscellaneous coverage, 398
   types of companies, 398

Automobile insurance, policy cancellation, 402
   premium retrievers, 401
   uninsured motorist endorsement, 397
Automobiles, 300
   buying an automobile, 307
   buy or lease, 316
   cost of ownership, 303-319
   financing, 68, 71-73, 312
   insurance, 315, 395-403

Balanced portfolio, 63
Bank loans, 69
   check reserve accounts, 71
   credit cards, 71
   discounting a note, 70
   single-payment loans, 70
   small loans, 70
   unsolicited credit cards, 71
Barron's National Business and Financial Weekly, 207
Bold investment policy, 214
Bonds, 146-152
   blanket mortgage, 149
   bond analysis, 163
   bond indenture, 146
   bond rating services, 147
   callable, 152
   collateral trust, 149
   convertible, 152
   debentures, 147
   debt-equity ratio, 167
   first mortgage, 146
   guaranteed, 149
   junior, 147
   leverage, 167

Subject Index

Bonds, market analysis, 163
  receiver's certificates, 147
  second mortgage, 147
  senior, 147
  yields, 149
Bond yields, 149
  asset coverage, 164
  bond yield table, 150, 151
  callable bonds, 151
  current yield, 149
  yield to maturity, 149
Book value, 168
Brokerage houses, 190
  account executives, 191
  independent brokers, 190
  Merrill Lynch, Pierce, Fenner & Smith, Inc., 191
Brokerage services, 190-199
  "buy" orders, 192
  calls, 193
  commission rates, 195
  limited order, 192
  margin trading, 194
  odd-lot transactions, 192, 199
  open orders, 192
  puts, 193
  round lot, 192
  selling against the box, 195
  selling short, 195
  sell orders, 192
  stop-loss orders, 192
  straddles, 194
  "third market," 199
Budget administration, 31
  assembling data, 32
  budget schedules, tentative, 34
  setting up a budget, 32
Budget balance sheet, 33
Budgeting, 25-46
  administration of, 31, 32
  alternative costs, 29
  comparisons, 38
  by impoverished persons, 31, 32
  irregular incomes, 41
  maximizing satisfactions, 28
  by middle-income persons, 31, 42
  necessities, 42
  necessity for, 25
  prudent spending, 18
  rational choice, 29
  revisions, 37
  types of, 34

Budgeting, by upper-income persons, 31, 43
  wants, 25-28
Budgeting, bookkeeping, 37
  cash, 34
  check stubs, 36
  installment credit, 36
  types of, 34
Bull market, 173
Business organizations, corporations, 137
  capital structure, 139
  charter, 137
  corporate structure, 138
  limited liability, 137
  securities, 134
forms of, 134
  individual proprietorship, 135
    advantages, 135
    unlimited liability, 135
  partnership, 135
    advantages, 135
    disadvantages, 136
    mutual agency, 136
    unlimited liability, 136

Callable bonds, 151
Casualty Insurance, 387-403
Classified insurers, 390
Commercial banks, 103
  checking account as savings, 103
  Federal Deposit Insurance Corporation, 103
  savings accounts, 104
  service charges, 103
  time deposits, 104
Commodity markets, 200
  commodity exchanges, 200
  hedge, 200
  speculative commodities, 200
Common stocks, 154-158
  analysis, check list, 163
  book value, 62
  capital gains, 155
  debt-equity ratio, 154, 167
  leverage, 154, 167
  long on the market, 154
  market image, 168
  par value, 155
  price-earnings ratio, 167
  short-term capital gains, 155
  stock dividend, 156
  stock split, 155

Common stocks, voting rights, 156
Community property laws, 288
Conspicuous consumption, 27
Consumer Bulletin, 309
Consumer credit, 56
  cost of, 65
  credit outstanding, 56, 57
  see also Personal credit
Consumer finance companies, 71
  model Consumer Finance Act, 71
  shoppers' loans, 72
Consumer Reports, 309
Corporate form of business organization, 137
  capital structure, 139
  corporate securities, 138
    diversification, 141
    limited liability, 137
    significance to investors, 141
  corporate structure, 138
    parent corporation, 138
    subsidiary corporation, 138
  corporation charter, 137
  stockholders' equity, 139
Cost of consumer credit, 65
  annual percentage rate, 67
  constant-ratio formula, 67
    explanation of, 65
  dollar cost, 66
  hidden carrying charges, 60
  percentage rate, 65
  reasons for, 65
  residual interest, 67
  sales finance companies, 72
  service charge concept, 68
  simple interest, 66
Cost of medical care, 326-330
  coinsurance, 335
  doctors' fees, 327
  drug prices, 329
  hospital rates, 327
  increasing costs, 326
Counter-cyclical monetary and fiscal policies, 446-457
  built-in stabilizers, 447
  discretionary fiscal policy, 449
  fiscal policy, 447
  monetary policy, 447
Credit cards, 59
  bank credit cards, 59, 71
  general purpose, 59
  limited purpose, 59

Credit contracts, 62
  acceleration clause, 64
  accommodation paper, 64
  add-on clause, 64
  bailment lease, 63
  chattel mortgages, 63
  conditional sales contracts, 63
  co-signer agreements, 64
  installment sales agreements, 63
  owner's equity, 63
  prepayment clause, 65
  wage-assignment, 64
  wage-garnishment, 64
Credit institutions, 68-79
  bank loans, 70
  consumer finance companies, 71
  credit unions, 76
  industrial banks, 76
  pawnbrokers, 78
  remedial loan societies, 79
  sales finance companies, 72
Credit insurance, 74
Credit life insurance, 424
Credit unions, 109
  convenience, 109
  volume, 109
Cumulative preferred, 153

Debt adjusters, 30
Debt consolidation, 61
Debt counselors, 30
Debt-equity ratio, 167
Declining term insurance, 419
Distribution of securities, 181
  continuing market, 183
  direct to investment bankers, 181
  marketability, 184
  over-the-counter, 184
  secondary distribution, 183
  underwriting syndicates, 182
Dollar averaging, 173
Dower or curtesy, 289
Dow-Jones, 169, 234
DuPont, 160

Endowment insurance, 418
Engel's Law, 15, 42
Estate, disposition of, 492-515
  gifts, 512
  minimizing estate shrinkage, 514
  statute of descent and distribution, 492

Subject Index

Estate, taxes, 499-504
  will, importance of, 492
Estate planning, 489-515
  building an estate, 490
  foundations, 510
  objectives, 490
  trusts, 504-512
Estate taxes, 499-502
  computation of, 178
  federal estate tax, 499
  gross estate, 499
  marital deduction, 500
  net estate, 500
  state estate taxes, 502
  state inheritance taxes, 502
  tax shelters, 477, 478
Evolving concepts of investment, 92
  for durable goods purchases, 94
    borrowing to save and invest, 114
    enforced saving, 101
  earning assets, 93
Evolving concepts of saving, 92
  for contingencies, 94
  for durable goods purchases, 94
  for emergencies, 94
  for later spending, 93
  for permanent investment, 93
  personal reasons, 95
    builds character, 97
    builds funds, 97
    provides security, 98
  voluntary saving, 101
Extended coverage endorsement, 391, 393

Family-income rider, 416, 419
Family life cycle, 26
  full nest stage, 26
  newly built nest stage, 26
Financial advisory services, 209
Financial programs, financial security, 119
  investment programs, 119
Financial reporting services, 209
  Fitch Investment Service, 209
  Moody's, 209
  Standard and Poor's, 209
Financial responsibility laws, 396
Fire insurance, 391
Fitch Investment Service, 209
Forbes Magazine, 209
Ford Foundation, 511
Foundations, 510

Fraternal insurance companies, 430
Fundamental approach to security analysis, 156-169
  analysis of firms, 159
  analysis of industries, 157
  check list, 163
  special investment situations, 161

Garnishment, 30
Government bonds, 109
  Appreciation bonds, 110
  Freedom bonds, 110
  Income bonds, 110
  Series E, 110
  Series H, 110
  State and municipal, 112
  Treasury bills, 110
Government regulation, 212
  regulation of investment institutions, 210
Government services, 352-355
  expenditures, 354
  public expenditures, 354
  taxation, 355-381
    forms of, 357
    principles of, 355
Group health insurance, prepayment plans, 337-345
Group insurance, 424
Growth stocks, 126
  after-taxes, 126
  anticipated income, 126
  increment, 123
Guardian, duties of, 499

Health insurance, 331
  comprehensive medical expense, 335
  loss of income, 335
  major medical expense, 334
  prepayment plans, 337
    Blue Cross, 337
    Blue Shield, 339
    Independents, the, 341
Home investment as savings, 114
  "Sweat equity," 114
Homeowners A,B,C insurance policies, 393
Homeowners policies H-1 to H-5, 393
Housing, 245-290
  building codes, 255
  buying, selling, building, 276, 286
  buy or rent, 276
  cost of, 246, 259
  evaluating a house, 281

Subject Index

Housing, fashions in dwellings, 252
  finance, 92, 256, 264
  government's role in, 269, 276
  housing industry, the, 254
  insurance, 391-395
  maximum density standards, 251
  minimum floor space required, 249
  needs, 249
  operation and maintenance, 261
  sites, availability and use, 255
  supply of housing, 253
  titles, deeds, legal matters, 286
  types of dwellings, 256
Housing finance, 264-276
  Conventional loans, 272
  Federal Home Loan Bank, 275
  Federal Housing Administration, 269
  Federal National Mortgage Association, 274
  mortgage insurance, 270
  participation payments, 271
  state lending agencies, 275
  Veterans' Administration loans, 272

Income as an investment objective, 123
  increment, 124-126
  investment risks, 123
  yield, 124
Income management, 437-463
  business-cycle irregularities, 437
    deflation, 444
    inflation, 439
      cost-push, 440
      demand-pull, 441-444
Income tax, 364-380
  annuities and pensions, 375
  capital gains, 373
  exemptions, 379
  itemized deductions, 376
  medical and dental expenses, 378
  penalties and appeals, 380
Independent insurance companies (automobile), 399
Industrial insurance, 423
Installment credit, 60
  amortized, 60
  cost of, 65
  debt consolidation, 61
  installment loans, 61
  optional credit, 61
  sales finance, 62

Installment loans, 61
Insurable risks, 389
Insurance syndicate, 389
Investing in one's own future, 114
Investment, for durable goods, 93, 94
  earning assets, 93
  evolving concepts of, 92
  enforced saving, 95
  prior saving, 94
Investment companies, 105
  Boston trusts, 221
  classification of, 219
  closed-end, 222
  face-amount certificates, 226
  incorporated, 221
  investment management firms, 221
  investment trust, 221
  Massachusetts trusts, 221
  Mutual funds, 223, 226
  open-end, 222, 223
  proliferation of funds, 231
  regulated companies, 226
  typical companies, 226
  Unit trust, 226
Investment companies in evolution, 233
  accumulation plans, 235
    contractural plans, 236
    front-end load, 236
    level load, 236
    no load, 236, 237
  distribution companies, 235
  management firms, 234
  performance record, 233
  Securities and Exchange Commission, 237
  self regulation, 237
  sliding scale fees, 235
Investment Company Act of 1940, 219
Investment company portfolios, 227
  balanced fund, 228
  blue-chip fund, 229
  capital exchange funds, 232
  common stock fund, 228
  diversified fund, 228
  dual funds, 230
  growth funds, 229
  hedge funds, 231
  income funds, 229
  industry funds, 230
  leverage funds, 231
  special situation funds, 232
  specialized funds, 228
  "swap funds," 232

Subject Index   533

Investment information, 202
Investment programs, 118-150
  bold policy, 214
  growth stocks, 126
  income as an objective, 123
  investor's need for information, 213
  leave the market alone, 214
  primary investment program, 119
  small business, 127
Investment risks, 124-126
  business or functional, 125
  market risk, 125
  minimizing investment risks, 125
  money-rate risk, 125
  price-level risk, 125
Investment timing, 171

Jumping-juvenile policy, 423

Leverage, 167
Life insurance, 407-431
  cash surrender value, 425
  double indemnity insurance, 426
  extended term insurance, 426
  mortality tables, 408-409
  need for insurance, 407-412
  participating policies, 429
  policy loans, 425
  as a savings device, 112
  types of companies, 429
  types of policies, 412
Life Insurance Fact Book, 432, 433
Life insurance trusts, 508
Limited-payment life insurance, 416
Lloyds of London, 389

Managing a small business, 127-136
  accounting, 131-133
  failures, age of business, 136
Medicaid, 331
Medical care, 323-347
  cost of, 326-330, 342-344
  demand for, 324
  expenditures for, 324
  financing medical care, 330-343
  health insurance, 331-337
  medicare, 345
  preventive care, 325
  supply of, 325
Medicare, 345-347
Merrill Lynch, Pierce, Fenner and Smith, Inc., 191

Moody's Investment Service, Inc., 147, 209
Morris Plan Banks, 76
  savings certificates, 76
Mortgage-retirement policies, 419
Mortgages, 264-269
  amortized, 264
  closing costs, 268
  direct reduction, 264
  interest rates, 267
  long term, 283
  mortgage insurance, 270
  short term, 283
  source of loans, 266
Motor vehicle safety laws, 396
Multiple-line insurance, 391
Multiplier, the, 453
Mutual insurance companies, automobile, 398
  life insurance, 429
Mutual savings banks, 104
  safety of funds, 106
  savings accounts, 106
  volume of savings, 105

National Association of Home Builders, 249
National Association of Security Dealers, 211
National income accounting, 454
  the circular flow, 450
  income versus savings interrelationships, 451
  the multiplier, 453
  savings versus investment interrelationships, 452
National need for saved funds, 98
  for business expansion, 98, 445
  for government use, 99
  related to the circular flow, 99, 437-457
National Stock Exchange, 189
Nature of personal credit, 56
  credit rhythm, 59
  economic justification of, 74
  economic results, 79-82
    cyclical effects, 81
    personal consequences, 80
      credit buildup, 80
      credit prone, 80
      social responsibility, 80, 81
      standard of living, 81
    social consequences, 81
  imperfect market, 81
  usury, 77

New York Stock Exchange, 185
New York Stock Exchange Fact Book, 185
New York Times, 203

Ordinary life insurance, 415
Over-the-counter, 184

Paradox of thrift, 452
Participating preferred, 153
Pawnbrokers, 78
Permanent income hypothesis, 27
Permanent insurance, 415
Personal credit, 56-82
    constant ratio formula, 67
    cost of, 65
    debt adjusters, 30
    imperfect market, 81
    increasing use of, 56
    nature of, 56
    types of, 58
        credit cards, 59
        optional credit, 61
            retail sales credit, 58
            revolving credit, 60
            sales finance credit, 62
            slow billing, 60
            thirty-day charge accounts, 58
Personal expenditures, 14
    changing patterns of, 15
    discretionary spending, 18
    Engel's law, 15
    expenditure patterns, 17
Personal finance in wartime, 457-463
    credit controls, 460
    price controls, 461
    rationing, 461
Personal income, 4
    college education, importance of, 11
    distribution of, 7
    lifetime earnings, 10
    professions, preference for, 12
    rising personal incomes, 7
    sources of, 4
Point-and-figure charts, 169
Policy endorsements, 391
Preferred risk (automobile insurance), 400
Preferred stocks, 152
    analysis, check list, 163
    asset coverage, 164
    cumulative preferred, 153
        arrearage, 153
        versus noncumulative, 153

Preferred stocks, market image, 164
    participating preferred, 153
    preferential claim, on assets, 153
        on earnings, 153
Primary investment program, 119
    adequate insurance, 120
    commercial bank saving, 119
    government bonds, 121
    home ownership, 121
    liquidity of funds, 120
    low income investments, 122
    savings account, 121
Probate, 497
    administrator, duties of, 497
    executor, duties of, 497
    fees, 498
    guardian, duties of, 499
Property insurance, 391-395
Provident Loan Society, 79
Prudent spending, 45
Public transportation, 300
    cost of, 307
    federal subsidies, 303
    problems of, 301

Railroad stocks, 160
Rating bureaus, 399
Reciprocal companies, automobile insurance, 399
Regional stock exchanges, 189
Regulation of investment institutions, 210-214
    adequate disclosure, 212
    government regulation, 212
    inadequacy of regulation, 213
    listed securities, regulation of, 212
    manipulative activities, 212
    National Association of Security Dealers, 211
    Security and Exchange Commission, 212, 219, 237
    self regulation, 210
    stock exchange regulations, 211
Reinsurance, 389
Retirement programs, 469-484
    annuities, 471-481
    pension plans, 481-483
    planning for, 469
    social security, 471-476
    sources of income, 470
Russell Sage Foundation, 71

Subject Index

Sales finance companies, 72
  credit insurance, 74
  rates charged, 74
    economic justification, 74
    time-preference, 75
Saving, evolving concepts of, 92
  for contingencies, 94
  for durable goods, 94
  for emergencies, 94
  for later spending, 93
  personal reasons for, 95
    builds character, 97
    effect of thriftiness, 97
    provides security, 98
    voluntary saving, 95
Saving, personal, 88
  composition of, 90-92
  evolving concepts of, 92
  federal Reserve study of, 90
  financial assets and liabilities, 96
  oversaving, 100
  reasons for, 95-99
  size of savings, 90, 91
  undersaving, 100
Savings, life insurance as, 112, 406-431
  locked-in savings plan, 112
  as a savings device, 112
    advantages, 112
    disadvantages, 113
Savings and loan associations, 106
  Federal Savings and Loan Insurance Corp., 106
  investment certificates, 107
  passbook savings accounts, 107
  security of the funds, 107
  volume, assets, liabilities, 108
Savings devices, 100
  borrowing to save and invest, 114
  built-in savings, 102
  cash savings, 100
    a form of hoarding, 101
    safeguarding the funds, 101, 103, 107
  government bonds, 109
  home investments, 114, 245-290
  life insurance, 112, 407-431
  nonmonetary savings, 102
  one's own future, 114
  passbook accounts, 101
    involuntary savings, 101
    voluntary withholding, 101
Savings facilities, 88; *see also* Savings institutions

Savings institutions, 102
  commercial banks, 103
  credit unions, 109
  government bonds, 109
  life insurance, as savings, 112
  mutual savings banks, 104
  savings and loan associations, 106
Securities and Exchange Commission, 213, 219, 237
Slum clearance, 248
Small business investment, 126
  business experience, 129
  business survey, 129
  ease of entry, 128
  prospect of a profit, 133
  reasons for, 127
  success or failure, 127
  why businesses fail, 128
    adequacy of capital, 129
    managing a business, 131
Social security, 471-476
  benefits, eligibility for, 473
  old age and survivor's disability insurance, 476
  payments, 475
Special investment situations, 161
  financial reorganization, 162
  new era companies, 161
  old companies in new fields, 161
Standard and Poor's Corporation, 147, 209
Standard and Poor's 500 Stock Index, 234
Statute of descent and distribution, 492
Stock companies (insurance), automobiles, 398
  life insurance, 429
Stock exchanges, 184
  American Stock Exchange, 188
  continuing market for securities, 183
  marketability, 184
  National Stock Exchange, 189
  New York Stock Exchange, 185
  regional stock exchanges, 189
  traders, 184
  unregistered exchanges, 190
Straight life insurance, 415, 459
Survey Research Center, 248

Taxation, 355-381
  corporate income, 360
  equality of sacrifice, 356
  expediency, 356
  federal, 128

Taxation, gift and estate taxes, 360
   personal income, 358
   progressive, 357
   property tax, 362
   proportional, 357
   regressive, 357
   sales taxes, 363
   state and local, 357
Technical approach to security analysis, 169
   Dow-Jones theory, 171
   point-and-figure charts, 169
   wave cycles, 170
Tenancy, 288
Term insurance, 412-414
   advantages of, 413
   convertible, 413
   renewable, 413
   step-rate, 413
   unfavorable features, 414
Third market, 199
Thrift, paradox of, 452
Transportation, 297-318
   demand for, 298
      need for, 298
      social patterns, 299
   supply, 300
      automobiles, 300
      public transportation, 300
Trusts, 504-512
   custodian accounts, 509
   irrevocable, 506
   life insurance trusts, 508
   living trusts, 505
   revocable, 506
   testamentary, 508

Types of corporate securities, 146
   bonds, 146
   common stocks, 154
   preferred stocks, 152

Underwriting syndicates, 182
Unlicensed lenders, 77
   loan sharks, 77
   wage buying, 77
Utility and disutility, 48
   diminishing, 48
   marginal, 50
   point of indifference, 30

Wall Street Journal, 203
Wants, 25-27
   constellations of, 29
   discriminating tastes, 44
   family life cycle, 26
   gradations of, 25
   inadequate budgeting, 30
   insatiable, 25
   urgency of, 25
Whole life insurance, 415, 459
Wills, 492-499
   drawing up a will, 493
   importance of, 492
   probate, 497
   safeguarding of, 494

Yield of a bond, 149

Zero cost insurance, 415